Global Perspectives on Gender and Work

Global Perspectives on Gender and Work

Readings and Interpretations

EDITED BY JACQUELINE GOODMAN

ROWMAN & LITTLEFIELD PUBLISHERS, INC.
Lanham • Boulder • New York • Toronto • Plymouth, UK

Published by Rowman & Littlefield Publishers, Inc.
A wholly owned subsidiary of The Rowman & Littlefield Publishing Group, Inc.
4501 Forbes Boulevard, Suite 200, Lanham, Maryland 20706
http:/—www.rowmanlittlefield.com

Estover Road, Plymouth PL6 7PY, United Kingdom

British Library Cataloguing in Publication Information Available

Library of Congress Cataloging-in-Publication Data

Global perspectives on gender and work : readings and interpretations / edited by Jacqueline
Goodman.
   p. cm.
 Includes bibliographical references and index.
 ISBN 978-0-7425-5613-3 (cloth : alk. paper) — ISBN 978-0-7425-5614-0 (pbk. : alk. paper)
 1. Sexual division of labor—History. 2. Women employees—History. 3. Women—Social
conditions. I. Goodman-Draper, Jacqueline.
 HD6060.6.G56 2010
 331.4—dc22

                                        2009049994

Printed in the United States of America

Contents

Acknowledgments

Books always require the collective efforts of many. I would like to thank my first editor at Rowman & Littlefield, Jessica Gribble, who believed in this project and supported it throughout her tenure. I would also like to thank Susan McEachern, the editorial director at Rowman & Littlefield, who shepherded the project to its completion with patience and excellent guidance, for her enthusiasm and support. Additionally, I would like to thank Carrie Broadwell-Tkach, assistant editor at Rowman & Littlefield, who provided nothing short of calm assistance ever since she took up this project.

I would also like to thank Michael Waters, Kendall Taylor, Alex Goodman, Steve Goodman, Ben Goodman, and Marion Goodman for their great friendship and support throughout the process, as well as Sam and Rachel Draper for their humor, energy, and love as their mother struggled to combine family and work.

Finally, I would like to thank Jackie Rush, secretary of the Sociology and Politics departments at SUNY Potsdam, for her fastidious work, her tireless typing, editing, and overall organizational support. This book could not have been completed without her superlative skill and friendship.

Dividing the Labor: Marie and Michel Bastien, Native Montagnais-Naskapi of Northwest River, Labrador (photo by Richard Leacock, 1951)

Part I

ORIGINS OF THE GENDERED DIVISION OF LABOR

Men and women around the globe are segregated into different employment sectors and jobs. In the less-developed economies of Asia, sub-Saharan Africa, the Middle East, North Africa, and parts of Latin America and the Caribbean, women perform the majority of agricultural labor, while men predominate in industrial work. Women in these developing economies constitute 60–90 percent of the labor force in fresh produce and garment manufacture, as well as the majority in export processing zones. Women also remain globally concentrated in social and personal services, while men dominate the better-paid financial, business, and real estate services. Although 1.2 billion women and 1.8 billion men participated in the global labor force in 2007, women continue to perform the vast majority of household labor and family care (International Labor Organization 2004). When did such global divisions of labor between men and women emerge? Are they due to innate gendered traits (nature), or are there other explanations (variations on nurture) that might provide a more compelling answer?

The readings in Part I address the nature/nurture debate on three levels. They examine: 1) the basic notion of biological determinism of gender (nature); 2) the social construction of gender (nurture); and 3) the ways in which production relations give rise to varied social relations of gender. Research that investigates innate sex differences abounds, with conclusions that continue to evolve over time as new scientific findings emerge. In the nineteenth century, biologists believed that women's brains were too small for intellectual activities but large enough for household duties. In the 1960s sociobiologists argued that natural selection predisposed women to capacities for nurture and monogamy, while men were selected for leadership, aggression, and polygamy. More recent research suggests that women have a stronger connection between the two sides of the brain (a larger corpus callosum), hypothesizing that this might explain "women's intuition," as well as their greater ability to express emotions verbally compared to men. This research suggests that men have fewer such connections but excel in spatial tests, such as rotating three-dimensional objects in their minds, rendering them superior in map reading and other spatial skills. The implications of such research findings for social policy are limitless. If men have less ability to verbally express emotions, should they be prohibited from practicing psychiatry, social work, or health care? Similarly, if women lack ability in spatial visualization, should they be denied work as air traffic controllers, bus drivers, or architects?

Anne Fausto-Sterling addresses the pitfalls of biological determinism of sex differences in "The Problem with Sex/Gender and Nature/Nurture." She suggests we must stop searching for the ultimate biological causes of behavior, because they are not the Holy Grail we are seeking. "Neither naked sex nor naked culture exists" writes Fausto-Sterling. Both nature and nurture interact with each other at every stage of life's development, leading to ever-evolving organisms. "Instead of asking how anatomy limits function . . . ask how function shapes anatomy. To claim a biological difference is not to claim immutability" (Fausto-Sterling 2003, 125). Fausto-Sterling advocates a Developmental Systems approach, which denies there are two distinct sets of processes in development: one guided by genes and hormones, while another is guided by the environment. Instead, she argues that development is a "process of emergence" comprised of many influences, which cannot be reduced to a single cause. One example she provides is the very ability to see. In order for a completely functional set of eye-brain connections to be established in the newborn infant, light must be present after birth. Thus, "genetic activity . . . guides development by responding to external signals reaching specific cells at specific times" (Fausto-Sterling 2003, 128). In sum, Fausto-Sterling argues we must seek multiple influences in the development of gender differences, particularly important when formulating both research investigations and social policy.

Judith Lorber, in "'Night to His Day': The Social Construction of Gender," takes a different approach to the nature/nurture debate and argues that gender is a socially constructed concept. It is not biology that determines our destiny, she argues, but culture. Quoting Simone de Beauvoir, Lorber writes, "One is not born, but rather becomes a woman. . . . [C]ivilization produces this creature . . . which is described as feminine." Humans learn how to be men and women; they are not born that way. In China, from the tenth to the twentieth century, girls' feet were bound into deformed, three-inch stumps to become "feminine." In many Islamic societies girls undergo genital mutilation to render them culturally acceptable as potential marriage partners, and in the United States girls diet sometimes to their death or might undergo breast enlargement surgery to reach that "feminine" ideal. Similarly, American boys are taught to lift weights, act aggressively, and sometimes engage in violence to defend their socially constructed ideal of masculinity and honor.

Lorber illustrates these social constructions with the example of transsexual James Morris, a former mountain climber, soldier, and foreign correspondent, who held a high status as a male with these attributes in American society. When James became Jan Morris, the female travel writer, his status in society declined dramatically. Men treated her as a subordinate, and s/he began to learn helplessness. S/he found that men preferred women who were less verbal, less focused on themselves, and s/he complied. The same individual lost her previous social and economic status in the gender switch from man to woman. Lorber argues that gender is simply a way of structuring social life and becomes a major component in the construction of a society's stratification system.

In those societies where men are ranked higher, regardless of their actual contributions, their work and behaviors are more highly valued and rewarded. The gendered division of labor, according to Lorber, emerges from the needs of the social order for a reliable method of food production, and for the reproduction of the next generation. The ways in which these needs are met by each society remains a social construction.

Luigi Guiso et al. illustrate the conclusions of both Lorber and Fausto-Sterling in their article, "Culture, Gender, and Math," where they demonstrate that long-held beliefs about male genetic superiority over females in math is, in fact, inaccurate. In using data from more than two hundred seventy-six thousand fifteen-year-olds who took the international standardized tests in math, reading, science, and problem solving in over forty countries in 2003 (Programme for International Student Assessment), the authors found that the so-called gender gap in math is correlated with gendered access to education and other opportunities. Although globally boys outperform girls in math, the authors found that in countries that are deemed "gender equal" societies, such as Sweden, Iceland, and Norway, girls scored as well as or better than boys on math tests. The gender equality ratio was measured by World Economic Forum's Gender Gap Index (GGI), which reflects economic, political, and social well-being for females around the world. In Turkey, where the GGI indicates very low gender equality, boys do much better than girls on the math scores. While girls outperform boys in reading ability tests around the globe, both their reading and math scores show marked increase in those countries with a higher GGI index. These findings shed clear light on the biologically based explanation in rejecting nature as a determinant of gender differences, in favor of nurture.

Anthropologist Eleanor Leacock examines the possible origins of the gender division of labor, never assuming it is linked to innate biological differences. Instead, she suggests in "Montagnais Women and the Jesuit Program for Colonization" that it is connected to transformations in relations of production. She studied the Montagnais Naskapi hunter-gatherers of the Labrador Peninsula in the mid-twentieth century, along with studying seventeenth-century French Jesuit diaries, to conclude, as Frederick Engels maintained in *The Origin of the Family, Private Property and the State*, that production relations ultimately give rise to a specific set of social relations, between the sexes and otherwise.

The seventeenth-century diaries written by French missionaries attempting to "civilize the Montagnais" provide a window through which to view the economic and social life of the seventeenth-century Montagnais. French Jesuits recorded that both male and female Montagnais Naskapi contributed equitably to the subsistence needs of the entire band. Women gathered the daily subsistence requirements of fruits and vegetables and hunted small game, while men hunted large game, on a more infrequent basis, all distributed throughout the entire band. There was no private ownership of goods or hierarchical authority over others, and leadership was based on outstanding oral ability, not power, according to Jesuit Le Jeune. Leacock argues that comparable contributions to subsistence production resulted in egalitarian gender relations, values that troubled the Jesuits, who wrote of the ways they attempted to undermine the traditional gender values by instructing men to invoke their authority over women and children.

It was only when the Jesuits wanted furs and drew the Montagnais into the fur trade that the hunter-gatherers became less communal in their pursuits and the equitable division of labor between the sexes was weakened. Leacock suggests that once males became involved in the individual activity of fur trapping and trading, where someone else controlled production and the distribution of goods, the basis for inequality between individuals and genders emerged.

Subscribing to Engels' analysis, Leacock surmised that as men were recruited for this specialized economic activity, they gained unequal access to goods, and in the possible interest of passing on their wealth to heirs, the nuclear family emerged as the economic unit, separate from the larger band. While Montagnais men trapped furs, they could no longer hunt or fish, and they became dependent on trade. Women became increasingly excluded from the public sphere of access to resources, as they had to "care for" their husband and children, and were relegated to the private sphere of family. This transformation in production relations rendered women more economically dependent on males and, consequently, subordinate. The Montagnais' gendered division of labor began simply as an egalitarian way to organize the social order, according to Leacock, but was transformed into gender inequality as production relations metamorphosed into specialized, individual male economic activity, to the exclusion of women.

Heidi Hartmann also examines the origin of sexual division of labor and similarly relies on ethnographic data to make her argument in "Capitalism, Patriarchy, and Job Segregation by Sex" that the sexual division of labor may in fact be historically universal. She infers from the anthropological data that egalitarianism might have prevailed in our pre-state past because women and men sustained equal participation in the production and distribution of goods. However, this division of labor between men and women may in fact be the ultimate cause of inequality between men and women as well. Hartmann argues that economic interdependence between men and women in tribal societies was undermined by the rise of state societies, as the state sought to control the tribal resource base: land and labor power. Kings and lords of the state might have accomplished this by utilizing the traditional sexual division of labor, and the male tendency for greater power due to men's role in military ventures, to impose male authority over women and children. This would have bypassed traditional, tribal collective group rights. In return for relinquishing their labor and land, men might have been rewarded with empowerment in the nuclear family.

Hartmann suggests that patriarchy was solidified prior to the emergence of capitalism in the fifteenth to eighteenth centuries. Such male dominance was carried forward into the capitalist organization of industry as production was removed from the home and men became less dependent on women's production contributions. But the emergence of capitalism also threatened patriarchal control, as it brought women and children into the labor force, altering the nuclear family, the basis of male power over women. Male workers in the wage labor system, she argues, sought to maintain the sexual division of labor, since male dominance was primarily sustained through job segregation by sex in the capitalist economy. It enforced lower wages for women, which kept women dependent on men, and encouraged them to marry and perform domestic duties for husbands, while men benefited from both higher wages and the domestic division of labor. Women's unpaid domestic labor in turn weakened women's position in the labor market and sustained the unequal, gendered division of labor. In conclusion, the authors in Part I debunk biological determinism as the origin of the gendered division of labor. Instead they explore its causes and subsequent transformation into gendered inequality through an examination of comparative and ethnographic evidence, which reveals an intersection of economic, social, and political forces.

CHAPTER 1

The Problem with Sex/Gender and Nature/Nurture

Anne Fausto-Sterling

For a good century and a half, scientists, social scientists and politicians have appealed to biological difference to explain social inequality between men and women, people of African descent and Caucasians, members of different economic classes and people of different religions. In turn, a wide variety of scholars writing over a long period of time have critiqued these scientific claims (Russett 1989; Fausto-Sterling 2000). In the mid-1980s, I drew a composite picture gleaned from the writings of contemporary biological and social scientists: these writers claimed that women are naturally better mothers, while men are genetically predisposed to be aggressive, hasty and fickle. They may rape to pass on their genes. Women's lack of aggressive drive and native ability ensures that they will always earn less, thus guaranteeing equal pay discriminates against men (Fausto-Sterling 1992).

At the time, I critically examined the underlying scientific evidence, demonstrating its procedural and interpretive weaknesses. I also suggested that instead of setting nature against nurture we reject the search for root causes and substitute a more complex analysis in which an individual's capacities emerge from a web of mutual interactions between the biological being and the social environment. Although I had the right idea, the moment was not right to express it in terms that might unify biological scientists, sociologists, developmental psychologists, and feminists. I believe that now that moment of unification is upon us.

In the 1970s, feminist social scientists proposed a theory that created two categories: *sex*, the supposed biological essence that underlay gender and *gender* the social overlay that produced two different categories of being—men and women, through an ill-defined process of socialization. This theoretical approach had many virtues. It permitted the examination of differential treatment of boys and girls in school and men and women in the workplace. It opened the door to a virtual growth industry of cultural analysis examining the construction of gender ideology in the media and on the streets. But it also had a big drawback. Leaving "sex" in the realm of scientifically verifiable fact left feminism vulnerable to a new tide of biological difference. Indeed, that new tide is very much with us (see for example: Udry 2000; Wizemann and Pardue 2001).

For some, sex encroaches deep into the territory of social difference, while for others it is a minimal entity. If there is something that we could call "naked sex" (Kraus 2000)—that which is left when all gender is stripped away—we have to argue about for how much of gender difference it can account. If we leave naked sex to biologists and biologically oriented social scientists, we will find that the territory allotted to it is growing apace while the explanatory power of socially produced gender shrinks in proportion. In the sex versus gender model, biological sex is opposed to social sex. Nature is opposed to culture, the body becomes the recipient of culture, and gender becomes the content of culture. Worst of all, for those interested in social change, naked sex is often—albeit incorrectly—seen as immutable, while gender, is often, albeit incorrectly, seen as malleable. To the extent that the sex/gender analysis of social difference reinforces our view of the material body as a natural given, our feminist debate influences the structure of other struggles. Indeed, the biological debates about race and about sex have intersected and mutually constructed one another for a good two centuries (Russett 1989).

In *Sexing the Body: Gender Politics and the Construction of Sexuality* (Fausto-Sterling 2000), I detail several examples of how the biology-culture debate about the body plays out. Let me briefly pick one of these—an alleged sex difference in the structure of a part of the brain called the corpus callosum. Scientists have argued about whether or not there is a sex difference in the corpus callosum for more than 100 years. Some think that the (real) difference might explain sex/gender variation in verbal and spatial ability and that the knowledge of such difference should be used to shape educational policy. Others believe there is no difference. I use this scientific debate to think about how social arguments sustain scientific disputes, concluding that we will not resolve the *science* at issue until we have reached some form of consensus over the *social policy* at hand.

While the above insight is important, however, I want here to emphasize a different aspect of the problem. Suppose, hypothetically, someone proved beyond a doubt that a sex difference in the corpus callosum was clearly linked to verbal and spatial abilities. Would that mean that feminists adhering to the sex/gender distinction would have to agree that educators need to treat boys and girls differently when they teach maths and English? Would that force us to accept the argument that we cannot expect there to be more women engineers than the 9.2 per cent employed in the US workforce in 1977? At its worst, too strict an adherence to the sex/gender dualism puts us in just such a position. At its best, it leaves feminists in a position of constant defensiveness, with all of our energy focused on refuting or mitigating the latest findings of sex differences produced by biomedical researchers. Psychologist Susan Oyama refers to this as hauling "phenomena back and forth across the biological border" (Oyama 2000, 190). I, for one, am tired of being in this position, and this weariness has pushed me—and other theorists—to think differently about biology, culture, sex, and gender (see, for example, Birke 2003; Annandale 2003). In making new theory, we reclaim a defining position in the social debate about gender and we can direct our creativity towards breaking new pathways rather than fighting off the dogs that nip constantly at our heels.

I find especially helpful a set of approaches that I have gathered under the flag of Developmental Systems Theory, or DST for short. From the point of view of DST, neither naked sex nor naked culture exist. Findings of so-called biological difference do not imply a claim of immutability or inevitability. Consider once again the corpus callosum. Some scientists believe that this brain structure differs in men and women; others that it differs in left- and right-handers and yet others believe that it differs in gay and straight men (where it is really a stand-in for a gendered account of homosexuality). Elsewhere I write about the uncertain nature of these conclusions (Fausto-Sterling 1992; Fausto-Sterling 2000), but here I want to think about what it might mean if these claims were scientifically uncontestable. In bringing a DST approach to the claim of brain differences in adult men and women, the assertion of difference becomes a starting point. The interesting question is how the differences developed in the first place. For example, this possible difference in the adult corpus callosum is not present in the brains of small children. A DST researcher will want to design experiments to test hypotheses about how different experience leads to a divergence in brain development. Instead of asking how anatomy limits function, one asks how function shapes anatomy. To claim a biological difference is not to claim immutability.

New research questions become apparent when we turn matters around in this way. What childhood experiences and behaviours contribute to the developing anatomy of the brain? Are there particular developmental periods when a child's brain is more or less responsive to functional stimuli? How do nerve cells translate externally generated information into specific growth patterns and neural circuits? Answering these latter questions will require the skills of molecular biologists and cell biologists as well as psychologists, sociologists and cultural theorists. DST will not put basic biologists out of business, but will set their research in a different intellectual framework.

Just as a claim of biological difference does not imply immutability, a claim of socially induced difference does not necessarily imply malleability. For example, if differential social experience produces differences in brain anatomy and thus in brain function, later experiences would then be interpreted and integrated by a differently functioning brain. Change to a pre-differentiated state would be improbable. Many people consider it extremely difficult to change from being hetero- to homosexual or vice versa. But the fact that a particular form of sexual desire is hard to change does not mean that it hasn't been socially caused.

How, more specifically, can DST help to form a new research agenda which depends upon the mutual construction of sex and gender? Psychologists Esther Thelen and Linda Smith list some of the basic goals of developmental systems theory (Thelen and Smith 1994). The first is to understand the origins of novelty. Thelen and Smith discuss behavioural novelty—starting to crawl and then to walk for example, but I would like to use DST to elucidate the emergence by the age of two-and-a-half of gender differences in play and the ability to categorize self and others by gender. Infants are not born with these behaviours. Rather, the behaviours emerge during the first two to three years of life. We have a sketchy idea of the timing of such emergence but little in the way of coherent theory to explain our observations (Ruble and Martin 1998).

A second goal of DST is to reconcile global regularities with local variability. In the case of gender, this means understanding the emergence of general features recognizable as something we call gender, while at the same time incorporating into our story the enormous within-group variability.

A third goal of systems theory is to integrate developmental data at many levels of explanation. Consider Judith Butler's controversial and frequently misunderstood assertion that "gender ought not to be construed as a stable identity . . . rather, gender is an identity tenuously constituted in time, instituted in an exterior space through a *stylized repetition of acts*" (Butler 1990, 140; emphasis in the original). Butler was not thinking specifically about physiological mechanisms by which the body might materially incorporate gender. Nevertheless, a systems approach to the body insists that relatively stable states of being emerge from a process of repetitive trial and error. Thus Butler's notion of repeated performance, designed to describe gender development at the psychoanalytic level, could become a starting point to design studies aimed at understanding the material basis of gender. "Material basis" is here understood as a set of physiological and social expressions which emerge as individuals learn about social gender, practice it, and make it their own. That brain anatomy might itself develop in particular ways in response to such practice and repetition seems likely to me, but is a hypothesis that requires specification and testing.

Such an application of DST to Butler's ideas of performance also provide an answer to Pheng Cheah's critique of Butler (Cheah 1996). Cheah argues that Butler's account of gender development is philosophically wanting because it only applies to humans, a fact that leaves human gender critically unconnected to the rest of biology. Most biologists, however (myself included) view human biology—including sex/gender development—as falling along a continuum. DST can provide accounts of how gender materializes in the body that will work for all animals, not just humans. Granted there are some big discussions about consciousness and intentionality in non-human primates that must be held along the way. But stretching claims such as Butler's about repetitive performance to develop a systems account of the biological materialization of gender in humans, will open the door to understanding biological development more broadly, and confront untenable claims that human materiality differs fundamentally from that of other animals.

A fourth goal of developmental systems theory is to provide a biologically plausible yet non-determinist account of the development of behaviour. As Thelen and Smith write, "the boundaries between what is innate and what is acquired become so blurred as to be at the very least uninteresting compared to the powerful questions of developmental process" (Thelen and Smith 1994). A fifth goal is to understand how local processes, that is, what happens in a particular family or to a particular child or a particular random experience, can lead to global outcomes. For example, most children learn to walk. But the individual paths they take to that accomplishment can vary quite a lot.

A final goal for DST is to establish a theoretical basis for generating and interpreting empirical research that breaks out of the idea of adding up so much nature and so much nurture to create a final outcome. This means learning how to apply statistical systems that do not partition variance. (For critiques of the Analysis of Variance approach to the study of human difference see: Wahlsten 1990.)

Psychologists have most successfully applied DST to phenomena that have little to do with gender. Studying such applications, however, can help us to construct a research agenda aimed at explicating the emergence of gender in early childhood and its subsequent development throughout the life cycle. Consider how Thelen and her colleagues investigate the question of how we learn to walk. In the 1940s and 1950s, psychologists described the stages of learning to walk—up on all fours, crawling, standing, walking holding on, etc. They reasoned that each new stage directly reflected changes in the brain. But how can the millions of neurons, the wide variety of muscle contraction patterns, and the complex patterns of neuronal activity, ever result in a highly specific movement such as putting one leg in front of another? During development, individuals go through periods of instability as they incorporate new tasks—be they motor, cognitive or emotional. In an infant, seemingly random motor activity, for instance, eventually emerges into new and fairly stable forms of movement, first crawling, then walking.

A recent example illustrates why developmental systems theory has begun to replace more rigid accounts of stages of neuromuscular development. In 1992 pediatricians recommended that to minimize the danger of sudden infant death, infants be placed on their back (supine) or side to sleep rather than on their bellies (prone). Since the recommendation and a public education campaign, the percentage of US infants sleeping in the prone position has decreased from 70 per cent to 27 per cent. With that change has come another—a dramatic shift in the age at which infants reach motor milestones such as pulling to stand up, crawling, creeping and rolling from a prone to supine position (Davis *et al.* 1998). The observation that sleep position affects the timing of motor development makes perfect sense to a systems theorist, since neuromuscular development is an *effect* of use and experience. That both supine and prone sleepers learn to walk at about the same time may reflect the fact that by one year of age they have all developed the strength needed to sustain independent walking. But supine and prone sleepers don't attain that strength in exactly the same way or according to the same time schedule.

As long as the basic conditions—the force of gravity, the firmness of the ground, neuromuscular responses (indeed these are all part of the system of walking), remain stable, the ability to walk remains stable as well. But the stability is what DST theorists call "softly assembled." Walking, for example, is a flexible ability. We don't use exactly the same neuromuscular responses when walking on different substrates, yet we walk. Walking can take on different strides—ambling, strolling, fast-walking. It can adjust to an injury in a knee joint, etc. Softly assembled states can dissolve into new periods of instability and new types of stability can emerge from these seemingly chaotic events—learning to walk again following muscle atrophy or traumatic injury would be one such example.

Consider as another example, the development of the retina and the ability to see. The axons of nerve cells from the retina of each eye connect to a part of the brain known as the lateral geniculate nucleus. Some of the retinal axons from the right eye connect to the lateral geniculate nucleus of the left hemisphere while others connect to the right hemisphere, while the opposite is true for axons from the left eye. Within the lateral geniculate nucleus, axons from the two eyes terminate in separate alternating layers. There is also an additional level of organization in these projections called ocular dominance columns. Initially, neither the layering of these lateral geniculate nucleus axons from left to right nor the dominance columns are present, but via an active process of axon retraction and elaboration, eventually the adult connections emerge.

These events do not occur seamlessly in response to some internal logic of genes acting spontaneously inside cells. Rather, visual experience plays a key role. The firing of certain neurons strengthens their connections. Neuroscientists say "cells that fire together wire together, those that don't won't." The fact that light, entering the eye after birth is necessary for a completely functional set of eye-brain connections explains why it is so important to remove congenital cataracts no later than six months after birth (Le Grand *et al.* 2001).

In the development of vision, key features of developmental systems theory emerge. First, specific connections are not *programmed* by some genetic blueprint. Genetic activity, rather, guides development by responding to external signals reaching specific cells at specific times. Early in development these signals come from other cells while at a later time signals include spontaneous electrical activity generated by developing nervous tissue and, still later, light entering through the newborn and infant eye. A functional system emerges from a context-bound system in which seemingly random activity—that is spontaneous nerve firings and visual input—evolve into more highly structured form and function. Often these connections must happen during a critical window of development. One general point to be made is that different kinds of connections have different degrees of plasticity. Some critical windows reside only in one stage of the life cycle because that is the only time when (so far as we currently know) the entire system is constructed in a particular way. In some cases an end state can be produced by more than one initial starting point while in others only one initial starting point can produce an end state. Other systems, though, may be open to change more than once in a life cycle or may even be continuously modifiable during the life cycle. Thus a key notion of developmental systems theory is that there are periods of relative stability and other moments of great instability. During unstable moments important changes can occur which in turn resolve into new and stable form and function. An important future task for biologists and social scientists, working together, is to apply these concepts to gender formation during the life cycle.

How might DST apply to the analysis of sex and gender? Consider the uproar over biologist Simon LeVay's 1991 article reporting differences in the microanatomy of both male and female brains and in the brains of gay and straight men (LeVay 1991). The initial response from many of us was to point out the technical shortcomings of the study, but in a recent study some of these have been overcome. Neuroanatomist William Byne could not replicate the gay/straight differences that LeVay reported. But as had LeVay, Byne found measurable differences between men's and women's hypothalamuses (Byne *et al.* 2001). Given that his is the third independent report of this anatomical brain difference, I think we would be hard-pressed to deny the finding. But accepting the difference need not push us into a bio-determinist corner. Instead, we need to insist that scientists ask developmental and functional questions about the difference. Most importantly, we need to hammer home the point that differences found in adults arise during development.

This insistence opens the door for a theory and practice of what contemporary theorists call embodiment. Recall the DST concept of softly-assembled states. Although relatively stable, such states can dissolve into chaotic periods out of which new types of stability can emerge. Consider the conflict between the idea that homosexuality is inborn versus the thought that it is somehow learned after birth. Sometimes this argument resolves into a debate about whether the trait is unchangeable or whether it can be altered by force of will. There is bad thinking on both sides of this argument. For many homosexuals, same-sex attraction is a stable state of desire. If we think of that stability as being softly assembled, however, it becomes less surprising that it can sometimes become destabilized and after a period of disarray, some new quasi-stable form of desire can emerge.

Recent work on the nature of memory in rats can help us conceptualize my argument. Consider rats that have been fear-conditioned to associate a tone with an electric shock. At first, the conditioned response is unstable. It requires about six hours and some protein synthesis to consolidate. The memory associating a tone with shock, however, can be pushed out of what I will call its softly assembled state by preventing more protein synthesis at the time that memory is again evoked by playing the tone (Nader 2000). The conclusion from this experiment is that when a memory is drawn upon and then stored again, new memory proteins are made. In these experiments, memories become destabilized and open to revision for a brief period before a new period of stability begins.

The concept that memory can be revised during episodes of retrieval can be useful in thinking about homosexuality. Consider the statement by a gay person that they always remember being different. Perhaps they remember liking dolls instead of trucks (or for lesbians, liking trucks instead of dolls). If, during the evocation of memory, it is possible to edit and incorporate contemporary information, then memory itself becomes part of a system that produces the sexual preference or gender identity. The memories are perfectly real, but they become progressively adjusted, presumably throughout childhood and into adulthood, to take into account new experiences and newly available information. Surely it is possible for social and neuroscientists to collaborate in applying the study of memory processing and revision to the acquisition of gender identity and sexual orientation. Such applications have the potential to provide a dynamic account of embodiment rather than the less plausible view that some people are born with a homosexual homunculus which merely unfolds over a lifetime.

In light of my discussion of DST I propose a new research agenda for the study of sex and gender differences. First, we need to think more about individual differences than group averages. This means studying individual development and accepting the idea that there are many different individual paths to a global outcome. Feminist social theory contains rich work on the emergence of sex and gender differences, much of which examines mid- and late child development or adulthood. But we know little about the early emergence of difference. And it's the early emergence of difference that is often used as evidence for a biological cause for difference.

We can, however, say a few things about early development. At seven months, on average, infants respond differently to male and female voices. By nine months, they can tell the sexes apart largely on the basis of hair length. But other contributions to an infant's ability to discriminate sexes such as height and smell have not been well studied. Children can differentially label the sexes by about thirty months but they are better at labelling adults than they are at labelling other children. Children take quite a while before they use genitalia as clues to sex and before they are able to do this they rely heavily on hair cues. In the United States small children believe that figures with blond curly hair are female. Adolescents, but not younger children, use dynamic clues, such as running or sitting to identify gender (Ruble and Martin 1998).

The racial specificity of such findings make future, culturally specific studies imperative. Most studies of early development of gender perception have been done on white middle-class children in America and the entire question of constructing culturally neutral accounts of gender difference continues to vex feminist theory. Indeed, a central component of a feminist social science research agenda must be to examine the early development of gender constructs and behaviours in different cultures and in different socio-economic groups and within different ethnic and racially-defined communities. If we develop process-based theories of human development rather than relying on averages and statistical norms, we will have fewer problems including human variation in our accounts of gender development.

After children learn to identify gender they then develop a separate concept—that gender is constant and stable. At first children don't necessarily believe that "once a girl always a girl." It takes a while for young children to develop the notion that, first, genitalia provide a reliable way of distinguishing between boys and girls and second that one of the implications of knowing about genital difference is that gender is fixed. The ages at which these two ideas develop—although certainly older than three years—have yet to be clearly resolved.

By about two-and-a-half years of age (white, middle-class American) children begin to show knowledge of gender stereotypes, about objects (dresses versus trousers, trucks versus flowers) and activities (active playing, passive playing, playing in the home-making corner, throwing a ball, playing with trucks). Although they know about these gendered stereotypes, social scientists have yet to assess which ones children learn first. I offer the above, abbreviated description of the development of gender awareness in children not as an account of how gender emerges, but rather as an invitation. I ask developmental systems theorists who have produced fascinating but non-gendered accounts of motor and cognitive development to use DST to think about gender. Similarly, I request social scientists who study gender to break away from the traditional biological, psychoanalytic, cognitive social learning or gender schema approaches. Instead, I encourage them to look at the trajectory that I've sketched above, fill in important gaps, and begin to use developmental systems theory to understand the process by which gender emerges at very young ages. How does it stabilize? What might contribute to its destabilization, and how does it restabilize and change during the process of an entire life cycle?

At the same time I invite feminist theorists in the humanities to revisit the social sciences with a new developmental systems theory vision. This is the impulse of the current vogue of the term embodiment among feminist theorists. Embodiment suggests a process by which we *acquire* a body rather than a passive unfolding of some preformed blueprint. Beginning to understand that the world works via systems will enable us to specify more clearly the links between culture and the body and to understand how nature and nurture, sex and gender are indivisible concepts. Finally, the political fallout from these ideas remains to be addressed. We—and here I mean feminist political theorists—need to think harder about how engaging with the world of sex and gender from a DST point of view will affect our strategies for social change.

CHAPTER 2

"Night to His Day"
THE SOCIAL CONSTRUCTION OF GENDER

Judith Lorber

Talking about gender for most people is the equivalent of fish talking about water. Gender is so much the routine ground of everyday activities that questioning its taken-for-granted assumptions and presuppositions is like thinking about whether the sun will come up.[1] Gender is so pervasive that in our society we assume it is bred into our genes. Most people find it hard to believe that gender is constantly created and re-created out of human interaction, out of social life, and is the texture and order of that social life. Yet gender, like culture, is a human production that depends on everyone constantly "doing gender" (West and Zimmerman 1987).

And everyone "does gender" without thinking about it. Today, on the subway, I saw a well-dressed man with a year-old child in a stroller. Yesterday, on a bus, I saw a man with a tiny baby in a carrier on his chest. Seeing men taking care of small children in public is increasingly common—at least in New York City. But both men were quite obviously stared at—and smiled at, approvingly. Everyone was doing gender—the men who were changing the role of fathers and the other passengers, who were applauding them silently. But there was more gendering going on that probably fewer people noticed. The baby was wearing a white crocheted cap and white clothes. You couldn't tell if it was a boy or a girl. The child in the stroller was wearing a dark blue T-shirt and dark print pants. As they started to leave the train, the father put a Yankee baseball cap on the child's head. Ah, a boy, I thought. Then I noticed the gleam of tiny earrings in the child's ears, and as they got off, I saw the little flowered sneakers and lace-trimmed socks. Not a boy after all. Gender done.

Gender is such a familiar part of daily life that it usually takes a deliberate disruption of our expectations of how women and men are supposed to act to pay attention to how it is produced. Gender signs and signals are so ubiquitous that we usually fail to note them—unless they are missing or ambiguous. Then we are uncomfortable until we have successfully placed the other person in a gender status; otherwise, we feel socially dislocated. In our society, in addition to man and woman, the status can be *transvestite* (a person who dresses in opposite-gender clothes) and *transsexual* (a person who has had sex-change surgery). Transvestites and transsexuals carefully construct their gender status by dressing, speaking, walking, gesturing in the ways prescribed for women or men—whichever they want to be taken for—and so does any "normal" person.

For the individual, gender construction starts with assignment to a sex category on the basis of what the genitalia look like at birth.[2] Then babies are dressed or adorned in a way that displays the category because parents don't want to be constantly asked whether their baby is a girl or a boy. A sex category becomes a gender status through naming, dress, and the use of other gender markers. Once a child's gender is evident, others treat those in one gender differently from those in the other, and the children respond to the different treatment by feeling different and behaving differently. As soon as they can talk, they start to refer to themselves as members of their gender. Sex doesn't come into play again until puberty, but by that time, sexual feelings and desires and practices have been shaped by gendered norms and expectations. Adolescent boys and girls approach and avoid each other in an elaborately scripted and gendered mating dance. Parenting is gendered, with different expectations for mothers and for fathers, and people of different genders work at different kinds of jobs. The work adults do as mothers and fathers and as low-level workers and high-level bosses shapes women's and men's life experiences, and these experiences produce different feelings, consciousness, relationships, skills—ways of being that we call feminine or masculine.[3] All of these processes constitute the social construction of gender.

Gendered roles change—today fathers are taking care of little children, girls and boys are wearing unisex clothing and getting the same education, women and men are working at the same jobs. Although many traditional social groups are quite strict about maintaining gender differences, in other social groups they seem to be blurring. Then why the one-year-old's earrings? Why is it still so important to mark a child as a girl or a boy, to make sure she is not taken for a boy or he for a girl? What would happen if they were? They would, quite literally, have changed places in their social world.

To explain why gendering is done from birth, constantly and by everyone, we have to look not only at the way individuals experience gender but at gender as a social institution. As a social institution, gender is one of the major ways that human beings organize their lives. Human society depends on a predictable division of labor, a designated allocation of scarce goods, assigned responsibility for children and others who cannot care for themselves, common values and their systematic transmission to new members, legitimate leadership, music, art, stories, games, and other symbolic productions. One way of choosing people for the different tasks of society is on the basis of their talents, motivations, and competence—their demonstrated achievements. The other way is on the basis of gender, race, ethnicity—ascribed membership in a category of people. Although societies vary in the extent to which they use one or the other of these ways of allocating people to work and to carry out other responsibilities, every society uses gender and age grades. Every society classifies people as "girl and boy children," "girls and boys ready to be married," and "fully adult women and men," constructs similarities among them and differences between them, and assigns them to different roles and responsibilities. Personality characteristics, feelings, motivations, and ambitions flow from these different life experiences so that the members of these different groups become different kinds of people. The process of gendering and its outcome are legitimated by religion, law, science, and the society's entire set of values.

In order to understand gender as a social institution, it is important to distinguish human action from animal behavior. Animals feed themselves and their young until their young can feed themselves. Humans have to produce not only food but shelter and clothing. They also, if the group is going to continue as a social group, have to teach the children how their particular group does these tasks. In the process, humans reproduce gender, family, kinship, and a division of labor—social institutions that do not exist among animals. Primate social groups have been referred to as families, and their mating patterns as monogamy, adultery, and harems. Primate behavior has been used to prove the universality of sex differences—as built into our evolutionary inheritance (Haraway 1978). But animals' sex differences are not at all the same as humans' gender differences; animals' bonding is not kinship; animals' mating is not ordered by marriage; and animals' dominance hierarchies are not the equivalent of human stratification systems. Animals group on sex and age, relational categories that are physiologically, not socially, different. Humans create gender and age-group categories that are socially, and not necessarily physiologically, different.[4]

For animals, physiological maturity means being able to impregnate or conceive; its markers are coming into heat (estrus) and sexual attraction. For humans, puberty means being available for marriage; it is marked by rites that demonstrate this marital eligibility. Although the onset of physiological puberty is signaled by secondary sex characteristics (menstruation, breast development, sperm ejaculation, pubic and underarm hair), the onset of social adulthood is ritualized by the coming-out party or desert walkabout or bar mitzvah or graduation from college or first successful hunt or dreaming or inheritance of property. Humans have rituals that mark the passage from childhood into puberty and puberty into full adult status, as well as for marriage, childbirth, and death; animals do not (van Gennep 1960). To the extent that infants and the dead are differentiated by whether they are male or female, there are different birth rituals for girls and boys, and different funeral rituals for men and women (Biersack 1984, 132–33). Rituals of puberty, marriage, and becoming a parent are gendered, creating a "woman," a "man," a "bride," a "groom," a "mother," a "father." Animals have no equivalents for these statuses.

Among animals, siblings mate and so do parents and children; humans have incest taboos and rules that encourage or forbid mating between members of different kin groups (Lévi-Strauss 1956, [1949] 1969). Any animal of the same species may feed another's young (or may not, depending on the species). Humans designate responsibility for particular children by kinship; humans frequently limit responsibility for children to the members of their kinship group or make them into members of their kinship group with adoption rituals.

Animals have dominance hierarchies based on size or on successful threat gestures and signals. These hierarchies are usually sexed, and in some species, moving to the top of the hierarchy physically changes the sex (Austad 1986). Humans have stratification patterns based on control of surplus food, ownership of property, legitimate demands on others' work and sexual services, enforced determinations of who marries whom, and approved use of violence. If a woman replaces a man at the top of a stratification hierarchy, her social status may be that of a man, but her sex does not change.

Mating, feeding, and nurturant behavior in animals is determined by instinct and imitative learning and ordered by physiological sex and age (Lancaster 1974). In humans, these behaviors are taught and symbolically reinforced and ordered by socially constructed gender and age grades. Social gender and age statuses sometimes ignore or override physiological sex and age completely. Male and female animals (unless they physiologically change) are not interchangeable; infant animals cannot take the place of adult animals. Human females can become husbands and fathers, and human males can become wives and mothers, without sex-change surgery (Blackwood 1984). Human infants can reign as kings or queens.

Western society's values legitimate gendering by claiming that it all comes from physiology—female and male procreative differences. But gender and sex are not equivalent, and gender as a social construction does not flow automatically from genitalia and reproductive organs, the main physiological differences of females and males. In the construction of ascribed social statuses, physiological differences such as sex, stage of development, color of skin, and size are crude markers. They are not the source of the social statuses of gender, age grade, and race. *Social statuses* are carefully constructed through prescribed processes of teaching, learning, emulation, and enforcement. Whatever genes, hormones, and biological evolution contribute to human social institutions is materially as well as qualitatively transformed by social practices. Every social institution has a material base, but culture and social practices transform that base into something with qualitatively different patterns and constraints. The economy is much more than producing food and goods and distributing them to eaters and users; family and kinship are not the equivalent of having sex and procreating; morals and religions cannot be equated with the fears and ecstasies of the brain; language goes far beyond the sounds produced by tongue and larynx. No one eats "money" or "credit"; the concepts of "god" and "angels" are the subjects of theological disquisitions; not only words but objects, such as their flag, "speak" to the citizens of a country.

Similarly, gender cannot be equated with biological and physiological differences between human females and males. The building blocks of gender are *socially constructed statuses*. Western societies have only two genders, "man" and "woman." Some societies have three genders—men, women, and *berdaches* or *hijras* or *xaniths*. Berdaches, hijras, and xaniths are biological males who behave, dress, work, and are treated in most respects as social women; they are therefore not men, nor are they female women; they are, in our language, "male women."[5] There are African and American Indian societies that have a gender status called *manly hearted women*—biological females who work, marry, and parent as men; their social status is "female men" (Amadiume 1987; Blackwood 1984). They do not have to behave or dress as men to have the social responsibilities and prerogatives of husbands and fathers; what makes them men is enough wealth to buy a wife.

Modern Western societies' *transsexuals* and *transvestites* are the nearest equivalent of these crossover genders, but they are not institutionalized as third genders (Bolin 1987). Transsexuals are biological males and females who have sex-change operations

to alter their genitalia. They do so in order to bring their physical anatomy in congru-
ence with the way they want to live and with their own sense of gender identity. They
do not become a third gender; they change genders. Transvestites are males who live
as women and females who live as men but do not intend to have sex-change surgery.
Their dress, appearance, and mannerisms fall within the range of what is expected
from members of the opposite gender, so that they "pass." They also change genders,
sometimes temporarily, some for most of their lives. Transvestite women have fought
in wars as men soldiers as recently as the nineteenth century; some married women,
and others went back to being women and married men once the war was over.[6] Some
were discovered when their wounds were treated; others not until they died. In order
to work as a jazz musician, a man's occupation, Billy Tipton, a woman, lived most of
her life as a man. She died recently at seventy-four, leaving a wife and three adopted
sons for whom she was husband and father, and musicians with whom she had played
and traveled, for whom she was "one of the boys" (*New York Times* 1989).[7] There have
been many other such occurrences of women passing as men to do more prestigious
or lucrative men's work (Matthaei 1982, 192–93).[8]

Genders, therefore, are not attached to a biological sub-stratum. Gender boundaries are breachable, and individual and socially organized shifts from one gender to
another call attention to "cultural, social, or aesthetic dissonances" (Garber 1992,
16). These odd or deviant or third genders show us what we ordinarily take for
granted—that people have to learn to be women and men. Men who cross-dress for
performances or for pleasure often learn from women's magazines how to "do femininity" convincingly (41–51). Because transvestism is direct evidence of how gender
is constructed, Marjorie Garber claims it has "extraordinary power . . . to disrupt, expose, and challenge, putting in question the very notion of the 'original' and of stable
identity" (16).

Gender Bending

It is difficult to see how gender is constructed because we take it for granted that it's
all biology, or hormones, or human nature. The differences between women and men
seem to be self-evident, and we think they would occur no matter what society did.
But in actuality, human females and males are physiologically more similar in appearance than are the two sexes of many species of animals and are more alike than different in traits and behavior (Epstein 1988). Without the deliberate use of gendered
clothing, hairstyles, jewelry, and cosmetics, women and men would look far more
alike.[9] Even societies that do not cover women's breasts have gender-identifying clothing, scarification, jewelry, and hairstyles.

The ease with which many transvestite women pass as men and transvestite men
as women is corroborated by the common gender misidentification in Westernized
societies of people in jeans, T-shirts, and sneakers. Men with long hair may be addressed as "miss," and women with short hair are often taken for men unless they
offset the potential ambiguity with deliberate gender markers (Devor 1987, 1989).
Jan Morris, in *Conundrum*, an autobiographical account of events just before and just

after a sex-change operation, described how easy it was to shift back and forth from being a man to being a woman when testing how it would feel to change gender status. During this time, Morris still had a penis and wore more or less unisex clothing; the context alone made the man and the woman:

> Sometimes the arena of my ambivalence was uncomfortably small. At the Travellers' Club, for example, I was obviously known as a man of sorts—women were only allowed on the premises at all during a few hours of the day, and even then were hidden away as far as possible in lesser rooms or alcoves. But I had another club, only a few hundred yards away, where I was known only as a woman, and often I went directly from one to the other, imperceptibly changing roles on the way—"Cheerio, sir," the porter would say at one club, and "Hello, madam," the porter would greet me at the other. (1975, 132)

Gender shifts are actually a common phenomenon in public roles as well. Queen Elizabeth II of England bore children, but when she went to Saudi Arabia on a state visit, she was considered an honorary man so that she could confer and dine with the men who were heads of a state that forbids unrelated men and women to have face-to-unveiled-face contact. In contemporary Egypt, lower-class women who run restaurants or shops dress in men's clothing and engage in unfeminine aggressive behavior, and middle-class educated women of professional or managerial status can take positions of authority (Rugh 1986, 131). In these situations, there is an important status change: These women are treated by the others in the situation as if they are men. From their own point of view, they are still women. From the social perspective, however, they are men.[10]

In many cultures, gender bending is prevalent in theater or dance—the Japanese kabuki are men actors who play both women and men; in Shakespeare's theater company, there were no actresses—Juliet and Lady Macbeth were played by boys. Shakespeare's comedies are full of witty comments on gender shifts. Women characters frequently masquerade as young men, and other women characters fall in love with them; the boys playing these masquerading women, meanwhile, are acting out pining for the love of men characters.[11] In *As You Like It,* when Rosalind justifies her protective crossdressing, Shakespeare also comments on manliness:

> Were it not better,
> Because that I am more than common tall,
> That I did suit me all points like a man:
> A gallant curtle-axe upon my thigh,
> A boar-spear in my hand, and in my heart
> Lie there what hidden women's fear there will,
> We'll have a swashing and martial outside,
> As many other mannish cowards have
> That do outface it with their semblances.
>
> (I, i, 115–22)

Shakespeare's audience could appreciate the double subtext: Rosalind, a woman character, was a boy dressed in girl's clothing who then dressed as a boy; like bravery, masculinity and femininity can be put on and taken off with changes of costume and role (Howard 1988, 435).[12]

M Butterfly is a modern play of gender ambiguities, which David Hwang (1989) based on a real person. Shi Peipu, a male Chinese opera singer who sang women's roles, was a spy as a man and the lover as a woman of a Frenchman, Gallimard, a diplomat (Bernstein 1986). The relationship lasted twenty years, and Shi Peipu even pretended to be the mother of a child by Gallimard. "She" also pretended to be too shy to undress completely. As "Butterfly," Shi Peipu portrayed a fantasy Oriental woman who made the lover a "real man" (Kondo 1990b). In Gallimard's words, the fantasy was "of slender women in chong sams and kimonos who die for the love of unworthy foreign devils. Who are born and raised to be perfect women. Who take whatever punishment we give them, and bounce back, strengthened by love, unconditionally" (Hwang 1989, 91). When the fantasy woman betrayed him by turning out to be the more powerful "real man," Gallimard assumed the role of Butterfly and, dressed in a geisha's robes, killed himself: "because 'man' and 'woman' are oppositionally defined terms, reversals . . . are possible" (Kondo 1990b, 18).[13]

But despite the ease with which gender boundaries can be traversed in work, in social relationships, and in cultural productions, gender statuses remain. Transvestites and transsexuals do not challenge the social construction of gender. Their goal is to be feminine women and masculine men (Kando 1973). Those who do not want to change their anatomy but do want to change their gender behavior fare less well in establishing their social identity. The women Holly Devor called "gender blenders" wore their hair short, dressed in unisex pants, shirts, and comfortable shoes, and did not wear jewelry or makeup. They described their everyday dress as women's clothing: One said, "I wore jeans all the time, but I didn't wear men's clothes" (Devor 1989, 100). Their gender identity was women, but because they refused to "do femininity," they were constantly taken for men (1987; 1989, 107–42). Devor said of them: "The most common area of complaint was with public washrooms. They repeatedly spoke of the humiliation of being challenged or ejected from women's washrooms. Similarly, they found public change rooms to be dangerous territory and the buying of undergarments to be a difficult feat to accomplish" (1987, 29). In an ultimate ironic twist, some of these women said "they would feel like transvestites if they were to wear dresses, and two women said that they had been called transvestites when they had done so" (31). They resolved the ambiguity of their gender status by identifying as women in private and passing as men in public to avoid harassment on the street, to get men's jobs, and, if they were lesbians, to make it easier to display affection publicly with their lovers (Devor 1989, 107–42). Sometimes they even used men's bathrooms. When they had gender-neutral names, like Leslie, they could avoid the bureaucratic hassles that arose when they had to present their passports or other proof of identity, but because most had names associated with women, their appearance and their cards of identity were not conventionally congruent, and their gender status was in constant jeopardy.[14] When they could, they found it easier to pass as men than to try to change the stereotyped notions of what women should look like.

Paradoxically, then, bending gender rules and passing between genders does not erode but rather preserves gender boundaries. In societies with only two genders, the gender dichotomy is not disturbed by transvestites, because others feel that a transvestite is only transitorily ambiguous—is "really a man or woman underneath." After sex-change surgery, transsexuals end up in a conventional gender status—a "man" or a "woman" with the appropriate genitals (Eichler 1989). When women dress as men for business reasons, they are indicating that in that situation, they want to be treated the way men are treated; when they dress as women, they want to be treated as women:

> By their male dress, female entrepreneurs signal their desire to suspend the expectations of accepted feminine conduct without losing respect and reputation. By wearing what is "unattractive" they signify that they are not intending to display their physical charms while engaging in public activity. Their loud, aggressive banter contrasts with the modest demeanor that attracts men. . . . Overt signalling of a suspension of the rules preserves normal conduct from eroding expectations. (Rugh 1986, 131)

For Individuals, Gender Means Sameness

Although the possible combinations of genitalia, body shapes, clothing, mannerisms, sexuality, and roles could produce infinite varieties in human beings, the social institution of gender depends on the production and maintenance of a limited number of gender statuses and of making the members of these statuses similar to each other. Individuals are born sexed but not gendered, and they have to be taught to be masculine or feminine.[15] As Simone de Beauvoir said: "One is not born, but rather becomes, a woman . . . ; it is civilization as a whole that produces this creature . . . which is described as feminine" (1953, 267).

Children learn to walk, talk, and gesture the way their social group says girls and boys should. Ray Birdwhistell, in his analysis of body motion as human communication, calls these learned gender displays *tertiary sex characteristics* and argues that they are needed to distinguish genders because humans are a weakly dimorphic species—their only sex markers are genitalia (1970, 39–46). Clothing, paradoxically, often hides the sex but displays the gender.

In early childhood, humans develop gendered personality structures and sexual orientations through their interactions with parents of the same and opposite gender. As adolescents, they conduct their sexual behavior according to gendered scripts. Schools, parents, peers, and the mass media guide young people into gendered work and family roles. As adults, they take on a gendered social status in their society's stratification system. Gender is thus both ascribed and achieved (West and Zimmerman 1987).

The achievement of gender was most dramatically revealed in a case of an accidental transsexual—a baby boy whose penis was destroyed in the course of a botched circumcision when he was seven months old (Money and Ehrhardt 1972, 118–23). The child's sex category was changed to "female," and a vagina was surgically constructed when the child was seventeen months old. The parents were advised that they could successfully raise the child, one of identical twins, as a girl. Physicians assured them that the child was too young to have formed a gender identity. Children's sense of which gender they belong to usually develops around the age of three, at the time that they start to group objects and recognize that the people around them also fit into categories—big, little; pink-skinned, brown-skinned; boys, girls. Three has also been the age when children's appearance is ritually gendered, usually by cutting a boy's hair or dressing him in distinctively masculine clothing. In Victorian times, English boys wore dresses up to the age of three, when they were put into short pants (Garber 1992, 1–2).

The parents of the accidental transsexual bent over backward to feminize the child—and succeeded. Frilly dresses, hair ribbons, and jewelry created a pride in looks, neatness, and "daintiness." More significant, the child's dominance was also feminized:

> The girl had many tomboyish traits, such as abundant physical energy, a high level of activity, stubbornness, and being often the dominant one in a girls' group. Her mother tried to modify her tomboyishness: "I teach her to be more polite and quiet. I always wanted those virtues. I never did manage, but I'm going to try to manage them to—my daughter—to be more quiet and lady-like." From the beginning the girl had been the dominant twin. By the age of three, her dominance over her brother was, as her mother described it, that of a mother hen. The boy in turn took up for his sister, if anyone threatened her. (Money and Ehrhardt 1972, 122)

[. . .]

Many cultures go beyond clothing, gestures, and demeanor in gendering children. They inscribe gender directly into bodies. In traditional Chinese society, mothers bound their daughters' feet into three-inch stumps to enhance their sexual attractiveness. Jewish fathers circumcise their infant sons to show their covenant with God. Women in African societies remove the clitoris of prepubescent girls, scrape their labia, and make the lips grow together to preserve their chastity and ensure their marriageability. In Western societies, women augment their breast size with silicone and reconstruct their faces with cosmetic surgery to conform to cultural ideals of feminine beauty. Hanna Papanek (1990) notes that these practices reinforce the sense of superiority or inferiority in the adults who carry them out as well as in the children on whom they are done: The genitals of Jewish fathers and sons are physical and psychological evidence of their common dominant religious and familial status; the genitals of African mothers and daughters are physical and psychological evidence of their joint subordination.[16]

[. . .]

For human beings there is no essential femaleness or maleness, femininity or masculinity, womanhood or manhood, but once gender is ascribed, the social order constructs and holds individuals to strongly gendered norms and expectations. Individuals may vary on many of the components of gender and may shift genders temporarily or permanently, but they must fit into the limited number of gender statuses their society recognizes. In the process, they re-create their society's version of women and men: "If we do gender appropriately, we simultaneously sustain, reproduce, and render legitimate the institutional arrangements. . . . If we fail to do gender appropriately, we as individuals—not the institutional arrangements—may be called to account (for our character, motives, and predispositions)" (West and Zimmerman 1987, 146).

> The gendered practices of everyday life reproduce a society's view of how women and men should act (Bourdieu [1980] 1990). Gendered social arrangements are justified by religion and cultural productions and backed by law, but the most powerful means of sustaining the moral hegemony of the dominant gender ideology is that the process is made invisible; any possible alternatives are virtually unthinkable.[17] (Foucault 1972; Gramsci 1971)

For Society, Gender Means Difference

The pervasiveness of gender as a way of structuring social life demands that gender statuses be clearly differentiated. Varied talents, sexual preferences, identities, personalities, interests, and ways of interacting fragment the individual's bodily and social experiences. Nonetheless, these are organized in Western cultures into two and only two socially and legally recognized gender statuses, "man" and "woman."[18] In the social construction of gender, it does not matter what men and actually do; it does not even matter if they do exactly the same thing. The social institution of gender insists only that what they do is *perceived* as different.

If men and women are doing the same tasks, they are usually spatially segregated to maintain gender separation, and often the tasks are given different job titles as well, such as executive secretary and administrative assistant (Reskin 1988). If the differences between women and men begin to blur, society's "sameness taboo" goes into action (Rubin 1975, 178). At a rock and roll dance at West Point in 1976, the year women were admitted to the prestigious military academy for the first time, the school's administrators "were reportedly perturbed by the sight of mirror-image couples dancing in short hair and dress gray trousers," and a rule was established that women cadets could dance at these events only if they wore skirts (Barkalow and Raab 1990, 53).[19] Women recruits in the U.S. Marine Corps are required to wear makeup—at a minimum, lipstick and eye shadow—and they have to take classes in makeup, hair care, poise, and etiquette. This feminization is part of a deliberate policy of making them clearly distinguishable from men Marines. Christine Williams quotes a twenty-five-year-old woman drill instructor as saying: "A lot of the recruits who come here don't wear makeup; they're tomboyish or athletic. A lot of them have the preconceived idea that going into the military means they can still be a tomboy. They don't realize that you are a *Woman* Marine" (1989, 76–77).[20]

[. . .]

Gender Ranking

Most societies rank genders according to prestige and power and construct them to be unequal, so that moving from one to another also means moving up or down the social scale. Among some North American Indian cultures, the hierarchy was male men, male women, female men, female women. Women produced significant durable goods (basketry, textiles, pottery, decorated leather goods), which could be traded. Women also controlled what they produced and any profit or wealth they earned. Since women's occupational realm could lead to prosperity and prestige, it was fair game for young men—but only if they became women in gender status. Similarly, women in other societies who amassed a great deal of wealth were allowed to become men—"manly hearts." According to Harriet Whitehead (1981):

> Both reactions reveal an unwillingness or inability to distinguish the sources of prestige—wealth, skill, personal efficacy (among other things)—from masculinity. Rather there is the innuendo that if a person performing female tasks can attain excellence, prosperity, or social power, it must be because that person is, at some level, a man. . . . A woman who could succeed at doing the things men did was honored as a man would be. . . . What seems to have been more disturbing to the culture—which means, for all intents and purposes, to the men—was the possibility that women, within their own department, might be onto a good thing. It was into this unsettling breach that the berdache institution was hurled. In their social aspect, women were complimented by the berdache's imitation. In their anatomic aspect, they were subtly insulted by his vaunted superiority. (108)

In American society, men-to-women transsexuals tend to earn less after surgery if they change occupations; women-to-men transsexuals tend to increase their income (Bolin 1988, 153–60; Brody 1979). Men who go into women's fields, like nursing, have less prestige than women who go into men's fields, like physics. Janice Raymond, a radical feminist, feels that transsexual men-to-women have advantages over female women because they were not socialized to be subordinate or oppressed throughout life. She says:

> We know that we are women who are born with female chromosomes and anatomy, and that whether or not we were socialized to be so-called normal women, patriarchy has treated and will treat us like women. Transsexuals have not had this same history. No man can have the history of being born and located in this culture as a woman. He can have the history of *wishing* to be a woman and of *acting* like a woman, but this gender experience is that of a transsexual, not of a woman. Surgery may confer the artifacts of outward and inward female organs but it cannot confer the history of being born a woman in this society. (1979, 114)

[. . .]

For one transsexual man-to-woman, however, the experience of living as a woman changed his/her whole personality. As James, Morris had been a soldier, foreign correspondent, and mountain climber; as Jan, Morris is a successful travel writer. But socially, James was far superior to Jan, and so Jan developed the "learned helplessness" that is supposed to characterize women in Western society:

> We are told that the social gap between the sexes is narrowing, but I can only report that having, in the second half of the twentieth century, experienced life in both roles, there seems to me no aspect of existence, no moment of the day, no contact, no arrangement, no response, which is not different for men and for women. The very tone of voice in which I was now addressed, the very posture of the person next in the queue, the very feel in the air when I entered a room or sat at a restaurant table, constantly emphasized my change of status.
>
> And if other's responses shifted, so did my own. The more I was treated as woman, the more woman I became. I adapted willy-nilly. If I was assumed to be incompetent at reversing cars, or opening bottles, oddly incompetent I found myself becoming. If a case was thought too heavy for me, inexplicably I found it so myself. . . . Women treated me with a frankness which, while it was one of the happiest discoveries of my metamorphosis, did imply membership of a camp, a faction, or at least a school of thought; so I found myself gravitating always towards the female, whether in sharing a railway compartment or supporting a political cause. Men treated me more and more as junior, . . . and so, addressed every day of my life as an inferior, involuntarily, month by month I accepted the condition. I discovered that even now men prefer women to be less informed, less able, less talkative, and certainly less self-centered than they are themselves; so I generally obliged them. (1975, 165–66)[21]

Components of Gender

By now, it should be clear that gender is not a unitary essence but has many components as a social institution and as an individual status.[22]

As a social institution, gender is composed of:

Gender statuses, the socially recognized genders in a society and the norms and expectations for their enactment behaviorally, gesturally, linguistically, emotionally, and physically. How gender statuses are evaluated depends on historical development in any particular society.

Gendered division of labor, the assignment of productive and domestic work to members of different gender statuses. The work assigned to those of different gender statuses strengthens the society's evaluation of those statuses—the higher the status, the more prestigious and valued the work and the greater its rewards.

Gendered kinship, the family rights and responsibilities for each gender status. Kinship statuses reflect and reinforce the prestige and power differences of the different genders.

Gendered sexual scripts, the normative patterns of sexual desire and sexual behavior, as prescribed for the different gender statuses. Members of the dominant gender have more sexual prerogatives; members of a subordinate gender may be sexually exploited.

Gendered personalities, the combinations of traits patterned by gender norms of how members of different gender statuses are supposed to feel and behave. Social expectations of others in face-to-face interaction constantly bolster these norms.

Gendered social control, the formal and informal approval and reward of conforming behavior and the stigmatization, social isolation, punishment, and medical treatment of nonconforming behavior.

Gender ideology, the justification of gender statuses, particularly, their differential evaluation. The dominant ideology tends to suppress criticism by making these evaluations seem natural.

Gender imagery, the cultural representations of gender and embodiment of gender in symbolic language and artistic productions that reproduce and legitimate gender statuses. Culture is one of the main supports of the dominant gender ideology.

For an individual, gender is composed of:

Sex category to which the infant is assigned at birth based on appearance of genitalia. With prenatal testing and sex-typing, categorization is prenatal. Sex category may be changed later through surgery or reinspection of ambiguous genitalia.

Gender identity, the individual's sense of gendered self as a worker and family member.

Gendered marital and procreative status, fulfillment or nonfulfillment of allowed or disallowed mating, impregnation, childbearing, kinship roles.

Gendered sexual orientation, socially and individually patterned sexual desires, feelings, practices, and identification.

Gendered personality, internalized patterns of socially normative emotions as organized by family structure and parenting.

Gendered processes, the social practices of learning, being taught, picking up cues, enacting behavior already learned to be gender-appropriate (or inappropriate, if rebelling, testing), developing a gender identity, "doing gender" as a member of a gender status in relationships with gendered others, acting deferent or dominant.

Gender beliefs, incorporation of or resistance to gender ideology.

Gender display, presentation of self as a certain kind of gendered person through dress, cosmetics, adornments, and permanent and reversible body markers.

For an individual, all the social components are supposed to be consistent and congruent with perceived physiology. The actual combination of genes and genitalia, prenatal, adolescent, and adult hormonal input, and procreative capacity may or may not be congruous with each other and with sex category assignment, gender identity, gendered sexual orientation and procreative status, gender display, personality, and work and family roles. At any one time, an individual's identity is a combination of the major ascribed statuses of gender, race, ethnicity, religion, and social class, and the individual's achieved statuses, such as education level, occupation or profession, marital status, parenthood, prestige, authority, and wealth. The ascribed statuses substantially limit or create opportunities for individual achievements and also diminish or enhance the luster of those achievements.

Gender as Process, Stratification, and Structure

A a social institution, gender is a process of creating distinguishable social statuses for the assignment of rights and responsibilities. As part of a stratification system that ranks these statuses unequally, gender is a major building block in the social structures built on these unequal statuses.

As a *process,* gender creates the social differences that define "woman" and "man." In social interaction throughout their lives, individuals learn what is expected, see what is expected, act and react in expected ways, and thus simultaneously construct and maintain the gender order: "The very injunction to be a given gender takes place through discursive routes: to be a good mother, to be a heterosexually desirable object, to be a fit worker, in sum, to signify a multiplicity of guarantees in response to a variety of different demands all at once" (Butler 1990, 145). Members of a social group neither make up gender as they go along nor exactly replicate in rote fashion what was done before. In almost every encounter, human beings produce gender, behaving in the ways they learned were appropriate for their gender status, or resisting or rebelling against these norms. Resistance and rebellion have altered gender norms, but so far they have rarely eroded the statuses.

Gendered patterns of interaction acquire additional layers of gendered sexuality, parenting, and work behaviors in childhood, adolescence, and adulthood. Gendered norms and expectations are enforced through informal sanctions of gender-inappropriate behavior by peers and by formal punishment or threat of punishment by those in authority should behavior deviate too far from socially imposed standards for women and men.

Everyday gendered interactions build gender into the family, the work process, and other organizations and institutions, which in turn reinforce gender expectations for individuals.[23] Because gender is a process, there is room not only for modification and variation by individuals and small groups but also for institutionalized change (Scott 1988, 7).

As part of a *stratification* system, gender ranks men above women of the same race and class. Women and men could be different but equal. In practice, the process of creating difference depends to a great extent on differential evaluation. As Nancy Jay (1981) says: "That which is defined, separated out, isolated from all else is A and pure. Not-A is necessarily impure, a random catchall, to which nothing is external except A and the principle of order that separates it from Not-A" (45). From the individual's point of view, whichever gender is A, the other is Not-A; gender boundaries tell the individual who is like him or her, and all the rest are unlike. From society's point of view, however, one gender is usually the touchstone, the normal, the dominant, and the other is different, deviant, and subordinate. In Western society, "man" is A, "wo-man" is Not-A. (Consider what a society would be like where woman was A and man Not-A.)

The further dichotomization by race and class constructs the gradations of a heterogeneous society's stratification scheme. Thus, in the United States, white is A, African American is Not-A; middle class is A, working class is Not-A, and "African-American women occupy a position whereby the inferior half of a series of these dichotomies converge" (Collins 1990, 70). The dominant categories are the hegemonic ideals, taken so for granted as the way things should be that white is not ordinarily thought of as a race, middle class as a class, or men as a gender. The characteristics of these categories define the Other as that which lacks the valuable qualities the dominants exhibit.

In a gender-stratified society, what men do is usually valued more highly than what women do because men do it, even when their activities are very similar or the same. In different regions of southern India, for example, harvesting rice is men's work, shared work, or women's work: "Wherever a task is done by women it is considered easy, and where it is done by [men] it is considered difficult" (Mencher 1988, 104). A gathering and hunting society's survival usually depends on the nuts, grubs, and small animals brought in by the women's foraging trips, but when the men's hunt is successful, it is the occasion for a celebration. Conversely, because they are the superior group, white men do not have to do the "dirty work," such as housework; the most inferior group does it, usually poor women of color (Palmer 1989).

Freudian psychoanalytic theory claims that boys must reject their mothers and deny the feminine in themselves in order to become men: "For boys the major goal is the achievement of personal masculine identification with their father and sense of secure masculine self, achieved through superego formation and disparagement of women" (Chodorow 1978, 165). Masculinity may be the outcome of boys' intrapsychic struggles to separate their identity from that of their mothers, but the proofs of masculinity are culturally shaped and usually ritualistic and symbolic (Gilmore 1990).

The Marxist feminist explanation for gender inequality is that by demeaning women's abilities and keeping them from learning valuable technological skills, bosses preserve them as a cheap and exploitable reserve army of labor. Unionized men who could be easily replaced by women collude in this process because it allows them to monopolize the better paid, more interesting, and more autonomous jobs: "Two factors emerge as helping men maintain their separation from women and their control of technological occupations. One is the active gendering of jobs and people. The second is the continual creation of sub-divisions in the work processes, and levels in work hierarchies, into which men can move in order to keep their distance from women" (Cockburn 1985, 13).

Societies vary in the extent of the inequality in social status of their women and men members, but where there is inequality, the status "woman" (and its attendant behavior and role allocations) is usually held in lesser esteem than the status "man." Since gender is also intertwined with a society's other constructed statuses of differential evaluation—race, religion, occupation, class, country of origin, and so on—men and women members of the favored groups command more power, more prestige, and more property than the members of the disfavored groups. Within many social groups, however, men are advantaged over women. The more economic resources, such as education and job opportunities, are available to a group, the more they tend to be monopolized by men. In poorer groups that have few resources (such as working-class African Americans in the United States), women and men are more nearly equal, and the women may even outstrip the men in education and occupational status (Almquist 1987).

As a *structure,* gender divides work in the home and in economic production, legitimates those in authority, and organizes sexuality and emotional life (Connell 1987, 91–142). As primary parents, women significantly influence children's psychological development and emotional attachments, in the process reproducing gender. Emergent sexuality is shaped by heterosexual, homosexual, bisexual, and sadomasochistic patterns that are gendered—different for girls and boys, and for women and men—so that sexual statuses reflect gender statuses.

When gender is a major component of structured inequality, the devalued genders have less power, prestige, and economic rewards than the valued genders. In countries that discourage gender discrimination, many major roles are still gendered; women still do most of the domestic labor and child rearing, even while doing full-time paid work; women and men are segregated on the job and each does work considered "appropriate"; women's work is usually paid less than men's work. Men dominate the positions of authority and leadership in government, the military, and the law; cultural productions, religions, and sports reflect men's interests.

In societies that create the greatest gender difference, as Saudi Arabia, women are kept out of sight behind walls or veils, have no civil rights, and often create a cultural and emotional world of their own (Bernard 1981). But even in societies with less rigid gender boundaries, women and men spend much of their time with people of their own gender because of the way work and family are organized. This spatial separation of women and men reinforces gendered differentness, identity, and ways of thinking and behaving (Coser 1986).

Gender inequality—the devaluation of "women" and the social domination of "men"—has social functions and a social history. It is not the result of sex, procreation, physiology, anatomy, hormones, or genetic predispositions. It is produced and maintained by identifiable social processes and built into the general social structure and individual identities deliberately and purposefully. The social order as we know it in Western societies is organized around racial ethnic, class, and gender inequality. I contend, therefore, that the continuing purpose of gender as a modern social institution is to construct women as a group to be the subordinates of men as a group. The life of everyone placed in the status "woman" is "night to his day—that has forever been the fantasy. Black to his white. Shut out of his system's space, she is the repressed that ensures the system's functioning" (Cixous and Clement [1975] 1986, 67).

The Paradox of Human Nature

To say that sex, sexuality, and gender are all socially constructed is not to minimize their social power. These categorical imperatives govern our lives in the most profound and pervasive ways, through the social experiences and social practices of what Dorothy Smith calls the "everyday/everynight world" (1990, 31–57). The paradox of human nature is that it is *always* a manifestation of cultural meanings, social relationships, and power politics; "not biology, but culture, becomes destiny" (Butler 1990, 8). Gendered people emerge not from physiology or sexual orientation but from the exigencies of the social order, mostly, from the need for a reliable division of the work of food production and the social (not physical) reproduction of new members. The moral imperatives of religion and cultural representations guard the boundary lines among genders and ensure that what is demanded, what is permitted, and what is tabooed for the people in each gender is well known and followed by most (Davies 1982). Political power, control of scarce resources, and, if necessary, violence uphold the gendered social order in the face of resistance and rebellion. Most people, however, voluntarily go along with their society's prescriptions for those of their gender status, because the norms and expectations get built into their sense of worth and identity as a certain kind of human being, and because they believe their society's way is the natural way. These beliefs emerge from the imagery that pervades the way we think, the way we see and hear and speak, the way we fantasize, and the way we feel.

There is no core or bedrock human nature below these endlessly looping processes of the social production of sex and gender, self and other, identity and psyche, each of which is a "complex cultural construction" (Butler 1990, 36). *For humans, the social is the natural.* Therefore, "in its feminist senses, gender cannot mean simply the cultural appropriation of biological sexual difference. Sexual difference is itself a fundamental— and scientifically contested—construction. Both 'sex' and 'gender' are woven of multiple, asymmetrical strands of difference, charged with multifaceted dramatic narratives of domination and struggle" (Haraway 1990, 40).

Notes

1. Gender is, in Erving Goffman's words, an aspect of *Felicity's Condition*: "any arrangement which leads us to judge an individual's . . . acts not to be a manifestation of strangeness. Behind Felicity's Condition is our sense of what it is to be sane" (1983, 27). Also see Bem 1993; Frye 1983, 17–40; Goffman 1977.

2. In cases of ambiguity in countries with modern medicine, surgery is usually performed to make the genitalia more clearly male or female.

3. See J. Butler 1990 for an analysis of how doing gender *is* gender identity.

4. Douglas 1973; MacCormack 1980; Ortner 1974; Ortner and Whitehead 1981; Yanagisako and Collier 1987. On the social construction of childhood, see Ariès 1962; Zelizer 1985.

5. On the hijras of India, see Nanda 1990; on the xaniths of Oman, Wikan 1982, 168–86; on the American Indian berdaches, W. L. Williams 1986. Other societies that have similar institutionalized third-gender men are the Koniag of Alaska, the Tanala of Madagascar, the Mesakin of Nuba, and the Chukchee of Siberia (Wikan 1982, 170).

6. Durova 1989; Freeman and Bond 1992; Wheelwright 1989.

7. Gender segregation of work in popular music still has not changed very much, according to Groce and Cooper 1989, despite considerable androgyny in some very popular figures. See Garber 1992 on the androgyny. She discusses Tipton on pp. 67–70.

8. In the nineteenth century, not only did these women get men's wages, but they also "had male privileges and could do all manner of things other women could not: open a bank account, write checks, own property, go anywhere unaccompanied, vote in elections" (Faderman 1991, 44).

9. When unisex clothing and men wearing long hair came into vogue in the United States in the mid-1960s, beards and mustaches for men also came into style again as gender identifications.

10. For other accounts of women being treated as men in Islamic countries, as well as accounts of women and men cross-dressing in these countries, see Garber 1992, 304–52.

11. Dollimore 1986; Garber 1992, 32–40; Greenblatt 1987, 66–93; Howard 1988. For Renaissance accounts of sexual relations with women and men of ambigious sex, see Laqueur 1990, 134–39. For modern accounts of women passing as men that other women find sexually attractive, see Devor 1989, 136–37; Wheelwright 1989, 53–59.

12. Females who passed as men soldiers had to "do masculinity," not just dress in a uniform (Wheelwright, 1989, 50–78). On the triple entendres and gender resonances of Rosalind-type characters, see Garber 1992, 71–77.

13. Also see Garber 1992, 234–66.

14. Bolin describes how many documents have to be changed by transsexuals to provide a legitimizing "paper trail" (1988, 145–47). Note that only members of the same social group know which names are women's and which men's in their culture, but many documents list "sex."

15. For an account of how a potential man-to-woman transsexual learned to be feminine, see Garfinkel 1967, 116–85, 285–88. For a gloss on this account that points out how, throughout his encounters with Agnes, Garfinkel failed to see how he himself was constructing his own masculinity, see Rogers 1992.

16. Paige and Paige (1981, 147–49) argue that circumcision ceremonies indicate a father's loyalty to his lineage elders—"visible public evidence that the head of a family unit of their lineage is willing to trust others with his and his family's most valuable political asset, his son's penis" (147). On female circumcision, see El Dareer 1982; Lightfoot-Klein 1989; van der Kwaak 1992; Walker 1992. There is a form of female circumcision that removes only the prepuce of the clitoris and is similar to male circumcision, but most forms of female circumcision are far more extensive, mutilating, and spiritually and psychologically shocking than the usual form of male circumcision. However, among the Australian aborigines, boys' penises are slit and kept open, so that they urinate and bleed the way women do (Bettelheim 1962, 165–206).

17. The concepts of moral hegemony, the effects of everyday activities (praxis) on thought and personality, and the necessity of consciousness of these processes before political change can occur are all based on Marx's analysis of class relations.

18. Other societies recognize more than two categories, but usually no more than three or four (Jacobs and Roberts 1989).

19. Carol Barkalow's book has a photograph of eleven first-year West Pointers in a math class, who are dressed in regulation pants, shirts, and sweaters, with short haircuts. The caption challenges the reader to locate the only woman in the room.

20. The taboo on males and females looking alike reflects the U.S. military's homophobia (Bérubé 1989). If you can't tell those with a penis from those with a vagina, how are you going to determine whether their sexual interest is heterosexual or homosexual unless you watch them having sexual relations?

21. See Bolin 1988, 149–50, for transsexual men-to-women's discovery of the dangers of rape and sexual harassment. Devor's "gender blenders" went in the opposite direction. Because they found that it was an advantage to be taken for men, they did not deliberately cross-dress, but they did not feminize themselves either (1989, 126–40).

22. See West and Zimmerman 1987 for a similar set of gender components.

23. On the "logic of practice," or how the experience of gender is embedded in the norms of everyday interaction and the structure of formal organizations, see Acker 1990; Bourdieu [1980] 1990; Connell 1987; Smith 1987.

CHAPTER 3

Culture, Gender, and Math

Luigi Guiso, Ferdinando Monte, Paola Sapienza, Luigi Zingales

The existence,[1] degree,[2] and origin[3,4] of a gender gap (difference between girls' and boys' scores) in mathematics are highly debated. Biologically based explanations for the gap rely on evidence that men perform better in spatial tests, whereas women do better in verbal recall ones.[1,5,6] However, the performance differences are small, and their link with math test performance is tenuous.[7] By contrast, social conditioning and gender-biased environments can have very large effects on test performance.[8]

To assess the relative importance of biological and cultural explanations, we studied gender differences in test performance across countries.[9] Cultural inequalities range widely across countries,[10] whereas results from cognitive tests do not.[6] We used data from the 2003 Programme for International Student Assessment (PISA) that reports on 276,165 15-year old students from 40 countries who took identical tests in mathematics and reading.[11,12] The tests were designed by the Organization for Economic Co-operation and Development (OECD) to be free of cultural biases. They are sufficiently challenging that only 0.6% of the U.S. students tested perform at the 99th percentile of the world distribution.

Girls' math scores average 10.5 lower than those of boys (2% less than the mean average score for boys), but the results vary by country (see figure 3.1): in Turkey, -22.6, whereas, in Iceland, 14.5. A similar variation exists in the proportion of girls over boys who score above 95%, or 99% of the country-level distribution.[13]

The gender gap is reversed in reading. On average, girls have reading scores that are 32.7 higher than those of boys (6.6% higher than the mean average score for boys), in Turkey, 25.1 higher and in Iceland, 61.0 higher (figure 3.1). The effect is even stronger in the right tail of the distribution. In spite of the difference in levels, the gender gap in reading exhibits a variation across countries similar to the gender gap in math. Where girls enjoy the strongest advantage in reading with respect to boys, they exhibit the smallest disadvantage (sometimes even an advantage) in math. The correlation between the average gender gaps in mathematics and reading across countries is 0.59.[14]

To explore the cultural inputs to these results, we classified countries according to several measures of gender equality. 1) The World Economic Forum's Gender Gap

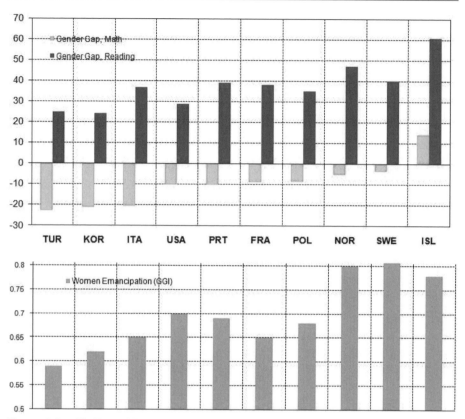

Figure 3.1.   Math and Reading Gender Gaps.

Note: In more gender-equal cultures, the math gender gap disappears and the reading gender gap becomes larger. **(Top)** Gender gaps in mathematics (light) and reading (dark) are calculated as the difference between the average girls' score and the average boys' score. A subset of countries is shown here (see SOM for complete data set and calculations). In many countries, on average, girls perform more poorly than boys in mathematics. In all countries, girls perform better than boys in reading. The gender gap in mathematics and reading correlates with country measures of gender status within the culture, one of which measures is the GGI **(bottom)**. Larger values of GGI point to a better average position of women in society. Besides USA, the countries are abbreviated as their first three letters, except for PRT, Portugal, and ISL, Iceland.

Index (GGI)[10] reflects economic and political opportunities, education, and well-being for women (see figure 3.1). 2) From the World Values Surveys (WVSs),[15] we constructed an index of cultural attitudes toward women based on the average level of disagreement to such statements as: "When jobs are scarce, men should have more right to a job than women." 3) The rate of female economic activity reflects the percentage of women age 15 and older who supply, or are available to supply, labor for the production of goods and services. 4) The political empowerment index computed by the World Economic Forum[8] measures women's political participation, which is less dependent on math skills than labor force participation. These four measures are highly correlated.[16]

We find a positive correlation between gender equality and gender gap in mathematics. If Turkey, a low gender-equality country (GGI=0.59), were characterized by the degree of gender equality manifested in Sweden (GGI=0.81), our statistical model suggests that the mean score performance in mathematics of girls relative to boys would increase by 23 points, which would eliminate the Turkish gender gap in math (See table 3.1). In more gender-equal countries, such as Norway and Sweden, the math gender gap disappears. Similar results are obtained when we use the other indicators of women's roles in society. These results are true not only at the mean level, but also in the tail of the distribution.[17] In Iceland, the ratio of girls to boys who score above the 99th percentile of the country distribution in math scores is 1.17.

There are many unobserved reasons why countries may differ in a way that affects the math gender gap. Without appropriate controls, we run the risk of capturing a spurious correlation between the unobserved factors and our measures of gender equality. We reran our regression at the student level, inserting a dummy variable for each country, to control for unobserved heterogeneity.[18] The interaction between gender and GGI index remains statistically significant at the 1% confidence level in a two-tailed t test, which suggests that the correlation between gender equality and girls' math scores is not driven by unobserved heterogeneity. This interaction between gender gap and GGI remains significant even when we insert an interaction between gender and log of GDP per capita, which suggests that the improvement in math scores is not just related to economic development, but to the improvement of the role of women in society.

To investigate whether the disappearance of math gender gap in some countries translates into an overall improvement of girls or is simply limited to mathematics scores, we correlated reading performance differences with measures of women's equality (table 3.1). In countries where women are more emancipated, girls' comparative advantage in reading widens. Comparing Turkey (GGI=0.59) and Sweden (GGI=0.81), we see an increase in the mean score performance of girls relative to boys in reading by 18 points, which almost doubles Turkey's reading gap in favor of girls.

To verify that these results are not driven by biological differences across countries, we analyzed whether they persist in populations that have a similar or identical evolutionary history. To assess history, we used a genetic distance measure[19,20] based on the frequency of each allele across DNA polymorphisms.

According to this measure, there are 13 European countries with genetic distance equal to zero and 26 European countries with genetic distance less than 100.[21] When we restrict the regression of the table (above) to either one of these two groups, our findings are substantially unchanged.[22]

These results suggest that the gender gap in math, although it historically favors boys, disappears in more gender-equal societies. The same cannot be said for how boys score in mathematics compared with how boys score in readings. Boys' scores are always higher in mathematics than in reading, and although the difference between boys' math and boys' reading scores varies across countries, it is not correlated with the GGI index or with any of the other three measures of gender equality.[23] Hence, in countries with a higher GGI index, girls close the gender gap by becoming better in both math and reading, not by closing the math gap alone. The gender gap in reading,

Table 3.1. Differences in Test Scores Correlated with Indicators of Gender Inequality

	LHS: Gender Gap Test Score, Math				LHS: Gender Gap in Test Score, Reading			
Women Emancipation (GGI)	105.49*** (26.92)				83.56*** (30.43)			
AVG. WVS indicators		13.21* (7.06)				16.39* (8.46)		
Female economic activity rate			0.45*** (0.14)				0.34** (0.15)	
Gross tertiary enrolment, female/male ratio				8.74* (4.65)				13.61*** (4.57)
Log GDP per capita, 2003	−6.56*** (2.40)	1.09 (2.26)	−3.12 (1.93)	−1.35 (2.01)	−2.23 (2.71)	0.52 (2.71)	−0.56 (2.15)	0.36 (1.98)
Constant	−19.62 (20.01)	−57.16** (23.27)	−2.75 (17.72)	−7.84 (19.80)	−3.02 (22.62)	−16.09 (27.90)	21.49 (19.80)	12.81 (19.48)
Observations	37	32	39	38	37	32	39	38
R-squared	0.32	0.15	0.23	0.10	0.20	0.14	0.12	0.21

Culture affects the gap. More gender-equal cultures are associated with reducing the negative gap in math and further enlarging the positive gap in reading in favor of women. Test scores are positively correlated with indicators of gender equality in society (GGI, WVSs, see text). Economic conditions are accounted for by per capita Gross Domestic Product (GDP). The correlation persists among high achievers on both tests. The constant is where the regression line intercepts the y axis, representing the amount the dependent y (gender gap) will be when all the independent variables are set to 0. LHS, left-hand side variable in the least-squares regression anaylsis. *$P<0.05$;**$P<0.01$.

which favors girls and is apparent in all countries, thus expands in more gender-equal societies. Similarly, although the gender gaps in all math subfields decrease in societies with more gender equality, the difference between the gender gap in geometry (where the boys' advantage relative to the girls' is the biggest) and arithmetic (where the boys' advantage relative to the girls' is the smallest) does not.[24]

This evidence suggests that intra-gender performance differences in reading versus mathematics and in arithmetic versus geometry are not eliminated in a more gender-equal culture. By contrast, girls' underperformance in math relative to boys is eliminated in more gender-equal cultures. In more gender-equal societies, girls perform as well as boys in mathematics and much better than them in reading. These findings shed some light on recent trends in girls' educational achievements in the United States, where the math gender gap has been closing over time.(2)

Notes

1. L. V. Hedges, A. Nowell, *Science* 269 (1995): 41.

2. C. Goldin, L. F. Katz, I. Kuziemko. *Journal of Economic Perspectives* 20, 133 (2006).

3. C. P. Benbow, J. C. Stanley, *Science* 210 (1980): 1262.

4. "The Science of Gender and Science: Pinker vs. Spelke, a Debate." *Edge* 160 (May 10, 2005). www.edge.org/documents/archive/edge160.html#d.

5. S. Baron-Cohen, *The Essential Difference: Men, Women, and the Extreme Male Brain.* London: Allen Lane, 2003.

6. D. Kimura, *Sex and Cognition.* Cambridge, MA: MIT Press, 1999.

7. E. S. Spelke. *American Psychologist* 60 (2005): 950.

8. D. Halpem, J. Wai, A. Saw. Pp. 48–72 in *Gender Differences in Mathematics* edited by A. M. Gallagher and J. C. Kaufman. New York: Cambridge University Press, 2005.

9. Materials and methods are available as supporting material on *Science* Online.

10. R. Hausmann, L. D. Tyson, S. Zahidi. *The Global Gender Gap Report.* Geneva, Switzerland: World Economic Forum, 2006.

11. OECD, Programme for International Student Assessment (PISA), 2nd Assessment (OECD, Paris, 2003).

12. PISA includes originally 41 countries; we drop Liechtenstein because it contains only 165 observations, which makes problematic any calculation of the tail of the distribution. All other countries have at least 639 observations.

13. Supporting online material www.sciencemag.org/cgi/content/full/320/5880/1164/DC1 Figure S2A.

14. Ibid. Figure S4.

15. R. Inglehart et al., "World Values, Surveys and European Values Surveys, 1981–1984, 1990–1993, and 1995–1997" (Computer files; Interuniversity Consortium for Political and Social Research, Ann Arbor, MI, 2000), distributed by ICPSR.

16. Supporting online material, Table S2.

17. Ibid. Table S3.

18. Ibid. Table S4.

19. This measure was originally computed at the population level by L. L. Cavalli-Sforza, P. Menozzi, A. Piazza. *The History and Geography of Human Genes.* Princeton, NJ: Princeton University Press, 1996.

20. This measure has been mapped on modern countries by E. Spolaore, R. Wacziarg, "The Diffusion of Development." Centre for Economic Policy Research Discussion Paper 5630. London: CEPR, 2006.

21. Supporting online material, Table S5.

22. Ibid. Table S6.

23. Ibid. Table S7A.

24. Ibid. Table S7B.

CHAPTER 4

Montagnais Women and the Jesuit Program for Colonization[1]

Eleanor Leacock

During the sixteenth century, the St. Lawrence valley was the scene of French and English competition for furs, especially for beaver which was used in the manufacture of hats. Sporadic trade of furs between native peoples and European fishermen was old, possibly preceding Columbus's first voyage; for when Cartier sailed up the St. Lawrence in 1534, the people he met were familiar with European vessels, products, and interest in furs. By midcentury, ships were coming to the area for the sole purpose of trading, and during the latter part of the century several companies competed unsuccessfully for a monopoly of the trade.

In 1559, a permanent French trading post was established at Tadoussac, downriver from Quebec, chosen by Champlain to be the headquarters of New France and founded in 1608. Three Rivers, further up the St. Lawrence, was established in 1617. Champlain was welcomed by the Algonkins and Montagnais.[2] They saw in him an ally in their warfare with the Iroquois, who, armed with weapons obtained from the Dutch, were raiding north and west for furs. Champlain's main interest was in gaining access to the interior trade through making alliances with Huron and Algonkin middlemen. He agreed to join the Algonkins and Montagnais in a retaliatory expedition against the Iroquois and was led, in the process, to the "discovery" of Lake Champlain. His way west, however, was persistently blocked by friendly noncooperation on the part of both Algonkins and Hurons. They were not eager to relinquish a middleman status that yielded a steady supply of iron tools, utensils (especially copper kettles), clothing, grain, and dried fruit.

Meanwhile, the number of trading vessels sailing up the St. Lawrence increased. Champlain wrote in 1611 that the Indians waited until several arrived before bringing out their furs, so that competition for them would push up their price. An average annual harvest of 15,000 to 20,000 beaver in the first years of the seventeenth century rose to 80,000 by 1670. By that time, the Iroquois had defeated and virtually annihilated the Hurons, the French were about to cede Canada to the English, and the English "company of adventurers" was opening up another route to the west with its post, Rupert's House, on Hudson's Bay. As the interest in furs pushed west, the northern and eastern parts of the Labrador Peninsula remained relatively distant from its influence. Not until the nineteenth century did the Hudson's Bay Company begin setting up posts in the Labrador interior.

Several missionaries accompanied Champlain on his first trips, but missionizing did not begin in earnest until 1632, when Quebec, temporarily occupied by the English, had been regained by the French. The traders were interested in the Indians as a source of furs. By contrast the mission, under the able leadership of the Jesuit Paul Le Jeune was committed to converting them to Christianity, resocializing them, and transforming them into settled farmers, citizens of New France. The Jesuits first worked intensively with the Montagnais-Naskapi, but soon began to pin their hopes on the populous, agricultural Hurons. When the Iroquois decimation of the Hurons dashed these hopes, some Jesuits remained to work with their Montagnais converts, but the main missionizing drive was over

What was the status of Montagnais-Naskapi women in the early seventeenth century when the French were establishing a foothold in the upper St. Lawrence valley? As is often the case, a look through accounts written at the time yields contrasting judgments. One may read that "women have great power. . . . A man may promise you something and if he does not keep his promise, he thinks he is sufficiently excused when he tells you that his wife did not wish him to do it" (Thwaites 1906, 5:179). Or one may read that women were virtual slaves.

> The women . . . besides the onerous role of bearing and rearing the children, also transport the game from the place where it has fallen; they are the hewers of wood and drawers of water; they make and repair the household utensils; they prepare food; they skin the game and prepare the hides like fullers; they sew garments; they catch fish and gather shellfish for food; often they even hunt; they make the canoes, that is skiffs of marvelous rapidity, out of bark;[3] they set up the tents wherever and whenever they stop for the night—in short, the men concern themselves with nothing but the more laborious hunting and the waging of war. . . . Their wives are regarded and treated as slaves. (2:77)

Fortunately, the ethnohistorical record for the Montagnais-Naskapi is full enough so that contradictions between two statements such as these can be resolved. The view that the hard work of native American women made them slaves was commonly expressed by European observers who did not know personally the people about whom they were writing. The statement about female authority, however, was written by a man who knew the Montagnais-Naskapi well and recognized that women controlled their own work and made decisions accordingly. Paul Le Jeune, superior of the Jesuit mission at Quebec, had spent a winter in a Montagnais lodge in order to learn the language and understand the culture of the people he was supposed to convert and "civilize." He commented on the ease of relations between husbands and wives in Montagnais society, and explained that it followed from "the order which they maintain in their occupations," whereby "the women know what they are to do, and the men also; and one never meddles with the work of the other" (5:133). "Men leave the arrangement of the household to the women, without interfering with them; they cut and decide and give away as they please without making the husband angry. I have never seen my host ask a giddy young woman that he had with him what became of the provisions, although they were disappearing very fast" (6:233).

Le Jeune sought to change this state of affairs, and he reported to his superiors in Paris on his progress in "civilizing" the Montagnais-Naskapi through what became a fourfold program. First, he saw permanent settlement and the institution of formally recognized chiefly authority as basic. "Alas!" he wrote, "If someone could stop the wanderings of the Savages, and give authority to one of them to rule the others, we would see them converted and civilized in a short time" (12:169). Second, Le Jeune stressed the necessity of introducing the principle of punishment into Montagnais social relations. Third, central to Le Jeune's program was education of Montagnais-Naskapi children. "How necessary it is to educate the children of the Savages," he stated. "We shall have them at last if they see that we do not send them to France" (5:137).

> If we had a good building in Kebec, we would get more children through the very same means by which we despair of getting them. We have always thought that the excessive love the Savages bear their children would prevent our obtaining them. It will be through this very means that they will become our pupils; for, by having a few settled ones, who will attract and retain the others, the parents, who do not know what it is to refuse their children, will let them come without opposition. And, as they will be permitted during the first few years to have a great deal of liberty, they will become so accustomed to our food and our clothes, that they will have a horror of the Savages and their filth. (9:103)

As the quotation suggests, Montagnais-Naskapi culture posed a stumbling block for the Jesuits, in that the Montagnais did not practice corporeal punishment of children. Le Jeune complained, "The Savages prevent their instruction; they will not tolerate the chastisement of their children, whatever they may do, they permit only a simple reprimand" (5:197). Le Jeune's solution was to propose removing the children from their communities for schooling: "The reason why I would not like to take the children of one locality in that locality itself, but rather in some other place, is because these Barbarians cannot bear to have their children punished, even scolded, not being able to refuse anything to a crying child. They carry this to such an extent that upon the slightest pretext they would take them away from us, before they were educated" (6:153–55).

Fourth, essential to Le Jeune's entire program was the introduction of European family structure, with male authority, female fidelity, and the elimination of the right to divorce. Lecturing a man on the subject, Le Jeune said the man "was the master and that in France women do not rule their husbands" (5:179). The independence of Montagnais women posed continual problems for the Jesuits. Le Jeune decided that:

> . . . it is absolutely necessary to teach the girls as well as the boys, and that we shall do nothing or very little, unless some good household has the care of this sex; for the boys that we shall have reared in the knowledge of God, when they marry Savage girls or women accustomed to wandering in the

> woods will, as their husbands, be compelled to follow them and thus fall
> back into barbarism or to leave them, another evil full of danger. (5:145)

Le Jeune's account of his problems, successes, and failures in introducing hierarchical principles into the ordering of interpersonal relations among the Montagnais-Naskapi affords a clear record of the personal autonomy that was central to the structure and ethics of their society—an autonomy that applied as fully to women as to men.

Montagnais-Naskapi Economy and Decision Making

The Montagnais-Naskapi lived by hunting and trapping wild game—caribou, moose, beaver, bear, hare, porcupine and water fowl—by fishing, and by gathering wild berries and other vegetable foods. Like foraging peoples everywhere, they followed a regular pattern of seasonal movement according to the provenience of the foods on which they depended. The Montagnais with whom Le Jeune worked summered on the shores of the St. Lawrence River, where groups of several hundred people gathered to fish, socialize, and make and repair canoes, snowshoes, and other equipment. In the fall, groups of some 35 to 75 people separated out to ascend one or another of the rivers that emptied into the St. Lawrence. During the winter hunting season, these bands might split up into smaller groups in order to spread out over a wide area in search of game. However, they kept in touch with each other so that if some were short of food, they could turn to others for help (Leacock 1969).

The smallest working unit was the group that lived together in a large conical lodge—some ten to twenty people, or, in Western terms, several nuclear families. In early times, as later, residential choices were probably flexible, and people moved about in accord both with personal likes and dislikes and with the need for keeping a reasonable balance in the working group between women and men and young and old. Upon marriage, however, a man ideally moved into his wife's lodge group (Thwaites 1906, 31:169). Accordingly, mentions of a Montagnais man's family might include the man's wife's sister, or a son-in-law, or a father-in-law (6:125, 9:33, 14:143–45). Yet three brothers and their wives shared the lodge in which Le Jeune lived. Le Jeune is silent about the relationships among the wives who, judging from hunting-group compositions in recent times, could easily have been sisters or parallel cousins.[4] In any case, Le Jeune's diary shows that the arrangement was not permanent.

Ethnographic evidence as well as the *Jesuit Relations* indicates that decisions about movements were made by the adult members of whatever group was involved. There is no question about women's importance in making such decisions. In fact, one recorder stated that "the choice of plans, of undertakings, of journeys, of winterings, lies in nearly every instance in the hands of the housewife" (68:93). Individuals might be chosen as spokespersons to mediate with the French, but such "chiefs" held no formal authority within the group. Le Jeune noted that "the Savages cannot endure in the least those who seem desirous of assuming superiority over the others; they place all virtue in a certain gentleness or apathy" (16:165).

> They imagine that they ought by right of birth, to enjoy the liberty of wild ass colts, rendering no homage to anyone whomsoever, except when they like. They have reproached me a hundred times because we fear our Captains, while they laugh at and make sport of theirs. All the authority of their chief is in his tongue's end; for he is powerful insofar as he is eloquent; and, even if he kills himself talking and haranguing, he will not be obeyed unless he pleases the Savages. (6:243)

Le Jeune was honest enough to state what he saw as the positive side of Montagnais egalitarianism:

> As they have neither political organization, nor office, nor dignities, nor any authority, for they only obey their Chief through good will toward him, therefore they never kill each other to acquire these honors. Also, as they are contented with a mere living, not one of them gives himself to the Devil to acquire wealth. (6:231)

In his final judgement, however, Le Jeune remained bound by his culture and his missionizing commitment: "I would not dare assert that I have seen one act of real moral virtue in a Savage. They have nothing but their own pleasure and satisfaction in view" (6:239–41).

The Jesuit Program For Changing Montagnais Marriage

As indicated above, Le Jeune's original assumption—that he could win the Montagnais to Christianity through converting the men—changed when he learned how far Montagnais family structure was from that of the French. He realized that he would have to give special attention to women as well as men if he was to eliminate the Montagnais' unquestioned acceptance of divorce at the desire of either partner, of polygyny, and of sexual freedom after marriage.

"The young people do not think that they can persevere in the state of matrimony with a bad wife or a bad husband," Le Jeune wrote. "They wish to be free and to be able to divorce the consort if they do not love each other" (16:41). And several years later: "The inconstancy of marriages and the facility with which they divorce each other, are a great obstacle to the Faith of Jesus Christ. We do not dare baptize the young people because experience teaches us that the custom of abandoning a disagreeable wife or husband has a strong hold on them" (22:229).

Polygamy was another right that women as well as men took for granted: "Since I have been preaching among them that a man should not have more than one wife, I have not been well received by the women; for, since they are more numerous than the men, if a man can only marry one of them, the others will have to suffer. Therefore this doctrine is not according to their liking" (12:165). And as for the full acceptance of sexual freedom for both women and men, no citation can be more telling of the gulf between French and Montagnais society than Le Jeune's rendition of a Montagnais rebuff.

> I told him that it was not honorable for a woman to love any one else except her husband, and that this evil being among them, he himself was not sure that his son, who was there present, was his son. He replied, "Thou hast no sense. You French people love only your own children; but we all love all the children of our tribe." I began to laugh, seeing that he philosophized in horse and mule fashion. (6:255)

Converts to Christianity wrestled with the dilemmas posed by the French faith. A recently married young man wished to be faithful to his wife, but felt himself "inclined toward infidelity." Deeply disturbed by his criminal wish, he entreated to be imprisoned or publicly flogged. When his request was refused, "He slips into a room near the Chapel and, with a rope that he finds, he beats himself so hard all over the body that the noise reaches the ears of the Father, who runs in and forbids so severe a penance" (22:67). The adoption of severe punitiveness both towards the self and others was reported by Le Jeune.

> The most zealous Christians met during the winter, unknown to us, in order to confer together upon the means of keeping themselves in the faith. One of them, in making an address, said that he thought more highly of prayers than of life, and that he would rather die than give them up. Another said that he wished he might be punished and chastised in case he forfeited the word he had given to God. A third claimed that he who should fall into any error must be put into prison and made to fast for four days without eating or drinking. The acts of justice that they see from time to time exercised on delinquents give them these ideas. (20:143)

Upon hearing the news, the fathers informed the converts that "they proceeded with too much severity; that mildness had more power over souls than force." The zealots argued, however, that the first among them who committed a fault, "however inconsiderable, should suffer imprisonment and fasting." This so frightened "the weak," Le Jeune continued, that "the report spread among the unbelievers that the Christian Savages had chains and bonds all ready to bind the refractory." Le Jeune concluded, "Some pagans told us they were risking the ruin of everything and that the Savages would kill one another. All this consoled us much, for we took pleasure in seeing the union of the Christians; it is much easier to temper fervor than it is to kindle it" (20:143).

Women and children alike suffered punishment at the hands of the converts. "A young Christian, getting into a passion, beat his wife, who had insolently provoked him," Le Jeune wrote. The man then repented of his sin and went to the chapel to pray to God for mercy. Le Jeune had the couple brought to him. "They were properly reprimanded," he reported, "especially the woman, who was more guilty than her husband" (18:155). As for the children,

> . . . they are all in an incredible state of satisfaction at having embraced
> the Faith. "We punish the disobedient" said they. A young girl who would
> not go to the nets, where her father sent her, was two days without food
> as a punishment for her disobedience. Two boys, who came late to prayers
> in the morning were punished by having a handful of hot cinders thrown
> upon their heads with threats of greater chastisement in case the offenses
> were repeated. (18:171)

Several Christians even had a drunken, young, pagan relative thrown into prison—in
Le Jeune's view, "an act fit to astonish all those who know the customs of the Savages,
who cannot endure that any one should touch their kinsmen; but God has more power
than nature" (20:153).

In 1640, eight years after Le Jeune's arrival in New France and the setting up of
a Jesuit mission, the governor called together a group of influential Montagnais men,
and "having recommended to the Christians constance in their marriages—he gave
them to understand that it would be well if they should elect some chiefs to govern
them" (18:99). Accordingly, the Montagnais sought advice from the Jesuits, who
supervised the election of three captains. The men then "resolved to call together the
women, to urge them to be instructed and to receive holy Baptism." The women were
used to holding councils of their own to deal with matters of concern to them and
reported surprise at being lectured to by the men.

> Yesterday the men summoned us to a council, but the first time that women
> have ever entered one; but they treated us so rudely that we were greatly
> astonished. "It is you women," they said to us, "who keep the Demons
> among us; you do not urge to be baptized . . . when you pass before the
> cross you never salute it, you wish to be independent. Now know that you
> will obey your husbands and you young people know that you will obey
> your parents, and our captains and if any fail to do so, we will give them
> nothing to eat." (18:107)

Women's responses ranged from zealous compliance to rebelliousness. An incident
illustrating compliance with a husband's wishes, and suggesting the internalization of
guilt, occurred when a Christian woman joined some "games or public recreation" of
which her husband did not approve.

> Having returned, her husband said to her, "If I were not a Christian, I would
> tell you that, if you did not care for me you should seek another husband to
> whom you would render more obedience; but having promised God not to
> leave you until death, I cannot speak to you thus, although you have of-
> fended me." This poor woman asked his forgiveness, without delay, and on
> the following morning came to see the Father who had baptized her, and said
> to him, "My Father, I have offended God, I have not obeyed my husband; my
> heart is sad; I greatly desire to make my confession of this." (18:35)

Other women continued to have lovers, to solicit married men to take a second
wife, and to defy or leave their husbands. One convert complained, "My wife is always

angry; I fear that the Demons she keeps in my cabin are perverting the good that I received in holy Baptism." Le Jeune wrote of this man,

> Another time his wife aimed a knife at his thigh, and he, evading the blow, had only his robe injured, in which this Megera made a great slash. Thereupon he came to us; meeting some Savages on the way, he began to laugh. "See," said he, "the anger of her who considers me her servant; she thought she would be able to irritate me, but I have more power over myself than to fall into passion at the anger of a woman."

Le Jeune added, "It is strange what Enemies the Savages are of anger, and how this sin shocks them," and continued,

> I know not what this simple man has done to win her over to God. "If thou wilt believe," he said to her, "I will love thee above all things; I will wait upon thee in all thy needs, I will even perform the little duties that the women do, I will go for water and wood; I will love thee more than myself." He pinched his arm and said to her, "Dost thou see this flesh? I do not love it; it is God whom I love, and those who believe in him. If thou are not willing to obey him thou must go away from me; for I cannot love those who do not love God."
>
> His wife derided him: "Dost thou not see that we are all dying since they told us to pray to God? Where are thy relatives? Where are mine? The most of them are dead. It is no longer a time to believe." (20:195–97)

Another particularly revealing incident offers an important comment on Montagnais ethics, and indicates the growing distance between the missionized Montagnais, with their acceptance of corporeal punishment, and the unconverted. A Jesuit called some "chief men" together and, after commending them on putting a stop to "the disorderly conduct that occasionally occurred among them," expressed astonishment at their permitting a young baptized woman to live apart from her husband. The captain responsible for her replied that "he had tried all sorts of means to make her return to her duty and that his trouble had been in vain; that he would, nevertheless, make another effort." The Jesuit Father counseled him to consult his people and decide upon what was to be done for such disobedience. "They all decided upon harsh measures. 'Good advice,' they said, 'has not brought her to her senses; a prison will do so.' Two Captains were ordered to take her to Kebec and . . . have her put in a dungeon." The woman fled, but they caught her and tied her to take her by canoe to Kebec. At this

> some Pagan young men, observing this violence, of which the Savages have a horror, and which is more remote from their customs than Heaven is from Earth, made use of threats, declaring that they would kill any one who laid a hand on the woman. But the Captain and his people, who were Christians, boldly replied that there was nothing that they would not do or endure, in order to secure obedience to God. Such resolution silenced the infidels.

To avoid being imprisoned, the woman "humbly begged to be taken back to Saint Joseph, promising thence forward she would be more obedient." Le Jeune stated,

> Such acts of justice cause no surprise in France, because it is usual there to proceed in that manner. But, among these peoples . . . where everyone considers himself from birth, as free as the wild animals that roam in their great forest . . . it is a marvel, or rather a miracle, to see a peremptory command obeyed, or any act of severity or justice performed.
>
> Some Savages, having heard that in France, malefactors are put to death, have often reproached us, saying that we were cruel—that we killed our own countrymen; that we had no sense. They asked us whether the relatives of those who were condemned to death did not seek vengeance. The Infidels still have the same ideas; but Christians are learning, more and more, the importance of exercising Justice. (22:81–85)

Shortly afterwards, another act of violence towards a woman again threatened to provoke conflict between Christian and "pagan" Montagnais, and again called for commendation on the part of the recorder (in this instance not Le Jeune, but Bartholemy Vimont). The Christian relatives of a young woman agreed in family council to beat her for speaking to a suitor against her parents' wishes: "We are taught that God loves obedience. We see the French practicing it; they have such a regard for that virtue that, if any one of them fail in it, he is punished. Parents chastise their own children, and masters their servants."

One of the relatives beat the girl and lectured other girls who had gathered: "This is the first punishment by beating that we have inflicted upon anyone of our Nation. We are resolved to continue it, if any one among us should be disobedient." Vimont commented:

> During the previous year the new Christians had a Savage put in prison. This year they have done more, for this last punishment seems to me very severe to be the first. Those who know the freedom and independence of these peoples, and the horror they have of restraint or bondage, will say that a slight touch of Heaven and a little grace are stronger and more powerful than the cannons and arms of kings and monarchs, which could not subdue them.

The angry suitor appealed to his father, who threatened the Christian Indians. They defended their action, saying that his son had not been affronted and that he should be satisfied with the girl's punishment. At this, Governor Montmagny had the suitor called in and, through an interpreter, warned the young man to be careful, saying he would consider any attack on the Christian Indians to be a personal attack upon him (22:115–27).

Long-Range Impact of the Jesuit Program

One must ask how fairly the *Jesuit Relations* can be used to evaluate the success of the Jesuit program for conversion and resocialization of the Montagnais-Naskapi. After all, the Jesuit fathers were, in effect, soliciting continued support for their work, and they spent many pages describing the piety of their converts. Furthermore, they drew heavily on second-hand reports from adherents to the mission who doubtless presented themselves in a favorable light when repeating conversations and describing incidents. However, as seen by quotations above, both Jesuits and converts reported fully and convincingly on the views and actions of the unconverted. There is no reason to doubt the evidence the *Relations* offer of the conflicting ideologies that caused profound social disruption for the group as a whole and deep psychological turmoil for those individuals, both women and men, who made an often agonizing decision to give up traditional beliefs and practices and adhere to new codes of conduct and commitment. Therefore, although they do not reveal the actual extent of conversion that took place among the Montagnais-Naskapi during the seventeenth century, the *Jesuit Relations* document in detail what is more significant: the nature of responses to the Jesuit program, ranging from zealous dedication, through formal conversion, that might well involve backsliding, to indifference, and finally, to active hostility.

With respect to female-male relations, premarital chastity, male courtship, monogamy, and marital fidelity became accepted as ideal behavioral norms by dedicated converts. In 1639, Le Jeune wrote of the "evil custom" whereby a man who was courting a woman would go to her to make love at night, and he advised the girls to refer their suitors to the Jesuits (16:61). Several years later Vimont reported that an old woman, "touched by the fear of God," gave the names of young unmarried lovers, who protested that such "suits of marriage" were "customary among them." The young people were lectured by their elders to "declare your affections to your parents; take their advice and that of the Father. . . . Make your visits by day and not by night; the faith and the prayer forbid this custom (24:139). Some people, Vimont reported, had already adopted a new form of courtship, whereby a suitor would send a girl a bark painting of a young couple "holding each other by the hand, in the position that they assume in Church when they get married." A girl who was rejecting her suitor would send the drawing back (22:71).

In keeping with the reciprocity of Montagnais-Naskapi female-male relations, converted men accepted the same standards as were enjoined on women. Le Jeune wrote that he had heard on good authority "that some shameless women, who have approached some men at night and solicited them to do evil in secret, received for answer only these words: 'I believe in God, I pray to him every day; he forbids such actions, I cannot commit them'" (16:61). Nor would a "worthy captain" take a second wife, even when solicited by the woman herself, but answered, "You come too late, I have given my word to God I cannot gainsay it. I will obey him; I have said to him, 'I will obey thee' and I will do it" (16:145).

The influence, direct and indirect, of formulating such ideals as these was enhanced by the Jesuit work with children. Le Jeune wrote,

> We have done so much for these poor unbelievers that they have given us some of their daughters, which seems to me an act of God. . . . These little girls are dressed in the French fashion; they care no more for the Savages than if they did not belong to their Nation. Nevertheless, in order to wean them from their native customs, and to give them an opportunity of learning the French language, virture and manners, that they may afterwards

assist their countrywomen, we have decided to send two or three to France, to have them kept and taught in the house of hospital nuns. . . . Oh if we could only send a certain one who is to remain in the house of which I have spoken. . . . The child has nothing savage about her except her appearance and color; her sweetness, her docility, her modesty, her obedience, would cause her to pass for a wellborn French girl, fully susceptible of education.

Le Jeune followed this entry with a reference to his wish for a building in Quebec, where three classes could be lodged, "the first of little French children, of whom there will be perhaps twenty or thirty Pupils; the second, of Hurons; the third, of Montagnes" (9:103).

For their part, the Montagnais expressed resentment that their presentation of children to the French was not reciprocated. A "captain" complained "One does not see anything else but little Savages in the houses of the French; there are little boys there and little girls—what more do you want? . . . You are continually asking for our children, and you do not give yours; I do not know any family among us which keeps a Frenchman with it" (9:233).

The contrast between the Montagnais attitude towards sharing children and that of the French was expressed by Le Jeune's statement that "they think they are doing you some great favor in giving you their children to instruct, feed and dress" (5:197). Perhaps no incident in the *Relations* more poignantly reveals the cultural distance to be spanned by Montagnais converts than that in which a French drummer boy hit a Montagnais with his drumstick, drawing blood. The Montagnais onlookers took offense, saying, "Behold, one of thy people has wounded one of ours; thou knowest our custom well; give us presents for this wound." The French interpreter countered, "Thou knowest our custom; when any of our number does wrong, we punish him. This child has wounded one of your people; he shall be whipped at once in thy presence." When the Montagnais saw the French were in earnest about whipping the boy,

> they began to pray for his pardon, alleging he was only a child, that he had no mind, that he did not know what he was doing; but as our people were nevertheless going to punish him, one of the Savages stripped himself entirely, threw his blanket over the child and cried out to him who was going to do the whipping; "Strike me if thou wilt, but thou shalt not strike him," And thus the little one escaped. (5:219)

This incident took place in 1633. How was it possible that scarcely ten years later, adults could be beating, withholding food from, and even, if the report is accurate, doing such things as throwing hot ashes on children and youths? Above, I have referred to the punitiveness toward the self and others that accompanied the often tormented attempt on the part of converts to reject a familiar set of values and replace it with another. This psychological response is familiar. To say this, however, merely presses the next question: Why did some Montagnais feel so strongly impelled to make this attempt? The answer is that the Jesuits and their teachings arrived in New France a full century after the economic basis for unquestioned cooperation, reciprocity, and respect for individual autonomy began to be undercut by the trading of furs for European goods. On the basis of new economic ties, some Montagnais-Naskapi were interested in attaching themselves to the mission station and the new European settlement, thereby availing themselves of the resources these offered. By the same token, some were prepared to accept the beliefs and ritual practices of the newcomers, and to adopt—or attempt to adopt—new standards of conduct.

Elsewhere, I have documented the process whereby the stockpiling of furs for future return, to be acquired when the trading ships arrived, contradicted the principle of total sharing based on subsistence hunting, fishing, and gathering (Leacock 1954). The process has subsequently been well described for the Canadian sub-Arctic generally, and it has been pointed out that parallel processes are involved when a horticultural people becomes involved in exchange relations with a market economy (Murphy and Steward 1955).

At the same time that the fur trade was undercutting the foundation for Montagnais-Naskapi values and interpersonal ethics, the terrible scourge of epidemic disease, the escalation (or introduction) of warfare, and the delusion of relief from anxiety offered by alcohol were also undermining Montagnais-Naskapi self-assurance. Alfred Goldsworthy Bailey (1969) has described the effects of these developments in a review of the conflict between European and eastern Algonkian cultures during the sixteenth and seventeenth centuries. Fear of disease, particularly smallpox which raged in the decade after the priests' arrival, was only equaled by fear of the Iroquois. The prolonged and intricate torture of Iroquois prisoners, into which women entered with even more zeal than men, was a grim expression of profound fearfulness and anger. Alcohol, which temporarily elated the spirits, led to fights around the European settlement; in 1664 there is reference to a case of rape committed under its influence (48:227).

This is not to say, however, that Montagnais-Naskapi society as a whole was thoroughly disrupted. The violence that occurred around the European settlement contrasts not only with the friendliness, gaiety, and lack of quarreling that Le Jeune described during the winter he spent in the interior in 1633–34, but also with the general cooperativeness and good will—albeit laced with raucous banter and teasing— that characterized Montagnais-Naskapi life in later centuries in the rest of the Labrador Peninsula. Quebec was, after all, a gateway to the North American interior, and fur-trading posts and mission stations pushed ever westward. The nonracist policy of building a French colony in part with resocialized Indians was abandoned and replaced by a hardening color line. In time, all Montagnais-Naskapi became Catholic, but without the close supervision of the Jesuits, they retained established religious practices and added Catholic sacraments and prayer. During the summer of 1951, the "shaking-tent rite," in which a religious practitioner converses with the gods, both gaining useful information and entertaining an audience in the process, was still being practiced in eastern Labrador.

The pace of change in most of the Labrador Peninsula was slow, as Indians living far from centers of early settlement and trade gradually became drawn into a fur-trapping economy. In the summer of 1950, I was able to document the final stages of transition in southeastern Labrador, at a time when the next major change was about to transform life for French and English fishermen and fur-trappers as well as

Montagnais-Naskapi hunter-trappers; a railroad was being built into a huge iron mine deep in the north-central part of the peninsula. When I was there, conditions in the north woods were still such that the traditional Montagnais-Naskapi ethic of cooperativeness, tolerance, and nonpunitiveness remained strong.

What about the relations between women and men? As in seventeeth century accounts, one can still find contrasting judgements. Burgesse (1944) has written that:

> labour is fairly equitably divided between the sexes under the economic system of the Montagnais. Each sex has its own particular duties but, within certain limits, the divisions between the types of work performed are not rigid. A man would not consider it beneath his dignity to assist his wife in what are ordinarily considered duties peculiar to the woman. Also, women are often enough to be seen performing tasks which are usually done by men. On being questioned in regard to this aspect of their economics, the Montagnais invariably reply that, since marriage is a union of co-equal partners for mutual benefit, it is the duty of the husband to assist his wife in the performance of her labors. Similarly, it is the duty of the wife to aid the husband. . . .
>
> The Montagnais woman is far from being a drudge. Instead she is a respected member of the tribe whose worth is well appreciated and whose advice and counsel is listened to and, more often than not, accepted and acted upon by her husband. (4–7)

Earlier, and by contrast, Turner had written:

> The sexes have their special labors. Women perform the drudgery and bring home the food slain by their husbands, fetching wood and water, tanning the skins, and making them into clothing. The labor of erecting the tents and hauling the sleds when on their journey during the winter falls upon them, and, in fact, they perform the greater part of the manual labor. They are considered inferior to men, and in their social life they soon show the effects of the hardships they undergo. (1894:271)

One could take these statements at face value as reflecting differences between two Montagnais-Naskapi bands, for the first statement refers to the southerly Lake St. John people and the second to the Ungava people of the north. However, the continuation of Turner's account reveals realities of Ungava life that contradict his formal statement.

> An amusing incident occurred within a stone's throw of Fort Chimo. An Indian had his clothes stripped from him by his enraged wife. She then took the tent from the poles, leaving him naked. She took their property to the canoe, which she paddled several miles upstream. He followed along the bank until she relented, whereupon their former relations were resumed, as though nothing had disturbed the harmony of their life. The man was so severely plagued by his comrades that for many days he scarcely showed his head out of the tent (Ibid.).

Translating the incident into the terms of political economy, women retained control over the products of their labor. These were not alienated, and women's production of clothing, shelter, and canoe covering gave them concomitant practical power and influence; despite formal statements of male dominance that might be elicited by outsiders. In northern Labrador in the late nineteenth century, dependence on trading furs for food, clothing, and equipment was only beginning. Band cohesion was still strong, based on the sharing of meat, fish, and other necessities and on the reciprocal exchange of goods and services between women and men.

By the middle of this century, the economic balance had tipped in favor of ultimate dependence upon the fur trade (and, in many cases, wage labor) throughout the entire Labrador Peninsula. The Montagnais-Naskapi lived in nuclear family units largely supported by the husband and father's wages or take from the trap line. Nonetheless, the resources of the land were still directly used, were still available to anyone, were acquired cooperatively insofar as it was most practical, and were shared. Furthermore, partly through their own desire and partly in accord with the racist structure of Western society, the Montagnais-Naskapi maintained their status as a semi-autonomous people and were not separated into an elite minority versus a majority of marginal workers. Thus, a strong respect for individual autonomy and an extreme sensitivity to the feelings of others when decisions were to be made went with a continuing emphasis on generosity and cooperativeness, which applied to relations between as well as within the sexes.

In my own experience living in a Montagnais-Naskapi camp, I noted a quality of respectfulness between women and men that fits Burgesse's characterization. I also observed such behavior as an ease of men with children, who would take over responsibility even for infants when it was called for, with a spontaneity and casual competence that in our culture would be described as "maternal." Nonetheless, men were "superior" in ways commonly alluded to in anthropological literature. The few shamans who still practiced their art (or admitted practicing it to an outsider) were men; band chiefs were men; and patrilocality was both an ideal and statistically more common among newlyweds than matrilocality. In short, Montagnais-Naskapi practice at this time fitted what is considered in the anthropological literature to be usual for people who live (or have recently lived) by direct acquisition and use of wild products: strongly egalitarian, but with an edge in favor of male authority and influence.

Seventeenth century accounts, however, referred to female shamans who might become powerful (Thwaites 1906:6:61; 14:183). So-called "outside chiefs," formally elected according to government protocol to mediate with white society, had no more influence within the group than their individual attributes would call for (Leacock 1958); and matrilocality had only recently given way to patrilocal postmarital residence (Leacock 1955). As markedly different as Montagnais-Naskapi culture continued to be from Western culture, the ethnohistorical record makes clear that it had been constantly restructuring itself to fit new situations and that the status of women, although still relatively high, had clearly changed.

Notes

1. This article is based in large part on a paper written in collaboration with Jacqueline Goodman (Leacock and Goodman 1976). An ethnohistorical summary of Montagnais-Naskapi culture in the seventeenth century can be found in Leacock *Myths of Male Dominance.* Monthly Review Press, 1981.

2. The anthropological term for the native population of the Labrador Peninsula, exclusive of the Eskimo, is "Montagnais-Naskapi." At times I shall use the simpler "Montagnais," a name applied by the French to the various groups that summered on the north shore of the St. Lawrence River. Like the Algonkins, the Montagnais are an Algonkian-speaking people.

3. Actually, men usually made canoe frames, and women covered them, though either sex could do both if necessary.

4. Parallel cousins are the children of two sisters or two brothers (and their spouses). Children of a brother and a sister (and their spouses) are called "cross-cousins." As is common in many kin-based societies, the Montagnais-Naskapi terms for parallel cousins were the same as for siblings, while the terms for cross-cousins, who were desirable marriage partners, connoted something like "sweetheart" (Strong 1929).

CHAPTER 5

Capitalism, Patriarchy, and Job Segregation by Sex

Heidi Hartmann

The division of labor by sex appears to have been universal throughout human history. In our society the sexual division of labor is hierarchical, with men on top and women on the bottom. Anthropology and history suggest, however, that this division was not always a hierarchical one. The development and importance of a sex-ordered division of labor is the subject of this paper. It is my contention that the roots of women's present social status lie in this sex-ordered division of labor. It is my belief that not only must the hierarchical nature of the division of labor between the sexes be eliminated, but the very division of labor between the sexes itself must be eliminated if women are to attain equal social status with men and if women and men are to attain the full development of their human potentials.

The primary questions for investigation would seem to be, then, first, how a more sexually egalitarian division became a less egalitarian one, and second, how this hierarchical division of labor became extended to wage labor in the modern period. Many anthropological studies suggest that the first process, sexual stratification, occurred together with the increasing productiveness, specialization, and complexity of society; for example, through the establishment of settled agriculture, private property, or the state. It occurred as human society emerged from the primitive and became "civilized." In this perspective capitalism is a relative latecomer, whereas patriarchy,[1] the hierarchical relation between men and women in which men are dominant and women are subordinate, was an early arrival.

I want to argue that, before capitalism, a patriarchal system was established in which men controlled the labor of women and children in the family, and that in so doing men learned the techniques of hierarchical organization and control. With the advent of public-private separations such as those created by the emergence of state apparatus and economic systems based on wider exchange and larger production units, the problem for men became one of maintaining their control over the labor power of women. In other words, a direct personal system of control was translated into an indirect, impersonal system of control, mediated by society-wide institutions. The mechanisms available to men were (1) the traditional division of labor between the sexes, and (2) techniques of hierarchical organization and control. These mechanisms were crucial in the second process, the extension of a sex-ordered division of labor to the wage-labor system, during the period of the emergence of capitalism in Western Europe and the United States.

The emergence of capitalism in the fifteenth to eighteenth centuries threatened patriarchal control based on institutional authority as it destroyed many old institutions and created new ones, such as a "free" market in labor. It threatened to bring all women and children into the labor force and hence to destroy the family and the basis of the power of men over women (i.e., the control over their labor power in the family).[2] If the theoretical tendency of pure capitalism would have been to eradicate all arbitrary differences of status among laborers, to make all laborers equal in the marketplace, why are women still in an inferior position to men in the labor market? The possible answers are legion; they range from neoclassical views that the process is not complete or is hampered by market imperfections to the radical view that production requires hierarchy even if the market nominally requires "equality."[3] All of these explanations, it seems to me, ignore the role of men—ordinary men, men as men, men as workers—in maintaining women's inferiority in the labor market. The radical view, in particular, emphasizes the role of men as capitalists in creating hierarchies in the production process in order to maintain their power. Capitalists do this by segmenting the labor market (along race, sex, and ethnic lines among others) and playing workers off against each other. In this paper I argue that male workers have played and continue to play a crucial role in maintaining sexual divisions in the labor process.

Job segregation by sex, I will argue, is the primary mechanism in capitalist society that maintains the superiority of men over women, because it enforces lower wages for women in the labor market. Low wages keep women dependent on men because they encourage women to marry. Married women must perform domestic chores for their husbands. Men benefit, then, from both higher wages and the domestic division of labor. This domestic division of labor, in turn, acts to weaken women's position in the labor market. Thus, the hierarchical domestic division of labor is perpetuated by the labor market, and vice versa. This process is the present outcome of the continuing interaction of two interlocking systems, capitalism and patriarchy. Patriarchy, far from being vanquished by capitalism, is still very virile; it shapes the form modern capitalism takes, just as the development of capitalism has transformed patriarchal institutions. The resulting mutual accommodation between patriarchy and capitalism has created a vicious circle for women.

My argument contrasts with the traditional views of both neoclassical and Marxist economists. Both ignore patriarchy, a social system with a material base. The neoclassical economists tend to exonerate the capitalist system, attributing job segregation to exogenous *ideological* factors, like sexist attitudes. Marxist economists tend to attribute job segregation to capitalists, ignoring the part played by male workers and the effect of centuries of patriarchal social relations. In this paper I hope to redress the balance. The line of argument I have outlined here and will develop further below is perhaps incapable of proof. This paper, I hope, will establish its plausibility rather than its incontrovertibility.

[. . .]

Anthropological Perspectives on the Division of Labor by Sex

[. . .]

According to Lévi-Strauss, culture began with the exchange of women by men to cement bonds between families—thereby creating *society*.[4] In fact Lévi-Strauss sees a fundamental tension between the family (i.e., the domestic realm in which women reside closer to nature) and society, which requires that families break down their autonomy to exchange with one another. The exchange of women is a mechanism that enforces the interdependence of families and that creates society. By analogy, Lévi-Strauss suggests that the division of labor between the sexes is the mechanism which enforces "a reciprocal state of dependency between the sexes."[5] It also assures heterosexual marriage. "When it is stated that one sex must perform certain tasks, this also means that the other sex is forbidden to do them."[6] Thus, the existence of a sexual division of labor is a universal of human society, though the exact division of the tasks by sex varies enormously.[7] Moreover, following Lévi-Strauss, because it is men who exchange women and women who are exchanged in creating social bonds, men benefit more than women from these social bonds, and the division of labor between the sexes is a hierarchical one.[8]

While this first school of anthropological thought, the "universalists," is based primarily on Lévi-Strauss and the exchange of women, Chodorow, following Rosaldo and Ortner, emphasizes women's confinement to the domestic sphere. Chodorow locates this confinement in the mothering role. She constructs the universality of patriarchy on the universal fact that women mother. Female mothering reproduces itself via the creation of gender-specific personality structures.[9]

Two other major schools of thought on the origins of the sexual division of labor merit attention. Both reject the universality, at least in theory if not in practice, of the sex-ordered division of labor. One is the "feminist-revisionist" school which argues that we cannot be certain that the division of labor is male supremacist; it may be separate but equal (as Lévi-Strauss occasionally seems to indicate), but we will never know because of the bias of the observers which makes comparisons impossible. This school is culturally relativist in the extreme, but it nevertheless contributes to our knowledge of women's work and status by stressing the accomplishments of females in their part of the division of labor.[10]

The second school also rejects the universality of sex-ordered division of labor but, unlike relativists, seeks to compare societies to isolate the variables which coincide with greater or lesser autonomy of women. This school, the "variationist," is subdivided according to the characteristics members emphasize: the contribution of women to subsistence and their control over their contribution, the organization of tribal versus state societies, the requirements of the mode of production, the emergence of wealth and private property, the boundaries of the private and public spheres.[11] A complete review of these approaches is impossible here, but I will cite a few examples from this literature to illustrate the relevance of these variables for the creation of a sex-ordered division of labor.

Among the !Kung, a hunting and gathering people in South West Africa, the women have a great deal of autonomy and influence.[12] Draper argues that this is the result of (1) the contribution of 60–80 percent of the community's food by the women and their retention of control over its distribution; (2) equal absence from the camp and equal range and mobility of the male hunters and the female gatherers (the women are not dependent on the men for protection in their gathering range); (3) the flexibility of sex roles and the willingness of adults to do the work of the opposite sex (with the exception that women did not hunt and men did not remove nasal mucous or feces from children!); (4) the absence of physical expression of aggression; (5) the small size (seventeen to sixty-five) of and flexible membership in living groups; (6) a close, public settlement arrangement, in which the huts were situated in a circle around the campfire.

In the late 1960s when Draper did her fieldwork, some of the !Kung were beginning to settle in small villages where the men took up herding and the women agriculture, like other groups (e.g., the Bantu) who were already settled. The agriculture and the food preparation were more time consuming for the women than gathering had been and, while they continued to gather from time to time, the new agricultural pursuits kept the women closer to home. The men, in contrast, through herding, remained mobile and had greater contact with the world outside the !Kung: the Bantus, politics, wage work, and advanced knowledge (e.g., about domesticated animals). These sex roles were maintained with more rigidity. Boys and girls came to be socialized differently, and men began to feel their work superior to the women's. Men began to consider property theirs (rather than jointly owned with the women), and "[r]anking of individuals in terms of prestige and differential worth ha[d] begun. . . ."[13] Houses, made more permanent and private, were no longer arranged in a circle. The women in particular felt that the group as a whole had less ability to observe, and perhaps to sanction, the behavior of people in married couples. Doubtless these changes occurred partly because of the influence of the male-dominated Western culture on the !Kung. The overall result, according to Draper, was a decrease in the status and influence of women, the denigration of their work, and an increase, for women, in the importance of the family unit at the expense of the influence of the group as a whole. The delineation of public and private spheres placed men in the public and women in the private sphere, and the public sphere came to be valued more.

Boserup, in *Woman's Role in Economic Development,* writes extensively of the particular problems caused for women when Third World tribal groups came into contact with Western colonial administrations.[14] The usual result was the creation or strengthening of male dominance as, for example, where administrations taught men advanced agricultural techniques where women were farmers, or schooled men in trading where women were traders. The Europeans encouraged men to head and support their families, superseding women's traditional responsibilities. Previous to colonization, according to Leavitt: "In regions like Africa and Southeast Asia, where shifting agriculture and the female farmer predominate, the women work very hard and receive limited support from their husbands, but they also have some economic independence, considerable freedom of movement, and an important place in the community. . . . In traditional African marriages the woman is expected to support herself and her children and to feed the family, including her husband, with the food she grows."[15] [. . .]

Europeans also entrusted local governance to male leaders and ignored women's traditional participation in tribal society. That the women had highly organized and yet nonhierarchical governmental structures, which were unknown and ignored by the colonists, is illustrated by the case of the Igbo in Nigeria. Allen reports that Igbo women held *mikiri*, or meetings, which were democratic discussions with no official leaders and "which articulated women's interests *as opposed to* those men."[16] The women needed these meetings because they lived in patrilocal villages and had few kinship ties with each other, and because they had their own separate economic activities, their own crops, and their own trading, which they needed to protect from men. When a man offended the women, by violating the women's market rules or letting his cows into the women's yam fields, the women often retaliated as a group by "sitting on a man"—carrying on loudly at his home late at night and "perhaps demolishing his hut or plastering it with mud and roughing him up a bit."[17] Women also sometimes executed collective strikes and boycotts. With the advent of the British administrators and their inevitably unfavorable policies toward women, the Igbo women adapted their tactics and used them against the British. For example, in response to an attempt to tax the women farmers, tens of thousands of women were involved in riots at administrative centers over an area of 6,000 square miles containing a population of 2 million people. The "Women's War," as it was called, was coordinated through the market *mikiri* network.[18] Allen continues to detail the distintegration of the *mikiri* in the face of British colonial and missionary policies.

In a study of a somewhat different process of state formation, Muller looks at the decline of Anglo-Saxon and Welsh tribal society and the formation of the English nation-state, a process which occurred from the eighth to the fifteenth century. Muller writes:

> The transition from tribe to state is historically probably the greatest watershed in the decline in the status of women. . . . This is not to deny that in what we call "tribal," that is, pre-state, society there is not a wide variation in the status of women and even that in certain pre-state societies, women may be in what we would consider an abject position *vis à vis* the men in that society. . . . We believe that the causes for these variations in status can be found, as in the case of State Societies, in the material conditions which give rise to the social and economic positions therein.[19]

Muller stresses that, in the Welsh and Anglo-Saxon tribes, "the right of individual maintenance was so well entrenched that these rights were not entrusted to a patriarchal head of a nuclear family, but were, rather, vested in the larger social group of the *gwely* [four-generation kinship group]."[20] Both men and women upon adulthood received a share of cattle from the *gwely*. The cattle provided their personal maintenance and prevented an individual from becoming dependent upon another. Thus, although in the tribal system land inheritance was patrilineal and residence patrilocal, a married woman had her own means of economic subsistence. Women were political participants both in their husbands' and in their natal lineages. Like a man, a woman was responsible for her children's crimes, and she and her natal lineages (*not* her spouse's) were responsible for her crimes. Tribal customs were, however, undermined by the emergence of the state. ". . . we can observe the development of public—as opposed to social—male authority, through the political structure imposed by the emerging state. Since the state is interested in the alienation of the tribal resource base—its land and its labor power—it finds it convenient to use the traditional gender division of labor and resources in tribal society and places them in a hierarchical relationship both internally (husband over wife and children) and externally (lords over peasants and serfs)."[21] The king established regional administrative units without regard to tribal jurisdictions, appointed his own administrators, bypassed the authority of the tribal chiefs, and levied obligations on the males as "heads" of individual households. Tribal groups lost collective responsibility for their members, and women and children lost their group rights and came under the authority of their husbands. Woman's work became private for the benefit of her husband, rather than public for the benefit of the kin group. As Muller points out, there must have been tendencies evident in tribal society that created the preconditions for a hierarchical, male-dominated state, for it was not equally likely that the emerging state would be female. Among these tendencies, for example, were male ownership of land and greater male participation in military expeditions, probably especially those farther away.[22]

This summary of several studies from the third school of anthropology, the variationist school, points to a number of variables that help to explain a decrease in woman's social status. They suggest that increased sexual stratification occurs along with a general process of social stratification (which at least in some versions seems to depend on and foster an increase in social surplus—to support the higher groups in the hierarchy). As a result, a decrease in the social status of woman occurs when (1) she loses control of subsistence through a change in production methods and devaluation of her share of the division of labor; (2) her work becomes private and family centered rather than social and kin focused; and/or (3) some men assert their power over other men through the state mechanism by elevating these subordinate men in their families, using the nuclear family against the kin group.[23] In this way the division of labor between men and women becomes a more hierarchical one. Control over women is maintained directly in the family by the man, but it is sustained by social institutions, such as the state and religion.

The work in this school of anthropology suggests that patriarchy did not always exist, but rather that it emerged as social conditions changed. Moreover, men participated in this transformation. Because it benefited men relative to women, men have had a stake in reproducing patriarchy. Although there is a great deal of controversy among anthropologists about the origins of patriarchy, and more work needs to be done to establish the validity of this interpretation, I believe the weight of the evidence supports it. In any case, most anthropologists agree that patriarchy emerged long before capitalism, even if they disagree about its origins.

In England, as we have seen, the formation of the state marks the end of Anglo-Saxon tribal society and the beginning of feudal society. Throughout feudal society the tendencies toward the privatization of family life and the increase of male power within the family appear to strengthen, as does their institutional support from church and state. By the time of the emergence of capitalism in the fifteenth through eighteenth centuries, the nuclear, patriarchal peasant family had become the basic production unit in society.[24]

The Emergence of Capitalism and the Industrial Revolution in England and the United States

The key process in the emergence of capitalism was primitive accumulation, the prior accumulation that was necessary for capitalism to establish itself.[25] Primitive accumulation was a twofold process which set the preconditions for the expansion of the scale of production: first, free laborers had to be accumulated; second, large amounts of capital had to be accumulated. The first was achieved through enclosures and the removal of people from the land, their subsistence base, so that they were forced to work for wages. The second was achieved through both the growth of smaller capitals in farms and shops amassed through banking facilities, and vast increases in merchant capital, the profits from the slave trade, and colonial exploitation.

The creation of a wage-labor force and the increase in the scale of production that occurred with the emergence of capitalism had in some ways a more severe impact on women than on men. [. . .] In the 1500s and 1600s, agriculture, woolen textiles (carried on as a by-industry of agriculture), and the various crafts and trades in the towns were the major sources of livelihood for the English population. In the rural areas men worked in the fields on small farms they owned or rented and women tended the household plots, small gardens and orchards, animals, and dairies. The women also spun and wove. A portion of these products were sold in small markets to supply the villages, towns, and cities, and in this way women supplied a considerable proportion of their families' cash income, as well as their subsistence in kind. In addition to the tenants and farmers, there was a small wage-earning class of men and women who worked on the larger farms. Occasionally tenants and their wives worked for wages as well, the men more often than the women.[26] As small farmers and cottagers were displaced by larger farmers in the seventeenth and eighteenth centuries, their wives lost their main sources of support, while the men were able to continue as wage laborers to some extent. Thus women, deprived of these essential household plots, suffered relatively greater unemployment, and the families as a whole were deprived of a large part of their subsistence.[27]

In the 1700s, the demand for cotton textiles grew, and English merchants found they could utilize the labor of the English agricultural population, who were already familiar with the arts of spinning and weaving. The merchants distributed materials to be spun and woven, creating a domestic industrial system which occupied many displaced farm families. This putting-out system, however, proved inadequate. The complexities of distribution and collection and, perhaps more important, the control the workers had over the production process (they could take time off, work intermittently, steal materials) prevented an increase in the supply of textiles sufficient to meet the merchants' needs. To solve these problems first spinning, in the late 1700s, and then weaving, in the early 1800s, were organized into factories. The textile factories were located in the rural areas, at first, in order both to take advantage of the labor of children and women, by escaping the restrictions of the guilds in the cities, and to utilize waterpower. When spinning was industrialized, women spinners at home suffered greater unemployment, while the demand for male handloom weavers increased. When weaving was mechanized, the need for handloom weavers fell off as well.[28]

In this way, domestic industry, created by emerging capitalism, was later superseded and destroyed by the progress of capitalist industrialization. In the process, women, children, and men in the rural areas all suffered dislocation and disruption, but they experienced this in different ways. Women, forced into unemployment by the capitalization of agriculture more frequently than men, were more available to labor, both in the domestic putting-out system and in the early factories. It is often argued both that men resisted going into the factories because they did not want to lose their independence and that women and children were more docile and malleable. If this was in fact the case, it would appear that these "character traits" of women and men were already established before the advent of the capitalistic organization of industry, and that they would have grown out of the authority structure prevailing in the previous period of small-scale, family agriculture. Many historians suggest that within the family men were the heads of households, and women, even though they contributed a large part of their families' subsistence, were subordinate.[29]

We may never know the facts of the authority structure within the preindustrial family, since much of what we know is from prescriptive literature or otherwise class biased, and little is known about the point of view of the people themselves. Nevertheless, the evidence on family life and on relative wages and levels of living suggests that women were subordinate within the family. [. . .] Moreover, the history of the early factories suggests that capitalists took advantage of this authority structure, finding women and children more vulnerable, both because of familial relations and because they were simply more desperate economically due to the changes in agriculture which left them unemployed.[30]

The transition to capitalism in the cities and towns was experienced somewhat differently than in the rural areas, but it tends to substantiate the line of argument just set out: men and women had different places in the familial authority structure, and capitalism proceeded in a way that built on that authority structure. [. . .] Men, usually the heads of the production units, had the status of master artisans. For though women usually belonged to their husbands' guilds, they did so as appendages; girls were rarely apprenticed to a trade and thus rarely become journeymen or masters. Married women participated in the production process and probably acquired important skills, but they usually controlled the production process only if they were widowed, when guilds often gave them the right to hire apprentices and journeymen. [. . .]

[. . .]

In the seventeenth and eighteenth centuries the family industry system and the guilds began to break down in the face of the demand for larger output. Capitalists began to organize production on a larger scale, and production became separated from the home as the size of establishments grew. Women were excluded from participation in the industries in which they had assisted men as they no longer took place at home, where married women apparently tended to remain to carry on their domestic work. Yet many women out of necessity sought work in capitalistically organized industry as wage laborers. When women entered wage labor they appear to have been at a disadvantage relative to men. First, as in agriculture, there was already a tradition of lower wages for women (in the previously limited area of wage work). Second, women appear to have been less well trained than men and obtained less desirable jobs. And third, they appear to have been less well organized than men.

[. . .]

Thus, the capitalistic organization of industry, in removing work from the home, served to increase the subordination of women, since it served to increase the relative importance of the area of men's domination. But it is important to remember that men's domination was already established and that it clearly influenced the direction and shape that capitalist development took. As Clark has argued, with the separation of work from the home men became less dependent on women for industrial production, while women became more dependent on men economically. From a position much like that of the African women discussed in Part I above, English married women, who had supported themselves and their children, became the domestic servants of their husbands. Men increased their control over technology, production, and marketing, as they excluded women from industry, education, and political organization.[31]

When women participated in the wage-labor market, they did so in a position as clearly limited by patriarchy as it was by capitalism. Men's control over women's labor was altered by the wage-labor system, but it was not eliminated. In the labor market the dominant position of men was maintained by sex-ordered job segregation. Women's jobs were lower paid, considered less skilled, and often involved less exercise of authority or control.[32] Men acted to enforce job segregation in the labor market; they utilized trade-union associations and strengthened the domestic division of labor, which required women to do housework, child care, and related chores. Women's subordinate position in the labor market reinforced their subordinate position in the family, and that in turn reinforced their labor-market position.

[. . .]

Notes

1. I define patriarchy as a set of social relations which has a material base and in which there are hierarchical relations between men, and solidarity among them, which enable them to control women. Patriarchy is thus the system of male oppression of women. Rubin argues that we should use the term "sex-gender system" to refer to that realm outside the economic system (and not always coordinate with it) where gender stratification based on sex differences is produced and reproduced. Patriarchy is thus only one form, a male dominant one, of a sex-gender system. Rubin argues further that patriarchy should be reserved for pastoral nomadic societies as described in the Old Testament where male power was synonomous with fatherhood. While I agree with Rubin's first point, I think her second point makes the usage of patriarchy too restrictive. It is a good label for most male-dominant societies (see Gayle Rubin, "The Traffic in Women," in *Toward an Anthropology of Women*, ed. Rayna Reiter [New York: Monthly Review Press, 1975]). Muller offers a broader definition of patriarchy "as a social system in which the status of women is defined primarily as wards of their husbands, fathers, and brothers," where wardship has economic and political dimensions (see Viana Muller, "The Formation of the State and the Oppression of Women: A Case Study in England and Wales," mimeographed [New York: New School for Social Research, 1975], p. 4, n. 2). Muller relies on Karen Sacks, "Engels Revisited: Women, the Organization of Production, and Private Property," in *Woman,*

Culture and Society, ed. Michelle Z. Rosaldo and Louise Lamphere (Stanford, Calif.: Stanford University Press, 1974). Patriarchy as a system between and among men as well as between men and women is further explained in a draft paper, "The Unhappy Marriage of Marxism and Feminism: Towards a New Union," by Amy Bridges and Heidi Hartmann.

2. Marx and Engels perceived the progress of capitalism in this way, that it would bring women and children into the labor market and thus erode the family. Yet despite Engels's acknowledgment in *The Origin of the Family, Private Property, and the State* (New York: International Publishers, 1972), that men oppress women in the family, he did not see that oppression as based on the control of women's labor, and, if anything, he seems to lament the passing of the male-controlled family (see his *The Condition of the Working Class in England* [Stanford, Calif.: Stanford University Press, 1968], esp.161–64).

3. See Richard C. Edwards, David M. Gordon, and Michael Reich, "Labor Market Segmentation in American Capitalism," draft essay, and the book they edited, *Labor Market Segmentation* (Lexington, Ky.: Lexington Books, 1973) for an explication of this view.

4. Claude Lévi-Strauss, "The Family," in *Man, Culture and Society*, ed. by Harry L. Shapiro (New York: Oxford University Press, 1971).

5. Lévi-Strauss, "The Family," 348.

6. Lévi-Strauss, "The Family," 347–48. "One of the strongest field recollections of this writer was his meeting, among the Bororo of central Brazil, of a man about thirty years old: unclean, ill-fed, sad, and lonesome. When asked if the man was seriously ill, the natives' answer came as a shock: what was wrong with him?—nothing at all, he was just a bachelor. And true enough, in a society where labor is systematically shared between men and women and where only the married status permits the man to benefit from the fruits of woman's work, including delousing, body painting, and hair-plucking as well as vegetable food and cooked food (since the Bororo woman tills the soil and makes pots), a bachelor is really only half a human being" (p. 341).

7. For further discussions of both the universality and variety of the division of labor by sex, see Melville J. Herskovits, *Economic Anthropology* (New York: W. W. Norton & Co., 1965), esp. chap. 7; Theodore Caplow, *The Sociology of Work* (New York: McGraw-Hill Book Co., 1964), esp. chap. 1.

8. For more on the exchange of women and its significance for women, see Rubin.

9. Nancy Chodorow, *Family Structure and Feminine Personality: The Reproduction of Mothering* (Berkeley: University of California Press, forthcoming). Chodorow offers an important alternative interpretation of the Oedipus complex (see her "Family Structure and Feminine Personality" in *Woman, Culture, and Society*).

10. Several of the articles in the Rosaldo and Lamphere collection are of this variety (see particularly Collier and Stack). Also, see Ernestine Friedl, "The Position of Women: Appearance and Reality," *Anthropological Quarterly* 40, no. 3 (July 1967): 97–108.

11. For an example of one particular emphasis, Leavitt states: "The most important clue to woman's status anywhere is her degree of participation in economic life and her control over property and the products she produces, both of which factors appear to be related to the kinship system of a society" (Ruby B. Leavitt, "Women in Other Cultures," in *Woman and Sexist Society*, ed. Vivian Gornick and Barbara K. Moran [New York: New American Library, 1972] 396). In a historical study which also seeks to address the questions of women's status, Joanne McNamara and Suzanne Wemple ("The Power of Woman through the Family in Medieval Europe: 500–1100," *Feminist Studies* 1, nos 3–4 [Winter-Spring 1973]: 126–41) emphasize the private-public split in their discussion of women's loss of status during this period.

12. Patricia Draper, "!Kung Women: Contrasts in Sexual Egalitarianism in Foraging and Sedentary Contexts," in *Toward an Anthropology of Women*.

13. Draper "!Kung Women," 108.

14. Ester Boserup, *Woman's Role in Economic Development* (London: George Allen & Unwin, 1970).

15. Leavitt, 412, 413.

16. Judith Van Allen, "'Sitting on a Man': Colonialism and the Lost Political Institutions of Igbo Women," *Canadian Journal of African Studies* 6, no. 2 (1972): 169.

17. Van Allen, "Sitting on a Man," 170.

18. Van Allen, "Sitting on a Man," 174–75. The British naturally thought the women were directed in their struggle by the men, though very few men participated in the riots.

19. Muller, 1. I am very grateful to Viana Muller for allowing me to summarize parts of her unpublished paper.

20. Muller, 14.

21. Muller, 25.

22. The examples of the !Kung, the Igbo, the Anglo-Saxons, and the groups discussed by Boserup all suggest that the process of expansion of state or emerging-state societies and the conquest of other peoples was an extremely important mechanism for spreading hierarchy and male domination. In fact, the role of warfare and imperialism raises the question of whether the state, to establish itself, creates the patriarchal family, or the patriarchal family creates the state (Thomas Vietorisz, personal communication). Surely emerging patriarchal social relations in prestate societies paved the way for both male public power (i.e., male control of the state apparatus) and the privatization of patriarchal power in the family. Surely also this privatization—and the concomitant decline of tribal power—strengthened, and was strengthened by, the state.

23. This point is stressed especially by Muller but is also illustrated by the !Kung. Muller states: "The men, although lowered from clansmen to peasants, were elevated to heads of nuclear families, with a modicum of both public power [through the state and religion] and a measure of private power through the decree of Church-State that they were to be lords over their wives" (35).

24. Both Hill and Stone describe England during this period as a patriarchal society in which the institutions of the nuclear family, the state, and religion, were being strengthened (see Christopher Hill, *Society and Puritanism* [New York: Schocken Books, 1964] esp. chap. 13; Lawrence Stone, *The Crisis of the Aristocracy, 1558–1641*, abridged ed. [New York: Oxford University Press, 1967], esp. chap. 11). Recent demographic research verifies the establishment of the nuclear family prior to the industrial revolution (see Peter Laslett, ed., *Household and Family in Time* [Cambridge: Cambridge University Press, 1972]). Because of limitations of my knowledge and space, and because I sought to discuss, first, the concept and establishment of patriarchy and second, its transformation in a wage-labor society, I am skipping over the rise and fall of feudal society and the emergence of family-centered petty commodity production and focusing in the next section on the disintegration of this family-centered production, creation of the wage-labor force, and the maintenance of job segregation in a capitalist context.

25. See Karl Marx, "The So-called Primitive Accumulation," in *Capital*, 3 vols. (New York: International Publishers, 1967), vol. 1, pt. 8; Stephen Hymer, "Robinson Crusoe and the Secret of Primitive Accumulation," *Monthly Review* 23, no. 4 (September 1971): 11–36.

26. Women and men in England had been employed as agricultural laborers for several centuries. [Alice] Clark found that by the seventeenth century the wages of men were higher than women's and the tasks done were different, though similar in skill and strength requirements (Alice Clark, *The Working Life of Women in the Seventeenth Century* [New York: Harcourt, Brace & Howe, 1920], 60). Wages for agricultural (and other work) were often set by local authori-

ties. These wage differentials reflected the relative social status of men and women and the social norms of the time. Women were considered to require lower wages because they ate less, for example, and were expected to have fewer luxuries, such as tobacco (see Clark and Pinchbeck throughout for substantiation of women's lower standard of living). Laura Oren has substantiated this for English women during the period 1860–1950 ("The Welfare of Women in Laboring Families: England, 1860–1950," *Feminist Studies* 1, nos. 3–4 [Winter–Spring 1973]: 107–25).

27. The problem of female unemployment in the countryside was a generally recognized one which figured prominently in the debate about poor-law reform, for example. As a remedy, it was suggested that rural families be allowed to retain small household plots, that women be used more in agricultural wage labor and also in the putting-out system, and that men's wages be adjusted upward (see Ivy Pinchbeck, *Women Workers and the Industrial Revolution, 1750–1850*, 69–84).

28. See Stephen Marglin, "What Do Bosses Do? The Origins and Functions of Hierarchy in Capitalist Production," *Review of Radical Political Economics* 6, no. 2 (Summer 1974): 60–112, for a discussion of the transition from putting out to factories. The sexual division of labor changed several times in the textile industry. Hutchins writes that the further back one goes in history, the more was the industry controlled by women. By the seventeenth century, though, men had become professional handloom weavers, and it was often claimed that men had superior strength or skill—which was required for certain types of weaves or fabrics. Thus, the increase in demand for handloom weavers in the late 1700s brought increased employment for men. When weaving was mechanized in the factories women operated the power looms, and male handloom weavers became unemployed. When jenny and waterframe spinning were replaced by mule spinning, supposedly requiring more strength, men took that over and displaced women spinners. A similar transition occurred in the United States. It is important to keep in mind that as a by-industry, both men and women engaged in various processes of textile manufacture, and this was intensified under putting out (see Pinchbeck 1969, chaps. 6–9).

29. See Clark; Pinchbeck; E. P. Thompson, *The Making of the English Working Class* (New York: Vintage Books, 1963).

30. In fact, the earliest factories utilized the labor of poor children, already separated from their families, who were apprenticed to factory owners by parish authorities. They were perhaps the most desperate and vulnerable of all.

31. See Clark, chap. 7. Eli Zaretsky ("Capitalism, the Family, and Personal Life," *Socialist Revolution*, nos. 13, 14 [1973]), follows a similar interpretation of history and offers different conclusions. Capitalism exacerbated the sexual division of labor and created the *appearance* that women work for their husbands; in reality, women who did domestic work at home were working for capital. Thus according to Zaretsky the present situation has its roots more in capitalism than in patriarchy. Although capitalism may have increased the consequence for women of the domestic division of labor, surely patriarchy tells us more about why men didn't stay home. That women worked for men in the home, as well as for capital, is also a reality.

32. William Lazonick argues in his dissertation, " Marxian Theory and the Development of the Labor Force in England" (Ph.D. diss., Harvard University, 1975), that the degree of authority required of the worker was often decisive in determining the sex of the worker. Thus handloom weavers in cottage industry were men because this allowed them to control the production process and the labor of the female spinners. In the spinning factories, mule spinners were men because mule spinners were required to supervise the labor of piecers, usually young boys. Men's position as head of the family established their position as heads of production units, and vice versa. While this is certainly plausible, I think it requires further investigation. Lazonick's work in this area (see chap. 4, "Segments of the Labour Force: Women, Children, and Irish") is very valuable.

All Family Members Worked: French Peasant Women Post-WWI (image courtesy of U.S. National Archives and Records Administration, 1917–1920)

Part II

GENDER AND WORK IN HISTORY

In 1984 the Equal Employment Opportunity Commission (EEOC) brought a suit against Sears, Roebuck and Co. for sex discrimination in their hiring and promotion practices. Although the case contained a myriad of political conflicts of interest, Judge John Nordberg found that Sears did not discriminate against women in the 1986 case. An interesting aspect of the trial was the contested expert testimony presented by two well-known feminist historians: Rosalind Rosenberg and Alice Kessler-Harris.[1]

Rosenberg, testifying for Sears, argued that men and women have historically placed different values on work and family. She testified that Sears did not discriminate against women by not employing them in higher-paid commission sales positions, because work outside the home is, and always has been, subordinate to family needs for women. Contemporary gender roles, she argued, are the modern equivalent of the seventeenth-century farm family division of labor, where women provided nurturing and family necessities, while men performed field work. Women, she argued, are more relationship centered, less competitive, and less self-confident, while men are more focused on work, derive their self-worth from work, and are more aggressive and competitive.

In contrast, Kessler-Harris, testifying for the EEOC, argued that women have historically functioned in almost every capacity now assumed to be male, always a function of whether there is a sufficient male labor force available at the right price. Kessler-Harris contended that wherever economic opportunity exists, women have always sought the employment. When those economic opportunities disappeared, women have been more likely to conform to prevailing notions of domesticity, an ideology that employers have used to regulate female participation in the workforce (Milkman).

The historical debate surrounding gendered values and work is explored in the articles of Part II. Joan Scott and Louise Tilly, in "Women's Work and the Family in Nineteenth Century Europe," challenge Rosenberg's perspective that working women constitute a historical anomaly, and that "women's proper place" is one of economic dependency and idealized femininity. In evaluating labor-force statistics from the nineteenth and twentieth centuries in England, France, and Italy, Scott and Tilly found that women of lower strata always worked, and this was in fact a significant aspect of their moral construct. The authors found a continuity of values and attitudes toward gender and work, which have adapted to changing historical circumstances.

Scott and Tilly maintain that among the working and peasant classes in preindustrial Europe, the household was the central economic unit. Family members were interdependent, providing mutual aid to one another, and all were expected to work for the household. Married women generally tended animals and the family garden, and marketed surplus dairy, poultry, and vegetables, while men worked in the fields. Married women held power in this family economy due to their role managing the household. Wives of farmers and craftsmen kept business accounts, purchased goods in the marketplace, and often acted as primary traders as well. Daughters were sent out to work as domestic servants, agricultural laborers, or apprentices to weavers and seamstresses, giving their earnings over to their parents.

With the rise of industrialization, the location and nature of work were transformed, according to Scott and Tilly, but a continuity of values persisted. Unmarried women and girls were recruited by rural silk and textile mills, still sending their wages home. The preindustrial household as economic unit was slowly undermined, however, as the workplace became physically separated from the home. Permanent migration of family members also served to weaken the family economy. The ideology of individualism emerged alongside this economic transformation, replacing family well-being with individual welfare as preeminent. First sons, then daughters, began to keep their own wages. As men entered the factories and formed unions, they fought for the "family wage" and pushed women out of the public arena and into the domestic sphere, rendering them dependent on men for allowances. In sum, Scott and Tilly argue that preindustrial values upholding the significance of women's work were sustained throughout history yet adapted to change over time.

Ruth Schwartz Cowan, in "Housewifery: Household Work and Household Tools under Pre-Industrial Conditions," corroborates Scott and Tilly's analysis of preindustrial gendered work in Europe with a focus on the United States. She argues that the very terms "housewife" and "husband" between the thirteenth and eighteenth centuries refer to those men and women who derived their status from working in and on their house and their land: the emergent middle class. Cowan contends that these preindustrial American husbands and wives worked hard physically and were interdependent in their subsistence roles. Although a sexual division of labor existed, it had no particular rationale. Men made cider and mead, while women made ale, beer, and wine. Women planted and tended vegetables and herbs, while men planted and tended grain, corn, or wheat. Women made and mended clothing from cloth, while men made and mended clothing from leather (shoes, jackets, breeches). Men did some tasks that required brute strength, such as pounding corn and hauling wood, while women also performed tasks requiring strength, such as doing laundry and making soap from lye and tallow. Some tasks were performed by both: weaving, milking cows, and carrying water.

The rise of industrialization in nineteenth-century America ushered in the most profound shift in this gendered agriculturally based economic interdependence, as workplaces were separated from "home places." Cowan suggests that social constructions of masculinity and femininity accompanied this economic shift toward industrialization, and might have served the interests of powerful segments of society. To identify women with "home," emotional warmth, morality, and passivity might have met the needs of ministers, who needed an audience for their sermons; of manufacturers, who needed markets for their goods; of mill owners, who needed pliant workers for their factories; and of newly wealthy men, who wanted wives of leisure ("ladies"), to symbolize their wealthy status. Cowan would disagree with Rosenberg's notion that woman's relationship-centered status is "natural." Rather she argues it was created.

The American experience of black men and women under slavery was both a reflection of the above analyses of gendered work, and its antithesis, according to Jacqueline Jones in "Black Women, Work, and the Family under Slavery." For slave owners, the institution of slavery was an economic and political system designed to extract as much labor from slaves as possible, through force. Whenever possible most slave owners ignored their own belief systems about the sexual division of labor. Slave women were forced to work fourteen-hour days alongside their brothers, fathers, and husbands, building fences, pitching hay, repairing roads, picking cotton and tobacco, plowing, hoeing, and caring for animals. A small percentage of slave women and children worked in the plantation owners' houses full-time, caring for the owners' children at all hours of the day and night, cooking, doing laundry, hauling water, cleaning, ironing, and serving every need and whim of the white owners, and often subjected to rape by the white male head of household.

Within slave family quarters, however, Jones argues, black men and women reproduced the sexual division of labor found in white colonial society. Into the nineteenth century slave women spun thread, wove cloth, made dyes for cloth, grew food for their family, and did most of the child care. Men in the slave quarters collected firewood, made shoes, constructed tools, built furniture, and hunted small animals. Some West African patterns of work and knowledge survived in American slave quarters as well. Certain West African tribes brought with them their cultural traditions of cultivating rice, cotton, and indigo, with women playing major roles in food production and the delivery of household services for their own families.

Although slave men and women maintained relative equality with one another due to their common absence of rights to property and acquisition of wealth (prohibiting men from attaining a level of patriarchy comparable to white men), slave women still worked doubly hard. They were not only laborers, but also reproducers of the slave owners' property: children. Jones illustrates the significance of this point with the way in which violence was meted out to pregnant slave women. A special hole was dug in the earth to protect her pregnant belly, while the rest of her body was exposed to endure the lash. In sum, Jones elucidates the ways in which African American slaves both reflected, and were prevented from adhering to, the dominant gendered values toward work during slavery.

Alice Kessler-Harris, in "The Paradox of Motherhood," brings the debate about gendered values toward work into the late nineteenth and early twentieth century and focuses on the role of the state. She argues that a paradox emerged in the United States in which the concept of motherhood became an object of protection in the workplace, yet women who became mothers had no job protection at all. In the 1908 case of *Muller v. Oregon,* the court argued that the state had an interest in protecting the present and future roles of "mothers of the race." As a result, women's hours and places of work were subsequently regulated, since all women were viewed as "potential mothers," requiring protection for their future offspring.

The result of this legislation was to perpetuate stereotypic assumptions about women: they were frail in their constitution, unable to work long hours or nights, and their primary role was to meet the needs of the family. Protective labor legislation was passed in thirty-nine out of forty-eight states between 1908 and 1920, regulating women's work hours. This set up the construct of motherhood versus work, rather than motherhood and work, in which maternity legislation could have emerged. There were no alternative proposals for child-care centers, paid parental leave, or increased police patrols to accommodate night work. In addition, male workers remained unprotected from low wages and dangerous work conditions they had to endure, resulting from unfettered capitalism, until the 1930s.

The American labor movement, interested in saving jobs for men and organizing male workers, campaigned for a "family wage," in which men would be paid enough to support the family as a whole, eliminating women's need to work at all. Middle-class women reformers concerned about sustaining "traditional" healthy families also fought for reduced hours of women's work, as well as night work restrictions.

The result of the protective labor legislation was, according to Kessler-Harris, that women remained protected only as potential mothers, not as workers or individuals. The construction of citizenship for women was rooted in the notion of the state's right to protect only motherhood and family roles. Thus, in contrast to Rosenberg's contention that women have always held family values as the primary determinant in their choice of work, Kessler-Harris argues that political and judicial factors have historically constrained women's economic opportunities for work, rendering it feasible or not to conjoin with family.

Note

1. Ruth Milkman, "Women's History and the Sears Case," *Feminist Studies* 12, no. 2 (1986): 375–400.

CHAPTER 6

Women's Work and the Family in Nineteenth-Century Europe

Joan W. Scott and Louise A. Tilly

[. . .]

Why did women work in the nineteenth century and why was the female labor force predominantly young and single? To answer these questions we must first examine the relationship of these women to their families of origin (the families into which they were born), not to their families of procreation (the family launched at marriage). We must ask not only how husbands regarded their wives' roles, but what prompted families to send their *daughters* out into the job market as garment workers or domestic servants.

The parents of these young women workers during industrialization were mostly peasants and, to a lesser extent, urban workers. When we examine the geographic and social origins of domestic servants, one of the largest groups of women workers, their rural origins are clear. Two-thirds of all the domestic servants in England in 1851 were daughters of rural laborers. For France, we have no aggregate numbers, but local studies suggest similar patterns. In his study of Melun, for example, Chatelain found that in 1872, 54 percent of female domestic servants were either migrants from rural areas or foreigners.[1] Theresa McBride calculated that in Versailles from 1825 to 1853, 57.7 percent of female domestic servants were daughters of peasants. In Bordeaux, a similar proportion obtained: 52.8 percent. In Milan, at the end of the nineteenth century, servants were less likely to be city-born than any other category of workers.[2]

If cultural values were involved in the decisions of rural and lower class families to send their daughters to work, we must ask what values they were. [. . .] [William] Goode assumes that the idea of "woman's proper place," with its connotations of complete economic dependency and idealized feminity is a traditional value.[3] In fact, it is a rather recently accepted middle-class value not at all inconsistent with notions of "the rights and responsibilities of the individual." The hierarchical division of labor within the family which assigned the husband the role of breadwinner and the wife the role of domestic manager and moral guardian emerged clearly only in the nineteenth century and was associated with the growth of the middle class and the diffusion of its values.[4] On the other hand, as we will demonstrate at length below, traditional ideas about women held by peasant and laboring families did not find feminine and economic functions incompatible. In the pre-industrial Europe described by Peter Laslett and in contemporary pre-modern societies studied by anthropologists,[5] the household or the family is the crucial economic unit. Whether or not all work is done at home, all family members are expected to work. It is simply assumed that women will work, for their contribution is valued as necessary for the survival of the family unit. The poor, the illiterate, the economically and politically powerless of the past operated according to values which fully justified the employment of women outside the home.

[. . .]

Our examination of the evidence on women's work in the nineteenth century has led us to a different understanding of the process which led to the relatively high employment of women outside the home in nineteenth-century Europe. The model we use posits a continuity of traditional values and behavior in changing circumstances. Old values coexist with and are used by people to adapt to extensive structural changes. This assumes that people perceive and act on the changes they experience in terms of ideas and attitudes they already hold. These ideas eventually change, but not as directly or immediately as Goode and Engels would have us believe. Behavior is less the product of new ideas than of the effects of old ideas operating in new or changing contexts.[6]

Traditional families then, operating on long-held values, sent their daughters to take advantage of increased opportunities generated by industrialization and urbanization. Industrial development did not affect all areas of a given country at the same time. Rather, the process can best be illustrated by an image of "islands of development" within an underdeveloped sea, islands which drew population to them from the less developed areas.[7] The values of the less developed sector were imported into the developing sector and there were extended, adapted and only gradually transformed.

As peasant values were imported, so was the behavior they directed. And work for the wives and daughters of the poor was a familiar experience in pre-industrial societies. No change in values, then, was necessary to permit lower class women to work outside the home during the nineteenth century. Neither did industrialization "emancipate" these women by permitting more of them to work outside the home. And, given the fluctuations in the size of the female labor force especially, it is difficult to see any direct connection between the work of peasant and working-class women and the political enfranchisement of all women.

[. . .]

Commentators on many different areas of Europe offer strikingly similar descriptions of peasant social organization. Anthropologists and social historians seem to agree that regardless of country "the peasantry is a pre-industrial social entity which carries over into contemporary society specific elements of a different, older, social structure, economy and culture." The crucial unit of organization is the family "whose solidarity provides the basic framework for mutual aid, control and socialization." The family's work is usually directed to the family farm, property considered to belong to the group rather than to a single individual. "The individual, the family and the farm appear as an indivisible whole." "Peasant property is, at least *de facto*, family property. The head of the family appears as the manager rather than the proprietor of family land."[8]

These descriptions of Eastern European peasants are echoed by Michael Anderson in his comparison of rural Lancashire and rural Ireland early in the nineteenth century. He suggests that in both cases the basis of "functional family solidarity . . . was the absolute *interdependence* of family members such that neither fathers nor sons had any scope for alternatives to the family as a source of provision for a number of crucially important needs."[9] Italian evidence confirms the pattern. Although in late nineteenth-century Lombardy a kind of *frérèche* (brothers and their families living together and working the land together) was a frequent alternative to the nuclear family, the household was the basic unit of production. All members of the family contributed what they could either by work on the farm, or, in the case of women and the young, by work in nearby urban areas or in rural textile mills. Their earnings were turned over to the head of the household; in the case of brothers joined in one household, the elder usually acted as head. He took care of financial matters and contractual relationships in the interests of all.[10] For Normandy in the eighteenth century, Gouesse's recent study has described the gradual evolution of reasons given for marriage when an ecclesiastical dispensation had to be applied for. At the end of that century, reasons such as "seeking well-being," or "desire to live happily" became more common. Gouesse considers these differences of expression rather superficial; what all these declarations meant, although few stated this explicitly, was that one had to be married in order to live. "The married couple was the simple community of work, the elementary unit." In nineteenth-century Brittany, "all the inhabitants of the farm formed a working community . . . linked one to the other like the crew of a ship."[11]

Despite differences in systems of inheritance and differences in the amount of land available, the theory of the peasant economy developed by Chayanov for nineteenth-century Russia applies elsewhere. The basis of this system is the family, or more precisely the household—in Russia, all those "having eaten from one pot." It has a dual role as a unit of production and consumption. The motivations of its members, unlike capitalist aims, involve "securing the needs of the family rather than . . . making a profit." The family's basic problem is organizing the work of its members to meet its annual budget and "a single wish to save or invest capital if economic conditions allow."[12]

Members of the family or household have clearly defined duties, based in part on their age and their position in the family and in part on their sex. Sex role differentiation clearly existed in these societies. Men and women not only performed different tasks, but they occupied different space.[13] Most often, although by no means always, men worked the fields while women managed the house, raised and cared for animals, tended a garden and marketed surplus dairy products, poultry and vegetables. There was also seasonal work in the fields at planting and harvest times.[14] [. . .]

Women labored not only on the farm, but at all sorts of other work, depending in part on what was available to them. In most areas their activity was an extension of their household functions of food provision, animal husbandry and clothing making. Documentation of this can be found in almost every family monograph in the six volumes of Le Play's *Les ouvriers européens.* There was the wife of a French vineyard worker, for example, whose principal activity involved the care of a cow. "She gathers hay for it, cares for it and carries its milk to town to sell." Another wife worked with her husband during harvest seasons and "washed laundry and did other work . . . for farmers and landowners in the neighborhood." She also wove linen "for her family and for sale." Other women sewed gloves or clothing; some took in infants to nurse as well.[15] In the regions surrounding the silk-weaving city of Lyon, the wives and daughters of farmers tended worms and reeled silk.[16] Similarly, in Lombardy, seasonal pre-occupation with the care of the hungry worms filled the time of women and children in the household.[17]

[...]

The role women played in the family economy usually gave them a great deal of power within the family. Scattered historical sources complement the more systematic work of contemporary anthropologists on this point. All indicate that while men assume primacy in public roles, it is women who prevail in the domestic sphere. Hufton even suggests they enjoyed "social supremacy" within the family.[18] Her suggestion echoes Le Play's first-hand observation. In the course of his extensive study of European working-class urban and rural families (carried out from the 1840s–70s), he was struck by the woman's role. "Women are treated with deference, they often . . . exercise a preponderant influence on the affairs of the family (*la communauté*)." [...]

The key to the woman's power, limited almost exclusively, of course, to the family arena, lay in her management of the household. In some areas, wives of craftsmen kept business accounts, as did the wives or daughters of farmers.[19] Their familiarity with figures was a function of their role as keeper of the household's accounts, for the woman was usually the chief buyer for the household in the market place and often the chief trader as well. Primitive as was the accounting these women could do, it was a tool for dealing with the outside world. Working-class women also often held the purse strings, making financial decisions, and even determining the weekly allowance their husbands received for wine and tobacco.

[...]

It is important here to stress that we speak here of married women. Whatever power these women enjoyed was a function of their participation in a mutual endeavor, and of the particular role they played as a function of their sex and marital status. Their influence was confined to the domestic sphere, but that sphere bulked large in the economic and social life of the family. In this situation, women were working partners in the family enterprise.

Daughters were socialized early, in lower-class families, to assume family and work responsibilities. "Daughters . . . begin as soon as their strength permits to help their mother in all her work."[20] Frequently they were sent out of the household to work as agricultural laborers or domestic servants. Others were apprenticed to women who taught them to weave or sew. In areas of rural Switzerland where cottage industry was also practiced, daughters were a most desirable asset. It was they who could be spared to spin and weave while their mothers worked at home; and they gave their earnings "as a matter of course to the economic unit, the maintenance of whose property had priority over individual happiness."[21] Whatever her specific job a young girl early learned the meaning of the saying, "woman's work is never done." And she was prepared to work hard for most of her life. [....]

Women's work was in the interest of the family economy. Their roles, like those of their husbands, brothers and fathers, could be modified and adjusted to meet difficult times or changing circumstances. [...]

This means that traditional families employed a variety of strategies to promote the well-being of the family unit. Sometimes the whole family hired itself out as farm hands, sometimes this was done only by men, at other times by one or more children. [. . .]

Similar examples can be drawn from non-farming families as well. The first industrial revolution in England broke the unity of home and workshop by transferring first spinning and then weaving into factories. Neil Smelser's study of *Social Change in the Industrial Revolution* shows, however, that in the first British textile factories the family as a work unit was imported into the mills. "Masters allowed the operative spinners to hire their own assistants . . . the spinners chose their wives, children, near relatives or relatives of the proprietors. Many children, especially the youngest, entered the mill at the express request of their parents."[22] This extension of the family economy into factories in early industrialization declined after the 1820s, of course, with the increased differentiation and specialization of work. But the initial adjustment to a changed economic structure involved old values operating in new settings.

[. . .] Long before the nineteenth century, lower-class families had sent their daughters out to work. The continuation of this practice and of the values and assumptions underlying it is evident not only in the fact of large numbers of single women working but also in the age structure of the female labor force, in the kinds of work these women did and in their personal behavior.

The fact that European female labor forces consisted primarily of young, single women—girls, in the language of their contemporaries—is itself an indication of the persistence of familial values. Daughters were expendable in rural and urban households, certainly more expendable than their mothers and, depending on the work of the family, their brothers. When work had to be done away from home and when its duration was uncertain, the family interest was best served by sending forth its daughters. Domestic service, the chief resort of most rural girls, was a traditional area of employment. It was often a secure form of migration since a young girl was assured a place to live, food, and a family. There were risks involved also; servant unemployment and servant exploitation were real. Nevertheless, during the nineteenth century, though many more girls were sent into service and moved farther from home than had traditionally been the case, the move itself was not unprecedented. Domestic service was an acceptable employment partly because it afforded the protection of a family and membership in a household.[23]

This was true not only of domestic service, but of other forms of female employment. In Italy and France, textile factory owners attempted to provide "family" conditions for their girls. Rules of conduct limited their activity, and nuns supervised the establishments, acting as substitute parents. *In loco parentis* for some factory owners sometimes even meant arranging suitable marriages for their female operatives.[24] [. . .]

Domestic service, garment-making and even textile manufacturing, the three areas in which female labor was overwhelmingly concentrated, were all traditional areas of women's work. The kind of work parents sent their daughters to do, in other words, did not involve a radical departure from the past. [. . .]

As parents sent daughters off with traditional expectations, so the daughters attempted to fulfill them. Evidence for the persistence of familial values is found in the continuing contributions made by working daughters to their families. If in some cases factories sent the girls' wages to their parents, in others, girls simply sent most of their money home themselves. In England, it was not until the 1890s that single working girls living at home kept some of their own money.[25] [. . .]

In Lancashire "considerable contact was maintained" between migrants and their families. Money was sent home, members of the family were brought to the city to live by family members who had "travelled" and sometimes even "reverse migration" occurred.[26] [. . .]

The cultural values which sent young girls out to work for their families also informed their personal behavior. The increase, noted by historians and demographers, in illegitimate birth rates in many European cities from about 1750 to 1850 can be seen, paradoxically, as yet another demonstration of the persistence of old attitudes in new settings.[27] Alliances with young men may have begun in the city as at home, the girls seeking potential husbands in the hope of establishing a family of their own. The difference, of course, was that social customs that could be enforced at home, could not be in the city. [. . .]

The loneliness and isolation of the city was clearly one pressure for marriage. So was the desire to escape domestic service and become her own mistress in her own home as her mother had been. The conditions of domestic service, which usually demanded that servants be unmarried, also contributed to illicit liaisons and led many a domestic to abandon her child. This had long been true; what was different in nineteenth-century Europe was that the great increase in the proportions of women employed in domestic service outstripped increased employment in manufacturing. This meant that more women than ever before, proportionately, were employed in this sector, which was particularly liable to produce illegitimate children.

Yet another motive for marriage was economic. Girls in factories were said to be fairly well-paid, but most girls did not work in factories. Women in the needle trades and other piece-work industries barely made enough to support themselves. (Wages constantly fluctuated in these consumer product trades and declined after the 1830s in both England and France. Women in these trades were also paid half of what men received for comparable work, often because it was assumed that women's wages were part of a family wage, an assumption which did not always correspond with reality.[28]) In the rural households they came from, subsistence depended on multiple contributions. The logical move for a single girl whose circumstances took her far from her family and whose wages were insufficient either to support herself or to enable her to send money home, would be to find a husband; together they might be able to subsist.

[. . .]

Even among prostitutes, many of whom were destitute or unemployed servants and piece-workers, a peculiar blend of old and new attitudes was evident. In pre-industrial society, lower-class women developed endless resources for obtaining food for their families. Begging was not unheard of and flirtations and sexual favors were an acknowledged way of obtaining bread or flour in time of scarcity. Similarly, in nineteenth-century London, prostitutes interviewed by Mayhew explained their "shame" as a way of providing food for their families. One, the mother of an illegitimate boy, explained that to keep herself and her son from starving she was "forced to resort to prostitution." Another described the "glorious dinner" her solicitations had brought. And a daughter explained her prostitution to the author of *My Secret Life* as her way of enabling the rest of the family to eat: "Well, what do you let men fuck you for? Sausage rolls?" "Yes, meat-pies and pastry too."[29]

Not all single working girls were abandoned with illegitimate children, nor, despite the alarm of middle-class observers, did most become prostitutes. Many got married and most left the labor force when they did. Both the predominance of young single girls in the female labor force and the absence of older married women reflect the persistence of traditional familial values. When they married, daughters were no longer expected to contribute their wages to their parents' household.

[. . .]

Whether they worked outside the home or not, married women defined their role within the framework of the family economy. Married working-class women, in fact, seem almost an internal backwater of pre-industrial values within the working-class family. Long after their husbands and children had begun to adopt some of the individualistic values associated with industrialization, these women continued the self-sacrificing, self-exploitative work that so impressed Le Play and that was characteristic of the peasant or household economy. Surely this (and not the fact that "husbands gave purpose to married women among the poor") is the meaning of the testimony of a woman from York cited by Peter Stearns: "If there's anything extra to buy such as a pair of boots for one of the children, me and the children goes without dinner—or mebbe only 'as a cop o' tea and a bit o' bread, but Him allers takes 'is dinner to work, and I never tell 'im."[30] As long as her role is economically functional for her family, familial values make sense for the lower-class woman. And the role of provider and financial manager, of seamstress and occasional wage earner was economically functional for a long time in working class families.

Perhaps most illustrative is this case history which embodies the collective portrait we have just presented. Francesca F. was born in about 1817 in a rural area of Moravia and remained at home until she was 11.[31] She had a typical childhood for a girl of her class. She learned from her mother how to keep house and help on the farm, and she learned at school how to read, write, figure and, most important of all, sew. At eleven, she was sent into domestic service in a neighboring town. She worked successively in several different houses, increasing her earnings as she changed jobs. At one house she acquired a speciality as a seamstress. She saved some money, but sent most of it home, and she returned home (to visit and renew her passport) at least once a year.

Until her eighteenth year, Francesca's experience was not unlike young girls' of earlier generations. Her decision to "seek her fortune in Vienna," though, began a new phase of her life. With the good wishes of her parents, she paid her coach passage out of her savings and three days after she arrived she found a job as a maid. She lived with the bourgeois family she worked for for six months. Then she left for a better position which she held until her master died (six months). Yet another job as a domestic lasted a year.

At twenty, attracted by the opportunities for work available in a big city and tired of domestic service, she apprenticed herself to a wool weaver. He went bankrupt after a year and she found yet another job. That one she quit because the work was unsteady and she began sewing gloves for a small manufacturer. Glove-making was a prospering piece-work industry and Francesca had to work "at home." Home was a boarding house where she shared her bed with another working girl of "dubious character." Unhappy with these arrangements, Francesca fortunately met a young cabinet maker, himself of rural origin with whom she began living. (The practice of sleeping with one's fiancé was not uncommon in rural Moravia according to Le Play.) She soon had a child whom she cared for while she sewed gloves, all the while saving money for her marriage. (Viennese authorities at this time required that workers show they could support a family before they were permitted to marry. The task of accumulating savings usually fell to the future bride.)

Three years after she met the cabinet-maker, they were married. Francesca paid all the expenses of the wedding and provided what was essentially her own dowry—all the linens and household furnishings they needed. The daughter of rural peasants, Francesca was now the mother of an urban working-class family. Although the care of her children and the management of her household consumed much of her time, she still managed to earn wages in 1853, by doing the equivalent of 125 full days of work, making gloves. (Although it amounted in Le Play's calculation to 125 days, Francesca sewed gloves part of the day during most of the year.)

As long as piece-work was available to her, Francesca F. could supplement her husband's wage with her own work. With the decline of such domestic work, however, and the rise of factories, it would become increasingly difficult for the mother of five young children to leave her household responsibilities in order to earn a wage. Economic conditions in Vienna in the 1850s still made it possible for Francesca to fulfill the role expected of a woman of the popular classes.

Traditional values did not persist indefinitely in modern or modernizing contexts. As families adapted customary strategies to deal with new situations they became involved in new experiences which altered relationships within the family and the perceptions of those relationships. As the process of change involved retention of old values and practices, it also transformed them, but in a more gradual and complex manner than either Goode or Engels implied.

The major transformation involved the replacement of familial values with individualistic ones. These stressed the notion that the individual was owner of him- or herself rather than a part of a social or moral whole.[32] They involved what Anderson calls "an instrumental orientation" of family members to their families "requiring reciprocation for their contribution in the very short run."[33] These attitudes developed differently in different places depending in part on specific circumstances. Nonetheless, the evidence indicates an underlying similarity in the process and the final outcome. Sons first, and only later daughters, were permitted to keep some of their earnings. They were granted allowances by their parents in some cases; in others a specified family contribution was set, in still others the child decided what portion of her pay she would send home (and it diminished and became increasingly irregular over time). Anderson points out that in Preston, high factory wages of children reversed normal dependencies and made parents dependent on their children. The tensions created by the different priorities of parents and children led to feuds. And in these situations children often left home voluntarily and gladly and "became unrestrained masters of their destiny."[34]

Long distance and permanent migration also ultimately undermined family ties. And the pressures of low wages and permanent urban living, the forced independence of large numbers of young girls, clearly fostered calculating, self-seeking attitudes among them. They began to look upon certain jobs as avenues of social and occupational mobility, rather than as a temporary means to earn some money for the family. Domestic service remained a major occupation for women until the twentieth century in most of Europe. (In fact, in the mid-nineteenth century the number of women employed as domestics increased tremendously.) Nonetheless, as it embodied traditional female employment, a position as a servant also began to mean an opportunity for geographic and occupational mobility. Once the trip to the city and the period of adjustment to urban life had been accomplished under the auspices of service, a young girl could seek better and more remunerative work.[35] Her prospects for marrying someone who made better money in the city also increased immeasurably.

Their new experiences and the difficulties and disillusionment they experienced clearly developed in young women a more individualistic and instrumental orientation. They lived and worked with peers increasingly. They wanted to save their money for clothes and amusements. They learned to look out for their own advantage, to value every penny they earned, to place their own desires and interests above those of their families.

Decreased infant mortality and increased educational opportunity also modified family work strategies. And instead of sending all their children out to work for the family welfare, parents began to invest in their children's futures by keeping them out of the work force and sending them to school. (Clearly this strategy was adopted earlier for sons than daughters—the exact history of the process remains to be described.) The family ethic at once sponsored intergenerational mobility and a new individualistic attitude as well.[36]

A number of factors, then, were involved in the waning of the family economy. They included the location of job opportunities, increased standards of living and higher wages, proximity to economic change, increased exposure to and adherence to bourgeois standards as chances for mobility into the bourgeoisie increased, ethnic variations in work patterns and family organization, and different rates of development in different regions and different countries. All of these factors contributed to the decline of the family as a productive unit and to the modification of the values associated with it. The decline can be dated variously for various places, classes and ethnic groups. It reached the European peasant and working classes only during the nineteenth century, and in some areas, like Southern Italy, rural Ireland and rural France, not until the twentieth century. The usefulness of the family model as a unit of analysis for social relationships and economic decision making, however, has not disappeared.[37]

[. . .] The rising standard of living and increased wages for men, which enabled them to support their families, made it less necessary for married women to work outside the home. (In early industrialization, such work also exacted great costs in terms of infant and child mortality.)[38] Even for single women, economic change reduced traditional work opportunities, while new jobs opened up for those with more education. After World War I, for example, domestic service was much less important as an area of employment for young women. A smaller number of permanent servants who followed that occupation as a profession replaced the steady stream of young women who had constituted the domestic servant population.[39] The rise of factory garment production seems to have limited work available for women in Milan and elsewhere.[40] On the other hand, the growth of new jobs in expanding government services, in support services for business, in commerce, in health services and in teaching provided work opportunities, primarily for single women, especially for those with at least a basic education.[41]

There is evidence also that women's role in the household, whether as wives or as daughters, was modified with time. In Britain, women in working-class families began to lose control over finances early in the twentieth century, but the process was not complete until World War II. Working girls began to receive spending money of their own only at the end of the nineteenth century. After about 1914, more and more single girls kept more and more of their wages, and wives began to receive a household allowance from their husbands, who kept the rest and determined how it was spent.[42] The rhetoric of some working-class organizations also suggests a change in ideas about family roles. Labor unions demanded higher wages for men so that they could support families and keep their wives at home. Some socialist newspapers described the ideal society as one in which "good socialist wives" would stay at home and care for the health and education of "good socialist children."[43]

The changes that affected women's work and women's place in the family late in the nineteenth and in the twentieth centuries are subjects which are virtually unexplored by historians. They cannot be understood, however, apart from the historical context we have presented. It was European peasant and working-class families which experienced at first hand the structural changes of the nineteenth century. These experiences were anything but uniform. They were differentiated geographically, ethnically and temporally and they involved complex patterns of family dynamics and family decision making. The first contacts with structural change in all cases, however, involved adjustments of traditional strategies and were informed by values rooted in the family economy. It is only in these terms that we can begin to understand the work of the vast majority of women during the nineteenth century. We must examine *their* experience in the light of *their* familial values and not our individualistic ones. The families whose wives and daughters constituted the bulk of the female labor force in western Europe during most of the nineteenth century simply did not value the "rights and responsibilities of the individual" which Goode invokes. Their values cannot be logically or historically tied to the political enfranchisement of women. [. . .]

Notes

1. Abel Chatelain, "Migrations et domesticité feminine urbaine en France, XVIII siècle-XX siècle," *Revue historique economique et sociale* 47 (1969): 521; E. Royston Pyke, *Golden Times* (New York, 1970), 156.

2. Theresa McBride, "Rural Tradition and the Process of Modernization: Domestic Servants in Nineteenth Century France," unpublished doctoral dissertation, Rutgers University, 1973,

85; Louise A. Tilly, "The Working Class of Milan, 1881–1911," unpublished doctoral dissertation, University of Toronto, 1974, 129–30.

3. William Goode, *World Revolution and Family Patterns* (New York, 1963).

4. Philippe Ariès, *Centuries of Childhood: A Social History of Family Life*, translated by Robert Baldick (London, 1962); J. A. Banks, *Prosperity and Parenthood. A Study of Family Planning Among the Victorian Middle Classes* (London, 1954); J. A. and Olive Banks, *Feminism and Family Planning in Victorian England* (New York, 1964) all associate the idea of these separate feminine characteristics with the middle class. John Stuart Mill made a compelling argument for granting political equality to women while recognizing feminine preferences and qualities which distinguish women from men. See J. S. and H. T. Mill, *Essays on Sex Equality*, Alice Rossi, ed. (Chicago, 1971). For analysis of hierarchical patterns see Susan Rogers, "Woman's Place: Sexual Differentiation as Related to the Distribution of Power," unpublished paper, Northwestern University, April, 1974.

5. Peter Laslett, *The World We Have Lost* (New York, 1965). Among the many anthropological and historical studies of pre-industrial societies are George Foster, "Peasant Society and the Image of the Limited Good," *American Anthropologist* 67 (April 1965): 293–315; Conrad Arensberg and Solon Kimball, *Family and Community in Ireland* (Cambridge, Mass., 1968); Ronald Blythe, *Akenfield, Portrait of an English Village* (New York, 1968); Edgar Morin, *The Red and the White: Report from a French Village* (New York, 1970); Mack Walker, *German Home Towns: Community, State and General Estates, 1648–1871* (Ithaca, New York, 1971).

6. Our notion is a variation of the one presented by Bert Hoselitz: "On the whole, the persistence of traditions in social behavior . . . may be an important factor mitigating the many dislocations and disorganizations which tend to accompany rapid industrialization and technical change." Bert Hoselitz and Wilbert Moore, *Industrialization and Society* (New York, 1966), 15.

7. W. Arthur Lewis, "Economic Development with Unlimited Supplies of Labour," in A. N. Agarwala and S. P. Singh, eds., *The Economics of Underdevelopment* (New York, 1963), 408.

8. Teodor Shanin, "The Peasantry as a Political Factor," in T. Shanin, ed., *Peasants and Peasant Societies: Selected Readings* (Penguin Books, 1971), 241–4. A similar analysis of the peasant family in mid-twentieth century can be found in Henri Mendras, *The Vanishing Peasant: Innovation and Change in French Agriculture*, translated by Jean Lerner (Cambridge, Mass., 1970), 76: "The family and the enterprise coincide: the head of the family is at the same time the head of the enterprise. Indeed, he is the one because he is the other . . . he lives his professional and his family life as an indivisible entity. The members of his family are also his fellow workers."

9. Michael Anderson, *Family Structure in Nineteenth Century Lancashire* (Cambridge, 1971), 96.

10. "Giunta per la Inchiesta Agraria e sulle condizioni della Classe agricola, *Atti*", Rome, 1882, Vol. VI, Fasc. II, 552, 559, Fasc. III, 87, 175–6, 373, 504, 575.

11. Y. Brekilien, *La vie quotidienne des paysans en Bretagne au XIXe siècle* (Paris, 1966), 37. Jean-Marie Gouesse, "Parenté, famille et marriage en Normandie aux XVIIe et XVII siècles," *Annales, Economies, Sociétés, Civilisations* 27e Année (July–October 1972), 1146–7.

12. Basile Kerblay, "Chayanov and the Theory of Peasantry as a Specific Type of Economy," in Teodor Shanin, ed., *Peasants and Peasant Societies, op. cit.*, 151, and *A. V. Chayanov on the Theory of Peasant Economy*, Daniel Thorner, Basile Kerblay and R. E. F. Smith, eds. (Homewood, Ill., 1966), 21, 60. See also Henriette Dussourd, *Au même pot et au meme feu: etude sur les communautés familiales agricoles du centre de la France* (Moulins, 1962).

13. For the most part, men worked outside the home. They performed public functions for the family and the farm. Women, on the other hand, presided over the interior of the household and over the private affairs of family life. Separate spheres and separate roles did not, however, imply discrimination or hierarchy. It appears, on the contrary, that neither sphere was subordinated to

the other. This interpretation is, however, still a matter of dispute among anthropologists. See Lucienne A. Roubin, "Espace masculin, espace feminin en communauté provencale," *Annales, E. S. C.* 26 (March–April, 1970), 540; Rogers (1974), *op. cit.*, and Rayna Reiter, "Men and Women in the South of France: Public and Private Domains," unpublished paper, 1973, New School for Social Research.

14. Pinchbeck, Part I, *passim.*; Alain Girard et Henri Bastide, "Le budget-temps de la femme mariée á la campagne," *Population* 14 (1959): 253–84.

15. Frederick Le Play, *Les Ouvriers Européens,* 6 vols. (Paris, 1855–78), Vol. 6, 145, 127, and Vol. 5, 261, respectively.

16. Arthur Dunham, *The Industrial Revolution in France* (New York, 1935), 170.

17. Marie Hall Ets, *Rosa, The Life of an Italian Immigrant* (Minneapolis, 1970).

18. Olwen Hufton, "Women in Revolution, 1789–1796," *Past and Present* 53 (1971): 93; Susan Rogers, "Female Forms of Power and the Myth of Male Dominance: A Model of Female/Male Interaction," unpublished paper, 1973; Rémi Clignet, *Many Wives, Many Powers: Authority and Power in Polygynous Families* (Evanston, 1970); Ernestine Friedl, "The Position of Women: Appearance and Reality," *Anthropological Quarterly* 40 (1967): 97–108; Evelyn Michaelson and Walter Goldschmidt, "Female Roles and Male Dominance Among Peasants," *Southwestern Journal of Anthropology* 27 (1971): 330–52; Rayna Reiter, "Modernization in the South of France: the Village and Beyond," *Anthropological Quarterly* 45 (1972): 35–53; Joyce Riegelhaupt, "Salaoio Women: An Analysis of Informal and Formal Political and Economic Roles of Portuguese Peasant Women," *Anthropological Quarterly* 40 (1967): 127–38. See also Olwen Huften, "Women and the Family Economy in Nineteenth Century France," unpublished paper, University of Reading, 1973.

19. That sometimes management roles implied literacy as well is indicated in a manuscript communicated to us by Judith Silver Frandzel, University of New Hampshire. It is the account book of a farm in Besse-sur-Barge, Sarthe, undated but from the 1840s, kept exclusively by the daughter of the family. She lists everything, from sale of animals and land to purchase of handkerchiefs, kitchen utensils or jewelry, for which money was spent or received.

20. Le Play, Vol. 3, 111.

21. Rudolf Braun, "The Impact of Cottage Industry on an Agricultural Population," in *The Rise of Capitalism*, edited by David Landes (New York, 1966), 63.

22. Neil Smelser, *Social Change in the Industrial Revolution: An Application of Theory to the British Cotton Industry* (Chicago, 1959), 188–9.

23. Chatelain, 508.

24. Ets, 87–115; Italy, Ufficio del Lavoro, *Rapporti sulli ispezione del lavoro (1 dicembre 1906–30 giugno (1908),* pubblicazione del Ufficio del Lavoro, Serie C, 1909, 64, 93–4, describes the dormitories and work arrangements in north Italian textile mills; Evelyne Sullerot, *Histoire et sociologie du travail féminin* (Paris, 1968), 91–4; Michelle Perrot, *Les Ouvriers en Gréve, France 1871–1890* (Paris, 1974), 213, 328. Recent interpretations of similar American cases are to be found in John Kasson, "The Factory as Republican Community: The Early History of Lowell, Mass.," unpublished paper read at American Studies Convention, October 1973, and Alice Kessler Harris, "Stratifying by Sex: Notes on the History of Working Women," working paper, Hofstra University, 1974.

25. Peter Stearns,"Working Class Women in Britain, 1890–1914," in Martha Vicinus, ed., *Suffer and Be Still* (Blommington, Indiana, 1972), 110.

26. Anderson, 153.

27. Cf. Edward Shorter, "Illegitimacy, Sexual Revolution and Social Change in Europe, 1750–1900," *Journal of Interdisciplinary History* 2 (1971): 237–72; "Capitalism, Culture and Sexuality: Some Competing Models," *Social Science Quarterly* (1972): 338–56; "Female

Emancipation, Birth Control and Fertility in European History," *American Historical Review* 78 (1973): 605–40.

28. Charles Booth, *Life and Labour of the People of London* (London, 1902); Eileen Yeo and E. P. Thompson, *The Unknown Mayhew* (New York, 1972), 116–80; France, Direction du Travail, *Les associations professionelles ouvriéres*, Vol. 4 (1903), 797–805; P. Leroy-Beaulieu, *Le travail des femmes au XIXe siècle* (Paris, 1873), 50–145.

29. Yeo and Thompson, 141, 148, 169; E. M. Sigsworth and J. J. Wylie, " A Study of Victorian Prostitution and Veneral Disease," in Vicinus, cited above, 81.

30. Stearns, 104.

31. Le Play, Vol. V, 9, 16–17, 45, 50–4.

32. C. B. MacPherson, *The Political Theory of Possessive Individualism, Hobbes to Locke* (Oxford paperback, 1964), 3.

33. Anderson, 131–2.

34. Ibid.

35. Theresa McBride, "Rural Tradition and the Process of Modernization: Domestic Servants in Nineteenth Century France," unpublished doctoral dissertation, Rutgers University, 1973, 85; Chatelain makes a similar point.

36. For an important discussion of changes in family strategies, see Charles Tilly, "Population and Pedagogy in France," *History of Education Quarterly* (Summer 1973): 113–28.

37. See for example Marc Nerlove, "Economic Growth and Population: Perspectives on the 'New Home Economics,'" unpublished draft, Northwestern University, 1973.

38. Margaret Hewitt, *Wives and Mothers in Victorian Industry* (London, 1958), 99–122 and Appendix I. For France, see the debate surrounding the passage of Loi Roussel in 1874, regulating wet nursing.

39. Chatelain; McBride, 20. Domestic service continued, at the same time, to be the channel of geographic mobility of small rural population groups, sometimes in international migration streams.

40. Louise A. Tilly, "Women at Work in Milan, Italy—1880–World War I," paper presented to the American Historical Association annual meeting, December 28, 1972.

41. Lee Holcombe, *Victorian Ladies at Work* (Hamden, Conn., 1973), 216.

42. Stearns, 116.

43. These particular attitudes were expressed in *Le Reveil des Verriers* in an article published in 1893, entitled "La Femme socialiste," but they are representative of many such attitudes expressed in the working class press. See M. Guilbert, "La Presence des femmes dans les professions: incidences sur l'action syndicale avant 1914," *Le Mouvement Social* 63 (1968): 129. For Italy, see *La Difesa delle Lavoratrici* (a socialist newspaper for women) May, 11, 1912, for a socialist view of women's role as mothers. See also Theodore Zeldin, *France, 1848–1945*. Vol. I. *Ambition, Love and Politics* (Oxford, 1973), 346.

CHAPTER 7

Housewifery

HOUSEHOLD WORK AND HOUSEHOLD TOOLS UNDER PRE-INDUSTRIAL CONDITIONS

Ruth Schwartz Cowan

Etymology can illuminate some of the murkier realms of social history. *Housewifery* has had a long history; in English the word can be traced back as far as the thirteenth century. Women have always cooked, laundered, sewed, and nursed children; but it was not until the thirteenth century, when the feudal period was ending and the capitalist organization of society just beginning, that some of the women who did these chores were given the name, and the very special social status, of "housewives."[1] Housewives were the spouses of "husbands"; and husbands, as the compound character of the name implies, were people whose work was also focused on the house (*hus* is the older spelling of our *house*) to which they were "bonded"—houses that they either rented or owned that were, in some socially identifiable sense, their own. Thus husbands and housewives both derived their status from the existence of their house and its associated land—the man because he had some title to it, and the woman because she was married to him. Husbands and housewives were not aristocrats and did not govern large households that employed and gave shelter to dozens, even hundreds, of people; neither were they transient laborers residing, if they resided at all, under roofs that belonged to other people. Housewives and husbands were among the first occupants of that singular social niche—the middle class. They worked the land (hence the term *husbandry* for what we would now call *farming*), and they made independent decisions about the disposition of livestock and tools that were in their possession. Any economic security they had they achieved by working together and *husbanding* their resources. The success of these early independent agricultural families, the yeomanry, depended on the hard labor of both men and women, as this bit of doggerel from the introduction to a popular sixteenth-century domestic manual makes clear:

> In jest and in earnest, here argued ye finde,
> That husband and huswife together must dwell,
> And thereto the judgement of wedded mans mind,

That husbandrie otherwise speedeth not well:
So somewhat more now I intende for to tell,
Of huswiferie like as of husbandrie told,
How huswifelie huswife helps bring in the golde.[2]

The labor that was called "housewiferie" from the thirteenth to the eighteenth centuries acquired a new name, "housework," in the nineteenth; the *Oxford English Dictionary* gives 1841 for the earliest date of its appearance in England and 1871 for the United States.[3] The nineteenth century was the period when industrialization began in England and the United States. Prior to industrialization the word *housework* would probably have been nonsensical since—with the exception of seamen, miners, soldiers, and peddlers—almost all people worked in or on the grounds of a house, their own, or someone else's. One of the most profound effects of industrialization was, and is, the separation of "work places" from "home places"—and the attendant designation of the former as the "place" for men and the latter as the "domain" of women—the set of ideas and behavior which was called, in the nineteenth century, the doctrine of "separate spheres."[4] This physical and ideological separation of men from women created novel conditions for the performance of women's traditional work, and a new word was coined as testimony to the change. *Housewifery* was too firmly rooted in the older, more rural world, peopled by families of yeoman farmers, artisans, and merchants. *Housework* belongs to the nineteenth and, later, the twentieth centuries—the world of workers, managers, and "sales personnel."

Housewifery and the Doctrine of Separate Spheres

Social and intellectual historians have described with considerable skill the nineteenth-century transition from pre- to post-industrial conditions. They have shown us precisely when the doctrine of separate spheres developed, and have also identified the behavioral, moral, emotional, and political consequences of the doctrine that justify calling it not just a doctrine but an ideology. The physical artifact "home" came to be associated with a particular sex, "women"; with a particular emotional tone, "warmth"; with a particular public stance, "morality"; and with a particular form of behavior, "passivity"; while at the very same time, "work" became associated with "men," "hardheartedness," "excitement," "aggression" and "immorality." Some historians have also suggested that these new sets of social definitions served the interests of certain powerful segments of society: manufacturers who needed markets for the goods they were producing, mill owners who needed tractable workers for their factories, ministers who needed audiences for their sermons, political leaders who needed to stabilize their electorates, and the newly rich men who needed to be able to cement their status with the mortar of elaborate hospitality that only homebound wives could provide.

[. . .]

Household Tools and Household Work

Any effort to describe the technological systems of cooking, cleaning, and laundering in the eighteenth and nineteenth centuries is fraught with difficulty. At different
times and in different places women labored under widely variant conditions. Some
were rich, and others were poor; some lived in times of turmoil, and others in times of
peace. Some had easy access to markets, and others were isolated on unpopulated frontiers; some had many children, others few; some were lazy, and others compulsive—
the list could go on endlessly. Technological and supply systems differed from place
to place; some economies were based on corn; others on wheat, tobacco, cotton, or
mineral goods. Some households burned wood; some, coal; some, peat; some, dried
sod; some, dried dung. Some people hauled their water from running brooks; some
collected it in rain barrels; some pumped it from wells; and some purchased it from
peddlers. Some people kept cows and were thereby able to make their own butter and
cheese; some purchased theirs from neighbors or shopkeepers. Some women baked
their own bread, others made their dough and brought it to a neighbor's oven for baking; some brought it to a bakeshop, others purchased theirs readymade. It is not easy
to generalize about what it was like to be engaged in cooking, cleaning, and laundering
under such vastly different conditions.

One way would be to work backward from some sample end product and to describe the technological systems and the work processes that would have been necessary
to produce it under various sets of conditions; for this purpose it is essential to choose
some end product that is both common to people living under variant conditions and
central to their lives. Most travelers' accounts of the meals eaten by Americans in those
centuries mention the ubiquity of some kind of "stew"—meat and vegetables cooked,
for a long time, in a liquid. Here, for example, is a traveler's account of the daily diet
of prosperous Dutch families living in Albany, New York, in the 1750s, but it is fairly
representative (give or take a different beverage, a different grain, or a different kind
of meat and vegetables) of what one can read about people living a century before or a
century after in places as diverse as Maine, Maryland, and Michigan:

> Their breakfast here in the country was as follows: they drank tea . . . and
> with the tea they ate bread and butter and radishes. . . . They sometimes
> had small round cheeses (not especially fine tasting) on the table, which they
> cut into thin slices and spread upon the buttered bread. . . . At noon they
> had a regular meal, meat served with turnips and cabbage. In the evening
> they made a porridge of corn, poured it as customary into a dish, made a
> large hole in the center into which they poured fresh milk. . . . This was
> their supper nearly every evening. After that they would eat some meat left
> over from the noonday meal, or bread and butter with cheese. If any of the
> porridge remained from the evening, it was boiled with buttermilk in the
> morning . . . and to this they added either syrup or sugar.[5]

Before the twentieth century, most people ate an extraordinarily unvaried diet;
conditions of weather, crop cycles, and transportation were such that, day in and day
out, only a very few foods were available, although what was available might change

with the season. The lengthy menus and eight-paragraph recipes that are sometimes trotted out as exemplars of cooking in the "good old days," are actually derived from documents left by people who were exceedingly rich, or they represent the stuff from which great feasts and celebrations were made. Ordinary people ate bread, cheese, butter, porridges, eggs, raw fruits and vegetables in season, preserved fruits and vegetables out of season (in the form, for example, of applesauce, jams, relishes, and pickles), all of it washed down by beer, cider, milk, tea, or coffee (rarely water as that was often undrinkable). When fresh meats were available, they were frequently roasted; otherwise, pork, lamb, and beef were either fried (as with bacon) or cooked for a long time in a liquid (in part to lessen the effects of whatever preservation process had been used). Conditions of household routine were such that the simplest and least exerting forms of cooking had to be utilized most frequently; hence the ubiquity and centrality of those classic "one-pot" dishes, soup and stew.

[. . .]

Let us begin by imagining that this particular pottage was being prepared in the home of a young childless couple living on a small farm in Connecticut in the middle of the eighteenth century, a farm that was as yet too small to require hired help in the fields or in the house, but was large enough to supply the basic needs of wife and husband. To butcher the animal from which the meat was to come, the husband would have used a set of knives made of wood and iron. This being Connecticut, the water to be used in preparation and cleaning would likely have come from a nearby stream and would have been carried to the house in a bucket made of wood, although the staves might have been girdled in iron or leather. The housewife would have put the meat and water into a large iron kettle, and this kettle would have been suspended over the fireplace on an iron lugpole (fifty years earlier it might have been made of green wood) inserted into the mortar of the chimney (lacking a lugpole, the housewife could have used a trammel or a crane made of iron, standing on the floor of the hearth). The fuel for the fire would be hardwood logs, cut, hauled, chopped, and stacked by her husband. The fuel would sit on iron or brass andirons in a fireplace constructed either of bricks or local fieldstones; as masons were not then common (or inexpensive), the likelihood is that her husband had constructed the fireplace himself. If the housewife had been following standard practice on these matters, the herbs and vegetables that were added to the stew would have come from a kitchen garden that she had planted and tended herself (although, when plowing in the spring, her husband might have turned over the soil if it was particularly wet and heavy). The grain that went into the stew for thickening might have been corn or wheat—and, unlike the herbs and vegetables, would have been the product of male, rather than female, labor. The husband would have superintended the growing of it as well as its subsequent processing; had it been corn, he would have husked it and scraped the kernels from the ear; if wheat, he would have supervised the cutting, threshing, and winnowing, although the housewife might have helped. If they had a hand mill (made of stone) for either form of grain, he would have pushed it or managed the draft animals doing the pushing; and if the grain was to be taken to a local water mill to be ground (which would have been the most likely choice in Connecticut in this period), he would have hauled it in a cart drawn by the same draft animals. Skimming and stirring were tasks that the housewife performed with wooden spoons; the spoons themselves had most likely been whittled by the husband during the previous winter when there was little work to be done in the fields. The salt (and other spices, had she had them) would have to have been purchased, as they could not have been made from locally available materials. Once made, the stew would have been served up in wooden trenchers (also whittled by hand), which then would have been wiped clean with a rag (which, at this date, would most likely have come from cloth imported from England, but which could also have been American homespun, although not of this particular housewife's manufacture, since the couple were too early in their life cycle to be able to afford either a loom or the time required for weaving). The last task remaining to the housewife would have been the cleaning of the kettle, accomplished with some water, perhaps some sand, a rag, and a brush that she had made herself, as its name implies, from branches and twigs.

This brief scenario illustrates two important points. First, under the conditions that prevailed in the American colonies during the eighteenth century, the work processes of cooking required the labor of people of both sexes; cooking itself may have been defined as women's work (which it was), but cooking could not be done without prior preparation of tools and foodstuffs, and a good deal of that prior preparation was, as it happens, defined as men's work. Second, acquisition of a technological system of cooking (the fireplace, andirons, pots, and accessory implements) required that there be some contact between the household and the market economy in which it was embedded. Even as simple a household as this one could not have been entirely self-sufficient, for it needed some surplus of cash or goods with which to purchase tools or raw materials that were essential for subsistence. To put this latter point in its baldest form, you cannot cook without a pot, and pots have to be purchased because only skilled artisans have the requisites for making them.

Had I focused on any other meal of the day or on any of the other tasks included in the standard definitions of housewifery—cleaning, laundering, care of infants, care of the ill, manufacture of clothing—these two points would have remained valid generalizations. Buttermaking required that someone had cared for the cows (and, at least among several of the ethnic groups that first settled these shores, this was customarily men's work), and that someone had either made or purchased a churn. Breadmaking required that someone had cared for the wheat (men's work) as well as the barley (men's work) that was one of the ingredients of the beer (women's work) that yielded the yeast that caused the bread to rise. Men grew the flax that women eventually spun into linen, and also had to "brake" it (crushing the fibers in a special, exceedingly heavy instrument) before it could be spun. Women nursed and coddled infants; but men made the cradles and mowed the hay that, as straw, filled and refilled the tickings that the infants lay on. Women scrubbed floors, but men made the lye with which they did it. If the tools used in any of these tasks had been purchased, the household would have had to have some surplus product to exchange for them; if not then the tools would have been made at home by men (with the possible exception of brooms used for sweeping and brushes for scrubbing), since working in wood and leather and metal was defined as men's work. If an eighteenth-century woman had attempted housekeeping without the assistance of a man (or of a good deal of cash with which to purchase the services of men), she would most likely have had markedly to lower her standard of living, to undertake tasks for which she had little training, and to work herself into a state of utter exhaustion—all of which conditions would have seriously endangered her health and probably her life. A similar fate would have befallen a man under the same circumstances had he tried to farm without the help of a woman. Small wonder that most people married and, once widowed, married again. Under the technological and economic conditions that prevailed before industrialization, survival at even a minimally comfortable standard of living required that each household contain adults (or at least grown children) of both sexes, and that each household have some minimal ability to participate in the market economy, at the very least so as to be able to acquire and maintain its tools.

The Household Division of Labor

The division of labor by sex in household work seems to have no rhyme or reason to it, but it was unquestionably a real fact of social existence before industrialization, just as it is today. Men made cider and mead (a drink made from fermented honey); women made beer, ale, and wine (except among the French, where the men made wine). Women mended clothing that was made out of cloth, but men mended clothing—particularly shoes, breeches, and jackets—that was made out of leather. Women had some tasks with which they filled the interstices of their days (sewing, spinning), but so did men (chopping wood and whittling). Men had some tasks that were thought to require brute strength (pounding corn, hauling wood), but so did women (doing the wash or making soap from tallow and lye). A few tasks appear to have been sexually neutral: weaving, milking cows, carrying water, and paring apples or potatoes were chores that, according to the available records, both men and women regularly undertook as the need arose.

Under duress, of course, people were capable of breaking out of their stereotypical roles. If a man was ill or disabled or away from home, a woman could go out to cut down the wheat or feed the cows; similarly, if a woman was unable to work at butchering time, a man could salt the beef or prepare the fat for tallow. But men and women were not well trained to undertake the tasks assigned to members of the opposite sex and consequently could not perform them expertly. The tasks may seem simple when viewed by people, like us, who do not have to perform them; but they were far from simple to the people whose sustenance depended on them; a winter of starvation could result from one small mistake.

An experience of this sort was related by Rebecca Burlend, a Yorkshire peasant woman, who immigrated to Illinois with her husband in 1831 and consequently experienced a kind of trip backward in time, from farming in a locale that was just experiencing the changes wrought by industrialization to farming under conditions that were essentially pre-industrial. The Burlends came to this country with few possessions and little money; they lacked almost all the tools they needed for farming. As there were sugar maples on the property on which they settled, they learned to tap the trees for sap and sold the resultant syrup to a local merchant in exchange for a few hoes and an axe. With the hoes (and the loan of one day's plowing from a neighbor with a plow and a team) they planted wheat their first spring. When the crop was ready for harvesting, they visited another neighbor and borrowed two sickles from him; but on the trip home Mr. Burlend fell on one of the sickles and so badly wounded his leg that he was in danger of dying for several days. When this danger was past, it was clear that he would not be able to stand for several weeks and consequently could not bring in the crop:

> Our wheat was quite ripe, indeed almost ready to shake, and if not cut soon, would be lost. We had no means of hiring reapers, and my husband could not stir out. I was therefore obliged to begin myself. . . . I worked as hard as my strength would allow . . . and in little more than a week had it all cut down. . . . But the wheat was still unhoused, and exposed to the rays of the burning sun, by which it was in danger of being dried so as to waste on the slightest movement. Having neither horses nor waggon, we here encountered another difficulty. The work however could not be postponed. . . . My partner had by this time so far recovered as to be able to move about . . . *and thus he came to the door to shew me how to place the sheaves in forming the stack.*[6] [Author's italics]

Although she had lived and worked on farms for her entire life, Rebecca Burlend did not know how to perform the final stages of reaping wheat; had her husband had not been there to advise her, she was certain that the entire crop would have been lost. People had to be under considerable duress, however, to step out of their accustomed sex roles, as Rebecca Burlend did. As her own testimony, and other first-hand accounts of such situations attest ("we had no means of hiring reapers"), the more usual solution to such a dilemma would have been to hire someone of the appropriate sex to perform the task in the absence of a partner: a "hired girl" to mind the children while a mother was ill or if she had died; a "hired man" to do the butchering or the plowing or the repair of fences if a man was disabled or away from home.

Young men and young women received from parents, relatives, and employers the training that they needed to perform their adult work. Children learned their work-related sex roles by becoming assistants to their parents and by being sent to the homes of relatives when need or circumstance made such an arrangement desirable. A young boy might be "given" to his grandparents if they needed help, or a young girl "lent" to neighbors with many small children to care for; a country niece might be boarded with a city uncle so that she could go to school and help her aunt, or a young city cousin invited to visit in the country to help bring in the harvest. [. . .]

Conclusion

[. . .]

The young couple, similarly, reminds us that although housework was socially defined as "women's work," in reality the daily exigencies of agrarian life meant that men and women had to work in tandem in order to undertake any single life-sustaining chore. The relations between the sexes were reciprocal: women assisted men in the fields, and men assisted women in the house. Women were responsible for cooking, cleaning, laundry, and infant care, just as men were responsible for plowing, sowing, mowing and horse (or oxen, or cow, or pig) care; and all of these chores were essential.

Finally, the tools with which the chores were done—the hoes and axes and pails and pots—seem to us simple devices, but they actually involved a household in complex relations with the market economy in which it was embedded. As self-sufficient as people may have been, they could not cut themselves off entirely from the artisans who made and repaired metal products or from the merchants who transported salt and lime and other household staples over long distances.

In addition, and somewhat ironically, the poorer people were, the fewer the tools they had; and the fewer the tools they had, the more likely they were to be dependent upon the vagaries of the market to provide them with the commodities—food, clothing, and shelter—that were needed for basic subsistence. Thus, our imaginary young couple in Connecticut, if they had wanted to improve their standard of living, would have been well advised to work hard, sustain each other, and take good care of their tools. Their grandchildren, or perhaps their great grandchildren, having passed over the great divide of industrialization would require different advice.

Notes

1. This analysis is based upon the entries for *housewife* and *husband* in *The Oxford English Dictionary* (Oxford, England, 1933). The earliest date given for *housewife* is 1225 and for *husband*—in the sense of a spouse to a housewife—1290.

2. Thomas Tusser [1577]. The verse comes from a poem by Tusser, "The Authours Dialogue between two Bachelors, of wiving and thriving by Affirmation and Objection," which Tusser used as the introduction to a work, "The points of Huswiferie," that he added to his earlier work, *Five Hundred Pointes of Good Husbandrie* [1573]. I have quoted it from the edition edited by W. Payne and Sidney Herrtage (London, 1878), 158.

3. See the entry under *housework* in *A Supplement to the Oxford English Dictionary* (Oxford, England, 1976). Significantly, the earlier volumes of the dictionary do not contain an entry for this word, presumably because the etymological research for those volumes was undertaken during the nineteenth century at a time when the word had not yet passed into frequent use.

4. Many social historians have commented on the origin and impact of this doctrine. On the development of the doctrine of separate spheres, see Carl Degler, *At Odds: Women and the Family in American History* (New York, 1980); Nancy Cott, *Bonds of Womanhood: "Women's Sphere" in New England, 1780–1835* (New Haven, 1977); Ann Douglas, *The Feminization of American Culture* (New York, 1978); Kathryn Kish Sklar, *Catherine Beecher: A Study in American Domesticity* (New Haven, 1973); Barbara Welter, *Dimity Convictions: American Women in the Nineteenth Century* (Columbus, Ohio, 1976); and Susan Strasser, *Never Done: A History of American Housework* (New York, 1982), chap. 10.

5. Peter Kalm, *Travels in North America* [1753], translated from Swedish into English by John Reinhold Forster [1770], revised and edited by Adolph B. Benson [1937], and reissued in facsimile of the 1937 edition (New York, 1964), vol. I, 602.

6. Rebecca and Edward Burlend, *A True Picture of Emigration* [London, 1848], edited by Milo Milton Quaife [1937] and reissued in facsimile of the 1937 edition (New York, 1968), 91–92.

CHAPTER 8

Black Women, Work, and the Family under Slavery

Jacqueline Jones

The burdens shouldered by slave women represented in extreme form the dual nature of all women's labor within a patriarchal, capitalist society: the production of goods and services and the reproduction and care of members of a future work force. The antebellum plantation brought into focus the interaction between notions of women *qua* "equal" workers and women *qua* unequal reproducers; hence a slaveowner just as "naturally" put his bondwomen to work chopping cotton as washing, ironing, or cooking. Furthermore, in seeking to maximize the productivity of his entire labor force while reserving certain domestic tasks for women exclusively, the master demonstrated how patriarchal and capitalist assumptions concerning women's work could reinforce one another. The "peculiar institution" thus involved forms of oppression against women that were unique manifestations of a more universal condition. The following discussion focuses on female slaves in the American rural South between 1830 and 1860—cotton boom years that laid bare the economic and social underpinnings of slavery and indeed all of American society.[1]

Under slavery, blacks' attempts to maintain the integrity of family life amounted to a political act of protest, and herein lies a central irony in the history of slave women. In defiance of their owners' tendencies to ignore gender differences in making work assignments in the fields, the slaves whenever possible adhered to a strict division of labor within their own households and communities. This impulse was exhibited most dramatically in patterns of black family and economic life after emancipation. Consequently, the family, often considered by feminists to be a source (or at least a vehicle) of women's subservience, played a key role in the freed people's struggle to resist racial and gender oppression, for black women's full attention to the duties of motherhood deprived whites of their power over these women as field laborers and domestic servants.[2]

Interviewed by a Federal Writers Project (FWP) worker in 1937, Hannah Davidson spoke reluctantly of her experiences as a slave in Kentucky: "The things that my sister May and I suffered were so terrible. . . . It is best not to have such things in our memory." During the course of the interview she stressed that unremitting toil had been the hallmark of her life under bondage. "Work, work, work," she said; it had consumed all her days (from dawn until midnight) and all her years (she was only eight when she began minding her master's children and helping the older women with their spinning). "I been so exhausted working, I was like an inchworm crawling along a roof. I worked till I thought another lick would kill me." On Sundays, "the only time they had to themselves," women washed clothes and some of the men tended their small tobacco patches. As a child she loved to play in the haystack, but that was possible only on "Sunday evening, after work."[3]

American slavery was an economic and political system by which a group of whites extracted as much labor as possible from blacks through the use or threat of force. A slaveowner thus replaced any traditional division of labor that might have existed among blacks before enslavement with a work structure of his own choosing. All slaves were barred by law from owning property or acquiring literacy skills, and although the system played favorites with a few, black females and males were equal in the sense that neither sex wielded economic power over the other. Hence property relations—"the basic determinant of the sexual division of labor and of the sexual order" within most societies[4]—did not affect male-female interaction among the slaves themselves. To a considerable extent, the types of jobs slaves did, and the amount and regularity of labor they were forced to devote to such jobs, were all dictated by the master.

For these reasons, the definition of slave women's work is problematical. If work is any activity that leads either directly or indirectly to the production of marketable goods, then slave women did nothing *but* work.[5] Even their efforts to care for themselves and their families helped to maintain the owner's work force and to enhance its overall productivity. Tasks performed within the family context—childcare, cooking, and washing clothes, for example—were distinct from labor carried out under the lash in the field or under the mistress's watchful eye in the Big House. Still, these forms of nurture contributed to the health and welfare of the slave population, thereby increasing the actual value of the master's property (that is, slaves as both strong workers and "marketable commodities"). White men warned prospective mothers that they wanted neither "runts" nor girls born on their plantations, and slave women understood that their owner's economic self-interest affected even the most intimate family ties. Of the pregnant bondswomen on her husband's large Butlers Island (Georgia) rice plantation, Fanny Kemble observed, "they have all of them a most distinct and perfect knowledge of their value to their owners as property," and she recoiled at their obsequious profession, obviously intended to delight her: "Missus, tho' we no able to work, we make little niggers for Massa." One North Carolina slave woman, the mother of fifteen children, used to carry her youngest with her to the field each day, and "when it get hungry she just slip it around in front and feed it and go right on picking or hoeing," symbolizing in one deft motion the equal significance of her productive and reproductive functions to her owner.[6]

It is possible to divide the daily work routine of slave women into three discrete types of activity. These involved the production of goods and services for different groups and individuals, and included women's labor that directly benefitted, first, their families, second, other members of the slave community, and third, their owners. Although the master served as the ultimate regulator of all three types of work, he did not subject certain duties related to personal sustenance (that is, those carried out in the slave quarters) to the same scrutiny that characterized fieldwork or domestic service.

[. . .]

In his efforts to wrench as much field labor as possible from female slaves without injuring their capacity to bear children, the master made "a noble admission of female equality," observed one abolitionist sympathizer, with bitter irony. Slaveholders had little use for sentimental platitudes about the delicacy of the female constitution when it came to grading their "hands" according to physical strength and endurance. Judged on the basis of a standard set by a healthy adult man, most women probably ranked as three-quarter hands; yet there were enough women like Susan Mabry of Virginia, who could pick four or five hundred pounds of cotton a day (150 to 200 pounds was considered respectable for an average worker), to remove from a master's mind all doubts about the ability of a strong, healthy woman field worker. As a result, he conveniently discarded his time-honored Anglo-Saxon notions about the types of work best suited for women, thereby producing many "dreary scenes" like the one described by northern journalist Frederick Law Olmsted: during winter preparation of rice fields on a Sea Island plantation, a group of black women, "armed with axes, shovels and hoes . . . all slopping about in the black, unctuous mire at the bottom of the ditches." Although pregnant and nursing women suffered from temporary lapses in productivity, most slaveholders apparently agreed with the (in Olmsted's words) "well-known, intelligent, and benevolent" Mississippi planter who declared that "labor is conductive to health; a healthy woman will rear most children." In essence, the quest for an "efficient" agricultural work force led slaveowners to downplay gender differences in assigning adults to field labor.[7]

Together with their fathers, husbands, brothers, and sons, black women were roused at four a.m. and spent up to fourteen hours a day toiling out of doors, often under a blazing sun. During the winter they performed a myriad of tasks necessary on nineteenth-century farms of all kinds: repairing roads, pitching hay, burning brush, and setting up post and rail fences. Like Sara Colquitt of Alabama, most adult females "worked in de fields every day from 'fore daylight to almost plumb dark." During the busy harvest season, everyone was forced to labor up to sixteen hours at a time—after sunset by the light of candles or burning pine knots. Miscellaneous chores occupied men and women around outbuildings regularly and indoors on rainy days. Slaves of both sexes watered the horses, fed the chickens, and slopped the hogs. Together they ginned cotton, ground hominy, shelled corn and peas, and milled flour.[8]

Work assignments for women and men differed according to the size of a plantation and its degree of specialization. However, because cotton served as the basis of the southern agricultural system, distinct patterns of female work usually transcended local and regional differences in labor-force management. Stated simply, most women spent a good deal of their lives plowing, hoeing, and picking cotton. In the fields the notion of a distinctive "women's work" vanished as slaveholders realized that "women can do plowing very well and full well with the hoes and equal to men at picking."[9]

[...]

Slaveholders often reserved the tasks that demanded sheer muscle power for men exclusively. These included clearing the land of trees, rolling logs, and chopping and hauling wood. However, plantation exigencies sometimes mandated women's labor in this area too; in general, the smaller the farm, the more arduous and varied was women's fieldwork. Lizzie Atkins, who lived on a twenty-five-acre Texas plantation with only three other slaves, remembered working "until slam dark every day"; she helped to clear land, cut wood, and tend the livestock in addition to her other duties of hoeing corn, spinning thread, sewing clothes, cooking, washing dishes, and grinding corn. One Texas farmer, who had his female slaves haul logs and plow with oxen, even made them wear breeches, thus minimizing outward differences between the sexes. Still, FWP interviews with former slaves indicate that blacks considered certain jobs uncharacteristic of bondswomen. Recalled Louise Terrell of her days on a farm near Jackson, Mississippi: "The women had to split rails all day long, just like the men." Nancy Boudry of Georgia said she used to "split wood just like a man." Elderly women reminisced about their mothers and grandmothers with a mixture of pride and wonder. Mary Frances Webb declared of her slave grandmother, "in the winter she sawed and cut cord wood just like a man. She said it didn't hurt her as she was strong as an ox." Janie Scott's description of her mother implied the extent of the older woman's emotional as well as physical strength: She was "strong and could roll and cut logs like a man, and was much of a woman."[10]

[...]

At times, a woman would rebel in a manner commensurate with the work demands imposed upon her. "She'd git stubborn like a mule and quit." Or she took her hoe and knocked the overseer "plum down" and "chopped him right across his head." When masters and drivers "got rough on her, she got rough on them, and ran away in the woods." She cursed the man who insisted he "owned" her so that he beat her "till she fell" and left her broken body to serve as a warning to others: "Dat's what you git effen you sass me." Indeed, in the severity of punishment meted out to slaves, little distinction was made between the sexes: "Beat women! Why sure he [master] beat women. Beat women jes' lak men." A systematic survey of the FWP slave narrative collection reveals that women were more likely than men to engage in "verbal confrontations and striking the master but not running away," probably because of their family and childcare responsibilities.[11]

[...]

No slave woman exercised authority over slave men as part of their work routine, but it is uncertain whether this practice reflected the sensibilities of the slaveowners or of the slaves themselves. Women were assigned to teach children simple tasks in the house and field and to supervise other women in various facets of household industry. A master might "let [a woman] off fo' de buryings 'cause she know how to manage de other niggahs and keep dem quiet at de funerls," but he would not install her as a driver over people in the field. Many strong-willed women demonstrated that they commanded respect among males as well as females, but more often than not masters perceived this as a negative quality to be suppressed. One Louisiana slaveholder complained bitterly about a particularly "rascally set of old negroes"—the better you treat them the worse they are." He had no difficulty pinpointing the cause of the trouble, for "Big Lucy, the leader, corrupts every young negro in her power." On other plantations women were held responsible for instigating all sorts of undesirable behavior among their husbands and brothers and sisters. On Charles Colcock Jones's Georgia plantation, the slave Cash gave up going to prayer meeting and started swearing as soon as he married Phoebe, well-known for her truculence. Apparently few masters attempted to coopt high-spirited women by offering them positions of formal power over black men.[12]

In terms of labor-force management, southern slaveowners walked a fine line between making use of the physical strength of women as productive workers and protecting their investment in women as childbearers. These two objectives—one focused on immediate profit returns and the other on long-term economic considerations—at times clashed, because women who spent long hours picking cotton, toiling in the fields with heavy iron hoes, and walking several miles a day sustained damage to their reproductive systems immediately before and after giving birth. For financial reasons, slaveholders might have "regarded pregnancy as almost holy," in the words of one medical historian. But they frequently suspected their bondwomen (like "the most insufferable liar" Nora) of shamming illness—"play[ing] the lady at your expense," as one Virginia planter put it. These fears help to account for the reckless brutality with which owners forced women to work in the fields during and after pregnancy.[13]

Work in the soil thus represented the chief lot of all slaves, female and male. In the Big House, a division of labor based on both gender and age became more apparent, reflecting slaveowners' assumptions about the nature of domestic service. Although women predominated as household workers, few devoted their energies full time to this kind of labor; the size of the plantation determined the degree to which the tasks of cleaning, laundering, caring for the master's children, cooking, and ironing were specialized. According to Eugene Genovese, as few as 5 percent of all antebellum adult slaves served in the elite corps of house servants trained for specific duties. Of course during the harvest season all slaves, including those in the house, went to the fields to make obeisance to King Cotton. Thus the lines between domestic service and fieldwork blurred during the day and during the lives of slave women. Many continued to live in the slave quarters but rose early in the morning to perform various chores for the mistress—"up wid de fust light to draw water and help as house girl"—before heading for the field. James Claiborne's mother "wuked in de fiel' some, an' aroun' de house sometimes." Young girls tended babies and waited on tables until they were sent outside—"mos' soon's" they could work—and returned to the house years later, too frail to hoe weeds but still able to cook and sew. The circle of women's domestic work went unbroken from day to day and from generation to generation.[14]

Just as southern white men scorned manual labor as the proper sphere of slaves, so their wives strove (often unsuccessfully) to lead a life of leisure within their own homes. Those duties necessary to maintain the health, comfort, and daily welfare of white slaveholders were considered less women's work than black women's and black children's work. Slave mistresses supervised the whole operation, but the sheer magnitude of labor involved in keeping all slaves and whites fed and clothed (with different standards set according to race, of course) meant that black women had to supply the elbow grease. For most slaves, housework involved hard, steady, often strenuous labor as they juggled the demands made by the mistress and other members of the master's family. Mingo White of Alabama never forgot that his slave mother had shouldered a work load "too heavy for any one person." She served as personal maid to the master's daughter, cooked for all the hands on the plantation, carded cotton, spun a daily quota of thread, wove and dyed cloth. Every Wednesday she carried the white family's laundry three-quarters of a mile to a creek, where she beat each garment with a wooden paddle. Ironing consumed the rest of her day. Like the lowliest field hand, she felt the lash if any tasks went undone.[15]

[. . .]

Between the ages of six and twelve, black girls and boys followed the mistress's directions in filling woodboxes with kindling, lighting fires in chilly bedrooms in the morning and evening, making beds, washing and ironing clothes, parching coffee, polishing shoes, and stoking fires while the white family slept at night. They fetched water and milk from the springhouse and meat from the smokehouse. Three times a day they set the table, helped to prepare and serve meals, "minded flies" with peacock feather brushes, passed the salt and pepper on command, and washed the dishes. They swept, polished, and dusted, served drinks and fanned overheated visitors. Mistresses entrusted to the care of those who were little more than babies themselves the bathing, diapering, dressing, grooming, and entertaining of white infants. In the barnyard black children gathered eggs, plucked chickens, drove cows to and from the stable, and "tended the gaps" (opened and closed gates). (In the fields they acted as human scarecrows, toted water to the hands, and hauled shocks of corn together.) It was no wonder that Mary Ella Grandberry, a slave child grown old, "disremember[ed] ever playin' lack chilluns do today."[16]

In only a few tasks did a sexual division of labor exist among children. Masters always chose boys to accompany them on hunting trips and to serve as their personal valets. Little girls learned how to sew, milk cows and churn butter, and attend to the personal needs of their mistresses. As tiny ladies-in-waiting they did the bidding of fastidious white women and of girls not much older than they. Cicely Cawthon, age six when the Civil War began, called herself the mistress's "little keeper": "I stayed around, and waited on her, handed her water, fanned her, kept the flies off her, pulled up her pillow, and done anything she'd tell me to do." Martha Showvely recounted a nightly ritual with her Virginia mistress. After she finished her regular work around the house, the young girl would go to the woman's bedroom, bow to her, wait for acknowledgment, and then scurry around as ordered, lowering the shades, filling the water pitcher, arranging towels on the washstand, or "anything else" that struck the woman's fancy.[17]

Sexual exploitation of female servants of all ages (described in graphic detail by Harriet Jacobs in Lydia Maria Child's *Incidents in the Life of a Slave Girl*) predictably antagonized white women. Jealousy over their husbands' real or suspected infidelities resulted in a propensity for spontaneous violence among many. Husbands who flaunted their adventures in the slave quarters increased the chance that their wives would attack a specific woman or her offspring. Sarah Wilson remembered being "picked on" by the mistress, who chafed under her husband's taunts; he would say, "'Let her alone, she got big, big blood in her,' and then laugh."[18]

A divorce petition filed with the Virginia legislature in 1848 included a witness's testimony that the master in question one morning told his slave favorite to sit down at the breakfast table "to which Mrs. N [his wife] objected, saying . . . that she (Mrs. N) would have her severely punished." Her husband replied "that in that event he would visit her (Mrs. N) with a like punishment. Mrs. N then burst into tears and asked if it was not too much for her to stand." This husband went to extreme lengths to remind his spouse of slave-mistress Mary Chesnut's observation that "there is no slave, after all, like a wife." In the black woman the mistress saw not only the source of her own degradation, she saw herself—a woman without rights, subject to the impulses of an arrogant husband-master.[19]

To punish black women for minor offenses, mistresses were likely to attack with any weapon available—a fork, butcher knife, knitting needle, pan of boiling water. Some of the most barbaric forms of punishment resulting in the mutilation and permanent scarring of female servants were devised by white mistresses in the heat of passion. As a group they received well-deserved notoriety for the "veritable terror" they unleashed upon black women in the Big House.[20]

Interviews with former slaves suggest that the advantages of domestic service (over fieldwork) for women have been exaggerated in accounts written by whites. Carrying wood and water, preparing three full meals a day over a smoky fireplace or pressing damp clothes with a hot iron rivaled cotton picking as back-breaking labor. Always "on call," women servants often had to snatch a bite to eat whenever they could, remain standing in the presence of whites, and sleep on the floor at the foot of their mistress's bed (increasing the chances that they would sooner or later be bribed, seduced, or forced into sexual relations with the master). To peel potatoes with a sharp knife, building a fire, or carrying a heavy load of laundry down a steep flight of stairs required skills and dexterity not always possessed by little girls and boys, and injuries were common. Chastisement for minor infractions came with swift severity; cooks who burned the bread and children who stole cookies or fell asleep while singing to the baby suffered every conceivable form of physical abuse, from jabs with pins to beatings that left them disfigured for life. The master's house offered no shelter from the most brutal manifestations of slavery.[21]

For any one or all of these reasons, black women might prefer fieldwork to housework. During his visit to a rice plantation in 1853, Olmsted noted that hands "accustomed to the comparatively unconstrained life of the negro-settlement detest the close control and careful movements required of the house servants." Marriage could be both a means and an incentive to escape a willful mistress. Jessie Sparrow's mother wed at age thirteen in order "to go outer de big house. Dat how come she to marry so soon." Claude Wilson recalled many years later that "his mother was very rebellious toward her duties and constantly harassed the "Missus" about letting her work in the fields with her husband until finally she was permitted to make the change from the house to the fields to be near her man." Other women, denied an alternative, explored the range of their own emotional resources in attempting to resist petty tyranny; their "sassiness" rubbed raw the nerves of mistresses already harried and high-strung. A few servants simply withdrew into a shell of "melancholy and timidity."[22]

The dual status of a bondwoman—a slave and a female—afforded her master a certain degree of flexibility in formulating her work assignments. When he needed a field hand, her status as an able-bodied slave took precedence over gender consider-ations, and she was forced to toil alongside her menfolk. At the same time, the master's belief that most forms of domestic service required the attentions of a female reinforced among slave women the traditional role of woman as household worker.

[. . .]

Much of the work black women did for the slave community resembled the co-lonial system of household industry. Well into the nineteenth century throughout the South, slave women continued to spin thread, weave and dye cloth, sew clothes, make soap and candles, prepare and preserve foods, churn butter, and grow food for the fam-ily table. Slave women mastered all these tasks with the aid of primitive equipment and skills passed on from grandmothers. Many years later, blacks of both sexes exclaimed over their slave mothers' ability to prepare clothing dye from various combinations of tree bark and leaves, soil and berries; make soap out of ashes and animal skins; and fashion bottle lamps from string and tallow. Because of their lack of time and materi-als, black women only rarely found in these activities an outlet for creative expression, but they did take pride in their resourcefulness and produced articles of value to the community as a whole.[23]

Black women's work in home textile production illustrates the ironies of com-munity labor under slavery, for the threads of cotton and wool bound them together in both bondage and sisterhood. Masters (or mistresses) imposed rigid spinning and weaving quotas on women who worked in the fields all day. For example, many were forced to spin one "cut" (about three hundred yards) of thread nightly, or four to five cuts during rainy days or in the winter. Women of all ages worked together, and chil-dren of both sexes helped to tease and card wool, pick up the loom shuttles, and knit. In the flickering candlelight, the whirr of the spinning wheel and the clickety-clack of the loom played a seductive lullaby, drawing those who were already "mighty tired" away from their assigned tasks.[24]

In the quarters, group work melded into family responsibilities, for the communal spirit was but a manifestation of primary kin relationships. Here it is possible only to outline the social dynamics of the slave household. The significance of the family in relation to the sexual division of labor under slavery cannot be overestimated: out of the mother-father, wife-husband nexus sprang the slaves' beliefs about what women and men should be and do. Ultimately, the practical application of those beliefs (in the words of Genovese) "provided a weapon for joint resistance to dehumanization."[25]

The two-parent, nuclear family was the typical form of slave cohabitation regard-less of the location, size, or economy of a plantation; the nature of its ownership; or the age of its slave community. Because of the omnipresent threat of forced separation by sale, gift, or bequest, this family was not "stable." Yet in the absence of such sepa-rations, unions between husbands and wives and parents and children often endured for many years. Marital customs, particularly exogamy, and the practice of naming children after the mother's or father's relatives (the most common pattern was to name a boy after a male relative) revealed the strong sense of kinship among slaves. House-holds tended to be large; Herbert G. Gutman found families with eight living children to be quite common. Out of economic considerations, a master would encourage his work force to reproduce itself, but the slaves welcomed each new birth primarily as "a social and familial fact." A web of human emotions spun by close family ties—affection, dignity, love—brought slaves together in a world apart from whites.[26]

In their own cabins, the blacks maintained a traditional division of labor between the sexes. Like women in almost all cultures, slave women had both a biological and a social "destiny." As part of their childbearing role, they assumed primary responsibility for childcare (when a husband and wife lived on separate plantations, the children remained with their mother and belonged to her master). Women also performed operations related to daily household maintenance—cooking, cleaning, tending fires, sewing and patching clothes.[27]

Fathers shared the obligations of family life with their wives. In denying slaves the right to own property, make a living for themselves, participate in public life, or protect their children, the institution of bondage deprived black men of access to the patriarchy in the larger economic and political sense. But at home, women and men worked together to support the father's role as provider and protector. In the evenings and on Sundays, men collected firewood; made shoes; wove baskets; constructed beds, tables, and chairs; and carved butter paddles, ax handles, and animal traps. Other family members appreciated a father's skills; recalled Molly Ammonds, "My pappy made all de furniture dat went in our house an' it were might' good furniture too," and Pauline Johnson echoed, "De furn'chure was ho-mek, but my daddy mek it good an' stout." Husbands provided necessary supplements to the family diet by hunting and trapping quails, possums, turkeys, rabbits, squirrels, and raccoons, and by fishing. They often assumed responsibility for cultivating the tiny household garden plots allotted to families by the master. Some craftsmen, like Bill Austin's father, received goods or small sums of money in return for their work on nearby estates.

These familial duties also applied to men who lived apart from their wives and children, even though they were usually allowed to visit only on Saturday night and Sunday. Lucinda Miller's family "never had any sugar, and only got coffee when her father would bring it to her mother" during his visits. The father of Hannah Chapman was sold to a nearby planter when she was very small. Because "he missed us and us longed for him," she said many years later, he tried to visit his family under the cover of darkness whenever possible. She noted, "Us would gather round him an' crawl up in his lap, tickled slap to death, but he give us dese pleasures at a painful risk." If the master should happen to discover him, "Us could track him de nex' day by de blood stains," she remembered.[28]

Hannah McFarland of South Carolina well remembered the time when the local slave patrol attempted to whip her mother, "but my papa sho' stopped dat," she said proudly. Whether or not he was made to suffer for his courage is unknown; however, the primary literature of slavery is replete with accounts of slave husbands who intervened, at the risk of their own lives, to save wives and children from violence at the hands of white men. More often, however, fathers had to show their compassion in less dramatic (though no less revealing) ways. On a Florida plantation, the Minus children often rose in the morning to find still warm in the fireplace the potatoes "which their father had thoughtfully roasted and which [they] readily consumed." Margrett Nickerson recalled how her father would tenderly bind up the wounds inflicted on her by a maniacal overseer; in later years, her crippled legs preserved the memory of a father's sorrow intermingled with her own suffering.[29]

[. . .]

Though dimmed by time and necessity, the outlines of African work patterns endured among the slaves. As members of traditional agricultural societies, African women played a major role in producing the family's food as well as in providing basic household services. The sexual division of labor was more often determined by a woman's childcare and domestic responsibilities than by any presumed physical weakness. She might engage in heavy, monotonous fieldwork (in some tribes) as long as she could make provisions for nursing her baby; that often meant keeping an infant with her in the field. She cultivated a kitchen garden that yielded a variety of vegetables consumed by the family or sold at market, and she usually milked the cows and churned butter.[30]

West Africans in general brought with them competencies and knowledge that slaveowners readily exploited. Certain tribes were familiar with rice, cotton, and indigo cultivation. Many black women had had experience spinning thread, weaving cloth, and sewing clothes. Moreover, slaves often used techniques and tools handed down from their ancestors—in the method of planting, hoeing, and pounding rice, for example. Whites frequently commented on the ability of slave women to balance heavy and unwieldy loads on their heads, an African trait.[31]

The primary difficulty in generalizing about African women's part in agriculture stems from the fact that members of West African tribes captured for the North American slave trade came from different hoe-culture economies. Within the geographically limited Niger Delta region, for example, women and men of the Ibo tribe worked together in planting, weeding, and harvesting, but female members of another prominent group, the Yoruba, helped only with harvest. In general, throughout most of sub-Saharan Africa (and particularly on the west coast), women had primary responsibility for tilling (though not clearing) the soil and cultivating the crops; perhaps this tradition, combined with work patterns established by white masters in this country, reinforced the blacks' beliefs that cutting trees and rolling logs was "men's work." In any case, it is clear that African women often did fieldwork. But because the sexual division of labor varied according to tribe, it is impossible to state with any precision the effect of the African heritage on the slaves' perceptions of women's agricultural work.[32]

The West African tradition of respect for one's elders found new meaning among American slaves; for most women, old age brought increased influence within the slave community even as their economic value to the master declined. Owners, fearful lest women escape from "earning their salt" once they became too infirm to go to the field, set them to work at other tasks—knitting, cooking, spinning, weaving, dairying, washing, ironing, caring for the children. (Elderly men served as gardeners, wagoners, carters, and stocktenders.) But the imperatives of the southern economic system sometimes compelled slaveowners to extract from feeble women what field labor they could. In other cases they reduced the material provisions of the elderly—housing and allowances of food and clothing—in proportion to their decreased productivity.[33]

[. . .]

The story of slave women's work encapsulates an important part of American history. For here in naked form, stripped free of the pieties often used in describing white women and free workers at the time, were the forces that shaped patriarchal capitalism—exploitation of the most vulnerable members of society, and a contempt for women that knew no ethical or physical bounds. And yet slave women demonstrated "true womanhood" in its truest sense. Like Janie Scott's mother who was "much of a woman," they revealed a physical and emotional strength that transcended gender and preached a great sermon about the human spirit.

Notes

1. On women's "productive-reproductive" functions and the relationship between patriarchy and capitalism, see Joan Kelly, "The Doubled Vision of Feminist Theory: A Postscript to the 'Women and Power' Conference," *Feminist Studies* 5, no. 1 (1979): 216–27; Heidi Hartmann, "Capitalism, Patriarchy, and Job Segregation by Sex," and Zillah Eisenstein, "Developing a Theory of Capitalist Patriarchy and Socialist Feminism," and "Some Notes on the Relations of Capitalist Patriarch," in *Capitalist Patriarchy and the Case for Socialist Feminism,* ed. Zillah R. Eisenstein (New York: Monthly Review Press, 1979); Annette Kuhn and Ann Marie Wolpe, "Feminism and Materialism," and Veronica Beechey, "Women and Production: A Critical Analysis of Some Sociological Theories of Women's Work," both in, *Feminism and Materialism: Women and Modes of Production,* eds. Annette Kuhn and Ann Marie Wolpe (London: Routledge & Kegan Paul, 1978).
    Several scholars argue that the last three decades of the antebellum period constituted a distinct phase in the history of slavery. Improved textile machinery and a rise in world demand for cotton led to a tremendous growth in the American slave economy, especially in the lower South. A marked increase in slave mortality rates and family breakups (a consequence of forced migration from upper to lower South) and a slight decline in female fertility rates indicate the heightened demands made upon slave labor during the years 1830–60. See Paul E. David et al., *Reckoning with Slavery: A Critical Study in Quantitative History of American Negro Slavery* (New York: Oxford University Press, 1976), 99, 356–57; Jack Erickson Eblen, "New Estimates of the Vital Rates of the United States Black Population During the Nineteenth Century," *Demography* 11 (1974): 307–13.

2. For example, see Kelly, "Doubled Vision," 217–18, and Eisenstein, "Relations of Capitalist Patriarchy," 48–52, on the regressive implications of family life for women. But Davis notes that the slave woman's "survival-oriented activities were themselves a form of resistance." Angela Davis, "Reflections on the Black Woman's Role in the Community of Slaves," *Black Scholar* 3 (Dec. 1971): 7.

3. Interviews with former slaves have been published in various forms, including George P. Rawick, ed., *The American Slave: A Composite Autobiography*, 41 vols., series 1 and 2, supp. series 1 and 2 (Westport Conn.: Greenwood Press, 1972, 1978, 1979); Social Science Institute, Fisk University, *Unwritten History of Slavery: Autobiographical Accounts of Negro Ex-Slaves* (Washington, D.C.: Microcards Editions, 1968); Charles L. Perdue, Jr., Thomas E. Borden, and Robert K. Phillips, *Weevils in the Wheat: Interviews with Virginia Ex-Slaves* (Charlottesville: University Press of Virginia, 1976); John B. Cade, "Out of the Mouths of Ex-Slaves," *Journal of Negro History* 20 (1935): 294–337.

The narratives as a historical source are evaluated in Paul D. Escott, *Slavery Remembered: A Record of Twentieth-Century Slave Narratives* (Chapel Hill: University of North Carolina Press, 1978), 3–18 ("the slave narratives offer the best evidence we will ever have on the feelings and attitudes of America's slaves"); Martia Graham Goodson, "An Introductory Essay and Subject Index to Selected Interviews from the Slave Narrative Collection" (Ph.D. dissertation, Union Graduate School, 1977); and C. Vann Woodward, "History from Slave Sources," *American Historical Review* 79 (1974): 470–81.

The Davidson quotation is from Rawick, ed., *American Slave*, Ohio Narrs., series 1, vol. 16, 26–29. Hereafter, all references to this collection will include the name of the state, series number, volume, and page numbers. The other major source of slave interview material taken from the FWP collection for this paper—Perdue et al.—will be referred to as *Weevils in the Wheat*.

4. Joan Kelly-Gadol, "The Social Relations of the Sexes: Methodological Implications of Women's History," *Signs* 1 (1976): 809–10, 819.

5. For discussions of women's work and the inadequacy of male-biased economic and social scientific theory to define and analyze it, see Joan Acker, "Issues in the Sociological Study of Women's Work," in Ann H. Stromberg and Shirley Harkess, eds. *Women Working: Theories and Facts in Perspective* (Palo Alto, Calif.: Mayfield, 1978), 134–61; and Judith K. Brown, "A Note on the Division of Labor by Sex," *American Anthropologist* 72 (1970): 1073–78.

6. Miss. Narrs., supp. series 1, pt. 2, vol. 7, 350; Okla. Narrs., supp. series 1, vol. 12, 110; Davis, "Reflections on the Black Woman's Role," 8; Frances Anne Kemble, *Journal of a Residence on a Georgian Plantation in 1838–1839* (London: Longman, Green, 1863), 60, 92.

7. Kemble, *Journal of a Residence*, 28; Lewis Cecil Gray, *History of Agriculture in the Southern United States*, vol. 1 (Washington, D.C.: Carnegie Institution, 1933), 533–48; *Weevils in the Wheat*, 199; Fla. Narrs., series 1, vol. 17, 305; Charles S. Sydnor, *Slavery in Mississippi* (Gloucester, Mass.: P. Smith, 1965), 20; Frederick Law Olmsted, *A Journey in the Seaboard Slave States* (New York: Dix and Edwards, 1856), 470; Frederick Law Olmsted, *A Journey in the Back Country* (New York: Mason Brothers, 1860), 59.

8. Olmsted, *Slave States*, 387; Ala. Narrs., series 1, vol. 6, 87. Work descriptions were gleaned from the FWP slave narrative collection (*American Slave* and *Weevils in the Wheat*) and Gray, *History of Agriculture*. Goodson ("Introductory Essay") has indexed a sample of the interviews with women by subject (for example, "candlemaking," "carding wool," "field work," "splitting rails").

9. *Weevils in the Wheat*, 26; Gray, *History of Agriculture*, 251; planter quoted in Leslie Howard Owens, *This Species of Property: Slave Life and Culture in the Old South* (New York: Oxford University Press, 1976), 39.

10. Texas Narrs., supp. series 2, pt. 1, vol. 2, 93–94; Miss. Narrs., supp. series 1, pt. 1, vol. 6, 235–36, and pt. 2, vol. 7, 404; Tex. Narrs., series 1, pt. 3, vol. 5, 231; Ind. Narrs., series 1, vol. 6, 25; Ga. Narrs., series 1, pt. 1, vol. 12, 113; Okla. Narrs., series 1, vol. 7, 314; Ala. Narrs., series 1, vol. 6, 338.

11. Ala. Narrs., series 1, vol. 6, 46; Fla. Narrs., series 1, vol. 17, 185; *Weevils in the Wheat*, 259, 216; Va. Narrs., series 1, vol. 16, 51; Escott, *Slavery Remembered*, 86–93. Escott includes an extensive discussion of resistance as revealed in the FWP slave narrative collection and provides data on the age, sex, and marital status of resisters and the purposes and forms of resistance. Herbert G. Gutman argues that the "typical runaway" was a male, aged sixteen to thirty-five years. Gutman, *The Black Family in Slavery and Freedom, 1790–1925* (New York: Pantheon, 1976), 264–65. See also Mary Ellen Obitko, "Custodians of a House of Resistance: Black Women Respond to Slavery," in *Women and Men: The Consequences of Power*, eds. Dana V. Hiller and Robin Ann Sheets (Cincinnati: Office of Women Studies, University of Cincinnati, 1977); Owens, *This Species of Property*, 38, 88, 95.

12. Fla. Narrs., series 1, vol. 17, 191; Bennet H. Barrow, quoted in Gutman, *Black Family*, 263; Robert S. Starobin, ed., *Blacks in Bondage: Letters of American Slaves* (New York: New Viewpoints, 1974), 54.

In his recent study, *The Slave Drivers: Black Agricultural Labor Supervisors in the Antebellum South* (Westport, Conn.: Greenwood Press, 1979), William L. Van DeBurg examines the anomalous position of black (male) drivers in relation to the rest of the slave community.

13. Todd L. Savitt, *Medicine and Slavery: The Diseases and Health Care of Blacks in Antebellum Virginia* (Urbana: University of Illinois Press, 1978), 115–20, planter quoted in Owens, *This Species of Property*, 38–40; planter quoted in Olmsted, *Slave States*, 190; Kemble, *Journal*, 121. Cf. Deborah G. White, "'Ain't I a Woman?': Female Slaves in the Antebellum South" (Ph. D. Dissertation, University of Illinois-Chicago Circle, 1979), 77–86, 101, 155–60.

14. Eugene Genovese, *Roll, Jordan, Roll: The World of Slaves Made* (New York: Random House, 1974), 328, 340; Ala. Narrs., series 1, vol. 6, 273; Miss. Narrs., supp. series 1, pt. 2, vol. 7, 400; Tex. Narrs., series 1, pt. 3, vol. 5, 45. Recent historians have emphasized that the distinction between housework and fieldwork was not always meaningful in terms of shaping a slave's personality and self-perception or defining her or his status. See Owens, *This Species of Property*, 113; Escott, *Slavery Remembered*, 59–60.

15. Ala. Narrs., series 1, vol. 6, 416–17. In her study of slave mistresses, Anne Firor Scott gives an accurate description of their numerous supervisory duties, but she ignores the fact that most of the actual manual labor was performed by slave women. See *The Southern Lady: From Pedestal to Politics, 1830–1930* (Chicago: University of Chicago Press, 1970), 31.

16. The FWP slave narrative collection provides these examples of children's work, and many more. Ala. Narrs., series 1, vol. 6, 157; Genovese, *Roll, Jordon, Roll*, 502–19; Owens, *This Species of Property*, 202.

17. Ga. Narrs., supp. series 1, pt. 1, vol. 3, 185; *Weevils in the Wheat*, 264–65; S.C. Narrs., series 1, pt. 4, vol. 3, 257.

18. Okla. Narrs., series 1, vol. 7, 347; White, "Ain't I a Woman?" 210–15; L. Maria Child, ed., *Incidents in the Life of a Slave Girl, Written By Herself* (Boston: L. Maria Child, 1861).

19. James Hugo Johnston, *Race Relations in Virginia and Miscegenation in the South, 1776–1860* (Amherst: University of Massachusetts Press, 1970), 247; Mary Boykin Chesnut, *A Diary from Dixie*, ed. Ben Ames Williams (Cambridge: Harvard University Press, 1980), 49.

20. Fla. Narrs., series 1, vol. 17, 35. For specific incidents illustrating these points, see *Weevils in the Wheat*, 63, 199; Okla. Narrs., series 1, vol. 7, 135, 165–66; Tenn. Narrs., series 1, vol. 16, 14. Slave punishment in general is discussed in Escott, *Slavery Remembered*, 42–46; Owens, *This Species of Property*, 88; Savitt, *Medicine and Slavery*, 65–69; See Herbert G. Gutman and Richard Sutch, "Sambo Makes Good, or Were Slaves Imbued with the Protestant Work Ethic?" in *Reckoning with Slavery*, David et al., 55–93; Frederick Douglass, *Narrative of the Life of Frederick Douglass, An American Slave* (Cambridge: Harvard University Press, 1960), 60–61. These examples indicate that Anne Firor Scott is a bit sanguine in suggesting that although southern women were sensitive to the "depravity" of their husbands, "it may be significant that they did not blame black women, who might have provided convenient scapegoats. The blame was squarely placed on men." See Anne Firor Scott, "Women's Perspectives on the Patriarchy in the 1850s," *Journal of American History* 61 (1974): 52–64.

21. Genovese, *Roll, Jordan, Roll*, 333–38. See, for example, the document entitled "A Seamstress Is Punished," in Gerda Lerner (ed.), *Black Women in White America: A Documentary History* (New York: Random House, 1972), 18–19.

22. Olmsted, *Slave States*, 421; S.C. Narrs., series 1, pt. 4, vol. 3, 126; Fla. Narrs., series 1, vol. 14, 356; Escott, *Slavery Remembered*, 64; Kemble, *Journal*, 98; Genovese, *Roll, Jordan, Roll*, 346–47.

23. The FWP slave narrative collection contains many descriptions of slaves engaged in household industry. Alice Morse Earle details comparable techniques used by white women in colonial New England in *Home Life in Colonial Days* (New York: Macmillan, 1935).

24. See, for example, S.C. Narrs., series 1, pt. 3, vol. 3, 15, 218, 236; Tex. Narrs., series 1, pt. 3, vol. 5, 20, 89, 108, 114, 171, 188, 220; Miss. Narrs., supp. series 1, pt. 1, vol. 6, 36.

25. Genovese, *Roll, Jordan, Roll*, 319.

26. Gutman, *Black Family*, 75. Escott points out that masters and slaves lived in "different worlds,": *Slavery Remembered*, 20. This paragraph briefly summarizes Gutman's pioneering work.

27. Davis, "Reflections on the Black Woman's Role," 7.

28. Gutman, *Black Family*, 142, 67–68, 267–78; Genovese, *Roll, Jordan, Roll*, 318, 482–94; S.C. Narrs., series 1, pt. 3, vol. 3, 192; Miss. Narrs., supp. series 1, pt. 2, vol, 7, 380–81.

29. Okla. Narrs., series 1, vol. 7, 210; Escott, *Slavery Remembered*, 49–57, 87; Owens, *This Species of Property*, 201.

30. For theoretical formulation of the sexual division of labor in preindustrial societies, see Brown, "A Note on the Division of Labor by Sex."

31. Peter Wood, *Black Majority: Negroes in Colonial South Carolina from 1670 Through the Stono Rebellion* (New York: Knopf, 1974), 59–62; P. C. Lloyd, "Osi fakunde of Ijebu," in Philip D. Curtin (ed.), *Africa Remembered: Narratives by West Africans from the Era of the Slave Trade* (Madison: University of Wisconsin Press, 1967), 236; Marguerite Dupire, "The Position of Women in a Pastoral Society," in *Women of Tropical Africa*, ed. Denise Paulme (Berkeley: University of California Press, 1963), 76–80; Olaudah Equiano, "The Life of Olaudah Equiano or Gustavus Vassa the AfricanWritten by Himself," in *Great Slave Narratives*, ed. Arna Bontemps (Boston: Beacon Press, 1969), 7–10; Kemble, *Journal*, 42; Elizabeth Ware Pearson, ed., *Letters from Port Royal Written at the Time of the Civil War* (Boston: W. B. Clarke, 1906), 58, 106.

32. Melville J. Herskovits, *The Myth of the Negro Past* (New York: Harper & Bros., 1941), 33–85; Wood, *Black Majority*, 179, 250; Hermann Baumann, "The Division of Work According to Sex in African Hoe Culture," *Africa* 1 (1928): 289–319.

On the role of women in hoe agriculture, see also Leith Mullings, "Women and Economic Change in Africa," in *Women in Africa: Studies in Social and Economic Change*, eds. Nancy J. Hafkin and Edna G. Bay (Stanford: Stanford University Press, 1976), 239–64; Sylvia Leith-Ross, *African Women: A Study of the Ibo of Nigeria* (New York: Praeger, 1965), 84–91; Ester Boserup, *Woman's Role in Economic Development* (New York: St. Martin's Press, 1970), 15–36; Jack Goody and Joan Buckley, "Inheritance and Women's Labour in Africa," *Africa* 63 (1973): 108–21. No tribes in precolonial Africa used the plow.

33. Olmsted, *Slave States*, 433; Gray, *History of Agriculture*, 548; Kemble, *Journal*, 164, 247; Douglass, *Narrative*, 76–78. According to Genovese, the ability of these elderly slaves "to live decently and with self-respect depended primarily on the support of their younger fellow slaves" (*Roll, Jordan, Roll*, 523); White "Ain't I a Woman?" 49; Miss. Narrs., supp. series 1, pt. 1, vol. 6, 242.

CHAPTER 9

The Paradox of Motherhood

NIGHT WORK RESTRICTIONS IN THE UNITED STATES

Alice Kessler-Harris

Among Western industrial countries, the United States was a late-comer to maternal protection. It did not pass national legislation to protect women's jobs in the weeks before and after childbirth until 1993. With the exception of New York, where a provision for paid job leaves and medical insurance for pregnant working women was discussed and then defeated in 1919, the states have also largely ignored the issue of maternity leaves for most private-sector workers.

Considering that concern for the welfare of mothers has dominated the discussion of protection for women workers in the United States, the absence of maternity leaves, which constitute the backbone of protective labor legislation in most other countries, is puzzling. In the early twentieth century, when the search for protection became a legislative priority, advocates of maximum hours, night work regulation, and safety and health measures rooted their arguments in the need to protect the family roles of women. At the same time, independent of the workplace, reformers struggled to address high levels of infant mortality through clinics for pregnant women and young children, and they argued successfully for mothers' pensions that would permit some mothers of small children to stay out of the work force.[1] Yet neither in this early period nor until very recently has maternal protection for women in the workplace ever seriously entered the U.S. legislative agenda.[2]

The silence about maternity legislation can hardly be explained as a function of the peculiarities of American labor legislation, which, until the 1930s, was rooted in gender differences. Gender-neutral legislation, offering minimal protections to industrial workers without regard to their sex, did not emerge in the United States until the late 1930s. Before that, with few exceptions, protective labor legislation was designed for women only. The exceptions involved the conditions of federal and some state and municipal employees, as well as workers whose health and safety affected public well-being. The hours of railway workers, for example, were reduced by federal law, and those of miners were reduced by many states because of the danger that exhausted workers might hurt passengers or other workers. However, in a precedent-setting 1905 case the U.S. Supreme

Court refused to allow New York State to regulate the hours of bakers because there was nothing intrinsically unhealthful in allowing bakers to work as long as they wished.[3]

While this case and others effectively stymied gender-neutral laws, legislation specific to women progressed rapidly. Between 1908 and 1920 an astonishingly wide array of laws emerged from state after state. Thirty-nine of the forty-eight states regulated hours for women; thirteen states and the District of Columbia passed minimum wage laws; sixteen states passed laws that expressly forbade night work for women. Because the progress of this legislation varied from state to state and because its impact has been well documented, I will not summarize it here.[4] Rather, I want to focus on the larger meaning of this body of legislation by looking at the case of night work laws.

License for the several states to regulate women's right to work under conditions of their own choosing derived from the U.S. Supreme Court's decision in the 1908 case of *Muller v. Oregon*. There the Court sharply distinguished between what was appropriate for men and what was desirable for women. Arguing that the state had an interest in women's present and future roles as actual mothers and as "mothers of the race," the Court upheld Oregon's effort to reduce the hours of women workers.[5] It thereby inscribed into precedent the notion that women, all of whom could be viewed as potential mothers, constituted a separate class and a proper subject for legislative action. For the next three decades, the basis of American protective legislation resided in women's capacity to become mothers. But no effort was made to address one of the central issues of motherhood: the difficulty of giving birth and of holding down a job at the same time. In sharp contrast to the frequent discussions of maternal and infant health, concern for maternity leaves for wage-earning women rarely entered the agendas of state legislators or female reformers.

Part of the explanation for this curious gap may lie in how the debate over protective legislation was constructed in the United States. First, in contrast to most countries, the debate was not primarily the province either of political parties or of the labor movement. No socialist or social democratic party was powerful enough to dominate the debate; neither of the leading parties (Republican or Democratic) took on the issues as a national cause; and the struggling trade union movement was too weak to provide leadership. For most of the first two decades of the twentieth century, the dominant American Federation of Labor resisted efforts to legislate on behalf of men and acquiesced reluctantly and ambivalently to efforts to legislate for women. Trade union leaders believed that the only real protection for workers derived from effective organization, and they convinced themselves that if male workers were unionized and earned a family wage, women would not have to work at all. In the meantime, union leaders offered lukewarm support for the efforts of groups like the Women's Trade Union League and the National Consumers' League to pass legislation for women only.

The failure of political and working-class leadership left the legislative initiative in the hands of a loose coalition of mostly female reformers. For the most part, the campaign for protective legislation was led on a state-by-state basis by middle-class women who possessed a vision of family as traditional as that of trade union men. Recent discussions of Florence Kelley and the National Consumers' League suggest that the political coalitions they formed to campaign for reduced hours, night work laws, and minimum wages for women led the drive to regulate women's paid labor.[6] Their efforts derived from concern for family life, and their strategies were shaped by the constraints of the legislative and judicial systems rather than by the agendas of poor working women.[7]

A second critical factor in the U.S. experience was the role of the courts. The legal debate over protective labor legislation intersected two discussions in U. S. law. The first, from the perspective of labor, was the conflict between the doctrine of freedom of contract and that of the police power of the state. By the late nineteenth century it had become pretty much settled law that the courts would not interfere with a worker's "individual right" to negotiate with an employer. This doctrine, known as "freedom of contract," held that every citizen had the right to decide when and under what circumstances he or she would work. Since, in the judgment of the courts, a practical equality existed between employer and employee, legislation that would impinge on the contractual relation was held unconstitutional. The state could intervene by regulating hours, wages, and working conditions only when it perceived the public interest or the general welfare to be at stake. In practice, court interpretations deprived even well-intentioned lawmakers of the opportunity to legislate for workers, except when the health of the worker was threatened in such a way as to damage public well-being. The police power of the state could thus be used to limit freedom of contract only in special circumstances.

Because she belonged to a class of people who could become mothers, a female worker turned out to be a special circumstance. From the perspective of family law, the state perceived, and the courts upheld, a primary interest in the family. They had, by the end of the nineteenth century, constructed an image of married women as individuals entitled to limited citizenship rights. Yet this class of citizens had particular claims on the courts by virtue of its role in preserving family life.[8] The entry of large numbers of women into the industrial labor force compelled legislatures and the courts to consider how women could simultaneously exercise the freedom of contract implicit in citizenship and demand the protection of the police power of the state to preserve their own health and that of their present and future families. At the heart of this debate lay the meaning of womanhood itself.

As in most other countries, debates over social legislation took place in the ferment surrounding a rapid industrialization process. [. . .] A massive influx of immigrants (some 20 million from foreign countries, and some 11 million from rural to urban areas in the United States between 1870 and 1920) made industrial workers particularly vulnerable. The process and its ideological justifications led to deteriorating working and living conditions for all workers and created special concerns about whether or not family life among the least skilled and most vulnerable might deteriorate to the point where the poor would no longer be trained to participate in the labor force. These concerns were exacerbated by the increasing numbers of women drawn into wage labor. By 1900, women constituted 25 percent of industrial workers. Though relatively few married women were employed (perhaps 6 percent) in 1900, they represented about 15 percent of all women workers.

Political, judicial, and economic parameters together heavily influenced the nature of the discourse on protective labor legislation. This discourse, which ultimately shaped visions of what was possible in the legislative sphere, created the paradoxical situation in which the idea of motherhood became the object of protection in the workplace, while women who became mothers derived no job protection at all.

The debate around prohibiting night work, which began in the United States in the late nineteenth century, provides a useful illustration of how this paradox came about. As part of the movement for shorter hours, the debate over night work added complexity to an already difficult issue. Historically, the debate emerged from discussion regarding maximum hours. Restricting night work was a heuristic device designed to encourage employers to obey the shorter hours legislation just beginning to emerge and to facilitate its enforcement.[9] Contemporary reformers understood that their efforts to reduce the daily hours of women wage-earners would be stymied if women worked split shifts or if they took a second job. To solve the problem, reformers called for prohibiting night work altogether. Their efforts quickly found justification in a range of arguments about the importance of family and the humane effects of shorter hours. Like arguments against the long working day, those formulated to prohibit women's work at night frequently confronted the equally salient issue of male night work. Though reformers were often sympathetic to laws that might have prohibited night work for men as well as women, legal precedent and a hostile judiciary vitiated this possibility. Thus, the moral effort to ensure that no one would work at night confronted the legal conviction that the work of adults could not be regulated. To resolve this stand-off required exaggerating gender differences and placing the qualities of women, not social justice for workers, in the forefront of the debate.

At the time of the Bern conference in 1906 (to which the United States did not send delegates because the individual states were empowered to legislate working conditions), only four of the forty-eight states had laws restricting the employment of women at night.[10] In one of these (New York), the state's highest court would declare night work laws unconstitutional in 1907. The Bern conference's resolution restricting women's night work seems to have had little effect on U.S. legislation.[11] No other states even attempted to restrict night work until after the U.S. Supreme Court declared in 1908 that women were in effect wards of the state, whose prior interest in their health and mothering capacity permitted intervention.[12] In the aftermath of this decision, several states included the regulation of night work among their laws restricting women's work. But even by 1918, only twelve states had such laws, as compared with the forty-two that had adopted maximum hour laws for women workers.[13]

[. . .]

Even that number exaggerates the kinds of protection women could expect. The laws varied dramatically from state to state as to the hours during which restrictions applied and the industries covered and exempted. For example, Indiana, Massachusetts, and Pennsylvania covered only manufacturing plants; South Carolina covered only retail stores; Ohio regulated night work for female ticket sellers; and Washington singled out elevator operators.[14] Even states with stringent regulations permitted exceptions: nurses, hotel workers, and those employed at seasonal agricultural and cannery labor were most frequently allowed to work at night. But other states, in no discernible pattern, thought it unnecessary to restrict the hours of women employed, for example, as domestics, actors and performers, or cloakroom attendants. Some exempted store workers for the two weeks before Christmas; others refused to restrict women who worked in small towns no matter what their occupation.[15] Most regulations prohibited work from 10 p.m. until 6 a.m. Massachusetts denied textile mills the right to employ women from 6 p.m. until 6 a.m. but allowed other businesses to utilize women during the evening hours. Some rural states with almost no industrial workers, such as North Dakota and Nebraska, passed restrictive night work laws, while heavily industrialized states like Illinois refused to do so. The Women's Bureau of the Department of Labor, surveying with some dismay this chaotic array of legislation in 1924, concluded that night work legislation was "found not only in a much smaller number of States than is legislation limiting the daily and weekly hours of work[,] but in many States which have both types of legislation, the night-work laws cover a much smaller group of industries or occupations."[16]

The wide array of laws, and the refusal of many states to adopt them, may reflect the fact that relatively few women earned their livings at night. A 1928 Women's Bureau study of twelve states found that on the average slightly more than 2 percent of all female wage earners worked during the night hours.[17] [. . .]

[Yet] these women were crucially placed. Among the night workers, as the Women's Bureau noted, "all but a negligible proportion were in the years of development or of highest childbearing capacity, the years precisely when all the characteristic injuries of night work are most disastrous."[18] [. . .]

These figures stand in sharp contrast to the female work force as a whole in 1920, less than 15 percent of which was married,[19] and probably no more than one-third of whom were mothers of small children. The problem, then, was that night work confronted a reluctant legislative and court system with what to do about working mothers. This phenomenon shaped the debate, structuring perceptions of the work force as a whole and leading to a formulation of gender distinctions that encouraged both the continuing exclusion of males from legislative protection and legislative silences about women who became mothers during their working years.

An examination of the rhetoric of the debate around night work that occurred in the late nineteenth and early twentieth centuries appears to explain how this happened. The debate locates itself in three areas: in the effort to modify harsh working conditions for all workers, regardless of sex; in the creation and precise definition of an idealized version of women (a universal woman); and in the problem of how to regulate competition in the labor force. [. . .]

Since the discussion of night work arose from an effort to restrict the role of capital and to humanize its uses in the treatment of all workers, night work legislation, like other protective legislation, initially was meant to incorporate an apparently gender-neutral concept of workers. Eliminating night work was necessary to increase the possibility of leisure, to allow full family lives, to provide access to education, and to encourage effective participation in political citizenship. These arguments continued through the first decades of the twentieth century.

Night work, it was argued, was not good for any worker. Thus, the secretary of the male Bakery and Confectionery Workers International Union used the following language to condemn it. Night work, he suggested, was "one of the greatest evils against humanity." Its deleterious effect on bakers "makes them dissatisfied and warps and spoils their dispositions because they are prevented from enjoying proper rest which they can not get during the day. Furthermore they are prevented from sharing in the joys of family life or the opportunities of educating themselves for a better station in life."[20] Note that the deleterious consequences are said to detract only from the lives of individuals, not specifically men alone. Contrast this with the language used in Josephine Goldmark's influential 1912 study, *Fatigue and Efficiency*, which identified the negative features of night work in gender-neutral terms. The "characteristic and invariable effects" of night work, she argued, were "the loss of sleep and sunlight," with its "inevitable physiological deficits." But, she continued, the evil effects of night work on everyone's health produced in women the additional problems of "loss of appetite, headache, anaemia, and weakness of the female functions."[21] With few exceptions, advocates of night work legislation turned arguments for its abolition into special pleadings for women. A typical article in the *American Journal* of *Public Health* would begin by asserting, "I am not in favor of night work for anybody," and then turn to the particular ill effects of night work on women.[22]

Failing to establish effective legal grounds for regulating capital's ability to buy labor, reformers turned to women as examples of what the state might appropriately do and sometimes offered them up as the vanguard of state activity. This discussion was inevitably influenced by the sharpening conflict over definitions of womanhood. Calling attention to the problem of night work for women in particular presented the issue as a social problem that could and did require state intervention, for the state, as many reformers pointed out, did not hesitate to exercise its police power when public health was at stake. This strategy at first stumbled on the roadblock of freedom of contract—defined as a right of citizenship.

While even the most ardent reformers hesitated to infringe on the citizenship rights of men, those of women proved to be much more vulnerable. When the issue first emerged in the landmark case of *Ritchie v. The People,* the court held that "if one man is denied the right to contract under the law as he has hitherto done under the law, and as others are still allowed to do by the law, he is deprived of both liberty and property." It struck down an effort to regulate women's hours as a "purely arbitrary restriction upon the fundamental right of the citizen to control his or her own time and faculties."[23] But within five years, women's citizenship rights came under pressure. In 1905, Pennsylvania's highest court allowed the state to regulate women's hours, asserting that "the fact that both parties are of full age and competent to contract does not necessarily deprive the state of the power to interfere when the parties do not stand upon an equality, or when the public health demands that one party to the contract shall be protected against himself." The state, the court added presciently, "retains an interest in his welfare, however reckless he may be."[24] The male adjective aside, we should not let this warning to womankind go unheeded. Later events were to sustain the court's notion that women's citizenship rights were vulnerable to legislative and judicial determinations about the public health, with or without the consent of the women involved. What was at issue, then, was not whether women needed the protection but whether to sustain state intervention required a modification of women's rights.

[...]

Because protective labor legislation relied on a special effort to restrict the citizenship rights of one class of people, the hope that it would serve as a vanguard—an example that would be followed by regulations for all workers—seemed doomed before it began. The discourse over night work quickly transformed what might have been a general struggle into a woman's issue, constructing contrasting pictures of gendered citizenship rights, organizational capacity, and natural and social circumstances.

How this happened can best be explained by looking at the rhetoric that formed the core of the debate over a period of more than two decades. Taken as a whole, the rhetoric creates a concept of an ideal, or universal, woman. To make the case for special legislation for women required riding roughshod over class, race, and ethnic distinctions and ignoring questions of life cycles and personal choice. The debate situated all women within a single framework defined as "natural" and located within childbearing and childrearing functions. It sought to portray a world in which these attributes dominated—and therefore justified the sacrifice of all others. The words of the New York State court that in 1914 articulated the standard for all other night work decisions drew on and extended the decision in *Muller v. Oregon.* Night work in factories, as contrasted with day labor, wrote the court, "substantially affects and impairs the physical condition of women and prevents them from discharging in a healthful and satisfactory manner the peculiar functions which have been imposed upon them by nature." The court offered little sympathy to the many women who did not exercise these functions, suggesting that such differences among women did not tempt it to modify the decision. Moreover, the court acknowledged that "this statute in its universal application to all factories will inflict unnecessary hardships on a great many women who neither ask nor require its provisions by depriving them of an opportunity to earn a livelihood by perfectly healthful labor although performed during some of the hours of the night."[25] But, the court insisted, such women should turn to the legislature, not the courts, for relief, for the prerogative of defining public welfare lay in legislative hands.

If this decision did not repeat the language of the public debate, it and the 1908 U.S. Supreme Court decision that sealed approval of all such restrictions certainly reaffirmed what would by the mid-1920s become a prevailing theme. That debate, firmly rooted in the traditional family and in women's place within it, identified women in terms of their family roles and articulated the expectation that they would reproduce. The debate was conducted as if all women were mothers or potential mothers. The evil effects of night work, on both men and women, receded in the face of its consequences for those who would bear or care for children. Rather, legislatures attempted to persuade the courts that women's health in particular required state intervention. Drawing heavily on the research utilized by successful European advocates of night work prohibitions, American supporters painted a distressing picture. Their language invoked the female's "delicate organism" and cited at length the injuries to women's reproductive systems, menstrual cycles, and general vitality that the state had a special interest in guarding. Inevitably, women's physical capacities were described as being far less than those of men. "No-one doubts," wrote the judge who issued the opinion in *The People v. Schweinler* (1914), "that as regards bodily strength and endurance [a woman] is inferior. . . . As healthy mothers are essential to vigorous offspring," he continued, "the physical well-being of women becomes an object of public interest and care in order to preserve the strength and vigor of the race."[26]

Advocates did not fail to add, nor courts to take notice of, the social burdens imposed on women by household tasks. Women's double day, suggested Frances Perkins, then the Industrial Commissioner of New York State, provided the rationale for protection. "Night work," she argued, "bears with special severity on women who under these conditions tend to work all night and discharge family and home duties most of the day."[27] Louis Brandeis and Josephine Goldmark, in their brief to the court hearing the New York State case on night work legislation, wrote that "Women who work in factories are not thereby relieved from household duties—from cooking, washing, cleaning and looking after their families,"[28] and the court concurred. Housework, it noted in its favorable ruling, filled "most of the day" for those who worked at night.[29]

[. . .]

In general, however, the effects of poverty and malnutrition and the debility caused by overwork were identified as the peculiarly gendered consequences of night work. Infant mortality and higher morbidity rates for working women were widely laid at its door. "It goes without saying," Brandeis and Goldmark dismissively wrote in their New York State brief, "that many other factors besides the mother's employment contribute to a high infant mortality, such as poverty, inadequate attendance at birth, wrong feeding, bad sanitation, and the like."[30] Though studies conducted by the U.S. Children's Bureau confirmed European research that demonstrated an overwhelming relationship between infant mortality and father's wages, arguments that an increase in male wages might solve some of the problems of malnutrition and long hours fell on deaf ears.

[. . .]

The unspoken text that appealed to the legislative instinct was the helplessness of women engaged in night work. What kinds of women would abandon their homes and children to such depravity? The literature described them as foreigners: "Poles, Hungarians and Russians," women who "speak little English" and were "always willing to work overtime." They were also "poor negro women" employed as substitutes for boys; or they were the "lintheads" of the southern textile industry.[31]

The language used to describe women's night-time experiences affirmed their helplessness. Louise Kindig, the twenty-three-year-old woman who tested the constitutionality of New York State's night work law in 1913 was described as "a frail girl" who "represented hundreds of working women who, night after night are employed in the factories and workshops of New York." Like other such women, Kindig was "forced to go outside for meals at midnight"[32] and was "turned into the streets at a late hour of night or at early dawn."[33] Women night workers were "ignorant women" who could "scarcely be expected to realize the dangers not only to their own health, but to that of the next generation from such inhuman usage."[34]

This message was eagerly, even anxiously perpetuated by male and female reformers for whom protective labor legislation, and particularly restrictions on night work, seemed to respond to a need to regulate a chaotic labor market. Here the emphasis shifted to the need to protect the male provider role, both in its economic aspects and in its social assumptions of patriarchal entitlements. Employers, union men, and reformers, as well as some wage-earning women, debated efforts to restrict night work and sometimes unilaterally limited women's ability to work at night as a function of implicit understandings about who should support the family and what constituted an appropriate job. The discussions here reflect and affirm a sense of entitlement on the part of males that turns women's refusal to submit to regulation into selfish acts that threaten to undermine the family.

Assumptions about male roles may explain why so few women worked at night to begin with—partly out of their own expectations and partly out of what the Women's Bureau described in 1928 as "an astonishingly strong feeling among employers in industry against the employment of women at night, irrespective of legal regulation."[35] These feelings, affirmed by union men, were not independent of generally shared assumptions about female roles. Lurid sketches of opportunities for immoral behavior inherent in female work at night, accusations that unscrupulous employers fed their female workers "liquor and narcotics to overcome exhaustion," and the conviction that the bad character of some night workers would infect even decent women—all these conspired to construct an image of night work that negated the possibilities of respectable family life.[36]

Opponents of night work restrictions adopted the same language but gave it a different twist. Conceding that family life was the most important issue at stake in whether or not legislation should be passed, they constructed images of sturdy, self-supporting women who used the extra income they could earn at night to support families in modest comfort. They repeated such stories as that of the female elevator operator whose family situation deteriorated when she lost her relatively comfortable job only to end up as a poorly paid charwoman. They circulated hardship stories of skilled women printers who could no longer keep their families after they lost their night jobs. Waitresses who could not work at night when the tips were highest complained that the hatcheck girls and cabaret singers, who were exempted from the law, were less likely to have children and families in need.[37]

The language of male prerogative and of family values translated directly into the work force. Elizabeth Faulkner Baker, in a thoughtful discussion of the problem, noted that both sides of the argument understood that if legislation passed, then "men will always be preferred . . . leaving women to earn a scanty living out of the left-over jobs—a part of the luckless mass of underpaid, unskilled and unorganized workers who toil long and hope little."[38] Such job segregation would inevitably follow night-work restrictions because whole categories of jobs would be removed from female competition.

Perhaps more significant in the long run, the explicit rejection by unionized men of the need for protective legislation was sustained and supported by a false perception of the role of trade unions that played off images of women's weaknesses. One popular magazine, for example, advocated night-work restrictions for women because "working women and girls, less able to organize for self protection need, if they are to fulfill the functions of motherhood, to be protected against the exploitation of their physical and mental life by a greedy and inhuman industrialism."[39] In 1907, perhaps 12 percent of America's urban male workers belonged to unions—a figure that rose to nearly 20 percent during World War I and then declined again in the 1920s. Not until the mass-organizing drives of the mid-1930s did the proportion of organized men in industry reach even 25 percent. Still, advocates of night work insisted that women needed the protection of laws to offset a protection already negotiated by men. Frances Perkins, for example, noted that women who were poorly organized could not be expected to reproduce the experience of men who had "in many instances created excellent in-dustrial conditions for themselves without legislation and through the medium of the trade union and the strike."[40]

Distinguishing men from women in this way preserved benefits for the rela-tively few, mostly skilled men who were union members—a boon to which working men were not insensitive. For example, when New York's unionized female printers, deprived of their night jobs under state law in 1914, petitioned the legislature for relief, they were opposed by a significant proportion of the membership of their own union. When in 1921 an exception was made in women's favor, union men and foremen placed obstacles in the paths of their return to their old jobs.[41] Despite a Women's Bureau finding that streetcar conducting was healthful outdoor work, the New York State legislature refused to grant an exemption when male workers fought against it. As a result, 83 percent of New York City's female streetcar conductors lost their jobs.

A rhetoric that obscured male needs and took its stance from questionable depic-tions of the character and lives of women concealed some of the larger issues of the debate. Though reformers frequently raised questions about the efficiency of running factories late at night, such questions did not enter the agenda until the discussion broadened in the 1930s. Rather, manufacturers thought about the problem in terms of control of the work force, constructing images of women that accorded with their own and with community perceptions of present and future labor force needs. Generally, it was easier to play the sexes off against each other than to exclude one sex or the other. "Night work for women," concluded Agnes de Lima," is fostered by the low wage scale for men, coupled with a comparatively high wage level for women which tempts them to enter the industry."[42]

This very cursory, tentative examination of the rhetoric surrounding night work legislation in the United States reveals a public culture in which men and women differ dramatically in their possession of citizenship rights. Night work, equally evil for men and women, was regulated only for women (albeit ambivalently) because their claims to citizenship rights were subject to public perceptions of appropriate behavior for females in family life. Such perceptions inhered in women's role in social reproduction and in the characteristics of person and physique assumed to be necessary to fulfill that role. Assumptions about women's roles and attributions to them of qualities that inhibited their capacity to function effectively in the work force turned the debate over night work into a discussion of women's functions. In the face of this onslaught against women's physical stamina and character, other alternatives such as nurseries for children, minimum wages for men, and police patrols for dangerous streets became invisible. The shape of the debate, framed in terms of settled assumptions about motherhood and domesticity, contributed to the passage of laws that exacerbated differences between men and women. Rooting legislation in this manner did more than characterize and disadvantage women; it discredited protective legislation for men. The unspoken message that legislation was necessary for the weak and inferior implied that only the weak and inferior would seek it. Mature adult males could be left to the mercy of an unencumbered capitalism.

Equally important, the particular construction of citizenship that facilitated legislation for women was rooted in the states' right to protect motherhood and family roles, not in a woman's right to protect her job. The discourse that made such a division possible created a vision of motherhood that precluded an amalgam of wagework and mothering in the public mind and therefore mitigated against maternity leaves to protect jobs and instead supported maternal protections that saved babies. A rhetoric that reduced women who worked to inadequate mothers left little room for policies that might allow mothers more rights at work. Instead, it encouraged ways of removing mothers from the work force through such devices as mothers' pensions.

What emerged in the late nineteenth and early twentieth century was at best a limited and hard-fought consensus on social reproduction and women's place in it. But it was costly. To assert woman's primary roles as childbearer and childrearer meant subsuming her role as provider. The result was that women's individual rights as citizens were regulated on behalf of motherhood. The powerful images invoked in the debate enabled the public to accept the loss of economic rights for women in favor of the states' desire to protect the rights of all women to be mothers. Consistent with the judicial antagonism against economic rights for all workers, as well as with the preferences of American industry, the courts did not protect the rights of women as workers. Instead, they offered women, conceived in terms of motherhood, the right not to work at all, setting up a contradiction between motherhood and work that made asking for maternity legislation all but inconceivable.

Notes

1. Joanne Goodwin, "An American Experiment in Paid Motherhood: The Implementation of Mothers' Pensions in Early Twentieth Century Chicago," *Gender and History* 4 (Autumn 1992): 323–42; Molly Ladd-Taylor, *Raising a Baby the Government Way: Mothers' Letters to the Children's Bureau, 1915–1932* (New Brunswick: Rutgers University Press, 1986), and *Mother-Work: Women, Child Welfare, and the State, 1890–1930* (Urbana: University of Illinois Press,

1994); and Theda Skocpol, *Protecting Soldiers and Mothers: The Political Origins of Social Policy in the United States* (Cambridge: Harvard University Press, 1993).

2. New York State provides perhaps the only exception to this. For a discussion of the New York legislative debates of 1917–19, when a maternity benefit proposal went down to defeat see Beatrix Hoffman, "Insuring Maternity: Women Reformers and the New York Health Insurance Campaign, 1916–20" (ms. in author's possession).

3. The case is *Lochner* v. *New York*, 198 U.S. 45 (1905). A good discussion of law in relation to American workers can be found in William Forbath, *Law and the Shaping of the American Labor Movement* (Cambridge: Harvard University Press, 1991). The standard discussion of law in relation to gender is in Leo Kanowitz, *Sex Roles in Law and Society: Cases and Materials* (Albuquerque: University of New Mexico Press, 1973).

4. A summary and discussion of this legislation can be found in Alice Kessler-Harris, *Out to Work: A History of Wage-earning Women in the United States* (New York: Oxford University Press, 1982), chap. 7. See also Judith Baer, *The Chains of Protection: The Judicial Response to Women's Labor Legislation* (Westport, Conn: Greenwood Press, 1978).

5. *Muller v. Oregon*, 208 U. S. 412 (1908).

6. Skocpol, *Protecting Soldiers and Mothers*; Kathryn Kish Sklar, *Florence Kelley and the Nation's Work: The Rise of Women's Political Culture, 1830–1900* (New Haven: Yale University Press, 1995).

7. Vivien Hart, *Bound by Our Constitution: Women, Workers, and the Minimum Wage* (Princeton: Princeton University Press, 1994), suggests that the shaping strategy was a desire to avoid the constraints of rigid judicial interpretation of the U.S. Constitution.

8. Michael Grossberg, *Governing the Hearth: Law and the Family in Nineteenth-Century America* (Chapel Hill: University of North Carolina Press, 1985), 300.

9. See, for example, discussions of New York and Massachusetts in Clara M. Beyer, *History of Labor Legislation for Women in Three States*, Bulletin of the Women's Bureau, No. 66 (Washington, DC.: Government Printing Office, 1929); and Elizabeth Faulkner Baker, *Protective Labor Legislation, with Special Reference to Women in the State of New York* (New York: Columbia University Press, 1925), 236.

10. These were Massachusetts (1890), Indiana (1894), Nebraska (1898), and New York (1903). See Mary D. Hopkins, *The Employment of Women at Night*, Bulletin of the Women's Bureau, No. 64 (Washington, D.C.: Government Printing Office, 1928), 2.

11. There is certainly evidence, however, that American reformers and legislators were aware of it. For example, when the New York State law came under judicial scrutiny in 1913–14, *The Survey*, an important outlet for the reform community, reported that in drafting the original law, members of a Factory Investigation Commission had "availed themselves of the recorded experience of the fourteen European nations who in 1906 met in Bern, Switzerland, to sign an international treaty prohibiting night work for women in industrial establishments" ("Progress of the New York Women's Night Work Case," 32 [June 12, 1914]: 169). The 1906 Bern Convention shows up frequently in the literature of reformers who refer to it as a mark of civilization. For example, *The Survey* frequently compared the lack of night work laws in the United States with those in Europe: "This tardy progress is in striking contrast to the action of the fourteen civilized countries of Europe which have, since 1906, by international treaty prohibited the night work of women" ("Night Work Law Tested in New York State," 31 [Dec. 24, 1913]: 343). Similar references can be found in the editorial pages of *The Charities and the Commons*, for example, in contrasting "the European movement towards total prohibition of women's nightwork in industrial establishments—representatives of all the civilized governments, having met twice during the past two years to draw up international agreements on the

subject—and the indifference to such protection in this country" ("Night Work: Women and the New York Courts," 17 [Dec. 1906]: 183.

12. Nancy Erickson sees this decision as less dramatic than is typically the case ("*Muller v. Oregon* Reconsidered: The Origins of a Sex-based Doctrine of Liberty of Contract," *Labor History* 30 [Spring 1989]: 230–31.

13. *State Laws Affecting Working Women*, Bulletin of the Women's Bureau, No. 40 (Washington, D.C.: Government Printing Office, 1924), 5.

14. *State Laws Affecting Working Women*, 5.

15. "Regulation of Women's Working Hours in the United States," *American Labor Legislation Review* 8 (December, 1918): 345–54.

16. *State Laws Affecting Working Women*, 5.

17. Hopkins, *The Employment of Women at Night*, 6 acknowledges the possibility of an undercount.

18. Hopkins, 10.

19. African-American women are a significant exception. Since the vast majority of them were excluded from industrial work and were occupied in domestic service and agricultural work, they would, in any event, not have been covered by this legislation. See U.S. Department of Labor, *Negro Women in Industry*, Bulletin of the Women's Bureau, No. 20 (Washington, D.C.: Government Printing Office, 1922).

20. Charles Iffland, "Reasons Why Night Work Should Be Abolished in Bakeries," *American Federationist* 26 (May 1919): 408.

21. Josephine Goldmark, *Fatigue and Efficiency: A Study in Industry* (New York: Charities Publication Committee, 1912), 266.

22. Emery Hayhurst, M.D., "Medical Argument against Night Work Especially for Women Employees," *American Journal of Public Health* 9 (1919): 367.

23. 155 Ill. 98 (1895), 105.

24. 15 PA Superior Court, 5 (1900), 17; and see *People v. Williams*, 184 N.Y. 131 (1907).

25. *People v. Schweinler Press*, 214 N.Y. 395 (1915), 400, 409.

26. Ibid., 401, 402.

27. Frances Perkins, " Do Women in Industry Need Special Protection?" *The Survey* 55 (Feb. 15, 1926): 531.

28. "A Summary of the 'Facts of Knowledge' Submitted on Behalf of the People," in National Consumer's League, *The Case against Night Work for Women* (New York: National Consumer's League, 1914), A10.

29. *People v. Schweinler Press*, 403.

30. "A Summary of the 'Facts of Knowledge,'" A10.

31. Agnes de Lima, *Night Working Mothers in Textile Mills: Passaic, New Jersey* (National Consumer's League and the Consumer's League of New Jersey, Dec. 1920), 5; *Wage-earning Women in Stores and Factories*, vol. 5 of *Report on Condition of Women and Child Wage Earners in the United States*, 214; Goldmark, *Fatigue and Efficiency*, 275.

32. "Night Work Law Tested in New York State," 343.

33. *Annual Report of the Consumers' League of New York* (1906), 19, cited in Baker, "Do Women in Industry Need Special Protection?" 239.

34. "Progress of the New York Women's Night Work Case," 169.

35. *Summary: The Effects of Labor Legislation on the Employment Opportunities of Women*, Bulletin of the Women's Bureau, No. 68 (Washington, D.C.: Government Printing Office, 1928), 15.

36. See Hopkins, *The Employment of Women at Night*, 57. For a discussion of glass workers and decent women, see "Fighting Women's Night Work in Rhode Island," *The Survey* 36 (Feb. 13, 1916): 48.

37. Rheta Childe Dorr, "Should There be Labor Laws for Women? No," *Good Housekeeping* 81 (Sept. 1925): 52ff.

38. Elizabeth Faulkner Baker, "Do Women in Industry Need Special Protection?" *The Survey* 55 (Feb. 15, 1926): 531.

39. "Night Work: Women and the New York Courts," 183.

40. Perkins, "Do Women in Industry Need Special Protection?" 530.

41. Baker, "Do Women in Industry Need Special Protection?" 532; Beyer, *History of Labor Legislation for Women.*

42. De Lima, *Night Working Mothers in Textile Mills*, 16.

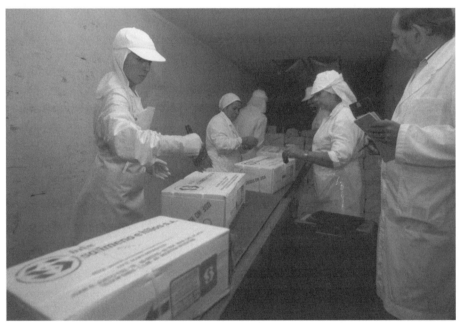

Gender Inequality in the Factory: Male Manages All-Female Workforce in a Frozen Fish Packing Plant, Argentina, 1995 (© International Labour Organization)

Part III

GENDER, WAGES, AND INEQUALITY

Why are women paid less than men for comparable as well as the same work? What does this have to do with occupational sex segregation, caregiving, human capital, and overall inequality? The readings in Part III address these and other questions. The first selection, "Still A Man's Labor Market: The Long-Term Earnings Gap," by Ashley English and Ariane Hegewisch, suggests that there has been progress toward narrowing the gender wage gap in the United States, from fifty-nine cents to the man's dollar in 1960, to seventy-seven cents by 2008. Nevertheless, they caution that this refers only to full-time workers, excluding half of all women. Over the fifteen-year period of their study, women on average earned $273,592, compared to $722,693 for men on average, constituting a 62 percent wage gap. Although women are closing the education and skill gap with men in the United States, data from 2005 show that within each racial and ethnic category, men still maintain higher weekly median earnings than women. Compared to men, Asian American women earn the highest wage of eighty-seven cents to the man's dollar; black women earn seventy-two cents, and Hispanic or Latina women earn fifty-nine cents to the man's dollar (U.S. Census Bureau, Current Population Survey, 2006 Annual Svc & Ec. Supplement).

English and Hegewisch contend that there are several explanations for the earnings disparity: 1) occupational sex segregation, 2) fewer hours of work offered in the female sector versus the male sector, 3) discrimination in the labor market, and 4) unequal social norms regarding family care and paid work. Both men and women face a striking degree of occupational sex segregation worldwide, although there is tremendous variation in how societies assign jobs to each gender. For example, the percentage of female clerical workers in the United States is 96.5 percent, while in Bulgaria it is 84.5 percent, compared to 3.1 percent in Pakistan and 39.2 percent in the Virgin Islands. In the United States service work is female dominated, while in Turkey it is predominantly male. In the United States manufacturing work is male dominated, while in Japan production jobs are gender integrated (Cartmill 1999).

Despite this global variation in occupational sex segregation, female-dominated occupations in the United States are characterized by 22 percent fewer work hours than male-dominated occupations, regardless of whether a male or a female performs the work. Males in female-dominated occupations still earn more than women, however. Female secretaries and administrative assistants, for example, earn 83.4 percent of what male clerical workers earn; female registered nurses (RNs) earn 86.6 percent of male RNs' earnings; and female elementary and middle-school teachers earn 87.6 percent of male schoolteachers' income (Institute for Women's Policy Research 2009).

One explanation for this pay disparity is "statistical discrimination," where employers discriminate against individual female employees based on real or imagined distinctions they perceive about the group's characteristics. Such assumptions might be that women work only for "pin money" to do their hair and nails, while their husbands earn the true family wage. Or, employers might believe that women choose to work fewer hours in order to spend more time with family, or that they will leave the workforce early to have babies and raise children. Such assumptions are often used to justify payment of lower wages to women. While in some instances such assumptions may have validity, it becomes statistical discrimination when they are attached to the entire female labor force.

A "taste for discrimination," in contrast, means that employers simply do not like specific groups of people and will therefore treat potential employees from these racial or gender groups as inferior. They might offer low wages, no promotions, and inadequate work conditions, or simply not hire them for high-level positions.

Christine Williams illustrates specific ways in which discrimination reveals itself in her study of the retail industry. Her piece, "The Social Organization of Toy Stores," focuses on two stores, Diamond Toys, a unionized store in an upscale urban shopping area, and the Toy Warehouse, a non-union store in a "bad neighborhood." Despite a female majority in each workforce, senior management positions in both retail stores were held only by white males. Employees at Diamond Toys were 60 percent white, with no black male employees, while the workforce at Toy Warehouse was 60 percent African American. African American men and women at the Toy Warehouse held lower-status and back-room jobs, such as cleaners, stockers, and security guards, while young, white, or light-skinned females and Asian American men were hired to work in the front of the store as cashiers.

Williams suggests that conventional economic theories provide inadequate explanations for the gender and race stratification she found in the two separate workplaces. Human capital theory, for example, argues women freely choose lower-level, lower-paid jobs that require minimal levels of education and skill based on their future fertility decisions. Knowing they will depart the workforce to have babies and raise children, they choose not to invest in more education. The market in turn chooses from these potential workers based on their education and skill qualifications. In contrast, the discrimination and structural inequality approach claims that differential opportunity exists for women and minorities in education and work due to discrimination, thus prohibiting racial and/or gendered groups from reaching their desired economic and social goals.

Williams rejects these conventional approaches as inadequate and argues instead that racial and gendered power and authority on the shop floor is a complex "matrix of domination," one comprised of a multitude of interactions between consumers, workers, coworkers, and management. She borrows Leslie Salzinger's concept of "interpolation" to explain this. Management creates an image of the "right" physical characteristics for each job based on presumed consumer preferences, and workers generally internalize these constructs as acceptable. Cashier jobs at the Toy Warehouse are portrayed as "female jobs," for example, belonging to white or light-skinned women. A few men were occasionally assigned to work as cashiers in the electronics department. But when a black male was asked during a staffing shortage to work at the cash register in a non-electronics department, he actually resisted, believing it would threaten his masculinity, elucidating this concept of "interpolation." Williams found that male workers deliberately erected barriers to keep women out of their jobs in an effort to create all-male bastions, which "help them preserve their masculinity."

In contrast, Diamond Toys employed both men and women as cashiers, but management otherwise segregated the employees by gender and race. Only women sold dolls and stuffed animals, while men sold sporting goods and electronics. The low-status, low-paid cleaning jobs were almost entirely Latino/a; the clerks were white, Asian, or Latino/a; and the directors were all white males. White employees generally did not speak to the nonwhite cleaning staff at Diamond Toys, thus preserving their status distinction of "white privilege" as well.

To overcome gender and race inequality in the workplace, Williams contends that it is necessary to integrate the racialized and gendered hierarchy of jobs, a difficult task as employers believe customers prefer these hierarchies, and employees are socialized to internalize them as well.

Nancy Folbre addresses the way in which such cultural norms have historically contributed to women's lower wages and status. In "The Milk of Human Kindness," Folbre argues that as individual women specialized in child rearing and other forms of care, they became more dependent on men for economic assistance. She presents the divergent economic arguments of liberal feminism and social feminism as possible alternative solutions to this inequity. The former, liberal feminism, focused on attaining greater individual rights for women in the world of work, politics, and economy as the means to increased status and income. In contrast, social feminism purported that human beings have an obligation to care for one another. Instead of women striving to diminish their caregiving role and simply replicating individualist, market principles (i.e., becoming more like men), women should work to incorporate caregiving into the marketplace.

Folbre concludes that in order for women to overcome their wage handicap, caregiving must become gender neutral, shared equitably between men and women, and remunerated at a fair market price. Such a shift in cultural norms and practices, she argues, will eliminate the deleterious social and economic effects of gendered caregiving.

A movement toward greater pay equity policy occurred in 2009 with the Lilly Ledbetter case. Lilly Ledbetter had worked for nearly two decades as a supervisor at a Goodyear Tire plant in Alabama, only to discover, through an anonymous note in her mailbox, that her male colleagues had been paid much more than her for many years. She brought an Equal Employment Opportunity Commission (EEOC) complaint against Goodyear, which went all the way to the Supreme Court. She lost her case when the court ruled 5–4 in *Ledbetter v. Goodyear* that employees can file a wage discrimination complaint only within 180 days of the date of the payroll decision.

After this verdict, Congress passed the Lilly Ledbetter Fair Pay Act, signed by President Obama, which expanded the statute of limitations. Although Ledbetter herself did not benefit from the new legislation, it breathed new life into the Equal Pay Act of 1963, a law that provides equal pay for equal work in the same workplace (Stolberg 2009). Title VII of the Civil Rights Act, which prohibits compensation discrimination on the basis of race, color, religion, sex, national origin, age, or disability, also gained new life with the Ledbetter legislation. Unlike the Equal Pay Act, Title VII does not require the claimant's job to be substantially equal to that of the higher-paid person, nor does it require that the claimant work in the same establishment as the higher-paid individual.

Legislation such as the above makes it easier for women to claim pay discrimination based on sex without retaliation. Some policy experts argue, however, that pay inequity will be eliminated only when workers are allowed to discuss their wages openly, employers conduct salary equity studies, and equal pay and equal opportunity legislation is enforced (Institute for Women's Policy Research 2009). Others contend both occupations and caregiving must become fully gender-integrated in order to achieve wage equality.

CHAPTER 10

Still a Man's Labor Market: The Long-Term Earnings Gap

A REPORT ON THE WAGE GAP AND ITS IMPLICATIONS FOR WOMEN, FAMILIES, AND THE LABOR MARKET

Ashley English and Ariane Hegewisch

This Research-in-Brief summarizes *Still a Man's Labor Market: The Long-Term Earnings Gap*, a report by Stephen J. Rose, Rose Economic Consulting, and Heidi Hartmann, Institute for Women's Policy Research (IWPR), published by IWPR in 2004. The report uses data from a 15-year longitudinal study (from the Panel Study of Income Dynamics) and shows that over that period women earned 62 percent less than men, or only 38 cents for every dollar men earned. This is less than half of the more conventional measure of the pay gap based on year-round earnings of full-time workers for a single year, which stands at 23 percent, or 77 cents for every male dollar earned. This new measure shows the costs over time for women and their families of the continued unequal division of family labor, with women having to make most of the adjustments of time in the labor market to perform family work. The report provides a detailed analysis of the gendered patterns in the labor market, showing that women are much more likely than men to have persistently low earnings; that women and especially men continue to work disproportionately in occupations where the majority of workers are of their own sex; that across the board men's jobs involve longer working hours than women's jobs, but that the pay premium for male jobs far exceeds the additional hours worked. The report also shows that over the period studied women were more likely to experience growth in earnings than men, but the earnings gap remained large.

Rose and Hartmann suggest that this reinforcing cycle of inequality in the labor market and in the distribution of domestic work, which results in low pay for women, is particularly damaging to the growing number of female-headed households. The authors end by suggesting a number of policy solutions that would close the wage gap and prevent women and their families from further losses due to the accumulated effect of the wage gap.

Introduction

Many argue that women's prospects in the labor market have steadily increased and that any small remaining gap in earnings between women and men is not significant.

They see the remaining differences as the result of women's own choices, or they argue that with women now graduating from college at a higher rate than men, and with the economy continuing its shift toward services, work and earnings differences between women and men may disappear entirely.

It is true that women have made progress relative to men. Women's labor force participation has risen rapidly; women have made progress in many occupations that previously were bastions of men; the wage gap has narrowed by more than one-third since 1960, from women earning 59 cents for every dollar earned by men, to 77 cents now. Yet this measure, by virtue of including only those who worked full-time for at least 50 weeks per year, excludes almost half of all women. While women's and men's work and careers have become more similar, important differences remain. Women are much more likely than men to reduce or interrupt their time in paid work to deal with family responsibilities, resulting in a dramatic impact on their earnings. Figure 10.1 shows that over a 15-year period less than half of all women (48.5 percent) had earnings in each of the 15 years, compared with 6 of 7 (84 percent) men; 3 of 10 women report four or more years without earnings (compared with 1 of 20 men). Women are also more likely to work fewer hours per year, working on average 500 hours fewer per year (or 22 percent less) than men, even when only men and women who have earnings in each year are compared.

This division of responsibility for family care results in very different wages and hours of work for men and women. Over the 15 years, the more likely a women is to have dependent children and be married, the more likely she is to be a low earner and have fewer hours in the labor market. The opposite holds for men: marriage and dependent children make it much more likely that a man has higher earnings and works longer hours.

When actual earnings are accumulated over many years for all men and women workers, the losses to women and their families due to the wage gap are large and can be devastating. The average woman earned only $273,592 while the average man earned $722,693, leaving a gap of 62 percent over the 15-year period.

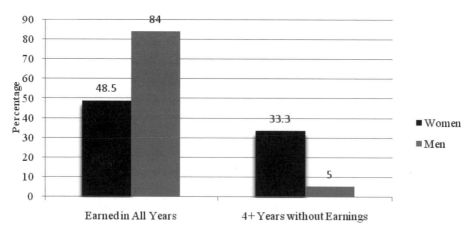

Figure 10.1. Women's and Men's Years with Earnings, 1983–1998
Source: Rose and Hartmann 2004, page 11; based on the Panel Study of Income Dynamics.

Methodology and Data

The report is based on an analysis of the Panel Study of Income Dynamics (PSID). The PSID is a longitudinal data set that tracks a representative sample of households over time. This analysis uses data from 1983 to 1998 and includes all prime-age workers (26 to 59 years old) who have at least one year of positive earnings during that period and who have provided information on labor market activity for each of the 15 years: 1,614 women and 1,212 men. All earnings have been converted into 1999 dollars.

Low Earnings as a Persistent Characteristic of Women's Paid Work

The earnings gap is not simply explained by women having less time in paid work. Hour per hour, including only those women and men with the strongest labor market attachment who had earnings every single year, in this study women still earn only 69.6 cents of each dollar earned per hour by men (see Table 10.1).

Again including only those with the strongest labor force attachment, women are significantly more likely to have low earnings (less than $15,000 annually—just above the poverty line for a family of three in 1999) than men. One in three women had four or more years with earnings below this threshold, compared with one in fourteen men.

Table 10.1. The Long-Term Labor Market Experience of Women and Men: Earnings, Work Hours, and Years Out of the Labor Force, 1983–1998

Number of Years Out of Labor Force	Shares	15 Year Averages[a]		Hourly Wage[b]	Hourly Wage Ratio[b]
		Annual Earnings	Annual Hours		
Females					
All Prime-age Females	100.0	$21,363	1,498	$12.82	60.0
None	48.5	$29,507	1,766	$15.72	69.6
1	10.2	$19,341	1,513	$12.25	72.3
2 or 3	11.8	$14,868	1,376	$10.56	75.6
4 or more	29.5	$11,280	1,100	$9.25	63.8
Males					
All Prime-age Males	100.0	$49,068	2,219	$21.38	
None	84.0	$52,510	2,260	$22.60	
1	7.5	$36,867	2,210	$16.94	
2 or 3	4.8	$28,777	2,062	$13.97	
4 or more	3.7	$21,896	1,524	$14.50	

Notes: [a]Zero earnings years are not included, i.e., averages for earnings and hours are calculated only for years when work is reported. Weighted data are used to calculate all figures.
[b]Hourly wages are person-weighted rather than hour-weighted so that each person's wage counts equally in the calculations regardless of how few or many hours the person worked. The hourly wage ratio is calculated as 100 × women's average hourly wages/men's average hourly wages.
Source: Rose and Hartmann 2004, page 9; based on the Panel Study of Income Dynamics.

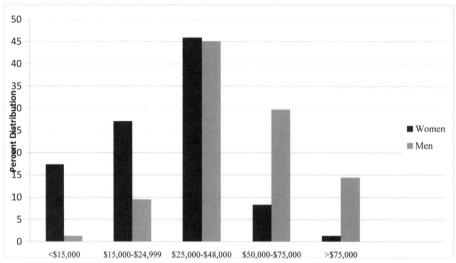

Figure 10.2. The Distribution of Annual Earnings among Women and Men with Strong Labor Force Attachment, 1983–1998
Note: For those with earnings in every year. Weighted data are used to calculate all figures.
Source: Rose and Hartmann 2004, page 11; based on the Panel Study of Income Dynamics.

Over the whole 15 years only a tiny minority of men (1.3 percent) fail to average at least $15,000 per year, compared with 17.7 percent of strongly attached women (see Figure 10.2). Ninety percent of those who average less than $15,000 per year are women.

The average annual earnings for most men and most women (with earnings in each of 15 years) were in the range of $25,000 to $49,999. But for men, that is virtually the bottom of the salary range: 44.5 percent of men earned more than $50,000 annually. For women, it's the top; only 9.6 percent of women on average earned more than $50,000 per year (see Figure 10.2).

Sources of the Wage Gap

However the wage gap is calculated, it is important to note that men's and women's earnings differ for many reasons including: discrimination in the labor market, discrimination in pre-labor market preparation (education/training programs), unequal societal norms at home, and the constrained decisions men and women make about work and home issues, which often result in women working fewer hours when they work and taking several years out of the labor market. Table 10.2 decomposes the wage gap to show these effects. Many economists believe the "remaining unexplained gap" can include the effects of discrimination.

Sex Segregation in the Labor Market

Women also face a striking degree of sex segregation in the labor market—women work in predominantly "women's jobs" and men in predominately "men's jobs," that is,

Table 10.2. Reasons for the Long-Term Earnings Gap[a] between Men and Women, 1983–1998

Women on average earn less than men over 15 year period (Earnings gap):	62.1%
Gap due to differences in number of years out of the labor force:	18.3%
Gap due to differences in hours worked when working:	15.8%
Remaining unexplained gap	28.0%

Note: [a]The earnings gap = 100 − the earnings ratio.
Source: Rose and Hartmann 2004, page 22; based on the Panel Study of Income Dynamics

in jobs where the majority of workers are of one sex. To investigate this division and its impact on earnings further, the report divides jobs into three tiers or clusters—"elite" jobs, "good" jobs, and "less-skilled" jobs. Within each tier, occupations are classified as either male dominated or female dominated, thus resulting in six clusters (Table 10.3). For both genders, approximately 58 percent of strongly attached workers, those with earnings in all 15 years, work consistently in a *single* one of the six career occupational clusters (spending at *least* 12 of 15 years in that cluster). The remaining 42 percent have mixed work histories, mainly rotating among jobs in the bottom two tiers. At least 75 percent of workers are of one gender within each of the six tiered gender clusters. Male and female pairs of occupations within each tier require an equivalent level of education and skills. The three male clusters account for half of all male workers; less than one in ten men (8 percent) work in the female dominated clusters; the remaining male workers had mixed work experience. Women are a little less likely to work in a cluster dominated by their own sex than men (44 percent) and more likely than men to work in a job where the majority of workers are of the other sex (15 percent)—not surprisingly, given that male dominated jobs traditionally pay more.

In each tier, women's jobs pay significantly less than their male counterparts. This is so even though both sets of occupations tend to require the same level of educational preparation; it also holds when only full-time workers (at least 1,750 hours—35 weeks for at least 50 weeks per year) are included.

Table 10.3. A Three-Tiered Labor Market (Sample Occupations)

	Women's Jobs (75% or more female)	Men's Jobs (75% or more male)
Elite Jobs Managerial/Professional	Teachers Nurses	Business Executives Scientists Doctors Lawyers
Good Jobs Supervisors, Blue Collar Craftspeople, Technicians, Clerical	Secretaries	Skilled blue-collar work Police Firefighters
Less-Skilled Jobs Sales clerks, Food work, Personal/Service work, Unskilled blue collar work	Sales Clerks Personal Service Work	Factory Jobs

Source: Rose and Hartmann 2004, page 39.

Moreover, both men and women earn more in the male sector of each tier than their counterparts do in the female sector in the same tier, indicating a premium for working in male-typed jobs, and conversely, a penalty for working in female-typed jobs. (In the elite tier, women actually earn less per hour in male jobs than female jobs, as shown in Table 10.5, yet their annual earnings are higher in the male jobs because women in men's jobs work more hours; despite slightly lower hourly earnings, their overall earnings opportunities may be better in the male sector.) Yet men tend to earn more than women in all tiers. In the highest paid tier, male elite jobs, men on average earned $74,877 compared with $51,085 for full-time female workers (in 1999 dollars).

Significant Differences in Hours of Work

Another striking difference between male and female dominated jobs is in the number of hours worked on average per year. Male dominated jobs, and jobs where neither sex is in a clear majority, have significantly more work hours per year than female dominated jobs (see Table 10.4) at each level. This also holds for each gender—women in male dominated jobs on average work longer than women in female dominated jobs, and men in female dominated jobs work fewer hours on average than men in male dominated jobs. This suggests that the occupational difference in work hours goes beyond mere "preference" by individual men and women and reflects a more systematic adjustment in hours to the gendered norm in the division of family labor.

The differences in average annual hours are partly a reflection of the greater likelihood for women to work reduced hours (less than 1,750 hours per year). Yet the differences are also stark when only those men and women working full-time are included (those who work at least 35 hours per week for 50 weeks per year, see Table 10.4). Men in elite male or elite female jobs typically work over an hour more per week than women in similar jobs. Men in "good" female jobs on average work over three hours more per week than women in similar jobs. The pattern is less clear in the less skilled jobs.

Yet the difference in hours does not account for the earnings gap. As can be seen from Table 10.5, men out earn women hour by hour, even when only women with the strongest labor market attachment are included.

Table 10.4. Hours Worked by Continuously Employed Women and Men by Career Occupational Groups, 1983–1998

| | Male Sector | | | Female Sector | | |
| | Women | | Men | Women | | Men |
Tier	All	Full-Time	All	All	Full-Time	All
Elite Jobs	2,154	2,264	2,332	1,705	2,117	2,158
Good Jobs	2,247	2,469	2,221	1,860	1,989	2,156
Less-Skilled Jobs	1,871	2,018	2,199	1,670	2,279	2,016

Notes: ªAs there is not much difference in the distribution across occupational groups between men who work full-time and all men (because most men work full-time), data are not reported separately for men who work full-time.
Source: Rose and Hartmann 2004, page 15; based on the Panel Study of Income Dynamics.

Table 10.5. Earnings of Continuously Employed Women and Men by Career Occupational Average Hourly Wages

Earnings of Continuously Employed Women and Men[a] by Career Occupational Cluster

Average Hourly Wages

Tier	Female Sector[b]			Male Sector[b]			Increase for Women If Move to Male Sector
	Women	Men	Ratio	Women	Men	Ratio	
Elite Jobs	$22.85	$24.28	0.94	$22.56	$32.11	0.70	−1.2%
Good Jobs	$15.47	$22.16	0.70	$18.76	$22.65	0.83	21.2%
Less-skilled Jobs	$10.54	$16.03	0.66	$12.55	$16.20	0.77	19.0%

Notes: [a] Analysis includes workers aged 26 to 59 with earnings in all 15 years of the study period.
[b] Male (female) sector jobs are defined as those having a majority male (female) workforce.
Source: Rose and Hartmann 2004, page 15; based on the Panel Study of Income Dynamics.

Better Wage Growth over Time for Women than Men

One disadvantage of averaging male and female earnings data over the 15-year period is that such an average cannot show whether earnings disparities were higher at the beginning than at the end of the period. The earnings gap between women and men during the period from 1983 to 1998 was significantly smaller than for the previous 15-year period, a reflection of women spending fewer years out of the labor market and gaining more education and skills. To analyze whether the earnings gap has narrowed further during the period, the authors compute an average annual change rate in earnings for each worker (with at least two years of earnings). The analysis divides workers into three age groups at the start of the period, to check whether the pattern for younger women significantly differs from older women, and then estimates annual growth rates over the period for men and women. The normal assumption is that over time average earnings will increase as workers progress through their careers and gain seniority and skills, but earnings, of course, might also stall or decline.

The analysis shows significant gender differences, with men on average being less likely to have seen earnings growth over the period (58 percent of men compared to 73 percent of women) and more likely to have had an actual decline in earnings (26 percent of men compared to 19 percent of women) (Figure 10.3). Younger men (those aged 26 to 31 in 1983) tended to do better than older men (39 to 45 years) but even in this age group one-third had no or negative earnings growth. Younger women also did better than older women, with "only" one-fifth of them having stable or decreasing earnings compared with 44 percent of women in the older cohort.

This finding of stagnating or declining earnings for men over time corresponds to other studies. As the manufacturing sector struggled during the 1980s, many men

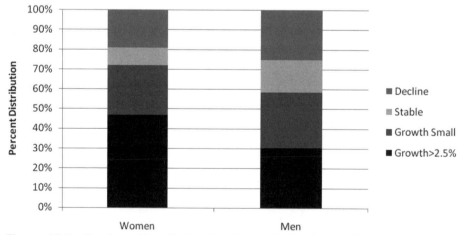

Figure 10.3. Earnings Growth for Continuously Employed Men and Women, 1983-1998.

Source: Rose and Hartmann 2004, page 23; based on the Panel Study of Income Dynamics.

experienced stagnating or falling earnings. Women's earnings rose both because they were in a better place in the labor market and because they increased their education and their labor market attachment. While the generally narrowing pay gap is encouraging, it is important to keep two caveats in mind: women started at such a low level that it was relatively easy to move up; and women with work interruptions likely had to start again at a much reduced level before they experienced large earning gains. Yet even though women are catching up, progress is slow and the pay gap continues to be substantial and unlikely to narrow much further without major policy adjustments.

Wives Who Earn More than Their Husbands

While much of the data confirms that men generally earn more than women, this does not hold for all couples. Among the group of women who had earnings in each year, and were married for the whole period (about one-third of all women in the sample), 15 percent out earned their husbands (even if often the difference was not large). Hourly wages are higher than their husbands' for almost one-quarter of the women in this group (although, because hours might be lower, not all of them had higher average annual earnings). And, even though different working patterns mean that women earn less over the long term, among college educated women more than 85 percent had higher hourly earnings than their husbands in at least one year of the survey period.

Self-Reinforcing but Increasingly Unstable Gendered Division of Labor

Although women have made some gains relative to men, progress has stalled since the early 1990s. The gender gap in earnings has a major influence on families' life opportunities, on their likelihood of experiencing poverty, on older women's retirement security, and on single mothers' ability to provide for their children's care and education. Married women continue to be at least partially insulated from the impact of women's low earnings through their connection to higher earning men. Yet most families would have a higher standard of living if women's wages and lifetime earnings were higher. Single mothers, and their families, with no other household income to make up for the lower earnings available in most women's jobs, are particularly penalized. Furthermore, women's low life-time earnings can have devastating effects in old age by preventing women from building up sufficient resources for retirement. Widowed, divorced, or never married women over age 65 share high poverty rates of approximately 20 percent.

Gender differentiation in the labor market is self-reproducing. When students express interest in non-traditional jobs, they are often not encouraged to pursue the appropriate career preparation by guidance counselors. Employers may pay women less because they believe women are more likely to leave work. They may structure jobs to provide part-time hours because they believe women are dependent on jobs with shorter work hours. Without subsidized child care, many families are left to their own resources to combine family care with paid work. When the husband out earns the wife, it makes greater economic sense for the wife, as the lower earner, to provide more or all of the child care because less income is lost if the lower-earner cuts back her work.

This gendered division of labor is self-reinforcing. Yet it is also arguably increasingly unstable and unsustainable. Men and women spend growing portions of their lives unmarried. Women's expectations are changing and they are demanding more independence and greater economic security throughout life, whether they are single or married. Women are closing the graduate school gap with men. Women have begun to outnumber men in law and medical schools and have increased their numbers substantially in business schools. But even though progress has been considerable over the last few decades, at the current speed of change it would still take 50 years for women to close the pay gap. Policy makers need to develop new policy interventions that can help break the vicious cycle that makes women trade down their progress at work and makes men lose out on family time.

Policy Implications

There is not a single cause, and hence no single solution, that will deliver equality to men and women in the labor market. The factors contributing to the long-term pay gap include continued direct discrimination in the labor market; the undervaluation of work typically performed by women; the lack of systematic work family supports; the particular disadvantages faced by the growing number of women-headed households; the marriage penalties in the tax system; the under-representation of women in higher paying occupations; and poor working conditions in the labor market especially for lower skilled jobs. A program responding to these problems needs to include:

- **Policies that reduce sex discrimination in the labor market:** Providing more resources to oversight agencies including the Equal Employment Opportunity Commission and the Office of Federal Contract Compliance would strengthen the enforcement of equal opportunity laws and lead to resolving complaints more quickly. Developing new Equal Employment Opportunity remedies to address the comparable worth problem could require employers to show that comparable jobs are paid fairly, using tools such as job evaluation systems.
- **Policies that make it easier to combine paid work with family work:** Affordable, good quality early care and education for children has many benefits, including making it easier for lower income mothers to stay in the workforce. New policies are needed to make workplaces more family-friendly, including more flexible hours and job-guaranteed paid leaves for sickness and family care, the elimination or capping of mandatory overtime, a shorter standard work week, and the increased availability of better quality, reduced hours jobs. Last but not least, encouraging men to use family leave and reduce their work hours—and tackling discrimination faced by men who take up family leave or adjust hours to deal with family care—will help change the double-standard in parenting that places the responsibility for it on women.

- **Education and training policies to increase women's presence in higher paying jobs:** Increasing resources for non-traditional skills training, improving access to vocational training especially for single mothers, and improving career counseling and information available to girls and young women still in school are all important as there are still too many women who have been discouraged from pursuing higher education and/or job training for occupations that are not traditionally held by women.

- **Policies to increase the support for women-headed households:** Families headed by single mothers who face discrimination and lower earnings in the labor market are much more likely to live in poverty. Female-headed households need increased support in the forms of improved access to the income of non-custodial fathers after divorce, improved child care support, and improved access to vocational training and education programs designed to make it possible for single mothers to participate.

- **Policies to reduce the "marriage penalty":** Reducing the bias in income taxes and Social Security benefits on the secondary earner in a marriage will reduce the disincentives that depress the work effort of the lower earning member of a married couple.

- **Policies to tackle the low-wage labor market:** Policies that raise the minimum wage and provide resources for its proper enforcement and programs that encourage increased unionization will provide higher wages and increased access to benefits for low-wage workers, who are disproportionately female.

CHAPTER 11

The Social Organization of Toy Stores

Christine L. Williams

[...]

Retail jobs, like other jobs in the service sector, have grown in number and changed dramatically over the past decades. Service jobs gradually have replaced manufacturing jobs as part of the general deindustrialization of the U.S. economy. This economic restructuring has resulted in boom times for wealthy American consumers as the prices for many commodities have dropped (a consequence of the movement of production overseas). It has also resulted in an erosion of working conditions for Americans in the bottom half of the economy, including service workers. Retail jobs have become increasingly "flexible," temporary, and part-time. Over the past decades, workers in these jobs have experienced a loss of job security and benefits, a diminishment in the power of unions, and a lessening of the value of the minimum wage (McCall 2001). Yet while most retail workers have lost ground, the giant corporations they work for have enjoyed unprecedented prosperity and political clout.

George Ritzer (2002) aptly uses the term *McJobs* to describe the working conditions found in a variety of service industries today. The word is a pun on McDonald's, the fast-food giant that introduced and popularized this labor system. McJobs are not careers; they are designed to discourage long-term commitment. They have short promotion ladders, they provide few opportunities for advancement or increased earnings, and the technical skills they require are not transferable outside the immediate work environment. They target sectors of the labor force that presumably don't "need" money to support themselves or their families: young people looking for "fun jobs" before college; mothers seeking part-time opportunities to fit around their family responsibilities; older, retired people looking for the chance to get out of the house and to socialize.[1] However, this image does not resonate with the increasing numbers of workers in these jobs who are struggling to support themselves and their families (Ehrenreich 2001; Talwar 2002). The marketing of McJobs on television commercials for Wal-Mart and fast-food restaurants obscures the harsh working conditions and low pay that contribute to the impoverished state of the working poor.

In addition to contributing to economic inequality, jobs in the retail industry are structured in ways that enhance inequality by gender and race. Although all retail workers are low paid, white men employed in this industry earn more money than any other group.[2] Overall, about as many men as women work in retail trades, but they are concentrated in different kinds of stores. For example, men make up more than three quarters of workers in retail jobs selling motor vehicles, lumber, and home and auto supplies, while women predominate in apparel, gift, and needlework stores (U.S. Bureau of Labor Statistics 2004).

In both stores where I worked, the gender ratio was about 60:40, with women outnumbering men. I was surprised that so many men worked in these toy stores. In my admittedly limited experience, I associated women with the job of selling toys. But I learned that because of the way that jobs are divided and organized, customers usually don't see the substantial numbers of men who are working there too.

Retail work is also organized by race and ethnicity. Ten percent of all employees in the retail trade industry are African American, and 12 percent are of Hispanic origin, slightly less then their overall representation in the U.S. population. But again, whites, African Americans, and Latina/os are likely to work in different types of stores. For example, African Americans are underrepresented (less than 5 percent) in stores that sell hardware, gardening equipment, and needlework supplies and overrepresented (more than 15 percent) in department stores, variety stores, and shoe stores. Similarly Latina/os are underrepresented (less than 6 percent) in bookstores and gas stations and overrepresented (more than 16 percent) in retail florists and household appliance stores (U.S. Bureau of Labor Statistics 2004).[3]

The two stores where I worked had radically different racial compositions. Sixty percent of the workers at the Toy Warehouse were African American, and 60 percent of those at Diamond Toys were white. Only three African Americans, all women, worked at Diamond Toys. No black men worked at that store. In contrast, only four white women (including me) worked at the Toy Warehouse. In this chapter, I explore the reasons for this and other dramatic differences in the organization of these toy stores.

Sociologists have long recognized the workplace as a central site for the reproduction of social inequalities. Studies of factory work in particular have shown us how race and gender hierarchies are reproduced through the social organization of the work.[4] I argue that the labor process in service industries is equally important for understanding social inequality, even though this sector has not come under the same degree of scrutiny by sociologists.[5] I demonstrate how the working conditions at the two stores perpetuate inequality by class, gender, and race. The jobs are organized in such a way as to benefit some groups of workers and discriminate against others.

The stores where I worked represent a range of working conditions in large retail trade establishments. Although both were affiliated with national chains and both were in the business of selling toys, Diamond Toys was unionized and the Toy Warehouse was not. The union protected workers from some of the most egregious aspects of retail work. But, as I will show, the union could not overcome the race, gender, and class inequalities that are reproduced by the social organization of the industry.

Stratified Selling

[...]

The hierarchy of jobs and power within the stores was marked by race and gender. In both stores the directors and assistant directors were white men. Immediately below them were managers, who were a more diverse group, including men and women, whites and Latinas/os, and, at the Toy Warehouse, an African American woman (Olive). There were far more managers at Diamond Toys than at the Toy Warehouse; I met at least ten managers during my time there, versus only two at the Toy Warehouse.

The next layer of the hierarchy under managers were supervisors, who were drawn from the ranks of associates. They were among those who had the most seniority and thus the most knowledge of store procedures, and they had limited authority to do things like void transactions at the registers. All of the supervisors at Diamond Toys were white and most were men, while at the Toy Warehouse supervisors were more racially diverse and most were women. It took me a long time to figure out who the supervisors were at the Toy Warehouse. Many of those I thought were supervisors turned out to be regular employees. They had many of the same responsibilities as supervisors, but, as I came to find out, they were competing with each other for promotion to this position. When I asked why they were acting like supervisors, it was explained to me that the Toy Warehouse wouldn't promote anyone before he or she was proficient at the higher job. This policy justified giving workers more responsibilities without more pay. At Diamond Toys, in contrast, job descriptions were clearer and were enforced.

Associates were the largest group of workers at the stores (sometimes referred to as the staff). They included men and women of all races and ethnic groups and different ages, except at Diamond Toys, where I noted that there were no black men. Despite the apparent diversity among the staff, there was substantial segregation by race and gender in the tasks they were assigned. Employees of toy stores are divided between back- and front-of-house workers. The back-of-house employees and managers work in the storage areas, on the loading docks, and in the assembly rooms. In both stores where I worked, the back-of-house workers were virtually all men. The front-of-house workers, the ones who interacted with customers, included both men and women. But there, too, there was job segregation by gender and race, although, as I will discuss, it was harder to discern and on occasion it broke down.

There were two other jobs in the toy store: security guards and janitors, both of whom were subcontracted workers. Both the Toy Warehouse and Diamond Toys employed plainclothes security guards who watched surveillance monitors in their back offices and roamed the aisles looking for shoplifters. At the Toy Warehouse, the individuals who filled those jobs were mostly African American men and women, while only white men and women were hired for security at Diamond Toys. Finally, all of the cleaners at the two stores were Latinas. They were recent immigrants who didn't speak English.

What accounts for the race and gender segregation of jobs in the toy store? Conventional economic theory argues that job segregation is the product of differences in human capital attainment. According to this view, the marketplace sorts workers into jobs depending on their qualifications and preferences. Because men and women of different racial/ethnic groups possess different skills, aptitudes, and work experiences, they will be (and indeed should be) hired into different jobs. Economists generally see this process as benign, if not beneficial, in a society founded on meritocracy, individual liberty, and freedom of choice (Folbre 2001).

In contrast, when sociologists look at job segregation, they tend to see discrimination and structural inequality (Reskin and Roos 1990). Obtaining the right qualifications for a high-paying job is easier for some groups than others. Differential access to college education is an obvious example: society blocks opportunities for poor people to acquire this human capital asset while smoothing the path for the well-to-do. But the sociological critique of job segregation goes deeper than this. Sociologists argue that the definitions of who is qualified and what it means to be qualified for a job are linked to stereotypes about race and gender. Joan Acker (1990) argues that jobs are "gendered," meaning that qualities culturally associated with men (leadership, physical strength, aggression, goal orientation) are built into the job descriptions of the higher-status and higher-paid occupations in our economy. Qualities associated with women (dexterity, passivity, nurturing orientation) tend to be favored in low-paying jobs. In addition to being gendered, jobs are racialized. Black women have been subjected to a different set of gendered stereotypes than white women. Far from being seen as delicate and passive, they have been perceived as dominant, insubordinate, and aggressive (Collins 2000). Those who make hiring decisions draw upon these kinds of racialized stereotypes of masculinity and femininity when appointing workers to specific jobs.

Leslie Salzinger (2003) has examined how this job placement works in manufacturing plants along the U.S.-Mexico border. She uses the concept of "interpellation" to describe how managers imagine a specific, embodied worker in each job and how workers come to see themselves in these imaginings. Workers, in other words, typically consent to and embrace the stereotypes, since their opportunities depend on their conformity to these managerial imaginings. She shows that to get a job on the assembly line, young women workers have to represent themselves as docile, dexterous, and unencumbered by family responsibilities. They really have no choice: to get a job they must become the embodiment of their bosses' stereotypes. Eventually, she argues, the line between the stereotype and the authentic self blurs.

This process may be exacerbated in interactive service work, where employers carefully pick workers who "look right" for the corporate image they attempt to project to the public. A recent court case against Abercrombie & Fitch illustrates this. A suit was brought against the retailer by Asian Americans and Latinas/os who said they were refused selling jobs because "they didn't project what the company called the A & F look (Greenhouse 2003). Although the company denied the charge, the suit brings to light the common retail practice of matching employees with the image the company is seeking to cultivate. More egregious examples are found in sexualized service work, as in the case of Hooters restaurants (where only buxom young women are hired), and in theme parks like Disney, notorious for its resistance to hiring African Americans (Loe 1996; Project on Disney 1995).

[. . .]

My experience illustrates this process of interpellation and resistance. I was hired to be a cashier at both toy stores. I didn't seek out this job, but this was how both managers who hired me envisioned my potential contribution. Only women were regularly assigned to work as cashiers at the Toy Warehouse, and I noticed that management preferred young or light-skinned women for this job. Some older African American women who wanted to work as cashiers had to struggle to get the assignment. Lazelle, for example, who was about thirty-five, had been asking to be put on register over the two months she had been working there. She had been assigned to be a merchandiser. Merchandisers retrieved items from the storeroom, priced items, and checked prices when the universal product codes (UPCs) were missing. Lazelle finally got her chance at the register the same day that I started. We set up next to each other, and I noticed with a bit of envy how much more competent and confident on the register she was compared to me. (Later she told me she had worked registers at other stores, including fast-food restaurants.) I told her that I had been hoping to get assigned to the job of merchandiser. I liked the idea of being free to walk around the store, engage with customers, and learn more about the toys. I had mentioned to Olive that I wanted that job, but she had made it clear that I was destined for cashiering and the service desk (and later, to my horror, computer accounting). Lazelle looked at me as if I were crazy. Merchandising was generally considered to be the worst job in the store because it was so physically taxing. From her point of view I had been assigned the better job, no doubt because of my race, and it seemed to her that I wanted to throw that advantage away.[6]

The preference for whites in the cashier position reflected the importance of this job in the store's general operations. In discount stores like the Toy Warehouse, customers had few opportunities to interact and consult with salesclerks. Most shoppers at the Toy Warehouse knew they were on their own in the stores and rarely asked salesclerks for their advice on purchases. The cashier was the only human being that the customer was guaranteed to contact, giving the role enormous symbolic—and economic—importance for the organization. At the point of sale, transactions could break down if the customers were not treated in accordance with their expectations. The preference for white and light-skinned women as cashiers should be interpreted in this light: in a racist and sexist society, such women are generally believed to be the friendliest and most solicitous group and thus best able to inspire trust and confidence.[7]

Personally, I hated working as a cashier. I thought it was a difficult, stressful, and thankless job. Learning to work a cash register is much like learning to use a new computer software package. Each store seems to use a different operating system. After working at these jobs I started to pay attention to every transaction that I made as a customer in a store, and I have yet to see the same computer system twice. The job looks simple from the outside, but because of the way it is organized cashiers have no discretionary power, making them completely dependent on others if anything out of the ordinary happens. Like every large store, the places where I worked used UPCs on the merchandise, and we scanned these with a laser instead of entering prices into the register. Managers had a special key that they could use to override the UPC, but the cashiers did not, which caused a great deal of frustration to customers. If the customer knew the price of an item but the UPC tag was missing, we would have to search for the item in the inventory code book (at Diamond Toys) or page a merchandiser (at the

Toy Warehouse) to go find another one with the tag in place so we could scan it into the register. If customers changed their minds midtransaction, we would have to call a manager to void their purchase. If they asked for a small discount on damaged merchandise, we had to ask the manager. If they didn't have the money to cover a purchase, the register would freeze up and we would have to call the manager. We couldn't even open up our registers to make change for the gum ball machine. Customers would often treat us like morons because we couldn't resolve these minor and routine situations on our own, but we were given no choice or autonomy.

[. . .]

Talwar (2002) notes in her study of fast-food restaurants that African American men are sometimes preferred as cashiers during the nighttime hours, especially in dangerous neighborhoods. This is presumed to offer some protection for the registers in case of attempted robbery. Here again we see how the image of "cashier" is linked to managers' race and gender stereotypes regarding the qualifications for the job. At the Toy Warehouse, African American men were not routinely assigned to the register at any time of day or night, but they were used to perform a security function in the evening. When the store closed at the end of the day, Olive would make an announcement over the public intercom instructing two black men to "clear the store" and "check the bathrooms." This was often said in a menacing way to scare the stragglers into leaving, especially if it had to be repeated more than once. This task assignment drew upon and bolstered stereotypes about the strength and inherent aggressiveness of African American men.

Cashiers did perform some security tasks at the Toy Warehouse. In addition to being responsible for requesting pulls, we were expected to check the customers' bags and receipts whenever the alarm sounded at the front door. The alarm was set off when people left the store with merchandise affixed with security tags that had not been properly deactivated. This happened approximately every ten minutes. Half of the people who set off the alarm turned around immediately to offer proof that they were not guilty of anything, and the other half just continued walking out the door. We tended to ignore both groups. We were usually too busy with other customers to stop and check the ones who came back into the store, so we just waved them out. We certainly were not going to run after customers who continued walking out. If they had indeed stolen any merchandise, we weren't about to expose ourselves to the potential danger of a physical confrontation. I thought that this should have been the job of a uniformed security force, but Olive told me that a uniformed guard would damage the store's image as a welcoming and happy place.

A few men were regularly assigned to work as cashiers at the Toy Warehouse, but this happened only in the electronics department. The electronics department was cordoned off from the rest of the store by a metal detector gate intended to curtail theft. All of the men with this regular assignment were Asian American. They had sought out this assignment because they were interested in computers and gaming equipment. Working a register in that section may have been more acceptable to them in part because the section was separated from the main registers and in part because Asian masculinity—as opposed to black or white masculinity—is often defined through technical expertise. My sense was that the stereotypical association of Asian American men with computers made these assignments desirable from management's perspective as well.

Occasionally men were assigned to work the registers outside the electronics department, but this happened only when there were staffing shortages or scheduling problems. [. . .] On [one] occasion, I had observed Deshay [a twenty-five-year-old African American], skillfully evade the assignment to work register. Deshay normally worked as a merchandiser, and he also worked in the storeroom unloading boxes from the delivery trucks. I noticed when he was called to the register because I had never seen an African American man work there. Olive called Deshay to her office over the walkie-talkie (without telling him why—if he had known why, he later told me, he wouldn't have responded to the page). Next thing I saw him with a register drawer, and he was told to start counting it out in preparation for cashiering. He took the till over to the service desk, and I turned around for a moment and he was gone! Eventually I caught up with him in the break room and asked him what happened. I said, "That was some disappearing act!" He told me, with mounting exasperation and anger, that he did not want to work register, he was not hired to work register, he had too many other jobs to do, and if they forced him to work register he would file a lawsuit against them. He didn't say outright that cashiering was a lousy job, my guess is, because that was the job I was doing.

This is another example of interpellation. Deshay had come to see himself in managerial stereotypes about the appropriate roles for black men. But I think that another reason Deshay didn't want to cashier was that he felt his masculinity was at stake. For many men, work functions as outward proof of their masculine identity (Williams 1989, 1995). Their poise, their sense of strength, and even their heterosexuality are challenged when they do "women's work." Even though there is nothing inherently feminine about working a cash register, management had defined the job as "women's work," and Deshay was eager to distance himself from any job considered "feminine." This psychological incentive fit in with managerial goals. In this way, workplaces draw on gender to "manufacture consent"—that is, to make workers complicit in the social organization that management prefers.

[. . .]

The stores exploited young men's insecurity in their masculinity by assigning them to jobs that required them to do a great deal of heavy lifting. They had to move freight and deliver large items (like baby car seats, play sets, and bikes) to the front of the store and occasionally out to the customer's car. Several men told me that the physical aspect of their work wore them out and meant that their jobs in retail could only be temporary. But at the same time they took a great deal of pride in these tasks. Because the tasks were defined as masculine, they seemed to experience a boost in self-esteem for accomplishing them.

[. . .]

Crossing over is a different experience for men and women. When a job is identified as masculine, men often will erect barriers to women, making them feel out of place and unwanted, which is what happened to Chandrika. In contrast, I never observed women trying to exclude men or marginalize men in "their" jobs. On the contrary, men tried to exclude themselves from "women's work." Job segregation by gender is in large part a product of men's efforts to establish all-male preserves, which help them to prove and to maintain their masculinity (Williams 1989). Management colludes in this insofar as they share similar stereotypes of appropriate task assignments for men and women or perceive the public to embrace such stereotypes. But they also insist on employee "flexibility," the widespread euphemism used to describe their fundamental right to hire, fire, and assign employees at will. At the Toy Warehouse, employees were often threatened that their hours would be cut if they were not "flexible" in terms of their available hours and willingness to perform any job. But in general managers shared men's preferences to avoid register duty unless no one else was available.

How and why a specific job comes to be "gendered" and "racialized," or considered appropriate only for women or for men, or for whites or nonwhites, depends on the specific context (which in the case of these toy stores was shaped—but not determined—by their national marketing strategies. Thus, in contrast to the Toy Warehouse, Diamond Toys employed both men and women as cashiers, and only two of them were African American (both women). At the Toy Warehouse, most of the registers were lined up in the front of the store near the doors. Diamond Toys was more like a department store with cash registers scattered throughout the different sections. The preference for white workers seemed consistent with the marketing of the store's workers as "the ultimate toy experts." In retail service work, professional expertise is typically associated with whiteness, much as it is in domestic service (Wrigley 1995).

Although both men and women worked the registers, there was gender segregation by the type of toy we sold. Only women were assigned to work in the doll and stuffed animal sections, for example, and only men worked in sporting goods and electronics. Also, only women worked in gift wrap. Some sections, like the book department, were gender neutral, but most were as gender marked as the toys we sold.

This gender segregation occasionally would break down at Diamond Toys, and men would be assigned to work in the women's sections when enough women weren't available. At Diamond Toys, Carl, a thirty-year-old white man, once had to work backup with me in dolls. He performed the role in a completely campy style, swishing around the floor and answering the phone with "Barbie speaking!" Carl, who normally didn't act this way, was parodying the assumed homosexuality of any man interested in dolls (and, indeed, many of the high-end Barbie customers were gay). Turning the role into a joke made his temporary assignment seem more palatable and less inconsistent with his masculinity.

The most firmly segregated job in the toy store was the job of cleaner. As I have noted, only Latinas filled these jobs. I never witnessed a man or a woman of different race/ethnicity in them. (The reasons for the segregation of Latinas into cleaning jobs have been explored by Hondagneu-Sotelo 2001.) There were different degrees of integration and acceptance of the cleaners at the two stores. Estella, who was the only cleaner at the Toy Warehouse, was well integrated among the associates. The staff appreciated the hard work she did: it was, after all, a truly Herculean effort to keep that store clean. In contrast, the three Latina cleaners at Diamond Toys seemed alienated from the rest of the staff. Few people ever talked to them. I thought at first that this was because most of the associates couldn't speak Spanish, but I noticed that hardly anyone even said hello. I would often observe them in the break room sitting alone with no one to talk to. Angie, a twenty-seven-year-old Latina associate, told me that she thought people were mean to the cleaners and ignored them because they were Hispanic. Because I spoke Spanish I could break that norm. In fact, once I was talking to Rosario, a cleaner from Costa Rica, and Lisa, a twenty-five-year-old Latina who worked in the back office, walked by. She looked startled and asked me if I spoke Spanish. I said yes, and she said, "But I thought you were, uh, white." It amazed her that a white person could and would speak to the janitors. In addition to preserving masculinity, then, job segregation helped to preserve the privileges of whiteness. Ignoring the cleaners promoted a status distinction between "their" jobs and the work of "regular" employees.

[. . .]

Conclusion

[. . .]

In this chapter, I have argued that the social organization of work in large toy stores also contributes to class, gender, and race inequalities. The Toy Warehouse, which had a predominately African American staff, paid extremely low wages, offered few benefits, and demanded "flexible" workers who made no scheduling demands. The store was segregated by race and gender, with white men in the director positions and African American women in managerial and supervisory roles. Among the staff, only white and light-skinned women and Asian American men were regularly assigned to cashiering positions, and only men (of all racial/ethnic groups) worked in the back room unloading and assembling the toys. African American men and women filled the positions of security guards, stockers, and gofers.

Because Diamond Toys was unionized, it offered better pay than the Toy Warehouse (but not a "living wage"), and its employees received health care and vacation benefits. Schedules were posted in advance, legally mandated breaks were honored, and career ladder promotions were available. For all of these reasons, a union does make a positive difference for workers.

But unions are not a panacea for all of the problems of retail work. Historically, unions have not successfully redressed exclusionary hiring and promotion policies that favor whites over racial/ethnic minorities and men over women; some even claim that unions have made these problems worse (Lichtenstein 2002). Thus Diamond Toys was even more firmly segregated than the Toy Warehouse, as evidenced by the complete absence of black men. The predominately white staff at Diamond Toys was headed by white men in the director positions and mostly white men and women in managerial, supervisory, and security roles. The white, Latina/o and Asian American clerks were divided up on the floor by gender, with men selling mostly boys' toys and women selling baby toys and girls' toys. In both stores, Latinas monopolized the subcontracted cleaning roles. Thus, even though selling toys at Diamond Toys was a better job than selling toys at the Toy Warehouse, it was a highly segregated and exclusionary workplace. Even with a union, working at Diamond Toys would not qualify as a "good job."

[. . .]

In addition to changing toy stores' economic organization, restructuring their jobs is necessary to alter their gender and race dynamics. As I have argued, the hierarchical and functional placement of workers according to managerial stereotypes results in advantages for white men and (to a lesser extent) white women and disadvantages for racial/ethnic minority men and women. These stereotypes are perhaps more deeply entrenched than low wages, based as they are on perceptions of customer preferences. Consumers therefore have a role in pressing for changes in these job assignments. But in my view, the struggle for equal access to "bad jobs" is hardly worth an organized effort. There is little point in demanding equal access to jobs that don't support a family. Similarly, career ladders have to be created before equal opportunities for advancement are demanded. The fight against racism and sexism, then, should be folded into efforts to economically upgrade these jobs. The goal of restructuring jobs in toy stores, and in retail work in general, should be self-sufficiency—and hope—for all workers, regardless of race or gender.

Notes

1. This is not the "ideal worker" sought by employers at the fast-food restaurants in Harlem studied by Katherine Newman (1999). She found that young people under twenty-two were disproportionately rejected for job openings in the mid-1990s. More than half of new hires were older than twenty-three. Nevertheless, the retail and fast-food industries continue to justify their low wages and meager benefits on the basis of this "ideal worker" who doesn't "need" their job to support himself or herself economically. This is how Wal-Mart justifies its minimal payment of employee health care benefits. After a series of news reports lambasting the store for its failure to provide health care coverage for most workers, a Wal-Mart spokesperson maintained that most of those who are not covered by Wal-Mart benefits are "senior citizens on Medicare, students covered by their parents' policies, or employees with second jobs or working spouses" (Abelson 2004, A13). This is the historic argument for not paying living wages to women—they don't really "need" the money from their work because they are members of families with access to a male wage (see Kessler-Harris 1990). This argument justifies unequal pay for equal work (which is illegal under Title VII) and undermines all workers' rights to fair compensation.

2. Men make more money than women in most occupations. Among sales workers employed in the general category "retail and personal services," men earn on average $488 per week, and women earn $325, a ratio of .67. (These numbers are the 2002 median weekly earnings of full-time workers.) If we take out workers employed in some of the most gender-segregated stores (those selling motor vehicles, apparel, furniture, appliances, hardware, and parts), men earn on average $466 per week, and women earn $353, a ratio of .76. (This reflects the income of workers in the category "Sales workers, other commodities.") This information is from U.S. Bureau of Labor Statistics (2002).

3. The National Association for the Advancement of Colored People (NAACP) issued a report in 2003 claiming that the retail trade industry, compared to other industries, is especially notorious for discriminating against African Americans. This report, which ranked forty-five

large retail companies on employment opportunities, marketing procurement, community reinvestment, and charitable donations, gave the industry a "D" average (compared to "C" for the lodging, telecommunications, and banking industries).

4. See Burawoy (1980), Freeman (2000), Hossfeld (1990), Milkman (1997), and Salzinger (2000).

5. Notable exceptions include Hochschild (1983), Leidner (1993), Glazer (1993), and Talwar (2002). I speculate that the production focus of most sociology is due to the association of retail work with consumption, long considered women's work, instead of production, which is generally considered a higher-status male domain. Lizabeth Cohen (2003) argues that this split is a legacy of the Progressive Era, when the two issues were uncoupled politically, with women spearheading movements for consumer rights and men spearheading movements for worker rights.

6. Although I was hired to be a cashier, my actual job involved many other tasks. When there were no customers ready to check out, I was on the floor helping customers find things, giving them advice, straightening shelves, returning merchandise to its proper location, and so on. My job involved constant interacting, chatting, joking, complaining, and goofing off with other staff members, not only while we were doing our jobs, but also while we were on break and while we were straightening the store after closing.

7. Robert Zussman's careful reading of this text inspired this insight, for which I am grateful.

CHAPTER 12

The Milk of Human Kindness

Nancy Folbre

> If you're lonely, I will call.
> If you're poorly, I will send poetry.
> I love you.
> I am the milkman of human kindness.
> I will leave an extra pint.
>
> —Billy Bragg

[. . .]

In our culture, milk often serves as a metaphor for kindness, and motherhood embodies both. Partly as a result, our ideals of love and care for others have often been defined differently for women and men. When I graduated from high school in 1969, I was warned not to seem too smart or too ambitious. Some family friends capped this advice with a quotation from Shakespeare: "Be good, sweet girl, and let those who will be clever." I remember my mother giving me a big wink. As someone who had reconciled herself to goodness, she secretly urged me on to mischief. Over time, I've seen discomfort about female accomplishments diminish. Norms of appropriate behavior for women have changed.

In a 1977 poll, about two-thirds of the Americans surveyed agreed that "It is much better for everyone if the man is the achiever and the woman takes care of the home and family." By 1998, only one-third agreed: the proportions had reversed.[1] Women are now far more likely to work outside the home than they were twenty-five years ago. Partly as a result, they are less bound by family obligations, with more permission—indeed, encouragement—to pursue their own interests. Men's work hasn't changed nearly as much. The amount of time they devote to housework and child care has increased by a negligible amount.

This chapter explores the connections between masculinity, femininity, self-interest, and care for others. In the United States today, men and women have equal rights before the law. With respect to the care of children and other dependents, however, our cultural norms still reflect greater expectations for women than for men. Economic theory offers vivid examples of this cultural double standard. The history of feminism reflects a sustained effort to challenge it.

Liberal feminism has demanded greater individual rights for women. Social feminism has demanded greater social obligations, especially for men. For reasons that have to do with our economic system, as well as our political history, liberal feminism has enjoyed relatively more success in the United States than in the more traditional societies of Europe. Its very success has contributed to a dilemma. Women know they can benefit economically by becoming achievers rather than caregivers. They also, know, however, that if all women adopt this strategy, society as a whole will become oriented more toward achievement than care.

> Most advice books for men concern money and sex and say virtually nothing about caring for their elderly parents or small children. Books for women, such as Helen Gurley Brown's *Having It All* or Sonya Freeman's *Smart Cookies Don't Crumble*, now also glamorize a life for women that is relatively free of the burden of care.
>
> —Arlie Hochschild, "Ideals of Love" in Karen V. Hansen
> and Anita Corey, eds., *Families in the U. S.: Kinship
> and Domestic Politics*

Coercion and Care

It is often assumed that women are naturally more altruistic than men, especially toward their own offspring. Biologists borrow an economic concept, pointing out that mothers have a greater biological "investment" in children than fathers do, since they carry the fetus within their body and nourish the infant with milk from their breasts. Maternal love, however, has always had limits. The varied circumstances in which we have evolved have forced mothers to make hard choices, to evaluate the effect that one child might have on another child's—and on her own—chances of survival.[2]

Any time that costs and benefits are taken into account, outcomes hinge on who pays the costs and who enjoys the benefits. Precisely because mothers pay a disproportionate share of the costs, fathers often worry less than mothers about the prospect of too many offspring. Furthermore, the more that women specialize in child rearing, the more dependent they become on adult men for assistance. As a result, fathers generally acquire power along with the responsibility for caring for their families. The biological division of labor sets the stage for an array of social and cultural forms of control over women, some of which may give patriarchal societies an edge over more egalitarian societies.[3]

Conservative social thinkers, including many economists, insist that women are naturally suited to child care, and that this, in turn, gives them a comparative advantage in providing care to others, including the sick and elderly. Specialization, after all, increases efficiency. But specialization also affects the development of human capabilities and the exercise of bargaining power. In the short run, it may be efficient for one country to specialize in producing sugar and bananas while another country specializes in producing computers and guns. In the long run, however, the country that specializes in producing sugar and bananas is unlikely to be able to defend its own borders or develop its own technology. The same may be said of a person who specializes in rearing children and taking care of other dependents.

Historical scholarship details the many laws that gave fathers and husbands property rights over daughters and wives, enforced male control over female wealth and income, restricted women's access to education and systematically excluded them from access to lucrative jobs.[4] It is difficult to explain why such coercive rules evolved, if not because of some big differences between what men wanted women to do and what women would have chosen on their own. A nineteenth-century Prussian law actually gave husbands the right to determine how long their wives should breast-feed their infants.[5]

In some areas of the world, women's relative position has improved over the last two centuries. Economic development and technological change have increased the importance of brains—including women's brains—relative to brawn. Equally important has been the decline in fertility and the shift of focus from the quantity of children to the quality of their upbringing. Looking back, it seems pretty clear that traditional patriarchal rules did more than increase women's specialization in child rearing. They also increased women's specialization in the provision of other kinds of care services. Economic dependence made women's welfare contingent on the welfare of their fathers and husbands—a powerful incentive to pay attention to other people's needs. Those who are denied a cultural conception of themselves as individuals may not even think of themselves as separate persons.[6]

Many systematic forms of violence seem designed to decrease women's ability to perform directly productive work. Foot-binding in ancient China made it difficult for women to walk. Strict rules of exclusion, such as purdah in many Islamic countries, limit women's opportunity to earn a market income. Genital mutilation, still practiced in many areas of Africa, poses serious risks to women's health. Domestic violence, still rife in many areas of Europe and the United States, makes it more difficult for a wife or mother to get dinner on the table and children off to school. All these practices lower productivity and enforce subordination, encouraging women to put others' needs above their own.

Of course, you can't force somebody to love you. Subordination doesn't always lead to high quality care. It can create tension, resentment, even fury. Greek mythology tells of Medea, so angered by her husband Jason's betrayal that she murdered their two sons and served them up for dinner. Less extreme threats have often given women informal power. We value love most when it is freely given. People who have a voice in defining their commitments to other people probably fulfill those commitments more gracefully. Allowing women new choices improves the quality of care and, in this respect, everybody benefits.

But choice is a funny thing, affected by both moral values and by social pressures. Often what we choose depends on what we think other people will choose. It's harder to stay honest if we see other people cheating. It's harder to engage in teamwork if other team members are shirking. It's harder to take on responsibilities for the care of other people if those responsibilities don't seem to be shared. This is why too much choice—or too little social coordination of choice—can lead to outcomes that can be just as problematic as having no choice at all.

Work versus Care

In the seventeenth century, a number of English political theorists began to argue that men should govern themselves rather than automatically accept the authority of a king. They also laid the conceptual foundation for an economy based on contract rather than coercion. John Locke emphasized two basic economic principles. First, a man should have ownership of himself; no one else should have dominion over him. Second, a man should be allowed to claim the products of his own labor, thus guaranteeing incentives for him to work hard and well.

None of these principles were initially extended to anyone except adult male citizens. The notion that women should have a right to vote was thought preposterous. The idea that they should have control over their own decisions was also ruled out. Fathers had authority over daughters until they married. Once married, women were required to obey their husbands. Women exercised some choice over whom they would marry but a decision not to marry at all was impractical, given the restrictions on their access to education or well-paid work. As to the right of control over the products of their own labor—the main product of women's labor was children, and female control over grown sons would have violated men's presumed right to self-determination.[7]

In retrospect, this double standard seems as outrageous as it is inconsistent. At the time, however, it was justified by the claim that women's activities—primarily, caring for children and other dependents—did not amount to real work. Unlike men's activities, they did not involve the rational calculation of costs and benefits or responses to economic incentives. Rather, what women did was both instinctive and moral, performed for natural and God-given reasons. Women who declined to accept this responsibility were treated as unnatural and wicked.

Although such views were widely held, they were by no means universal. Early critics of the double standard pointed out that women seemed to be penalized, rather than rewarded, for assuming the responsibilities of motherhood. Mary Astell, a largely self-educated merchant's daughter who eked out a living for herself as a writer, issued in 1694 a salvo entitled *A Serious Proposal to the Ladies for the Advancement of Their True and Greatest Interest*. Astell played famously upon the inconsistencies of John Locke's theory, pointing out that it was a bit difficult to understand how, if kings had no God-given authority over their subjects, men could claim God-given authority over their wives.

She complained that men seemed to consider the nursing of children as low and despicable even though no activity deserved more honor, or greater thanks and rewards.[8] Astell located the source of women's subordination in their responsibilities for care: "Such the generous offices we do them: Such the ungenerous returns they make us."[9] About a hundred years later, Mary Wollstonecraft would pick up the argument in *A Vindication of the Rights of Women*. Few people realize that feminism as an intellectual tradition reaches to the beginnings of liberal political theory. It may not have received much attention or respect at the time, but it was present, foreshadowing things to come.

[. . .]

Separate Spheres

In my family, the men took charge of making money while the women figured out ways to give it away. I remember my mother, a restless housewife, taking on sizable responsibilities for the local Junior League, the United Fund, and the Girl Scouts. She died of cancer when I was eighteen, and my father remarried about a year later. My second mom was a high-powered businesswoman who helped start a small manufacturing firm, but lost interest once it was bought out by a multinational corporation. She then turned her attention and her energy to running a local San Antonio philanthropy.

The family that my father worked for had a similar division of labor. Mr. Mac's aunt, Leta McFarlin Chapman, grew up in a small Texas town named Pecan Grove where she attended school with a number of Native Americans. She always claimed that the experience had given her a lifelong concern for minority groups and under-privileged people in general. Over her lifetime, she gave well over a hundred million dollars to churches, colleges, and hospitals—far exceeding her nephew's generosity.

The notion that women should be more altruistic than men has a long history. In the nineteenth century, it became a virtual obsession. The growth of capitalism increased the scope of impersonal exchange, particularly the sale of labor power to strangers in return for wages. This process created enormous apprehensions. Would society become so atomistic, so competitive, so individualistic that it would fall apart? Conservatives like Edmund Burke urged a return to feudal principles of respect for royal and paternal authority. Socialists like Robert Owen began to imagine new forms of social organization based on the family writ large, in which men and women would work together as brothers and sisters.[10]

A more common response to apprehension about the growth of markets was the romanticization of family life. By devoting themselves to their husbands and children, women could hold civilization together. In both Britain and the United States, a burgeoning literature of domesticity explained how women could become angels of the home. No one painted a more panoramic view of this process than Catherine Beecher and Harriet Beecher Stowe, whose 1869 book *The American Woman's Home* became so popular that it remained a textbook for my own grandmother's generation.

The Beecher sisters sought to create home as a haven in a heartless world. Women's greatest mission, they argued, is "self-denial."[11] They didn't believe that women were innately altruistic, but rather that they were destined to preserve the values of the home so threatened by the impersonal business world. "A man that has been drawn from the social ties at home and has spent his life in the collisions of the world," Catherine Beecher explained, "seldom escapes without the most confirmed habits of cold and revolting selfishness."[12] Only a devoted wife and mother could civilize such a man and buffer the disruptive effects of competition on society as a whole.[13]

The Beecher sisters focused on women's moral obligations. Other advocates of this "separate spheres" approach recognized the need to ensure that women would not be distracted from their historical mission. In the late nineteenth century the famous English economist Alfred Marshall praised the efficiency of the forces of supply and demand in the labor market—as far as men were concerned. He explicitly warned that higher wages for women in the labor market might tempt them to neglect their duties as wives and mothers.[14] As a professor at Cambridge he opposed admitting women to study for degrees because they might become more preoccupied with developing their own capabilities than those of their future children.[15] He attributed the declining birth rate in England—which he considered a serious problem—to "women's selfish desire to resemble men."[16]

The separate spheres doctrine was appealing to economists for a variety of reasons. It relieved them of the responsibility for analyzing love and altruism, while reiterating their principles of morality. It excused them from considering the economics of family life, without suggesting that this aspect of life was unimportant. Most conveniently, the separate spheres doctrine helped men explain just why they should be self-interested, while women should be altruistic. It was, for them, a comfortable way of seeking the best of both worlds.

[. . .]

Crybabies

The last two decades of the twentieth century witnessed a conservative backlash against feminism, driven by a fear that women were becoming less altruistic. Rush Limbaugh panics at the thought of women acting in their own self-interest, explaining that women's jobs are to "establish enduring values that are crucial to the continuation of mankind."[17] George Gilder proclaims that the beautiful thing about femininity is its "civilizing" influence.[18] Allan Bloom argues that the American mind is doomed unless men take responsibility for achievement, and women take responsibility for care.[19] It's quite flattering, really, until you realize the dimensions of the burden. Civilization is not entirely women's responsibility.

This kind of conservatism demeans men by assuming that they can't possibly help out. The argument seems to be that women must not stop behaving in traditional ways, because men are incapable of offering more love and tenderness. The sacrifice of mothers—but not fathers—is held forth as an imitation of Christ. Conservative activist Connie Marshner asks: "How can we possibly imitate the Creator in our relationships if we can't learn from our mothers to give of ourselves, to offer ourselves in love to another, and to control our fleshly impulses for the sake of another?"[20] Marshner wants women to be more unselfish than men—a double standard that seems inconsistent with her own Christian ideals.

Much of the rage about abortion reflects a larger anxiety about maternal care. According to the so-called pro-life perspective, women shouldn't have a choice to care or not to care for a developing fetus. From the so-called pro-choice perspective, such a choice is crucial to the meaning as well as the quality of caring. Anti-abortion activists are often explicit in their attacks on what they consider female selfishness. As one doctor put it, "I think women's lib is on the wrong track. I think they've got every [possible] gripe and they've always been that way. The women have been the superior people. They're more civilized, they're more unselfish by nature, but now they want to compete with men at being selfish. And so there's nobody to give an example, and what happens is that men become more selfish."[21] Here's that anxiety again, that fear that men simply can't be altruistic unless women are more so.

In 1993, a journalist named Barbara Dafoe Whitehead wrote an article entitled "Dan Quayle Was Right."[22] The brouhaha started when then–Vice President Quayle criticized an episode of the television show *Murphy Brown* in which the heroine, played by Candice Bergen, decided to have a child out of wedlock. Never mind that the child had actually been conceived while Murphy was married to his father. Television was undermining family values by sanctioning divorce and holding a single mother up as a positive role model. Whitehead took up Quayle's campaign on a more serious intellectual level, arguing that public policy should explicitly discourage divorce and births out of wedlock.

She told a joke that pretty well captures the fear our society feels about the loss of feminine altruism. Two female praying mantises are having a conversation in the garden. The first one says, "It's tough being a single parent, tougher than I thought." "Yeah," says the second. "Maybe we shouldn't have eaten our husbands after all." The lesson is that women should stop being bloodthirsty feminists and return to our traditional self-sacrificing roles as wives and mothers. While we're at it, maybe we should also ask for a big pay cut as child care workers, secretaries, nurses, and teachers. That way, we could help out in the business world as well as at home.

[. . .]

Trucks versus Dolls

In an era of rapid social change it is genuinely difficult to define our values. Feminists have long struggled with a dilemma framed as "equality" versus "difference." Should women concentrate on attaining success in male terms, demanding the right to compete? Or should women value the qualities that make them different from men and try to reduce the ways in which society penalizes femininity? Liberal feminists have often fought for the right to behave in more masculine ways. Social feminists have often fought for rules that would require men to take on more traditionally feminine responsibilities both within the family and beyond.

In the United States, at least, a liberal and highly individualist form of feminism has prevailed. Everybody has heard of "Take-Your-Daughter-to-Work Day," an event promoted by the Ms. Foundation to encourage young women to think about their careers. No one has ever heard of "Teach-Your-Son-How-to-Babysit Day." Even women who earn considerably more than their husbands seldom persuade their guys to put more hours into family work. Highly educated women are moving into traditionally

masculine professions. But men recognize that moving into traditionally female occupations would probably entail a significant loss of pay and status. It takes courage and
conviction for a man to go to nursing school.

Our culture continues to define care in feminine terms. Perhaps as a result, many
women feel uncomfortable with the notion that masculine ideals are somehow better
than feminine ones. It's a view that has been nicely summarized by a bumper sticker:
"Women who want to be as good as men lack ambition." Some people think that girls
should be encouraged to play with blocks and trucks rather than dolls, the better to
compete with boys. But as one reader put it in a letter to the *New York Times*, "If we
continue to promote 'rewardable' skills over those related to nurturing, who's going to
take care of us when we're too old, young or sick to be out pursuing rewards?"[23]

Of course, if women are going to pursue this strategy, we must ourselves continue
to play with dolls. And that is a risky business. A lot of feminist economists are down-
right opposed to it. "I just don't see any good evidence for the 'difference' perspective,"
says Myra Strober of Stanford University. "It glorifies existing stereotypes of female
behavior." Barbara Bergmann of American University strongly opposes any efforts to
count housework as part of the Gross Domestic Product, one proposal for valuing a
"different" kind of contribution: "Anything that romanticizes housework and childcare," she growls, "is bad for women."[24] Strober and Bergmann are right—unless and
until we can distribute responsibilities for care more equally and reward caring more
generously. The challenge for social feminists is to show how we might do this—in
practice as well as in theory.

Sharing Care

There is nothing natural or inevitable about the way we associate femininity with
altruism. Most fathers also care for their children. They change diapers, get up in
the night to warm their babies' bottles, and go to work to earn the money to buy
the milk and bicycles and computers their children need. Nowadays fathers are being encouraged to play a more direct role. Sharing care for children, however, is not
enough. Other dependents, including the sick and the elderly, require attention. Most
adults need to be cared for in the emotional sense, even if not in the economic sense
of relying on another to take responsibility for them. Our need for love may ebb and
flow, but sometimes it comes in tidal waves. As the biologist Franz de Waal explains,
"Absorption of parental care into adult human relationships is evident from the widespread use of infantile names (such as 'baby') for mates and lovers. . . ."[25] Traditionally,
scientists have drawn a sharp distinction between altruism toward kin and toward
non-kin.[26] More recently, they have begun to argue there is a continuum, rather than
a gulf.[27] Kinship, after all, is a relative concept. Human beings share a common genetic
heritage. Altruism toward immediate kin fosters altruism toward others who are less
closely related. We are often altruistic toward our mates, who share responsibility for
our actual or potential offspring. Our brothers, sisters, nephews, and nieces, as well as
our children, share our genes and will combine them with those of other people when
they have children of their own. Kin-based altruism reinforces our concerns about the

future. Worrying about the future impels us to worry about those who will inhabit it, alongside our immediate kin.

Emotional connections to other people reinforce reciprocity and trust. Groups that elicit solidarity from their members may be able to out-compete those that don't. Organizations often refer to their members as symbolic kin. Feminists appeal to a larger concept of "sisterhood." Trade union members, like fraternities and sororities, frequently refer to each other as "brothers and sisters." Patriots vow to love the mother country or the fatherland, and so on.

Empathy for other people is a powerful force—so powerful, in fact, that we often take steps to avoid letting it develop.[28] Is empathy a siren song? According to Greek mythology, Odysseus knew that his boat would be passing by the island of the sirens, whose beautiful voices tempted sailors to hurl themselves into the surf and approach them, only to be dashed against the rocks. A famously wise man, he filled his sailors' ears with wax to deafen them, but devised a way to safely listen to the music himself. He instructed his sailors to bind him to the mast and to refuse to release him until the boat had passed the island. The preemptive measure protected him against loss of self-control as he swooned with pleasure from the song.

Maybe Homer misleads us. Maybe the surf is not so dangerous after all. Maybe the sailors could use a bit of a swim, and seeing the sirens face to face would make Odysseus a better man. We might want to listen for the music—even turn up the volume—instead of shutting it out. There are ways of encouraging empathy for others, rather than trying to repress it. To come back to the gendered double standard: if we can reinforce caring behavior in women, we can also reinforce it in men. Doing so, however, will be costly. That's why we need some good economists on the case.

> Instead of importing into the household principles from the marketplace, perhaps we should export to the wider society the relations suitable for mothering persons and children.
>
> —Virginia Held, "Mothering versus Contract" in
> Jane J. Mansbridge, ed., *Beyond Self-Interest*

Unacceptable Choices

Many feminists have fought patriarchy with individualism, demanding new rights for women and conducting a process of consciousness-raising that has encouraged women to become more assertive. That the results can be uncomfortable and inconvenient for men is obvious. It is becoming increasingly apparent that there can also be some negative consequences for dependents, such as children, the sick, and the elderly. Patriarchy was not simply a means of privileging men. It was also a means of ensuring an adequate supply of care. By increasing the pressure on women to be altruistic toward members of their families and communities, it helped to minimize the retaliatory logic that can lead to the War of All Against All.

We cannot base our critique of impersonal market-based society on some romantic vision of a past society as one big happy family. In that family, Big Daddy was usually in control. Today, patriarchal coercion is unacceptable. On the other hand, pure selfish individualism is both ugly and unviable. Without at least some altruism, we cannot reproduce ourselves. If we believe we have obligations to care for one another, we should decide what these are and how they should be enforced. Since we can't depend entirely on human nature and/or divine assistance, some rewards and punishments will probably be required. The milk of human kindness does not flow from some natural, inexhaustible source. Nor is it produced according to the laws of supply and demand.

Notes

1. Numbers based on analysis of the General Social Survey. See Lee Badgett, Pamela Davidson, Nancy Folbre, and Jeannette Lim, "Breadwinner Dad, Homemaker Mom. An Interdisciplinary Analysis of Changing Gender Norms in the United States, 1977–1998" (Department of Economics, University of Massachusetts, Amherst, MA, August 2000).

2. Sara Blaffer Hrdy, *Mother Nature: A History of Mothers, Infants, and Natural Selection* (New York: Pantheon, 1999).

3. For more discussion of this possibility see Nancy Folbre, *Who Pays for the Kids? Gender and the Structures of Constraint* (New York: Routledge, 1994).

4. Folbre, *Who Pays for the Kids?*

5. August Bebel, *Women and Socialism*, trans. Daniel De Leon (New York: Schocken Books, 1971).

6. Amartya Sen, "Gender and Cooperative Conflicts," in *Persistent Inequalities: Women and World Development*, ed. Irene Tucker (New York: Oxford University Press, 1990), 123–49. Feminist theorist Joan Tronto also points out that robbing individuals of opportunities to effectively pursue their self-interest may encourage them to live through others, using caring as a substitute for more selfish gratification. See her "Beyond Gender Differences to a Theory of Care," *Signs: Journal of Women in Culture and Society* 12, no. 4 (Summer 1987): 647, 650.

7. Mary O'Brien, *The Politics of Reproduction* (Boston: Routledge and Kegan Paul, 1981); Lorenne M. G. Clark and Lynda Lange, *The Sexism of Social and Political Theory: Women and Reproduction from Plato to Nietzsche* (Toronto: University of Toronto Press, 1979); John Locke, *Two Treatises of Government*, ed. Peter Laslett (Cambridge University Press, 1967).

8. Mary Astell, "The Hardships of the English Laws in Relation to Wives," in Vivien Jones, ed., *Women in the Eighteenth Century* (New York: Routledge, 1990), 225.

9. Astel, "The Hardships of the English Laws."

10. Nancy Folbre, "Socialism, Feminist and Scientific," in *Beyond Economic Man*, eds. Marianne Ferber and Julie Nelson (Chicago: University of Chicago Press, 1993).

11. Catherine Beecher and Harriet Beecher Stowe, *The American Woman's Home* (New York: J. B. Ford and Company, 1869), 19.

12. Kathryn Kish Sklar, *Catherine Beecher: A Study in American Domesticity* (New York: Yale University Press, 1973), 87.

13. Sklar, *Catherine Beecher*, 156.

14. Alfred Marshall, *Principles of Economics*, 8th ed. (London: Macmillian, 1930), 685, 715.

15. David Reisman, *Alfred Marshall's Mission* (New York: St. Martin's Press, 1990), 210.

16. W. Pigou, *Memorials of Alfred Marshall*, "Letter to Louis Dumur, July 2, 1909" (New York: A. M. Kelley, 1966), 459–61.

17. Rush Limbaugh, *The Way Things Ought to Be* (New York: Pocket Books, 1992), 201.

18. George Gilder, *Sexual Suicide* (New York: Quadrangle, 1973) and *Wealth and Poverty* (New York: Basic Books, 1981).

19. Allan Bloom, *The Closing of the American Mind: How Higher Education Has Failed Democracy and Impoverished the Souls of Today's Students* (New York: Simon and Schuster, 1987).

20. Connie Marshner, *Can Motherhood Survive? A Christian Looks at Social Parenting* (Brentwood, TN: Wolgemuth and Hyatt, 1990), 195. See also Linda Kintz, *Between Jesus and the Market: The Emotions That Matter in Right-Wing America* (Durham, NC: Duke University Press, 1997).

21. Cited in Kristin Luker, *Abortion and the Politics of Motherhood* (Berkeley: University of California, 1984), 163.

22. Barbara Dafoe Whitehead, "Dan Quayle Was Right," *The Atlantic Monthly*, 271, no. 4 (April 1993): 47–84.

23. Linda Jordan, "Dolls versus Trucks," *New York Times*, 19 April 1993.

24. Barbara Presley Noble, "Male, Female Leadership Styles Hot Subject of Controversy," *Springfield Union*, August 18, 1993, 35.

25. Franz de Waal, *Good Natured: The Origins of Right and Wrong in Humans and Other Animals* (Cambridge, MA: Harvard University Press, 1996), 43.

26. E. O. Wilson, *Sociobiology: The New Synthesis* (Cambridge, MA: Harvard University Press, 1975).

27. In addition to de Waal, *Good Natured*, see Elliot Sober and David Sloan Wilson, *Unto Others: The Evolution and Psychology of Unselfish Behavior* (Cambridge, MA: Harvard University Press, 1998).

28. Daniel C. Batson, "How Social an Animal? The Human Capacity for Caring," *American Psychologist* 45, no. 3 (March 1990): 344.

Breaking the Professional Glass Ceiling (© International Labour Organization)

Part IV

GENDER, MANAGEMENT, AND THE PROFESSIONS

The former president of Harvard University, Dr. Larry Summers, triggered a firestorm in 2005 when he sought to explain the gender gap among science professors at top-tier American universities. Although women hold 29 percent of science and engineering positions in American educational institutions, they fill only 15 percent of those positions at the top fifty research universities. Summers noted that "the most likely explanations are 1) women are just not so interested as men in making the sacrifices required by high-powered jobs, 2) men may have more 'intrinsic aptitude' for high-level science, and 3) women may be victims of old-fashioned discrimination." "In my own view," he states, "their importance probably ranks in exactly the order that I just described" (Ripley 2005).

This speech set off a national discussion on gender and the professions. Data revealed that major changes had occurred in the sciences, as American women received only one of every ten science and engineering PhDs in the 1970s, whereas by 2005 women earned one-third of all science doctorates. Outside of academia, in America's private and government sectors, women held 23 percent of science and engineering positions in 2005 (Amanda Ripley 2005). Women's enrollment in engineering increased in other parts of the world as well between 1991–2001: from 5.7 to 8.8 percent in Uganda, from 4 to 11.7 percent in Iran, from 9.5 to 14 percent in Italy, from 12 to 19 percent in Canada, and from 12.2 to 25.6 percent in Tunisia (Wirth 2002).

Despite this global progress, the Glass Ceiling Commission in the United States found that American women persist in hitting their heads on a glass ceiling at the workplace, comprised of invisible, artificial barriers that block women from attaining senior positions. Women constituted 49.9 percent of the total American workforce in 2009 yet were only 8 percent of the top managers, 2 percent of senior management in Fortune 500 companies, and less than 13 percent of corporate board members. Women's presence in law increased from 14.4 percent in 1975 to 40.3 percent in 2003, yet they constituted only 16 percent of all U.S. law partners (EEOC 2003). Similarly, women comprised 25 percent of all physicians in 2002, compared to 7.6 percent in 1970, yet remain underrepresented in academic and leadership positions in medicine: women were 10 percent of department chairs, 16 percent of full professors, and 11 percent of medical school deans (Nancy Groves 2008). Glass ceilings prevail in other countries as well, as evidenced by France, where women comprise only 5 percent of the executive workforce; Germany, where they comprise less than 11 percent of supervisory board members; and Britain, where the number of senior female executives in 2004 totaled seventeen at the top one hundred corporations, to cite a few examples (*The Economist* 2005; Schonberger 2006).

Not only do women bump up against glass ceilings, but they also confront "glass walls": invisible barriers that concentrate women in specific sectors. According to a UN Report in 2000, Sweden has the highest percentage of women in managerial and administrative positions at 59 percent, yet they remain primarily in the lower-paid public sector (UN Report 2000). Forty-two percent of women executives, administrators, and managers in the United States are located in the lower-paid service sector, and in the UK, 50 percent of senior women managers are located in dead-end personnel departments.

What are the causes and effects of glass ceilings and walls for women and minorities in management and the professions? Do these invisible barriers lead to occupational sex and race segregation, or do individuals freely choose their own positions in the workplace? These and other questions are addressed by the readings in Part IV, primarily centered around three perspectives: discrimination, human capital, and organizational structure (examined in other contexts throughout the book). First, discrimination theorists argue that glass ceilings and walls emanate from employers' use of statistical discrimination in their hiring practice, where employers use sex (and/or race) as a proxy for an individual's potential productivity. They might presume women will leave work more often due to family responsibilities, or they might believe women are less capable than men of higher-order thinking in such fields as science, engineering, or neurosurgery. Such employer beliefs serve to impose invisible barriers upon women's career choices and advancement. Second, the human capital theorists argue that women's position in the occupational hierarchy is due to their free choice, a choice based on whether the occupation will accommodate their future childbearing plans. Those women who know they will leave the workforce to have children will not invest time or resources to develop their human capital, and thus choose jobs that do not require high levels of skill or education. According to this view, women do not pursue high-powered professional or managerial positions, because it is financially irrational to invest in an expensive education, knowing that they will soon withdraw from the workforce to bear and raise children. Instead, they choose low-paid, part-time, low-mobility positions that will not interfere with their family responsibilities. And third, some organizational structure theorists argue that men's and women's reactions to the workplace are not specifically gendered. Rather, their behaviors in the organization are based on their occupational category, minority or majority status, and position at work.

The readings in Part IV address divergent aspects of these theoretical approaches. Rosabeth Moss Kanter examines two American corporations in "The Impact of Hierarchical Structures on the Work Behavior of Women and Men" and argues that men and women respond similarly to the structural conditions of their work. If opportunity and power (or lack thereof) are available in their job, both men and women will act to enhance their power and opportunity within the organization. If they are located in a dead-end position, with no opportunity for advancement or greater responsibility at work, both men and women will refocus their energies on activities outside of work, such as family or leisure. If an individual is in the numerical minority within the workplace (a member of any group that represents less than 15 percent of the workforce), that token minority will be more susceptible to stereotyping and feel strong pressure to conform to the norms of the dominant group's work culture. Any minority, regardless of race or sex, will react similarly to this structural position in the workplace. Thus, Kanter contends that the salient factor in determining workplace behaviors is organizational structure, not gender.

Jennifer Pierce investigates Kanter's argument in "Women and Men as Litigators: Gender Differences on the Job" with data from a male-dominated law firm. She found that male litigators exaggerated differences between themselves and female litigators by discussing stereotypically masculine subjects, such as sports or drinking. Pierce contests Kanter's conclusion on the behavior of minorities in organizations, finding that female litigators demonstrated three alternative responses to their minority status. Some women lawyers practiced an "ethic of care" (Gilligan 1982), in which they sought to maintain empathy in their work and client relationships to ensure no one is hurt. Others practiced "an ethic of care" only in their office relationships, and not in the courtroom, where they exhibited the typical adversarial behavior characterized by male litigators. The third group of female lawyers adopted an aggressive, conflictual style more characteristic of male lawyers in both the office and the courtroom. Hence, Pierce argues that in a sex-segregated profession such as law, gender shapes the responses of both men and women (albeit with variations) within the context of the occupational structure and varied gender identities of those in the minority.

Christine Williams also examines Kanter's argument on the behavior of numerical minority groups within the professional workplace in "The Glass Escalator: Hidden Advantages for Men in the 'Female' Professions." She studied the male experience in four female-dominated professions: nursing, librarianship, grade-school teaching, and social work. Williams found that men in these occupations, although in the minority, were able to maintain their own personal style on the job and did not conform to the female dominant work culture. In fact the men experienced a male "escalator" effect to the top of the hierarchy within these professions. Not only did the men avoid the glass ceiling, but their masculinity had the reverse effect: it was viewed positively by both colleagues and superiors in these professions, resulting in higher wages and promotions.[1] Williams found that the effects of anti-female sexism outweighed the effects of tokenism when men entered nontraditional, female-dominated professions. The only form of discrimination these men faced was from outside the occupation. The public often presumed the men were gay and ascribed a diminished status to them because of their employment in female-typed occupations.

Sharon Collins, in "Black Mobility in White Corporations: Up the Corporate Ladder But Out on a Limb," considers the role of race tokenism within organizations, specifically the ways in which the job mobility of professional African Americans is affected in predominantly white corporations, regardless of gender. She counters the human capital theory, which suggests African Americans climb the corporate ladder with equal speed and agility as whites, based on their skills, education, and individual preferences. Instead, Collins found that discrimination operates within organizations to sideline black men and women into "racialized" jobs, such as affirmative action, community relations, and urban affairs positions. These "racialized" jobs are dead-end and have stunted African American skill development, rendering African Americans ineligible for other top corporate positions. In sum, whether they attempt to conform to the dominant white work culture or not, Collins argues that human capital deficits are foisted upon token African Americans in the white corporation through a structure of "racialized" job assignments, which impose further barriers to their advancement.

Yen Le Espiritu, in "Gender and Labor in Asian Immigrant Families," investigates the ways in which race- and sex-segregated work affects professional Asian immigrants in the United States. She contends that despite human capital and economic resources, all classes of Asian immigrant women in the United States face racial discrimination at work, compounded by gendered subordination within the patriarchal Asian family at home. An increased number of Asian women emigrated to the United States as a result of 1965 immigration laws, which encouraged unification of immigrant families. Although many Asian immigrants became scientists, engineers, and health-care professionals (between 1988 and 1990, two-thirds of foreign nurses and 60 percent of foreign physicians in the United States were from Asia), job opportunities for highly educated Asians remained limited. This resulted in an increase in Asian self-employment. Le Espiritu argues that statistical discrimination played a role in steering less-educated Asians into low-wage work: janitorial work and cooking for men, and garment work, electronic assembly, child care, and domestic work for women.

Although professional Asian men with high levels of education face racial discrimination and lower wages in the workplace, husbands in self-employed Asian families remain the sole legal owners of the family business and maintain control over the finances. This contributes to the subordination of Asian women. Despite the wife's labor in the family business, she is unpaid and is expected to perform the double shift: domestic tasks, such as cooking and cleaning, for the husband, in the business as well as at home.

In sum, the readings in Part IV address the multiplicity of ways in which gender and race interpenetrate the structure and culture of professional occupations and organizations.

Note

1. Such an assertion is supported by wage data, which show that men earn higher wages than women for the same work in female-dominated professions, as noted in Part III. In heavily female-dominated professions, such as elementary- and middle-school teaching, 81.7 percent female, women earn 10 percent less than male schoolteachers. In registered nursing, 91.6 percent female, women earn 8 percent less than male nurses. Female physicians and surgeons earn 39 percent less than their male counterparts, female lawyers earn 22 percent less than comparable male jurists, and female college and university educators earn 21 percent less than their male counterparts (U.S. Department of Labor Statistics, 2007).

CHAPTER 13

The Impact of Hierarchical Structures on the Work Behavior of Women and Men

Rosabeth Moss Kanter

This paper makes the case for an absence of sex differences in work behavior, arguing instead that work attitudes and work behavior are a function of location in organizational structures. The structures of opportunity (e. g., mobility prospects) and power (e. g., influence upward), along with the proportional representation of a person's social type, define and shape the ways that organization members respond to their jobs and to each other. In hierarchical systems like large corporations, the relative disadvantage of many women with respect to opportunity and power results in behaviors and attitudes (such as limited aspirations, concern with co-worker friendships, or controlling leadership styles) that are also true of men in similarly disadvantaged positions. The structure of power in organizations, rather than inherent sexual attitudes, can also explain why women sometimes appear to be less preferred as leaders. It is concluded that it is not the nature of women but hierarchical arrangements that must be changed if we are to promote equity in the workplace.

This paper proposes that structural conditions, particularly those stemming from the nature of hierarchy, shape apparent "sex differences" in the workplace and in organizations. Findings about behavior of and toward women in organizations can be explained by a number of structural variables that *also* can account for the behavior of and toward men in similar situations. This conclusion has been reached after field work in two corporations, interviews with "token" women in professional and management positions and secretaries and secretarial supervisors, and an extensive review of the social psychological and sociological literatures on work orientations and leadership behavior.

Underlying this analysis is a conception of an organization as a total system. Occupations, work behavior, and work relations are too often studied as if they exist in a vacuum—each occupation or office or departmental unit considered as an isolated entity—and not within complex systems that define the position of interacting parties with respect to larger distributions of opportunity, power, and numerical ratios of social types. The hierarchical systems in which most work relations occur define which people are mobile, which will advance, which positions lead to other positions, and how many opportunities for growth and change occur along a particular chain of positions. Organizational systems also define a network of power relations outside of the authority vested in formal positions; the power network defines which people can be influential beyond the boundaries of their positions. Finally, the distribution of social types and social characteristics among personnel in different positions (and especially such ascribed characteristics as age, race, and sex) define whether people of a given type are relatively rare or relatively common.

These three structural variables—the opportunity structure, the power structure, and the sex ratio—shape the behavior of women in organizations, just as they shape the behavior of men. If women sometimes have lower aspirations, lesser involvement with work, and greater concern with peer group relations—so do men in positions of limited or blocked mobility. If women are sometimes less preferred as leaders, generate lower morale among subordinates, and use directive-interfering leadership styles—so are men with relatively little organizational or system-wide power. If women in managerial or professional positions are sometimes isolated, stereotyped, overly visible, and cope by trying to limit their visibility—so are men who are "tokens" and therefore rare among a majority of another social type.

In other words, structural position can account for what at first glance appear to be "sex differences" and perhaps even explain more of the variance in the behavior of women and men. It becomes important to understand how women and men get distributed across structural positions and how this differential distribution affects behavior—not how women differ from men. In this analysis, sex is one criterion for social placement, one sorting mechanism among others, that accounts for which positions and roles are considered appropriate for people. Women may be more likely to face discrimination than men, and more women than men may be found at the bottom of opportunity and power hierarchies. If given opportunity, women may more often find themselves alone among other sex peers. But the behavior of women at the bottom (or alone) should be seen as a function of *being* at the bottom, and not primarily as a function of being a woman.

This paper considers two structural effects of hierarchical systems on behavior: the opportunity structure and the power structure. It deals primarily with the behavioral consequences of disadvantaged positions. To explain fully the behavior and problems of women in more advantaged positions requires the introduction of the third variable, the sex ratio, for women more highly placed in hierarchies are often "tokens" in groups numerically dominated by men; the effects of tokenism on women and men is discussed at length elsewhere (Kanter 1975a, 1993).

Work Orientations, Aspirations, and Location in an Opportunity Structure

It is tempting to conclude, on the basis of research evidence and common-sense observations, that women's work orientations, on the average, differ from those of men's. Isn't this, after all, compatible with the "primary" socialization of women for family roles and men for work roles? Women, this thesis goes, tend to be less involved in their work and committed to it than men, interrupting their careers whenever they can; they are more concerned about their relationships with other people than the task or reward aspects of their jobs; and they have lower levels of aspiration. I review some of the evidence for these statements below. But I also argue, instead, that all of these findings can be explained by the nature of the *opportunity structure* in which people find themselves in an organization, whether they are men or women. People in low-mobility or blocked-mobility situations tend to limit their aspirations, seek satisfaction in activities outside of work, dream of escape, and create sociable peer groups in which interpersonal relationships take precedence over other aspects of work. When women occupy low-mobility positions, they tend to exhibit these characteristics; since most of the women studied in organizations tend to be disadvantageously placed in the organization's opportunity structure, they confirm the generalizations made about "women's organizational behavior." Yet, when we observe *men* disadvantageously located in the opportunity structure, they tend to demonstrate the same characteristics. What one line of thought considers a "sex difference," I consider a structural phenomenon. (See Laws 1976, for a psychological version of a similar argument.) This is consistent with the prevalent finding in organizational behavior that people at upper levels of organizations tend routinely to be more motivated, involved, and interested in their jobs than those at lower levels (Tannenbaum et al., 1974, 1).

OPPORTUNITY AND LIMITED ASPIRATIONS

The evidence for women's more limited aspirations and greater concern with peer relationships comes from a variety of sources. Several studies conclude that women more than men tend to be concerned with local and immediate relationships, remaining loyal to the local work group even as professionals, rather than identifying with the field as a whole and aspiring to promotions which might cause them to leave the local environment. Several studies of male professionals in organizations have found a correlation between professionalism and a "cosmopolitan" rather than a "local" orientation, using Merton's terms. The one exception was a study of nurses by Bennis and colleagues (1958b). In this *female* group, the more professionally oriented nurses "did not differ from others in their loyalty to the hospital, and they were *more* apt than others, not less, to express loyalty to the local work groups" (Blau and Scott 1962, 69). While Blau and Scott conclude that this is due to the limited visibility of the nurses' professional competence, it is also compatible with the response of people to a professional opportunity structure characteristic of nursing which does not offer much mobility out of the current organization and in which good peer relationships are likely to be an important component of competent work performance. Similarly, Costantini and Craik (1972) found that women politicians in California were oriented intraparty and locally more than men, while the men were much more often oriented toward higher office. The difference in the opportunity structures for women and men in politics at the time this research was carried out is well known, making the women's preferences understandable on structural rather than characterological grounds.

In a recent dissertation research project on a major corporation, Homall (1974) surveyed 111 non-exempt (i.e., hourly) employees on their attitudes toward promotion. Using an expectancy-value theory, she found that men show greater motivation to be promoted than women and perceive greater overall desirability and likelihood of the possible consequences following a promotion. The men also perceived themselves to be more competent in basic managerial skills than the women did and to receive more encouragement from superiors to improve and advance. But newer employees were also more likely than older to show high motivation for promotion, and the better educated more likely than the more poorly educated, indicating that not only sex but also other characteristics affecting the employee's real advancement opportunities played a part in the results.

Homall also found that *neither* men nor women *reported* perceiving many real advancement opportunities for themselves. Yet, in this company, like most, the differences in the *actual* opportunities for men and women, and the mobility hierarchies in which they are located, are quite striking and dramatic. About two-thirds of the women non-exempts in the company unit from which the sample was drawn were secretaries. The secretarial hierarchy is a short one, with increased rank reflecting the status of the boss rather than the secretary's work, and leading to executive secretary as the highest position. Until recently, practically no executive secretary was ever promoted into the exempt (salaried) ranks, and those promoted represent a miniscule proportion of either secretaries or exempt personnel. The other women in Homall's sample were predominantly clerks in dead-end jobs. It is not surprising that the aspirations of women in such an organizational situation should be limited, that they should not think highly of their own management skills, and that they should turn to other sources of satisfaction. Indeed, in a study of the values of 120 occupational groups, secretaries (the only predominantly female category studied) were unique in placing their highest priorities on security, love, responsibility and happiness—not job advancement (Sikula 1973). The men in Homall's sample, on the other hand, were a much smaller proportion of the non-exempt population. The majority worked as accounting clerks or in the international exports department in a customer relations function that led directly into the exempt ranks of the company. Their mobility prospects were strong.

There is evidence that, in general, the jobs held by most women workers tend to have shorter chains of opportunity associated with them, to contain fewer advancement opportunities. In a study of 11 industries employing about 17% of the U.S. work force, (motor vehicles and parts, basic steel, communications, department and variety stores, commercial banking, insurance carriers, and hotels and motels), a consulting group found that as the amount of progression possible in non-supervisory jobs increased—the number of steps of opportunity it contained—the proportion of women declined markedly (Grunker et al., 1970). Women represented 46% of all non-supervisory workers, but they were a whopping 64% of workers in the "flattest" jobs (least advancement opportunities) and a miniscule 5% of workers in the highest opportunity jobs (13).

Thus, the Homall results and others showing women's "lower" work involvement and aspirations can be more profitably read as reflecting a response on both the part of employees and their managers to the worker's placement in an opportunity structure. Those who are disadvantageously placed limit their aspirations and are less likely to be perceived as promotable, thus completing a vicious cycle. Those who are more advantageously placed are likely to maintain higher aspirations and to be encouraged in keeping them. The sex-typing of jobs in this major corporation, like others, means that a *social structural effect* might be misleadingly interpreted as a sex difference. My own interviews, in the same company Homall studied, with women who are advantageously placed in a high-mobility opportunity structure (as sales personnel in a hierarchy that regularly leads directly to management positions) indicates that they are highly motivated and aspire to top management positions.

But it is not only women who respond to blocked mobility by limiting their aspirations, lowering work commitment, and dreaming of escape. Men poorly placed in an opportunity structure tend to behave in similar ways. A number of classic studies of male blue-collar workers indicate that work commitment and aspirations are both low where advancement opportunities also are low. Dubin (1956) concluded that work is not a "central life interest" of industrial workers. Chinoy's (1955) study of automobile workers revealed some interesting parallels between the men's response to their work and that of female clerical workers or the telephone company women observed by Langer (1970). The younger men, first, tended to define their jobs as temporary and, instrumentally, as means to immediate out-of-work pleasure through the purchase of consumer goods. Hope for or interest in promotion was extremely limited, especially for those men over 35. When workers hoped for "better" jobs, they tended to mean those that were easier or cleaner, rather than those that advanced them in the hierarchy. Almost four-fifths had at some time contemplated leaving; they dreamed of escape into their own small business. As Riesman put it: "Chinoy's interviews show work to be regarded as a form of daily part-time imprisonment, through which one pays off the fines incurred by one's pursuit of the good, or rather the 'good time,' life at home and on vacations" (1955, xix).

Other research confirms this finding. Purcell (1960) studied male workers in three meat packing plants. Around half were negative about their chances for advancement, and many denied that they would ever *want* to be foremen. Bonjean and his associates (1967) also found that individuals with negative mobility perceptions tend to have low aspirations. Where work is boring or repetitive and chances for mobility low, people tend to develop little attachment to work and seek their major satisfactions in the family realm. They also seek to leave the organization whenever possible. Mayer and Goldstein (1964) and others offer evidence that the "interrupted career" pattern is true for men as well as women; blue-collar men leave organizations to start small businesses and then return when (as is statistically likely) the business fails.

CONCERN WITH PEER GROUP RELATIONSHIPS

Along with more limited aspirations, women are said to be more concerned than men with interpersonal relationships on the job, more involved with other people than with the intrinsic nature of the task. In attitudinal studies attempting to distinguish job aspects motivating increased performance ("motivating" factors) from those merely preventing dissatisfaction ("hygiene" factors), attitudes toward interpersonal relations with peers constituted the only variable differentiating men and women. (The women in two major studies include those in both relatively high-level and relatively low-level jobs.) For women, peer relationships were a motivational factor, spurring them on, whereas for men they were only a hygiene factor, which the men would miss if it were not there but which did not push them to perform (Davis 1967, 35–36).[1] One of the few significant sex differences found by University of Michigan researchers in their national survey of the attitudes of 1472 working men and women lay also in this area. More women (68%) than men (61%) indicated that it was very important to them that their coworkers be friendly and helpful (Crowley, Levitin, and Quinn 1973). And Johnston (1975), in a more limited survey of workers in an Australian soap factory, found that men and women differed in the reasons they most often gave for liking their jobs. Women mentioned "coworkers are friendly" with greatest frequency; "the job is interesting" came in second, tied with "the immediate boss is kind." For men, the listing was nearly reversed. "The job is interesting" received the most frequent mentions, with friendly coworkers tied for second place, and the kind boss coming in fifth.

Some laboratory studies also suggest that the tendency of more women than men to be concerned with the quality of relationships affects those women's behavior and performance. Female game-playing strategy, in a series of experiments, tended on the average to be "accommodative," including rather than excluding, and oriented toward other people rather than toward winning, whereas the male strategy was more often "exploitative" and success-oriented (Vinacke 1959; Uesugi and Vinacke 1963). But even here, later investigators have challenged the sex differences interpretation and offered an explanation based on situational characteristics. Lirtzman and Wahba (1972) have pointed out that the Vinacke experiments used minimally competitive social games with uncertainty and risk reduced once coalitions were formed, permitting any sort of partnership relationship. In their own experiments, using a highly competitive game with high uncertainty about the consequences of behavior, sex differences disappeared. Women as well as men behaved competitively, aggressively, and exploitatively, trying to maximize their chances of winning. In other words, the context shapes organizational behavior. A concern with relationships tends to arise for women in low-risk, low-uncertainty environments, where opportunities will not be lost if one accommodates to others.

The opportunity structure is an important part of the context that defines for organization members how important good, accommodative relationships with peers ought to be, and whether or not minimizing peer relations in favor of competition or distance has a "pay-off" in mobility. High-mobility situations foster rivalry, instability in the composition of work groups, comparisons upward in the hierarchy, and concern with intrinsic aspects of the job. Low-mobility situations, however—those characteristic of most of the working women studied—foster camaraderie, stably composed groups, and more concern with extrinsic rewards, social and monetary. In a classic piece of sociological analysis, Merton (1968, 233) argued that amount of upward mobility as an institutionalized characteristic of a social system generates either vertical or horizontal orientations. When people face favorable advancement opportunities, they compare themselves upward in rank, with one foot already out of the current peer group in the process he called "anticipatory socialization." Unfavorable advancement opportunities, on the other hand, lend themselves to comparison with peers, and concern with peer solidarity. Pennings' (1970) study of white collar workers with high or low mobility opportunities (measured by promotion rates) offers confirmation. The importance attached to intrinsic job characteristics, to the nature of the job itself as opposed to such external factors as relationships with coworkers, varied with promotion rates.

Work-value orientations and the importance of interpersonal relations, then, are a function of the structure of opportunity facing people in different parts of the organization by virtue of the category into which they fall. There is evidence that men as well as women turn to relationships with work peers as an alternative interest when mobility opportunities are limited or blocked. Under such circumstances, men, like women, form strong peer groups that value solidarity and loyalty within the group and look with suspicion upon fellow workers who identify or interact with anyone outside the group. One example is the men in the bank wiring room group in the Hawthorne studies (Roethlisberger and Dickson 1939) who created a strong peer group which restricted work output. Burns' (1955) observations of a factory in an uncertain, changing environment, showed dramatically the differences in interpersonal orientations of low- and high-mobility men. The older men, considered "over the hill" and in positions outside of the main career advancement ladders, formed "cliques" oriented toward protection and reassurance; these peer groups represented, to Burns, organized retreats from occupational status into the realm of intimacy. The younger men, on the other hand, who still had opportunities, formed a very different kind of group, "cabals" which plotted an increase in their status. The younger men oriented themselves around power, while the older ones substituted intimacy and support. Tichy (1973) hypothesizes that in no-mobility systems friendship needs are the primary pressure for group formation, and that lack of ability to envision other rewards in the future encourages people to seek more immediate socio-emotional rewards in the present situation.

A laboratory study of communication in experimentally created hierarchies offers supportive evidence for the importance of peer relationships in low-opportunity situations. Cohen (1958) put male subjects into high-power (management-like) or low-power (subordinate-like) task groups, varying the opportunity structure for the two low-power groups. One condition offered no opportunities for mobility into the high-power group; the other created the possibility for mobility during the experimental situation. The mobile groups showed greater concern with task, suppressed irrelevant communications, were less critical of the upper groups, and were more oriented toward the high-power groups than toward members of their own peer group. They were careful about criticism, stayed more with the task, and tended to be less attracted to members of their own group than to the high-power people. The non-mobiles, on the other hand, centered their affect and attention on the members of their own group, neglecting the high-power people, because "for them, communication and interaction cannot be instrumental to mobility" (Cohen 1958, 49). The non-mobiles were also significantly more likely to feel that their "social validity" was received from their own rather than the upper group, to send "cohesiveness-building content" to their own group, and to be openly critical of the upper group.

Tichy has further theorized that the peer groups formed by non-mobile people tend to quickly become closed:

> Members of no-mobility organizations tend not to be interested in instrumental relationships, since they offer very little possibility of changing the individual's status in any way; once a member is satisfactorily adapted to a clique, he is under no pressure to look for other relationships. This tends to create cliques which are closed. (1973, 205–6)

As a member of a closed peer group, the individual is under further pressure to remain loyal to the immediate group of workmates and to see leaving the group, even for a promotion, as an act of "disloyalty." We can speculate with some confidence that the rare man who is offered an advancement opportunity out of a low-mobility peer group will experience some of the same conflict as the rare secretary who is ambivalent about the promotion she is offered because it will mean "leaving her friends." (For a woman, the conflict is probably more severe, because as she rises in an organization she is likely to find fewer and fewer female peers, whereas men find a male peer group at every level of the system.)

And thus the circle is closed. Initial placement in an opportunity structure helps determine whether a person will develop the aspirations and orientations that make further mobility possible. Women in low-mobility organizational situations develop attitudes and orientations said to be characteristic of "women as a group" but which can more profitably be seen as human responses to blocked opportunities. (Some of these responses, of course, may have positive rather than negative social value.)

Leadership Attitudes, Behavior, and the Power Structure

There is no research evidence that yet proves a case for sex differences in either leadership aptitude or style. A wide variety of investigations, from field studies of organizations to paper-and-pencil tests, indicate that the styles of men and women vary over the same range, and there are no conclusive sex-related preferences (Crozier 1965, 126; Day and Stogdill 1972; Rousell 1974; Bartol 1974, 1975). In an organizational simulation using college students, Bartol found that sex of the leader did not by itself affect follower satisfaction, even when female leaders were characterized by high dominance, a trait most likely to "offend" male subordinates (Bartol, 1974, 1975).

Even attempts to prove that women leaders are perceived and evaluated differently from men—a not unlikely occurrence—have resulted in very few significant results. In a study of high school departments, Rousell (1974) found that teachers' ratings of their department heads' aggressiveness, suggestibility, and professional knowledge did not discriminate between the sexes. Bartol and Butterfield (1974) asked subjects to make judgments about male and female leaders exhibiting a variety of styles. The evaluations of men and women did not differ significantly on most variables, including such critical ones as "production emphasis," but there was a tendency to give higher ratings to men than to women when they "initiated structure" and higher to women than men when they showed "consideration," demonstrating some propensity for raters to "reward" people for sex-role-appropriate behavior. Rosen and Jerdee (1973) used a different set of categories but had nearly identical results. Students and bank supervisors judged stories involving male and female leaders using four different styles. The "reward" style was rated somewhat more effective when used by men, but the "friendly-dependent" style (which the researchers hoped would capture a female stereotype) was rated high for *either* sex when used with the opposite sex. The use of "threat" was considered ineffective for both sexes, though there was a slight but not significant tendency to let men get away with it more than women. Thus, sex-role stereotypes seem to play only a very small role, if any, in responding to the style of a leader, and leadership styles themselves do not show much differentiation by sex.

On the other hand, there is considerable evidence for a general cultural attitude that men make better leaders. A large number of studies have concluded that neither men nor women want to work for a woman (although women are somewhat more ready to do so than men, and people who have already worked under a woman are much likelier to be favorable toward doing so). In a 1965 *Harvard Business Review* survey of 1000 male and 900 female executives, for example, an educated and experienced sample, over two thirds of the men and nearly one fifth of the women reported that they themselves would not feel comfortable working for a woman. Very few of either sex (9 percent of the men and 15 percent of the women) felt that *men* feel comfortable working for a woman; and a proportion of the male respondents said that women did not belong in executive positions. A total of 51 percent of the men responded that women were "temperamentally unfit" for management, writing comments such as, "They scare male executives half to death . . . As for an efficient woman manager, this is cultural blasphemy . . ." (Bowman, Worthy, and Greyser 1965). At the same time, there is a prevalent stereotype of the "woman boss" as rigid, petty, controlling, and too prone to interfere in personal affairs of subordinates. (See Laird 1942. My own interviews confirm this stereotypic picture.)

It is too easy to explain these findings only by reference to abstract notions of sex discrimination. Here, too, I want to invoke a structural explanation that can account for a preference for male leaders and for women's occasional use of authoritarian-controlling leadership styles. Both of these phenomena are understandable given the current distribution of men and women in the power structure of organizations. The nature of the power structure of the organization as a *total* system can account for (a) which leaders are preferred and considered effective by subordinates; and (b) which leaders are likely to use and be perceived as using overly directive, overly interfering styles.

LEADERSHIP EFFECTIVENESS AND POWER POSITION

What makes leaders effective with subordinates? Attempts to distinguish more effective and less effective styles have generally failed, in part because there are trade-offs associated with emphasizing one or another forms of supervision, as early studies of authoritarian, democratic, and laissez-faire leaders showed. While human relations skills are considered important if coupled with a production emphasis, the evidence is mixed enough to permit few conclusions about leader traits alone (Tannenbaum 1966, 78–9). Marcus and House (1973), for example, tried to differentiate instrumental and expressive exchanges between superiors and subordinates as a way to predict interaction and group process. The distinction was not ultimately very useful. Subordinates reported getting about equally as much job-related information whether the leaders tended to be instrumental or expressive, and they found very little relationship between styles of leadership behavior and subordinate group process. This is one of a number of studies that fail to demonstrate that leader strategy alone makes much difference and, as I have already indicated, there is no firm evidence that men and women differ in characteristic choice of style anyway.

But what *does* seem to make a difference is the leader's own position in the power structure of the wider organizational system. Early theory in organizational behavior assumed a direct relation between leader behavior and group satisfaction and morale, as if each organizational sub-group existed in a vacuum. However, Pelz (1952) discovered in the early 1950s that perceived influence *outside* the work group and upward in the organization was a significant intervening variable. He compared high- and low-morale work groups to test the hypothesis that the supervisor in high-morale groups would be better at communicating, more supportive, and more likely to recommend promotion. Yet, when he analyzed the data, the association seemed to be nonexistent or even reversed. In some cases, supervisors who frequently recommended people for promotion and offered sincere praise for a job well done had *lower* morale scores. The differentiating variable that Pelz finally hit upon was whether or not the leaders had power outside and upward: influence on their own superiors and how decisions were made in the department as a whole. The combination of good human relations *and* power was associated with high morale. Human-relations skills and low power (a likely combination for women leaders) sometimes had negative effects on morale.

High external status, sometimes taken as a shorthand symbol for potential or actual power and influence also contributes to leader effectiveness. It adds a power base outside of the legitimate authority vested in the current office. Subordinates are more likely to inhibit aggression and negativity toward a demanding person of higher than lower status (Thibaut and Riecken 1955). People who come into a group with higher external status tend to be liked more, talk more often, and receive more communications (Hurwitz, Zander, and Hymovitch 1968). Leaders with higher-status characteristics are generally assumed to be capable of greater influence in other parts of the organization. This gives people of higher credentials and higher-status ascribed characteristics an obvious initial advantage over those with lesser assets, and, to belabor the obvious, gives men an edge over women on this variable.

An advantageous location in the power structure has real as well as symbolic pay-offs. It gives leaders more rewards to dispense to subordinates, as they may have more claim over the resources of the organization. It means that the leader can more effectively back up both promises and threats and can, indeed, make changes in the situation of subordinates. Such organizational power comes from several factors that are themselves structural: (a) close contact and good relations with other power-holders in the system; (b) advantageous location in the opportunity structure and favorable mobility prospects. The first guarantees influence through present relations and present interactions; the second through bets about future increases in power, giving subordinates a chance to capitalize on the success of a "comer" in the organization (see Stein, 1976).

Women are currently likely to be disadvantaged on both grounds and thus less likely to act as though they have, and be perceived by subordinates as having, organizational power. In business organization, those systems in which the most negative attitudes toward working for women are consistently expressed, women are both numerically rare and structurally isolated as managers or supervisors of any kind. Statistically, they represent about three percent of all managers and officials in the most recent U.S. census, but even within this category they tend to be concentrated in staff rather than line positions where they often lack supervisory responsibility (Kanter 1975b). Accumulating evidence indicates that women leaders, under such circumstances, may be excluded from the informal network of organization managers (Cussler 1958), just as they may be excluded from the influential networks of professional peers in male-dominated professions (Epstein 1970). Even if she occupies a leadership position, then, a woman may have less influence in the wider organizational situation because of her rarity and isolation, and this may interfere with her effective exercise of leadership, with subordinate satisfaction, or with the likelihood of subordinates to prefer her to a man, *regardless* of her own style or competence. This proposition may account for evidence of the importance of a male sponsor in the success of woman executives (Cussler 1958; Hennig 1970). A high-status man bringing a woman leader up behind him may provide the visible sign needed by subordinates that the woman does have influence outside and upward. While sponsors serve multiple functions (such as coaching and socialization in the informal routines), the "reflected power" they offer may be even more important for women that for men who are protégés. Indeed, the dozen women I interviewed who are the first to sell industrial chemicals (on a sales force of over 300) reported that their influence with customers is partly a function of how much their manager indicates he will back up and support their decisions. They can be more effective at selling if they look like they have organizational power.

POWER, POWERLESSNESS, AND LEADERSHIP STYLE

Leaders with favorable mobility prospects are also likely to please their subordinates more than those who appear stuck. Here there is a complex interaction between leader power, leader behavior, and subordinate perception. People well-placed in the opportunity structure are already likely to be paying more attention to those upward in the organization and to be less critical of them, and thus to be making the connections that give them organizational power. They are also likely to be less rigid, directive, and authoritarian than low-mobility leaders (Hetzler 1955). And, they offer more opportunity to subordinates to move up right along with them. Under such circumstances, we can guess that leader actions are likely to be seen as helping rather than hindering the group's performance and that morale would be high.

The only significant sex-linked difference found in a study of high school department heads lay in just these group climate characteristics, and they can be traced directly to differences in the organizational power of the men and women leaders, even though the researcher does not herself make this interpretation. Rousell (1974) studied 205 teachers and 40 department heads, 25 male and 15 female, working with small departments of roughly equal sex distribution. Departments headed by men were perceived as higher in "esprit and intimacy"—a good indicator of morale—and those headed by women in "hindrance"—an indicator that the leader was seen as getting in the way rather than promoting subordinates' interests. But mobility prospects and the likelihood that leaders would be moving up in the organization also appear to have been very different for the men and the women. For one thing, there were no women *above* the level of department head in the whole county. Secondly, the women seemed to have risen to their last position. They had moved to this position more slowly than the men (they were older, more experienced, and had spent a longer time in their previous positions) and they had more limited aspirations (one-seventh of the women, as contrasted with half of the men expressed a desire for further promotions).

Levenson (1961) has also suggested that the fact of promotability itself influences style of supervision and subordinate attitudes, evoking good leadership practices. *Promotable* supervisors are more likely to adopt a participatory style in which they share information, delegate, train, and allow latitude and autonomy—in order to show that they are not indispensable in their current jobs and to fill the vacancy created by their promotion with someone they have trained. *Unpromotable* supervisors, on the other hand, may try to retain control and restrict the opportunities for their subordinates' learning and autonomy, as they themselves are not moving up, and a capable subordinate represents a serious replacement threat.

Thus, when people in "middle management" positions have lower advancement potential and a less favorable position in the power structure (because of their age, ascribed characteristics, or present achievements), they tend to "take it out" on their subordinates in the form of greater directiveness and increased control. So do people who feel relatively powerless or relatively insecure in their jobs. In other words, under these circumstances, more likely to be encountered by women than by men, *men as well as women* begin to act in those ways said to characterize the negatively stereotyped "woman boss."

Hetzler (1955) conducted an attitude survey of male Air Force officers. He found that leaders of lower status and advancement potential favored more directive, rigid, and authoritarian techniques of leadership, seeking control over subordinates. Subordinates were their primary frame of reference for their own status assessment and enhancement, and so they found it important to "lord it over" group members, just as some women have complained women supervisors do to them. They also did not help talented members of the group get ahead (perhaps finding them too threatening), selecting immediate assistants of mediocre rather than outstanding talent. A series of laboratory experiments confirm these field observations. People who find themselves relatively powerless, because they lack confidence in their own abilities, or because they encounter resistance from their targets of influence, tend to use more coercive rather than persuasive power (Goodstadt and Kipnis 1970). Furthermore, the "psychologically powerless"—as people who know they are going no further in an organization are likely to be—are more likely to use coercive power to elevate their own sense of worth and dignity, especially when their control over subordinates is threatened by someone's "poor attitude" (Goodstadt and Hjelle 1973).

Finally, people who feel vulnerable and insecure are most likely to be authoritarian-controlling leaders. The behavior attributed to women supervisors is likely to be characteristic of new and insecure supervisors generally. Gardner (1945) noted this during World War II when the demands of war production brought women into formerly all-male positions. Even women, he observed, complained that women supervisors were unfriendly, too critical, too concerned with petty details, and too strict in disciplining them. But Gardner concluded that newly promoted men given supervisory jobs without sufficient training also showed these tendencies:

> Any new supervisor who feels unsure of himself, who feels that his boss is watching him critically, is likely to demand perfect behavior and performance from his people, to be critical of minor mistakes, and to try too hard to please his boss. A woman supervisor, responding to the insecurity and uncertainty of her position as a woman, knowing that she is being watched both critically and doubtfully, feels obliged to try even harder. And for doing this she is said to be "acting just like a woman." (Gardner 1945, 270–1)

We again come full circle. Those favorably placed in the power structure are more likely to be effective as leaders and thus likely to gain even more power. The attitudes toward women leaders in organizations where they are most likely to have an unfavorable position in the power structure, despite the authority of their office, become understandable not just as an example of sex discrimination but as an example of a general organizational process that can also affect men. If some women respond, as some men do, by turning to control over subordinates as their internal measure of "success," this reaction is also understandable as a response, to structural circumstances.

Conclusion

It is time to move beyond "sex differences" and "sex roles" in our understanding of the observed behavior of women in organizations, and to return to classic and emerging social psychological and structural theories that explain behavior as a function of position in a network of hierarchical relations. By looking at the larger organizational context in which relationships and interactions occur, we can account for the behavior of both men and women who find themselves in similar positions in an opportunity or power structure or in a similar sex ratio. Tannenbaum and colleagues reach this conclusion in another context in their study of 50 plants in 5 nations: that social structure rather than interpersonal relations is the more substantial basis for understanding outcomes such as the distribution of reactions and adjustments within a system (1974, 205).

We thus avoid the "blame the victim" approach that locates explanations for work behavior in dispositions in the individual (whether planted there by temperament or socialization). The real villain of the piece in a structuralist model turns out to be the very nature of hierarchy. Complex organizations whose opportunity and power structures routinely disadvantage some kinds of people (whether women or men) are likely to generate the behavioral consequences of such disadvantaging. On the other hand, the creation of a class of advantaged who are offered the prospects for increasing their opportunities and power does not itself always lead to desirable consequences, for those people may become more involved with the politics of climbing than with the human side of the organization or the personal side of life.

The structuralist perspective that I have outlined here suggests a different kind of social policy and intervention strategy for the elimination of sex discrimination than the "sex differences" or "sex roles" schools of thought (Kanter 1976a). Instead of retraining women (or men) as individuals to acquire work-appropriate behavior, attitudes, and motivation, or providing different models of socialization, change strategies would focus on the structure of the organization as a total system. It is much easier, of course, to approach the individual, the family, or the school with change policies and research programs, as these are relatively small and powerless elements of the society compared to work organizations. But I argue that it is those complex organizations that more critically shape the prospects for the work life of adults, and it is thus those systems we must investigate and understand. It is the nature, form, and degree of hierarchy that should bear the burden of change.

Note

1. While the dual-factor theory of motivation has been challenged recently, these results stand independently of the theory.

CHAPTER 14

Women and Men as Litigators
GENDER DIFFERENCES ON THE JOB

Jennifer Pierce

In *The Merchant of Venice*, Portia poses as a male judge in an attempt to bring the plea for mercy into the halls of justice. Rejecting a binary logic of justice in which one party wins and another loses, Portia argues instead for a resolution to a legal dispute in which none of the parties will be harmed. Carol Gilligan refers to Portia's stance as an illustration of morality based on what she calls an "ethic of care" (1982, 105). In her early study of moral reasoning, Gilligan finds that women consistently pose moral questions in a "different voice" than men do.[1] In their attempts to resolve moral dilemmas and issues of responsibility, Gilligan's women, like Portia, are concerned with maintaining relationships so that no one will be hurt, whereas men are concerned with abstract notions of universal rights and justice. More recently, in their study of women and men lawyers, Gilligan's colleagues, Dana Jack and Rand Jack (1988, 1989), find that despite variations in behavior between women, as a group women are more likely than men to express a caring orientation in the practice of law.

In contrast to the empirical findings of Gilligan et al., sociologist Rosabeth Moss Kanter (1977, 1978) finds that women lawyers and managers as tokens or the numerical minority in their occupational group feel strong pressures to conform to existing masculine norms within the workplace and as a consequence minimize, rather than emphasize, whatever differences exist between them and the dominant group. Other studies on token women in male-dominated professions and occupations have confirmed Kanter's thesis (Williams 1989; Spangler, Gordon, and Pipkin 1978). These contradictory sets of findings raise the central questions for consideration in this chapter: Do women trial lawyers conform to male-defined norms of the adversarial role or do they speak in a Portia-like dissatisfaction with the male voice?

I observed that some women litigators practiced an ethic of care in the resolution of legal disputes, others adopted the adversarial model for the courtroom and a more care-oriented approach in the office, and a small minority conformed to the male model. To make sense of these findings, I reject the "either-personality-or-social-structure" construction of the Gilligan-Kanter debate and argue instead that gender shapes the experiences of women in the legal profession at the structural level at the same time that women and men as litigators reproduce gender at the micro-level of interactions and identity. [. . .]

Compared to men, women as a group are less likely to embrace the adversarial model in all aspects of their work, instead expressing a caring orientation toward others, either in the resolution of legal conflicts and/or in relations with staff in the office. Here, I introduce West and Zimmerman's (1987) concept of "doing gender" as the mediating behavioral link between the structural and individual levels of analysis. In my argument, women litigators, as token members of a male-dominated profession, do not passively conform to the norms of the adversarial model. Instead, they actively construct an emotional style that is consistent with their notion of gender-appropriate behavior. Furthermore, their choice of doing gender is informed in some way by their identity and sense of self as relational or feminine. [. . .]

Structural Differences and Boundary Heightening

[. . .]

Not only do men predominate in numbers and in their positions of power, but private elite law firms represent in Epstein's words, "the quintessential upper-class male culture." "Nowhere is the 'old boy' network so characteristic of the formal and informal structure of an occupation as in the 'establishment bar'" (1983, 178). Recent articles in the legal trade press, such as the *National Law Journal* and *American Bar Association Journal*, suggest that little has changed since Epstein conducted her study in the late seventies (Hazard 1988; Salaman 1988; Bay 1989; Jordan 1989).[2] In a California study conducted by the State Bar Women in Law Committee, 88 percent of the women surveyed believed there is a "subtle pervasive gender bias" in the legal profession, and two-thirds of the respondents said that women are not accepted by their male peers (Bay 1989). Hearings conducted by the American Bar Association Commission of Women in the Profession drew similar conclusions (Salaman 1988). Commenting on these findings, executive vice-president of the American Bar Association, Jill Wine-Banks stated,

> Discrimination is perhaps more dangerous now. It is more invidious because people know enough not to be so blatant in their behavior. They're much more careful about what they say. But what they think remains. (quoted in Salaman 1988)

These studies as well as my own suggest that women still have a hard time gaining admission to the old-boy network. One area in which women lawyers continue to face exclusionary practices is informal socializing with male colleagues. In large law firms, such socializing is an important mechanism for obtaining interesting or important cases and information and for garnering trust and political capital with influential partners. Kanter (1977) argues that token members of an occupational group are less likely to be included in informal socializing. This is frequently the case for women attorneys in this study, such as Kelly, a thirty-five-year-old associate from Bonhomie Corporation:

> My supervisor is so disengaged [from me]. But there is an underlying un-
> spoken camaraderie between him and the male associates. There is just no
> way for me to crack through it. They play golf together, go on long bicycle
> trips together. . . .I'm never included.

Leslie, a twenty-nine-year-old associate, said:

> I dislike the "macho" atmosphere [at informal social events]. I went once,
> and all the associates were trying to see who could drink the most beer.
> Maybe they did it because I was there. I don't know, but I never went
> again.

Another woman said that when she first started working at Bonhomie, she "went out
for drinks with the boys" but found the talk always turned to baseball. "I thought 'Oh,
no. Here they go again.'"

These examples suggest not only that women are often excluded from all-male informal social groups but that even when they were included they still felt they did not
belong. The response of their male colleagues exemplifies what Kanter calls "boundary
heightening," that is, the exaggeration of differences by the dominant group between
themselves and tokens. Male lawyers exaggerate the differences between women lawyers and themselves by talking about stereotypical male topics such as sports when
women are present and by turning social events such as after-hours drinks into compe-
titions. Such behavior serves, consciously or not, to underscore the differences between
women and men, thereby constantly reminding the women that they are different and
do not fit in.

Another way that male attorneys remind women they are not part of the "male
culture" is by deflating women's occupational status. When Sandra Day O'Connor
graduated from Stanford Law School in the early 1960s with a distinguished academic
record, no employer was willing to hire her at a law firm except as a legal secretary
(Morello 1986). Rhode (1988) notes that O'Connor's experience was not uncommon
at that time. Today, such discriminatory hiring practices are illegal.[3] Women are no
longer denied jobs as attorneys; however, they are frequently mistaken for secretaries.
Many of the women I interviewed expressed anger and annoyance at such incidences.
Jeanette, a thirty-two-year-old associate said:

> I'd been with the firm for about eight months with James [a partner] when
> Jerry [another partner] came up to me and asked me to type something. I
> looked surprised and said, "I'm an attorney, not a secretary." I actually sat
> next to this man at a litigation department luncheon [for attorneys] the
> week before, so I knew he knew me. He laughed and said with a conspirato-
> rial wink, "Oh yeah, but don't all women know how to type." He sauntered
> down the hall. I was furious.

[. . .] Another means of heightening boundaries between male and female
attorneys is through sexual harassment. The sexualization of women is perhaps the
most blatant way to exaggerate differences between the sexes. Recent studies of the
legal profession suggest that sexual harassment is much more common than was once

supposed.[4] Many of the women lawyers I interviewed reported incidences of unwanted sexual invitations, attention, and behavior. For example, Gabriella, a twenty-six-year-old associate, was harassed by a male partner at a firm cocktail party who was notorious for such behavior; she slapped him in response.

> Everyone else knew about George, but I was new, I didn't know to avoid him. So, when he tried to grab my breasts, I didn't even think, I just came out swingin. . . . It was so humiliating. Then, afterwards . . . the snide remarks, the knowing glances, the comments, "How's your left hook?" It was the second public humiliation.

Another young women lawyer, Nancy, described the sexual harassment she experienced with a judge for whom she had clerked her first year out of law school:

> He used to flirt and talk to me all day long. Most of the time I just tried to ignore it. . . . Finally, one day he said to me, "Nancy, do you work out?" I said, "Why do you ask?" He said, "I'm wondering what you look like in a sweatsuit." I replied, "Keep your sexual fantasies to yourself!" Later, I reported him to the court. They had gotten tons of complaints and told me [the judge] specifically requested female law clerks. . . . They never did anything about it.

[. . .]

Not only is the culture of law firms strongly male, but the model of the professional career itself is distinctly male. In her classic article, "Inside the Clockwork of Male Careers," Hochschild (1975) argues that academic institutions support careers that are implicitly based on the male life cycle. If the male professor has a family, the underlying assumption is that his wife will devote her time and energy to managing the potential disruption this could create in his career. Hochschild writes: "Other things being equal, the university rewards the married, family-free man" (67). Law professor Geoffrey Hazard makes a similar argument about the legal profession:

> This model of a professional career is distinctly male, and does not work for most women. Apart from everything else in life, a woman's biological clock has a different setting. Most women who become lawyers follow the same pathway as men until they complete college at about age 21. . . . Only a few women these days are firmly committed to having no children . . . a decision male lawyers need not impose on themselves. If women wish to keep open the option of having children, they face strategic choices in relating professional career to personal life. (Hazard 1988, 24)

The clockwork of male careers played itself out in the legal department at Bonhomie Corporation and at Lyman, Lyman and Portia. Although Bonhomie had an eight-week maternity-leave policy, many women lawyers complained that while men were able to obtain part-time work assignments for "health reasons," they were unable to work part-time after having a baby. Mary, a woman lawyer and a single mother, confronted the managing partner with this double standard. He told her that "the men had families to support." On the other hand, the private firm had no official maternity-leave policy. "They do it on a case-by-case basis," explained Jessie, a young woman in her sixth month of pregnancy. She added, "I have no idea what's going to happen after I have the baby. The management committee hasn't decided my case yet. I am facing this big transition in my life, and I don't even know if I will have a job after I have the baby." Deborah Rhode sarcastically describes management's viewpoint about this issue: "The prevailing view at some firms is that 'having a baby is a personal decision, rather like vacationing in Tahiti' and unworthy of significant organizational support" (1989, 1185).

Gendered Feeling Rules

The double standard posed for women by the "quintessential male culture" of the law can also be seen by looking at the divergent "feeling rules" men and women face about appropriate display of emotional labor. [. . .] [There are] two main components of the gamesmanship required of litigators—intimidation and strategic friendliness. Unlike male attorneys, women encounter a double bind in the aggressive component of emotional labor. At NITA and both law firms, women attorneys were criticized for being "too nice to the witnesses," "not forceful enough," "too bashful," and "unaggressive," at the same time that they were admonished for being "too aggressive." Men, on other hand, were sometimes criticized for being "too aggressive" and not listening carefully to the witness but were more likely to be praised for their ruthlessness. This double bind emerged not only in the aggressive component of gamesmanship, but in its less confrontational—though equally manipulative—form, strategic friendliness. For example, when male attorneys used cajoling and placating strategies to achieve an instrumental end, they received support and encouragement from their colleagues. Women who adopted similar tactics, were accused of using their "feminine wiles" to get their way with the witness or opposing counsel.

Underlying such attitudes is a gendered division of emotional labor, in which men are expected to be aggressive, manipulative, and instrumental, and women are not. Women who display these qualities are regarded as "unladylike," "domineering," "strident," and "shrill." In her classic study on women lawyers, Epstein (1983) suggests such women violate the cultural myth of the "good woman."

> A pervading myth about women is that they possess or should possess higher moral standards than men. . . . In the view that women are good or ought to be so, "good" usually translates as "too good"—too good for politicking and therefore governing, too good to make deals and therefore to enter business, too good to be tough-minded and therefore to make good scientists, physicians, or lawyers. (1983, 268-69)

The myth of the good woman suggests that women lawyers, like women in other occupations, are expected to express care and concern for others. However, because gamesmanship requires intimidation, manipulation, and artifice, women lawyers are placed in a constant double bind between the requirements of the role of the "good woman" and the role of the adversary.

The double bind posed by the aggressive component of gamesmanship is evident in a presentation made by a young woman lawyer at the National Institute for Trial Advocacy. Amanda performed a confrontational cross-examination of the witness, badgering him until he began to admit that he wasn't absolutely sure about the date of the incident in question. Amanda, however, had one mannerism that the teacher did not like—her smile. At the end of one of the leading questions, "You don't remember what you did on August 28th, do you, Mr. Jones?" she smiled. In his comments at the end of her presentation, the teacher said that her smile detracted from the seriousness and aggressiveness of the cross-examination. He told her half-seriously and half-jokingly that if she smiled again, he would hold her in "contempt of court." His advice to Amanda was to "lose the smile and be more forceful."

[. . .]

In the afternoon session, when Amanda went back to class, she did another cross-examination. This time she didn't smile at all, and instead hammered away at the witness with question after question, looking serious and stern. This time, the teacher told her that her cross-examination was "dull, lacking animation and interest." As Amanda herself said afterwards, "I feel like I can't win. If I smile, I'm not aggressive enough. If I'm aggressive and don't smile, I'm boring. What am I supposed to do to be a good lawyer?"

This question plagued many of the women lawyers in this study. They found that if they were polite to the witnesses they cross-examined, they were criticized for not being forceful enough. When they became more aggressive, they were admonished for "overplaying it" or "being phoney." Lyn, a pleasant young woman associate, was censured in her performance evaluation for not being "tough enough" because she "got along too well with opposing counsel." Similarly, the male attorneys in Leslie's office thought she "wasn't tough enough to go to court," despite the fact that she had won the moot court competition in law school and been a debate champion in college. Both women found that when they tried to be more assertive, they were described as "too hyper" or "too shrill." As one of the NITA's female teachers astutely observed, "Unlike men, women lawyers have to find a balance in the courtroom between being forceful, but not being too shrill."

[. . .]

Other women lawyers were censured for their aggressive behavior, though none as severely as Chris. For example, in a litigation department meeting, Anne described the tactics she had used in a recent deposition. In her cross-examination, the plaintiff claimed that he knew the defendant had lied to him on the phone. Anne successfully showed that the plaintiff couldn't know this.

Q: How did you know she was lying?

A: She, her voice volume changed.

Q: How did her voice change?

A: Well, if you're trained into the art of recognizing people's responses, I felt that I recognized that she got upset, that they went, came into light.

Q: Mr. Diamond, what training have you received in interpreting changes in people's voice patterns?

A: I have studied psychology books myself, and I have daily contact with tons of people in the performance of my job.

Q: What psychology books have you read which have discussed the interpretation of voice pattern?

A: Several.

Q: Could you identify these?

A: Not specifically, specific to the subject, but specific to the methods of lie detectors, and I know that one of the forms of recognition is when someone's lying or he's been confronted with an unpleasant situation, there is sweatiness. There's change in the resistance of the skin, sweatiness, redness.

Q: Were you speaking to the defendant face-to-face during this conversation?

A: No, over the telephone.

Q: Didn't you say that you thought the defendant was lying?

A: Yes.

Q: And, didn't you say that sweatiness is a sign that someone may be lying?

A: Yes.

Q: Tell me, Mr. Diamond, how did you detect sweatiness over the telephone?

A: Uh.

Q: That's all for today.

At the conclusion of her story, Anne repeated the phrase, "Tell me, Mr. Diamond, how did you detect sweatiness over the telephone?" in a stern, serious voice. Several attorneys laughed. One man curtly responded, "Well, we'd better not call Anne up for a date." More laughter followed his comment. Rather than supporting Anne's strategy, his remark undermined her presentation by sexualizing her as a potential "date" rather than congratulating her as a professional colleague, and thereby rendering problematic her behavior in the deposition. The "joke" also reflects a hierarchical pattern. In her article, "Laughter among Colleagues," Rose Laub Coser (1960) argues that in interactions between superiors and subordinates, superordinates such as male residents initiate jokes, while female nurses "receive" them. In this case, the joke is initiated by a male at his female colleague's expense, thus, serving to put Anne in her place as a woman.

[. . .]

Doing Gender: Variation and Continuity

The male-dominated structure of the legal profession, as well as the gendered nature of "feeling rules," sets the limits for gender-appropriate emotional labor for male and female litigators. Men as a group were more likely to follow the dictates of the adversarial model and to refrain from developing social relationships with support staff. On the other hand, women were less likely to embrace the adversarial model wholeheartedly, instead performing a relational form of emotional labor emphasizing a caring orientation toward others, either in the adjudication of legal disputes or in office working relations. Women and men did not conform precisely to these limits but rather varied in the degree to which they performed gender appropriate emotional labor. Much like the women lawyers in Jack and Jack's (1988) study, women's behavior in this study also varied. At Lyman, Lyman and Portia and in the legal department at Bonhomie Corporation, women's emotional labor fell along a continuum ranging from those who sought to reshape the adversarial role to fit their caring orientation (26 percent), those who "split the role" (58 percent), and those who minimized the feminine self by adopting the male model (16 percent).[5] Men also varied in how closely they adopted the strategies of gamesmanship. Some wholeheartedly embraced the adversarial role (40 percent), others did it but expressed a more distanced relation to it (50 percent), and a small minority rejected the model altogether (10 percent).

RESISTING AND RESHAPING THE ADVERSARIAL ROLE

Women lawyers who attempted to reshape the adversarial role to fit their caring orientation expressed a strong dissatisfaction with the traditional adversarial role. Twenty-six percent of women fell into this category. They paid more than "lip service" to their expressed values by actively seeking to incorporate alternatives to gamesmanship in their daily practice. Like the feminist lawyers Epstein interviewed, these women were dedicated to social goals rather than making money and valued egalitarian relationships with colleagues and with support staff (Epstein 1983, 139–40).[6] Men in this category were also critical of the adversarial role and its emotional requirements. Although they attempted to reshape the adversarial role, they did little to challenge hierarchical working relations with support staff in the office.

The following conversation between two lawyers illustrates the feelings expressed by women in the first group:

> *Tom*: Dealing with the aggressive role is purely personal. If people aren't aggressive by nature, they won't be good litigators. If I had to I could persuade any client to do whatever I wanted. . . .
>
> *Linda*: But isn't that unethical? You have to inform clients of the downside as well. . . . [*Later, in a private conversation*] Tom's partially correct, you sometimes do have to be aggressive to survive. But the majority of lawyers aren't cutthroat. There are other possible ways to resolve problems.

[. . .]

The difference in these approaches is reminiscent of Carol Gilligan's (1982) early findings on gender differences in moral development. In her study, Gilligan finds that men tend to resolve moral dilemmas using a language of rights and responsibilities and an abstract notion of justice. Men identify the legal issue, balance the rights of each party, and declare one the winner. By contrast, women utilize an "ethic of care," considering the needs of all the parties involved as well as their relationships, and attempt to find a solution that will satisfy everyone, rather than selecting a winner and a loser. Thus, Gilligan finds that women are more concerned with how moral dilemmas are resolved.

Many of the women I interviewed expressed concern for how legal disputes were resolved. Margaret, a young associate at the private firm, expressed a Gilliganesque concern about her working relationship with opposing counsel:

> I don't give into being aggressive, rude, and snotty to get the best results. You don't have to stand up to opposing counsel by screaming on the phone, for example. You can always hang up. . . . They can't win by playing hard-ball all the time. Being a feminine woman and being reasonable, that's how I see myself. Howard, the partner I work for, adopts the adversarial relationship. That's not me. I don't know what happened before in this case I'm working on or why it had accelerated to such an ugly state. I decided to be reasonable. Now opposing counsel calls me and says, "Look Margaret, I don't trust Howard, but I trust you, I think we can work this out."

In this way, Margaret found an alternative to the aggressive and manipulative aspects of gamesmanship. Her particular style emphasizes mutual trust and respect rather than suspicion and combativeness. This style carried over into her working relations with secretaries and paralegals as well.

> I think it's really important to develop working relationships out of mutual respect. I've seen too many attorneys treat their secretaries badly—like they're not people, like they don't matter. But they do matter, it does matter. Every time you treat someone like that, you hurt them, and you hurt yourself. It's a process of dehumanization, and it works both ways.

Gail, another young woman lawyer, found yet another way to deal with her dissatisfaction with the adversarial model:

> When I first came to the legal department, [senior counsel] made it clear I was on the "fast track." After a couple of years under a supervisor who gave me complete autonomy without any kind of psychic reward, I felt burned out. I wasn't contributing to society, plus all the stress and long hours. I decided at that point to find personal satisfaction. I got off the sixty-hour-week fast track. I took a three-month leave of absence. I came back to work part-time. I work [here] four days a week and do pro bono work on Fridays—I work for legal services for kids. I need to do it!

In her pro bono work, Gail found a way to satisfy her interests in the human side of the job: "I can't relate to the psychic manipulation and gamesmanship. When I go to work on Fridays, I feel like I'm doing real work for real people with real problems. I don't have to puff myself up or put other people down. It's about real life."

Other women attorneys also expressed concern with the quality of the procedure for resolving legal disputes and the quality of legal relationships and actively sought alternative means to adjudicate legal conflicts. For instance, Jessie, a young associate, described a situation she tried to resolve in a novel fashion. The case involved a plaintiff and defendant who had formerly been friends. One had sued the other for breach of contract in a business arrangement. The plaintiff refused to agree to any of the settlement negotiations. The case had dragged on for several years with repeated depositions, discovery motions, and settlement conferences. Initially, the plaintiff always seemed eager to settle, but in the end, he refused every offer. After days of reviewing the files and reading deposition transcripts, Jessie developed a theory about the bitter antagonism between the two parties and decided to try it out.

She called a preliminary settlement conference between the plaintiff and the defendant. She sat them both down in the conference room and said,

> I've read through the files thoroughly and I see this case as a simple breach of contract. What I don't understand completely is the animosity between the two of you. Mr. Smith has agreed to pay you a considerable sum of money for your loss, Mr. Henry. And you refuse the offer time and time again. It strikes me that you're angry with Mr. Smith about something unrelated to the lawsuit. I wonder if you could tell me what it's about?

This question was followed by a long silence. Jessie added,

> I realize that this is unorthodox Mr. Henry, but I have a feeling that the only way you two can ever resolve this dispute is if we get to the bottom of this antagonism between the two of you. If you prefer not to discuss it, I'll respect your wishes.

Mr. Henry finally said, "You really want to know?" Jessie nodded. He went on, "He married my ex-wife!" Mr. Smith said, "What! You left her for someone else. You left her! I didn't know you cared about what she did." The interchange continued for some time, with exclamations, accusations, and laughter on both sides. Finally, Jessie brought the discussion back to business. "Would you be willing to accept Mr. Smith's offer?" Mr. Henry agreed.

Jessie's approach contrasts sharply to the adversarial model. Rather than focusing only on her client's interests, she attempted to create a resolution by considering the interests of all the parties involved. Furthermore, her relationship to the plaintiff was not purely instrumental and manipulative, but one of genuine interest and concern. She wanted to get to the bottom of things, and she believed that a more personal approach would work: "People think I am a pushover because I'm nice and pleasant. But sometimes I think practicing law can be different if you're pleasant and treat people with respect."

Jessie sought not only to transform the practice of law, but to break down hierarchical relations in the office:

> A lot of lawyers think because they have a law degree, they're smarter than everyone else. I've never suffered from that delusion. I value what everyone on my team has to offer. . . . If Joan [a secretary] tells me I did something wrong, I listen. She's been in the office longer than I have and she knows a lot of things I don't. . . . The practice of law encourages hierarchical thinking. If we break that down, we can be better lawyers, better people.

By reshaping the adversarial role to fit their more relational orientation, these women contradict Kanter's findings on female tokens. Rather than conforming to the male model, these women self-consciously reject the binary win-lose structure of adversarial practice and construct alternative forms of practice that value mutual trust and respect in relationships. Their active participation in creating a more caring orientation within the legal profession serves as both a critique of and a challenge to the male-defined adversarial role. Furthermore, their emphasis on "real" relationships undermines one of the major assumptions of gamesmanship, that is, that relations with others are a game in which people are treated as objects. Rather than deny the subjectivity of the other, these women recognize the other as an authentic subject.[7]

Some men in this category also expressed serious misgivings about the adversarial role. Patrick, for example, criticized many lawyers for their tendency to behave like "assholes." By contrast, he wanted to practice law in a less adversarial way—one influenced by Eastern philosophy.

> I do martial art, aikido. I like to live that as my personal lifestyle. In aikido, you overcome your opponents without being an asshole, but understanding their interests. Let's try to resolve both interests, rather than winning is everything. I think that I am new enough as an attorney that I don't know how well it works in practice. I think that you can apply it to other parts of your life, you know making compromises and not being adversarial.
> *Do you think you will be successful with that attitude?*
> Successful? I don't know. I would like to think that I could be successful with this attitude. I can't see it some other way. If this profession demands that I become an asshole and I realize that I become an asshole, I would make a change, because this is just a job. I don't think enough people are concerned with resolving conflict this way. For them, it is zero-sum, win-lose. And it's a real ego investment, too. I think a lot of people want to win for the sake of winning.
> *Have you ever put this into practice at the office?*
> Maybe, I am naive, but I was in a dispute in a banking case. There was a situation where I could have said "fuck you" to opposing counsel, but I didn't. When it was clear that I was not going to do this through reason, I just said, "I can't do it, I'm sorry."

Unlike lawyers who adopt a guerrilla-warfare mentality, Patrick endorses the Eastern philosophy of aikido to describe his position. Rather than trying to overcome opponents by force, he wants to "understand their interests" and "resolve the interests from both sides." Such a concern appears quite Gilliganesque. However, though highly critical of the combative aspects of the adversarial role, his seemingly relational stance did not extend to his working relationships in the office. He was friendly with secretaries and paralegals, but he made no effort to create friendships with them, insisting instead on "professional relationships." Furthermore, paralegals reported that Patrick frequently "pulled rank"—that is, he was quick to remind them that he was the lawyer. While Patrick's critique of the adversarial model is quite similar to that of the women in this category, it did not extend to his behavior in other working relationships in the office.

[. . .]

SPLITTING THE ROLES VERSUS DISTANCING

In their study on women lawyers, Jack and Jack (1988) found that some women lawyers "split" the lawyering role by living up to the demands of the professional role and, at the same time, maintaining their personal caring morality. They accomplished this by splitting their roles at home and at work, adopting an adversarial role at work but embracing a caring ethic at home. In my research, women also split roles, but in a different way. The second group of female lawyers (58 percent of women) assimilated to the masculine norms of gamesmanship in their dealings with opposing counsel and with clients, but their actions and feelings in the office often belied this stance. Some adopted a combative style with opposing counsel but treated staff and colleagues with concern and/or respect. Others utilized gamesmanship but often expressed strong feelings of guilt and dissatisfaction. On the other hand, men in the second group distanced themselves from the adversarial role. Unlike men in the first group, who criticized the combative aspect of the adversarial role, these men were not critical but instead expressed a curiously detached relationship to the emotional requirements of the job.

[. . .]

Jeanette was another litigator who had a reputation for being "tough." Watching her practice her "mock trial," I was struck by the contrast between her angry demeanor in the courtroom and her typically pleasant presentation of self in the office. While opposing counsel was presenting his side of the case, she rolled her eyes dramatically, scowled, and made faces suggesting to the jury that she thought the other lawyer was an idiot. When it was her turn to cross-examine the witness, she utilized a confrontational approach, simultaneously questioning and berating the witness.

In the office Jeanette's behavior took on a more relational tone. She planned surprise birthday parties for all the secretaries, paralegals, and lawyers on her team, and often baked the cake herself. During the holiday season, she personally delivered Christmas cards and candy canes to all the people who worked for her. Moreover, when I left the legal department she made a special effort to take me out to lunch to thank me for all the work I had done for her. Jeanette defended her behavior in this way:

> I really like my secretary. She's great. Our friendship is important to me. . . .
> [But] some lawyers have lectured me on my lack of professionalism. You
> know, [she adopts a deep voice] "It's not professional to be friends with your

secretary." To me, that's a male attitude. If I were professional all the time,
I wouldn't have any friends at all.

Again, we can see that Jeanette self-consciously rejects what she considers to be the
male-defined professional stance for office etiquette, opting instead for more personal
relationships.

Yolanda, the "queen of sanctions," also fell into this category. Despite her no-
nonsense attitude in the courtroom and her reputation at the courthouse, in the office
Yolanda was attentive and friendly in personal interactions. During department meetings, she was usually one of the few attorneys who chatted and joked with paralegals.
She made an effort to include people in conversations, doing what Pamela Fishman
(1978) calls "interaction work." Moreover, unlike the other women attorneys, Yolanda
freely discussed make-up, clothes, jewelry, and dieting in public situations. During one
meeting, she described at great length a new leather mini-skirt she had bought and
where she planned to wear it. When senior counsel cast a disapproving glance in her
direction, she shot back, "I'm just trying to liven things up, Sam. These meetings are so
dull!" Everyone laughed. Again, her attention to personal interactions belies the more
aggressive style she develops in the courtroom.

Yolanda describes these different presentations of self:

> What I do in court, I do because I have to. I'm a damn good litigator and
> I'm not afraid to be tough. In the office, I can be Yolanda and joke around
> and talk to people. That's when I get to be myself.

[. . .]

Many of the women I interviewed who fell into the second category were aware of
the conflict between their personal morality and the adversarial role. Yolanda described
it in this way:

> Personal relationships are important to me. I like my colleagues, I like my
> secretary. And then there's court, I love going to court. I like drama, getting
> dressed up, playing the role. But sometimes it's hard. When I worked for
> the district attorney's office, I prosecuted a lot of poor people, Black people.
> As an African-American woman, I had problems with that. People were
> always telling me, "Yolanda, you're not down for the community." I didn't
> like thinking about that, that's why I got out. Now, I defend the company,
> it's different.
>
> *How is it different?*
>
> I don't prosecute poor people any more. But the conflict is still there, it's
> just not as great. Now I defend Bonhomie and we all know what a pristine,
> innocent, and pure-as-snow company it is. [*Laughs.*] I don't like knowing
> what I do hurts people.

[. . .]

By splitting roles between conforming to masculine norms of gamesmanship in
relations with opposing counsel and clients and adopting a caring orientation in the
office, the behavior of the women in the second category contradicts Kanter's thesis

about the behavior of token women. While these women seemingly conform to the masculine norms, thereby making themselves less visible in Kanter's formulation, their behavior toward support staff and colleagues in the office and the expression of their Gilliganesque concern for relationships suggests that they have not fully assimilated the masculine demands of the profession. Their behavior and expressed feelings underscore instead a fundamental conflict between the adversarial role and their personal feelings about the importance of relationships, civility, and fair play.

Like these women, the male lawyers in the second group accepted adversarial tactics in the courtroom. However, they did not split roles—their behavior did not take a more relational tone in the office. They did not pursue friendships with secretaries, remember birthdays of colleagues or support staff, bake cakes, or buy flowers. Nor did they embrace the adversarial model enthusiastically. Instead, they expressed a distanced attitude toward their courtroom behavior. One lawyer commented dryly on his use of adversarial tactics: "I put on my mask for battle. I parry, I thrust. I score. It's like fencing." His lack of affect contrasts sharply with lawyers who describe their victories and strategies with vigor and enthusiasm. Similarly, Nathan, another lawyer, said, "I've done it so many times, it's like going through the motions. I turn on when I go to court. When I come back to the office, I shut down. It's a male thing." Another lawyer described the emotional dimension of the job as "the lubricant. It's like oiling a bicycle wheel to keep it from squeaking." These men perform the requisite emotional labor in the courtroom, but they appeared to remove themselves from it. By distancing themselves, they have created an additional component to emotional labor. Not only do they treat other people as objects to manipulate, but they seem to regard their own feelings and behavior in the same way.

[. . .]

TALK LIKE A LAWYER, THINK LIKE A LAWYER, ACT LIKE A LAWYER

The third and smallest group of women lawyers (16 percent) emulated the behavior of aggressive male litigators in the courtroom and in the office. Jack and Jack describe this type of woman lawyer as one who "accepted the male model and tried to mold herself to fit its dictates" (1988, 269). In their study, women who fell in this category "minimize the caring self . . . [and made themselves] talk like a lawyer, think like a lawyer, act like a lawyer (1988, 270). This particular model of behavior has been encouraged in popular advice books and articles written for career women (Harragan 1977; Strachan 1984). For example, in an article in the American Bar Association Journal, a female attorney advises women who want to succeed in a "man's world" to establish themselves as committed and competent professionals by doing top quality work, working long hours, and never shirking late hours or weekend projects. In addition, she suggests rejecting any association with the traditional female role:

> Don't go home to cook dinner—or if you do, don't tell anyone. Keep your personal life in the background. . . . Never make excuses based on the needs of a spouse or children. Dress and talk in a conservative and professional manner.

> . . . Dress like a lawyer. Don't chew gum. When called "dear" or flirted with
> in business meetings or professional situations, respond only with entirely
> professional business-like statements, so that all communications are placed
> on and remain on a highly professional plane. [And finally] Don't think of
> yourself, or allow anyone to think of you, as anything but a hard driving,
> capable lawyer. (Strachan 1984, 94–95; passage reordered from original)

The women who fell into the third category closely adhered to the male standard
for success. Not only did they adopt hardball tactics in the courtroom, but unlike
women lawyers who reshaped or split the adversarial role, they maintained "professional working relationships" with their secretaries and paralegals. Kathryn, for example, said, "I'm not friends with my secretary and I don't intend to be. It's simply a
working relationship." And another asked rhetorically, "Why should I be friends with
her? She's my secretary." In addition, these women strongly rejected seeing themselves
as women lawyers. Kathryn believed, "Being a woman is just not an issue. I never think
that because I happen to be a woman, blah, blah, blah will happen." Such a gender-
neutral view carried over to her experience of discrimination:

> Discrimination? Sometimes clients will say that it's odd to have a woman
> on the case. But I don't pay attention to that. You just get in there, roll up
> your sleeves, and you do the work. I worked hard, I put in the hours and I
> made partner. In fact, I was the first woman partner in this department. But
> being a woman had nothing to do with it.

Candace, another partner from the private firm, echoed Kathryn's sentiment about
discrimination:

> Of course, it bothers me. So does nuclear war. But the bottom line is that
> I can't do anything about it. All day long, this client avoids phone calls be-
> cause he thinks women are incompetents. Hell, it bothers me, but I can't let
> myself dwell on it, because dwelling on it just depresses me. So I focus on
> my work. That's what women have to do, work and work hard!
>   *It sounds like you use a lot of energy to keep these feelings beneath the sur-*
> *face.*
>   To survive I have to *not* think about all these things. If I did I would go
> crazy.

Both these women deny discrimination is a significant factor, though in slightly different ways. Candace acknowledges its existence but doesn't let herself dwell on it and
focuses instead upon her work. Kathryn simply refuses to pay attention to it. For both
women, "hard work" is viewed as the key to their success—being a woman has nothing to do with it.
    [. . .]
The women in the third category most closely approximate Kanter's predictions
about the behavior of tokens. However, these women also represented the smallest group
of women lawyers numerically—only 16 percent fell into this category. Moreover, while
these women have conformed outwardly to the male model, they have strong feelings

about the personal costs such conformity has entailed, feelings that are related to gender. It is femininity that is put in a box and tucked away or denied.

These styles are similar to the behavior of men in the third group who emphatically embraced the adversarial model. They considered aggression and strategic friendliness to be central and acceptable parts of the job. Bill, a young associate explained, "I do my best work when I hate the other side. The more obnoxious they are, the harder I work against them." Bill has no interest in changing the nature of the relationship with opposing counsel. He doesn't believe that you can trust the other side and has no interest in trying. "They lie all the time—that's the way it is."

In addition, the men in this category strongly reject alternatives to the adversarial model. When I asked one man whether he had ever utilized any means to resolve disputes other than adversarial tactics, he responded, "That's pie in the sky. Everyone can't win. There are winners and losers in litigation. It's zero-sum. And I want my client to win." Similarly, when I asked a partner what he liked best about his job, he said:

> Winning for sure. Of course, you usually only win part of the case, not the whole thing. But winning is definitely emotionally satisfying—it's emotionally satisfying to know you did it.

[. . .]

For these men, conforming to the adversarial model does not pose any personal costs. Whereas women in this category felt that adopting the adversarial role involved suppressing their gender identity, men saw the role as a natural extension of their masculinity. For example, John asserts later in the same interview, "No offense, but [women] just don't have the balls to be tough litigators. It's just one of those things that men do better. Women are good at writing briefs." Similarly, Bill not only embraces the adversarial role but describes it as "something men get into." "You've got to be tough and ruthless. Most women can't do that."

In this section, I have shown that female attorneys perform a more varied range of emotional labor. Existing theoretical accounts do not adequately explain the variation in the behavior of these women lawyers. While Kanter's proposition that women conform to male norms of the legal profession describes the behavior of women in the third group, it does not account for those who split roles or those who reshaped the adversarial model. Similarly, Gilligan's social psychological theory explains why some women created alternative, caring practices of lawyering, but it does not explain why others did not. How then can we explain the variation in behavior?

To answer this question, the experiences of women attorneys must be theorized as a dynamic relationship between occupational structure, behavior, and identity. Gender is an integral part of this analysis. In my explanation, gender shapes the experiences of women lawyers at the level of occupational structure while legal workers reproduce gender in their interactions with one another. At the structural level, female litigators find themselves a token minority in a male-dominated occupation, encountering a professional socialization and a career track based on a male model of success. They must contend with boundary heightening, and they face contradictory messages about the appropriate display of emotional labor: when they adopt gamesmanship strategies they are criticized for "unladylike" and "shrill" behavior, but when they are "nice" or "pleasant," they are judged "not tough enough" to be good lawyers.

The double bind women attorneys invariably experience explains, in part, the variation in their behavior. There are simply no clear-cut "feeling rules" for women lawyers. Nor is there any one form of acceptable emotional labor for them. Whether they closely adhere to the adversarial model or not, they garner criticism, disapproval, and even ostracism. However, assuming that structure determines behavior in a simple one-to-one relationship denies agency to social actors and neglects the continuous and reciprocal relationship between the two levels of analysis. To improve upon this theoretical weakness, I view the masculinized structure of the legal profession as setting limits on female litigators' behavior. Some women attorneys cross over these boundaries, others move within and around them, and still others remain safely inside the lines.

Regardless of which strategy women select, their negotiation within these limits poses a nagging question: How can I be a lawyer and at the same time be a woman? Answering this question entails choosing behavior congruent with their notions of gender-appropriate behavior—which is not necessarily the same thing as behaving in traditionally female ways. Socialization in a masculinized profession has provided these women with life experiences as well as an education that provides them an array of choices for "doing gender" (West and Zimmerman 1987). Women lawyers who split roles do gender in accordance with professional norms in the courtroom and with their conceptions of feminine behavior in the office. Those who adopt a more relational orientation reshape the adversarial role to be consistent with their notions of how law ought to be practiced and their sense of how women as traditional caregivers should do law. Finally, even the women who adopt the role of the professional combatant do gender by accepting the advice for women lawyers that encourages them to establish themselves as competent professionals and to downplay their association with the traditional female role. Ironically, this group of women sought to be lawyers and women by minimizing the feminine side of themselves.

[. . .]

Notes

1. In her more recent work with Lyn Brown, *Meeting at the Crossroads*, Gilligan modifies her earlier position, arguing that adolescent girls sometimes use many moral voices rather than only one. While the variation Brown and Gilligan document is consistent with the findings in this chapter, I see my theoretical account as distinctive. I am concerned with a specific set of theoretical questions regarding the reproduction of gender at micro- and macro-levels of analysis, but Brown and Gilligan's work, though interesting and evocative, is primarily descriptive.

2. Epstein also draws this conclusion in the epilogue to the 1993 edition of her book *Women and Law*.

3. See Rhode (1989) for a detailed review of changes in law that have affected women's paid labor-force employment.

4. The extent of sexual harassment within the profession has been reported by academic studies (Rosenberg, Perlstadt and Phillips 1993; MacCorquodale and Jensen 1993) as well as by studies conducted by the legal profession itself (Butler 1989; Lewin 1989; Margolick 1990a).

5. These percentages were calculated by adding together the number of women trial lawyers in each law firm and dividing the total by the number of women who fell into each category. The total number of women litigators in both firms was nineteen. Five women (approximately 26 percent) fell into the first category, "Resisting and Reshaping the Adversarial Role." Eleven women (58 percent) fell into the second category, "Splitting the Roles"; and three women (16 percent) fell into the third. I utilized the same method to determine the percentages of male attorneys in each category.

6. Only a few of the women I interviewed in this category identified themselves as feminists. Most opted for what Stacey (1991) terms a post-feminist description of their political identity which takes the form, "I believe in equal opportunity, but I am not a feminist. . . ."

7. This is similar to what Jessica Benjamin calls "mutual recognition" or "the necessity of recognizing as well as being recognized by the other" (1989, 23).

CHAPTER 15

The Glass Escalator

HIDDEN ADVANTAGES FOR MEN
IN THE "FEMALE" PROFESSIONS

Christine L. Williams

This paper addresses men's underrepresentation in four predominantly
female professions: nursing, elementary school teaching, librarianship, and
social work. Specifically, it examines the degree to which discrimination
disadvantages men in hiring and promotion decisions, the work place culture, and in interactions with clients. In-depth interviews were conducted
with 99 men and women in these professions in four major U.S. cities.
The interview data suggest that men do not face discrimination in these
occupations; however, they do encounter prejudice from individuals outside their professions. In contrast to the experience of women who enter
male-dominated professions, men generally encounter structural advantages
in these occupations which tend to enhance their careers. Because men face
different barriers to integrating nontraditional occupations than women
face, the need for different remedies to dismantle segregation in predominantly female jobs is emphasized.

The sex segregation of the U.S. labor force is one of the most perplexing and tenacious problems in our society. Even though the proportion of men and women in
the labor force is approaching parity (particularly for younger cohorts of workers)
(U.S. Department of Labor 1991, 18), men and women are still generally confined
to predominantly single sex occupations. Forty percent of men or women would have
to change major occupational categories to achieve equal representation of men and
women in all jobs (Reskin and Roos 1990, 6), but even this figure underestimates the
true degree of sex segregation. It is extremely rare to find specific jobs where equal
numbers of men and women are engaged in the same activities in the same industries
(Bielby and Baron 1984).

Most studies of sex segregation in the work force have focused on women's experiences in male-dominated occupations. Both researchers and advocates for social
change have focused on the barriers faced by women who try to integrate predominantly male fields. Few have looked at the "flip-side" of occupational sex segregation:
the exclusion of men from predominantly female occupations (exceptions include
Schreiber 1979; Williams 1989; Zimmer 1988). But the fact is that men are less likely
to enter female sex-typed occupations than women are to enter male-dominated jobs

(Jacobs 1989). Reskin and Roos, for example, were able to identify 33 occupations in which female representation increased by more than nine percentage points between 1970 and 1980, but only three occupations in which the proportion of men increased as radically (1990, 20–21).

In this paper, I examine men's underrepresentation in four predominantly female occupations—nursing, librarianship, elementary school teaching, and social work. Throughout the twentieth century, these occupations have been identified with "women's work"—even though prior to the Civil War, men were more likely to be employed in these areas. These four occupations, often called the female "semi-professions" (Hodson and Sullivan 1990) today range from 5.5 percent male (in nursing) to 32 percent male (in social work). (See Table 15.1.) These percentages have not changed substantially in decades. In fact, as Table 15.1 indicates, two of these professions—librarianship and social work—have experienced declines in the proportions of men since 1975. Nursing is the only one of the four experiencing noticeable changes in sex composition, with the proportion of men increasing 80 percent between 1975 and 1990. Even so, men continue to be a tiny minority of all nurses.

Although there are many possible reasons for the continuing preponderance of women in these fields, the focus of this paper is discrimination. Researchers examining the integration of women into "male fields" have identified discrimination as a major barrier to women (Jacobs 1989; Reskin 1988; Reskin and Hartmann 1986). This discrimination has taken the form of laws or institutionalized rules prohibiting the hiring or promotion of women into certain job specialties. Discrimination can also be "informal," as when women encounter sexual harassment, sabotage, or other forms of hostility from their male co-workers resulting in a poisoned work environment (Reskin and Hartmann 1986). Women in nontraditional occupations also report feeling stigmatized by clients when their work puts them in contact with the public. In particular, women in engineering and blue-collar occupations encounter gender-based stereotypes about their competence which undermine their work performance (Epstein 1988; Martin 1980). Each of these forms of discrimination—legal, informal, and cultural—contributes to women's underrepresentation in predominantly male occupations.

The assumption in much of this literature is that any member of a token group in a work setting will probably experience similar discriminatory treatment. Kanter

Table 15.1. Percent Male in Selected Occupations, Selected Years

Profession	1990	1980	1975
Nurses	5.5	3.5	3.0
Elementary teachers	14.8	16.3	14.6
Librarians	16.7	14.8	18.9
Social workers	31.8	35.0	39.2

Source: U.S. Department of Labor Bureau of Labor Statistics. *Employment and Earnings* 38:1 (January 1991), Table 22 (Employed civilians by detailed occupation), 185; 28:1 (January 1981), Table 23 (Employed persons by detailed occupation), 180; 22:7 (January 1976), Table 2 (Employed persons by detailed occupation), 11.

(1977), who is best known for articulating this perspective in her theory of tokenism, argues that when any group represents less than 15 percent of an organization, its members will be subject to predictable forms of discrimination. Likewise, Jacobs argues that "in some ways, men in female-dominated occupations experience the same difficulties that women in male-dominated occupations face" (1989, 167), and Reskin contends that any dominant group in an occupation will use their power to maintain a privileged position (1988, 62).

However, the few studies that have considered men's experience in gender atypical occupations suggest that men may not face discrimination or prejudice when they integrate predominantly female occupations. Zimmer (1988) and Martin (1988) both contend that the effects of sexism can outweigh the effects of tokenism when men enter nontraditional occupations. This study is the first to systematically explore this question using data from four occupations. I examine the barriers to men's entry into these professions; the support men receive from their supervisors, colleagues and clients; and the reactions they encounter from the public (those outside their professions).

Methods

I conducted in-depth interviews with 76 men and 23 women in four occupations from 1985–1991. Interviews were conducted in four metropolitan areas: San Francisco/ Oakland, California; Austin, Texas; Boston, Massachusetts; and Phoenix, Arizona. These four areas were selected because they show considerable variation in the proportions of men in the four professions. For example, Austin has one of the highest percentages of men in nursing (7.7 percent), whereas Phoenix's percentage is one of the lowest (2.7 percent) (U.S. Bureau of the Census 1980). The sample was generated using "snowballing" techniques. Women were included in the sample to gauge their feelings and responses to men who enter "their" professions.

Like the people employed in these professions generally, those in my sample were predominantly white (90 percent).[1] Their ages ranged from 20 to 66 and the average age was 38. The interview questionnaire consisted of several open-ended questions on four broad topics: motivation to enter the profession; experiences in training; career progression; and general views about men's status and prospects within these occupations. I conducted all the interviews, which generally lasted between one and two hours. Interviews took place in restaurants, my home or office, or the respondent's home or office. Interviews were tape-recorded and transcribed for the analysis.

Data analysis followed the coding techniques described by Strauss (1987). Each transcript was read several times and analyzed into emergent conceptual categories. Likewise, Strauss' principle of theoretical sampling was used. Individual respondents were purposely selected to capture the array of men's experiences in these occupations. Thus, I interviewed practitioners in every specialty, oversampling those employed in the *most* gender atypical areas (e.g., male kindergarten teachers). I also selected respondents from throughout their occupational hierarchies—from students to administrators to retirees. Although the data do not permit within group comparisons, I am reasonably certain that the sample does capture a wide range of experiences common to men in these female-dominated professions. However, like all findings based on qualitative data, it is uncertain whether the findings generalize to the larger population of men in nontraditional occupations.

In this paper, I review individuals' responses to questions about discrimination in hiring practices, on-the-job rapport with supervisors and co-workers, and prejudice from clients and others outside their profession.

Discrimination in Hiring

Contrary to the experience of many women in the male-dominated professions, many of the men and women I spoke to indicated that there is a *preference* for hiring men in these four occupations. A Texas librarian at a junior high school said that his school district "would hire a male over a female."

> *I:* Why do you think that is?
>
> *R:* Because there are so few, and the . . . ones that they do have, the library directors seem to really . . . think they're doing great jobs. I don't know, maybe they just feel they're being progressive or something, [but] I have had a real sense that they really appreciate having a male, particularly at the junior high. . . . As I said, when seven of us lost our jobs from the high schools and were redistributed, there were only four positions at junior high, and I got one of them. Three of the librarians, some who had been here longer than I had with the school district, were put down in elementary school as librarians. And I definitely think that being male made a difference in my being moved to the junior high rather than an elementary school.

Many of the men perceived their token status as males in predominantly female occupations as an *advantage* in hiring and promotions. I asked an Arizona teacher whether his specialty (elementary special education) was an unusual area for men compared to other areas within education. He said,

> Much more so. I am extremely marketable in special education. That's not why I got into the field. But I am extremely marketable because I am a man.

In several cases, the more female-dominated the specialty, the greater the apparent preference for men. For example, when asked if he encountered any problem getting a job in pediatrics, a Massachusetts nurse said,

> No, no, none. . . . I've heard this from managers and supervisory-type people with men in pediatrics: "It's nice to have a man because it's such a female-dominated profession."

However, there were some exceptions to this preference for men in the most female-dominated specialties. In some cases, formal policies actually barred men from certain jobs. This was the case in some rural Texas school districts, which refused to hire men in the youngest grades (K–3). Some nurses also reported being excluded from positions in obstetrics and gynecology wards, a policy encountered more frequently in private Catholic hospitals.

But often the pressures keeping men out of certain specialties were more subtle than this. Some men described being "tracked" into practice areas within their professions which were considered more legitimate for men. For example, one Texas man described how he was pushed into administration and planning in social work, even though "I'm not interested in writing policy; I'm much more interested in research and clinical stuff." A nurse who is interested in pursuing graduate study in family and child health in Boston said he was dissuaded from entering the program specialty in favor of a concentration in "adult nursing." A kindergarten teacher described the difficulty of finding a job in his specialty after graduation: "I was recruited immediately to start getting into a track to become an administrator. And it was men who recruited me. It was men that ran the system at that time, especially in Los Angeles."

This tracking may bar men from the most female-identified specialties within these professions. But men are effectively being "kicked upstairs" in the process. Those specialties considered more legitimate practice areas for men also tend to be the most prestigious, better paying ones. A distinguished kindergarten teacher, who had been voted city-wide "Teacher of the Year," told me that even though people were pleased to see him in the classroom, "there's been some encouragement to think about administration, and there's been some encouragement to think about teaching at the university level or something like that, or supervisory-type position." That is, despite his aptitude and interest in staying in the classroom, he felt pushed in the direction of administration.

The effect of this "tracking" is the opposite of that experienced by women in male-dominated occupations. Researchers have reported that many women encounter a "glass ceiling" in their efforts to scale organizational and professional hierarchies. That is, they are constrained by invisible barriers to promotion in their careers, caused mainly by the sexist attitudes of men in the highest positions (Freeman 1990).[2] In contrast to the "glass ceiling," many of the men I interviewed seem to encounter a "glass escalator." Often, despite their intentions, they face invisible pressures to move up in their professions. As if on a moving escalator, they must work to stay in place.

A public librarian specializing in children's collections (a heavily female-dominated concentration) described an encounter with this "escalator" in his very first job out of library school. In his first six-months' evaluation, his supervisors commended him for his good work in storytelling and related activities, but they criticized him for "not shooting high enough."

> Seriously. That's literally what they were telling me. They assumed that because I was a male—and they told me this—and that I was being hired right out of graduate school, that somehow I wasn't doing the kind of management-oriented work that they thought I should be doing. And as a result, really they had a lot of bad marks, as it were, against me on my evaluation. And I said I couldn't believe this!

Throughout his ten-year career, he has had to struggle to remain in children's collections.

The glass escalator does not operate at all levels. In particular, men in academia reported some gender-based discrimination in the highest positions due to their universities' commitment to affirmative action. Two nursing professors reported that they felt their own chances of promotion to deanships were nil because their universities viewed the position of nursing dean as a guaranteed female appointment in an otherwise heavily male-dominated administration. One California social work professor reported his university canceled its search for a dean because no minority male or female candidates had been placed on their short list. It was rumored that other schools on campus were permitted to go forward with their searches—even though they also failed to put forward names of minority candidates—because the higher administration perceived it to be "easier" to fulfill affirmative action goals in the social work school. The interviews provide greater evidence of the "glass escalator" at work in the lower levels of these professions.

Of course, men's motivations also play a role in their advancement to higher professional positions. I do not mean to suggest that the men I talked to all resented the informal tracking they experienced. For many men, leaving the most female-identified areas of their professions helped them resolve internal conflicts involving their masculinity. One man left his job as a school social worker to work in a methadone drug treatment program not because he was encouraged to leave by his colleagues, but because "I think there was some macho shit there, to tell you the truth, because I remember feeling a little uncomfortable there . . . ; it didn't feel right to me." Another social worker, employed in the mental health services department of a large urban area in California, reflected on his move into administration:

> The more I think about it, through our discussion, I'm sure that's a large part of why I wound up in administration. It's okay for a man to do the administration. In fact, I don't know if I fully answered a question that you asked a little while ago about how did being male contribute to my advancing in the field. I was saying it wasn't because I got any special favoritism as a man, but . . . I think . . . because I'm a man, I felt a need to get into this kind of position. I may have worked harder toward it, may have competed harder for it, than most women would do, even women who think about doing administrative work.

Elsewhere I have speculated on the origins of men's tendency to define masculinity through single-sex work environments (Williams 1989). Clearly, personal ambition does play a role in accounting for men's movement into more "male-defined" arenas within these professions. But these occupations also structure opportunities for males independent of their individual desires or motives.

The interviews suggest that men's underrepresentation in these professions cannot be attributed to discrimination in hiring or promotions. Many of the men indicated that they received preferential treatment because they were men. Although men mentioned gender discrimination in the hiring process, for the most part they were channelled into more "masculine" specialties within these professions, which ironically meant being "tracked into better paying and more prestigious specialties.

Supervisors and Colleagues: The Working Environment

Researchers claim that subtle forms of work place discrimination push women out of male-dominated occupations (Jacobs 1989; Reskin and Hartmann 1986). In particular, women report feeling excluded from informal leadership and decision-making networks, and they sense hostility from their male co-workers, which makes them feel uncomfortable and unwanted (Carothers and Crull 1984). Respondents in this study were asked about their relationships with supervisors and female colleagues to ascertain whether men also experienced "poisoned" work environments when entering gender atypical occupations.

A major difference in the experience of men and women in nontraditional occupations is that men in these situations are far more likely to be supervised by a member of their own sex. In each of the four professions I studied, men are overrepresented in administrative and managerial capacities, or, as is the case of nursing, their positions in the organizational hierarchy are governed by men (Grimm and Stern 1974; Phenix 1987; Schmuck 1987; Williams 1989; York, Henley and Gamble 1987). Thus, unlike women who enter "male fields," the men in these professions often work under the direct supervision of other men.

Many of the men interviewed reported that they had good rapport with their male supervisors. Even in professional school, some men reported extremely close relationships with their male professors. For example, a Texas librarian described an unusually intimate association with two male professors in graduate school:

> I can remember a lot of times in the classroom there would be discussions about a particular topic or issue, and the conversation would spill over into their office hours, after the class was over. And even though there were . . . a couple of the other women that had been in on the discussion, they weren't there. And I don't know if that was preferential or not. . . . It certainly carried over into personal life as well. Not just at the school and that sort of thing. I mean, we would get together for dinner . . .

These professors explicitly encouraged him because he was male:

> I: Did they ever offer you explicit words of encouragement about being in the profession by virtue of the fact that you were male? . . .
>
> R: Definitely. On several occasions. Yeah. Both of these guys, for sure, including the Dean who was male also. And it's an interesting point that you bring up because it was, oftentimes, kind of in a sign, you know. It wasn't in the classroom, and it wasn't in front of the group, or if we were in the student lounge or something like that. It was . . . if it was just myself or maybe another one of the guys, you know, and just talking in the office. It's like . . . you know, kind of an opening-up and saying, "You know, you are really lucky that you're in the profession because you'll really go to the top real quick, and you'll be able to make real definite improvements and

changes. And you'll have a real influence," and all this sort of thing. I mean, really, I can remember several times.

Other men reported similar closeness with their professors. A Texas psychotherapist recalled his relationships with his male professors in social work school:

> I made it a point to make a golfing buddy with one of the guys that was in administration. He and I played golf a lot. He was the guy who kind of ran the research training, the research part of the master's program. Then there was a sociologist who ran the other part of the research program. He and I developed a good friendship.

This close mentoring by male professors contrasts with the reported experience of women in nontraditional occupations. Others have noted a lack of solidarity among women in nontraditional occupations. Writing about military academies, for example, Yoder describes the failure of token women to mentor succeeding generations of female cadets. She argues that women attempt to play down their gender difference from men because it is the source of scorn and derision.

> Because women felt unaccepted by their male colleagues, one of the last things they wanted to do was to emphasize their gender. Some women thought that, if they kept company with other women, this would high-light their gender and would further isolate them from male cadets. These women desperately wanted to be accepted as cadets, not as *women* cadets. Therefore, they did everything from not wearing skirts as an option with their uniforms to avoiding being a part of a group of women. (Yoder 1989, 532)

Men in nontraditional occupations face a different scenario—their gender is construed as a *positive* difference. Therefore, they have an incentive to bond together and empha-size their distinctiveness from the female majority.

Close, personal ties with male supervisors were also described by men once they were established in their professional careers. It was not uncommon in education, for example, for the male principal to informally socialize with the male staff, as a Texas special education teacher describes:

> Occasionally I've had a principal who would regard me as "the other man on the campus" and "it's us against them," you know? I mean, nothing really that extreme, except that some male principals feel like there's nobody there to talk to except the other man. So I've been in that position.

These personal ties can have important consequences for men's careers. For example, one California nurse, whose performance was judged marginal by his nursing supervi-sors, was transferred to the emergency room staff (a prestigious promotion) due to his personal friendship with the physician in charge. A Massachusetts teacher acknowl-edged that his principal's personal interest in him landed him his current job.

I: You had mentioned that your principal had sort of spotted you at your previous job and had wanted to bring you here [to this school]. Do you think that has anything to do with the fact that you're a man, aside from your skills as a teacher?

R: Yes, I would say in that particular case, that was part of it. . . . We have certain things in common, certain interests that really lined up.

I: Vis-à-vis teaching?

R: Well, more extraneous things—running specifically, and music. And we just seemed to get along real well right off the bat. It is just kind of a guy thing; we just liked each other . . .

Interviewees did not report many instances of male supervisors discriminating against them, or refusing to accept them because they were male. Indeed, these men were much more likely to report that their male bosses discriminated against the *females* in their professions. When asked if he thought physicians treated male and female nurses differently, a Texas nurse said:

I think yeah, some of them do. I think the women seem like they have a lot more trouble with the physicians treating them in a derogatory manner. Or, if not derogatory, then in a very paternalistic way than the men [are treated]. Usually if a physician is mad at a male nurse, he just kind of yells at him. Kind of like an employee. And if they're mad at a female nurse, rather than treat them on an equal basis, in terms of just letting their anger out at them as an employee, they're more paternalistic or there's some sexual harassment component to it.

A Texas teacher perceived a similar situation where he worked:

I've never felt unjustly treated by a principal because I'm a male. The principals that I've seen that I felt are doing things that are kind of arbitrary or not well thought out are doing it to everybody. In fact, they're probably doing it to the females worse than they are to me.

Openly gay men may encounter less favorable treatment at the hands of their supervisors. For example, a nurse in Texas stated that one of the physicians he worked with preferred to staff the operating room with male nurses exclusively—as long as they weren't gay. Stigma associated with homosexuality leads some men to enhance, or even exaggerate their "masculine" qualities, and may be another factor pushing men into more "acceptable" specialties for men.

Not all the men who work in these occupations are supervised by men. Many of the men interviewed who had female bosses also reported high levels of acceptance—although levels of intimacy with women seemed lower than with other men. In some cases, however, men reported feeling shut-out from decision making when the higher administration was constituted entirely by women. I asked an Arizona librarian whether men in the library profession were discriminated against in hiring because of their sex:

> Professionally speaking, people go to considerable lengths to keep that kind of thing out of their [hiring] deliberations. Personally, is another matter. It's pretty common around here to talk about the "old girl network." This is one of the few libraries that I've had any intimate knowledge of which is actually controlled by women. . . . Most of the department heads and upper level administrators are women. And there's an "old girl network" that works just like the "old boy network," except that the important conferences take place in the women's room rather than on the golf course. But the political mechanism is the same, the exclusion of the other sex from decision making is the same. The reasons are the same. It's somewhat discouraging . . .

Although I did not interview many supervisors, I did include 23 women in my sample to ascertain their perspectives about the presence of men in their professions. All of the women I interviewed claimed to be supportive of their male colleagues, but some conveyed ambivalence. For example, a social work professor said she would like to see more men enter the social work profession, particularly in the clinical specialty (where they are underrepresented). Indeed, she favored affirmative action hiring guidelines for men in the profession. Yet, she resented the fact that her department hired "another white male" during a recent search. I questioned her about this ambivalence:

> *I:* I find it very interesting that, on the one hand, you sort of perceive this preference and perhaps even sexism with regard to how men are evaluated and how they achieve higher positions within the profession, yet, on the other hand, you would be encouraging of more men to enter the field. Is that contradictory to you, or . . . ?
>
> R: Yeah, it's contradictory.

It appears that women are generally eager to see men enter "their" occupations. Indeed, several men noted that their female colleagues had facilitated their careers in various ways (including mentorship in college). However, at the same time, women often resent the apparent ease with which men advance within these professions, sensing that men at the higher levels receive preferential treatment which closes off advancement opportunities for women.

But this ambivalence does not seem to translate into the "poisoned" work environment described by many women who work in male-dominated occupations. Among the male interviewees, there were no accounts of sexual harassment. However, women do treat their male colleagues differently on occasion. It is not uncommon in nursing, for example, for men to be called upon to help catheterize male patients, or to lift especially heavy patients. Some librarians also said that women asked them to lift and move heavy boxes of books because they were men. Teachers sometimes confront differential treatment as well, as described by this Texas teacher:

As a man, you're teaching with all women, and that can be hard sometimes. Just because of the stereotypes, you know. I'm real into computers . . . and all the time people are calling me to fix their computer. Or if somebody gets a flat tire, they come and get me. I mean, there are just a lot of stereotypes. Not that I mind doing any of those things, but it's . . . you know, it just kind of bugs me that it is a stereotype, "A man should do that." Or if their kids have a lot of discipline problems, that kiddo's in your room. Or if there are kids that don't have a father in their home, that kid's in your room. Hell, nowadays that'd be half the school in my room (laughs). But you know, all the time I hear from the principal or from other teachers, "Well, this child really needs a man . . . a male role model" (laughs). So there are a lot of stereotypes that . . . men kind of get stuck with.

This special treatment bothered some respondents. Getting assigned all the "discipline problems" can make for difficult working conditions, for example. But many men claimed this differential treatment did not cause distress. In fact, several said they liked being appreciated for the special traits and abilities (such as strength) they could contribute to their professions.

Furthermore, women's special treatment sometimes enhanced—rather than poisoned—the men's work environments. One Texas librarian said he felt "more comfortable working with women than men" because "I think it has something to do with control. Maybe it's that women will let me take control more than men will." Several men reported that their female colleagues often cast them into leadership roles. Although not all savored this distinction, it did enhance their authority and control in the work place. In subtle (and not-too-subtle) ways, then, differential treatment contributes to the "glass escalator" men experience in nontraditional professions.

Even outside work, most of the men interviewed said they felt fully accepted by their female colleagues. They were usually included in informal socializing occasions with the women—even though this frequently meant attending baby showers or Tupperware parties. Many said that they declined offers to attend these events because they were not interested in "women's things," although several others claimed to attend everything. The minority men I interviewed seemed to feel the least comfortable in these informal contexts. One social worker in Arizona was asked about socializing with his female colleagues:

> *I:* So in general, for example, if all the employees were going to get together to have a party, or celebrate a bridal shower or whatever, would you be invited along with the rest of the group?
>
> *R:* They would invite me, I would say, somewhat reluctantly. Being a black male, working with all white females, it did cause some outside problems. So I didn't go to a lot of functions with them . . .
>
> *I:* You felt that there was some tension there on the level of your acceptance . . . ?

> R: Yeah. It was OK working, but on the outside, personally, there was some tension there. It never came out, that they said, "Because of who you are we can't invite you" (laughs), and I wouldn't have done anything anyway. I would have probably respected them more for saying what was on their minds. But I never felt completely in with the group.

Some single men also said they felt uncomfortable socializing with married female colleagues because it gave the "wrong impression." But in general, the men said that they felt very comfortable around their colleagues and described their work places as very congenial for men. It appears unlikely, therefore, that men's underrepresentation in these professions is due to hostility towards men on the part of supervisors or women workers.

Discrimination from "Outsiders"

The most compelling evidence of discrimination against men in these professions is related to their dealings with the public. Men often encounter negative stereotypes when they come into contact with clients or "outsiders"—people they meet outside of work. For instance, it is popularly assumed that male nurses are gay. Librarians encounter images of themselves as "wimpy" and asexual. Male social workers describe being typecast as "feminine" and "passive." Elementary school teachers are often confronted by suspicions that they are pedophiles. One kindergarten teacher described an experience that occurred early in his career which was related to him years afterwards by his principal:

> He indicated to me that parents had come to him and indicated to him that they had a problem with the fact that I was a male. . . . I recall almost exactly what he said. There were three specific concerns that the parents had: One parent said, "How can he love my child; he's a man." The second thing that I recall, he said the parent said, "He has a beard." And the third thing was, "Aren't you concerned about homosexuality?"

Such suspicions often cause men in all four professions to alter their work behavior to guard against sexual abuse charges, particularly in those specialties requiring intimate contact with women and children.

Men are very distressed by these negative stereotypes, which tend to undermine their self-esteem and to cause them to second-guess their motivations for entering these fields. A California teacher said,

> If I tell men that I don't know, that I'm meeting for the first time, that that's what I do, . . . sometimes there's a look on their faces that, you know, "Oh, couldn't get a real job?"

When asked if his wife, who is also an elementary school teacher, encounters the same kind of prejudice, he said,

> No, it's accepted because she's a woman. . . . I think people would see that
> as a . . . step up, you know. "Oh, you're not a housewife, you've got a career.
> That's great . . . that you're out there working. And you have a daughter, but
> you're still out there working. You decided not to stay home, and you went
> out there and got a job." Whereas for me, it's more like I'm supposed to be
> out working anyway, even though I'd rather be home with [my daughter].

Unlike women who enter traditionally male professions, men's movement into these jobs is perceived by the "outside world" as a step down in status. This particular form of discrimination may be most significant in explaining why men are underrepresented in these professions. Men who otherwise might show interest in and aptitude for such careers are probably discouraged from pursuing them because of the negative popular stereotypes associated with the men who work in them. This is a crucial difference from the experience of women in nontraditional professions: "My daughter, the physician," resonates far more favorably in most peoples' ears than "My son, the nurse."

Many of the men in my sample identified the stigma of working in a female-identified occupation as the major barrier to more men entering their professions. However, for the most part, they claimed that these negative stereotypes were not a factor in their own decisions to join these occupations. Most respondents didn't consider entering these fields until well into adulthood, after working in some related occupation. Several social workers and librarians even claimed they were not aware that men were a minority in their chosen professions. Either they had no well-defined image or stereotype, or their contacts and mentors were predominantly men. For example, prior to entering library school, many librarians held part-time jobs in university libraries, where there are proportionally more men than in the profession generally. Nurses and elementary school teachers were more aware that mostly women worked in these jobs, and this was often a matter of some concern to them. However, their choices were ultimately legitimized by mentors, or by encouraging friends or family members who implicitly reassured them that entering these occupations would not typecast them as feminine. In some cases, men were told by recruiters there were special advancement opportunities for men in these fields, and they entered them expecting rapid promotion to administrative positions.

> *I:* Did it ever concern you when you were making the decision to enter
> nursing school, the fact that it is a female-dominated profession?
>
> *R:* Not really. I never saw myself working on the floor. I saw myself pretty
> much going into administration, just getting the background and then
> getting a job someplace as a supervisor, and then working, getting up into
> administration.

Because of the unique circumstances of their recruitment, many of the respondents did not view their occupational choices as inconsistent with a male gender role, and they generally avoided the negative stereotypes directed against men in these fields.

Indeed, many of the men I interviewed claimed that they did not encounter negative professional stereotypes until they had worked in these fields for several years. Popular prejudices can be damaging to self-esteem and probably push some men out of these professions altogether. Yet, ironically, they sometimes contribute to the "glass escalator" effect I have been describing. Men seem to encounter the most vituperative criticism from the public when they are in the most female-identified specialties. Public concerns sometimes result in their being shunted into more "legitimate" positions for men. A librarian formerly in charge of a branch library's children's collection, who now works in the reference department of the city's main library, describes his experience:

> R: Some of the people [who frequented the branch library] complained that they didn't want to have a man doing the storytelling scenario. And I got transferred here to the central library in an equivalent job . . . I thought that I did a good job. And I had been told by my supervisor that I was doing a good job.
>
> I: Have you ever considered filing some sort of lawsuit to get that other job back?
>
> R: Well, actually, the job I've gotten now . . . well, it's a reference librarian; it's what I wanted in the first place. I've got a whole lot more authority here. I'm also in charge of the circulation desk. And I've recently been promoted because of my new stature, so . . . no, I'm not considering trying to get that other job back.

The negative stereotypes about men who do "women's work" can push men out of specific jobs. However, to the extent that they channel men into more "legitimate" practice areas, their effects can actually be positive. Instead of being a source of discrimination, these prejudices can add to the "glass escalator effect" by pressuring men to move *out* of the most female-identified areas, and *up* to those regarded more legitimate and prestigious for men.

Conclusion: Discrimination against Men

Both men and women who work in nontraditional occupations encounter discrimination, but the forms and consequences of this discrimination are very different. The interviews suggest that unlike "nontraditional" women workers, most of the discrimination and prejudice facing men in the "female professions" emanates from outside those professions. The men and women interviewed for the most part believed that men are given fair—if not preferential—treatment in hiring and promotion decisions, are accepted by supervisors and colleagues, and are well-integrated into the work place subculture. Indeed, subtle mechanisms seem to enhance men's position in these professions—a phenomenon I refer to as the "glass escalator effect."

The data lend strong support for Zimmer's (1988) critique of "gender neutral theory" (such as Kanter's [1977] theory of tokenism) in the study of occupational segregation. Zimmer argues that women's occupational inequality is more a consequence of sexist beliefs and practices embedded in the labor force than the effect of numerical underrepresentation per se. This study suggests that token status itself does not diminish men's occupational success. Men take their gender privilege with them when they enter predominantly female occupations; this translates into an advantage in spite of their numerical rarity.

This study indicates that the experience of tokenism is very different for men and women. Future research should examine how the experience of tokenism varies for members of different races and classes as well. For example, it is likely that informal work place mechanisms similar to the ones identified here promote the careers of token whites in predominantly black occupations. The crucial factor is the social status of the token's group—not their numerical rarity—that determines whether the token encounters a "glass ceiling" or a "glass escalator."

However, this study also found that many men encounter negative stereotypes from persons not directly involved in their professions. Men who enter these professions are often considered "failures," or sexual deviants. These stereotypes may be a major impediment to men who otherwise might consider careers in these occupations. Indeed, they are likely to be important factors whenever a member of a relatively high status group crosses over into a lower status occupation. However, to the extent that these stereotypes contribute to the "glass escalator effect" by channeling men into more "legitimate" (and higher paying) occupations, they are not discriminatory.

Women entering traditionally "male" professions also face negative stereotypes suggesting they are not "real women" (Epstein 1981; Lorber 1984; Spencer and Podmore 1987). However, these stereotypes do not seem to deter women to the same degree that they deter men from pursuing nontraditional professions. There is ample historical evidence that women flock to male-identified occupations once opportunities are available (Cohn 1985; Epstein 1988). Not so with men. Examples of occupations changing from predominantly female to predominantly male are very rare in our history. The few existing cases—such as medicine—suggest that redefinition of the occupations as appropriately "masculine" is necessary before men will consider joining them (Ehrenreich and English 1978).

Because different mechanisms maintain segregation in male- and female-dominated occupations, different approaches are needed to promote their integration. Policies intended to alter the sex composition of male-dominated occupations—such as affirmative action—make little sense when applied to the "female professions." For men, the major barriers to integration have little to do with their treatment once they decide to enter these fields. Rather, we need to address the social and cultural sanctions applied to men who do "women's work" which keep men from even considering these occupations.

One area where these cultural barriers are clearly evident is in the media's representation of men's occupations. Women working in traditionally male professions have achieved an unprecedented acceptance on popular television shows. Women are portrayed as doctors ("St. Elsewhere"), lawyers ("The Cosby Show," "L.A. Law"), architects ("Family Ties"), and police officers ("Cagney and Lacy"). But where are the male nurses, teachers and secretaries? Television rarely portrays men in nontraditional work roles, and when it does, that anomaly is made the central focus—and joke—of the program. A comedy series (1991–92) about a male elementary school teacher ("Drexell's Class") stars a lead character who *hates children*! Yet even this negative portrayal is exceptional. When a prime time hospital drama series ("St. Elsewhere") depicted a male orderly striving for upward mobility, the show's writers made him a "physician's assistant," not a nurse or nurse practitioner—the much more likely "real life" possibilities.

Presenting positive images of men in nontraditional careers can produce limited effects. A few social workers, for example, were first inspired to pursue their careers by George C. Scott, who played a social worker in the television drama series, "Eastside/Westside." But as a policy strategy to break down occupational segregation, changing media images of men is no panacea. The stereotypes that differentiate masculinity and femininity, and degrade that which is defined as feminine, are deeply entrenched in culture, social structure, and personality (Williams 1989). Nothing short of a revolution in cultural definitions of masculinity will effect the broad scale social transformation needed to achieve the complete occupational integration of men and women.

Of course, there are additional factors besides societal prejudice contributing to men's underrepresentation in female-dominated professions. Most notably, those men I interviewed mentioned as a deterrent the fact that these professions are all underpaid relative to comparable "male" occupations, and several suggested that instituting a "comparable worth" policy might attract more men. However, I am not convinced that improved salaries will substantially alter the sex composition of these professions unless the cultural stigma faced by men in these occupations diminishes. Occupational sex segregation is remarkably resilient, even in the face of devastating economic hardship. During the Great Depression of the 1930s, for example, "women's jobs" failed to attract sizable numbers of men (Blum 1991, 154). In her study of American Telephone and Telegraph (AT&T) workers, Epstein (1989) found that some men would rather suffer unemployment than accept relatively high paying "women's jobs" because of the damage to their identities this would cause. She quotes one unemployed man who refused to apply for a female-identified telephone operator job:

> I think if they offered me $1000 a week tax free, I wouldn't take that job. When I . . . see those guys sitting in there [in the telephone operating room], I wonder what's wrong with them. Are they pansies or what? (Epstein 1989, 577)

This is not to say that raising salaries would not affect the sex composition of these jobs. Rather, I am suggesting that wages are not the only—or perhaps even the major—impediment to men's entry into these jobs. Further research is needed to explore the ideological significance of the "woman's wage" for maintaining occupational stratification.[3]

At any rate, integrating men and women in the labor force requires more than dismantling barriers to women in male-dominated fields. Sex segregation is a two-way street. We must also confront and dismantle the barriers men face in predominantly female occupations. Men's experiences in these nontraditional occupations reveal just how culturally embedded the barriers are, and how far we have to travel before men and women attain true occupational and economic equality.

Notes

1. According to the U.S. Census, black men and women comprise 7 percent of all nurses and librarians, 11 percent of all elementary school teachers, and 19 percent of all social workers (calculated from U.S. Census 1980: Table 278, 1–197). The proportion of blacks in social work may be exaggerated by these statistics. The occupational definition of "social worker" used by the Census Bureau includes welfare workers and pardon and parole officers, who are not considered "professional" social workers by the National Association of Social Workers. A study by degreed professionals found that 89 percent of practitioners were white (Hardcastle 1987).

2. In April 1991, the Labor Department created a "Glass Ceiling Commission" to "conduct a thorough study of the underrepresentation of women and minorities in executive, management, and senior decision-making positions in business" (U.S. House of Representatives 1991, 20).

3. Alice Kessler-Harris argues that the lower pay of traditionally female occupations is symbolic of a patriarchal order that assumes female dependence on a male breadwinner. She writes that pay equity is fundamentally threatening to the "male worker's sense of self, pride, and masculinity" because it upsets his individual standing in the hierarchical ordering of the sexes (1990, 125). Thus, men's reluctance to enter these occupations may have less to do with the actual dollar amount recorded in their paychecks, and more to do with the damage that earning "a woman's wage" would wreak on their self-esteem in a society that privileges men. This conclusion is supported by the interview data.

CHAPTER 16

Black Mobility in White Corporations

UP THE CORPORATE LADDER BUT OUT ON A LIMB

Sharon M. Collins

More than 30 years of social and political pressure to diversify corporate personnel and management teams has resulted in more black managers but negligible gain for African American men in powerful decision-making jobs in corporate America. Against this backdrop, this paper asks if constraints on blacks' corporate progress are manufactured in the work process. Using in-depth career interviews with 76 black executives, I argue that the ability to achieve top jobs is shaped by a link between opportunity structure and human capital. The structure of black managerial achievement erodes black skills over time because of role constraints.

Spurred in part by threats of federal sanctions, white companies during the 1960s and 1970s incorporated a new echelon of college-educated blacks into previously closed managerial job and business-related professions (Farley 1984; Freeman 1981, 1976a, 1976b; Landry 1987). Indeed, the 1960s witnessed the reversal of a longstanding pattern of declining black-white income ratios with levels of education—and the ratio of black-to-white income rose most rapidly for managers. Employed black men, in particular, were in greater demand for prestigious occupations in the labor market. In 1960, only about 7 percent of non-white male college graduates were managers, compared with 18 percent of college-educated white men (Freeman 1976b). Between 1960 and 1970, the proportion of black male college graduates employed as managers increased almost twofold over the 1960 level (Freeman 1976b). And between 1970 and 1980, the number of black men holding executive, administrative, or managerial jobs increased each year at twice the rate of white men (Farley and Allen 1987).

Yet, even after more than 30 years of social and political pressure to diversify corporate manpower and management teams, the net result is more black managers but negligible gain for black men in the decision-making strongholds of white corporate America (Chicago Urban League 1977; Heidrick and Struggles 1979; Korn/Ferry 1986; Theodore and Taylor 1991). Despite gains in entry, African-Americans clearly stagnate in their climb up the managerial hierarchy, thereby failing to make inroads into key decision-making positions and in the racial redistribution of power.

Against a backdrop of sustained inequality in corporate job allocation, this paper asks whether constraints to blacks' corporate progress are manufactured in the work process. In the 1960s and 1970s, highly educated blacks experienced less discrimination in access to higher-paying corporate jobs, yet we know little about their careers. Nkomo and Cox (1990) examine macro-and micro-level variables related to job promotion; Kraiger and Ford (1985) focus on discrimination in performance evaluation; and others survey black managers' perceptions of corporate life (Jones 1986; Irons and Moore 1985). The responsibilities and assignments accorded black managers in the post-entry period are a crucial but neglected element for analysis.

This paper explores the problem of race and corporate mobility. It uses a unique data set: in-depth interviews with 76 of the most successful black executives employed in major Chicago-based white corporations in 1986. These black achievers in traditionally closed managerial occupations have had the greatest chance to enter into the higher echelons of organizations in functions tied to profitability. I explore the repercussions of a corporate division of labor on the career development of these managers.

Neoclassical economic theories and social structural explanations of race-based inequality in labor markets often are argued as oppositional insights. That is, human capital theory in economic literature and status attainment theory in sociology presume that economic progress among blacks is a color-blind function of supply-side characteristics such as education, ability, and individual preferences—not race conscious social forces and barriers. The lack of marketable skills, a dependent mentality, inferior education, and even relatively lower IQs are reasons for blacks' inability to gain parity with whites (Herrnstein and Murray 1994; Murray 1984; Smith and Welch 1983, 1986; Sowell 1983).

The opposing contention is that individuals' economic attainments are determined by structural aspects of the labor market. This alternate viewpoint attributes people's limited progress to the characteristics of their jobs (Doeringer and Piore 1971; Thurow 1975). Minorities and women, for example, fill occupational niches that are in decline or that do not lead to advancement (Ghiloni 1987; Kanter 1977; Reskin and Roos 1990). Consequently, powerful and prestigious jobs with career growth opportunities—managerial jobs, in particular—are much more likely to be filled by white men. In contrast, insights from my study of black managers in the white private sector cast social structure and human capital as interactive, not as mutually exclusive explanatory schemes.

In this paper, I illustrate how a link between opportunity structure and human capital shaped subjects' abilities to achieve top jobs. In general, I view the managerial division of labor as mediating human capital. Therefore, these factors interactively influence blacks' progress in executive arenas. First, I argue that Chicago corporations deployed highly educated black labor out of mainstream positions and into "racialized" jobs. These are jobs created or reoriented during the 1960s and 1970s to carry out pro-black governmental policies and mediate black-related issues for white-owned companies. Affirmative action, urban affairs, community relations, and purchasing jobs are examples. Next, I show the impact of filling these jobs on executives' upward mobility. Initially, these jobs annointed black job holders with positive status in a company, thus attracting black talent. Over time, however, this structure of opportunity under-developed the human capital that corporations value. Consequently, racialized jobs marginalized the job holder's skills and, thus, the job holder. Ultimately, occupants' probability of moving into, competing for, and/or performing in, corporate areas that lead to decision-making positions (that is, general management, sales/marketing, production, finance/accounting, and human resources) was greatly diminished.

The Study

I considered blacks to be "top executives" if: 1) they were employed in a banking institution and had a title of comptroller, trust officer, vice-president (excluding "assistant" vice president), president or chief officer; or 2) they were employed in a non-financial institution as department manager, director, vice president, or chief officer. In the mid-1980s, the respondents in this study held some of the more desirable and prestigious positions in Chicago's major corporations. About two-thirds (52) had the title of director or higher, including three chief officers, 30 vice presidents, and 19 unit directors. (The total includes three people with the title "manager" whose rank within the organization was equivalent to director.) The participants in this study were among the highest-ranking black executives in the country. Five of the executives interviewed were the highest-ranking blacks in corporations nationwide. Almost half (32) were among the highest-ranking blacks in a company's nationwide management structure.

To locate these managers, first I identified the 52 largest white corporations in Chicago using the *Chicago Reporter's* (1983, 1986) listing of industrials, utilities, retail companies, transportation companies, and banks. Second, I asked knowledgeable informants familiar with the white corporate community in Chicago to identify blacks who met the study criteria. These same informants also identified employees of the targeted companies who might be able to provide names of higher-level black officers. I then used snowball sampling to identify a total of 87 managers. Eleven people were not interviewed because they declined to participate, because of logistical problems, or because they did not meet my criteria. Using resumes respondents forwarded to me before the interview, I explored the characteristics of each executive's job, as well as each respondent's career development and promotional opportunities.

I distinguished two types of jobs held by blacks in white corporations: racialized and mainstream. A job was coded "racialized" when its description indicated an actual and/or symbolic connection to black communities, to black issues, or to civil rights agencies at any level of government. For example, one respondent was hired by the chief executive officer of a major retailer in 1968 specifically to eradicate discriminatory employment practices used in the personnel department. I coded this job "racialized" because it was designed to improve black opportunities in the company at a time when the federal government increasingly was requiring it.

In contrast, jobs in line and support areas that lack racial implications in a company were coded "mainstream." In this category, functions relate to constituencies, and neither explicit nor implicit connections to blacks could be found in the job description. A vice president and regional sales manager for a *Fortune* 500 company in the manufacturing and retail food industry provides an illustration of a career consisting of mainstream jobs. A *Fortune* 15 East Coast oil company hired this manager as a market researcher in 1961; his job involved marketing only to the total (predominantly white) consumer market, not to "special" (predominantly black) markets. He was not assigned to black territories as a salesman nor as a sales manager although, he said, "Those kinds of things even happen now [and once] happened a lot." This manager was not responsible for a predominantly black sales force, nor for sales and marketing to the black community when he managed geographical areas.

In this paper, the "mainstream" is the pipeline of line and support jobs leading to senior executive positions that oversee the strategic planning, human resource/personnel development, or production components of a company. For example, the manager just cited moved up the mainstream sales hierarchy from salesman to sales manager, from zone manager to district manager, from area manager to division manager and, finally, to his current position as a firm officer. Granted, the pipeline narrows as it moves upward, yet the flow of occupants into these jobs fills the executive vice president, senior vice president, group vice president, functional vice president, and corporate specialist slots that comprise company officers. The typical track to top jobs in major corporations is through profit-oriented positions, such as sales, operations, and finance or, to a lesser degree through personnel or public relations (Korn/Ferry 1990).

A Corporate Division of Labor

The corporate division of labor found among Chicago's top black executives is distinctly different than job patterns found among their white peers. In this study, African American executives with mainstream careers in the private sector stand out as the exception, not the rule. Only one-third (25) of the people I interviewed built careers that consisted entirely of mainstream jobs. On the other hand, 12 (16 percent) had one racialized job and about half (39) had two or more racialized jobs. One vice president and company director was a company ombudsman during the 1970s whose task was, he said, to "promote the visibility and good name" of the bank in the black community in Chicago. A second vice president built a career interspersed with black community relations jobs during the late 1960s and 1970s that, he said, "develop[ed] a good corporate citizenship image among blacks and . . . work[ed] with . . . local [black] agencies." A third vice president spent part of his tenure in an urban affairs job. He said:

> After the civil disorders, the riots . . . there was a tremendous movement . . . to have black [representation in the company]. Basically [my] job was to work with the [company] and come up with minority candidates.

To obtain a rough comparative illustration of black and white executive careers, I conducted an informal survey of top white executives by asking 20 CEOs of major Chicago private sector companies if they ever held affirmative action or urban affairs jobs. (I asked about these jobs specifically because they exemplify racialized jobs.) Only one had (or admitted having) a job in either of these areas. Some CEOs even seemed startled by the question. The CEO that had worked in urban affairs performed different tasks than those performed by my respondents. Although this man represented the company on several city-wide committees to improve race relations, his job, unlike the black executives I interviewed, was a part-time, temporary assignment, not a full-time, permanent position. The results of my informal survey suggest that—among the managerial elite in Chicago—blacks are likely to have held racialized jobs, but whites are not.

Disparate career patterns are not attributable to educational differences. Indeed, African American respondents' educational level closely parallel that of white male senior-level executives in 1986. Ninety-four percent of top executives in *Fortune* 500 companies surveyed by Korn/Ferry (1986) had bachelors' degrees, and 42 percent had graduate degrees. Eighty-nine percent of respondents in my study had at least a bachelor's degree when they entered the private sector. Over one-third (38 percent) earned advanced degrees. Moreover, their level of education is well above the median level of about one year of college for salaried male managers in 1960 and in 1970 (U.S. Bureau of Census 1960, 1973). In addition, slightly more than one-half of the black graduates I interviewed received their college degrees from predominantly white institutions.

Career differences are not extensions of respondents' ports of entry into the private sector. Almost one-half of 45 people who filled affirmative action and urban affairs jobs started in the corporate mainstream with line positions. Therefore, black but not white managerial careers reflect a race conscious interaction with skill and education that tracked black managers into administrative jobs that emerged during the 1960s and 1970s.

The career of one man, who was succeeding in his company but then moved into an urban affairs position, exemplifies this interaction between race and career tracking. Between 1964 and 1967 this man rapidly ascended through a series of supervisory and store management slots to become an area supervisor, a middle management position. At 23, his annual salary was more than doubled by a performance-based bonus. Yet, in the midst of this mainstream success (i.e., succeeding in the route typically traveled by the company's top executives), this man was asked to create an urban affairs program. The circumstances that led to this request were relatively straightforward: Civil rights activists had confronted the company with specific demands backed by the threat of a nationwide boycott; and the company viewed blacks as a sizeable proportion of its customer base. The respondent said, "Basically [my] job was to work with the licensee department and [come] up with minority candidates around the country to become [store owners]." After completing a strenuous series of meetings with the company's top executives—which included the head of personnel, a senior vice president, the head of licensing, the corporate legal council, and finally, the company president—he was offered, and he accepted, the assignment.

Within this operations-driven corporation, a manager with demonstrated talent for business operations generally would be considered a serious contender for a top-level mainstream position. From this perspective, slotting this man in an urban affairs job appears to be a frivolous use of talent. But in 1968, no other blacks worked at the company's corporate offices (save for one black janitor) and the company was vulnerable to racial protest. Deploying a black middle-level manager, a known commodity, into corporate urban affairs was a rational business decision. Indeed, a white vice president of personnel who worked in a major Chicago firm during the 1960s and 1970s noted that top management often filled newly created affirmative action positions with their best workers. He explained that this strategy signalled to the rank and file workers the seriousness of a company's commitment. Senior corporate managers believed that transferring an experienced black line manager into affirmative action would increase the credibility of this collateral role and enhance its effectiveness.

Black social and political unrest infused black managerial capacities with race-related purposes (Collins 1997). African Americans moved into urban affairs, affirmative action, and other racialized management jobs that required them to interact predominantly with black community organizations and/or to help white companies recruit black labor. A 53-year-old company director, who began his private sector managerial career in operations in a retail company, was deployed to set up the equal employment opportunity function for the company. He recalled that the perquisites accompanying the job were "very attractive [and] that was the place for us [blacks] to be."

Indeed, other occupants of affirmative action and urban affairs jobs who were recruited from mainstream line areas commented that black-oriented jobs appeared to be a route where talented blacks could advance rapidly. Senior-level white management, usually either senior vice presidents or chief executive officers, personally solicited 12 of the 22 recruits (55 percent) from the mainstream. Eleven (50 percent) were given salary increases, more prestigious job titles, and promises of future rewards. Nine people turned down the first attempt at recruitment because they evaluated the job to be a dead end, despite high pay and elevated titles, and were approached a second time by top management. A director of affirmative action and diversity took the job initially because, he said, "I remember the CEO saying, 'we want you to take this beautiful job. It's going to pay you all this money. It's going to make you a star.'"

Racialized Division of Labor and Mobility

What impact did this allocative process have on upward mobility in white corporations? To compare the advancement associated with racialized and mainstream careers, I selected 64 respondents employed in the white private sector at least since 1972 to construct a career typology.[1] Three types of managerial careers—mainstream, mixed, and racialized—emerged, based on the jobs that these executives held. Respondents having no racialized jobs in their careers were coded as having mainstream careers (24 of 64). Respondents whose careers incorporated at least one, but not a majority, of racialized jobs were coded as having mixed careers (22 of 64), the careers of those with a majority of racialized jobs were coded as racialized (18 of 64).

LOWERED JOB CEILINGS

By the mid-1980s, racialized respondents had advanced less than respondents in main-stream careers. The top executives (i.e., chief officers and senior vice presidents) spent most of their careers in mainstream areas. There was little difference in the executive job titles associated with mixed and mainstream careers, possibly because the vast majority of mixed careers had only one or two racialized jobs in them.

In contrast, 80 percent of racialized careers terminated with director or manager titles. Only 38 percent of the mainstream careers, and 46 percent of mixed careers terminated with those titles. Not one manager in a racialized career progressed above vice president.

Those who stayed in racialized jobs were ambitious people who saw themselves as doing the best they could, given blacks' historically limited job possibilities in white companies. One equal employment opportunity manager had post-graduate work in physics and engineering. He had been with the company eight years when the employee relations director approached him to set up the company's first affirmative action program. This man accepted the offer because, he said, "I wanted to get into management. That was the first and only opportunity that I felt I was going to get." This executive weighed the job's perquisites against the void in managerial opportunities for blacks in white firms. Racialized managerial positions appeared to be a way to sidestep the career stagnation common among the handful of blacks who previously attained management roles but remained trapped in low-level positions. In the 1970s, such jobs seemed to offer faster mobility, greater freedom and authority, and higher visibility and access to white corporate power brokers than mainstream jobs.

I asked an affirmative action director for a major retail company in Chicago if he ever tried to move back into the mainstream after he took on equal employment opportunity functions. To my surprise he said that he turned down a buyer's job with his first employer. He said, "I was stubborn at that point. No, I didn't want that." Given that buyers were key people in that organization and that the job was a stepping stone to higher-paying positions, his refusal signals the attractiveness of racialized positions in companies in the early 1970s. He said,

> Remember now, this [equal opportunity] stuff was exciting and there's a trap that you get into. Those of us who are in this kind of area talk about it all the time. It's kind of a golden handcuffs trap. We used to go on the convention circuit around the country . . . the Urban League and the NAACP, promoting our individual corporations. We were visible. We were representing the company. We had big budgets. I mean, you know, you go to every convention. And [you can] get yourself two or three suites and entertain all the delegates. You could spend $15,000 or $20,000 at a convention. I never had that kind of money to spend, to sign a check, so it was very attractive.

The economic rewards and social status that accompanied racialized positions were unimaginable luxuries to blacks—in this or any employment sector—in the years preceding federal legislation. With the benefit of hindsight, the affirmative action director explained:

> I believe that had I stayed in operations [I would have] continued to move up and that's where the clout is. But the opportunity just wasn't there [for blacks] when I started with that company.

After a slight pause he added, somewhat ruefully, "things changed and it is now."

Only four of 18 managers with racialized careers (22 percent) were the highest ranking black executive in a company's Chicago location. In contrast, 31 of 46 managers who had a majority of mainstream functions in their careers (72 percent) were the highest-ranking black executive in a Chicago company. Acknowledging advancement limitations associated with racialized jobs, respondents alternately described them as "dead end jobs [that had] no power," "nigger jobs," and "money-using" versus "money producing" jobs. The affirmative action director quoted above said that creating and administering the affirmative action function for his company was a misstep in his career:

> If I had to go back and do it all over again, I would not stay in affirmative action. Them that brings in the dollars is where the most opportunity is. I advise my sons . . . stay out of the staff functions, although those functions are very necessary.

He went on to name people who took different routes, and who he viewed—somewhat wistfully—as "making it."

Not coincidentally, a manager's position in the corporate division of labor in 1986 coincided with his level of optimism about his future in a company (see Kanter 1977, 135). About three-quarters of mainstream (19 of 26) but less than one-quarter of racialized respondents (4 of 20) believed in 1986 that their chances for a promotion or a lateral move leading to promotion in the company were "good" or "very good." Respondents in racialized careers in 1986 reported that they were at the end of their career ladders in white companies. Sixty-five percent (13 of 20) said there would be no additional moves for them in the company, neither lateral nor promotional. Moreover, their pessimism extended to their perceptions of their opportunities for upward mobility on the open job market. The director of affirmative action quoted above summarized this shared perception of future mobility: "ascension for me is over."

The white executive elite I interviewed informally shared the opinion that African-American managers in racialized jobs were "out of the mix," in other words, not in the running for top jobs in a company. The assessment of each group—black and white—is not surprising, because racialized jobs are predominantly support positions, although these jobs can be found in sales and operations areas.[2] White executives, in general, view support functions as one of the worst routes to top jobs in a company (Korn/Ferry 1990). Nkomo and Cox (1990) indicate line positions play a highly significant positive role in individuals' promotion success. Support jobs are less desirable than line jobs because they lack influence and have shorter and more limited chains of career opportunities (Kanter 1977). I suggest further that the chain of opportunity becomes even shorter when linked to a job with racial purposes. These jobs not only impose relatively lower career ceilings, they underdevelop the talents and skills that corporations value, and therefore marginalize the job holder.

LIMITED SKILL DEVELOPMENT

Pressures placed on companies by federal government legislation and by protests in urban black communities made racialized jobs valuable to companies. In placating blacks and buffering corporations from racial turmoil, racialized jobs were highly unstructured; employees handled new and unpredictable contingencies. More than 80 percent of first racialized jobs were created when the respondents filled them. Ultimately, however, this managerial division of labor undermined the development of black human capital. As job content evolved, racialized jobs became routine work centered on a narrow set of administrative tasks extracted from generalist personnel functions. One manager noted that his job in the 1970s involved recruiting blacks, but not whites, into a company. Another mentioned the job was essentially "[black] number counting." A third man said the company promoted him and increased his salary because he was serving a function. He admitted he was aware, even then, that his future in the company might be limited:

> You have a little stepladder . . . a logical progression [of personnel functions] you have to go through if you are to ever become a personnel director. I wasn't doing any of that. As far as I could see, the company wanted black folks to be my only responsibility.

The narrowness of the jobs' routines limited—not broadened—these people's development of knowledge and skills. An executive for a clothing manufacturer and retailer made this clear when he summarized his experience:

> [The company] sent me to Chicago for a week long workshop on affirmative action. In that one week I learned all I needed to know about affirmative action, and I haven't learned much since. It's the kind of field that nothing, well, a few laws might change, but the concept doesn't. You don't branch out. There's nothing, oh, now how can I explain it? There's not a lot of specialties . . . in affirmative action. You deal with 6 or 7 basic laws, or regulations and . . . once you know those there's not an awful lot more to learn. I'm serious about it. Since 1965 or 1972, I don't think I've learned very much more.

Racialized managers in the 1960s and 1970s initially were rewarded with mobility in their companies. Ultimately, however, they required little or no company investment for job preparation and training. This racialized structure of mobility, therefore, created and solidified career ceilings through a cumulative work experience. Although managers' status elevated when their departments, titles, and salaries grew, respondents weren't trained in other areas. When I asked managers for job descriptions associated with various promotions, one affirmative action manager in a segregated career dismissed the question, indicating that he was "essentially doing the same thing" in each affirmative action job, although the scope of each job and his title and grade-level changed. His report distinctly contrasts with those of respondents who were promoted in mainstream personnel. In the case of personnel executives, at least six distinct components of job experience were clearly delineated— including employee relations, employment, compensation and benefits, and labor relations.

In contrast, people who ascended racialized career ladders became more specialized and increasingly secluded from generalist management areas. One manager summarized the gulf between mainstream and racialized personnel in the following way:

> If you stay in affirmative action, when you go looking for a job you're going to be seen as the affirmative action person. And personnel jobs are bigger than that.

Narrowly defined racialized jobs rely on interpersonal skills and external relationships without building administrative skills and internal support networks important to advancement. For example, a manager in a manufacturing company described his urban affairs job as if he were an ambassador-at-large:

> I just moved about. Traveled. Everything was coming out of the community and I was there. I'd make 10, sometimes 12, meetings [in the black community] a day.

An executive in the food industry described his affirmative action job in a strikingly similar way:

> I spent most of my time in the [black] community trying to . . . let people know that there were jobs and positions available in this company. I did a lot of speaking with community groups.

An executive in a communications firm said, "Mostly I worked with local community agencies to get the word out that there were opportunities [in the company]."

A director of urban affairs linked his company with black civil rights and social service organizations and represented it in black-dominated settings. This college-educated man moved out of sales and became skilled at brokering the interest of his company, successfully "absorbing" the tensions between white companies and urban black constituencies. He said that in 1971:

> [My role was to] make [the company] look good. I did what they needed done to look good in the community. They utilized me in that fashion. For eleven years I was just their spook who sat by the door, and I understood that. Certainly I was, and I charged them well for it.

MARGINALIZED JOB HOLDERS

The structure of upward mobility became restrictive so that success in segregated areas prolonged these managers' career segregation. Prolonged career segregation, in turn, further undermined these executives' value in mainstream corporate functions. Promoting respondents in place created and solidified career barriers by conferring information about respondents' abilities. That is, racialized human capital became a factor in marginalizing respondents by limiting their value in mainstream corporate functions. People in segregated careers faced two alternatives for enhancing their chances for upward mobility: (1) to laterally move into an entirely different corporate area associated with mainstream planning, production, or human resources administration, or (2) to move laterally to the mainstream component of the racialized area (e.g., from community relations to public relations). People who specialized in affirmative action, community relations, and other race-related jobs were stymied in both routes by real or perceived limits to their usefulness in mainstream fields.

When an affirmative action manager (and one-time comptroller) tried to re-enter the corporate mainstream, she found she was locked into her racialized niche at each turn. She said:

> I tried to negotiate myself out [of affirmative action]. There didn't seem to be a lot of . . . future. I wanted to try to get back into merchandising at that point. Or go back into comptrolling or to go somewhere else in personnel. You know nothing ever came out of it. I even took a special class . . . to get accreditation in personnel, as a personnel generalist. Which I completed. [It] had absolutely no effect on me going anywhere. . . . It got to where the [job] level and the salary level to go and change fields is too high . . . to [be] able to sell me to someone else. The likelihood of me going outside of [affirmative action] at this point is pretty well zero.

The trade-off to rising in companies in racialized jobs that required specialized skills and external networks was that managers became cut off from the internal networks and skill-building that would enable them to move into, and then move up in, the corporation's job mainstream.

A community relations manager for a major electronics corporation—when noting that his company's commitment to urban affairs programs for blacks began to decrease noticeably in the 1980s—also illustrates this trade-off. Observing, as he put it, the "handwriting on the wall," he made multiple attempts to move out of his dissolving niche in the company and into a mainstream production area. He first attempted to get into production, and next into general administrative services. Describing these attempts he said:

> I was just not able to make that break. I talked to [people] in various divisions that I was interested in, and I got the lip service that they would keep [me] in mind if something opened up. As it happened, that just did not develop. I can never remember being approached by anyone. Nothing

[happened]—that I can really hang [onto] as an offer. People would ask, "have you ever run a profit and loss operation?"

Finally, he described himself as taking "hat in hand" and approaching senior management in 1982 to request duties he knew to be available in a general administrative area. He said:

> Frankly, this was an attempt to seize an opportunity. This time I went and I asked for a [new assignment]. We had some retirement within the company and some reorganization. I saw an opportunity to help myself. The urban affairs was shrinking. A number of jobs we created [in urban affairs] were completely eliminated. It just happened that the opportunity [to pick up administrative services] was there. It had a significant dollar budget and profit and loss opportunity . . . it was concrete and useful. So I asked for it.

Yet he was only temporarily successful in his attempt to exchange urban affairs for a more stable assignment in administrative services. One year later he was invited to resign from the company because of poor performance.

The story told by a second urban affairs manager—who tried a move to warehouse distribution in a retail company—reveals similar constraints. This manager was a department director, a position that was targeted to be cut from the company. This manager also discovered that the trade-off for rising in a company in urban affairs was an inability to shift into any mainstream corporate function. Here is his assessment:

> I was too old to do what you had to do to compete. . . . I was competing with 21 and 22 year olds to get into the system. They couldn't charge [my salary] to a store and have me doing the same thing the others [were] doing [for much less money]. You need the ground level experience. When I should have gotten it, I was busy running an affirmative action department.

Indeed, from a practical standpoint, retraining this individual would not reap a long-term benefit because of his age. Consequently, I asked this manager why he didn't move laterally into mainstream public relations, an area (apparently) he was more qualified to pursue. He responded:

> I thought about it very seriously. I wondered where I was going with the system. It came up quite often. I talked about it when first I accepted this job. And at the end. They told me, "We don't know. We'll have to get back to you." They never did.

That his superiors never got back to him "at the end" may reflect the fact that the organization needed him precisely where he was placed. Or, it may result from the fact that he lacked a skill base and/or his superiors perceived that his skills differed from those managers who had moved up the ladder in generalized public relations. The latter point is highlighted by the comments of a manager who failed in his attempt to transfer into compensation and benefits—precisely because his past concentration in affirmative action made him under-qualified for the job. He explained:

> I moved over . . . as director. Now, mind you, I'm going from a corporate
> [affirmative action] job . . . to . . . compensation and benefits. I told the
> chairman of the company I didn't have any experience in that field. I might
> not be his man.

In short, because of limited skills and career "track records," people who were concentrated in racialized roles lacked the human capital to compete in mainstream company areas. The same skills that once made them valuable now constrained them.

Discussion

Rather than viewing human capital and structure as mutually exclusive explanatory variables, these interviews illustrate that the organization of managerial job assignments and job allocation create human capital deficits. Human capital and the structure of management occupations are not independent phenomena; they interact to mediate labor market outcomes. In the case of black managers, human capital explains the existence of a supply of black labor that companies could draw from when confronted with governmental anti-bias pressures in the 1960s and 1970s. Yet, although human capital was a necessary ingredient for entry and initial job attainments, it does not sufficiently explain who competes for and succeeds in attaining organization power. For black managers, the structure of opportunities associated with the managerial assignments looms large as an additional explanatory variable. The relationship between human capital is circular: A race-based system of job allocation creates a deficit in on-the-job training and experience, and this structurally imposed deficit, in turn, leads to human capital deficits that create barriers to black advancement.

The talent and training that these managers initially brought to their occupations were filtered through a peripheral system of jobs and cumulative work experience. As respondents moved into—and then up through—racialized management assignments, they were locked out from mainstream management jobs. The devaluation of their abilities eventually constrained their progress in executive arenas.

The observations derived from this study have several implications. The first concerns the level of analysis. Studies that rely only on aggregate level data cannot explain black progress, or the lack of progress, without a supplementary closer look at the jobs African Americans hold. This study shows that individual skill and talent is embedded in, and brought forth by, a sequence of assignments in an ongoing work process. Both Althauser (1975, 143) and Freeman (1976b, 146) have commented on this. Althauser suggests the need to focus on characteristics of the jobs black men hold, just as attention is now given to the job holders' characteristics. Freeman further notes that the degree to which blacks are in token (i.e., black-related) jobs, the significance of blacks' gains may be overstated. More recently, Bielby and Baron (1984, 1986) show that analyses that use detailed occupational categories reveal more occupational segregation. Yet, there are few case studies on black professional and managerial careers.

The second implication concerns the more abstract problem of how inequality is manufactured. To the extent that blacks occupy jobs cut off from core company goals, they are held back from core skill development. The interaction between an individual and the work s/he does can evolve so that a worker matures or evolves in such a way that the worker is taken out of the running. When viewed through the lens of my analysis, the often noted—but rarely explored—high concentration of blacks in corporate support implies a process of deskilling highly-educated blacks through the absence of on-the-job profit-centered work experiences. How such a concentration occurred is a critical research question regarding the status of blacks in white collar occupations. In this study, the black managerial vanguard entering the white private sector was eased out of the running for top executive jobs via racialized careers because of a mix of corporate pressure, career naivete, and black's perceptions of race-related corporate barriers (Collins 1977).

Human capital and structural explanations of what influences black achievement generally correspond to functionalist and conflict perspectives in sociology. By extension, therefore, findings from this study are nested in a broad paradigm of inequality. Using a conflict perspective, career construction can be viewed as part of a process of social closure to defend the existing advantage of white managers (see Tomaskovic-Devey 1993). This idea is similar to Reskin and Roos's (1987) proposal that occupational sex segregation is best understood within the broader conceptual framework of status hierarchies. The corporate role in the allocation of jobs—and the assessment of their value—was not a function of objective or impersonal supply characteristics, but of a race-conscious employment discrimination. It is not clear that the subsequent deskilling of a black cohort depressed their wages, as Braverman (1973) suggested. Rather, this deskilling served a more pressing purpose. The problem for white corporate elites was how to incorporate protected groups of minorities while minimizing their impact on organizational culture and structure. The creation and allocation of racialized jobs was an efficient way to meet both goals. These jobs appeased governmental legislation and black demands for more economic resources, while reducing the threat of increased competition for managerial power in organizations along racial lines. Initially, racialized jobs had attractive characteristics that suggested they were important to a company—faster mobility, greater freedom, and high visibility to white power brokers, but over time, racialized functions became routinized and devalued. Ultimately, the peculiar evolution during the 1960s and 1970s of careers documented in this study diminished the black executive pool in Chicago corporations that could compete to manage mainstream units in the 1980s and beyond. Consequently, many respondents over the last three decades did not—and could not—blossom into black executives in powerful decision making roles.

Notes

1. I selected the base year 1972 because it takes about 15 to 20 years to reach upper management positions in the major companies in the non-financial sector of Chicago (Chicago Urban League 1977).

2. Sales functions involved helping white corporations orient products' positive images to black consumers. People in operations took on racialized functions when managing a predominantly black workforce and mediating black-white relationships in racially volatile employment settings.

CHAPTER 17

Gender and Labor in Asian Immigrant Families

Yen Le Espiritu

This article explores the effects of employment patterns on gender relations among contemporary Asian immigrants. The existing data on Asian immigrant salaried professionals, self-employed entrepreneurs, and wage laborers suggest that economic constraints and opportunities have reconfigured gender relations within contemporary Asian America society. The patriarchal authority of Asian immigrant men, particularly those of the working class, has been challenged due to the social and economic losses that they suffered in their transition to the status of men of color in the United States. On the other hand, the recent growth of female-intensive industries—and the racist and sexist "preference" for the labor of immigrant women—has enhanced women's employability over that of some men. In all three groups, however, Asian women's ability to transform patriarchal family relations is often constrained by their social positions as racially subordinate women in U.S. society.

Through the process of migration and settlement, patriarchal relations undergo continual negotiation as women and men rebuild their lives in the new country. An important task in the study of immigration has been to examine this reconfiguration of gender relations. Central to the reconfiguration of gender hierarchies is the change in immigrant women's and men's relative positions of power and status in the country of settlement. Theoretically, migration may improve women's social position if it leads to increased participation in wage employment, more control over earnings, and greater participation in family decision making (Pessar 1984). Alternatively, migration may leave gender asymmetries largely unchanged even though certain dimensions of gender inequalities are modified (Curtis 1986). The existing literature on migration and changing gender relations suggests contradictory outcomes whereby the position of immigrant women is improved in some domains even as it is eroded in others (Hondagneu-Sotelo 1994; Morokvasic 1984; Tienda and Booth 1991).

This article is a first attempt to survey the field of contemporary Asian immigrants and the effects of employment patterns on gender relations. My review indicates that the growth of female-intensive industries in the United States—and the corresponding preference for racialized and female labor—has enhanced the employability of some Asian immigrant women over that of their male counterparts and positioned them as coproviders, if not primary providers, for their families. The existing data also suggest that gender relations are experienced differently in different structural occupational locations. In contrast to the largely unskilled immigrant population of the pre-World War II period, today's Asian immigrants include not only low-wage service sector workers but also significant numbers of white-collar professionals. A large number of immigrants have also turned to self-employment (Ong and Hee 1994). Given this occupational diversity, I divide the following discussion into three occupational categories and examine gender issues within each group: the salaried professionals, the self-employed entrepreneurs, and the wage laborers.[1] Although changes in gender relations have been slow and uneven in each of these three groups, the existing data indicate that men's dependence on the economic and social resources of women is most pronounced among the wage laborers. In all three groups, however, Asian women's ability to transform patriarchal family relations is often constrained by their social position as racially subordinated women in U.S. society.

As a review of existing works, this article reflects the gaps in the field. Overall, most studies of contemporary Asian immigrants have focused more on the issues of economic adaptation than on the effects of employment patterns on gender relations. Because there is still little information on the connections between work and home life—particularly among the salaried professionals—the following discussion on gender relations among contemporary Asian immigrants is at times necessarily exploratory.

Immigration Laws, Labor Needs, and Changing Gender Composition

Asian Americans' lives have been fundamentally shaped by the legal exclusions of 1882, 1917, 1924, and 1934, and by the liberalization laws of 1965.[2] Exclusion laws restricted Asian immigration to the United States, skewed the sex ratio of the early communities so that men were disproportionately represented, and truncated the development of conjugal families. The 1965 Immigration Act equalized immigration rights for all nationalities. No longer constrained by exclusion laws, Asian immigrants began coming in much larger numbers than ever before. In the period from 1971 to 1990, approximately 855,500 Filipinos, 610,800 Koreans, and 576,100 Chinese entered the United States (U.S. Bureau of the Census 1992). Moreover, with the collapse of U.S.-backed governments in South Vietnam, Laos, and Cambodia in 1975, more than one million escapees from these countries have resettled in the United States. As a consequence, in the 1980s, Asia was the largest source of U.S. legal immigrants, accounting for 40% to 47% of the total influx (Min 1995b, 12).[3] In 1990, 66% of Asians in the United States were foreign born (U.S. Bureau of the Census 1993, Figure 3).

Whereas pre-World War II immigration from Asia was composed mostly of men, the contemporary flow is dominated by women. Women comprise the clear majority among U.S. immigrants from nations in Asia but also from those in Central and

South America, the Caribbean, and Europe (Donato 1992). Between 1975 and 1980, women (20 years and older) constituted more than 50% of the immigrants from China, Burma, Indonesia, Taiwan, Hong Kong, Malaysia, the Philippines, Korea, Japan, and Thailand (Donato 1992). The dual goals of the 1965 Immigration Act—to facilitate family reunification and, secondarily, to admit workers with special job skills—have produced a female-dominated flow. Since 1965, most visas have been allocated to relatives of U.S. residents. Women who came as wives, daughters, or mothers of U.S. permanent residents and citizens comprise the primary component of change (Donato 1992, 164). The dominance of women immigrants also reflects the growth of female-intensive industries in the United States, particularly in the service, health care, microelectronics, and apparel-manufacturing industries (Clement and Myles 1994, 26). Of all women in the United States, Asian immigrant women have recorded the highest rate of labor force participation (Gardner, Robey, and Smith 1985). In 1980, among married immigrant women between 25 and 64 years of age, 61% of Korean women, 65% of Chinese women, and 83% of Filipino women were in the labor force (Duleep and Sanders 1993). In 1990, Asian women had a slightly higher labor force participation rate than all women, 60% to 57% respectively (U.S. Bureau of the Census 1993, Figure 6).

Economic Diversity among Contemporary Asian Immigrants

Relative to earlier historical periods, the employment pattern of today's Asian Americans is considerably more varied, a result of both immigration and a changing structure of opportunity. During the first half of the 20th century, Asians were concentrated at the bottom of the economic ladder—restricted to retailing, food service, menial service, and agricultural occupations. After World War II, economic opportunities improved but not sufficiently for educated Asian Americans to achieve parity. In the post-1965 era, the economic status of Asian Americans has bifurcated, showing some great improvements but also persistent problems. The 1965 Immigration Act and a restructuring of the economy brought a large number of low-skilled and highly educated Asians to this country, creating a bimodalism (Ong and Hee 1994). [. . .] Asian Americans were overrepresented in the well-paid, educated, white-collar sector of the workforce and in the lower paying service and manufacturing jobs. This bimodalism is most evident among Chinese men: although 24% of Chinese men were professionals in 1990, another 19% were in service jobs.

Asian professional immigrants are overrepresented as scientists, engineers, and health care professionals in the United States. In 1990, Asians were 3% of the U.S. total population but accounted for close to 7% of the scientist and engineer workforce. Their greatest presence was among engineers with doctorate degrees, comprising more than one fifth of this group in 1980 and in 1990 (Ong and Blumenberg 1994, 169). Although Asian immigrant men dominated the fields of engineering, mathematics, and computer science, Asian immigrant women were also overrepresented in these traditionally male-dominated professions. In 1990, Asian women accounted for 5% of all female college graduates in the U.S. labor force but 10% to 15% of engineers and architects, computer scientists, and researchers in the hard sciences (Rong and Preissle 1997, 279–280).

In the field of health care, two thirds of foreign nurses and 60% of foreign doctors admitted to the United States during the fiscal years 1988 to 1990 were from Asia (Kanjanapan 1995, 18). Today, Asian immigrants represent nearly a quarter of the health care providers in public hospitals in major U.S. metropolitan areas (Ong and Azores 1994a, 139). Of the 55,400 Asian American nurses registered in 1990, 90% were foreign born (Rong and Preissle 1997, 279–280). The Philippines is the largest supplier of health professionals to the United States, sending nearly 25,000 nurses to this country between 1966 and 1985 and another 10,000 between 1989 and 1991 (Ong and Azores 1994a, 154). Due to the dominance of nurses, Filipinas are more likely than other women and than Filipino men to be in professional jobs. [. . .] In 1990, 20% of Filipino women but only 12% of Filipino men had professional occupations.

Responding to limited job opportunities, particularly for the highly educated, a large number of Asian Americans have also turned to self-employment. Asian immigrants are much more likely than their native-born counterparts to be entrepreneurs: In 1990, 85% of the Asian American self-employed population were immigrants (Ong and Hee 1994, 51). Korean immigrants have the highest self-employment rate of any minority and immigrant group (Light and Bonacich 1986). A 1986 survey showed that 45% of Korean immigrants in Los Angeles and Orange counties were self-employed. A survey conducted in New York City revealed an even higher self-employment rate of more than 50% (Min 1996, 48). Because another 30% of Korean immigrants work in the Korean ethnic market, the vast majority of the Korean workforce—three out of four Korean workers—is segregated in the Korean ethnic economy either as business owners or as employees of coethnic businesses (Min 1998, 17). The problems of underemployment, misemployment, and discrimination in the U.S. labor market have turned many educated and professional Korean immigrants toward self-employment (Min 1995a, 209). Based on a 1988 survey, nearly half of the Korean male entrepreneurs had completed college (Fawcett and Gardner 1994, 220).

Although some Asian immigrants constitute "brain drain" workers and self-employed entrepreneurs, others labor in peripheral and labor-intensive industries. The typical pattern of a dual-worker family is a husband who works as a waiter, cook, janitor, or store helper and a wife who is employed in a garment shop or on an assembly line. In a study conducted by the Asian Immigrant Women Advocates (AIWA), 93% of the 166 seamstresses surveyed in the San Francisco-Oakland Bay Area listed their husbands' jobs as unskilled or semiskilled, including waiter, bus boy, gardener, day laborer, and the like (Louie 1992, 9). Most disadvantaged male immigrants can get jobs only in ethnic businesses in which wages are low but in which only simple English is required (Chen 1992, 103). On the other hand, since the late 1960s, the United States has generated a significant number of sector service occupations—paid domestic work, child care, garment and electronic assembly—that rely primarily on female immigrant workers (Hondagneu-Sotelo 1994, 186–187). Due to the perceived vulnerability of their class, gender, ethnicity, and immigration status, Asian immigrant women—and other immigrant women of color—have been heavily recruited to toil in these low-wage industries. [. . .]Asian women of all ethnic groups were much more likely than Asian men to be in administrative support and service jobs.

Gender Relations among Salaried Professionals

Although the large presence of Asian professional workers is now well documented, we still have little information on the connections between work and home life—between the public and private spheres—of this population. The available case studies suggest greater male involvement in household labor in these families. In a study of Taiwan immigrants in New York, Hsiang-Shui Chen reports that the degree of husbands' participation in household labor varied considerably along class lines, with men in the professional class doing a greater share than men in the working and small-business classes (1992, 77). Although women still performed most of the household labor, men helped with vacuuming, disposing of garbage, laundry, dishwashing, and bathroom cleaning. In a survey of Korean immigrant families in New York, Pyong Gap Min found a similar pattern: younger, professional husbands undertook more housework than did men in other occupational categories, although their wives still did the lion's share (1998, 42–43). Professional couples of other racial-ethnic groups also seem to enjoy more gender equality. For example, Beatriz M. Pesquera (1993, 194) reports that Chicano "professional men married to professional women did a greater share than most other men." This more equitable household division of labor can be attributed to the lack of a substantial earning gap between professional men and women, the demands of the women's careers, and the women's ability to pressure their husbands into doing their share of the household chores (Hondagneu-Sotelo 1994; Hood 1983; Kibria 1993; Pesquera 1993). On the other hand, Chen (1992), Min (1998), and Pesquera (1993) all conclude that women in professional families still perform more of the household labor than their husbands do. Moreover, Pesquera reports that, for the most part, the only way women have altered the distribution of household labor has been through conflict and confrontation, suggesting that ideologically most men continue to view housework as women's work (1993, 185). These three case studies remind us that professional women, like most other working women, have to juggle full-time work outside the home with the responsibilities of child care and housework. This burden is magnified for professional women because most tend to live in largely White, suburban neighborhoods where they have little or no access to the women's social networks that exist in highly connected ethnic communities (Glenn 1986, 41; Kibria 1993).

Given the shortage of medical personnel in the United States, particularly in the inner cities and in rural areas, Asian women health professionals may be in a relatively strong position to modify traditional patriarchy. First, as a much sought-after group among U.S. immigrants, Asian women health professionals can enter the United States as the principal immigrants (Espiritu 1995, 21). This means that unmarried women can immigrate on their own accord, and married women can enter as the primary immigrants, with their husbands and children following as dependents. My field research of Filipino American families in San Diego suggests that a female-first migration stream, especially when the women are married, has enormous ramifications for both family relations and domestic roles. For example, when Joey Laguda's mother, a Filipina medical technologist, entered the country in 1965, she carried the primary immigrant status and sponsored Joey's father and two other sons as her dependents. Joey describes the downward occupational shift that his father experienced on immigrating to the United States: "My father had graduated in the Philippines with a bachelor's degree in criminology but couldn't get a job as a police officer here because he was not a U.S. citizen. So he only worked blue-collar jobs" (Espiritu 1995, 181). The experience of Joey's father suggests that Asian men who immigrate as their wives' dependents often experience downward occupational mobility in the United States, while their wives maintain their professional status. The same pattern exists among Korean immigrant families in New York: while Korean nurses hold stable jobs, many of their educated husbands are unemployed or underemployed (Min 1998, 52).

Moreover, given the long hours and the graveyard shifts that typify a nurse's work schedule, many husbands have had to assume more child care and other household responsibilities in their wives' absences. A survey of Filipino nurses in Los Angeles County reveals that these women, to increase their incomes, tend to work double shifts or in the higher paying evening and night shifts (Ong and Azores 1994b, 183–184). In her research on shift work and dual-earner spouses with children, Harriet Pressner (1988) finds that the husbands of night-shift workers do a significant part of child care; in all cases, it was the husbands who supervised the oft-rushed morning routines of getting their children up and off to school or to child care. Finally, unlike most other women professionals, Asian American nurses often work among their coethnics and thus benefit from these social support systems. According to Paul Ong and Tania Azores (1994b, 187), there are "visible clusterings of Filipino nurses" in many hospitals in large metropolitan areas. These women's social networks can provide the emotional and material support needed to challenge male dominance.

Despite their high levels of education,[4] racism in the workplace threatens the employment security and class status of Asian immigrant professional men and women. Even when these women and men have superior levels of education, they still receive economic returns lower than those of their White counterparts and are more likely to remain marginalized in their work organizations, to encounter a glass ceiling, and to be underemployed (Chai 1987; Ong and Hee 1994, 40–41; Yamanaka and McClelland 1994, 86). As racialized women, Asian professional women also suffer greater sexual harassment than do their Western counterparts due to racialized ascription that depicts them as politically passive and sexually exotic and submissive. In her research on racialized sexual harassment in institutions of higher education, Sumi Cho (1997) argues that Asian American women faculty are especially susceptible to hostile-environment forms of harassment. This hostile environment may partly explain why Asian American women faculty continue to have the lowest tenure and promotion rate of all groups (Hune and Chan 1997).

Racism in the workplace can put undue stress on the family. Singh, a mechanical engineer who immigrated to the United States from India in 1972, became discouraged when he was not advancing at the same rate as his colleagues and attributed his difficulties to job discrimination based on national and racial origins. Singh's wife,

Kaur, describes how racism affected her husband and her family: "It became harder and harder for my husband to put up with the discrimination at work. He was always stressed out. This affected the whole family" (Dhaliwal 1995, 78). Among Korean immigrant families in New York, the husbands' losses in occupational status led to marital conflicts, violence, and ultimately divorce. Some Korean men turned to excessive drinking and gambling, which contributed to marital difficulties (Min 1998, 52, 55). A Korean wife attributes their marital problems to her husband's frustration over his low economic status:

> Five years ago, he left home after a little argument with me and came back
> two weeks later. He wanted to get respect from me. But a real source of the
> problem was not me but his frustration over low status. (Min 1998, 54)

Constrained by racial and gender discrimination, Asian professional women, on the other hand, may accept certain components of the traditional patriarchal system because they need their husbands' incomes and because they desire a strong and intact family—an important bastion of resistance to oppression.

GENDER RELATIONS AMONG
SELF-EMPLOYED ENTREPRENEURS

Ethnic entrepreneurship is often seen as proof of the benefits of the enterprise system: If people are ambitious and willing to work hard, they can succeed in the United States. In reality, few Asian immigrant business owners manage to achieve upward mobility through entrepreneurship. The majority of the businesses have very low gross earnings and run a high risk of failure. Because of limited capital and skills, Asian immigrant entrepreneurs congregate in highly competitive, marginally profitable, and labor-intensive businesses such as small markets, clothing subcontracting, and restaurants (Ong 1984, 46). In an analysis of the 1990 census data, Ong and Hee (1994, 47) show that the median annual income of self-employed Asian Americans is $23,000, which is slightly higher than that of Whites ($20,000). But there is a great deal of variation in earnings: a quarter earn $10,400 or less, another quarter earn at least $47,000, and 1% earn more than $200,000 (1994, 55, n17). The chances for business failure appear particularly high for Southeast Asian immigrants; for every 20 businesses started by them each month, 18 fail during the first year (May 1987).

Given the labor-intensive and competitive nature of small businesses, women's participation makes possible the development and viability of family enterprises. Initially, women contribute to capital accumulation by engaging in wage work to provide the additional capital needed to launch a business (Kim and Hurh 1985). In a study of professional and educated Korean couples in Hawaii, Alice Chai (1987) found that Korean immigrant women resisted both class and domestic oppression by struggling to develop family businesses where they work in partnership with their husbands. Operating a family business removes them from the racist and sexist labor market and increases their interdependence with their husbands. Women also keep down labor costs by working without pay in the family enterprise (Kim and Hurh 1988, 154). Often, unpaid female labor enables the family store to stay open as many as 14 hours a day, and on weekends, without having to hire additional workers (Bonacich, Hossain, and Park 1987, 237). According to Ong and Hee, three quarters of Asian immigrant businesses do not have a single outside employee—the typical store is run by a single person or by a family (1994, 52).[5] Their profits come directly from their labor, the labor of their families, and from staying open long hours (Gold 1994). According to Ong and Hee, approximately 42% of Asian American business owners work 50 hours or more per week, and 26% work 60 hours or more per week (1994, 47). Finally, the grandmothers who watch the children while the mothers labor at the family stores form an additional layer of unpaid family labor that also supports these stores (Bonacich et al. 1987, 237).

Because of their crucial contributions to the family enterprise, wives are an economically valuable commodity. A 1996–1997 survey of Koreans in New York City indicates that 38% of the working women worked together with their husbands in the same businesses (Min 1998, 38–39). A study of Korean immigrants in Elmhurst, Illinois, indicates that "a man cannot even think of establishing his own business without a wife to support and work with" (Park 1989, 144). Yoon reports a similar finding among Korean businesses in Chicago and Los Angeles: Wives are the most important source of family labor (1997, 157). Corresponding changes in conjugal relationships, however, have been slow and uneven. Unlike paid employment, work in a family business seldom gives women economic independence from their husbands. She is co-owner of the small business, working for herself and for her family, but she is also unpaid family labor, working as an unpaid employee of her husband. It is conceivable that, for many immigrant women in small businesses, the latter role predominates. Min (1998) reports that in almost all cases, when a Korean husband and wife run a business, the husband is the legal owner and controls the money and personnel management of the business. Even when the wife plays a dominant role and the husband a marginal role in operating and managing the family business, the husband is still considered the owner by the family and by the larger Korean immigrant community (1998, 45–46). In such instances, the husbands could be the women's "most immediate and harshest employers" (Bonacich et al., 1987, 237).

Even though the family business, in some ways, is the antithesis of the separate gender spheres (men's public world of work and women's private world of domesticity), it can exacerbate dependency. Like housework, managing stores fosters alienation and isolation because it "affords little time and opportunity for women who run them to develop other skills or to establish close friendships" (Mazumdar 1989, 17). Also, living and working in isolation, immigrant entrepreneurs may not be as influenced by the more flexible gender roles of U.S. middle-class couples and thus seem to be slower than other immigrant groups to discard rigid gender role divisions (Min 1992). In most instances, women's labor in family businesses is defined as an extension of their domestic responsibilities. Kaur, a South Asian immigrant woman who manages the family grocery store, describes the blurred boundaries between home and work:

> I have a desk at home where I do my paperwork. This way I can be home
> when my daughters get home from school, and when my husband gets

home from work I can serve him dinner right away. . . . I bought a stove for the store on which I cook meals for my husband and children during the hours when business is slow at the store. . . . I try to combine my housework with the store work such as grocery shopping. When I go shopping I buy stuff for home and the store. (Dhaliwal 1995, 80)

The family's construction of Kaur's work as an extension of her domestic responsibilities stabilizes patriarchal ideology because it reconciles the new gender arrangement (Kaur's participation in the public sphere) with previous gender expectations and ideologies. Similarly, Min reports that in most Korean produce, grocery, and liquor stores that stay open long hours, wives are expected to perform domestic functions at work such as cooking for their husbands and, often, other employees (1998, 49).

When these small businesses employ coethnics, wages are low and working conditions dismal. Ong and Umemoto list some of the unfair labor practices endured by workers in ethnic businesses: unpaid wages and unpaid workers' compensation, violation of worker health and safety regulations, and violation of minimum wage laws (1994, 100). The exploitation of coethnic workers, specifically of women workers, is rampant in the clothing subcontracting business. Asian immigrant women comprise a significant proportion of garment workers. Asian immigrant men also toil in the garment industry but mostly as contractors—small-business owners who subcontract from manufacturers to do the cutting and sewing of garments from the manufacturers' designs and textiles. Because they directly employ labor, garment contractors are in a sense labor contractors who mobilize, employ, and control labor for the rest of the industry (Bonacich 1994).

As middlemen between the manufacturers and the garment workers, these contractors struggle as marginally secure entrepreneurs on the very fringes of the garment industry (Wong 1983, 365). The precarious nature of the business is indicated by the high number of garment factories that close each year (Ong 1984, 48; Wong 1983, 370).[6] Given the stiff business competition, Asian male contractors have had to exploit the labor of immigrant women to survive. The steady influx of female limited-English-speaking immigrants puts the sweatshop owner in an extremely powerful position. Because these women have few alternative job opportunities, the owners can virtually dictate the terms of employment: They can pay low wages, ignore overtime work, provide poor working conditions, and fire anyone who is dissatisfied or considered to be a troublemaker (Wong 1983, 370). In retaliation, various unionization and employment organizations such as AIWA have worked for the empowerment of immigrant Asian women workers in the garment industry as well as in the hotel and electronics industries (Lowe 1997, 275). It is important to stress that the problem of exploitation is not primarily gender- or ethnic-based but inherent in the organization of the garment industry. Embedded in a larger, hierarchically organized structure, Asian immigrant contractors both victimize the workers they employ and are victimized by those higher up in the hierarchy. The contracting system insulates the industry's principal beneficiaries—the manufacturers, retailers, and bankers—from the grim realities of the sweatshops and the workers' hostility (Bonacich 1994). Against these more dominant forces, Asian American men and women have, occasionally, formed a shared sense of ethnic and class solidarity that can, at times, blunt some of the antagonism in the contractor-worker relationship (Bonacich 1994, 150; Wong 1983, 370).

In sum, the burgeoning Asian immigrant small-business sector is being built, in part, on the racist, patriarchal, and class exploitation of Asian (and other) immigrant women. Barred from decent-paying jobs in the general labor market, Asian immigrant women labor long and hard for the benefit of men who are either their husbands or their employers or both—and in many cases, for the benefit of corporate America (Bonacich et al. 1987, 238). The ethnic business confers quite different economic and social rewards on men and women (Zhou and Logan 1989). Whereas men benefit economically and socially from the unpaid or underpaid female labor, women bear the added burden of the double work day. Thus, it is critical to recognize that the ethnic economy is both a thriving center and a source of hardship and exploitation for Asian immigrant women.

Gender Relations among the Wage Laborers

Of the three occupational groups reviewed in this article, gender role reversals—wives' increased economic role and husband's reduced economic role—seem to be most pronounced among the wage laborers. In part, these changes reflect the growth of female-intensive industries in the United States, particularly in the garment and microelectronics industries, and the corresponding decline of male-dominated industries specializing in the production and distribution of goods (Clement and Myles 1994, 26). As a consequence, Asian immigrant women with limited education, skills, and English fluency have more employment options than do their male counterparts. Since the late 1960s, a significant number of U.S. informal sector occupations have recruited primarily female immigrant workers. The garment industry is a top employer of immigrant women from Asia and Latin America. The growth of U.S. apparel production, especially in the large cities, has been largely driven by the influx of low-wage labor from these two regions (Blumenberg and Ong 1994, 325). In Los Angeles, Latin American immigrants (mainly from Mexico) and Asian immigrants (from China, Vietnam, Korea, Thailand, and Cambodia) comprise the majority of the garment work force; in New York, Chinese and Dominican workers predominate; and in San Francisco, Chinese and other Asians prevail (Loucky, Soldatenko, Scott, and Bonacich 1994, 345). The microelectronics industry also draws heavily on immigrant women workers from Asia (mainly Vietnam, the Philippines, South Korea, and Taiwan) and from Latin America (mainly Mexico) for its low-paid manufacturing assembly work (Green 1980; Katz and Kemnitzer 1984; Snow 1986). Of the more than 200,000 people employed in California's Silicon Valley microelectronics industry in 1980, approximately 50% (100,000 employees) were in production-related jobs; half of these production-related workers (50,000–70,000) worked in semiskilled operative jobs (Siegel and Borock 1982). In a study of Silicon Valley's semiconductor manufacturing industry, Karen Hossfeld reports that the industry's division of labor is highly skewed by gender and race. At each of the 15 subcontracting firms (which specialize in unskilled and semiskilled assembly work) that Hossfeld observed, between 80% and 100% of workers were Third World immigrants, the majority of whom were women (1994, 72). Based on interviews with employers and workers at these firms. Hossfeld concludes that "the lower the skill and pay level of the job, the greater the proportion of Third World immigrant women tends to be" (73).

In labor-intensive industries such as garment and microelectronics, employers prefer to hire immigrant women, as compared to immigrant men, because they believe that women can afford to work for less, do not mind dead-end jobs, and are more suited physiologically to certain kinds of detailed and routine work. The following comment from a male manager at a microelectronics subcontracting assembly plant typifies this "gender logic": "The relatively small size [of many Asian and Mexican women] makes it easier for them to sit quietly for long periods of time, doing small detail work that would drive a large person like [him] crazy"(Hossfeld 1994, 74). As Linda Lim (1983, 78) observes, it is the *comparative disadvantage* of women in the wage-labor market that gives them a comparative advantage vis-à-vis men in the occupations and industries where they are concentrated—so-called female ghettoes of employment." A White male production manager and hiring supervisor in a Silicon Valley assembly shop discusses his formula for hiring:

> Just three things I look for in hiring [entry-level, high-tech manufacturing operatives]: small, foreign, and female. You find those three things and you're pretty much automatically guaranteed the right kind of work force. These little foreign gals are grateful to be hired—very, very grateful—no matter what. (Hossfeld 1994, 65)

In Hawaii, Korean immigrant women likewise had an easier time securing employment than men did because of their domestic skills and because of the demand for service workers in restaurants, hotels, hospitals, and factories (Chai 1987). These examples illustrate the interconnections of race, class, and gender. On one hand, patriarchal and racist ideologies consign women to a secondary and inferior position in the capitalist wage-labor market. On the other hand, their very disadvantage enhances women's employability over that of men in certain industries, thus affording them an opportunity to sharpen their claims against patriarchal authority in their homes.

The shifts in women's and men's access to economic and social resources is most acute among disadvantaged Southeast Asian refugees (Donnelly 1994; Kibria 1993). The lives of the Cambodian refugees in Stockton, California, provide an example (Ui 1991). In Stockton, an agricultural town in which the agricultural jobs have already been taken by Mexican workers, the unemployment rate for Cambodian men is estimated to be between 80% and 90%. Unemployed for long periods of time, these men gather at the corners of the enclaves to drink and gamble. In contrast, Cambodian women have transformed their traditional roles and skills—as providers of food and clothing for family and community members and as small traders—into informal economic activities that contribute cash to family incomes. Women have also benefited more than men from government-funded language and job-training programs. Because traditionally male jobs are scarce in Stockton, these programs have focused on the education of the more employable refugee women (Ui 1991, 166–167). In particular, refugee women are trained to work in social service agencies serving their coethnics primarily in secretarial, clerical, and interpreter positions. In a refugee community with limited economic opportunities, social service programs—even though they are usually part-time, ethnic specific, and highly susceptible to budget cuts—provide one of the few new job opportunities for this population, and in this case, most of these jobs go to the women. Relying on gender stereotypes, social service agency executives have preferred women over men, claiming that women are ideal workers because they are more patient and easier to work with than men (169). Thus, in the Cambodian community of Stockton, it is often women, and not men, who have relatively greater economic opportunities and who become the primary breadwinners in their families. On the other hand, stripped of opportunities for employment, men often lose their "place to be" in the new society (170–171).

The shifts in the resources of immigrant men and women have challenged the patriarchal authority of Asian men. Men's loss of status and power—not only in the public but also in the domestic arena—places severe pressure on their sense of well-being, leading in some instances to spousal abuse and divorce (Luu 1989, 68). A Korean immigrant man describes his frustrations over changing gender roles and expectations:

> In Korea [my wife] used to have breakfast ready for me. . . . She didn't do it anymore because she said she was too busy getting ready to go to work. If I complained she talked back at me, telling me to fix my own breakfast. . . . I was very frustrated about her, started fighting and hit her. (Yim 1978, as cited in Mazumdar 1989, 18)

According to a 1979 survey, marital conflict was one of the top four problems of Vietnamese refugees in the United States (Davidson 1979, as cited in Luu 1989, 69). A Vietnamese man, recently divorced after 10 years of marriage, blamed his wife's new role and newfound freedom for their breakup:

> Back in the country, my role was only to bring home money from work, and my wife would take care of the household. Now everything has changed. My wife had to work as hard as I did to support the family. Soon after, she demanded more power at home. In other words, she wanted equal partnership. I am so disappointed! I realized that things are different now, but I could not help feeling the way I do. It is hard to get rid of or change my principles and beliefs which are deeply rooted in me.(Luu 1989, 69)

Loss of status and power has similarly led to depression and anxieties in Hmong males. In particular, the women's ability—and the men's inability—to earn money for households "has undermined severely male omnipotence" (Irby and Pon 1988, 112). Male unhappiness and helplessness can be detected in the following joke told at a family picnic: "When we get on the plane to go back to Laos, the first thing we will do is beat up the women!" The joke—which generated laughter by both men and women—drew upon a combination of "the men's unemployability, the sudden economic value placed on women's work, and men's fear of losing power in their families" (Donnelly 1994, 74–75).

The shifts in the resources of men and women have created an opportunity for women to contest the traditional hierarchies of family life (Chai 1987; Kibria 1993; Williams 1989, 157). Existing data indicate, however, that working-class Asian immigrant women have not used their new resources to radically restructure the old family system but only to redefine it in a more satisfying manner (Kibria 1993). Some cultural conceptions, such as the belief that the male should be the head of the household, remain despite the economic contributions of women. Nancy Donnelly (1994, 185) reports that although Hmong women contribute the profits of their needlework sales to the family economy, the traditional construction of Hmong women as "creators of beauty, skilled in devotion to their families, and embedded in a social order dominated by men" has not changed. In the following quotation, a Cambodian wife describes her reluctance to upset her husband's authority:

> If we lived in Cambodia I would have behaved differently toward my husband. Over there we have to always try to be nice to the husband. Wives don't talk back, but sometimes I do that here a little bit, because I have more freedom to say what I think here. However, I am careful not to speak too disrespectfully to him, and in that way, I think I am different from the Americans. (Welaratna 1993, 233)

The traditional division of household labor also remains relatively intact. In a study of Chinatown women, Loo and Ong (1982) found that despite their employment outside the home, three fourths of the working mothers were solely responsible for all household chores. In her study of Vietnamese American families, Kibria (1993) argues that Vietnamese American women (and children) walk an "ideological tightrope"—struggling both to preserve the traditional Vietnamese family system and to enhance their power within the context of this system. According to Kibria, the traditional family system is valuable to Vietnamese American women because it offers them economic protection and gives them authority, as mothers, over the younger generation.

For the wage laborers then, the family—and the traditional patriarchy within it—becomes simultaneously a bastion of resistance to race and class oppression and an instrument for gender subordination (Glenn 1986, 193). Women also preserve the traditional family system—albeit in a tempered form—because they value the promise of male economic protection. Although migration may have equalized or reversed the economic resources of working-class men and women, women's earnings continue to be too meager to sustain their economic independence from men. Because the wage each earns is low, only by pooling incomes can a husband and wife earn enough to support a family. Finally, like many ethnic, immigrant, poor, and working-class women, working-class Asian women view work as an opportunity to raise the family's living standards and not only as a path to self-fulfillment or even upward mobility as idealized by the White feminist movement. As such, employment is defined as an extension of their family obligations—of their roles as mothers and wives (Kim and Hurh 1988, 162; Pedraza 1991; Romero 1992).

Conclusion

My review of the existing literature on Asian immigrant salaried professionals, self-employed entrepreneurs, and wage laborers suggests that economic constraints (and opportunities) have reconfigured gender relations within contemporary Asian America society. The patriarchal authority of Asian immigrant men, particularly those of the working class, has been challenged due to the social and economic losses that they suffered in their transition to the status of men of color in the United States. On the other hand, the recent growth of female-intensive industries—and the racist and sexist "preference" for the labor of immigrant women—has enhanced women's employability over that of men and has changed their role to that of a coprovider, if not primary provider, for their families. These shifts in immigrant men's and women's access to economic and social resources have not occurred without friction. Men's loss of status in both public and private arenas has placed severe pressures on the traditional family, leading at times to resentment, spousal abuse, and divorce. For their part, Asian women's ability to restructure the traditional patriarchy system is often constrained by their social-structural location—as racially subordinated immigrant women—in the dominant society. In the best scenario, responding to the structural barriers in the larger society, both husbands and wives become more interdependent and equal as they are forced to rely on each other, and on the traditional family and immigrant community, for economic security and emotional support. On the other hand, to the extent that the traditional division of labor and male privilege persists, wage work adds to the women's overall workload. The existing research indicates that both of these tendencies exist, though the increased burdens for women are more obvious.

Notes

1. Certainly, these three categories are neither mutually exclusive nor exhaustive. They are also linked in the sense that there is mobility between them, particularly from professional to small-business employment (Chen 1992, 142). Nevertheless, they represent perhaps the most important sociological groupings within the contemporary Asian immigrant community (Ong and Hee 1994, 31).

2. The Chinese Exclusion Act of 1882 suspended immigration of laborers for 10 years. The 1917 Immigration Act delineated a "barred zone" from whence no immigrants could come. The 1924 Immigration Act denied entry to virtually all Asians. The 1934 Tydings-McDuffie Act reduced Filipino immigrants to 50 persons a year. The 1965 Immigration Law abolished "national origins" as a basis for allocating immigration quotas to various countries—Asian countries were finally placed on equal footing.

3. After Mexico, the Philippines and South Korea were the second- and third-largest source countries of immigrants, respectively. Three other Asian countries—China, India, and Vietnam—were among the 10 major source countries of U.S. immigrants in the 1980s (Min 1995b, 12).

4. According to the 1990 U.S. Census, 43% of Asian men and 32% of Asian women 25 years of age and older had at least a bachelor's degree, compared with 23% and 17%, respectively, of the total U.S. population (U.S. Bureau of the Census 1993, 4). Moreover, the proportion of Asians with graduate or professional degrees was higher than that of Whites: 14% versus 8% (Ong and Hee 1994). Immigrants account for about two thirds to three quarters of the highly educated population (Ong and Hee, 38–39).

5. For example, in Southern California, many Cambodian-owned doughnut shops are open 24 hours a day, with the husbands typically baking all night, while wives and teenage children work the counter by day (Akast 1993).

6. In New York City, more than a quarter of Chinatown garment shops went out of business between 1980 and 1981. Similarly, of the nearly 200 Chinatown garment shops that registered with California's Department of Employment in 1978, 23% were sold or closed by 1982 and another 8% were inactive (Ong 1984, 48).

*Navigating the Waters of Lower-Waged Work: Policewoman Handles the Beat (©
International Labour Organization)*

Part V

GENDER AND LOW-WAGED WORK

Is class still a valuable heuristic device for twenty-first-century analysis of gender and work in the global economy? In classic Marxist theory, class is defined by one's individual relation to the process of production. Owners of the process of production are referred to as the bourgeoisie, while wage laborers who sell their labor power to capitalists are known as the working class, or proletariat. Marx predicted that those in the working class, who share a common position of exploitation in the labor process, would eventually realize their shared economic and political interests with one another and join collective organizations (unions) to fight for their workplace rights against capital. This latter emergent process is referred to as the development of class consciousness.

A central criticism of this framework is its exclusion of gender, race, and ethnicity. The industrial warfare between workers and capital between 1876 and the 1930s consisted primarily of white males, in both the United States and Europe. Neither women nor persons of color were viewed as central to working-class struggles within this analysis. The role of family, community, ethnicity, and race all remained beyond its purview.

By the 1960s, Marxist feminists challenged this analysis and argued that these variables must be included in order to better understand social processes of change. Capitalists benefit from the unpaid domestic labor performed by women (the maintenance and reproduction of the future and current workforce), and women constitute a reserve army of labor, a supply of workers whom capitalists can bring into the workplace and expel as needed. This critique further argues capitalists have historically recruited workers based on their race, gender, and family status in order to pay them lower wages. Examples include hiring "expendable" Yankee farm girls in New England textile factories in the nineteenth century, South East Asian girls and women in the apparel industry in the twentieth century, and teenagers in fast-food shops in the twentieth and twenty-first centuries, all based on the presumption that these workers have no families to support and can therefore be paid a low wage.

To incorporate these findings as they relate to women, race, and ethnicity, new definitions of class emerged to include women's unpaid domestic labor, paid domestic

241

labor in other people's homes, and their confrontations with the state in family and community welfare. Karen Brodkin Sacks redefined *working class* to "encompass both waged and unwaged workers who are members of a community that is dependent upon waged labor but that is unable to reproduce itself on those wages alone" (Sacks 1989, 545). Hence, Sacks argues that class must be viewed as a collective relationship to the means of production, not an individual relationship. In addition, she suggests gender identities are inseparable from racial and class identities.

Other critics of class analysis, the "intersectionalists," argue that the focus on capital as the central, uniform force that structures social relations is insufficient. They suggest that a focus on power is a more discerning approach that lends itself more easily to understanding the ways in which different identities, such as race, class, nationality, and gender, shift over time and intersect with one another (Butler 1990). Butler argues that we cannot separate gender from the "political and cultural intersections in which it is invariably produced and maintained" (1990, 3). This approach critiques the notion that race, class, or gender categories are in some way separate and "essentialist," that is, that they exist eternally in nature. Rather, intersectionalists argue that these categories of identity have different meanings in different political and cultural contexts, changing in time and space. The readings in Part V address the multiplicity of gender, race, and ethnic identities of low-wage workers, examining these arguments through historic and ethnographic research.

Amel Adib and Yvonne Guerrier demonstrate the salience of the "intersectionality" approach in "The Interlocking of Gender with Nationality, Race, Ethnicity, and Class: The Narratives of Women in Hotel Work." They maintain the multiplicity of one's identities, such as nationality, race, gender, sexual identity, class, and religion, can be understood as 1) relational and 2) contextual. A relational identity refers to the comparison of one identity to another, and a contextual identity refers to the context in which an identity is constructed. The specific context in which an individual is situated will determine the roles, meanings, and expectations that a particular identity will carry.

In their article on hotel workers, the authors describe a case where a British chambermaid's nationality is most prominent. She is derogatively called a "tart" by the other chambermaids, who are majority Portuguese. In the context of this all-female environment, Adib and Guerrier found the hotel worker's nationality carried the heaviest identity weight. There was no gender unity or class consciousness here. In fact her sexuality was impugned by other women with this pejorative term, linked to both her class and nationality.

In another illustration, a Jamaican woman was hired into an all-female work area as the only nonwhite receptionist. In this context, the woman's race became her most significant identity. All the other Jamaican women who worked at the hotel were cleaners and viewed her as a traitor to her race for even accepting the position as receptionist. In addition, the white male hotel customers ignored her, speaking only to white receptionists for their needs. Thus, no racial solidarity was evinced in this context. The authors contend that different aspects of one's identity emerge as dominant in distinct times and places, and in relation to disparate groups in the workplace. This reveals the complexity of unequal power relations, as well as the difficulty in achieving class consciousness for social change.

Susan Martin similarly examines the interlocking relationship of identities, specifically, race and gender, within the police station in "'Outsider Within' the Station House: The Impact of Race and Gender on Black Women Police." She argues that race and gender identities interact within the structural organization of work to elicit differential power relations. Policing was historically identified as a white male occupation until 1972, when the Equal Employment Opportunity Act, an amendment to the Civil Rights Act of 1964, was passed, mandating the hiring of African American men and women. As police forces diversified, Martin found that each identity group subjectively experienced their position in the workplace differently, based on the identity category that others selected to focus on.

Some in the police force ascribed black, female police officers with the stereotypic gendered and racial identities of mammy, matriarch, welfare recipient, or "hot momma." Others assigned white policewomen with the stereotypic gendered identities of piety, purity, submissiveness, and domesticity. These racial and gendered images served to affect the actual power relations within the workforce. White women were frequently given administrative jobs within the station house and treated as "wives," according to Martin, while black policewomen often experienced hostility from their superiors and coworkers, lacking necessary backup from white male police officers while patrolling the streets. Since female officers most often worked together with male police officers, acceptance by the men became very important to them. This structural situation divided and conquered women police officers, undermining their potential unity. The women police officers criticized one another along the stereotypic gendered and racial lines, internalizing the dominant identity characterizations of white and black women. Such socially constructed gender and racial identities undermined the potential for gender and/or class unity within the police force.

In contrast to the authors of the above two selections, Dorothy Sue Cobble views class and gender as separate yet salient variables in understanding social change in the workplace and beyond. She writes in "When Feminism Had Class" that millions of working women joined the ranks of American labor unions in the 1940s and developed a gender and class consciousness that differed from that of their male colleagues as well as that of middle-class women. Unlike middle-class female reformers, who pursued an individualist, gender neutral, equal rights tradition through the National Women's Party, labor union women sought collective strategies to solve the problems of their class and gender. Unionized low-wage women sought to transform the nature of working-class jobs and to incorporate gender into the transformation.

Cobble demonstrates that American labor union women had a class consciousness yet did not always choose equal treatment with the men of their class in their strategy for change. They recognized women's unique contribution of reproductive labor to society, for which they sought compensation from both employers and the state. The low-wage working women pushed their unions to negotiate for better maternity leave and health coverage during childbirth. They supported protective labor legislation that limited the hours and places of work for women but fought to apply this legislation to men as well.

Asserting their class-conscious gender identity, these wage-earning women fought to de-gender the "family wage," insisting that women, not simply men, were heads of households and deserved wages that would support an entire family. Unionized men finally fought for equal pay for equal work as well in the 1930s, in order to prevent employers from replacing them with lower paid females, especially in the U.S. electrical trades and auto industry where it was a prevalent practice in the 1930s. They also fought for equal pay for comparable work and laid the groundwork for subsequent legislation, including the Equal Pay Act of 1963, the Pregnancy Discrimination Act of 1978, and the Family and Medical Leave Act of 1993.

Carla Freeman discusses the way in which low-wage working women constructed their gender identity in Barbados to affect class relations in an infomatics factory. In "Myths of Docile Girls and Matriarchs: Local Profiles of Global Workers," Freeman argues that the global capitalist "ideal" of a feminized, low-wage workforce is docile, cheap, and childless. Although there are large numbers of women available to be drawn into the labor market and then released, based on the needs of the employer (constituting a "reserve army of labor"), these women are neither docile nor childless, according to Freeman. They have emerged as a strong workforce, attaining many of their demands, based to a large extent on their social construction of womanhood, which does not match the "ideal" workforce envisioned by global employers.

Freeman suggests that women working in this low-wage economic sector of Barbados have drawn on a historic cultural concept of womanhood that contrasts with the Western concept of femininity as defined by their European colonizers, the Victorian "cult of domesticity." In the European construction, "true women" were deemed "respectable" in church and home, subordinate to their husbands, and symbols of their husbands' economic status.

The West Indian infomatics workers reconstituted this gender identity, retaining the cultural thread of respect and responsibility, but transforming it to conform to their historical need for economic stability, an integral component of West Indian womanhood. Given the fluctuations of male employment in Barbados, low-wage women needed to sustain their children through some form of paid labor. Thus the combination of wage work and motherhood evolved into essential components of West Indian notions of womanhood, a gender identity that was transferred to the workplace. This gender identity gave rise to a strong West Indian matriarchal infomatics worker who pushed back against employer regulations that workers remain childless and without the need for a "family wage." With state-supported maternity policies, global employers were compelled to meet the workers' demands, an illustration of Sacks's notion of class as a collective relationship to the means of production. This selection also exemplifies the "intersectionalist" concept of gender identity as linked to context and class, changing over time.

These readings raise questions about the ways in which workers shape the workplace, and the ways in which the workplace shapes them, in terms of interlocked identities, their consciousness of these identities, and the strategies they employ to make change in work and society.

CHAPTER 18

The Interlocking of Gender with Nationality, Race, Ethnicity and Class

THE NARRATIVES OF WOMEN IN HOTEL WORK

Amel Adib and Yvonne Guerrier

Whilst gender in the workplace has been extensively researched, investigation into how gender interacts with other factors such as ethnicity and class has been less explicitly considered. This article explores the interlocking of gender with other categories such as class, ethnicity, race and nationality in the context of hotel work. It draws on the narratives of women describing their experiences of working in hotels. Findings from this empirically based examination suggest that gendered and other representations at work are not constructed as a process of adding difference on to difference, where categories are considered as separate and fixed. Instead, what emerges is a negotiation of the many categories shaping identities at work, which exist simultaneously and shift according to context.

Introduction

In considering the nature of gendered identities, there is a growing wish to "expos[e] the alleged uniformity of gender" (Gherardi 1995, 19) and an interest in exploring the multiplicity and diversity of gendered identities in organizations. It is increasingly recognized that gendered identities are not fixed or unitary but are constructed through complex social processes and practices (Butler 1990; Collinson 1992; Gherardi 1995). The simultaneous and shifting nature of gendered identities has been particularly examined within analysis of masculinities in organizations, Collinson and Hearn suggesting that:

> . . . analyses need to reflect and explore the dynamic, shifting and often contradictory social relations and identities through which men's differences, and their perceptions of differences, are reproduced and transformed in organisational practices and power asymmetries. (1994, 9)

Gender as a concept can be analysed separately from others, but in practice, gender is played out in conjunction with other categories. In the extensive literature on women's experience of work, little attention has been paid to the ways in which other aspects of identity such as nationality, race, ethnicity or social class impinge on women's construction of their experiences. Part of the endeavour to explore the concept of gender as simultaneous and shifting necessitates its study in relation to these other categories.

This article explores the narratives of women at work within operative level jobs in the hotel industry. This industry, in line with the wider hospitality industry, employs a substantial proportion of women (Lucas 1995; Purcell 1993). There have been many studies that explore the experience of women in jobs in the hospitality and wider leisure industry (Adkins 1995; Hall 1993; Hochschild 1983; Hughes and Tadic 1998; Leidner 1993). The fact, however, that the modern hotel typically has a diverse workforce—men and women from diverse ethnic and national backgrounds serving an equally diverse range of guests—has been relatively neglected by researchers. In addition, hotels are structured around a range of work roles that carry different expectations about gender, race, ethnicity, and class. This diverse environment facilitates a discussion of the way gender identity interlocks with other categories in the context of work.

The Construction of Gender Identities as Shifting and Interlocking with Other Categories

While the relation of gender to other categories such as race, ethnicity, class and nationality is still under-researched, theorizatian is developing in disciplines such as cultural studies, critical race theories, labour process theories and feminist theories. This article outlines theories that explore how gender interlocks with other categories in order to shed light on the construction of gendered identities within the narratives of particular organizational members.

ESSENTIALISM AND THE CONCEPT OF DIFFERENCE

The concept of difference has been significant in theorization on the diversity of identities. In attempting to avoid essentialism, we can deal with diversity simply by fragmenting identities into multiple divisions: white women, Asian women, black women, bourgeois women, proletariat women, lesbian women, heterosexual women, mothers, non-mothers, urban women, rural women, and so on. However, rather than counteracting essentialism, this approach may, in fact, reduce identities to categories that are in danger of implying a fixed or naturalized notion. Guillaumin (1995) warns of the dangers of theorization on the basis of difference and explains that we can succeed in avoiding the trap of essentialism only by making explicit the processes of social construction that identify groups as different.

Theorists have drawn attention to the significance of the dualistic nature of differentiation. Hall explains:

> . . . identities are constructed through, not outside, difference. This entails
> the radically disturbing recognition that it is only through the relation of
> the Other, the relation to what it is not, to precisely what it lacks, to what
> has been called its *constitutive outside* that the "positive" meaning of any
> term—and thus its identity—can be constructed. (1996a, 4–5; original
> emphasis)

This theory is expanded in the work of Said (1978) who uncovers the relational
identity between Orientalism and the west. Said examines how western representations ascribe difference to other places and cultures. He argues that in the process of
negation, by identifying what is different; what is not, one simultaneously identifies
what is. So, by identifying what the Other is, the west identifies what *it* itself is. The
construction of the Orient within Eurocentric culture therefore reaffirms the sense of
what is European and western.

Said also argues that an ascription of difference is an ascription of reduction
(1978). By ascribing difference to the Orient, it is reduced to a relational identity to
the west and it loses a meaning in its own right. This reduction also brings with it a
notion of an essentialist, fixed and unchanging identity. The ascription of difference
acts, therefore, as a power relation, relying on a dualistic relationship of one "thing"
to another and constructed within a particular context which carries specific sets of
cultural assumptions.

In the theorization of identity, critiques of essentialism reveal the dangers of
interpreting identity as a set of separate and fixed differences added incrementally
one to another. These theories help identify two main aspects of the process of social
construction of identity, namely that identity construction is both relational and contextual. It is relational in the sense that identity construction engages in Othering, a
process which assumes a relationship of one identity to another. Identity construction
is contextual in that the context in which this process occurs shapes the meanings,
expectations and roles that particular identities carry. The relational and contextual
aspects of gendered identities are explored in this article through the narratives of
particular workers in the hotel context.

THE INTERLOCKING OF RACE WITH OTHER CATEGORIES

Like theorization on gender, critical race theorists and cultural studies theories reject
the liberal notion that interprets race, gender, ethnicity, class, and sexual orientation
as separate and essentialist categories (Alfieri 1997; Crenshaw et al., 1995; Delgado
1995). Within these disciplines the notion of intersectionality has been developed to
describe the interconnections and interdependence of race with other categories. Critical race theorists emphasize the significance of what they term the intersectionality of
social and cultural categories within systems of representations that construct racial
and gendered stereotypes (Crenshaw et al., 1995).

Black cultural political theories, in particular in the work of Hall, describe the
need for the recognition that the category "black" is a politically and culturally

constructed category used to represent a diverse range of positionalities in relation to social experience and cultural identities. Hall explains:

> . . . the end of the essential black subject also entails a recognition that the central issues of race is always historically in articulation, in a formation, with other categories and divisions and are constantly crossed and recrossed by the categories of class, of gender and ethnicity. (1996b, 444)

Hall calls for a new politics of representation that displaces hitherto stable political categories and avoids the pitfalls of essentialism and reductionism.

Brah (1996) believes that gender, race, ethnicity, sexuality and nationality are analytical categories that represent types of power relation and partly form identity. She argues that "the idea of power holds that individuals and collectivities are simultaneously positioned in social relations constituted and performed across multiple dimensions of differentiation: that these categories always operate in articulation" (1996, 242). The intersection of these specific types of power relation produces "a space of/for theoretical crossovers that foreground processes of power inscribing these interrelationalities; a kind of *theoretical creolisation*" (Brah 1996, 210; original emphasis).

The concept of intersectionality helps to create a theoretical space for analysing the interlocking of political categories. It also avoids essentialism and enables the significance of context to be explored. Intersectionality does not, however, remain a merely theoretical concept: it is also played out in practice. This article provides, through the narratives of individual workers, empirical examples of how the crossovers of gender with race, ethnicity and class are articulated in particular workplaces. Brah explains the significance of this type of investigation as follows:

> What is of interest is how these fields of power collide, enmesh and configure; and with *what effects*. What kinds of inclusions or exclusions does a *specific articulation of power* produce? That is, what patterns of equity or inequality are inscribed; what modes of domination or subordination are facilitated; what forms of pleasure are produced; what fantasies, desires, ambivalence and contradictions are sanctioned; or what types of political subjects positions are generated by the operations of given configurations of power? (Brah 1996, 248; original emphasis)

In our exploration of this data we explore the ways in which the intersectionality of gender, race, ethnicity, nationality and class are articulated. This article does not deal with the material effects of these interconnections, but rather the ways in which these are played out in the narratives of respondents. This article, therefore, explores through empirical data how gendered identities intersect with other categories in the context of hotel work.

THE INTERLOCKING OF GENDER WITH OTHER CATEGORIES

Whilst the term "intersectionality" is particularly used within discussions on race, the construction of gendered identities and its relationship with other categories is explored within some feminist analysis.

Dual systems theories have engaged in the interconnections between different systems of oppression, such as those relating to patriarchy and capitalism, to provide a structural analysis of the dual inequality of gender and class (Delphy and Leonard 1992; Walby 1986). These theories have been crucial in contextualizing the analysis of gender inequalities within a particular historical, social, political and economic setting.

At the level of the workplace, students of work have often analysed the interrelationship between gender identities and class. Studies such as Cockburn's analysis of printers and masculinity (1983) and Pollert's study of women and factory work (1981), for example, usefully acknowledge the interconnections of class and gender identities. These theories have, however, been criticized for implying that the systems of inequality are distinct from each other. Collinson and Hearn suggest that "the problem here is that dual systems theory must inevitably treat patriarchal and capitalist relations as somehow outside each other" (1996, 63).

Deconstructionist theories have also been influential. They provide a critique of particular types of identity politics and highlight the discursive construction of identities. They have enabled a debate over categories such as "woman" and a rejection of the binary assumptions underlying identity politics of masculine and feminine, even within feminism. Such theorization warns against separating out "gender" from its constitutive context in order to analyse it as though it were a separate category. For the purpose of this article, these arguments help to highlight the need for theorization of gender, not simply as a separate category that connects with other separate categories, but interlocked with race and class, for instance, as a *fusion*. Butler explains:

> [i]f one "is" a woman, that is surely not all one is; the term fails to be exhaustive, not because a pregendered "person" transcends the specific paraphernalia of its gender, but because gender is not always constituted coherently or consistently in different historical contexts, and because gender intersects with racial, class, ethnic, sexual and regional modalities of discursively constituted identities. As a result, it becomes impossible to separate out "gender" from the political and cultural intersections in which it is invariably produced and maintained. (1990, 3)

THE INDIVIDUAL AS SUBJECT IN THE PROCESS OF CONSTRUCTING IDENTITY

Empirical studies of the construction of identity in organizations are developing. In particular, critical labour process theorists examine the construction of identity, subjectivity and belonging to a workplace, from the point of view of the individual as subject. For example, Collinson argues for a need to consider "power as a positive as well as negative, and workers as subjects as well as objects of *class* and *gender* relations" (1992, 38; original emphasis). His perspective considers human beings simultaneously as both subjects and objects, so that, while individuals are shaped by institutional arrangements of power, they also make sense of these and their position within this context.

Collinson's work on masculinities explores the investment of workers in particular gendered and class discourses in a specific organizational setting (1992). He argues that this investment represents an individual's existentialist search to secure a unitary identity. Collinson's theory suggests that the contested nature of identity may be to do with the complex nature of "being," that is of being both part of and separate from the world around. Individuals attempt to make sense of the multiple social positions that they inhabit. For the purpose of this article, therefore, analysing how respondents, as subjects and objects of organizational context, construct meaning through narratives allows for an exploration of the systems of representation that shape identities.

One significant concept developed by critical labour process theorization is that of resistance (Collinson 1992; Jermier et al., 1994). What constitutes resistance has become an interesting debate (Edwards et al., 1995; Jermier et al., 1994). However, a broad definition is offered as "small-scale and informal means by which workers counter managerial control of the workplace" (Edwards et al., 1995, 283). In the process of examining workers' narratives and how they make sense of their position within organizations, the concept of resistance is a useful analytical tool for identifying the transformative power of individuals' narratives. With respect to identity construction within workers' narratives, resistance to organizational arrangements of power needs to be considered. However, as the critical literature on resistance argues, the multiplicity of the types of resistance and the contradictory nature of resistance itself suggests that workers' resistance can both reproduce as well as transform organizational arrangements and work role expectations.

THE SIGNIFICANCE OF THE WORKPLACE SETTING
IN THE PROCESS OF IDENTITY CONSTRUCTION

The organizational context in which identities are constructed is significant. Collinson and Hearn argue that place is significant to the exploration of shifting masculinities as follows:

> Multiplicity and diversity are relevant not only to the analysis of masculinity, but also to the different forms and locations of workplaces—the sites of work of masculinity. These sites will vary, for example, according to occupations, industry, culture, class and type of organization. These multiple masculinities interconnect with multiple sites. (1996, 66)

Placing this research within the location of hotels provides an empirical example of gender construction in a new setting, since hotel work has not previously been analysed in this way. Empirically informed studies of the complex ways in which gender is represented, constructed, reproduced and transformed within institutional arrangements help to examine the contingent nature of gender. This article analyses the representations of gender attempting to explore these in relation to institutional arrangements of hotels.

To the extent that hotels provide a "home away from home" by offering essentially domestic services on a commercial business, hotel work may be regarded as quintessentially women's work (Novarra 1980) where traditional gender roles at home are mirrored at work. However, as Purcell (1993) points out, hotel work is stigmatized because of its associations with personal servitude. Indeed much hotel work may be regarded as carrying a social taint because of this and thus may be defined as "dirty work" (Ashforth and Kreiner 1999; Hughes 1958). Women may predominate in certain hotel jobs, not so much because they are regarded as particularly appropriate for women, but because these jobs are regarded as appropriate only for those disadvantaged in the labour force. Certainly, the largest proportions of female workers are found in the lowest skill, lowest status and "dirtiest" hotel jobs. Thus, men tend to be employed as managers or in craft or semi-skilled positions (such as chefs), whilst women are found in "operative positions": chambermaids, cleaners, waiting and bar staff, unskilled cooks kitchen hands (Bagguley 1990; Lucas 1995).

The hotel workforce is, however, a diverse one in many ways. It comprises, for example, a high proportion of ethnic minority workers and migrant workers (Lucas 1995). One writer who, at least, speculates about this relationship between race, ethnicity and gender within hotel work is Adkins (1995). In her study of customer service work in the hospitality and leisure industries in the UK, she suggests that black women may be under-represented in such work because they cannot be represented as sexually attractive to (white, male) customers in the way that white women can. Thus white faces and white bodies are on show whilst black faces and bodies are kept behind the scenes.

This article focuses particularly on two categories of hotel work: the roles of receptionists and chambermaids. Both these jobs are undertaken predominantly by women. Reception work may be constructed as women's work in that it requires a substantial amount of emotional labour. The physical appearance and presentation of a woman on reception is important; she should be friendly, helpful and sexually attractive. If Adkins' proposition is correct, this is not just women's work but also white women's work.

By contrast, there is no assumption that chambermaids should deliver emotional labour or present an attractive appearance: indeed the maid is expected instead to be invisible or a "non-person" (Goffman 1959) who goes about her work without disturbing the guest. Chambermaiding is women's work to the extent that it is regarded as requiring domestic skills for which women are inherently skilled (Kinnaird et al., 1994). No attempt seems to have been made to reconstruct this work as requiring male skills when undertaken in the commercial rather than the domestic setting, as happened with food service and food preparation. It is "dirty work," in Hughes' terms (1958) in that it carries both a social and a physical taint—clearing up after guests. Whilst statistics are difficult to find, ethnic minority and migrant workers are clustered in the lowest graded work in the hospitality industry (Lucas 1995) and it is common to find that all the chambermaids in a hotel are drawn from the same ethnic minority or migrant group. While reception work is "respectable" women's work, therefore, chambermaiding is not constructed merely as women's work, but as work to be undertaken only by certain groups of women.

Methodology

[. . .] This article draws on the narratives of four respondents from a total of 15 in the initial study. They were chosen to represent accounts of how the respondents felt positioned in terms of gender, race, nationality, ethnicity, and class by both guests and co-workers.

The respondents are hotel management students from a London university, recently returned from a one-year industrial placement working in hotels as part of their degree requirements and who were all invited to participate in the study. The respondents took part on a voluntary basis.

[. . .]

The respondents worked as "normal" operative staff: receptionists, waitresses, chambermaids, and reservation staff as well as in duty management in hotels in the UK and abroad, ranging from two and five-star hotels. All the respondents in this study are in their 20s, except for one who is in her 40s.

The group of respondents in this study does not form a representative sample of hotel workers. [. . .] The interviews were semi-structured, using open-ended questions that covered chosen themes.

[. . .]

The Narratives

The narratives presented relate to experiences of women workers in relation to two categories of hotel job: that of the chambermaid and that of the receptionist. Both these roles are feminized but they carry very different expectations about the type of woman undertaking them and therefore provide examples of the complex ways in which race, nationality, and class interconnect with gender in the representations of women workers. The first narrative provides an example of how one individual makes sense of her position working as a chambermaid and uses nationality to differentiate between workers. Amy, a white British trainee in her early 20s, who worked as a chambermaid in Guernsey, explains:

> I hated housekeeping, because all the staff working in housekeeping were Portuguese and we didn't get on, they didn't speak English to me . . . [they] basically had this impression that all English girls are tarts . . . they just think they're slappers basically. . . . It was just the way they are with all English girls really, unless they get to know you socially, which they don't cause actually they don't mix with you, . . . it's the "them and us" thing, you know, they live together: they associate with Portuguese people; and then there are the English.

Amy's narrative highlights how, in this all-female environment, she sees nationality as the main category through which chambermaids are differentiated and form separate groups. The housekeeping context in which Amy finds herself makes her feel that she does not fit in. She also wishes to be treated differently due to her status as management trainee, as she describes when recounting a conversation she had with her manager:

> I said basically I wasn't meant to be a cleaner and I was a management trainee.

Amy's narrative illustrates how she constructs her identity as distinct from the other chambermaids using nationality (British, not Portuguese) and occupational class (management trainee, not chambermaid) as the two categories that mark her out. This example reflects the complex processes involved in identity building and differentiation within an all-female environment. The categories of nationality and class are used within Amy's narrative to negotiate Otherness and to make sense of who she is in relation to her colleagues.

Amy sees herself as a traveller in a strange world just as much as if she was working in an all-male environment. In fact, drawing on Gherardi's analysis of women in predominantly male work groups, Amy could be described as the "snake in the grass" (Gherardi 1995, 109). She appears to construct herself as an outsider who refuses to conform to what is expected of her in this situation. Certainly Amy's narrative suggests that she is "passing through" housekeeping: this is a transitional phase to better things and that she does not belong in housekeeping.

Amy also reports her colleagues as describing English women as "tarts" or "slappers," that is "dirty" women. This put-down is clearly gendered. However, it also interlocks with other categories. A connection is made, in this example, between sexual availability and nationality. The juxtaposition of "English" to "tart" suggests that what makes a woman a tart is her "Englishness." Amy highlights this intersection between gender and nationality in her narrative. According to Amy's narrative, the Portuguese maids describe someone as a tart according to their nationality. It is also interesting that, in relation to a job which may be defined as "dirty work" (Ashforth and Kreiner 1999; Hughes 1958) it carries a physical and social taint, Amy recalls a put-down which relates to Hughes' third form of taint: moral taint.

In this example of an all-female environment, gender is used in conjunction with nationality and class to form a variety of ways in which this chambermaid represents herself and other chambermaids. We see the tensions in workers' representations of themselves and others. Amy is a management trainee doing a "dirty" low-status job. She also relates to a culturally different group to that of the other chambermaids. She both represents herself and, in turn, reports being represented by the others, as different. Interestingly in an all-female environment, whilst the insult used to denigrate the Other is gendered, nationality is the discerning factor that separates and excludes one worker from the rest.

The issue of resistance is significant in Amy's rejection of an organizationally ascribed identity as low-status. Edwards et al. explain how resistance practices can be a means through which "employees often begin to construct an alternative, more positive sense of self, dignity and identity to that provided, prescribed or circumscribed by the organization" (1995, 284). Amy's narrative indeed rejects the ascribed organizational identity of chambermaids. She does, however, appear to want to be ascribed the organizational identity of management trainee and therefore her narrative resists one type of organizational identity in favour of another. Particularly by using the word "cleaner," Amy's reported narrative to her manager suggests that she is not best suited to do "dirty" work but instead she would be better employed doing something more "respectable."

In examining worker resistance to managerial control, critical labour process theorists have observed the contradictory nature of resistance and its often intrinsic link with consent (Collinson 1992; Edwards et al., 1995). The rejection within Amy's narrative of any identification with other maids represents, on the one hand, outward resistance to managerial control. However on the other hand, this resistance also implies consent to the idea that the context of chambermaiding is low-status.

In the interview Amy takes the opportunity to reaffirm her difference and her unsuitability to housekeeping. Her use of the phrase "them and us" reinforces her sense that she belongs in a separate camp to the chambermaids. Her narrative implies in fact that she, as separate to the other chambermaids, belongs with "them." We can conjecture that she may think that she belongs with the people working in the front-of-house who interact with the guests, rather than the chambermaids, who are hidden from view, foreign and not skilled enough to be interacting with guests. In addition, it might be that the very sexualized insult Amy recounts as referring to English women is a reference to the flaunting of sexuality insidiously present in the job of receptionist, a job in which mainly white English women are employed.

The issue of status and race or ethnicity is highlighted in the second example relating to chambermaids. Pauline, a Jamaican woman in her 40s who was the first black receptionist in an exclusive five-star London hotel, described the following incident:

> When I worked there I was asking things about colour . . . because when I started of course all the maids were black. . . . And a couple of them said to me, "Oh you're going to be our new housekeeper"; so I said, "No, actually, I'm gonna be working in reception." . . . And they said "Oh! How long has that taken?" so that prompted me to ask Beverley [Pauline's immediate manager], "Is there any reason why you've never had a black receptionist?" . . . She explained to me that she had never really thought about it to any degree, but she said, "I must say that when you came for your interview and I wanted to offer you the job, Mr. X [the general manager], he said 'I would love to employ her straight away but I just want to toss something up with the Head of Housekeeper. How do you think her life would be with the other girls, with the maids?'" That was his concern, which I thought was quite interesting . . . a black person in reception; there were all the black maids: would they try to make life a bit uncomfortable—in a way like, I would almost be seen as some sort of traitor: what was I doing there, why wasn't I in housekeeping? That was his concern, because they are quite a vociferous lot of girls, I mean, they say what they think.

Pauline's example, like Amy's, illustrates the expectations regarding who does what in the context of hotel work. They reflect the observation within hospitality literature that ethnic minority women are less likely to be employed front-of-house or in customer contact jobs in the service industry (Adkins 1995; Bagguley 1987; Lucas 1995). They also reflect the common practice that women workers from ethnic minorities are more prominent in jobs in which they are required to be nearly invisible to the customer. This may involve undertaking "dirty" tasks such as cleaning, as in the role of chambermaids.

The intersectionality of gender with race in Pauline's account of what happened when she entered reception appears to provide her with a sense that she does not quite belong there. Applied to Gherardi's analysis of women entering male occupations, Pauline's account of her experience indicates she identifies herself as a guest in a friendly culture (1995). Whilst she reports being welcomed in her new environment at reception by the managers, who she recalls expressing warmth at her arrival, she also recounts how they had made an exception in letting her work there. Her story describes being welcomed in as different and as an exception, based on her colour.

Pauline's example, therefore, illustrates how, within a female dominated working environment, the category of race is used to differentiate female workers. It appears from Pauline's narrative that race is the salient issue with regards to how she reports being identified in relation to others. It is her different colour that overrides her gender in raising questions regarding her suitability for the job of receptionist.

In addition, the interconnection of gender to race is interlocked with a third category of class. This is apparent in Pauline's report that the maids believed her to be the new housekeeper; that is to say, their boss, rather than another chambermaid. Pauline's demeanour suggests a middle-class background. Pauline, therefore, describes herself as being differentiated by her class from the chambermaids. This incident suggests there are multiple connections between gender, race, class and group belonging and provides an example of the multiple, simultaneous and shifting nature of identity construction. In one context, that of receptionists, Pauline is considered different because of her race, while in another she is different because of her class. The multiple and shifting nature of identity is also evident in the ambivalent feelings Pauline herself expresses about her position in relation to others. In particular, her choice of the word, "traitor," suggests that she may feel some ambivalence towards a job with a strong representation as "non-black." Pauline's example demonstrates the variety of identities that workers negotiate in the workplace and how these identities co-exist simultaneously and shift according to different work contexts.

Although Pauline did not encounter any problems with the chambermaids as she reports the general manager had feared, she did experience a disturbing incident of racism by a guest. She described her experience as follows:

> . . . a guest who had been coming to the hotel for several years and who was known to the managing director [came in]. His attitude towards me was hostile: I knew it and he knew it. There was nothing overt about his behaviour; he simply ignored me and spoke over my head to one of the managers as if I did not exist, had not spoken, and had not presented him with a registration card.

Pauline felt this guest treated her as though she were a non-person. Her experience of his refusal to engage in any contact with her reaffirms to her that she, as a black woman at reception, does not form part of his expectations of what a receptionist should be. Her description suggests he metaphorically moved her to the back regions, to where he could not see her.

Interestingly, another respondent, Rachel, describes being hurt by an incident that she also interpreted as racist. This time it came from a black guest who she believed preferred to deal with a black receptionist rather than herself. This incident occurred in the USA and the respondent was a young white Israeli woman working as a receptionist.

> *Rachel*: . . . what I did notice is that a lot of people—even with colour, especially American, you know—have very discrimination, racial discrimination and, you know, if you are one: if you were black or whatever and the person dealing with you was black; yes: they were happy to deal with you—the guest I mean: and when I tried to deal with someone, they weren't very pleasant to me.
>
> *Interviewer*: So a black person, you noticed, preferred to go to a black person?
>
> *Rachel*: Yeah, not everyone. I don't want to make generalizations but for the first time in my life I was actually approached by that and that really hurt. And there was a black person next to me and so, when they left, I said to him: I looked at him and I said, "Don't tell me that wasn't a racial thing, a racist thing." And he said, "No, you're right." He even noticed it so it wasn't like I was paranoid.

This example of perceived discrimination against a receptionist apparently mirrors Pauline's example. Rachel, however, as a white female, holds the "appropriate" attributes for this role whilst, it might be argued that the black male receptionist preferred by the guests holds "inappropriate" ones. Rachel reports her reaction as that of shock and disbelief; she needs to check her perceptions against those of her co-worker to ensure that she is not paranoid. An initial analysis would suggest an inversion of the normal process of discrimination which brings into focus Rachel's "whiteness": an attribute that would not normally mark her out. However, this incident follows a discussion in Rachel's narrative about her Israeli identity and the way that this affects her relations with the guests.

> I wouldn't speak Hebrew [though] I knew they [guests] were Israeli. I would hear them speaking and I wouldn't. The main reason why I don't is because, first of all, it happened to me once that I would speak and then they would say, "What, do you think I can't speak English? Why are you talking to me in Hebrew?" You know what I mean? And that's embarrassing. Um, and the second thing is that once they know you speak the same language they are going to bug you non-stop. "Oh, but, you know, you are one of us, you can do this for us," and I would try, but if my manager was there, I would say "no." You know, deal with other people as well. Which is right. I don't treat certain people [better] because they're from my country or whatever. I never did that, but I notice that other people did, in the front desk, a lot, and that was so wrong. And also, even my supervisor, she used to come up and say, not next to them, before they just arrived, she would say, "Oh Rachel, your family is here. Can you deal with them?"

Rachel expresses her ambivalence about being marked out, in her role as receptionist, as an Israeli. The incident in which she perceives she is discriminated against by a black guest is not, in this light, a mirror of Pauline's experience. For Pauline, working in a white work group, the racist incident and the description of her hiring is clearly constructed in terms of a black/white dichotomy. For Rachel, rather than a black/white dichotomy, her concern seems to be whether the workplace is blind to colour and ethnicity, as she believes it should be, or whether inevitably staff and guests favour, and are favoured by, their "families," be they Israeli or black. "Being black" in Rachel's narrative seems to be constructed in opposition to categories such as "being Israeli," whereas in Pauline's narrative it is clearly constructed in opposition to "being white." The context in which Pauline and Rachel worked: a five-star hotel in which all other receptionists were white, compared with a mid-market hotel with greater heterogeneity of receptionists; arguably helped to shape these constructions.

Another example where gender interconnects with ethnicity and class involves an incident of male to female sexual harassment. Maria, a Spanish woman in her early 20s working in a two-star hotel in Washington in the USA, was being sexually harassed by the chef, who was from El Salvador. She describes how she dealt with the situation:

> The chef was harassing all the girls . . . this guy asked me to go out [with him] . . . when I was going to ask for my lunch, I need to speak to him and he tell me, "OK, you be nice to me and I am going to be nice to you." I don't need to listen to this kind of thing! . . . One day I was speaking with him . . . and after this he was more nice with me and I think it is because he saw me, not like a woman, but like a sister because I was speaking, "Look, I am in the same situation" (the guy was from El Salvador): "I have the same crap from the people here, so don't make my life difficult, OK?" . . . The point is that we speak Spanish: he was from a different country; he came here to make a new life and this is what I was trying to do.

The interlocking of gender with ethnicity and with class is enacted in this narrative. Firstly, Maria describes how she counters unwanted sexual advances from the chef by emphasizing her ethnicity rather than her gender. Maria rejects being considered primarily as a woman and her representation of herself as instead belonging primarily to a particular ethnicity allows her to become a "sister," rather than a woman, to the chef. She renegotiates her gendered identity with the chef by appropriating her ethnicity. As his "sister," Maria implies she is sexually unavailable to him and should be protected, rather than abused. In this narrative, therefore, the interlocking of gender with ethnicity forms part of the gendered process of constructing identity and of differentiation within a particular gender.

In addition, and in conjunction with the intersection of gender with ethnicity, the category of class and social status also engages in the process of identity construction. Maria presents herself to the chef as belonging to the same social status as him due to their common immigrant economic and social circumstances. Maria is also a management trainee, which could set her apart from the other workers in terms of occupational class. However her remark ("I have the same crap from the people here"), suggests she aligns herself with disadvantaged groups in opposition to "the people here."

The process of identity construction in this example involves the fusion of gender ascription to ethnicity and class ascription, all of which interconnect with each other. The categories of gender, ethnicity and class are interdependent. They construct each other so that, in Maria's case, the self-representation of her ethnicity shapes that of her class and is, in turn, an attempt to reconstruct her identity in relation to gender as "sister" rather than "woman." This process reveals the negotiation of simultaneous categories and involves the interdependence of these categories in the construction of identities.

[. . .]

Conclusions

This article has focused on the narratives of women working within hotels. We have attempted to highlight some of the ways in which gender is interrelated with other characteristics within these narratives, in particular with race, ethnicity and class background. The narratives demonstrate the simultaneous and shifting nature of identity: at one point in the narrative the women's gender may be in the foreground and at the next point it may be her ethnic identity which is salient. They highlight the ways in which women differentiate themselves from other women at work. Collinson and Hearn comment, in relation to men at work, that "the unities that exist between men should not be overstated. They are often more precarious, shifting and instrumental than first appearances suggest" (1996, 72). The same may be said about women at work.

If the focus is just on gender in the study of women's construction of their identities at work, we argue that much of the complexity and ambiguity of that experience is lost. But how do we then incorporate these other categories of race, ethnicity, nationality and class, which help to form identity? As with gender, categories such as race and class reinforce structural power relationships so, for example, whilst being female lessens one's power within the organization, being a black or migrant female further lessens one's power and tends to "fit" one into particular types of backstage roles. However, the respondents do not seem to interpret their work experience in terms of one type of difference being added to another type of difference. Instead, their identities are fluid. Certain identities may be emphasized or downplayed as a form of resistance. Rachel resists her Israeli identity. Maria's narrative is an interesting example of a woman attempting to bring to the foreground aspects of her identity to her advantage.

[. . .]

In summary, this article contributes to the study of gender and organizations by providing empirical examples of the process by which gender interacts with other categories in specific narratives of hotel workers when exploring how individuals, as subjects, position themselves within institutional power arrangements. This endeavour is significant for two main reasons. Firstly, it provides empirical accounts of the complex ways that individuals make sense of themselves in the world of work. This enables the theorization of gender to be related to other categories that, in practice, co-exist with gendered identities. Secondly, in examining the process of the interlocking of gender with other categories, the article illustrates the complex nature of individuals' positioning according to the work context and the changing and relational character of the articulation of identity at work. This article illustrates that gendered and other representations at work do not represent a process of adding difference on to difference; where categories are considered as separate and fixed. Instead, what emerges from data is a negotiation of many categories that exist simultaneously and that shift according to context.

CHAPTER 19

"Outsider Within" the Station House

THE IMPACT OF RACE AND GENDER ON BLACK WOMEN POLICE

Susan E. Martin

Most of the research on the effects of discrimination on occupational behavior has focused either on race or gender, ignoring the unique social location of black females. Recent feminist scholarship has identified the need for an interactive model articulating the interlocking nature of racial and sexual systems of subordination. This paper examines the interactive effects of race and gender in one male-dominated occupation—police work. Based on in-depth interviews with 106 black and white officers and supervisors from five large municipal agencies, it explores the perspectives, experiences, and structural barriers black women officers face in dealing with white female and black and white male co-workers. This study finds that the combination of their race and gender statuses leads to both unique problems and perspectives for black women. The interaction of racism and sexism results in each form of expression modifying the nature and impact of the other.

In the past 30 years more women and persons of color have entered occupations previously limited to white men. Although some studies have examined the factors that have aided or hindered women's advancement into "non-traditional" occupations and others have focused on changes in the occupational status of blacks and other ethnic minorities, few have systematically focused on the interactive effects of race and gender on black women's occupational perspectives and behavior.

This paper examines how race and gender interact and affect the workplace status and perspectives of black women by closely examining one occupation long dominated by white males—police work. It explores how racism enlarges cleavages among women and how sexism divides black women and men, while police work itself, in controlling "the dangerous classes," contributes to these divisions. By focusing on these interlocking systems of oppression in one particular setting this paper seeks to expand understanding of the interconnections among these elements of an overarching structure of domination and resistance to it.

The Intersection of Race and Gender

[...]

Differences in class and occupational status intersect with those of race and gender in separating black and white women. Historically white middle-class women accepted and contributed to the domestic code that enabled them to slough off burdensome domestic work onto more oppressed groups of women. As service work moved from the home to institutionalized urban labor markets segmented by race and gender, the race and gender hierarchy also moved into public settings. This divergence in the experiences of black and white women with respect to access to power, their workplace activities, and their roles in their respective communities has contributed to black women's "acute consciousness of the interlocking nature of race and gender oppression" (Glenn 1992, 34–35).

Kanter's (1977) structural approach identifies power, opportunity, and group representation as key determinants of occupational behavior and work-related contingencies in work organizations. Inequalities in opportunities for mobility and the distribution of power within an organization lead some members toward success and consign others to failure. In addition, "tokens," whose type is underrepresented in majority-dominated groups, face barriers to occupational achievement including performance pressure, exclusion as "outsiders," and treatment according to familiar stereotypes.

Kanter's theory of tokenism was conceived as gender neutral and as broadly applicable to racial and other minorities. However, it ignores both the specific effects of sexism that male tokens do not suffer (Zimmer 1988; Williams 1992) and the effects of other dimensions of domination including race, class, sexual orientation, and age. As Acker (1990, 146) observes, neither mobility opportunities nor the organizations in which they are found are "gender neutral." Rather,

> advantage and disadvantage, exploitation and control, action and emotion, meaning and identity are patterned through and in terms of a distinction between male and female, masculine and feminine. Gender is not an addition to ongoing processes, conceived as gender neutral. Rather, it is an integral part of those processes.

Organizations are "gendered" in terms of physical and social divisions (e.g., job titles and physical space); symbols and images (e.g., language and dress) that explain and reinforce those divisions; interaction processes and patterns that enact dominance and submission (e.g., nonverbal "door ceremonies"); and the production of organizational identities that are gendered.

Furthermore, organizations are structured by racial divisions, stereotypes, and patterns of dominance and deference that intersect with gender distinctions. In one of the few studies examining these patterns of interaction that focused explicitly on black women, Collins (1990) identifies four stereotypes or "controlling images." In contrast to the key virtues of piety, purity, submissiveness, and domesticity to which white women have been encouraged to aspire, black women have been portrayed as mammies, matriarchs, welfare recipients, and "hot mommas." These images have maintained the political economy of domination by making racism, sexism, and poverty appear to be normal and inevitable. They have kept black women as "others," at the margins of society, while their labor market opportunities have been severely restricted to low paying service jobs (Collins 1990).

To provide a clearer picture of the interlocking effects of gender and race, this paper explores their impact on one occupation that traditionally has been monopolized by white men. While a fully interactive model would compare the experiences and perspectives of incumbents from all groups, this paper focuses on black women as the pivotal group in defining the commonalities and differences between: 1) black and white women in their experiences of sexism; and 2) black men and women in the face of racism, in police organizations which have long been dominated by and served the interests of dominant white men.

The Police and Discrimination

Police work has a long tradition of discriminatory selection criteria and assignment practices. Until recently, most black men were rejected by racially discriminatory selection procedures that excluded persons that did not "fit" (Gray 1976); those that became officers[1] walked foot beats in ethnic neighborhoods and were prohibited from arresting white offenders (Leinen 1984). Regardless of race, women were employed as "policewomen," got lower pay, and worked with "women, children, and typewriters" (Milton 1972).

In 1972, the Equal Employment Opportunity Act outlawed discrimination by public emloyers on the basis of race, color, religion, sex, or national origin. Since that time, most police agencies have altered discriminatory selection criteria related to education, age, height, and weight, as well as their use of arrest records, agility tests, and veterans' preference (Sulton and Townsey 1981). They have modified the agility tests and personal interview procedures that disproportionately eliminated women and the written examinations that disproportionately eliminated minority candidates; many departments now are guided by affirmative action plans.[2]

As a result, the representation of women and black men in policing has grown. By the end of 1986, in municipal departments serving populations of more than 50,000 people, white men comprised 72.2 percent of the sworn personnel, non-white men made up 19 percent, white women constituted 5.3 percent, and non-white women 3.5 percent. Although black women made up only 2.5 percent of all sworn officers, they constituted 31 percent of the female officers, whereas Black men comprised only 12.5 percent of male personnel (Martin 1990). Above the entry officer rank, the proportion of women police was 3.3 percent and that of black women a mere 1 percent.

While the door to the station house has opened to minority men and all women, both racist (Leinen 1984; Christopher et al. 1991) and sexist attitudes and behaviors remain widespread within police departments (Horne 1980; Hunt 1990; Martin 1980, 1990; Pike 1991). Nevertheless, in comparing the discrimination experienced by female and minority male officers, Pike (1991, 275) suggests that minority men do not challenge the "quintessential" police officer role in the same way women do. Stereotypes of black men fit into the traditional police model since they are seen as physically strong, street-wise, and masculine; their integration did not require organizational changes. In contrast, the integration of women required changes in facilities, uniforms, and physical training programs. In addition, the organizational stereotype of "what women are like" means that women are much less likely to match the ideal type of the officer and those that do risk being labeled "butch" or "bitch." None of these studies, however, has addressed the issue of the unique situation of black women officers and the interactive effects of racism and sexism.

Data Sources and Research Design

The data reported here come from case studies in five large municipal agencies that were part of a larger study designed to assess the current status of women in policing (Martin 1990). The case studies explored departmental policies and procedures for integrating women into policing and officers' perspectives on changes in the status of women over the past two decades.

[. . .]

The interviews were semi-structured, lasted about two hours, and explored a wide range of work issues. In four of the five sites, half of the interviews were conducted by the author (who is white) and half by a black female research associate.[3] When the interview schedule permitted a choice, we each interviewed persons of our own race in order to increase rapport and disclosure of potentially embarrassing information.

Officers' Perceptions of Discrimination

The interviews indicated that across the five case study departments the experience of discrimination is widespread but that officers differ in their perceptions of it both on the basis of gender and race.[4] These differences help explain why female officers rarely have acted in concerted political fashion, despite their common experience of sex discrimination, including sexual harassment.

Most of the female but only a minority of the male respondents believe that they had been victims of discrimination as police officers.[. . .] Sixty-eight percent of the black women and 80 percent of the white women reported encountering discrimination based on either race or sex, in contrast to 43 and 32 percent of the white and black men, respectively ($X^2=58.5$; df=9; p<.001). Yet white and black women differed in their experiences of discrimination. The majority of white women reported facing sex discrimination (77 percent) but were unlikely to believe they had been victims of racial discrimination (20 percent). Black women reported racial discrimination as the more frequent experience (61 percent) than sex discrimination (55 percent), although a substantial minority (48 percent) of the black women reported experiencing both. Black women also were much more likely than black men to report racial discrimination (24 percent compared with 61 percent).

Table 19.1.   Percentage of Case Study Police Officers That Experienced Discrimination by Gender and Race

Type of Discrimination	White Female (N=35)	Black Female (N=31)	White Male (N=21)	Black Male (N=17)
Sex only	60	7	10	—
Race only	3	13	19	24
Both race and sex	17	48	14	—
Neither	20	32	57	76
Total	100%	100%	100%	100%

Among the men, whites claimed to be victims of racial discrimination more frequently than blacks (43 percent versus 24 percent) and most of their complaints were related to racial discrimination (made by 33 percent). Complaints of sex discrimination came only from white men.[5]

Respondents also were asked whether they had benefited or been favored because of their race or sex. Black women were as likely as white women (36 percent versus 38 percent) to report being favored, but the former were more likely to believe they had benefited from both statuses while the white women felt favored only on the basis of their sex. A third of the black men but none of the white males believe they had been favored.

The meaning of discrimination varied among the four groups. Some whites, particularly the men, regard themselves as having been victimized by affirmative action programs which resulted in promotion of black men and women who scored lower than they did on the promotion exam. Male respondents never mentioned and women infrequently commented on the inequities that arise from assignments attributable to informal sponsorship by powerful mentors or from membership in "old boy networks." Thus the measure of "discrimination" is the decision-making process related to a specific opportunity or position, particularly when there are formalized rules that confer advantage to a class rather than individuals. In contrast, there is little recognition of inequities built into the organizational logic (Acker 1990) or the ways that decision rules related to policies, procedures, and systems of evaluations structure advantages or disabilities in ways that are both gendered and racially biased. If everyone competes according to the same formal criteria (whether or not these are appropriate, job related, or biased in some fashion), then there is no perception of discrimination. Conversely, when "the playing field is not level," persons are promoted "out of turn" or from a race or sex-based list, or an assignment is earmarked for a person of a particular race and/or gender, the decision is viewed as discriminatory.

Men, both black and white, also expressed indignation at the "discrimination" arising from women's "taking advantage" of their sexuality to gain sponsorship, protection, and coveted assignments. That as males, some men "took advantage" of informal "buddy" relationships and insider status and were involved in exchanges of other types of favors was ignored by the men and infrequently articulated by the women. Many women also were critical of those (other) women who exchanged sexual favors for job-related benefits. Although they recognized that this had a negative impact on women as a group, (and some observed that individually they had had to work harder because they did not "play"), few labeled it discrimination.

Affirmative Action Policies, Counting Rules, and the Intersection of Race and Sex

Given the presence of discrimination on the basis of both race and gender, how to "count" black females has an important effect on the implementation of affirmative action efforts. Clearly some individual black women have benefited, but in three of the case study departments the rules applied to counting in court orders and affirmative action plans have worked to black women's disadvantage.

This disadvantage was most strikingly illustrated by the legal battle over promotion procedures in the Chicago police department, as black men and white women protected their own interests at the expense of the black women. The department's hiring and promotion process came under supervision of the federal courts as a result of *U.S. v. City of Chicago.* In 1973, after a finding that the sergeant's promotional exam was discriminatory, the judge imposed quotas for promotions. The black women, as black plaintiffs, were represented by the Afro-American Police League and initially were drawn from the promotion list as blacks, regardless of gender. When the white women realized some black women were being promoted to sergeant ahead of them, however, they filed a claim asserting that all females should be treated as a single minority group. The judge ruled that black women could not be given double benefits. He asked the Afro-American League's legal representative whether it was acceptable to count the black women as women, not as blacks, for the purpose of the quota. Without consulting the women, the lawyer agreed.

Perhaps in accepting the change the lawyer recognized that he would increase the number of positions for which blacks were eligible. Alternatively, one might interpret his actions as knowingly undercutting the black women. While the change increased promotion opportunities for black men by removing the women from competition with them, it forced the black women to compete with the white women whose test scores were better than theirs (whereas those of black men were not). When the black women legally protested the decision several years later, the judge agreed that they had a valid complaint but ruled that it was "not timely." As one black woman observed, "Nobody was looking out for our interests."[6]

In another department, although black females now outnumber white females three to one, the affirmative action practice remains the promotion of one white woman for every black woman. In a third department, black women have been double counted, but the result in counting them twice is to shrink rather than expand either the quota for women or for minorities.

Despite these generally disadvantageous counting rules, the black women often have incurred the hostility of both white women and black men who feel that the black women have taken "their" places. Furthermore, when black females act in concerted fashion with black men, as the Chicago lawsuit illustrates, they have less power to share, lower status as women, and face being betrayed or undermined by their "allies" in the latter's quest for advantage.

Race and Gender Effects on Street Patrol Activities

The initial resistance to both racial integration and the assignment of women to police patrol was strong, organized, and sometimes life threatening (Bloch and Anderson 1974; Martin 1980; Leinen 1984; Hunt 1984). Such systematic harassment has largely ended. Nevertheless, both racism and sexism continue, although they are expressed in different ways. Many men—both white and black—still openly voice negative views of women as officers, prefer not to work with them, and alter their behavior when they have a female partner. In contrast, black men are accepted as capable officers, although racial politics abounds and seating at roll calls and most off-duty socializing remain racially separate. Overt expressions of racism, however, are taken seriously by command staff and have led to disciplinary actions in the departments in this study.

How do these patterns of racism and sexism affect black women officers' perceptual world, street patrol behavior, and opportunities for mobility? All rookie officers face a "reality shock" when they begin street patrol. This initial training period is important in developing skills and self-confidence and establishing a reputation. An officer who does not have or take opportunities to develop patrol skills due to limiting assignments, inadequate instruction, or overprotection is likely to be hesitant or fail to act in a confrontation. Such incompetent officers are regarded by others as potential dangers they are anxious to avoid, thus perpetuating the cycle of incompetence on patrol. Gender-based patterns of occupational socialization and expectations of patrol performance influence the way rookies respond, creating self-fulfilling prophecies for many women officers (Martin 1980).

These patterns are most visible for the first generation of women officers who faced organized resistance designed to drive them out of police work. They faced insufficient instruction, co-worker hostility, and the "silent treatment" that "made eight hours seem like eight days"; close and punitive supervision; exposure to danger and lack of backup; and paternalistic overprotection. As one black woman recounted:

> Males didn't want to work with females, and at times, I was the only female or black on the shift so I had to do a lot to prove myself. I was at the precinct 10 days before I knew I had a partner 'cause . . . (the men) called in sick and I was put in the station. The other white guys called the man who was assigned to work with me the 11th day and told him to call in sick. . . . He came in anyway.

Another noted:

> My first day on the North side, the assignment officer looked up and said, "oh shit, another fucking female." That's the way you were treated by a lot

of the men. The sergeant called me in and said the training officer doesn't want to ride with you but I've given him a direct order to work with you.

Although both white and black women were targets of the men's hostility, several black women observed differences in their treatment that reflect differences in the cultural images and employment experiences of black and white women. Historically, white women have been "put on a pedestal," idealized as frail, and spared from physical labor. In contrast, black women have assumed the "beast of burden" role (Dill 1979), performing heavy physical labor in fields, factories, and the homes of white women, as well as coming "to symbolize sexuality, prowess, and . . . embody the 'myth of the superwoman'" (Palmer 1983, 158). Faced with these dual images of womanhood, white women formed their identities around "good" womanhood, accepted their difference from black women, and adopted a sense of superiority, although, in reality, they were powerless, having accepted economic and psychological dependence on white men who control their sexuality.

On patrol, women tend to be treated according to those traditional patterns. In all five departments the initial cohorts of white women assigned to patrol, particularly those that were physically attractive or attached to influential white men, were more likely than black women to be "protected" from street patrol assignments by being given station house duty and rapid transfers to administrative units. As one woman noted,

> white women were put on a pedestal, treated like wives . . . (Many) got jobs doing typing for commanders and downtown assignments. They're high priced secretaries.

On street patrol too, there were and continue to be differences in expectations and treatment of black and white women. Patrol officers rely heavily on fellow officers for backup in dangerous situations; providing backup when another officer calls for help is a central norm of policing (Westley 1970). Police also may support, control, or sanction others by their willingness to "slide in" on calls to provide added police presence and by the speed with which they provide assistance.

Both the lack of reliable backup and overprotectiveness are likely to reduce an officer's willingness to take risks or display initiative. But the officer who fails to act appropriately is shunned as a "coward." And when such behavior is displayed by a woman, rather than being an individual failure, the stigmatizing label is generalized to all women.

Many of the white patrolmen are protective of white women, and the latter acquiesce by enacting the stereotyped roles of "pet," "mother," or "seductress" (Kanter 1977) to gain personal acceptance and backup. Black women also are told to remain "back covers" by male partners who do not expect them to perform as equals. When they defer to white men and accept a passive role, however, they cannot count on being protected as females and may instead be viewed as "lazy" (thereby fitting the "welfare mother" stereotype). A black woman explained:

> Black women don't expect to be nice to them (white men) because white males won't protect us on the street.

Another noted that when she had a white female partner, the white men backed them up; when she worked with a black partner the white men would not do so. Several stated they had faced outright racial harassment, illustrated by the following incident that occurred in 1977:

> My training officer and I went to a call. . . .When we got back, our car door was open and there was a cut out arrow from a sheet of paper taped to the window. The word "nigger" was written on the arrow which was pointing to my seat. My training officer told me not to pay attention to it, but it bothered me. I didn't report it; it wouldn't have done any good . . . but the incident let me know where I stood.

Black women face uncertainties related both to co-worker backup and to unpredictable responses of citizens to a black woman exercising authority. They also are aware of the historical role of the police as oppressors in the black community. These factors contribute to their reluctance to adopt the policing style characteristic of white men who are enthusiastic about "aggressive patrol" and seeking out crime and criminals. This difference in occupational perspective and role performance style was illustrated in interviews with two rookie officers for whom similar assignments to "the projects" posed starkly contrasting problems. The black female was troubled by responding to conflicts involving people she had grown up with and was embarrassed to learn intimate information about their lives. The white male burned out after acting as the macho enforcer zealously arresting for drug offenses persons he viewed as "animals" he had to fight "tooth and claw."

Non-Patrol Assignments and Station House Interaction

Inside the station, women face a hostile working environment filed with sexual propositions, pornographic material, and cursing (Martin 1980; Swerdlow 1989). Several black women asserted that they faced additional displays of deliberate disrespect shown to them as women by the men's use of language.[7] One black woman observed:

> White males generally have very little respect for black females, especially if they don't know you. . . . If a white female is around and they start their cursing, they'll say "excuse me." If a black female is around they don't stop. Their attitude is, "oh it is only a black female, who cares."

Black men also tend to be protective of women but black women cannot count as heavily on them for backup. First, they are fewer in number and, therefore, less available when needed. In addition, they face pressures from the white men (or shared their resistance to women on patrol), not to back the women up.

Interacting with these gender-based stereotypes, black women face widespread racial stereotypes as well as outright racial harassment. Stereotypically, blacks are assumed to be less knowledgeable, reliable, and able to manage power as supervisors. For example, a black female burglary detective observed that white men are reluctant to recognize her expertise. Precinct supervisors often call her unit for information. However, when she answers calls from white males they tend to argue with what she says. Another black woman asserted:

> A white male can goof off all day and nobody'd say a thing. But a woman, especially a black woman . . . has to work twice as hard.

Another woman did just that when she took over the administrative work of two sergeants who retired at the same time in her detective unit. Although she explained, "I had an advantage, I knew how to type," the difference was also one of attitude. The men would wait for a typist; she did the work herself, to assure that the records were current. While she observed, "now everything runs smoothly," her performance may also contribute to the subsequent "downgrading" of such administrative support positions and to their resegregation (Reskin and Roos 1990).

As part of the gendering of organizations, job tasks come to be "loaded with gender meanings" (Hall 1993, 454). Even before integration, not only was policing done by men and thus viewed as "men's work," police attached gendered meanings to various tasks and aspects of the job. Hunt (1984) observed that police symbolically construct their occupational world in terms of oppositional categories with masculine and feminine significance. "Real police work" is associated with the outside domain of the street where men engage in high status, dirty, dangerous crime fighting activities. In contrast, inside administrative work, formal rules, and cleanliness are associated with femininity. As women officers have moved into symbolically "feminine" inside positions, those jobs have become more strongly gender labeled and devalued in the eyes of male officers.

It probably was no accident that men in administrative support jobs emphasized their "masculine" policy and administrative responsibilities, letting the typing pile up rather than perform the task regarded as "women's work." As women gain these assignments, by using their "feminine" typing and office management skills to make the unit operate more efficiently, they also risk transforming the gender and racial meanings of the work so that it confers less prestige and authority.[8]

In some instances, the black women's combination of race and gender has made the nature of their problems ambiguous. One explained:

> Sometimes I couldn't tell if what I faced was racial or sexual or both. The black female is the last one on the totem pole in the department, so if things are okay you thank God for that.

A black female supervisor reported having problems with a white male subordinate who deliberately violated procedures. After he transferred, she learned that his new male supervisor also had problems with him,

> so it wasn't a female thing . . . but at the time I couldn't be sure. . . . I felt he was rebelling against me because I was a female lieutenant and a black lieutenant. I had a double whammy on me as female and black.

Facing the "double whammy," however, emboldened some black female supervisors to stand up to harassment and challenge the systemic racial and gender discrimination they perceived, perhaps because of their detachment from the informal work culture. Like Simmel's "marginal man" (sic), the black female has been the "outsider within" (Collins 1986). Nowhere is this truer than in the "macho" world of police work, where black women are separated both from many black male officers who have enthusiastically embraced its "crime fighting" activities and from white women by the latter's expectations of protection as stereotypic women. Having survived isolation and performance pressures as officers and as sergeants, they relished their access to power and sought to use it in broadly political ways.[9] Several told of challenging evaluation and assignment practices they regarded as racist, not simply for individual career advancement but on behalf of black officers. One black woman in a command position related the following:

> I took a beating for changing things (regarding race). Whites are tribal in this community 'cause they see all blacks as the enemy and as criminals. I understand their ethnocentrism . . . but cannot tolerate some of the stuff that was going on. When I insisted on doing things by the book there was rebellion. . . . Now they're on the right path but they call me 'that woman' because I caused them problems.

A female sergeant related the following experience. When she observed that blacks were receiving lower service ratings, regardless of their productivity, she began recording all activities for the unit. The next rating period, when the lieutenant called all sergeants in to justify their ratings, the whites and the black male sergeant had rated blacks lower than the whites; she rated females and blacks higher. The lieutenant refused to approve her ratings and demanded an explanation. She stated that her ratings were based on her six-month log on all officers' activities and threatened to file a grievance and let the records speak for themselves if the ratings were not changed. She added:

> The lieutenant sat back in his chair and said that in his 15 years as a lieutenant he'd never had a black officer challenge him. He wondered how long it would take for a black to speak up. He added it took guts, but that the service ratings would be changed.

A third black woman supervisor stated that she challenged the disproportionate number of detective positions held by white men after feeling empowered by the model provided by Jesse Jackson when he ran for president.

Dealing with Black Men

Although black women often have worked closely with black men to reduce the effects of racial discrimination, their relations with them also are strained by tensions and dilemmas associated with sexuality and competition for desirable assignments and promotions. Like white women, in the struggle for power and acceptance in policing, black males have sometimes allied with white men. The bases for their alliance, however, rest largely on their shared resistance to the integration of women into the "policemen's" world. Yet, the open hostility of black men to white women—particularly those with close personal bonds to white male police—always poses the threat of reprisals. Consequently, the black men appear to display less hostility to white than black women with whom they compete for positions and promotions earmarked "black" by affirmative action programs.

Illustrating such competition, a black woman observed that when she was promoted her black male peers suggested that she had taken "their" slot. Another noted, "if you speak up or show you can think for yourself . . . you have problems from black men." For example, a black female lieutenant told of being verbally abused by a white lieutenant. When she hung up on him, he called her commander to complain. When her black commander asked why she could not be nicer to the lieutenant, her response was, "The only thing that I hate more than a white man trying to run over me is a black man clearing the way."

Others recounted instances of sexual harassment and the dilemmas it posed in choosing between fighting for one's personal interests as a woman and recognition of a "larger" concern arising from racism and the need to preserve racial solidarity. One black woman observed, "The black men have assumed they could make sexual approaches to black women they would hesitate making to whites." Another reported:

> The worst harassment I got came from a black male lieutenant. . . . The only reason I didn't (file a sexual harassment suit) is because the lieutenant's black. I guess that makes me a racist but I looked at the overall problem it would have caused and how it would be played up in the press and didn't do it.

Elaborating on the competition theme, one woman mused:

> For some reason the black men tend to hurt us more (than white men). . . . Maybe they're afraid of us, although they won't admit it.

Several recounted instances of competition for scarce resources, from being denied lockers in the station house to jealousy regarding assignments. For example, a black woman asserted:

> The white commanders put white women on desk jobs for years. As soon as black females got desk assignments, however, the black guys complained.

Other black women, however, observed that they have had support from black men but poor treatment from whites. One stated, for example:

> Black males are generally good to work with but white males generally have very little respect for black females, especially if they don't know you.

In departments with a large proportion of black personnel or a black chief the effects of racism seem to diminish, but this tends to heighten black women's awareness of sex discrimination, particularly in the selection of members of the command staff:

> No woman in the department is considered capable of operating in the inner circle. . . . It's an exclusive club . . . and having a woman as the right

hand man (sic), the Chief would suffer ridicule from ranking men. They'd say "what can she offer," implying what is done by a woman can't be of value.

Ironically, she did not comment on the implied sexual innuendo.

Relations among Women Officers

All respondents agreed that there is little unity among the women. They are divided by divergent perspectives on occupational performance, gender enactment, racism, and by white men's success using a "divide and conquer" strategy, playing on the racism of white females and the sexism of black males. Consequently, most women do not see it in their best interest to organize.

All police must find a personal style that solves certain work-related problems: dealing with fear and danger; gaining citizen compliance; and relating to peers and supervisors. In addition, women officers must cope with discrimination, sexual harassment, gender stereotypes, and the interactional scripts that incorporate race and gender in what is considered appropriate behavior for a "policeman." They must negotiate an occupational identity and respond to the gender role stereotypes into which they are cast.

Martin (1980) observes that women officers are pressured to enact the police role either as *police*women or police*women*. The former behave in a manner that conforms to existing male behavioral norms and emphasizes being professional, dedicated, aggressive, and controlling even though this means acting "unladylike" and being labeled "dyke" or "bitch." The latter, in contrast, emphasize their femininity, adopt a less assertive policing style, and consequently fail to meet work-related expectations.

Most female respondents stated that they seek to negotiate an identity that allows them to maintain their femininity, succeed as officers, and gain individual acceptance as "just me." Nevertheless, most were critical of other women, including those who "behave like clinging vines" or "act mannish" on the job and those who "act like sluts" or "try to make their way around the department on knee pads" because each of these behaviors contributes to negative stereotyping that "rubs off on us."

Although some women—both white and black—have succeeded in creating a new "woman-cop" identity by combining valued masculine and feminine attributes and self definitions (Hunt 1984), the opportunities, options, and the way they arrived at their identities also are affected by racial scripts for policing styles and prevailing stereotypes of and structural constraints on black and white women.[10]

A few of the women belong to state or national women's law enforcement organizations, but efforts to organize the women in their own agencies have been short-lived or sporadic. Chicago is the only case study site with an active (but still fledgling) departmental women officers' organization, the Coalition of Law Enforcement Officers (CLEO). Formally open to all officers, CLEO is designed to address the concerns of black women officers through educational growth and support activities.[11] Commenting on a recent meeting held by CLEO, one white Chicago officer admiringly observed:

> White women won't be organized. (At the CLEO meeting) they were talk-
> ing about day care! . . . White women have the housewife syndrome; many
> black women are single, used to running a family, and are more assertive.
> . . . Black women have much more consciousness of abuse; white women
> are less aware of abuse as women.

Another white woman added:

> Black females are more militant and don't think white females are suffering.
> I wish they could see how white males treat white females.

[. . .]

Racism compounds the divisions among women. Several blacks noted that white
women are as racist as white men. For example, one woman stated:

> White females seem to think that minorities are totally incompetent, dirty,
> don't know what we are doing, and need to be led by the hand and told
> what exactly has to be done, so that we won't screw up anything. That's
> insulting to me.

Others recounted incidents of racism involving women. Some incidents were individual;
others involved organized actions such as that illustrated by the white women's legal action that blocked black women from accessing both their identities in *U.S. vs. Chicago*.

Joining a women's group, the men assert and white women perceive, means implicitly joining "them" (the other racial group) which makes you not part of "us." For
women of both races acceptance by the men (of the same race) is more important than
the support of other women, for both work-related and social reasons. Since women
usually work with men and depend on them for backup, their support is often a matter of life and death. Men have more experience, "muscle," and are available in greater
numbers than women officers. They also are the supervisors who have the power to
reward and punish. In addition, social activities including dating and marriages occur
along racial lines. Men of each race control women's on-duty behavior by threatening
them with social isolation.

Both white and black men have used racism to control the women of their race
and prevent women from unifying to address sex discrimination. A white female, for
example, said that when she rejected the sexual advances of a white male, he started the
rumor that she only slept with blacks. This attempt to assert white male control used
both racism and sexism: doubly impugning the woman's behavior as both "promiscuous" and "disloyal."

In departments where blacks have gained political and numerical power, overt racism has diminished. However, the salience of their oppression as women is heightened.
As one black female supervisor observed:

> They keep us competing, fat versus thin, old versus young, and women
> seem to fall for it. Getting unity is like pulling teeth. The women say (of a
> female supervisor who tries to counsel them), "she doesn't want to help us"
> and while the women are feuding, the men are moving up.

Conclusions

This study has sought to go beyond dichotomous approaches to understanding both race and gender that have characterized much of the study of racism and sexism. Instead of the prevailing "either/or" approach, it has sought to treat them as interlocking systems of oppression and has employed a "both/and" approach to focus on black women as a unique class or group. It has done so using a narrowly targeted in-depth strategy of examining workplace experiences and perceptions in an occupation long dominated by white men—policing. Such a strategy has both strengths and weaknesses.

On the positive side, police work provides rich opportunities for exploring interlocking dimensions of discrimination and black women's "unique angle of vision" (Collins 1990, 26). Gender is deeply embedded in the police culture, while historically police departments have excluded black officers and have served as enforcers of a system of racial injustice in the black community. Despite changes in the past two decades, the idealized image of the representative of the forces of "law and order" and protector who maintains "the thin blue line" between "them" and "us" remains white and male. As "outsiders within" black women's perspectives on policing challenges the prevailing notions, including the "naturalness" of the police role as it currently is enacted, and hints at an alternative vision of policing. Moreover, their experiences suggest the complexity of the interconnections of racism and sexism which themselves are parts of the larger "matrix of domination" (Collins 1990, 225). They also illustrate some of the ambiguities in distinguishing among the bases for differential treatment.

Domination occurs not only with respect to race and gender but class, age, sexual orientation, and ethnicity, and operates on three levels at which people experience and resist it: the individual; the group or community; and social system. Thus this examination has focused on only one cell of the matrix and explored it for only one particular occupation. Even in this narrowly focused effort, however, the reception of black and white women, and nature of the "discrimination" they experienced appears to have varied across specific work settings, depending on whether or not they were introduced as a result of legal action against the department as well as the racial and social climate in the study sites.

The in-depth strategy has the advantage of reducing the likelihood of either overgeneralization or oversimplification that have characterized studies of both racism and sexism. It suggests that experiences and perspectives are situated not only historically but within organizational and occupational contexts that vary. And, in studying an occupational or organizational setting in which both black and white men are present, it has expanded the "three-way relationship involving white men, white women, and women of color" in which "race and gender dynamics are played out" (Glenn 1992, 34) to give black men a role.

At the same time, it has excluded several important issues and elements of that matrix that should be noted. It "controlled" for several variables by ignoring or excluding them. The class backgrounds of the officers were presumed to be the same for black and white officers; this clearly is questionable and merits further study. Most of the persons that were interviewed were experienced officers and "successes" who had been promoted. The perspectives expressed by these black women may point to useful strategies for survival but understate the problems of "average" women officers, particularly those that left police work. The experiences of a wider segment of the occupational or organizational group also merit future exploration.

The data rest entirely on intensive interviews without observing actual behavior or gathering intensive personality measures. Since discrimination often is subtle, the findings illustrate the ways in which one may easily confuse whether "discrimination" is based on race, gender, age, experience, or personality style. Thus the "by the book" behavior of the female supervisor cited in this paper illustrates how a personality or interactional style that is offensive to others may elicit punishment or be perceived in race or gender terms.

The both/and conceptual perspective allows one to view all groups as having varying amounts of penalty and privilege in a single system that changes over time. White women are penalized by gender but privileged by their race. Depending on the context, an individual may be oppressor and member of an oppressed group or both simultaneously. For example, the interactions of white women officers with other police and with citizens most likely were affected by their age, rank, and by the authority of their office. Similarly, black men alternately were shown to act as mediators and oppressors of black women in "divide and conquer" politics characteristic of many organizational settings.

Assuming the perspective of persons who are multiple minorities illuminates the unique uncertainties and heightened consciousness that result, as well as the advancement strategies likely to be different from those of other groups. As "outsiders within" with limited expectations of climbing onto "the pedestal" or becoming "one of the boys," black women have been able to distance themselves from the occupational culture and adopt a more critical view of it as well as their place in it.

[. . .]

Notes

1. The term police officer has replaced policeman and policewoman as the generic term referring to sworn police personnel of all ranks. While the word "officer" sometimes is used to mean police at the lowest rank in a semi-military organization, I will use it in the generic sense unless otherwise specified.

2. By the end of 1986, 15 percent of the departments in cities serving populations of more than 50,000 were operating under court orders or consent decrees (most of these were in jurisdictions with populations over 250,000) and 42 percent had adopted voluntary affirmative action plans (Martin 1990). Only 4 percent of municipal agencies still had minimum height and weight standards as entry criteria (Fyfe 1986).

3. Personal contingencies prevented the research associate from leaving Washington D.C. to conduct the interviews in Phoenix. The proportion of blacks in that city and police department, however, is very small.

4. After relating their history of assignments and experiences during initial training, respondents were asked directly "Have you experienced discrimination on the basis of race or sex as members of the police department?" No definition of discrimination was provided but all

positive responses were probed. Even before getting to this question, however, many of the women described treatment by training officers, supervisors, and fellow officers that was subsequently described as discrimination or as sexual harassment. A separate question regarding both their definition and experience of sexual harassment was included late in the interview schedule (if the subject had not already been explored).

5. The low proportion of black men reporting discrimination is puzzling. Although it is possible that women's "radar" for detecting discrimination was more sensitive, a more likely explanation is that the interviews, focused largely on women in policing, led the black men to minimize discussion of their own experiences of racial discrimination. Furthermore, the higher proportion of white than black males to claim to have been a victim of discrimination suggests both a reluctance of some of the latter to discuss their experiences and the strength of the white backlash and resentment of affirmative action. The perception of being a victim of "reverse discrimination" was only expressed by respondents in the agencies with court ordered affirmative action policies including racial quotas for promotions. The acrimony over integration was particularly intense in Detroit where a powerful police union dominated by white men had initiated a number of lawsuits challenging several court ordered affirmative action policies.

6. This case clearly illustrates the problem of judicial treatment of black women's employment discrimination claims. If courts shifted from looking one at a time at "protected categories" to conceptualizing "black women" as a distinct class by Title VII of the Civil Rights Act it would a substantial impact on current antidiscrimination efforts (Scarborough 1989).

7. White men sometimes combined expressions of racism and sexism in their put downs of black women by evoking stereotypes of the latter's sexuality. The mechanism was strikingly displayed by a white male respondent in his interaction with the black female interviewer. In discussing the racial integration of the police work he strayed from the question to gratuitously assert:

> I can't accept it that it is acceptable for black women to have babies out of wedlock and give them over to the grandparents. These women prefer to date married men. They don't care how men treat them.

He responded to a question about how white females are accepted in policing saying:

> . . . On a par with black females. I don't want to offend you but if I was reincarnated, I wouldn't want to come back as a black female.

But of course he was deliberately offending, by making clear his stereotypic view of black women as both sexually promiscuous and willing victims of black men.

8. This energetic black woman also stated:

> Initially they (the men) couldn't stand the thought of you being around them; now all administrative units are run by females. Few men type so they seek out good females.

Similarly, an internal audit by the Chicago police determined that women held 53 percent of the "inside" permanent station assignments in violation of the seniority rules.

9. In addition to bringing structural changes, a high proportion of the black women related at least one instance of resisting oppression, bias, or discrimination at a personal level. For example one woman stated:

> When I was (assigned to work) at the jail I had a lieutenant who didn't like blacks period. . . . He wouldn't speak to me. One day I was the only one in the office and if he wanted to get out, I'd have

> to let him out (by opening the electronically-controlled door). I deliberately turned my back to him so he'd have to ask me to let him out. He stood five minutes before saying anything.

Nevertheless, ultimately she "won" by forcing him to recognize and address her as a fellow officer.

10. Examining the structural constraints on correctional officer role enactment, Zimmer (1986) found that they affected black and white in different ways. A woman who wanted to enact the "modified' (or police*woman*-like) style of work performance required protection from male co-workers and safe non-contact assignments from male supervisors. Since most co-workers and virtually all supervisors in the prisons were white men, they forced black women into direct contact assignment. The latter perceived this distribution of assignments as racial prejudice although it was due primarily to the lack of "connections" also faced by white women from urban areas who lacked ties to male supervisors. Harlan and O'Farrell (1982) also note that black women who entered traditionally male blue collar jobs in large industrial firms felt similarly disadvantaged vis-à-vis white women.

11. At the time the data were collected, CLEO was only 18 months old, had been inactive in its first year, and included only 55 members (out of approximately 1,000 women in the department, 455 of whom are black). Its continuation and success under a new leader are uncertain. Its focus on concerns of black women, however, may have removed one source of tension that has hampered organizing efforts in other departments.

CHAPTER 20

When Feminism Had Class

Dorothy Sue Cobble

Twenty-three-year-old Myra Wolfgang strode to the middle of one of Detroit's forty Woolworth's five-and-dime stores in 1937 and signaled for the planned sit-down strike of salesclerks and counter waitresses to begin. The main Woolworth's store was already on strike, and the Hotel Employees and Restaurant Employees Union (HERE) was threatening to escalate the shutdown to all the stores in Detroit. Wolfgang was an art school dropout from a Jewish Lithuanian immigrant family. A natural orator with a wicked wit, she had already given her share of soapbox speeches for radical causes as a teenager before settling down to union organizing in her early twenties. Nicknamed the "battling belle of Detroit" by the local media, she eventually became an international vice president of HERE. But in the 1940s and 1950s, Wolfgang ran the union's Detroit Joint Council, which bargained contracts for the thousands of union cooks, bartenders, food servers, dishwashers, and maids in Detroit's downtown hotels and restaurants. She relished a good fight with employers, particularly over issues close to her heart. A lifelong member of the National Association for the Advancement of Colored People (NAACP), she insisted, for example, on sending out racially integrated crews from the union's hiring hall in the late 1940s and 1950s, rejecting such standard employer requests as "black waiters only, white gloves required."

In the 1960s, Wolfgang, now in her fifties, led a sleep-in at the Michigan state-house to persuade legislators to raise the minimum wage. She also brought Hugh Hefner to the bargaining table to talk about the working conditions of Playboy bunnies at his Detroit club. HERE eventually won a national contract covering all the Playboy clubs by 1969, but Detroit was the first to go union. In the initial bargaining sessions in 1964, Wolfgang and her negotiating team debated with management over the exact length in inches of the bunny suit, that is, how much of the food server's body would be covered. They proposed creating rules not just for bunnies but for *customers*—rules such as "look but do not touch." And they challenged the Playboy practice of firing bunnies as they aged and suffered what management called "loss of bunny image," a somewhat nebulous concept according to the union but not in the eyes of the Playboy Club. Bunny image faded, Playboy literature warned, at the precise moment bunnies developed such employee defects as "crinkling eyelids, sagging breasts, crepey necks, and drooping derrieres."

These fascinating and somewhat atypical labor-management conversations came only after an extensive seven-month organizing campaign. Wolfgang launched her assault by sending her younger daughter, seventeen-year-old Martha, in as a union "salt," shortly after the Detroit club opened in 1963. She was promptly hired, despite being underage. Martha then fed Mom a steady diet of useful information, particularly about the club's wage policies, or rather its *no-wage* policies. Bunnies, it turned out, were expected to support themselves solely on customer tips. Wolfgang and her volunteers picketed the club, wearing bunny suits and carrying signs that read: "Don't be a bunny, work for money." They also secured favorable media coverage, lots of it. To the delight of scribbling reporters, Wolfgang "scoffed at the bunny costume as 'more bare than hare' and insisted that the entire Playboy philosophy was a 'gross perpetuation of the idea that women should be obscene and not heard.'"

I first stumbled across Wolfgang—or, better put, she reached out and grabbed me—when I came across her papers some years ago in the Walter P. Reuther labor archives in Detroit. It was not just her entertaining antics that kept me awake. I was intrigued by her *political philosophy*, particularly her gender politics. She considered herself a feminist, and she was outspoken about her commitment to end sex discrimination. Yet at the same time, Wolfgang lobbied against the Equal Rights Amendment (ERA) until 1972, and she led the national committee against repeal of woman-only state protective laws. She also accused Betty Friedan, author of the feminist best-seller *The Feminine Mystique* (1963) and the first president of the National Organization for Women (NOW), of demeaning household labor, romanticizing wage work, and caring not a whit about the needs of the majority of women. Indeed, in a 1970 Detroit debate between Wolfgang and Friedan hosted by Women's Studies at Wayne State University, things rapidly devolved into mutual name-calling. Friedan called Wolfgang an "Aunt Tom" for being subservient to the "labor bosses" and Wolfgang returned the favor, calling Friedan the "Chamber of Commerce's Aunt Tom."[1]

My curiosity roused, I set out to discover more about the Myra Wolfgangs of the post-Depression decades. I came to understand that there were multiple and competing visions of how to achieve women's equality in the so-called doldrum years[2]—the supposedly quiescent trough of feminist reform between the 1920s and the 1960s. Moreover, the Wolfgangs of the world, far from being oddities, were the *dominant* wing of feminism in that era. In other words, a feminism that put class and social justice at its core did not end with the Progressive-era generation of women reformers. Indeed, stimulated by the rise of a new labor movement in the 1930s and the heady experiences of World War II, it emerged refashioned and modernized by the end of the war. And significantly, unlike the social justice feminism of an earlier era, it was led by *labor* women, women who identified with and worked in the labor movement, arguably the largest and most powerful social movement of the period.

But why hasn't this history been told before? Why aren't the reform efforts of labor women part of the standard narrative of postwar labor and women's history? In part, the absence results from long-standing gender biases that are still operative among many historians of labor. Labor history as a field takes as its primary focus male workers and their activities in the public wage-earning arena. Gender as a category of historical analysis remains external to the narrative and theoretical frame.[3] Yet labor women also are missing from the history of American *feminism*. Indeed, the scholarship on American feminism has a class problem. The history of feminism is largely the story of the efforts of white middle class and elite women to solve their *own* problems. The efforts of working class and minority women to achieve gender justice, as *they* define it, are relegated to the historical margins, if they appear at all.[4]

The labor women reformers featured in this chapter also had a class problem, but theirs was of a different sort. The class problem for them was, in many ways, what I assume it is for many readers of this volume, that is, how to create a *new* politics of class—one that recognizes the multiplicity of class experience and that refuses to take any single class identity or location as representative of the whole. In pursuing their aims, they chose to work closely with the labor movement, and they embraced many of its fundamental tenets. But at the same time, they sought to create a *different* labor movement, one that would include women fully in its governance and in its agenda. In so doing, they were pioneering an alternative feminism, a feminism that took class seriously and that sought a gender equality that would meet the needs of the majority of women, not just the few. The history of this forgotten generation of women labor reformers can help us envision a new class politics and a new, more inclusive feminism, one that would once again have class.

The Other Labor Movement

We have much to learn from our foremothers, even those who lived, worked, and organized in that supposedly benighted prefeminist era before the 1960s. Their generation came of age in the midst of depression and war. Many were "Rosies" who took on wartime jobs and at the war's end supposedly returned to the home and embraced a conservative gender ideology centered on domesticity. Yet the majority of women war workers were working class and had jobs *before* the war. The majority also kept on working *afterward*. Many of these women turned their energies in the postwar decades to building unions and to making those unions more responsive to the needs of women.

The story of union growth in the 1930s is an oft-told tale. But for labor *women*, the 1940s proved just as crucial. The labor movement feminized substantially during the 1940s, adding millions of women to its ranks. The number of women in the labor movement skyrocketed in wartime and then plummeted immediately after the war, but what often gets lost is that the number rebounded in the late 1940s and then remained *far above* the 1930s levels in both *absolute* and *percentage* terms. By 1953, three million women were union members, a far cry from the eight hundred thousand who belonged in 1940, and the percentage of unionists who were women had doubled since 1940, reaching 18 percent. In addition, some two million women belonged to labor auxiliaries. Auxiliaries took in the wives, daughters, mothers, sisters, and, on occasion, "friends" of union men. By the 1940s, many of these women were also wage earners, albeit in unorganized sectors. Although not accorded the full rights and benefits of union membership in the international unions, central labor councils, and labor federations that issued their charters of affiliation, women auxiliary members defined themselves as an integral part of the labor movement, and they participated actively in its political and economic life.[5]

These women union and auxiliary members comprise an "other labor movement" as well as an "other women's movement." This "other women's movement," as Karen Nussbaum, the former head of the AFL-CIO Working Women's Department, enjoys pointing out, is still the largest women's movement in the country, registering over six million women, a fact not lost on the *Wall Street Journal*. In reporting the January 2002 release of U.S. government statistics on union membership, which revealed a 1 percent loss in male membership, down to nine and a half million, and a close to 1.5 percent gain in the number of women, up to almost seven million, the newspaper opened its story with the query "Women's Movement?"[6]

In addition to the rise in the number of women who belonged to unions, the 1940s witnessed the move of women into local, regional, and national *leadership* positions in the labor movement. This development should not be confused with gender parity in union leadership, by any stretch of the imagination. Nevertheless, the power and influence of women in unions increased, and a critical mass emerged of women union leaders who were committed to women's equality as well as to class and race justice. Myra Wolfgang was not alone. Many others made their mark as well: Esther Peterson, Dorothy Lowther Robinson, Gladys Dickason, and Anne Draper of the Amalgamated Clothing Workers of America (ACWA); Maida Springer-Kemp of the International Ladies' Garment Workers' Union (ILGWU); Mary Callahan and Gloria Johnson of the International Union of Electrical Workers (IUE); and a remarkable group of women at the United Auto Workers (UAW), including Caroline Dawson Davis, Lillian Hatcher, Millie Jeffrey, Olga Madar, and Dorothy Haener. Some of the most vocal and visionary labor feminists—women like Ruth Young, the first woman on the international executive board of the United Electrical Workers (UE), and Elizabeth Sasuly and Luisa Moreno of the Food, Tobacco, Agricultural, and Allied Workers of America (FTA)—disappeared from the public stage by the early 1950s, due in large part to cold war politics. But they were the exceptions, not the rule.[7]

It is impossible to give each of these women her due in a short essay. But let me offer two brief biographical sketches—one of Addie Wyatt of the United Packinghouse Workers of America (UPWA), and a second of Caroline Dawson Davis of the UAW. Hired in 1941 at Armour's meat-packing plant in Chicago, Mississippi-born Addie Wyatt, like many African American women in this period, had her first encounter with trade unionism during the war. It wasn't long before she filed her first grievance. The foreman had given her job to a newly hired white woman and reassigned her to a worse position on the "stew line." "I was very angry, and as I always did when there was something I didn't think was right, I spoke out." When the issue couldn't be resolved with the foreman, Wyatt and her union representative, a black woman steward, marched over to the plant superintendent's office. "What effect," Wyatt remembered thinking, could "two black women have talking to the two white, superior officers in the plant?" To her amazement, she and the steward won. Just as surprising was the union response when she got pregnant. The steward explained the union's maternity clause: Wyatt could take up to a year off and her job would be held for her. "I didn't really believe them. But I thought I'd try it, and I did get my job back." By the early 1950s, her local (UPWA 437), the majority of whose members were white men, elected her as vice president. Later, she took over the presidency of the local and ran successfully for the UPWA's national executive board on a platform emphasizing women's rights and the advancement of racial minorities. In 1954, she was appointed to the UPWA staff as the first black woman national representative, a position she held for the next thirty years.[8]

Caroline Dawson Davis, who headed the UAW Women's Department from 1948 until her retirement in 1973, grew up in a poor Kentucky mining family steeped in religion and unionism. In 1934, she got a job as a drill press operator in the same Indiana auto parts plant that had hired her father. Caroline Davis had a strong anti-authoritarian streak, and, like Addie Wyatt, had a bad habit of stepping in to stand up for anyone being mistreated. Both these traits propelled her toward union activity. "The worst thing about a job to me was authority," Davis once explained. "I loved people," she continued, and "I believed in people. I never saw the difference between someone who had a title and a lot of money, and Joe Doe and Jane Doe who swept floors and dug ditches." Thirty-year-old Davis helped organize her plant in 1941, was elected vice president of UAW Local 764 in 1943, and, shortly thereafter, "moved upstairs when the union president was drafted." By 1948, Davis had taken over the reins of the UAW Women's Department. A year earlier, *Life* magazine had run a feature story on "the strikingly attractive lady labor leader," accompanied by a four-page photo spread of Davis. In one photo, Davis lounges at home reading Freud, a thinker whose ideas, she explained to the interviewer, proved indispensable to running her local union. "If I hadn't been a union leader," Davis added, "I would have been a psychiatrist."[9]

The majority of labor feminists[10] came up from the shop floor and were from working class and poor backgrounds, women like Wyatt and Davis. Yet some came from decidedly elite families—not what I expected to find when I first began my research. A generation earlier, many politically engaged college women would have moved into settlement house work, or joined the National Consumers' League, or pursued a career in social welfare. But in the context of the 1930s, they gravitated toward the labor movement. By the 1940s many held union staff jobs as lobbyists and political action coordinators, as community service representatives, and as research and education directors. A few, like Esther Peterson, eventually moved into key government posts.

Perhaps the most influential labor feminist of her generation, Peterson grew up in Provo, Utah, where her father was the local school superintendent. She received her BA from Brigham Young University in 1927 and then pursued graduate work at Columbia Teachers College before being swept up in the dramatic labor struggles of the 1930s. She taught theater, physical education, and economics to working girls at the local YWCA, and she was on the faculty of the Bryn Mawr Summer School for Women Workers until the school closed its doors in 1938, after the faculty and their worker students persisted in such questionable activities as helping the college maids organize. Shortly before her fourth child was born in 1946, Peterson moved from the

Education Department of the ACWA to become its first Washington-based legislative representative. Then, in 1958, she became the AFL-CIO's first woman congressional lobbyist. As Peterson tells the story, she was assigned to John F. Kennedy, the junior senator from Massachusetts, because no one thought he would amount to much. Two years later, the newly elected president tapped her to direct the U.S. Women's Bureau. Eventually, she became the highest-ranking woman official in the Kennedy administration. She is often credited with playing a key role in the establishment of the president's Commission on the Status of Women (the first federal body devoted to assessing women's status and needs), the passage of the Equal Pay Act, and other significant federal breakthroughs of the early 1960s.[11]

Social Rights and Wage Justice

By the end of World War II, this group of women labor leaders had mapped out a broad-ranging and concrete social reform agenda that would guide them into the late 1960s. It also put them in opposition to the National Woman's Party (NWP), to the policies and principles being touted by conservative employers and politicians, and, at times, to the priorities advanced by their union brothers. They came together nationally at a series of U.S. Women's Bureau conferences held for trade union women leaders between 1944 and 1946, and they continued to socialize and work together for the next twenty-five years, first through the Women's Bureau Labor Advisory Committee, a group that served as a national think tank for top women in the labor movement from 1945 to 1953, and then through the National Committee for Equal Pay, which existed from 1953 to 1965, and other ad hoc coalitions.[12]

Like their opponents in the NWP, labor feminists recognized that discrimination against women *did* exist—an assumption not widely shared in the 1940s. Their goal was not to end *all* distinctions on the basis of sex, which they feared would be the result of the passage of the ERA. They sought only to end those distinctions that *harmed* women, that is, the "unfair" or "invidious" distinctions that amounted to discrimination. Some distinctions, they felt, actually benefited the majority of women, such as the woman-only state laws setting wage floors and hour ceilings. They wanted these protections extended to men; but until that happened, the laws should be retained. This conviction was a major source of labor feminists' opposition to the ERA.

Yet the battle over the ERA was not the only source of their alienation from the feminists in the NWP. Sex discrimination was a problem, they agreed, but it was not the *only* problem. Class, race, and other kinds of inequalities needed to be addressed as well. But how? Here again, labor feminists parted ways with the more individualist, equal rights feminist tradition often celebrated in current histories. Individual opportunity, access to the market, and equal treatment with men were important and necessary. But they were also *insufficient*, particularly for poor women. Working class women, like working class men, needed *more* than access to the market or the opportunity to move into the few positions at the top. They needed to *transform* the market *and* the nature of working class jobs. To effect this transformation, labor women looked to the state and to working class organizations.

Space precludes any kind of comprehensive history of labor feminists' reform efforts, but let me briefly describe their principal concerns. Making "no bones about the fact that there are certain things women need that men don't," labor feminists sought accommodation for women's reproductive labor from employers and the state. Pregnancy was not "developed by women for their entertainment," remarked one prominent labor feminist. It was a "social function" and as such should be borne by the community.[13] Labor feminists pushed unions to negotiate improved pregnancy and maternity leaves with job and income guarantees, health coverage for women during childbirth, and contract language that would give workers more control over their work schedules and more time off for family emergencies. Labor feminists also sought to expand disability and unemployment coverage to pregnant women and mothers, fought for tax reforms that would benefit families with dependents, and lobbied repeatedly for federally funded universal child care programs. When labor feminists testified before Congress in the 1940s and early 1950s on behalf of bills amending the Social Security Act, they argued for the importance of universal health care insurance, including the cost of childbirth, and they made a strong case for the sections of the bill that provided four months of paid maternity leave. Caring labor was as deserving of social wages and state benefits as any other work, they reasoned, and the right to a life apart from wage work was an important aspect of what they called "first-class economic citizenship" for women. "Women must not be penalized for carrying out their normal functions of motherhood," Esther Peterson told a convention of international government officials in 1958. But, she ruefully added, "the achievement of our real goal of adequate maternity leave with cash payment and medical and hospital insurance for all women workers is still ahead of us."[14]

These efforts are clearly forerunners to the work-family reforms that have become increasingly central to the current women's movement. Yet the core of the labor feminist work-family agenda still has not been incorporated into today's discussions. For theirs was a reform movement aimed at solving the problems of nonprofessional women. That meant, for them, finding *collective*, not *individual*, solutions to two crucial concerns: low wages and long hours.

The solution to raising women's wages that came to predominate by the end of the 1960s was to move women into higher-paying men's jobs. But this was not the primary strategy pursued by labor feminists. Rather, throughout the 1940s and 1950s they sought to upgrade and change the way the jobs held by the majority of women were valued and paid. The wage-setting systems used by employers undervalued women's skill, productivity, and responsibility, the labor feminists claimed, and a fundamental rethinking of employer pay practices was in order. In other words, when the comparable worth movement burst onto the national stage in the 1980s, resulting in millions of dollars of pay equity raises for secretaries, nurses, and others in underpaid pink-collar jobs, the idea was not new. It had a long historical pedigree rooted in the activism of union women of a generation earlier.

From the 1940s to the 1960s, labor women urged their unions to bargain, picket, and strike over the gender wage gap. They also launched a national legislative campaign for what they called "a fair rate for the job" or "equal pay for comparable work." They succeeded in passing new equal pay laws in eighteen states in the postwar decades, and, in 1945, they introduced a bill mandating equal pay for comparable work into Congress, reintroducing it every year until an amended version passed in 1963. But the amended version was a far cry from what labor women had envisioned. "Equal" had been substituted for "comparable" and the impact of the law diluted considerably. Women should be paid the same as men when they do the same work, the labor feminists had argued; they should also receive a fair and just wage when they do different jobs.

Yet labor feminists' approach to raising women's wages in this period was not limited to calls for equal pay. They also pursued higher wages for women by supporting the extension of collective bargaining to new groups of women, by lobbying for higher minimum wage statutes, and by resuscitating labor's long-standing claim to a "living wage"—or what some historians refer to as a "family wage." The labor movement's wage demands historically were gendered: if a single wage high enough to cover dependents could be achieved, it was often assumed that men would earn it and their wives would contribute to the family economy as homemakers. Rather than abandon the family wage, labor feminists wanted to degender it, to claim it for women as well as men. A just wage recognized dependency and acknowledged that, in many instances, a wage needed to support more than the individual wage earner. This is a particularly important point, given the ideological shift today toward a "market wage," or a wage supposedly determined solely by productivity or supply-and-demand calculations.

"What's after the family wage?" social theorist Nancy Fraser asked not too long ago.[15] Well, unfortunately, the answer does not appear to be a provider or family wage for all but a wage based on what economist Eileen Appelbaum calls an "unencumbered worker ideal." This false ideal and the low wage it justifies extends to women and increasingly to men a new myth of individualism, one that denies the reality of our social interdependence and sets up a false world of always able-bodied, perpetually self-reliant individuals—entities who exist apart from community, civic life, or caregiving responsibilities. This was not the world labor feminists sought.

Ending the "Long Hour Day"

The struggle over time in the postwar era was as gendered as the struggle over wages. Mary Anderson, the immigrant boot- and shoemaker who became the first director of the U.S. Women's Bureau in the 1920s, argued then that the problem of women's inequality would never be solved until the "long hour day" was eliminated. But by the 1940s, the labor movement was seeking time off not in the form of shorter *daily* hours, but in the form of a shorter workweek, a shorter work year and a shorter work life. In the postwar decades, the majority of unions bargained for and won paid vacations, paid sick leave, and paid retirement—what UAW president Walter Reuther called "lumps of leisure." Labor feminists, for their part, supported many of these union campaigns. At the same time, they continued to press for shorter *daily* hours, because the "lumps of leisure" approach did not do much for those juggling the "double day" of household and market work.

Rebuffed in the bargaining arena, labor feminists turned to legislation. They were optimistic that the Fair Labor Standards Act (FLSA), the federal law covering wages and hours that many had helped pass in 1938, could be strengthened. Yet the state hour laws that covered women only—some forty-three states had such laws in 1957—offered even better protection against the long hour day. Many state laws set ceilings on *daily* and *weekly* hours and forbid *any* work beyond those maximums. In contrast, the FLSA used the disincentive of time-and-a-half overtime pay after a forty-hour week to discourage long hours, but it did not forbid them. The FLSA approach, many thought, was an inadequate check on employer power and on the competitive market's relentless drive toward longer hours. Throughout the 1940s and 1950s, then, labor feminists sought to preserve existing state hour laws and, where possible, extend them to men. The opportunity to earn was important, they pointed out, but so was a work time policy that reined in market work and allowed for the right *not* to work as well as the right *to* work.

But the sex-based state hour laws were repealed, and no new effective mechanisms for limiting work time were identified. Rather, the FLSA became the nation's primary regulatory approach to limiting long hours. Recognized as increasingly problematic today, its weakness is certainly part of the reason why work hours in the United States are longer than in any other industrialized country.[16]

An Unfinished Agenda

At the risk of oversimplifying the rich and complex history of postwar social justice feminism, let me conclude by drawing attention to a few of the principles that I take to be both central to that movement and worth reclaiming by those contemplating a feminist class politics for the future. The labor feminists who led the other women's movement in the decades following the Depression articulated their own distinct and evolving vision of women's equality. They sought social as well as individual rights, and the reform agenda they championed—just wages, protection against long hours and overwork, and the social supports and job flexibility necessary to care for their families and communities—launched a debate over employment practices that carries on today. Yet the social and gender inequities they identified have not been resolved. Indeed, economic inequality is on the rise, and the burdens that once bore down largely on working class women—long hours, the incompatibility of parenting and employment, and the lack of societal support for caring labor—are increasingly the problems of everyone. Ending those inequities for the majority of women will depend on a new class politics emerging within the larger women's movement as well as within organized labor.

Such an effort could profitably take many of its pages from its mid-twentieth-century foremothers. The labor feminists whose stories are told here recognized multiple sources of inequality and injustice, and they tried to build a politics that addressed these problems *simultaneously*. Gender, race, and other identities were not add-ons to class experience but inseparable features of it. The question for labor feminists was not whether class or gender or race should be given priority, but how social movements can incorporate difference and how coalitions across difference can be sustained. For the labor movement, that meant understanding that workers come in all sizes and shapes, and that there is no *one* class identity or consciousness because there is no *one* worker.[17] For the women's movement, it meant understanding that women differ among themselves, that is, that there is no one experience of gender, of gender exploitation, or even of gender liberation. Labor feminists believed, as do I, that the strongest political bonds are those that grow out of acknowledging differences as well as commonalities.

Notes

1. Quotes from Dorothy Sue Cobble, *Dishing It Out: Waitresses and Their Unions in the Twentieth Century* (Urbana: University of Illinois Press, 1991), 12, 97–99, 128–30, 199–200; Edwin Lahey, "Myra, the Battling Belle of the Working-Man's Café Society," *Detroit Free Press*, July 24, 1966, 8–11; and Jean Maddern Pitrone, *Myra: The Life and Times of Myra Wolfgang, Trade Union Leader* (Wyandotte, MI: Calibre, 1980), 122–24. For more on Wolfgang, consult Dorothy Sue Cobble, *The Other Women's Movement*, 2–3, 31–33, 180–81, 188–90, 201–2.

2. Leila Rupp and Verta Taylor use the term "doldrums" to describe the postwar decades. They focus on the National Woman's Party as the predominant carrier of feminism in those years. See *Survival in the Doldrums: The American Women's Rights Movement, 1945 to the 1960s* (New York: Oxford University Press, 1987).

3. For a fuller discussion of the gender biases of labor history, see Ava Baron, "Gender and Labor History: Learning from the Past, Looking to the Future," in *Work Engendered: Toward a New History of American labor,* ed. Ava Baron (Ithaca, NY: Cornell University Press, 1991), 1–46.

4. For other scholarly work suggesting the need for new measures of "feminist consciousness," see for example, Evelyn Nakano Glenn, "From Servitude to Service work: Historical Continuities in the Racial Division of Paid Reproductive Labor," in *Unequal Sisters: A Multicultural Reader in U.S. Women's History*, 3rd., eds. Vicki L. Ruiz and Ellen Carol DuBois (New York: Routledge, 2000), 436–65; or Deborah King, "Multiple Jeopardy, Multiple Consciousness: The Context of a Black Feminist Ideology," *Signs* 14 (Autumn 1988): 42–72. When I use the term "working class," I do not mean to suggest a rigid dichotomous class categorization of society. I am simply referring to that majority group in society whose members' income, whether from their own market work or that of family members, derives primarily from nonsupervisory wages or salary.

5. Cobble, *The Other Women's Movement*, 15–25.

6. "Women's Movement?" *Wall Street Journal*, January 22, 2002, A1.

7. For biographical sketches of these and other labor women reformers, consult Cobble, *The Other Women's Movement*, 25–49. Oral histories of Esther Peterson, Maida Springer-Kemp, Mary Callahan, and other trade union women of their generation can be found most readily in Brigid O'Farrell and Joyce Kornbluh, *Rocking the Boat: Union Women's Voices, 1915–1975* (New Brunswick, NJ: Rutgers University Press, 1996).

8. Quotes from Addie Wyatt, "An Injury to One Is an Injury to All: Addie Wyatt Remembers the Packinghouse Workers Union," *Labor Heritage* 12 (Winter/Spring 2003): 26–27; interview with Addie Wyatt by Rick Halpern and Roger Horowitz, January 30, 1986, United Packinghouse Workers of America Oral History Project, State Historical Society of Wisconsin, Madison, Wisconsin. See also Cobble, *The Other Women's Movement*, 32–33, 201–3.

9. Quotes from interview with Caroline Davis by Ruth Meyerowitz, July 23, 1976, "The Twentieth Century Trade Union Woman: Vehicle for Social Change," oral history project, Institute of Industrial Relations, University of Michigan, Ann Arbor; "Lady Labor Leader: To Keep Labor Peace and Prosperity in an Indiana Factory, the Boss of Local 764 Just Acts Like a Woman," *Life*, June 30, 1947, 83–85. See also Cobble, *The Other Women's Movement*, 37–42, 182.

10. I consider them "feminists" because they recognized that women suffer disadvantages due to their sex and because they sought to eliminate sex-based disadvantages. I call them "labor feminists" because they articulated a particular variant of feminism that put the needs of working class women at its core, and because they championed the labor movement as the principal vehicle through which the lives of the majority of women could be bettered.

11. Cobble, *The Other Women's Movement*, 34–36, 151–64, 181–82; and Esther Peterson with Winifred Conkling, *Restless: The Memoirs of Labor and Consumer Activist Esther Peterson* (Washington, DC: Caring, 1995).

12. The following discussion is based on Cobble, *The Other Women's Movement*, chaps. 2–6.

13. Quote from transcript, "Conference of Trade Union Women, April 1945," Women's Bureau, U.S. Department of Labor, record group 86, National Archives and Record Center, Washington, DC.

14. Quote from Esther Peterson, "The Changing Position of Women in the Labor Force," in U.S. Department of Labor, *Labor Laws and Their Administration: Proceedings of the 41st Convention of the International Association of Governmental Labor Officials, Augusta, Georgia, August 24–28, 1958,* Bulletin 199 (Washington, DC: U.S. Government Printing Office, 1958), 22–23.

15. Nancy Fraser, "After the Family Wage: What Do Women Want in Social Welfare?" *Social Justice* 21 (Spring 1994): 80–86.

16. For more on the debate over time, see Cobble, *The Other Women's Movement*, 139–44, 171–73, 186–90; and Dorothy Sue Cobble, "Halving the Double Day: The Labor Origins of Work-Family Reform," *New Labor Forum* 12 (Fall 2003): 63–72.

17. For a fuller discussion of how labor is changing to meet the needs of women, see Dorothy Sue Cobble and Monica Bielski Michal, "'On the Edge of Equality'?: Working Women and the U.S. Labour Movement," in *Gender, Diversity, and Trade Unions: International Perspectives,* eds. Fiona Colgan and Sue Ledwith (London: Routledge, 2002), 232–56.

CHAPTER 21

Myths of Docile Girls and Matriarchs

LOCAL PROFILES OF GLOBAL WORKERS

Carla Freeman

Across the production floors of Data Air and Mulitext, amid colorful poulazzo skirt suits and the latest styles of hair weaves and fashion jewelry, scarcely a male voice is heard, or shirt and tie in view.[1] Why are the offshore data entry operations in Barbados, like a variety of multinational industries the world over, filled with women workers? Do these data processors match the international profile of the "ideal" offshore factory workers across the developing world? Simple though these questions appear, and consistent though the replies they prompt tend to be (among local and foreign corporate managers, development officers, and workers themselves), the answers are not self-evident. I begin this chapter by challenging the assumption that women around the world constitute a cheap, available, and therefore "ideal" and ready-made source of labor for multinational corporations aiming to cut costs by relocating production facilities abroad. By drawing on the historical realities of women's work in Barbados [. . .] and describing the current (and divergent) profiles of Barbadian informatics workers, I show that rather than "tapping reserves" of local women, multinational industries engage in complex and active processes of incorporation—actually creating ideal workers for particular sorts of offshore production.

This process of incorporation relies heavily on particular formulations of gender, and in particular, of femininity. The "young and malleable" "docile girl" is, without a doubt, the most idealized caricature of the global assembly line worker. Multinational industrialists and representatives from third world governments have for more than two decades recited a litany of rationales for why young, single, childless, and well-educated women represent the ideal labor force for their corner of global production. Indeed, they take for granted the abundant existence of precisely this type of female worker in nearly every part of the world.[2] The following comments are typical explanations, from both ends of the spectrum in the informatics industry in Barbados for why export industries hire predominantly women workers.

> I suppose the men would get frustrated just sitting there keying all the time; most men like to know they're moving around or delivering something. (Angela, an informatics worker, 1990)

> Women tend to do light assembly work which involves sitting and manipu-
> lating fine objects. Some persons claim that men don't have that good co-
> ordination. . . . I think it might more be a matter of aptitude, and aptitude
> is probably cultivated by your society and so on. A man is seen in movies
> and in real life doing things, moving and so on. A man is never seen sitting
> . . . especially on a line manipulating fine things. And he may not have the
> practice. . . . Women have had practice manipulating needles and doing fine
> intricate things, embroidery or cake icing, or being more delicate. And also
> they have smaller hands, so if you're going to manipulate fine things their
> physical structure may have some impact. . . . Whatever the reason is, it so
> happens that women tend to do data entry, garments, electronics assembly,
> and men tend to do heavier work. (Representative of the Barbados Indus-
> trial Development Corporation, 1990)

Such sentiments are echoed virtually everywhere across the global assembly line—from Mexico to the Philippines, even in contexts in which the patterns of recruitment have shown signs of change. The fact that these gendered rationales are given voice in Barbados presents a number of ironies, in the light of both historical and contemporary realities of women's work on this small Afro-Caribbean island.

[. . .]

Why Do Women Make "Ideal" Global Factory Workers?

Several excellent studies of the new international division of labor have shed light on the sorts of prerequisites sought by foreign companies establishing off-shore industries in developing countries (e.g., Fröbel, Heinrichs, and Kreye 1980; Harvey 1989; Henderson and Castells 1987; Sklair 1991). Among these are generous tax holidays, a peaceful political climate, the absence of trade union organization, low rent on production facilities, and well-appointed factory shells. In addition to these incentives multinationals have generally been drawn to regions where industrial, community, and family life are strongly influenced by patriarchal relations. Mention is often made by government development officers and corporate representatives of large and available pools of untapped female labor, with the promise that these women make up an ideal and previously ignored reservoir of malleable workers. In fact, cheap labor in the form of young women workers has been described as the single most important factor in the international movements of labor intensive industries, such as garments and electronics, and gender has played a fundamental role in constituting vast labor forces around the world.[3]

Women's youthful and strong bodies are advertised by industrialists and national government representatives around the world as ideally suited for meticulous work and long hours of tedious labor. Their fingers are described as nimble and dexterous and used to fine-detail work from traditional feminine arts of embroidery, sewing, and other needlecrafts. Women are presumed to possess a natural innocence, inexperience, and eagerness to learn that insure a temperament that is ideally suited, as well. Their positions within their families and within third world economies are also integral to many foreign companies' notions of their suitability. They are assumed to be socialized within "traditional," often rural households where patriarchal relations dictate obedient behavior on the part of daughters, and their employment may even have been arranged by a male member of the family. Their status as daughter, furthermore, is said to imply that while their wage will contribute to the household economy, it is not the primary source of support. Their single and childless status insures their availability and undivided sense of responsibility to work. Their youth and recent completion of secondary school (a requirement for many offshore industries at the upper tier of export production sectors, including informatics) implies that they are literate, disciplined to the rhythm of a regimented day, and first-time wage earners. In brief, these young women in terms both of "body" and "mentality," as individuals or as members of households, families, communities, and the international marketplace, have come to represent the quintessential off-shore assembly worker across the globe.

There is a long historical precedent for conceiving women workers as "reserve armies of labor." Following Karl Marx's lead, Harry Braverman (1974, 383) used this notion to describe the process of capital accumulation, whereby an industrial pool of labor can be incorporated or discarded as wage workers as required by capital. Braverman argues that with increased rationalization of a wide range of work (in both industrial and service areas) as well as increased geographical mobility of these jobs, larger numbers of workers are recruited into employed and then reserve armies of labor. The reserve army functions as a flexible reservoir of labor that responds to the demands of capital and now serves as a cheap labor source for expanding service industries. Recent work has turned attention to the fact that women have systematically been drawn into these footloose industries. Braverman (385) notes that "women form the ideal reservoir of labor for the new mass occupations. The barrier confining women to much lower pay scales is reinforced by the vast numbers in which they are available to capital." Women are presented as constituting massive pools of labor, patiently waiting for the tides of capital to pull them into wage work for the first time. And, by definition, women as low wage workers are logically concentrated in those industrial sectors of the economy undergoing rationalization.

[. . .] Why and how women's labor comes to be defined as "cheap" is, in fact, a complex process in which gender is created, contested, and refashioned in particular, culturally specific ways. Women are no more "naturally" cheap labor than they are "naturally" docile or nimble fingered relative to men. [. . .]

Historical analyses of labor and households have demonstrated that the incorporation of women workers into low-wage labor-intensive jobs is not a new phenomenon. Textile mills and factories of the early nineteenth century revealed similar patterns and rationales for hiring large numbers of women workers, as young "mill girls" formed the image of prototypic wage-earning women in expanding industrial enclaves (Tilly and Scott 1978, 63). The relationships, however, between international, local, and household economies, as well as between the state and individual, family, cultural, and corporate conceptions of female labor are historically, culturally, and industry specific (Hartmann 1976; Westwood 1985; Beechey 1987).

The informatics sector in Barbados raises two issues that prompted my persistent questioning of the portrait of the "docile girl" as the universal "ideal" worker in global industries. The first relates to recruitment. Given the clerical white-collar association with computer-based work, I wondered whether even higher educational levels and skills would be demanded than are required in traditional offshore industries and whether the emphasis on youth and first-time work status would continue to be preferred or assumed. Early reports of some other countries entering the offshore informatics business (e.g., Ireland and India) observed that data entry was not a strictly female domain.[4] When offshore data entry work first began in the Republic of Ireland in the late 1970s, a large proportion of men were hired as operators. Indeed, it is particularly noteworthy that in Data Air's sister plant in the Dominican Republic, roughly 40 percent of the operators are men performing virtually the same data entry jobs as their Bajan counterparts.[5] Informatics' predominantly feminine profile in the Barbadian context, therefore, needed explanation.[6] Would the introduction of this impressive computer-centered industry invite greater numbers of men to enter what have been largely female enclaves of offshore production? Related to this point, there has also been some suspicion that clerical workers represent a different (higher) class of workers than factory workers, and the distinction poses important questions in the light of the official placement of the data entry sector under the same umbrella as traditional export industries. In short, I wondered whether the informatics workers represent a group of women workers distinct from their counterparts in the garment and electronics assembly plants that surround them.

A second set of questions relates to the realm of gender ideology and practice in Barbados and the contradiction between the history of Afro-Caribbean women as workers and mothers whose dual roles have been important to Barbadian society and economy (as well as to defining womanhood itself) and the depiction by multinational corporations of third world workers' femininity as "docile and submissive." The portrait of West Indian femininity that emerges from a wide range of sources related to Afro-Caribbean culture—including ethnographic literature on kinship, social structure, and women's work, and fiction, poetry, and music by and about Caribbean women—is not that of the "docile and submissive" woman worker. More common, especially in the realm of labor, are portraits of strong, resilient, resourceful, and hardworking matriarchs, such as those honored by calypsonian Adonijah.

> Woman helped to build this nation
> She helped it advance,
> So when you sing, please give her a chance.[7]
> She cut the cane to make the sugar,
> Make parts for computer,
> Is doctor, teacher, lawyer.
> She can do more than dance.

It takes two, if we must go on,
Without woman, the human race is gone.
Jah, Jah, know what I sing is true.
Is time to give the woman her due.
(Chorus)
She is mother of our children, bearer of life,
My queen, my friend, my woman, my wife.
Come with me, hand in hand,
We will guide you to the promised land.

Ideal and Real Ideologies of Femininity and the Legacy of Reputation and Respectability

Virtually all accounts of gender ideologies in the Caribbean identify a gap between socially prescribed and ideal notions of masculinity and femininity and what goes on in the "real" lives of the majority of Afro-Caribbean people. [. . .] The combination of slavery's brutality (culturally and in every other sense) and the fact that for Caribbean societies like Barbados there existed no indigenous or "native" culture prior to colonization has led many cultural analysts to argue that women and men in this part of the world have faced an unparalleled struggle to counter the Western metropolitan culture of their masters—and for Barbadian women this has been the Victorian cult of femininity (Hodge 1982). According to Senior (1991, 41), "historically, the model for 'right behavior' for women in the Caribbean was an imported one—the model which emerged elsewhere in Western society: that of woman as a being whose purpose is derived from the existence of another, whether husband, father, or extended family, and whose locus is the home or household."

[. . .] Afro-Caribbean masculinity is said to draw its forms of expression (verbal wit and displays of male prowess and virility) and primary loci of activity (public spaces, such as rum shops and street corners) from African roots, and Afro-Caribbean femininity is depicted as mirroring the conventions of European womanhood.[8] If reputation is best demonstrated through informal, face-to-face, noninstitutional exchanges, respectability is best embodied in the interior domains and associated values of the church and home—Christian morality, propriety, and decorum.[9] [. . .]

In this study I see reputation and respectability, not as isolated, ideal types purely derived from their African/European origins, but rather as a persistent and fluid dialectic within contemporary creolized Caribbean culture. [. . .] [T]hroughout West Indian women's history the desire for and sheer necessity of economic independence has been an important dimension of identity and self-image has meant that even idealized prescriptions for femininity are imbued with the notion that independence and work are integral to womanhood. [. . .]

[Barbadian men] find themselves affronted by contemporary young women whom they describe as ambitious, aggressive, "flashy," and generally unrespectable.[10] Notably, women too express a romanticized view of the past in which men were breadwinners, and women could be housewives. Women's "independence" then, is presented by men as a threat to their rightful power and responsibility as patriarchs, and by women as a necessary manifestation of economic need and increased opportunity. Kathleen, a young lead operator at Data Air, reflects on the changes:

> My mother's mother was a maid at a lady's house not far from us. The other [grandmother] did the same line of work. My life is much better. In those days there were a lot of hardships compared with now. Things [now] are much easier. . . . Women are more independent now than then . . . you find women driving cars a lot more . . . they live by themselves with their kids without a man in the house. You find women working in industries and other different work places. . . . Before, I guess, the men used to provide for the women while they stayed at home but now the women are getting out and finding themselves jobs to support themselves without the help of a man. I guess it's okay to have a man around, but if push come to shove, I could handle it on my own, too.

[. . .] The idea of a strong black matriarch draws on the history of women in the Caribbean who shouldered much of the burden of slavery, incipient nationhood, and a modern political economy through their tenacity as mothers and workers.[11] On other occasions, praise for the "responsible high-tech worker" is rooted in what Wilson (1969) construed as a European formulation of femininity—that of the dependent daughter who diligently preserves the moral fabric of society, here, through hard work, a sense of propriety, a naturally patient disposition, and acute manual dexterity. This version of womanhood resonates with Wilson's description of respectability, with the notable exception of the workplace (rather than the home) in which it is enacted.[12] For this version of femininity, as for that of the matriarch, family and home are the motivating force behind the women's responsible performance as workers, and, thus, wage work is interpreted solely as an expression of familial obligation, in which wages constitute a vital contribution to household survival.[13] Both of these ideals present limitations and distortion, as well as apertures for creative expression and the possibility of redefinitions of "worker" and "woman" in the context of the informatics industry. [. . .]

Who Are the Informatics Workers?

CHARLENE

When I met Charlene, she was working at Data Air in the "lifts prep" department, sorting airline coupons for different destinations. She was twenty-five and had been employed at Data Air since the firm opened in 1983. During the first two years of work, she had developed a skin condition related to the carbon on the backs of the airline tickets and stopped working for eighteen months. During that time, she took a full-time correspondence course from the United States to learn BASIC and COBOL computer languages. "I wanted to find another job, but I think now that my navel string is buried in Data Air," she explained with a laugh. Charlene and her seven-year-old daughter lived with her grandparents, both retired now. Her grandfather had been an accountant and her grandmother a seamstress. When Charlene's mother emigrated to the United States to work as a baby-sitter, Charlene came to live with her grandparents, and "then when she came back I didn't want to go with her as such. I was so attached to my grandparents, so I stayed with them." Her mother works as an "executive housekeeper" at one of the expensive West Coast hotels, and her father works for the Barbados Transport Board. Charlene's relationship with her daughter's father ended a year ago, after a six-year visiting relationship. Her daughter's father helps to support her with monthly payments, and Charlene contributes to maintaining the household with her grandparents. "They own the house, so for the bills, they would put half and I put the other half." "I got my daughter the year before I came here and my grandparents took care of her and [her father's mother] took care of her. I worked part-time at the reservations desk at Sandy Lane [one of the island's top hotels] but I was always interested in computers from going to school at Queens College [one of Barbados's top schools]. So this was the first real opportunity for me to go into this. I went and did a little course with computers after I finished school. I had seven 0-levels and two As.[14] At first my family thought this was a good thing until they heard about the pay, and they said, 'What?' Why am I doing this job when I'm so qualified? But, it's what I like doing, so I think that's best. I want something in the computer field . . . computers are the money."

SANDRA

Sandra is new to Data Air. She is eighteen years old and finished school less than a year ago. After a few weeks of temporary work at a local branch of Woolworth's, she applied for the job here and was successful. She works as a claims approver in the new insurance division of Data Air. She lives with her mother, a brother, three sisters, twin nieces, and a nephew. Two other brothers live on their own, and her father lives close by with his wife and children. Her mother works as a maid for a Trinidadian woman who works for an international bank and travels a great deal. Sandra's mother cares for her employer's baby, cooks, and cleans her house. "I learnt a lot from her . . . she been in that business for long, cleaning and such. She is happy. I always say to myself, you should make for yourself your opportunities, because they will not pass your way again. Right now I am happy here. I have no plans for another job at the moment, but I am always looking for a higher post here—to be a lead—collecting and sharing out the work—or QR—quality reviewing the work—and supervisor or anything like that. One of my grandmothers . . . she worked on a plantation in St. John, and she would come down sometimes to visit on weekends or sometimes we would go and spend weekends up by her. To me, the sun out there real hot, and I can't take it on [working in the cane fields]. Where here, it be cold [. . . she shivers]." Sandra's brother works for the government-run National Conservation Corps, cleaning the parks and public facilities; one sister works in an electronics assembly plant, another baby-sits two little boys, and the last sister works as a domestic in a private home, like their mother. At home, Sandra says, "I do the cleaning and my biggest sister usually do the cooking, but if I get home first, I will start the cooking. My last sister, she washes, another helps clean the house. My brother do all the men's stuff around the house. . . . Every two weeks I give my mother [BDS] $40, put some in the bank [BDS $50] and then I buy any toiletries I need, clothes. I'll keep money to last me the other two weeks. Maybe I'll buy foodstuffs, snacks, maybe tinned foods to use to bring to work, underwear or shirts for my nephew or nieces."

ROSEMARIE

Rosemarie is a woman wise and responsible beyond her years. At twenty-seven she has become the head of her household, following the death of both of her parents in a span of three years. She lives with her seven-year-old son, two older brothers, a sister, and niece. The day I met her was Rosemarie's sixth "anniversary" at Data Air as a data processor. Describing her household, she says with resignation and in a somewhat weary tone, "I'm the backbone of it, so I must make sure that it's on par at all times. I'm probably making the least [money of all the siblings] but I contribute the most. That's the way my parents left it, so, after my mother died it was my father, and it was, you know, almost unwritten, but everyone assumed that since she was ill, I would run the household, and I've been doing it ever since. It's a lot on my shoulders. I do most of the cooking, most of the cleaning, most of everything [she laughs]! Everybody else do their own laundry and on the weekend, my sister take over the house. She has the weekends and bank holidays. We take meals together only on the weekends because during the week I am at home when they are at work. . . . I always work second shift. I find it's good because I find during the mornings I can get things done . . . and I get home normally at a quarter to 12. . . . We decided that we're all going to give BDS $200 each month and if there's extras then we divide it by four. I put $100 to the credit union each bi-weekly pay period to save. The house was owned by our parents. Our neighbors give us vegetables from their garden, and we have a few fruit trees. We're, each one of us, hoping to own our own homes as we get more economically able. My sister's twenty-three now [a clerical worker for the National Insurance office], I'm twenty-seven, my brother's twenty-nine [an auto repairman], and the other is thirty-one [a carpenter]. We all have dreams of moving on."

In Barbados's pink-collar enclave, competing portraits of women as ideal workers are increasingly evident. Charlene, Sandra, and Rosemarie demonstrate some of the variation in household configuration, age, life stage, and economic circumstance of the total labor force in this new arena. The new pink-collar workers are simultaneously and paradoxically described by their employers (and themselves) as strong, selfless, and hardworking, frequently the main breadwinners for their children, indeed, as the backbone of society; and they are depicted as materialistic consumers obsessed with fashion and appearances, clever and even mercenary in their strategies for deriving support and piecing together a living. This latter characterization of women frequently asserts that these "girls" are young, dependent on the support of their families, and drawn to these jobs for the "extra" pocket money they provide. As such, these competing profiles of femininity draw on the presumption of an apparently universal "docile girl" but also dramatically contradict this portrait with that of the "strong black matriarch." They echo the familiar notions that women are well suited to low-wage industrial work because they are structurally dependent and temperamentally malleable and simultaneously express equally well-entrenched West Indian gender stereotypes of female strength, fortitude, and guile.

The competing gender ideologies of the powerful matriarch and the docile girl underlie numerous rationalizations for changing divisions of labor and patterns of labor recruitment and are invoked at will to explain why women make ideal workers in one or another domain, or why women are not eligible for particular enclaves of work. For example, within the sugar industry, the belief that women do not have the technical skills and cannot handle the responsibility as well as the night work demanded by factory jobs has kept them out of the higher-paying and skilled areas of the industry (e.g., pan boiling) while in field work women are paid at a lower rate. The call for a middle-class femininity reminiscent of the nineteenth-century European cult of domesticity has at some moments led to the expulsion of Barbadian women from the waged labor force, and at other times the assertion of women's legendary tradition of hard work and physical strength has been the prevailing rationale for their incorporation into new realms of wage work.

These contradictory images of womanhood and femininity emerge in a particularly heightened manner within the offshore information industry, as they are marked by constant allusion to the impressive high-tech, white-collar appearance of these enterprises. When adopted into company rhetoric, these opposing profiles of women workers take on particular importance. On one hand, as implied above, and contrary to accounts of traditional offshore industries in other countries where the idealized profile of the multinational assembly worker has been a young, single, first-time worker, managers in informatics are now known to assert that hiring women who have children (married or single heads of households or not) creates a more reliable and hardworking labor force.[15] Mothers are believed to work harder and generally take their jobs more seriously because regardless of the assistance of their extended families and "child fathers," they are the primary breadwinners for their children. One manager of a data entry operation contemplated hiring women for four-hour shifts to encourage those with children to take the jobs. He thought that the shorter workday would ease their child care burden, and at the same time enable the employment of these superior, more responsible workers. In contrast to the traditional argument for a family wage, where a male head of household is paid at a higher rate on the basis of his breadwinning role, these female heads of household, however, are paid low wages despite their higher levels of responsibility and job commitment.[16] On the other hand, like their counterparts in other countries, local managers were also frequently heard describing the work force as consisting of young girls in their first job who are working essentially for pocket money.[17] In short, this is the familiar "pin-money" argument so used to describe women's work and to rationalize the low wages they receive. These rationales and explanations are invoked as needed to maximize continuity and reliability of the labor force and to minimize wages and overall labor costs. Women, too, echo these competing rationales, even when their own life circumstances directly counter them.

A Barbadian manager of a small data entry company gave the following comment to explain the predominance of women workers:

> One of the factors is that there are about three or four women to every man in Barbados. [He hesitates . . .] maybe you should check that out with the statistical department, but I think that's true. Many of the people out there are females that are unemployed, fairly intelligent people, and typing is a skill that somehow seemed to fit into a female society.

In fact, women have historically outnumbered men in Barbados (the 1990 census figures cite a male population of 123,000 and a female population of 135,000). However, this manager's gross exaggeration reflects his sense of the "cheap reservoir" of female labor created more by women's economic vulnerability than their numerical disproportion.[18] As in many other developing countries, women between the ages of 19 and 25 represent the highest proportion of the unemployed labor force.[19]

The rationales I heard for the unmistakably feminine profile of informatics were grounded in such phenomena as the nature of the production process (typing; performing sedentary and meticulous work), the economic circumstances of both the nation and the family (disproportionate numbers of women out of work and needing employment), and the physical and emotional qualities of femininity that make women well suited to this work over other kinds. These rationales for hiring young "school leavers" (those who have just finished secondary school) bear resemblances to the international characterization but also point to specific dimensions of Afro-Caribbean lower-class culture—in particular, that of its "matrifocal" kinship and household structure. In the Barbadian informatics sector, employers say, on one hand, that they hire young women because their subsistence needs are insured by the safety net of their families and they are "secondary" earners with little financial responsibility. Employers characterize the young women as energetic youth who are eager to work hard both to help their families and to satisfy their own materialistic desires. They do not assume that the women come from patriarchal or nuclear families but instead acknowledge the multiple and extended form Afro-West Indian families have historically taken. Nonetheless, the expectation that youth implies minimal economic responsibility even in the absence of a male breadwinner links these rationales to those commonly articulated across the global assembly line and reinscribes the assumption that low wages are acceptable in the light of young women's structurally dependent position. Departing further from the typical international rationale is the explanation these companies now assert for retaining older women. Mature women are assumed not only to be experienced in the work world and therefore well socialized within the corporate work ethic but also, as Afro-Caribbean women, to be mothers and therefore particularly responsible, dependable employees.

[. . .]

Families, Households, and Divisions of Labor

[. . .] Across the global assembly line, multinational corporations have recruited not just women workers but women workers whose femininity is defined, created, and asserted in particular, different ways. Barbadian women predominantly are recruited for and drawn to informatics as the "ideal" offshore workers for reasons that involve both ideological and economic realities surrounding work and gender. The relationship between these ideologies and realities is complex, and sometimes even contradictory. For example, Charlene, who was raised by her grandparents and now supports her young daughter with her wages from Data Air and some help from her daughter's father, also hopes that she will marry, raise two children, work, and eventually open her own business. Thus, she readily articulates the "ideal" rationale that women are the logical informatics workers because they are better suited physically to the work and do not need to earn a family wage, and at the same time she recounts the economic insecurity of raising a child and piecing together a living and a future for herself and her daughter. The fact that her wage is necessary to the maintenance of her household contradicts the male breadwinner myth that she also carries in her mind. Examples of such contradictions between women's own experiences and histories and the gendered ideologies and rationales they frequently expressed were numerous. They are testaments to the multiple models of womanhood and femininity that coexist not merely between local and global corporate managers or between managers and workers or between the "old guard" and the "new recruits" but in the minds of individual women themselves.

Bajan women are recruited into offshore informatics, not because they are naturally more docile, dexterous, and nimble fingered than men or because they are dependent daughters who need little money because they work merely for "extras" or, on the other extreme, because their status as mothers guarantees their superior work ethic and reliability. These women are incorporated into the informatics sector through the powerful deployment of gender ideologies—local and global—in which the work of processing data is conceived as feminine by virtually all of the actors involved. And, women are drawn to informatics because it is one of few expanding arenas within the nation's economy. For these women, informatics offers an appealing entree into the world of high tech and modernity, as well as the promise of a steady wage. In the process of their incorporation, the ideologies of femininity (both local and global) that construe them as docile, patient, responsible, and even mercenary are invoked and reinscribed in order to make them ideal workers for this new industry. Fundamental to the process is the very fact that femininity is not embodied within a single profile. And, just as the "docile girl" stereotype has simultaneously misrepresented and disciplined women, the idealization of the "matriarch" runs similar essentializing risks that distort the realities of Barbadian women's changing experiences.

While Hall and Peña both draw our attention to the strategic power of difference, they see this difference as merely part of capitalism's strategy and design.[20] What I am arguing here, however, is that women workers have been important actors in the process of defining and making use of difference. History, culture, and women's collective and individual will have all conspired to challenge informatics companies' prescription for "ideal" pink-collar workers. Their insistence, for example, that motherhood and wage work are both integral to womanhood, and the state's support of this reality through laws guaranteeing maternity leave, has led companies not only to abandon their insistence that workers be childless but also to embrace a new "ideal" profile of the "strong matriarch." In doing so, informatics firms find they can profit from this culturally induced flexibility, just as Hall and Peña imply. What their arguments miss, however, is the active participation played by women workers in this drama, in both defining and reconfiguring "difference" amid the advance of global capitalism.

The effects of introducing a counter "ideal" in the form of the powerful matriarch are themselves contradictory. On one hand, women have been able to keep jobs that may otherwise have been turned over to younger school leavers and thus may move into new life stages (as partners, mothers, and wives), retain their jobs, and experience simultaneously the autonomy of a working woman and the affirmation that comes from being a mother. In the context of their informatics jobs, their motherhood confers added esteem and flexibility, as well as economic burden. Their responsibility to their children makes them serious, committed workers who are reliable and loyal to their employer; the employer's recognition of this benefit also makes him or her sympathetic in the event of a child's illness or familial obligations that require flexibility in an otherwise highly regimented work environment. On the other hand, these "matriarchs" increasingly forgo the guarantee of support from their extended kin networks that they might have expected, as well as facilities such as day care and related affordable domestic services that a modern market might otherwise provide. As such, their pink-collar work and their domestic responsibilities place them not as truly independent, powerful matriarchs or "leaders with men as their lieutenants" (Errol Miller 1991, 283) but as Afro-Barbadian women who continue to bear the burden of a double (if not triple) day.

The adaptations and juggling acts women perform in order to maintain their wage work through changing stages of their own life cycles, often in conjunction with informal economic activities as well as domestic responsibilities, make it impossible to perceive them merely as pawns, or as cookie-cutter versions of a global worker in the multinational labor game. Simultaneously, the foreign corporations make strategic use of the variations in family constellation and range of cultural ideologies of femininity and womanhood, as they incorporate them (and maintain them) within their labor force. With their own ends in mind, women and corporations exercise strategies of adaptation and of creative flexibility in redefining the profiles of offshore pink-collar workers in the Barbadian context.

Notes

1. A popular style of wide skirtlike pants usually worn with a matching top or jacket.
2. Africa is a notable exception to this global characterization of sources of ideal women workers for multinational corporate investments.
3. Interestingly, low wages are not the fundamental attraction of Barbados for firms engaging in offshore informatics. Although relative wage differentials certainly contribute to the profits

that can be made by moving there, other factors are even more central, such as the island's technological infrastructure, educated labor force, tax structure for offshore investment, political stability, and support of this industry. Indeed, Barbados has relatively high wages in relation to its Caribbean neighbors (and competitors in the industry) and is therefore aiming for the high end of informatics work over rudimentary and lower-skilled data entry.

4. Jean Pyle's excellent work (1990) on state policies and female employment in Ireland reveals the culturally and historically specific nature of women's incorporation into new export industries. In contrast to well-documented cases of Singapore, Malaysia, the Philippines, and Mexico, where women constitute the vast majority of offshore industrial labor forces, women's (and in particular, married women's) incorporation into the Irish wage economy has been severely curtailed by state legislation surrounding family and reproductive rights as well as high fertility rates and patriarchal household relations that militate against women's independent decision making.

5. This is an intriguing fact, given the well-entrenched pattern of gender segregation in traditional multinational factories in the Dominican Republic (e.g., garments, electronics, food processing). Managers and workers in the Dominican Data Air speculated that the draw of the computer technology along with increasing unemployment and underemployment rates accounted for the presence of young men in this special case of free zone work. They also asserted that a high proportion of these young men are students in technical or university programs who perceive these jobs as a temporary vehicle for getting experience with computers and earning money to help pay for school books and supplies. Additionally, the implementation of labor laws protecting pregnant women, in the 1990s, may account for employers' preference for male workers in what had been considered feminine occupations.

6. There are recent indications of the gender profile of transnational workers shifting in other industries and other countries. In maquiladora industries on the Mexican border, where employers offer greater benefits to attract labor, more men have begun to be employed in traditionally female industries (Catanzarite and Strober 1993; Sklair 1993), and in Taiwan and South Korea, the governments are deliberately shifting the shape of export production toward higher technology, automation, heavier industries, and, thus, male workers (Ward and Pyle 1995, 46).

7. Adonijah is addressing other calypsonians, here, who tend to objectify women in their songs, presenting them in sexual terms, as seductresses, and in generally unflattering ways.

8. There are several problems with Wilson's elaboration of these values as constitutive of Caribbean life. He fails to address any external elements, political or other institutional structures that contribute to the shaping of social realities, and he overstates the purely feminine nature of "respectability." See Besson 1993; Miller 1994; Moses 1977; Pyde 1990; Sutton 1974; Yelvington 1995 for various critiques, commentary, and reformulations of Wilson's respectability and reputation paradigm.

9. This formation resonates with the *casa/calle* dualism of gendered space in Spanish and Mediterranean culture.

10. The coexistence of an illusory sense of a past in which women are seen to have complied with certain feminine ideals and an experience of the present in which women's defiance of these norms poses a problem for the "natural" order of things are themes that emerged in many popular forums during this fieldwork. A public forum was held entitled "Are Caribbean Males in Crisis?" in which much of the discussion focused on "dealing" with the "changes" brought about by women's increasing independence, "latchkey children," and the "decline of the extended family."

11. Interestingly, in these invocations of the strong matriarch image, the emphasis is on strength as it is tied to responsibility rather than power. One might argue that a matriarch

derives power in part through the labor over which she controls, for example, her children. It is possible that this dimension of the figure of the "matriarch" is less well developed in the context of informatics largely because these women are, with few exceptions, mothers of still very young children.

12. Again, this is also the prevailing ideology of femininity within multinational industries across the globe. Interestingly, Olwig (1993b, 163) describes that for Nevisian women who migrate to Britain, ironically, it is only by leaving home (migrating) that they are able to fulfill the ideals of femininity and domesticity prescribed by respectability, such as a nuclear family or a "proper home."

13. As Safa (1990, 94), Stolcke (1984, 286), and others have pointed out, the portrayal of the family as the primary locus of female domination and inequality becomes particularly problematic in the Caribbean context, where the family may as well be viewed as a locus of support, nurturance, and primary identification even for women who also work for wages. For example, Safa (94) found that women workers in the Dominican Republic and Puerto Rico considered their paid employment as part of their domestic identity since they saw their work as contributing to the survival of their families as opposed to their own autonomy or self-esteem. Family, for Caribbean women, then, must be viewed both as a significant locus of social identity and a potential site of patriarchal subordination. What is sometimes overlooked in all of this discussion is the fact that while wages from work may be vital to the survival of a woman's household (whether or not she is head of the household), women work for reasons other than just to support their families.

14. Seven ordinary, or 0-level certificates and two advanced, or A-level certificates is an impressive academic achievement and would probably satisfy the minimum requirements for attending university.

15. Peña (1987, 132) also notes this observation and practice on the part of managers in maquiladoras in Mexico.

16. As noted earlier, there has been a historical trend of wage differentials between typically male and typically female arenas of work in Barbados. For example, between jobs of comparable skill, a machine attendant and a "light" industry assembly operator, the former performed by men receives a median wage of U.S. $119 a week and the latter, by women, U.S. $75 a week.

17. Continuing along these lines, one manager said he had heard (and counted on the fact) that Barbadian women would make good workers because they bear the bulk of responsibility for their children alone, and therefore must be responsible to their employees. However, he argued instead that the matriarchal and extended family seems to provide young people with a guaranteed safety net, thereby obviating precisely the autonomy and sense of responsibility he had hoped to find. Free Trade Zone employers in the Dominican Republic are cited as similarly expressing shifting ideas about ideal labor recruitment. Safa notes (1995, 105) for example, that some prefer women with children because of their greater job commitment (dependency) while others engage in a wide variety of measures to circumvent the burden of maternity leave, ranging from distributing birth control pills free of charge to requiring pregnancy tests or requiring a sterilization certificate before a worker is hired.

18. The argument that women far outnumber men in Barbados has at some moments in history had greater truth than at others and depends on labor migration trends as noted in Freeman (2000, chapter 3).

19. In fact, it is commonly believed that the threat of unemployed women poses a greater social problem than the threat of unemployed men. One point of view often expressed in the popular press holds that unemployed women are somehow more dangerous to society than unemployed men. According to Victoria Durant-Gonzalez (1982, 4), whereas unemployed men are known to "lime" or "hang out" at rum shops and on the streets, women are believed

to be more likely to turn to prostitution and destroy the moral fabric of the society. On the other hand, employed women tend to make greater economic contributions to the support of their children and families, whereas men are more likely to "spend their income among more than one household and in the rum shops"(4). For this reason, and contradicting the former argument, one frequently hears that women's employment not only preserves the moral fabric of society but also insures that wages are "better" (or more altruistically) spent.

20. Leslie Sklair (1993, 172), too, offers a similar argument about the role of gender in configuring idealized global workers: "In the last resort it does not matter to capital whether it is employing men or women—capital is not sexist (nor racist, for that matter), though it does use sexism (and racism) to suit its purposes, which are the production of profits and the accumulation of private wealth."

Enslaved: Bargaining for a Child Domestic Worker in Nepal (© International Labour Organization)

Part VI

GENDER AND THE GLOBAL DIVISION OF LABOR

How do we explain the transnational networks and immigration patterns of hundreds of thousands of Latina women from less-developed countries (LDCs), such as Mexico, Sri Lanka, and the Philippines, to North America, Europe, and the oil-rich Middle East since the 1970s? Why have more Mexican women than men worked in the maquiladoras along the Mexican-American border? How is gender identity manipulated by managers in Chinese workplaces and internalized by workers? How do we explain the emigration of Sri Lankan women to the Middle East as domestic workers and their husbands' subsequent transformed gender identity? Finally, how do we explain the rise of contemporary sex slave labor and the sex trade in areas like Thailand? These and other questions are explored in Part VI.

The world has been enmeshed in a global economy in which women have played a major role in global chains of production over the past several decades. In the last decade more than two hundred million women joined the global labor force, constituting 60 to 90 percent of the labor force in garment and fresh-produce production, along with a large portion of labor in outsourced call centers and financial services. In LDCs, over two-thirds of women are in vulnerable employment. This feminized global supply chain "stretches from the woman sewing a skirt in South Asia or Latin America to the consumer buying it in an upscale department store in one of the world's metropolises . . . shaped by social norms and gender inequalities that can systematically disadvantage women" (UNIFEM 2009).

There are two salient opposing interpretations of globalization and the class- and gender-stratified division of labor. The pro-globalization position can be characterized by the following ideas: First, free markets, free trade, and free choices have given consumers of the world the opportunity to buy imported goods at low cost, thereby transferring power from political institutions to individuals. Second, free trade has exposed corporations to increased competition, therefore decreasing corporate power over consumers. And third, global inequality has decreased since the 1980s. Although the annual gross domestic product (GDP) of the twenty wealthiest countries of the world has doubled over the past forty years, when examining the purchasing power of the individuals in their own countries, inequality has decreased. Since multinational corporations pay 30 percent higher wages than corresponding employers within the same country, according to the pro-globalization argument, inequality between individuals in LDCs has declined (Norberg 2004).

Those who challenge the pro-globalization stance argue that first, free trade agreements such as NAFTA (North American Free Trade Agreement) have given transnational corporations increased power and profits, as the cost of doing business is diminished by low wages, low environmental standards, and lack of unions and regulations. Second, low- and middle-income countries saw a sharply slower rate of economic growth between 1980 and 2005 and increased global inequality, in large part due to pressure from the World Bank and International Monetary Fund (IMF) policies. In an effort to promote cheap exports from LDCs and investment opportunities for multinational corporations, the World Bank and the IMF offered loans to LDCs with the stipulation that the LDCs make "structural adjustments" to their economies in return. These adjustments included: a) cutbacks to government spending on health, education, and welfare; b) reliance on the market to set food prices; c) privatization of state enterprises, such as water, sewer, and electricity; and d) national specialization of one or two cash crops for export. As a result, LDCs have experienced economic instability, coerced emigration, and deteriorated living and work conditions (Hart-Landsberg 2006).

Proponents of the anti-globalization perspective argue that the result of such policies has been catastrophic for many of the world's poor and women. Local elites in many LDCs have welcomed multinational corporations to buy up land and build factories, enhancing their own wealth and power. At the same time, peasant families have become increasingly impoverished and subjected to harsh conditions, as they have generally been forced from the land to become either seasonal workers in the fields, factory workers in export processing areas, home-based workers, or migrants to the West or Middle East, where they work as domestics, servants, and sex workers. Children have frequently ended up on the streets or have been forced into low-wage or slave labor, as their parents can no longer afford to feed them or provide the fees necessary for school.

The readings in Part VI elaborate on the critique of globalization. In "New World Domestic Order," Pierrette Hondagneu-Sotelo pays particular attention to globalization and the transnational immigration of Latina and Caribbean women to the West. The combination of expanded corporate investment in the LDCs, free trade agreements, war, and political persecution in Latin America has pushed women from their local economies in the Caribbean, Mexico, and Central America into the United States and other postindustrial economies. At the time when Euro-American women were becoming more educated and rising in the professional classes, their male partners were not making significant enough contributions to the domestic sphere, leaving a gap to be filled in child care and other domestic tasks. Women from the less-developed world have provided the labor that fills this need. They often leave their own children and families to become domestic workers in North America, Europe, and the Middle East, facing racial and immigrant discrimination.

Immigrants in the United States have faced a backlash, and Latina women have been accused of causing a decrease in wages and employment opportunities for American citizens, as well as competition for welfare benefits. As a result, xenophobic legislation has been passed, such as California's Proposition 184 in 1994, which targeted Latina women and children, denying them access to public education and welfare. Although ultimately found to be unconstitutional, this legislation reflected and created an anti-immigrant climate, paving the way for anti-bilingual education campaigns and the 1996 Welfare Reform Act, which blamed the poor for their own plight and cut back their access to government supports.

Leslie Salzinger similarly examines the role of gender in transnational production in "Trope Chasing: Making a Local Labor Market." In the 1960s American, Asian, and Mexican investors established assembly plants (maquiladoras) along the U.S.-Mexican border, in duty-free "export processing zones," or EPZs. Components produced in the United States were assembled into products (clothing, car engines, and computers, for example) in the EPZs, then reimported into the United States. Taxes were imposed only on the value added outside the United States, reducing corporate costs immeasurably. In addition, Mexican men participated in a temporary, low-wage agricultural bracero program in the American Southwest between 1942 and 1964. This program, combined with subsequent Mexican economic crises, pushed married women with children into the maquiladoras' workforce.

Salzinger argues that gender shaped, and was shaped by, the labor market in the maquiladoras between the 1960s and 1980s. Young women constituted 80 percent of this workforce from the outset, as employers sought a "feminized" workforce. They defined *feminine* as docile, dextrous, obedient, tolerant of boredom, and nonmilitant. Employers even went so far as to hire gay or transvestite males in order to maintain a docile, "feminized" workforce, as they defined it. However, as economic conditions in Mexico worsened in the early 1980s, the previously "feminine" workforce became politicized. The value of the peso dropped in 1982, causing wages to decline, and women workers reacted in decidedly "unfeminine," militant ways. They protested, quit one factory to work in another, and left Mexico entirely for service work in the United States. Thus, the traditional notion of "femininity" as docility was challenged by women workers over time as they became more militant, politicized agents of their own destiny.

Pun Ngai examines the creation and manipulation of a stereotypically "feminine" factory workforce as well in "Imagining Sex and Gender in the Workplace." Shenzhen developed into a thriving economic development zone with massive domestic and foreign investment, where rural peasant women migrate to work in factories that produce goods for the rest of the world's consumption. Ngai argues that these women are torn between competing realities: they desire to participate in globalization and modernity themselves, living in the big cities and purchasing consumer goods. Yet at the same time, they are subject to discrimination as former rural peasants and sexualized factory discipline as female workers. The author describes how contemporary China has sought to control its female workers by sexualizing them, instilling in them a concept of "femininity" as docile and subordinate. Although former chairman Mao Zedong sought to desexualize all workers by not distinguishing their class or gender, today factory managers attempt to control women workers by continually reinforcing the significance of their "femaleness," or inferior status.

While Chinese assembly-line workers resist this form of class and gender control, they are simultaneously trapped by it, as they embody the very politics of gender identity imposed on them. Some seek to ameliorate their workplace exploitation and alienation through the consumption of highly "feminine" goods, such as lipstick and pretty clothes. They feel that by enhancing their "feminine" appeal, they will be able to land a high-paid factory manager as a marriage partner, who will permanently remove them from their rural poverty and enable them to reach a higher social and economic status. This phenomenon is so common that a Chinese word exists to describe it: *dagonmei* is defined as the tension between class identity as a factory worker and sexual identity as a "feminine" woman seeking marriage as a way out of poverty.

Michele Gamburd writes about the effect that globalization has on gender identity in Sri Lanka in "Breadwinners No More: Masculinity in Flux." Traditionally, the "ideal" Sri Lankan man has been portrayed as the family breadwinner. High male unemployment since the creation of free trade zones in the 1970s, however, has transformed this gender ideal and has led to soaring rates of female emigration to the Middle East, where Sri Lankan women have sought work in order to send wages back to their families. Seventy percent of the emigrating Sri Lankan women are married, separated, or divorced, but most have at least one child. Sri Lankan men have generally responded negatively to this social and economic upheaval, perceiving it as a threat to their masculinity. In response, many men have become alcoholic, which in turn has given rise to a new symbol of masculinity within the changed cultural context. Other men have responded by seeking work in heavy manual labor to recoup their masculine role, while still others have accepted the new economic reality and have taken over the domestic work in the home, traditionally perceived as "women's work." Some Sri Lankan men have bullied those whom they perceived as feminine. Others have accepted the changing economic landscape and have attempted to serve as cultural change agents, seeking to normalize these formerly female activities as now acceptably masculine.

Many Sri Lankan women involved in this transnational work in the Middle East have paid a huge price with their lives. Eighty-eight percent have suffered psychological abuse, 38 percent have endured physical abuse, and 11 percent have experienced threatened or actual rape or sexual assault. Sixty percent of these home workers have not received regular food, 34 percent have been imprisoned by their employers, unable to leave the house, and 91 percent have reported working an average seventeen hours a day, without time off. Eighty-one percent have not been paid regularly, and some not at all. Out of all the women who have left Sri Lanka each year for the Persian Gulf, 15–20 percent have returned home prematurely due to abuse and nonpayment of salary or have been drawn into human trafficking or prostitution in the Middle East. More than one hundred such women come home in coffins each year (Waldman 2005). The government of Sri Lanka has been reluctant to investigate these crimes as this labor migration is a major source of revenue. It was estimated in 2003 that it has generated more than one hundred billion dollars in remittances each year (Waldman 2005).

Kevin Bales's piece "Thailand: Because She Looks Like a Child" focuses on the rise of sexual slavery in Thailand. Although prostitution was rendered illegal in Thailand in 1960, shortly thereafter a Service Establishments law was passed that made "entertainment" a legitimate industry. During the 1960s and 1970s American soldiers were stationed in Thailand for R & R as a respite from the Vietnam War. After the troops left in the 1970s, the Thai government encouraged the creation of sex establishments to bring increased tourism to the country. International tourists (two-thirds of whom were unaccompanied men) increased from 2 million in 1981 to over 7 million in 1996. Sex tourism continues to be a major source of income, and for the greedy profiteers of this industry, slavery provides even greater financial rewards. Bales concentrates in particular on the emergence of contract slavery, in which a broker offers to pay a poor family a sum, such as two thousand dollars, for their daughter to allegedly work in a factory or restaurant. Parents relinquish their girls for a variety of reasons, such as extreme poverty, religious beliefs that profess a female child's subordinate status and debt to her parents, a desire to see their daughters employed, and sadly, the desire to attain luxury material goods for themselves.

Once the contract is signed between broker and family, the child learns she has been tricked, and instead of working in a factory, she is forced under threat of severe violence to work in a brothel, performing ten sex acts per night until she pays off her "debt" to the broker for her purchase price. Extreme violence enacted upon these girls ensures that they will not escape from the brothel, as it jolts them into a state of severe shock, preventing them from resisting enslavement. Identity papers are stolen from the young women by the brothel owner, and the girls are sleep deprived, malnourished, and isolated. It isn't until they become diseased that they are seen as disposable and are thrown out or used as sex slave brokers themselves.

Bales writes that overall, 89 percent of trafficked sex slaves have been raped and want to escape, 70–90 percent have been physically assaulted, and 68 percent meet the clinical criteria for post-traumatic stress disorder. Those who are most susceptible to being trafficked are children from impoverished families, as they or their parents face unemployment at home and perceive that there are better economic opportunities elsewhere. Children in war-torn societies, as well as those who come from traditions of "fostering," where a third or fourth child in a family is sent to live and work with a relative in an urban area, are also highly susceptible to being trafficked. Although Bales focuses on sex trafficking within a single country, transnationally, approximately six hundred thousand to eight hundred thousand men, women, and children are trafficked across borders each year; of these, approximately 80 percent are female and up to 50 percent are minors. The majority of transnational trafficked victims are destined for sexual exploitation (U.S. Department of State 2007).

The readings in Part VI illustrate the ways in which globalization has increased economic inequality within families from LDCs, and the often brutal consequences. They also elucidate the ways in which gender identities are used as a means of managerial control, worker resistance, and family adaptation within the contemporary global economy.

CHAPTER 22

New World Domestic Order

Pierrette Hondagneu-Sotelo

Contemplating a day in Los Angeles without the labor of Latino immigrants taxes the imagination, for an array of consumer products and services would disappear (poof!) or become prohibitively expensive. Think about it. When you arrive at many a Southern California hotel or restaurant, you are likely to be first greeted by a Latino car valet. The janitors, cooks, busboys, painters, carpet cleaners, and landscape workers who keep the office buildings, restaurants, and malls running are also likely to be Mexican or Central American immigrants, as are many of those who work behind the scenes in dry cleaners, convalescent homes, hospitals, resorts, and apartment complexes. Both figuratively and literally, the work performed by Latino and Latina immigrants gives Los Angeles much of its famed gloss. Along the boulevards, at car washes promising "100% hand wash" for prices as low as $4.99, teams of Latino workers furiously scrub, wipe, and polish automobiles. Supermarket shelves boast bags of "prewashed" mesclun or baby greens (sometimes labeled "Euro salad"), thanks to the efforts of the Latino immigrants who wash and package the greens. (In addition, nail parlors adorn almost every corner mini-mall, offering the promise of emphasized femininity for $10 or $12, thanks largely to the work of Korean immigrant women.) Only twenty years ago, these relatively inexpensive consumer services and products were not nearly as widely available as they are today. The Los Angeles economy, landscape, and lifestyle have been transformed in ways that rely on low-wage, Latino immigrant labor.

The proliferation of such labor-intensive services, coupled with inflated real estate values and booming mutual funds portfolios, has given many people the illusion of affluence and socioeconomic mobility. When Angelenos, accustomed to employing a full-time nanny/ housekeeper for about $150 or $200 a week, move to Seattle or Durham, they are startled to discover how "the cost of living that way" quickly escalates. Only then do they realize the extent to which their affluent lifestyle and smoothly running household depended on one Latina immigrant woman.

[. . .]

311

The Growth of Domestic Work

The increased employment of women, especially of married women with children, is usually what comes to mind when people explain the proliferation of private nannies, housekeepers, and housecleaners. As women have gone off to work, men have not picked up the slack at home. Grandmothers are also working, or no longer live nearby; and given the relative scarcity of child care centers in the United States, especially those that will accept infants and toddlers not yet toilet trained, working families of sufficient means often choose to pay someone to come in to take care of their homes and their children.

Even when conveniently located day care centers are available, many middle-class Americans are deeply prejudiced against them, perceiving them as offering cold, institutional, second-class child care.[1] For various reasons, middle-class families headed by two working parents prefer the convenience, flexibility, and privilege of having someone care for their children in their home. With this arrangement, parents don't have to dread their harried early-morning preparations before rushing to day care, the children don't seem to catch as many illnesses, and parents aren't likely to be fined by the care provider when they work late or get stuck in traffic. As the educational sociologist Julia Wrigley has shown in research conducted in New York City and Los Angeles, with a private caregiver in the home, parents feel they gain control and flexibility, while their children receive more attention.[2] Wrigley also makes clear that when they hire a Caribbean or Latina woman as their private employee, in either a live-in or live-out arrangement, they typically gain something else: an employee who does two jobs for the price of one, both looking after the children as a nanny and undertaking daily housekeeping duties. I use the term "nanny/housekeeper" to refer to the individual performing this dual job.

[. . .]

Los Angeles' dubious distinction is not hard to explain. All of the top-ranked cities in paid domestic work have large concentrations of Latina or Caribbean immigrant women, and Los Angeles remains the number-one destination for Mexicans, Salvadorans, and Guatemalans coming to the United States, most of whom join the ranks of the working poor. Moreover, Los Angeles is a city where capital concentrates. It is a dynamic economic center for Pacific Rim trade and finance—what Saskia Sassen, a leading theorist of globalization, immigration, and transnational capital mobility, refers to as a "global city." Global cities serve as regional "command posts" that aid in integrating the new expansive global economy. Though Los Angeles lacks the financial power of New York or London, it has a large, diversified economy, supported both by manufacturing and by the capital-intensive entertainment industry. The upshot? Los Angeles is home to many people with highly paid jobs. As Southern California businesses bounced back from the recession of the early 1990s, many already handsomely paid individuals suddenly found themselves flush with unanticipated dividends, bonuses, and stock options.[3] And as Sassen reminds us, globalization's high-end jobs breed low-paying jobs.[4]

Many people employed in business and finance, and in the high-tech and the entertainment sectors, are high-salaried lawyers, bankers, accountants, marketing specialists, consultants, agents, and entrepreneurs. The way they live their lives, requiring many services and consuming many products, generates other high-end occupations linked to gentrification (creating jobs for real estate agents, therapists, personal trainers, designers, celebrity chefs, etc.), all of which in turn rely on various kinds of daily servicing that low-wage workers provide. For the masses of affluent professionals and corporate managers in Los Angeles, relying on Latino immigrant workers has become almost a social obligation. After relocating from the Midwest to Southern California, a new neighbor, the homemaker wife of an engineer, expressed her embarrassment at not hiring a gardener. It's easy to see why she felt abashed. In New York, the quintessential service occupation is dog walking; in Los Angeles' suburban landscape, gardeners and domestic workers proliferate. And in fact, as Roger Waldinger's analysis of census data shows, twice as many gardeners and domestic workers were working in Los Angeles in 1990 as in 1980.[5] Mexicans, Salvadorans, and Guatemalans perform these bottom-rung, low-wage jobs; and by 1990 those three groups, numbering about 2 million, made up more than half of the adults who had immigrated to Los Angeles since 1965.[6] Hundreds of thousands of Mexican, Salvadoran, and Guatemalan women sought employment in Los Angeles during the 1970s, 1980s, and 1990s,[7] often without papers but in search of better futures for themselves and for their families. For many of them, the best job opportunity was in paid domestic work.

Mexican women have always lived in Los Angeles—indeed, Los Angeles *was* Mexico until 1848—but their rates of migration to the United States were momentarily dampened by the Bracero Program, a government-operated temporary contract labor program that recruited Mexican men to work in western agriculture between 1942 and 1964. During the Bracero Program, nearly 5 million contracts were authorized. Beginning in the 1970s, family reunification legislation allowed many former bracero workers to legally bring their wives and families from Mexico. Immigration accelerated, and by 1990 there were 7 million Mexican immigrants in the United States, concentrated most highly in Southern California. Structural changes in the economies of both Mexico and the United States also significantly affected this dynamic. Mexico's economic crisis of the 1980s propelled many married women with small children into the labor force, and with the maturation of transnational informational social networks—and especially the development of exclusive women's networks—it wasn't long before many Mexican women learned about U.S. employers eager to hire them in factories, in hotels, and in private homes.[8]

Unlike Mexicans, Central Americans have relatively new roots in Los Angeles. The Salvadoran civil war (1979-92) and the even longer-running conflicts in Guatemala (military campaigns supported by U.S. government aid) drove hundreds of thousands of Central Americans to the United States during the 1980s. Almost overnight, Los Angeles became a second capital city for both Salvadorans and Guatemalans. Estimates of this population, many of whose members cannot speak English and remain undocumented (and hence officially undercounted), vary wildly. The 1990 census counted 159,000 Guatemalans and 302,000 Salvadorans in the Los Angeles region, but community leaders believe that by 1994, the number of Salvadorans in Los Angeles alone had reached 500,000.[9] Central Americans came to the United States fleeing war, political persecution, and deteriorating economic conditions; and though the political violence had diminished by the mid-1990s, few were making plans to permanently return to their old homes.[10] There have been numerous careful case studies of Central American communities in the United States; among their most stunning findings is that wherever Central American women have gone in the United States, including San Francisco, Long Island, Washington, D.C., Houston, and Los Angeles, they predominate in private domestic jobs.[11]

The growing concentration of Central American and Mexican immigrant women in Los Angeles and their entry into domestic service came on the heels of local African American women's exodus from domestic work. The supply of new immigrant workers has helped fuel a demand that, as noted above, was already growing. That is, the increasing number of Latina immigrants searching for work in California, particularly in Los Angeles, has pushed down wages and made modestly priced domestic services more widely available. This process is not lost on the women who do the work. Today, Latina domestic workers routinely complain to one another that newly arrived women from Mexico and Central America are undercutting the rates for cleaning and child care.

[. . .]

Domestic Work Versus Employment

Paid domestic work is distinctive not in being the worst job of all but in being regarded as something other than employment. Its peculiar status is revealed in many occupational practices and in off-the-cuff statements made by both employers and employees. "Maria was with me for eight years," a retired teacher told me, "and then she left and got a real job." Similarly, many women who do this work remain reluctant to embrace it *as* work because of the stigma associated with it. This is especially true of women who previously held higher social status. One Mexican woman, formerly a secretary in a Mexican embassy, referred to her five-day-a-week nanny/housekeeper job as her "hobby."

As the sociologist Mary Romero and others who have studied paid domestic work have noted, this occupation is often not recognized as employment because it takes place in a private home.[12] Unlike factories or offices, the home serves as the site of family and leisure activities, seen as by their nature antithetical to work. Moreover, the tasks that domestic workers do—cleaning, cooking, and caring for children—are associated with women's "natural" expressions of love for their families. Although Catharine E. Beecher and Harriet Beecher Stowe in the late nineteenth century, like feminist scholars more recently, sought to valorize these domestic activities (in both their paid and unpaid forms) as "real work," these efforts past and present have had little effect in the larger culture.[13] Housecleaning is typically only visible when it is not performed. The work of wives and mothers is not seen as real work; and when it becomes paid, it is accorded even less regard and respect.

[. . .]

In part because of the idiosyncratic and emotional nature of caring work, and in part because of the contradictory nature of American culture, employers are equally reluctant to view themselves as employers. This, I believe, has very serious consequences for the occupation. When well-meaning employers, who wish to voice their gratitude, say, "She's not just an employee, she's like one of the family," they are in effect absolving themselves of their responsibilities—not for any nefarious reason but because they themselves are confused by domestic work arrangements. Even as they enjoy the attendant privilege and status, many Americans remain profoundly ambivalent about positioning themselves as employers of domestic workers. These arrangements, after all, are often likened to master-servant relations drawn out of premodern feudalism and slavery, making for a certain amount of tension with the strong U.S. rhetoric of democracy and egalitarianism.[14] Consequently, some employers feel embarrassed, uncomfortable, even guilty.

Maternalism, once so widely observed among female employers of private domestic workers, is now largely absent from the occupation; its remnants can be found primarily among older homemakers. When employers give used clothing and household items to their employees, or offer them unsolicited advice, help, or guidance, they may be acting, many observers have noted, manipulatively.[15] Such gestures encourage the domestic employees to work harder and longer, and simultaneously allow employers to experience personal recognition and validation of themselves as kind, superior, and altruistic. Maternalism is thus an important mechanism of employer power.

Today, however, a new sterility prevails in employer-employee relations in paid domestic work. For various reasons—including the pace of life that harries women with both career and family responsibilities, as well as their general discomfort with domestic servitude—most employers do not act maternalistically toward their domestic workers. In fact, many of them go to great lengths to minimize personal interactions with their nanny/housekeeper and housecleaners. At the same time, the Latina immigrants who work for them—especially the women who look after their employers' children—crave personal contact. They *want* social recognition and appreciation for who they are and what they do, but they don't often get it from their employers. I argue that while maternalism serves as a mechanism of power that reinscribes some of the more distressing aspects of racial and class inequality between and among women, the distant employer-employee relations prevalent today do more to exacerbate inequality by denying domestic workers even modest forms of social recognition, dignity, and emotional sustenance.

[. . .]

Moreover, scarcely anyone, employer or employee, knows that labor regulations govern paid domestic work. Lawyers that I interviewed told me that even adjudicators and judges in the California Labor Commissioner's Office, where one might go to settle wage disputes, had expressed surprise when informed that labor laws protected housecleaners or nanny/housekeepers working in private homes. This problem of paid domestic work not being accepted as employment is compounded by the subordination by race and immigrant status of the women who do the job.

Globalization, Immigration, and the Racialization of Paid Domestic Work

Particular regional formations have historically characterized the racialization of paid domestic work in the United States. Relationships between domestic employees and employers have always been imbued with racial meanings: white "masters and mistresses" have been cast as pure and superior, and "maids and servants," drawn from specific racial-ethnic groups (varying by region), have been cast as dirty and socially inferior. The occupational racialization we see now in Los Angeles or New York City continues this American legacy, but it also draws to a much greater extent on globalization and immigration.

In the United States today, immigrant women from a few non-European nations are established as paid domestic workers. These women—who hail primarily from Mexico, Central America, and the Caribbean and who are perceived as "nonwhite" in Anglo-American contexts—hold various legal statuses. Some are legal permanent residents or naturalized U.S. citizens, many as beneficiaries of the 1986 Immigration Reform and Control Act's amnesty-legalization program.[16] Central American women, most of whom entered the United States after the 1982 cutoff date for amnesty, did not qualify for legalization, so in the 1990s they generally either remained undocumented or held a series of temporary work permits, granted to delay their return to war-ravaged countries.[17] Domestic workers who are working without papers clearly face extra burdens and risks: criminalization of employment, denial of social entitlements, and status as outlaws anywhere in the nation. If they complain about their jobs, they may be threatened with deportation.[18] Undocumented immigrant workers, however, are not the only vulnerable ones. In the 1990s, even legal permanent residents and naturalized citizens saw their rights and privileges diminish, as campaigns against illegal immigration metastasized into more generalized xenophobic attacks on all immigrants, including those here with legal authorization. Immigration status has clearly become an important axis of inequality, one interwoven with relations of race, class, and gender, and it facilitates the exploitation of immigrant domestic workers.

Yet race and immigration are interacting in an important new way, which Latina immigrant domestic workers exemplify: their position as "foreigners" and "immigrants" allows employers, and the society at large, to perceive them as outsiders and thereby overlook the contemporary racialization of the occupation. Immigration does not trump race but, combined with the dominant ideology of a "color-blind" society, manages to shroud it.[19]

[. . .]

Regional racializations of the occupation were already deeply marked in the late nineteenth and early twentieth centuries, as the occupation recruited women from subordinate racial-ethnic groups. In northeastern and midwestern cities of the late nineteenth century, single young Irish, German, and Scandinavian immigrants and women who had migrated from the country to the city typically worked as live-in "domestic help," often leaving the occupation when they married.[20] During this period, the Irish were the main target of xenophobic vilification. With the onset of World War I, European immigration declined and job opportunities in manufacturing opened up for whites, and black migration from the South enabled white employers to recruit black women for domestic jobs in the Northeast. Black women had always predominated as a servant caste in the South, whether in slavery or after, and by 1920 they constituted the single largest group in paid domestic work in both the South and the Northeast.[21] Unlike European immigrant women, black women experienced neither individual nor intergenerational mobility out of the occupation, but they succeeded in transforming the occupation from one characterized by live-in arrangements, with no separation between work and social life, to live-out "day work"—a transformation aided by urbanization, new interurban transportation systems, and smaller urban residence.[22]

[. . .]

For Mexican American women and their daughters, domestic work became a dead-end job. From the 1880s until World War II, it provided the largest source of nonagricultural employment for Mexican and Chicana women throughout the Southwest. During this period, domestic vocational training schools, teaching manuals, and Americanization efforts deliberately channeled them into domestic jobs.[23] Continuing well into the 1970s throughout the Southwest, and up to the present in particular regions, U.S.-born Mexican American women have worked as domestics. Over that time, the job has changed. Much as black women helped transform the domestic occupation from live-in to live-out work in the early twentieth century, Chicanas in the Southwest increasingly preferred contractual housecleaning work—what Romero has called "job work"—to live-in or daily live-out domestic work.[24]

While black women dominated the occupation throughout the nation during the 1950s and 1960s, there is strong evidence that many left it during the late 1960s. The 1970 census marked the first time that domestic work did not account for the largest segment of employed black women; and the proportion of black women in domestic work continued to drop dramatically in the 1970s and 1980s, falling from 16.4 percent in 1972 to 7.4 percent in 1980, then to 3.5 percent by the end of the 1980s.[25] By opening up public-sector jobs to black women, the Civil Rights Act of 1964 made it possible for them to leave private domestic service. Consequently, both African American and Mexican American women moved into jobs from which they had been previously barred, as secretaries, sales clerks, and public-sector employees, and into the expanding number of relatively low-paid service jobs in convalescent homes, hospitals, cafeterias, and hotels.[26]

These occupational adjustments and opportunities did not go unnoticed. In a 1973 *Los Angeles Times* article, a manager with thirty years of experience in domestic employment agencies reported, "Our Mexican girls are nice, but the blacks are hostile." Speaking very candidly about her contrasting perceptions of Latina immigrant and African American women domestic workers, she said of black women, "you can feel their anger. They would rather work at Grant's for $1.65 an hour than do housework. To them it denotes a lowering of self."[27] By the 1970s black women in the occupation were growing older, and their daughters were refusing to take jobs imbued with servitude and racial subordination. Domestic work, with its historical legacy in slavery, was roundly rejected. Not only expanding job opportunities but also the black power movement, with its emphasis on self-determination and pride, dissuaded younger generations of African American women from entering domestic work.

[. . .]

Two factors of the late twentieth century were especially important in creating this scenario. First, as many observers have noted, globalization has promoted higher rates of immigration. The expansion of U.S. private investment and trade; the opening of U.S. multinational assembly plants (employing mostly women) along the U.S.-Mexico border and in Caribbean and Central American nations, facilitated by government legislative efforts such as the Border Industrialization Program, the North American Free Trade Agreement, and the Caribbean Basin Initiative; the spreading influence of U.S. mass media; and U.S. military aid in Central America have all helped rearrange local economies and stimulate U.S.-bound migration from the Caribbean, Mexico, and Central America. Women from these countries have entered the United States at a propitious time for families looking to employ house-cleaners and nannies.[28]

Second, increased immigration led to the racialized xenophobia of the 1990s. The rhetoric of these campaigns shifted focus, from attacking immigrants for lowering wages and competing for jobs to seeking to bar immigrants' access to social entitlements and welfare. In the 1990s, legislation codified this racialized nativism, in large part taking aim at women and children.[29] In 1994 California's Proposition 187, targeting Latina immigrants and their children, won at the polls; and although its denial of all public education and of publicly funded health care was ruled unconstitutional by the courts, the vote helped usher in new federal legislation. In 1996 federal welfare reform, particularly the Immigration Reform Act and Individual Responsibility Act (IRAIRA), codified the legal and social dis-enfranchisement of legal permanent residents and undocumented immigrants. At the same time, language—and in particular the Spanish language—was becoming racialized; virulent "English Only" and anti-bilingual education campaigns and ballot initiatives spread.

Because Latina immigrants are disenfranchised as immigrants and foreigners, Americans can overlook the current racialization of the job. On the one hand, racial hostilities and fears may be lessened as increasing numbers of Latina and Caribbean nannies care for tow-headed children. As Sau-ling C. Wong suggests in an analysis of recent films, "in a society undergoing radical demographic and economic changes, the figure of the person of color patiently mothering white folks serves to allay racial anxi-eties."[30] Stereotypical images of Latinas as innately warm, loving, and caring certainly round out this picture. Yet on the other hand, the status of these Latinas as immigrants today serves to legitimize their social, economic, and political subordination and their disproportionate concentration in paid domestic work.

Such legitimation makes it possible to ignore American racism and discrimina-tion. Thus the abuses that Latina domestic workers suffer in domestic jobs can be explained away because the women themselves are foreign and unassimilable. If they fail to realize the American Dream, according to this distorted narrative, it is because they are lazy and unmotivated or simply because they are "illegal" and do not merit equal opportunities with U.S.-born American citizens. Contemporary paid domestic work in the United States remains a job performed by women of color, by black and brown women from the Caribbean, Central America, and Mexico. This racialization of domestic work is masked by the ideology of "a color-blind society" and by the focus on immigrant "foreignness."

Global Trends in Paid Domestic Work

Just as paid domestic work has expanded in the United States, so too it appears to have grown in many other postindustrial societies—in Canada and in parts of Europe—in the "newly industrialized countries" (NICs) of Asia, and in the oil-rich nations of the Middle East. Around the globe Caribbean, Mexican, Central American, Peruvian, Sri Lankan, Indonesian, Eastern European, and Filipina women—the latter in disproportionately great numbers—predominate in these jobs. Worldwide, paid domestic work continues its long legacy as a racialized and gendered occupation, but today divisions of nation and citizenship are increasingly salient. Rhacel Parrefias, who has studied Filipina domestic workers, refers to this development as the "international division of reproductive labor," and Anthony Richmond has called it part of a broad, new "global apartheid."[31]

In the preceding section, I highlighted the inequalities of race and immigration in the United States, but we must remember that the inequality of nations is a key factor in the globalization of contemporary paid domestic work. This inequality has had three results. First, around the globe, paid domestic work is increasingly performed by women who leave their own nations, their communities, and often their families of origin to do it. Second, the occupation draws not only women from the poor socioeconomic classes but also women of relatively high status in their own countries—countries that colonialism made much poorer than those countries where they go to do domestic work. Thus it is not unusual to find middle-class, college-educated women working in other nations as private domestic workers. Third, the development of service-based economies in postindustrial nations favors the international migration of women laborers. Unlike in earlier industrial eras, today the demand for gendered labor favors migrant women's services.

[...]

Social Reproduction and New Regimes of Inequality: Transnational Motherhood

[...]

Since the early 1980s, thousands of Central American women and Mexican women in increasing numbers have left their children behind with grandmothers, with other female kin, with the children's fathers, and sometimes with paid caregivers while they themselves migrate to work in the United States. The subsequent separations of time and distance are substantial; ten or fifteen years may elapse before the women are reunited with their children. Feminist scholarship has shown us that isolationist, privatized mothering, glorified and exalted though it has been, is just one historically and culturally specific variant among many; but this model of motherhood continues to inform many women's family ideals.[32] In order to earn wages by providing child care and cleaning for others, many Latina immigrant women must transgress deeply ingrained and gender-specific spatial and temporal boundaries of work and family.

One precursor to these arrangements is the mid-twentieth-century Bracero Program, discussed above. This long-standing arrangement of Mexican "absentee fathers" coming to work in the United States as contracted agricultural laborers is still in force today, though the program has ended. When these men come north and leave their families in Mexico, they are fulfilling masculine obligations defined as breadwinning for the family. When women do so, they are entering not only another country but also a radical, gender-transformative odyssey. As their separations of space and time from their communities of origin, homes, children, and sometimes husbands begin, they must cope with stigma, guilt, and others' criticism.

The ambivalent feelings and new ideological stances accompanying these new arrangements are still in flux, but tensions are evident. As they wrestle with the contradictions of their lives and beliefs, and as they leave behind their own children to care for the children of strangers in a foreign land, these Latina domestic workers devise new rhetorical and emotional strategies. Some nanny/housekeepers develop very strong ties of affection with the children in their care during their long work-weeks, and even more grow critical of their employers. Not all nanny/housekeepers bond tightly with their employers' children (and they do so selectively among the children), but most of them sharply criticize what they perceive as their employers' neglectful parenting—typically, they blame the biological mothers. They indulge in the rhetoric of comparative mothering, highlighting the sacrifices that they themselves make as poor, legally disenfranchised, racially subordinate working mothers and setting them in contrast to the substandard mothering provided by their multiply privileged employers.

Notions of childhood and motherhood are intimately bound together, and when the contrasting worlds of domestic employers and employees overlap, different meanings and gauges of motherhood emerge. In some ways, the Latina transnational mothers who work as nanny/housekeepers sentimentalize their employers' children more than their own. This strategy enables them to critique their employers, especially the homemakers who neither leave the house to work nor care for their children every day. The Latina nannies can endorse motherhood as a full-time vocation for those able to afford it, while for those suffering financial hardships they advocate more elastic definitions of motherhood—including forms of transnational motherhood that may force long separations of space and time on a mother and her children. Under these circumstances, and when they have left suitable adults in charge, they tell themselves that "the kids are all right."

These arrangements provoke new debates among the women. Because there is no universal or even widely shared agreement about what constitutes "good mothering," transnational mothers must work hard to defend their choices. Some Latina nannies who have their children with them in the United States condemn transnational mothers as "bad women." In response, transnational mothers construct new measures to gauge the quality of mothering. By setting themselves against the negative models of mothering that they see in others—especially the models that they can closely scrutinize in their employers' homes—transnational mothers redefine the standards of good mothering. At the same time, selectively developing motherlike ties with other people's children allows them to enjoy the affectionate, face-to-face interactions that they cannot experience on a daily basis with their own children.

Social reproduction is not simply the secondary outcome of markets or modes of production. In our global economy, its organization among privileged families in rich nations has tremendous repercussions for families, economies, and societies around the world. The emergence of transnational motherhood underscores this point, and shows as well how new inequalities and new meanings of family life are formed through contemporary global arrangements in paid domestic work.

Point of Departure

As we have seen, no single cause explains the recent expansion of paid domestic work. Several factors are at work, including growing income inequality; women's participation in the labor force, especially in professional and managerial jobs; the relatively underdeveloped nature of day care in the United States—as well as middle-class prejudices against using day care; and the mass immigration of women from Central America, the Caribbean, and Mexico. We have also examined the cultural and social perceptions that prevent paid domestic work from being seen and treated as employment, and have observed how contemporary racialization and immigration affect the job. Yet simply understanding the conditions that have fostered the occupation's growth, the widely held perceptions of the job, or even the important history of the occupation's racialization tells us little about what is actually happening in these jobs today. How are they organized, and how do employers and employees experience them?

Jobs in offices, in factories, or at McDonald's are covered by multiple regulations provided by government legislation, by corporate, managerial strategies, by employee handbooks, and sometimes by labor unions; but paid domestic work lacks any such formal, institutionalized guides. It is done in the private sphere and its jobs are usually negotiated, as Judith Rollins puts it, "between women." More broadly, I argue, paid domestic work is governed by the parallel and interacting networks of women of different classes, ethnicities, and citizenship statuses who meet at multiple work sites in isolated pairs. While employer and employee individually negotiate the job, their tactics are informed by their respective social networks. Today, many employers in Los Angeles and many Latina immigrants are, generationally speaking, new to the occupation. Rather than relying on information passed down from their mothers, both employers and employees draw on information exchanged within their own respective networks of friends, kin, and acquaintances and, increasingly, on lessons learned from their own experiences to establish the terms of private, paid domestic work (hiring practices, pay scales, hours, job tasks, etc.). That employers rarely identify themselves as employers, just as many employees hesitate to embrace their social status as domestic workers, means that the job is not always regarded as a job, leading to problematic relations and terms of employment.

Although there are regularities and patterns to the job, contemporary paid domestic work is not monolithic. I distinguish three common types of jobs:[33] (1) *Live-in nanny/housekeeper.* The live-in employee works for and lives with one family, and her responsibilities generally include caring for the children and the household. (2) *Live-out nanny/housekeeper.* The employee works five or six days a week for one family, tending to the children and the household, but returns to her apartment, her own community, and sometimes her own family at night. (3) *Housecleaner.* The employee cleans houses, working for several different employers on a contractual basis, and usually does not take care of children as part of her job. Housecleaners, as Mary Romero's research emphasizes, work shorter hours and receive higher pay than do other domestic workers, enjoying far greater job flexibility and autonomy; and because they have multiple jobs, they retain more negotiating power with their employers.[34]

Notes

1. Child care centers in the United States evolved out of the poorhouses and settlement projects, and continue to be stigmatized as providing second-rate care (see Clarke-Stewart 1993; Wrigley 1995). Many parents don't like to take young children out of the home; and many Americans express a strong cultural preference for familial care, or for the one-on-one attention received in a private home and not in an institutional setting, for virtually all types of care giving (see Stone 1998).

2. Wrigley 1995.

3. In 1997 the California Department of Finance released information showing that the strong growth in personal income tax revenue, collected from the unprecedented number of individuals enjoying soaring stock dividends, bonuses, or profits in business partnerships, had far exceeded the expectations of state finance experts, pushing tax receipts almost $1 billion ahead of what had been anticipated for fiscal year 1996–97 (Flanigan 1997). Already by 1996, California's postrecessionary economy was producing what one reporter called "a bumper crop of new millionaires" and new entrants to the $100,000+ income bracket (L. Gordon 1998, A1). Stock options and capital gains drove up the number of California tax filers with adjusted gross incomes of $1 million or more from about 9,000 in 1994 to 15,000 in 1996. In the same period, Californians reporting incomes between $100,000 and $1 million increased by 32 percent to 777,000 (L. Gordon 1998, A20).

4. Saskia Sassen, in her pathbreaking book *The Global* City (1991), identifies London, Tokyo, and New York as the major centers for coordinating and controlling the global economy; but many have noted that Los Angeles belongs on this list, not as a center of high finance so much as an economy of entrepreneurial companies intimately connected to world markets.

5. Waldinger 1996.

6. See Waldinger and Bozorgmehr 1996:14–15.

7. According to one estimate, 144,415 Latina immigrant workers arrived in Southern California in the 1980s, and 142,827 before 1980. These figures, which include Latina immigrant workers ages 25 to 64 in 1990, were calculated by Dowell Myers and Cynthia Cranford (1998), using the year of immigration from the 1990 Census PUMS. It is widely acknowledged that the census routinely undercounts poor, minority, and immigrant populations who do not speak English; and when women are employed in "invisible" jobs—as private domestic workers, as vendors in the informal sector, or in sweatshop assembly—they are even less likely to be counted.

8. For research on Mexican immigration and social networks, see Massey et al. 1987; Hondagneu-Sotelo 1994. On Mexican women's labor force participation in Mexico, see Beneria and Roldan 1987; and de Oliveira 1990.

9. For 1994 estimates, see Jonas n.d.: n. 6. These high estimates continued to increase; by 1999 the *Los Angeles Times* reported that Southern California had become home to 750,000 residents with roots in El Salvador, and 500,000 first- and second-generation Guatemalans (Olivio 1999). See also Lopez et al. 1996; Ulloa 1998.

10. A survey of 300 Guatemalans and Salvadorans in Los Angeles and San Francisco, conducted after the peace accords were signed in El Salvador in 1992, found that only 9 percent had definite plans to return to Central America, probably influenced by the perception of economic stability and economic advantages for their children in the United States, their ties to family, jobs, and other institutions in the United States, and continued economic decline in Central America. See Chinchilla and Hamilton 1997.

11. See Hagan 1994; Repak 1995; Mahler 1995; Lopez, Popkin, and Telles 1996; Menjívar 1999.

12. As Romero explains (1992, 21–23), the inability to recognize paid domestic work as real work is predicated on the dichotomous separation between "work" and "family." "Housework," she notes, "does not fit the definitions of work as productive labor, it does not produce values which can be exchanged in the capitalist marketplace" (21). Romero also observes that "the same 'unskilled' tasks that consume housewives' daily energy and time are indeed considered productive labor when performed as paid work in the labor market . . . [in] laundries, restaurants, and day care centers" (23).

13. In the introduction to their book published in 1869, Catharine E. Beecher and Harriet Beecher Stowe explained that they sought "to elevate the honor and remuneration of [domestic] employment" (13), in both its paid and unpaid forms.

14. As Judith Rollins (1985, 48) notes, for early American settlers, "democratic ideas undermined comfort with the traditional paternalistic master-servant relationship," presenting "a contradiction between the value of egalitarianism and the actual class and caste stratification."

15. Rollins 1985; Kaplan 1987; Romero 1992.

16. The amnesty program allowed nearly 3 million formerly undocumented immigrants, mostly Mexican, to obtain legal permanent residency—what is colloquially called the "green card"; a huge upsurge in naturalization applications in the mid–1990s followed. For a discussion of U.S. immigration policies as they have affected Mexicans, see Baker et al. 1998.

17. For an analysis of legalization strategies among Salvadoran immigrants and advocates from the early 1980s to the late 1990s, see Coutin 1998. In the spring of 1999, President Clinton announced his support of legislation providing amnesty-legalization for Salvadorans and Guatemalans who can prove they have permanently resided in the United States since 1990. This legislation did not pass in 2000.

18. See Colen 1989; Hondagneu-Sotelo 1997.

19. On the ideology of a "colorblind" society, see Gotanda 1991 (cited in Kim 1999); Omi and Winant 1994.

20. Katzman 1981, 66–69; Sutherland 1981, 4–6.

21. Katzman 1981, 222, 278.

22. Glenn 1986, 103; Katzman 1981, 90.

23. See Romero 1992, 79–87; see also Garcia 1981; Deutsch 1987. The historian Albert Camarillo has described the occupational ghettoization of Mexicans and Chicanos (1979, 80): "Regardless of nativity and regardless of whether one was a second-generation descendant of Mexican-born parents or a first-generation descendant of one of the earliest Mexican settlers in California, the likelihood of upward mobility was almost nil."

24. Romero 1992.

25. Rollins 1985, 56; Glenn 1986, 266 n. 21; Powers 1990 (cited in Repak 1995, 57).

26. In a significant journal article, Glenn (1992) has referred to service jobs in institutional settings as commodified social reproduction. "Racial-ethnic women," she notes, "are employed to do the heavy, dirty, 'back-room' chores of cooking and serving food in restaurants and cafeterias, cleaning rooms in hotels and office buildings, and caring for the elderly and ill in hospitals and nursing homes, including cleaning rooms, making beds, changing bed pans, and preparing food. In these same settings white women are disproportionately employed as lower-level professionals (e.g., nurses and social workers), technicians, and administrative support workers to carry out the more skilled and supervisory tasks" (20).

27. Liddick 1973a; see also Liddick 1973b.

28. Although immigrant women from Korea, Taiwan, the Philippines, Vietnam, Cambodia, and China have also entered the United States in great numbers during this period, they enjoy greater employment opportunities because of their higher (on average) educational status, and their access to jobs in family businesses in ethnic enclaves and in the professions.

29. See Chang 1994. In a 1995 article I argue that Latina immigrants and their children were targeted because they were perceived as nonworkers whose social reproduction needs drain the public welfare system. Notions of race, class, gender, and generation were central to this xenophobic legislative effort.

30. Wong 1994, 69.

31. Parreñas 2000; Richmond 1994.

32. On the cult of domesticity and feminist "rethinking of the family," see Thorne and Yalom 1992; Glenn 1994. For a broader discussion of how women in Latin America are affected by notions of family rooted in industrialization and urbanization, as well as by Mexican cultural controlling images of *la Virgen de Guadalupe, la llorona,* and *la Malinche,* see Hondagneu-Sotelo and Avila (1997).

33. I have not included in this research project domestic workers who work as "companions" or in elder care, in part because those working in this sector are primarily Filipina immigrants who have backgrounds in nursing or other health professions or are home care workers, contracted and paid not privately by individual employers but by the state of California, with funds from a mix of federal, state, and local sources. In Los Angeles I met very few Latina immigrants who had worked in elder care or as *damas de compañía,* but this occupation may be more concentrated in popular retirement centers. As baby boomers age, the demand in paid domestic work may soon shift from nannies to companions of the elderly. For research on Latina immigrants working in the latter domestic jobs, see Ibarra 2000. For research on Filipinas working in elder care in Los Angeles, see Parreñas 2000. Women who work in for-profit cleaning firms are also omitted, because I have chosen to focus on private paid domestic work. For a study of cleaning firms, see Mendez 1998.

34. Romero 1992.

CHAPTER 23

Trope Chasing

MAKING A LOCAL LABOR MARKET

Leslie Salzinger

> Today, from Penang to Ciudad Juárez, young Third World
> women have become the new "factory girls," providing a vast pool
> of cheap labor for globetrotting corporations.
>
> Annette Fuentes and Barbara Ehrenreich

[. . .] In Ciudad Juárez, managers indeed began by hiring young women, thus defining and shaping the local labor market through citing transnationally generated images of productive femininity. Over time, however, the tenacity of the equation of femininity with offshore productivity created a shortage of precisely such subjects, increasing the price and undermining the docility of local women workers and discomfiting local patriarchal elites. Thus, the story of the maquila labor market in Juárez is not only one of the hyper-exploitation of young women workers, but of the drying up of the "vast pool of cheap labor," of maquila managers' ongoing struggles to manage workers who aren't who they expect them to be, and of Juárez elites' (highly compensated) discomfort with the process. In this context, gender certainly shapes the export-processing labor market, but not through transnationals' capacity to leverage the ineluctable productivity of young, third-world women. Rather, gender intervenes because it is the terrain upon which the question of who looks like a maquila worker, and who doesn't, is decided, thus establishing the context within which hiring takes place and production is initiated.

Unemployed Men, Women's Work

When the program which established Mexico's maquilas was put into place in 1965,[1] it was already framed in public, gendered rhetorics. Yet, seen with the clarity of hindsight, the gendering looks doomed from the outset, for the framework was all about masculinity.[2] For decades, the U.S. government *bracero* program had imported Mexican men to work in the fields of the southwestern United States. Domestic pressures in the United States brought this to a halt in 1965, leaving both countries worried about the impact of 200,000 returning—and jobless—braceros on Mexico's border state.[3] The guarantee of tax-free entrée into the United States for the products of Mexican export-processing factories was intended to alleviate this problem by encouraging the establishment of businesses that could hire returning male farmworkers. On the face of it, the program was a phenomenal success. In 1975, a decade after it was established, maquilas employed more than 67,000 workers,[4] almost entirely at the border. By early 1992, when I arrived, they provided work for seven and a half times that number.[5] Unfortunately for this scheme, however, the jobs were not going to returning braceros; in fact they were not going to men at all. From the outset, young women made up over 80 percent of maquila workers.[6] Investors, while increasingly willing to participate in the program as the years progressed, had arrived with their own ideas about whom to hire.[7]

By the time the maquila program was established, free trade zones were already operating in East Asia, explicitly advertising the virtues of their feminine labor force.[8] Managers coming into Mexico took for granted that they would hire women. A 1966 report by the consulting firm Arthur D. Little,[9] oft-cited as a "smoking gun" in discussions of the exploitative dimensions of maquila hiring practices, explicitly suggested hiring women in order to increase the number of potential workers and thereby increase employer leverage. More telling, however, is an early treatise for prospective maquiladora investors, which simply assumed the workforce would be female and went on to enumerate Mexican women's many attractions: "From their earlier conditioning, they show respect and obedience to persons in authority, especially men. The women follow orders willingly."[10] This set of assumptions operated on the shop floor as well as in public relations. In a particularly fascinating example of this managerial common sense in the program's early years, we find managers looking to hire gay men when women were unavailable—for example, when women were still prohibited from doing night work. Van Waas describes a manager who requested gay men "as queer and effeminate as possible" and commented, "If I can't have women, I'll get as close to them as I can."[11] Similarly, in Anarchomex, a manager with a long history in the industry describes his experience supervising "the pink line." "They worked well, like women. It was very famous, that line."

Managers such as these claimed to be describing Mexican femininity, if not Mexican women, but they were in fact doing something else. Along with their colleagues in Asia, they were developing a new set of meanings for "femininity" that freed it from its location within the family, even potentially from its connection to female bodes at all, and reconstituted it as a set of transferable characteristics, including cheapness, natural docility, dexterity, and tolerance of boredom.[12] In the process, their description became prescription, and the transnational trope of productive femininity became the new standard for maquila workers, women and men alike.

[. . .] In 1979, a union spokesman still described the many "little ladies" who "aspired" to work in the maquilas, adding that the quantity of female labor in the area was "inexhaustible."[13] In the same period, the manager of a General Electric plant in Juárez explained at a conference that, given the 25 percent unemployment rate, they were able to hire two or three of every twenty-five applicants.[14]

In marked contrast to the sanguinity of transnational managers about these desirable new workers, the preferential employment of young women in the maquilas elicited troubled discussions in local media and conversation about the erosion of "traditional" patriarchal structures.[15] These anxieties were—and are—particularly evident in Ciudad Juárez, where concerns about the industry's preference for women were sharpened by the city's economic dependence on the maquilas and its national reputation for deviant sexuality and gender roles. A city of roughly a million people,[16] Ciudad Juárez is geographically isolated within its home country, linked instead with its U.S. "twin city" El Paso, in the midst of a windy desert. As a result of this placement, the city was barely subsisting on the traditional border "industries" of cheap liquor and prostitution in 1965. It was hungry for jobs, and starving for "respectable" ones, when the maquila program was established.[17]

Early discussions of the program by local elites were imbued with anxieties about working-class women's sexuality. [. . .] A 1971 article, "The Maquiladora Plants and the Border Woman," encapsulated the city's conflicted attitude toward the industry's hiring practices. In quick succession, it worried about the high number of single mothers in the plants and the local scarcity of maids and lauded Mexican women's special aptitude for maquila work (comparable even to that of their Asian counterparts) and the plants' role in slowing the growth of prostitution in the city.[18] In these few lines, the article captured the mixture of pride and shame, as well as the close links between discussions of women's work and women's sexuality, which characterized, and continues to characterize, local discussions of women's work in the industry.

This elite ambivalence was only heightened by women workers' increasingly assertive self-presentation as their preferential employment continued. In interviews from the period, workers recounted newly found "independence" from formerly controlling fathers and husbands.[19] Writing in the early eighties, Fernández-Kelly described the emergent assertiveness of these young workers, including scaring away men who showed up at "their" bars by jeering at them.[20] That these developments provoked anxiety in the city[21] is evident in articles like two written in 1979 in Juárez and printed in both the *Los Angeles Times* and a major Mexico City paper. In huge letters, the first headline declaimed, "MAQUILADORAS: Evil Exploitation of Women's Work: Fracture Traditional Mexican Family Structure." The next day its sequel added, "FAILURE OF THE BIP [the maquila program] TO EMPLOY BRACEROS: A Labor Force That Displaces the Man as Breadwinner."[22]

The linked anxieties reverberating through this article about familial disintegration, male displacement, and female misplacement continued to echo through local media coverage throughout the seventies and early eighties. In 1972, a bureaucrat was quoted in a local paper complaining that the maquilas "hadn't served the function for which they'd been created" because they'd hired women rather than men.[23] Calls by union leaders and local intellectuals to hire men were constant; they claimed that only by employing men as well as women could the maquiladora industry halt the "assault on family unity."[24] Throughout the seventies, Juárez papers enthusiastically reported each new promise of the imminent advent of "heavy" industry, expressly geared to the employment of male workers.[25] The Belgian consul made headlines in 1977 by saying that he intended to encourage Belgian investment that would provide work for men.[26]

When a maquiladora "for men" finally opened in 1979, its eighty-eight new jobs received tremendous attention, and local unions continued to laud its existence despite a quickly earned and well-deserved notoriety for toxic work conditions.[27]

By 1980, promises of a surge in "men's jobs" had become more diffident. A local bureaucrat, discussing his "confidence" that "this year" the maquilas would hire men, added: "To be honest, we must recognize that as of now, nothing is guaranteed, and all we have is the faith that this will happen."[28] In 1981, in the context of an expanding industry that showed no sign of changing its employment practices, an article used one of many reports of the imminent arrival of men's jobs to express elite anxieties about the erosion of local working-class manhood. "The husband, without work, lives off his wife, either losing his value as man of the house, if he still has it to lose, or otherwise, openly establishing a gigolo's existence."[29]

Media coverage was almost as perturbed by the women working as by the men who weren't, worrying over women's new and unnatural "emancipation."[30] Local pundits discussed young women's "premature growth" and disproportionate authority in the home.[31] Newspaper headlines blared about the dangers of "liberated women" in the plants carrying venereal diseases to an unsuspecting public through unregulated prostitution.[32] A Justice of the Peace announced that divorces were increasing because male unemployment generated "a false independence among the women."[33] And public functionaries repeatedly appeared in the media to obsess about maquila workers as mothers, whether the issue was the impact of their "dissolute lifestyle" on the health of newborns or ambivalent reports of their "liberated" decisions to register illegitimate children.[34] In 1980, a union began offering self-improvement courses for women workers, "so women workers save their moral and human values."[35]

There is of course a certain irony here. Young women were brought into the maquilas as ineluctably "feminine" and addressed as such internally. In the process of referencing this purportedly homegrown personality, transnational managers frequently succeeded in constituting it in the factory. Nonetheless, young women in Juárez, often migrating from cities further south to work in the plants, were less and less likely to live in traditional patriarchal homes[36] and were increasingly expressive of this newfound freedom outside the factory.[37] Thus, as transnational managers celebrated women workers' familially induced suitability for the rigors of assembly, local elites worried over their increasing assertiveness in the home, and about their male counterparts' consequent displacement in both spheres.[38] The few Mexican plant managers, members of transnational and local communities alike, ultimately articulated a perspective which reflected both celebration and unease. Thus, their viewpoints occasionally diverged from that of their more numerous foreign counterparts. In the following period, as women workers' shop-floor docility came under suspicion as well, these differences would come to be significant.

When Women Stop Acting like "Women"

In the early eighties, the industry romance with its workers began to fade. The U.S. economy went into a downward spiral, and maquila workers immediately began to feel the effects, not only in decreased hiring, but in mass layoffs and enforced "time off." After years of double-digit growth, the number of workers employed by the plants in Juárez fell by 6 percent between 1981 and 1982. By 1982, formerly "docile" workers were losing patience. The years 1981 to 1983 saw a burst of worker "demands" against their employers before the labor board (the Junta de Conciliación y Arbitraje).[39] Local papers reported in June 1982 that there had already been more formal strike threats in six months than there had ever been before in a full year—.8 per maquila.[40]

In 1980 and 1981, two strikes became the focus of dramatic media coverage. In mid-1980, a conflict between two unions[41] erupted at Andromex (Salzinger 2003) and for seven months, the public was treated to the sight of women workers yelling at their bosses, barricadng themselves in the plant, and forcefully asserting their right to be heard. The following year, at Fashionmex, workers legitimately concerned that the company would close down without paying the legally required worker indemnifications took their complaints to local authorities, to the streets, and to the media. They marched through downtown handing out leaflets proclaiming "For the union of all maquila workers!!" and forcibly stopped a truck full of company products from leaving the city before workers were paid.[42] At the same time, a newly radicalized COMO (Center for the Orientation of Women Workers)[43] weighed in on the side of "working women" in general, supporting both the Fashionmex and Andromex struggles and loudly proclaiming working women's right to self-determination.

The maquilas responded to these challenges either by leaving town[44]—or, more commonly, by threatening to leave—or with highly publicized blacklists intended to keep out "conflictive people."[45]Although they complained loudly of worker intransigence, they showed no sign of reevaluating the gendering of their hiring strategies. Local media, on the other hand, narrated the developments through their usual troubled gendered lens. Thus, stories of maquila workers' resistance were imbued with sexual innuendoes and mockery. At the end of the Andromex conflict, one paper reported that weird unfeminine hairstyles and a hysterical woman worker running nude through the plant were "the last straw" for workers after a bad year.[46] Six months later, a cartoon of the women at Fashionmex showed them busty and mini-skirted, ooing and ahing over their union boss,[47] and the day a recount went in their favor, a local paper buried the victory—reporting it inside an edition whose red, inch-and-a-half front-page headlines screamed "PROSTITUTION IN THE MAQUILADORAS."[48]

Amid this charged context, 1982 brought a drastic peso devaluation—the first of a series that would follow over the upcoming decade. Between 1981 and 1982, the dollar value of the peso was cut in half, and average maquila wages fell from US$234.30 weekly to US$105.60[49] The following year, maquila employment in Juárez jumped 26 percent. Even more dramatic devaluations followed in 1986 and 1987. By the end of the decade, in dollar terms, the peso was worth a mere fraction of its value at the outset of the maquila program,[50] and maquila employment in Juárez had tripled.[51]

[. . .]

As the value of maquila wages fell, women workers who had become reliant on higher salaries looked elsewhere. Local newspapers reported them moving into better paying "men's jobs"[52] and crossing the border to "earn dollars."[53] It was this set of decisions which, in tandem with management's inflexibility on wages, produced the "shortage" so dramatically presented in personnel department accounts. This was occasionally recognized at the time. In May 1988, *Twin Plant News* tartly lectured its readers. "Many companies believe that [because of] the large number of maquila plants that have been started in the last few years . . . there aren't enough people to go around . . . we would like to point out . . . that the number of 'employable' operators is still larger than the number of vacancies."[54]

Transnational managers expected "feminine" workers. That meant workers who were as inherently cheap and docile as they were sexed. However, cheapness and pliancy are at least in part market products, and tight labor markets rarely produce them. Thus, despite maquila managers' experience of the grueling labor shortage of the eighties as something like a natural disaster, it was substantially of their own making. In defining the paradigmatic maquila worker as simultaneously cheap, female, and docile, they created a market which eventually undercut the conditions of existence for such a creature. Many young women were still willing to work in the plants, of course, but there were no longer enough to keep all industry lines running at once. Ultimately the demand for cheapness made some shift in the demographics of maquila workforces inevitable.

The rigidity of transnational management's image of an appropriate maquila worker not only diminished women worker's availability, it also eroded the "docility" of those available. The alarmism of the early eighties notwithstanding, maquila lines never came to a halt for lack of workers. However, in the context of high labor demand, idiosyncratic benefit packages virtually invited workers to shop around. Thus, although maquila wage policies did not stop production, they did produce turnover.[55] In February 1984, the head of AMAC (the maquiladora industry association) said as much when he dismissed the notion that there was a labor shortage on the border: "What is going on at this time . . . is that there are 7,000 unstable workers . . . [who] go from one industry to another to where it's most convenient for them to offer their services, and this is reflected in the plants that don't bring their benefits up to the level of their competitor."[56]

Women's growing leverage in the labor market produced a similar phenomenon on the line, and after years of calling the shots, managers found themselves at a disadvantage. A supervisor who'd been a worker in the seventies lamented the new order: "In the beginning it was marvelous, when the maquilas started, because you took care of your work, you knew there were 200,000 more willing to do it."[57] This comment, and others like it, were encapsulated in tropes that, like the labor shortage jokes, were repeated in interview after interview with personnel managers who had been in the industry during this period:[58] "They always knew they could get work on the other side of the street"; or, "All a supervisor needed to do was look at her crosswise and she was out the door." Newspaper reports of the period took the same exasperated tone. Early in 1983, one complained: "Due to the current scarcity of women workers in the maquiladoras . . . the women change employment when they feel like it."[59] Three months later, the same paper reported: "Yesterday, maquila operators were found enjoying the labor shortage facing the plants; they don't worry about arriving early or being fired. At the Juárez Monument, Guadalupe Cárdenas and Laura Lozano . . . commented that they were already late; both said that, because of the labor shortage, they couldn't fire them, and that's the way it is, because the one thing there's plenty of is work in all the factories."[60] Women workers' "bad behavior" was directed at new male workers as well as at their bosses. A frustrated union leader complained that the few men who entered the plants were forced out by catcalling women co-workers, who were gleefully taking advantage of their unusual numerical superiority.[61]

On the heels of women workers' increasing assertiveness, the first cracks in the maquila managers' implacable image of the "docile woman worker" emerged in the spring of 1983. Fresh from a year of shop-floor militance, and in the midst of soaring male unemployment rates,[62] Andromex's new Mexican plant manager was among the first to recognize that "docile" was as scarce as female in its current workforce, and to announce that he was hiring men.[63] By March of 1983, others were quietly following suit, although they were reluctant to admit publicly that they were breaking with tradition. The head of the CROC announced that several companies the union worked with "had seen themselves obliged to hire men." He refused to name them, commenting that if he did so, "they wouldn't hire them anymore."[64] Obviously, these companies were not the only ones. In June, men made up three of every five workers hired[65] although they would not make up this high a percentage of the total workforce until the end of the decade.

Despite the burst of men hired in 1983, management remained skeptical about the utility of men for assembly work. In a typical statement from the first uptick in hiring men, the union boss responsible for hiring for a group of maquilas commented: "The hiring of men is done with more rigorous selective criteria given that they are more disobedient, irresponsible, and prone to absences; distressingly, in Juárez, men already got used to not working."[66]

Newspaper ads from the first half of the decade reflected this attitude, continuing to request women.[67] By the end of the eighties, though, industry representatives were frantic. Turnover was well over 100 percent annually[68] and industry complaints about shortages and increasing training costs had reached a fever pitch.[69] Still focused on getting their hands on femininity, however embodied, a few plants hired transvestites. One manager recalled, "The need for people was so great that we had men who walked around the plant dressed as women," adding parenthetically, "We don't permit that anymore." Maquilas paid workers to bring in friends,[70] established "gentleman's agreements" not to hire workers who'd left previous jobs "without clear reasons,"[71] and even considered setting a single salary and benefit structure for the industry as a whole.[72] In this context, they began to publicly discuss broadening their worker profile for the first time, acknowledging the possibility of hiring men, albeit in the most disrespectful terms. Their first public statements on the subject coincided with assessments of the feasibility of contracting senior citizens and the handicapped,[73] and although discussions of these latter two groups were pitched in the most self-congratulatory terms,[74] the possibility of hiring men was consistently framed as a compromise. Although women are "more careful and responsible," commented the head of AMAC in 1988, men had also been found "acceptable."[75]

Not surprisingly, men responding to these mixed messages were slow to enter maquila doors. In the spring of 1983, amid reports of the first labor crisis in the maquilas, their pace drew the ire of the editors of a local paper. A picture of men sitting under the trees was glossed by the caption: "Despite the many maquiladora factory announcements soliciting male workers, it seems that the *juarenses* have declared war against work and prefer to face the heat in the shade of a tree."[76] In 1988, the head of AMAC reiterated these complaints, commenting that "despite the invitations to take positions, there are very few [men] who are interested in working."[77] Managerial ambivalence and male workers' responses meant that the proportion of women in the maquila workforce did not go into free fall. Rather, between 1982 and the end of the decade, the percentage of men increased between 2 and 6 percent yearly. It was not until 1988, in the third year of over 10 percent growth in the city's maquiladora workforce, that there was finally a surge of advertisements directed at men as well as women.[78] Not until the end of the decade did men constitute a stable 45 percent of the industry's direct local workforce.[79]

The causes and consequences of the inflow of men into maquila work have been much debated.[80] As cheap, docile, and female became an increasingly difficult combination to find among flesh-and-blood job applicants, one might have expected that the tenacious feminization of maquila work would erode, especially as thousands of men filled shop floors with no noticeable impact on industry productivity. Yet the trope of productive femininity, nourished by ongoing links to a larger transnational imaginary, remained in place.[81] In the fantasy world of "off-shore production," docile women continued to hold the microscope and thread the needle. Maquila managers, ongoing participants in a larger, transnational system of meanings and taken-for-granteds, continued to cite the "maquila-grade female" as a standard against which to measure maquila labor.[82] As a result, for the most part, men were hired, but marked upon entry as lacking, with complex consequences both for their own sense of self and for shop-floor control.

Increases in the number of men in the maquilas did little to assuage local unease over changing gender roles, as the industry's ongoing preference for women kept the spotlight on changing familial structures. In an emblematic moment in 1985, the Mexican president met with (female) maquila workers during a visit to the city. His response to their complaints about transportation, housing, and other public services was a revealing non sequitur: "The fact that a large portion [of maquila jobs] are filled by women is inducing changes in our social and productive life, phenomena with which we Mexicans were previously unfamiliar and which present us with challenges which we cannot always resolve quickly."[83]

Between the president's perturbed comments in 1985 and a 1991 hiatus in the industry's breakneck expansion,[84] local media kept track of working-class women and men's role failures and sexual trespasses with grim zeal. In the financial sphere, local newspapers worried over women moving into "men's jobs"[85] and turning down employment as maids.[86] In the social sphere, reports were even more persistent and damning. Women were joining gangs in which they were "as dangerous and aggressive as men."[87] They were drinking and carousing,[88] practicing "free love" and using condoms,[89] divorcing, and having children out of wedlock.[90] In a particularly acidic report, a large local daily reported that the city was increasingly seeing an "unusual discrimination" against northern—that is, local—women in favor of their counterparts from the south in the area of paid domestic work. "It's as if women from these latitudes have forgotten the ritual of 'bed making' and of 'homemade *mole*.'"[91] Young working-class men were less constant a target, but the few comments were saturated with disdain. Men weren't working because "they really didn't want to find work,"[92] yet their "machismo" led to divorces when their wives worked.[93] More damning still, they were engaging in "the oldest job in the world" in the service of their employed female counterparts, and their consequent "lack of restraint" was evident in their participation in beauty contests and "ladies' only nights."[94]

[. . .] As hundreds of managers sought ever more desperately after the iconic feminine maquila worker, she moved farther and farther out of reach, making hiring and labor control an ongoing challenge and leading to tremendous variety in managerial strategies throughout the industry in the decade which followed.

Proliferating Genders

The demographics of the maquila industry in its first decades and the public rhetoric of its plant managers over time suggest that early analysts got it right: the edifice of transnational production was built on the preconstituted cheapness and docility of third-world women workers. The demographic situation at the end of the eighties and later suggests that early analysts got it wrong: femininity was not an essential element in the structure of third-world assembly. In my opinion, neither of these interpretations captures the complexity of the situation. Certainly, global production does not depend on the existence of a fixed and pre-set "femininity." Just as surely, however, the trope of "femininity" does matter in transnational production's development. Both discourse and demographics provide important information about the way in which gender operates at work. The idea of femininity structured, and continues to structure, production in the maquilas. It provides the norm against which workers are assessed in hiring and labor control, both in terms of their fitness for the work and in terms of what is possible and acceptable to expect of them in production. As such, although "women" are not necessarily a cornerstone of global production, the idea of who they are continues to structure its daily operations and ongoing evolution.

In the Juárez maquila industry of the early nineties, when I arrived in the city, this structuring process was particularly evident. The difficulty of finding flesh-and-blood workers who approximated managerial images meant that each manager was left to himself to find a way to make sense and profits of an unexpected workforce. Thus, each shop floor became a tiny experiment, an arena where a fluid set of gendered meanings was fixed and harnessed in the service of shop-floor control—and occasionally in the service of its undoing (see Salzinger, Chapter 7).

In late 1991, the industry was contracting in response to a recession across the border, and the number of men had stabilized at close to half the workforce. In an interview, the head of AMAC explained male workers' ongoing presence at the end of the boom as a consequence of their metamorphosis from highly "problematic" into something very much like "maquila-grade females." "It was a process of acculturation for men to incorporate themselves into production . . . with the years they have changed; now they have a mentality oriented toward the industry."[95] Outside his office, opinions of male workers were far more varied and less sanguine, however.[96] Despite the thousands of men working in the maquilas, there was still no trope, no structure of meaning, within which "male maquila worker" made sense. At 45 percent, they remained the ubiquitous exception.

A decade after the introduction of men into maquila work, the meaning structures around productive femininity remained fully evident and remarkably firm—still providing the narrative framework within which most maquila managers imagined, hired, and supervised workers. Even in this period, roughly half the ads in local newspapers specified women only, and many still requested "*Señoritas*" and "*Damitas*." Although there were exceptions (see Salzinger, Chapter 6) most managers continued to treat women's dextrous fingers, malleability, and capacity to withstand routine as "facts of life," even in the face of massive evidence, even personal experience, to the contrary.

For individual managers, the persistence of the trope of the "maquila-grade female," alongside the ongoing scarcity of workers who fit that description, created the quandary of how to hire and discipline a shop-floor labor force in such a context and have the project make sense. Immersion in the dailiness of four maquilas in the area made it possible for me to track the highly varied ways in which they addressed this problem, and to see the multiple gendered processes behind the mystery of the industry's demographics. The managers of the plants I will describe below each created their own path through this set of challenges, some more successfully than others, but all making meaning, if not profits, along the way.

In Panoptimex, transnational managers committed to a factory that "looked right" went to great lengths to import a workforce that matched the industry image, thus giving birth to a shop floor full of simulacra they perceived as originals. In Particimex, a plant established outside the city precisely in order to access a home-disciplined female workforce, Mexican managers addressed women workers in a rhetoric that explicitly challenged their transnational colleagues' celebration of Mexican women's "traditional" docility. In Andromex, Mexican managers found their few remaining images of feminine pliancy shattered by women workers' shop-floor militance. In response, they restructured their hiring and labor control strategies around the image of an (implicitly male) "worker," regaining shop-floor control in the process. And finally, in Anarchomex, transnational managers, stuck both in Juárez and in the common sense of the maquila industry, inadvertently created a shop-floor struggle over the content of worker masculinity, much to the detriment of production quality.

Each of these arenas of production constitutes a case study in the operations of gender at work. No individual case is either "typical" or "representative." Instead, it is the uniqueness of each plant which is of interest and importance. In taking the measure of these idiosyncrasies, we come to see how a globally constituted rhetoric operates through local conditions and subjectivities, creating facts on the ground whose wide variability in no way diminishes their indebtedness to global forces. [. . .]

Notes

1. The Border Industrialization Program (BIP).
2. This was at best disingenuous, since Mexican bureaucrats had already visited East Asian export-processing plants employing young female labor (Pearson 1991).

3. Baird and McCaughan (1979); Van Waas (1981).

4. INEGI (1990).

5. INEGI (1996).

6. Fernández-Kelly (1983); Carrillo and Hernández (1985).

7. The reasons for the maquilas' initial decision to hire women was the source of extensive discussion among researchers during the industry's early years. One group of analysts (Carrillo and Hernández 1985; Van Waas 1981; Tiano 1987a; 1987b) looked to the market, explaining the decision to hire women as a conscious attempt to create an industrial reserve army. This argument was made most strongly by Van Waas, who argued that these jobs were not traditionally women's jobs either in the United States or Mexico, and that therefore their feminization within the BIP was necessarily due to structural rather than "cultural" processes. Another group of analysts focusing on the gender of jobs took the opposite approach, comparing maquila jobs not to similar jobs in the United States and Mexico, but to similar industries based in Asia. They argued that Asian export-processing jobs were defined as "women's jobs," and that Mexican bureaucrats explicitly modeled themselves upon these projects (Fernández-Kelly 1983; Iglesias 1985; Gambrill 1981; Pearson 1991). Although there is no question that some maquila investors considered the benefits of increasing the pool of available labor (Carrillo and Hernández 1985, 88), I would argue, with the latter group, that maquila jobs were predicated upon a gendered configuration of labor power.

8. The reason for women's initial predominance in East Asian assembly work is the subject of an extensive literature. Analysts generally attribute it to women's "cheapness" and attribute this in turn to their position in the family (Safa 1986; Pearson 1991; Standing 1989). Lutz (1988) focuses instead on the circulation of images of women's docility. Although I am not attempting to explain this larger historical phenomenon here, the data suggest that such explanations are less distinct than they appear, and that women's disproportionate share of low-wage assembly is due to the way in which their familial situation is understood, used, and reconstructed by capitalist processes.

9. See Fernández-Kelly (1983); Carrillo and Hernández (1985); and Van Waas (1982) for discussion of the infamous Arthur D. Little report.

10. Baerresen (1971), 36.

11. Van Waas (1981), 346.

12. Sklair (1993) aptly terms this structure of meanings a "litany" which both describes and enforces its perspective, 172.

13. *El Fronterizo*, June 13, 1979. All newspaper articles dated between 1974 and 1985 come from the Centro de Orientacíon de la Mujer Obrero (COMO) archives, located on the premises of the Colegio de la Frontera Norte, Ciudad Juárez, in the early nineties.

14. Baird and McCaughan (1979), 146–47.

15. Pablo Vila (2003) documents the pervasiveness of such discussions outside the formal media as well.

16. The actual number of people living in Ciudad Juárez is a matter of some dispute. The Mexican government—reputedly anxious to underestimate the population of a state controlled by the opposition—put it at roughly three-quarters of a million, whereas local business groups—interested in presenting a large, available workforce to prospective investors—put it at almost twice that number (Desarrollo Económico de Ciudad Juárez [1991]). This issue is so well documented that in a handbook for prospective maquila investors, the author provided two population figures for Juárez, commenting, "There is a wide divergence between official census figures (shown first) and reliable estimates (shown in parentheses)." Baerresen (1971), 31.

17. For an excellent history of the establishment of the maquila program in Juárez, see Van Waas (1981) and Martinez (1978). Today, Juárez dominates the maquila industry and the

industry dominates the city's economy. Although Tijuana has a larger number of maquila establishments, the Juárez industry has always been distinguished by the large size of its factories, which thus house the overwhelming bulk of Mexico's maquila employment. By the late eighties, maquilas employed 30 percent of Juárez's "economically active" population and 46 percent of its "economically active" women (Cruz Piñeiro 1990), and by 1990 its percentage of the overall EAP had risen to 35 percent (*El Diario de Juárez*, March 14, 1990). In the city, signs of maquila influence abound, from local government's obvious kowtowing to the industry, to private buses ferrying maquila workers to downtown bars on Friday afternoons, to coverage of the Señorita Maquiladora beauty contest in local newspapers' society pages.

18. *El Fronterizo*, September 2, 1971.

19. Iglesias (1985), 70.

20. Fernández-Kelly (1983), 133 and 139.

21. Martínez (1978), 134.

22. *Excélsior*, September 22 and 23, 1979.

23. *El Fronterizo*, October 10, 1972.

24. *El Fronterizo*, August 16, 1981 and September 12, 1981.

25. *El Correo*, June 24, 1974.

26. *El Correo*, August 27, 1977.

27. These work conditions were described by an ex-worker during a 1992 interview. They were also reported in *El Correo*, July 2, 1980. On December 17 and 18, 1980, *El Diario de Juárez* reported the story of a young male worker who was killed in the plant.

28. *El Fronterizo*, January 1, 1980.

29. *El Correo*, March 17, 1981.

30. Fernández-Kelly (1983), 133.

31. *El Correo*, April 22, 1974. In the same year, a series of articles refer to the large numbers of single mothers in the maquilas.

32. *El Mexicano*, August 5, 1981; *El Diario de Juárez*, August 11, 1981.

33. Unattributed clipping from the COMO archives, Ciudad Juárez, August 19, 1977.

34. *El Fronterizo*, April 17, 1978; *El Diario de Juárez*, June 30, 1978.

35. *El Correo*, May 22, 1980.

36. Reygadas (1992).

37. Although my fieldwork in Juárez did not focus on women's behavior outside the maquilas, I observed that young women workers, for the most part, controlled a good part of their salaries, and the disjuncture between the overall quiescence on shop floors and their increasing autonomy outside is difficult to miss.

38. See Wolf (1990) for an analysis of the variable impact of assembly work on women's community and familial roles. She reports divergent effects of factory work on young women's autonomy, dependent on the family structures and mores within which it takes place.

39. Carrillo (1985).

40. *El Diario de Juárez*, June 3, 1982.

41. Through the mid-eighties, the Juárez maquila industry was the scene of union conflicts over who would represent workers. Conflicts took place both between the two largest national unions, the CTM (Confederation of Mexican Workers) and the CROC (Regional Confederation of Workers and Peasants), and between them and the considerably smaller CRT (Revolutionary Confederation of Workers). The conflict at Andromex was between the CTM and one of its recently ousted leaders. He had established a local CRT branch and was attempting to reinsert himself into the Juárez union scene in this era by taking over CTM contracts. Roughly a third of Juárez maquilas were unionized in 1987 (Carrillo and Ramírez 1990). In those that were unionized, workers generally saw little benefit, as all three Centrals operated as company unions.

42. For an analysis of the "contract" see De la Rosa Hickerson (1979). Also see Carrillo and Hernández (1985), 158–64.

43. For detailed histories of COMO, see Young and Vera (1984); Yudelman (1987); Kopinak (1989); and Peña (1997).

44. Fashionmex, for instance, did ultimately flee the city, leaving wages unpaid.

45. *El Correo*, November 17, 1980.

46. *El Fronterizo*, December 29, 1980.

47. *El Diario de Juárez*, July 29, 1981.

48. *El Mexicano*, August 5, 1981.

49. Jiménez (1989), 417.

50. Sklair (1993), 40.

51. INEGI (1991, 1996).

52. *El Diario de Juárez*, July 2, 1985; June 8, 1986.

53. *El Diario de Juárez*, April 20, 1988.

54. *Twin Plant News* 3 (10), May 1988, 8.

55. Shaiken (1990, 99) reports that although maquilas "would clearly like to reduce turnover, they have structured work in a way where transience in the production work force has a minimal negative impact." The highly fragmented labor process he refers to here pervades the industry. Just as complaints about labor shortages must be understood within the context of the decision not to raise wages, so complaints about turnover must be understood within the context of the decision not to introduce seniority systems.

56. *El Diario de Juárez,* February 5, 1984.

57. Panoptimex supervisor, 1992.

58. Managerial interviews, 1992–93.

59. *El Universal,* November 10, 1983.

60. *El Universal,* February 17, 1984.

61. *El Fronterizo*, August 31, 1983. Senior women workers in Andromex also told me they had teased new male workers during this period.

62. On September 5, 1983, amid the maquila "labor shortage," Banamex announced that unemployment was soaring in the city as a whole (*El Fronterizo*).

63. *El Diario de Juárez*, June 11, 1983.

64. *El Diario de Juárez*, March 30, 1983.

65. *El Diario de Juárez*, August 23, 1983.

66. *El Diario de Juárez*, March 30, 1983.

67. Review of COMO archives.

68. By 1989, AMAC statistics were showing an average of a 144 percent turnover annually.

69. *El Diario de Juárez*, September 14, 1987; January 25, 1988; June 17, 1989; March 28, 1990; October 20, 1990.

70. *El Diario de Juárez*, April 1, 1989; November 29, 1989.

71. *El Diario de Juárez*, September 18, 1990.

72. *El Diario de Juárez*, October 11, 1990.

73. Not surprisingly, there is little evidence that either senior citizens or disabled workers were ever hired in large numbers.

74. *El Diario de Juárez*, May 27, 1989; November 29, 1989; August 27, 1990.

75. *El Diario de Juárez*, May 14, 1988.

76. *El Fronterizo*, May 31, 1983.

77. *El Diario de Juárez*, May 14, 1988.

78. Review of *El Diario de Juárez* archives.

79. INEGI (1991). These levels remained stable throughout the years of my fieldwork in the industry (INEGI 1996).

80. See, for example, De la O (1991, 1997), Quintero (1992), Jiménez (1989, 401–2), and Peña (1997), who focus on the gendering of work. They argue that low-level assembly work continues to be feminized, but that as the number of technical and other skilled jobs, traditionally understood as male, has increased, so has the number of men employed overall. Although they are undoubtedly correct about increases in the number of such jobs, the explanation cannot account for the surge in male workers in nontechnical, unskilled jobs throughout the industry (see Chapters 6 and 7). Brannon and Lucker (1989); Jiménez (1989); and Catanzarite and Strober (1993) emphasize market structure. Brannon and Lucker (1989) and Jiménez (1989, 403) argue that as the maquila boom demanded increasing numbers of workers, desperate employers became willing to hire previously unacceptable job applicants. Catanzarite and Strober (1993) argue that, following the economic crisis of 1982, as other, better paying possibilities disappeared, desperate male workers became willing to take previously unacceptably "feminine" maquila jobs. Here, I argue with Jiménez that gendered meanings structure and constitute the labor market; hence a complete explanation must include both types of analyses.

81. Catanzarite and Strober (1993) do in fact assert that, by the late eighties, maquila work was no longer feminized. My own research shows no support for this conclusion. In interviews, managers constantly referred to their preference for women workers, generally referencing their purportedly greater patience, tolerance for boredom, and shop-floor malleability.

82. See Salzinger 2003, chapter 2, note 10.

83. *El Diario de Juárez*, June 28, 1985.

84. A recession in the United States in 1991 halted industry expansion until the next peso devaluation in 1994, after I had finished my fieldwork.

85. *El Diario de Juárez*, July 2, 1985; June 8, 1986.

86. *El Diario de Juárez*, June 8, 1986; January 2, 1989.

87. *El Diario de Juárez*, June 7, 1989.

88. *El Diario de Juárez*, July 24, 1989.

89. *El Diario de Juárez*, December 20, 1989.

90. *El Diario de Juárez*, February 18, 1991.

91. *El Diario de Juárez*, January 2, 1989.

92. *El Diario de Juárez*, May 14, 1988.

93. *El Diario de Juárez*, February 18, 1991.

94. *El Diario de Juárez*, March 10, 1991.

95. This comment, made during a 1993 interview, is remarkably similar to Sklair's (1993) argument that "once the image of the 'ideal' maquila worker is institutionalized and accepted by the working-class along the border, the need to employ women in preference to men diminishes, and job opportunities for docile, undemanding, nimble-fingered, nonunion and unmilitant men open up" (173).

96. Managerial interviews, 1992–93.

CHAPTER 24

Imagining Sex and Gender in the Workplace

Pun Ngai

[. . .] It is this critique of gender, sex, and body—sometimes called the political anatomy—that provides the greatest insight for my own ethnography of the workplace (Foucault 1978). The biopower of the factory machine is not only interested in molding a general body but also a particular sexed body, a feminine body to fit the factory discipline.[1] In this chapter, I will try to link up the process of political anatomy in the workplace with the process of sexualizing female bodies and registering multiple feminine identities. [. . .]

Desiring Sexual Subjects

In Shenzhen, as well as in other economic development zones, stories about dagongmei in popular magazines such as *Shenzhen Ren* (Shenzhen people), *Nü Bao* (Women's magazine), *Dagongmei* (Working daughters), and *Wailaigong* (Migrant workers) were booming in popularity.[2] Tropes, metaphors, episodes, and story plots centered on imaginations and themes such as the struggle of life and death in the modern industrial world, changing attitudes toward sex, love, and marriage, and the desire to become a modern man or woman. These magazines helped create a variety of lively images of dagongmei. Not without exaggeration and exception, the working daughters were portrayed as sexual subjects who were prepared to leave their villages to look not only for jobs but also for love and men. Often cast in a sad tone, predicated on the difficulties of pursuing "true" love, the stories nevertheless provided a new construction of female subjectivity—one in which dagongmei were active and bold in seeking love, in contrast to the traditional image of submissive Chinese women. In a column in *Shenzhen Ren* (Shen, October 1994), titled "Special Economic Zone Cannot Take Care of Dagongmei's Love," several short stories appeared, as follows.

> *One Male Line Leader and Ten Line Girls*
> On her first day working on the packaging line, Ping said, "The male line leader is so handsome!" After working for two years in six factories, it was

the first time she had met a handsome line leader. Ping's words threatened the other nine girls on the same line, for the line leader had become the little prince of ten hearts.

The line leader was from Guangdong. He had not completed his university studies but instead had gone off to work. At 5'8" tall, he was not too fat and not too thin. He had light skin, wore glasses, and seemed mature and a little bit shy. His actions were sharp and his words generous; he played no favorites among the ten girls or said anything unnecessary to anyone. For what needed reproach, he reproached all. For what needed concern, he showed concern to all.

The ten love seeds sprouted at the same time. Those who were bold wrote love letters and sent gifts to him; those who were timid loved him secretly in their hearts. Among the line girls, a war of love was launched openly, seriously affecting production. The male line leader could not deal with the situation and was forced to leave the factory. Without a word to the line girls, he was gone.

One Foreman and Six Working Daughters

A foreman, named Lai, could not compete with the other boys in the company because he was short and quiet. From day to night he toiled hard on production. He was only age twenty-two, but the workers all called him "old boy" or "work maniac."

However, six pretty young women in the workplace all loved him. They had all written love letters to him and waited for his reply. But he never uttered a word, as if nothing had happened. Cing was the prettiest woman in the workplace. Unlike the other women, she was not disappointed by his lack of reply and never stopped writing letters to him. Every day, she was the first one on the shop floor and worked very hard to increase her output in order to attract foreman Lai's attention. Yet he still made no move.

Eventually, Cing was in despair and could not face her foreman. She quit her job and became a salesgirl in a hardware store. However, the foreman often came to the store to buy materials. She quit the job again and wrote to him: she would go somewhere he could not see her. She went to work in a big hotel as a waitress. Unfortunately, there was nowhere she could hide; every Sunday, the foreman went with the boss to have breakfast in the hotel. They met again . . .

Cing wrote another letter: "You don't love me. I can't see you again. I have to go." She left town.

One Boy Worker and a Woman Supervisor

Coming from Guangxi as a boy, it was not easy for little Tao to find a job in a craft factory. He worked as an assistant. He cleaned the shop floor and the toilets, and loaded materials and products. He received a lower wage than anyone else and often felt inferior. However, as the saying goes, a fool has more happiness. He received a love letter from Miss Chan, the famous production supervisor in the factory.

Little Tao was throbbing and could not believe it. Yet after a couple of letters from Miss Chan to "invade" him, he finally "surrendered."

They rented a flat and lived together. Miss Chan took the role of bread-winner. She paid for all little Tao spent and helped him to send money back home regularly . . .

Little Tao could never believe in the "love" he had found. Refusing to take advantages from the woman, he left quietly. His hot and sincere lover was in tears.

All of these stories are made up of desiring female subjects who are far more active than men in expressing and pursuing love. If conventional discourses continued to portray women as passive sexual objects waiting for men, popular culture favored the image of a modern, young working woman who challenges traditional sexual relations and takes an active role. Young Chinese rural women no longer stayed at home, following their parents' arrangements or waiting for a matchmaker to decide their fate. Instead, in the magazines they were encouraged to go out: to leave their villages and look for their own love and life. "Your body is your own," "Hold tight to love," and "Control your own fate"—all of these hidden messages were conveyed through popular culture and became mottos for modern female life. These liberating messages, on the surface, encouraged challenges to the traditional sense of Chinese women's lives and their defiance to the patriarchal family. However, at the same time they were ma-nipulated by the hegemonic project of modernity and power to produce laborers for private and transnational capital.

The Proliferation of Sex and Sexualized Bodies

The feminization of labor use in the industrial export processing zones in Shenzhen, as elsewhere in China and other developing countries, was often linked to a project of renegotiating women's space and power, as well as to a politics of reimagining sex and gender in general. These larger discourses and politics could provide new elements for subverting conventional norms and values, but also simultaneously leaving women's agency submerged in the new matrix of power and subjugation. When I look at the contemporary Chinese scene with its shifting images, it is characterized by the prolif-eration of sex talk, sexual discourse, consumerized and female images (Evans 1997). Signs of sex are everywhere, inviting us into a Baudrillardian (1993) world where fe-male bodies are commodified and fetishized to such an extent that only a mass grave of signs remain. Nudes, erotica, and all kinds of sexy, seduced female bodies, both West-ern and Chinese, are found in magazines, posters, newspapers, book covers, calendars, and even academic books and periodicals. On every street corner in Shenzhen, as in other Chinese cities, advertisements on the lampposts tell passers-by that some families have secret, local knowledge of an operation to heal sexual diseases. Stories of sex and violence, uncontrollable sex drives, and sex outside of marriage are voiced in novels,

video shows, TV programs, and films. Painting, other visual arts, and avant-garde
dance performances all focus on the theme of the "sexualized body." As Elisabeth Croll,
after her experience in numerous field trips to China over the past decades, states:

> The Reform period is thus marked by a new interest in the image and
> presentation of the feminine, focusing first on physical appearance and
> adornment. This is not surprising given that one of the most important
> characteristics distinguishing reform from revolution is the new interest in
> consumption, in consumer goods and in their style, colour, material and
> brand name, all of which have generated a new phenomenon—consumer
> desire. . . . The new interest in commodities and lifestyles has brought about
> a new relation between people and things, so that persons have become clas-
> sified not so much by their class background or "work" or occupation as pre-
> viously, as by the possession of objects or their evaluation, so that identity
> has become associated with lifestyle rather than class label. (1995, 151)

The all-pervasive interest in female bodies in reform China is conjured up by all-
powerful consumer desires, whose gazes are not only sexy but further sexualized. The
technology of consumption power, in contrast to production power, is not interested
in producing disciplined bodies but rather libidinous, lascivious, and lustful female
bodies. The calling of feminist politics in Chinese society,[3] paradoxically, meets with
the political maneuvers of sex and gender at the very moment when the Chinese
female body is highly regulated, twisted, and subsumed by capital and power in the
transnational period. The discourse of the Chinese body, presumed docile and gentle,
is turned upside down, not only for the use of production power but also for consumption capital. Now the Chinese body has to be vibrant, sexualized, seductive, and
liberated enough to release all forces of libido.

Shenzhen nightlife—nightclubs, karaoke, wine bars, and hair salons—has flour-
ished since the mid-1980s and is marked by its extravagant sexual appetite, especially
for female bodies. Workplaces where women were predominant—such as garment,
electronics, and shoe and toy factories—were often called "peach orchards" in popular
magazines and stories. The notion of peach orchards imaginatively evoked and signified female places of sex, love, and joy, in spite of the fact that it was a male-oriented
if not sexist metaphor of men pursuing erotic objects. While a workplace full of young
women might be an orchard of peaches for men, it was definitely not a world of joy
and happiness for women, at least not for the women workers at the Meteor factory.

[. . .]

Sex talk was also thriving in the workplace, and my coworkers always warned me
not to go to hair salons or hotels, especially small ones, because they were often places
for exchanging "illicit" sex. In the factory workers' eyes, *bei mei*, the girls of the north,
were prostituting bodies whose world was highly differentiated from working bodies,
dagongmei.[4] Young and beautiful girls from north China (the place they were from
was highly emphasized and then degraded), were told to wait in hotels and search for
men alone. The phone would ring late at night and ask for "lonely heart" services. In
contrast to a pure and productive dagongmei working in the factories, beimei, the term
denoting perverted Chinese female bodies, was invested with more abject and yet re-

bellious meanings. Beimei were younger, fresher, more lush and virginal, and therefore they were more sexually arousing and desirable, easily disrupting the patriarchal order of society. For my coworkers these prostituting bodies were not their "family resemblances," and even though these beimei were trapped in a situation of oppression worse than dagongmei, the unity of sisterhood was still highly segregated and exclusive.

Amidst beimei, in the process of sex trading regional disparity between the north and the south was again produced and reproduced. Sex was not only inscribed with inequalities between male and female but also marked with economic discrimination between north and south. Prostitutes were themselves hierarchically differentiated: those who came from richer areas were worth much more than those from poorer areas. These differences between and within women again spoke of a self-defeating project in arguing for a universal category of women. The politics of identity is always the politics of difference. These subjects should be seen as the effects of power and as discursive constructs with their own possibilities, through a process of signification, differentiation, and exclusion (Butler 1990).

The "sexy" scenes in open-door China make me wonder if global capital particularly needs sexualized subjects. It seems clear that where private and transnational capital goes there is a proliferation of sex trade and sex discourses in towns and cities. Time after time since the early 1990s the central Chinese government has launched antiporn movements in the cities. The official discourse continues to promote a regulatory model of sexuality, and according to Harriet Evans (1997, 156), state discourses on sexual issues are largely a response to changing popular beliefs and practices. Although no longer effective, never has the state lost its interest in regulating individual sexual conduct and marital behavior. With deflated and worn-out ideological apparatus, the failure of the central state to safeguard the "virginity" of Chinese society is all too plain to see. The local state, however, was far more tolerant, because they saw the sex industry closely linked to local economic development. As one local cadre in a southern Chinese town openly told me: "No sex, no video shows, no clubs, no hair salons, no restaurants, no hotels, no money!" Sex linked up the entire chain of economic activities, just as corruption facilitated political life in China. No sex, no money. In contemporary China, discourses on sex—official and civil, and at odds with each another—fight hard to grasp and produce the reality in which the real, although impossible, again becomes more artificial.

Invoking Sexual Subjects

It seems that for private and global capital, "sexualizing the subject" is crucial to the creation of the modernity project. The political technology of capital involves a series of maneuvers of hierarchization and division of society, of which sexual difference was one of the major regulatory targets. As noted above, dagongmei stands in contrast to gongren, the nonsexualized subject in Mao's era, and entails a process of sexualization within laboring bodies. Mei explicitly means a young woman and a sister. The feminization of labor has proceeded rapidly in Shenzhen and in other economic development zones, clearly illustrating that basic industrial laborers, especially cheap and unskilled workers, are mostly female. Male workers, dagongzai, are not excluded, but once they are needed they are given different positions in the sexual division of labor in the workplace, as we will see later. Labor is thus no longer taken as an unsexed body but as a gendered subject exhibiting itself more as a "sexual being" than as a "class being" in postsocialist China.

Sexualizing laboring bodies in this manner is a project of capital rather than the state. This can be seen if we compare the two social subjects: the gongren of Mao's period and the dagongmei/zai of today. With gongren, sexual difference was submerged and made redundant in socialist labor relations. Women were introduced into the "world of men," be it in light, heavy, or military industries. The official rhetoric proclaimed that women could hold up half the sky in socialist China; that they could do whatever men could do. In official regulatory practices sexual difference was diluted and made meaningless through propaganda and institutionalized arrangements. With the dissolution of socialist practices in general and the bankruptcy of state and collective enterprises in particular, the gongren subject was disappearing and the term became an outdated mode of everyday discourse, especially in south China. The disembodied world of industrial labor was to be sexualized; its sex was not to be veiled but had to be reinvented and regulated.

In the Meteor workplace it was not difficult to find that the regulation of a sexed body was fundamental to the control of labor. Given that the workplace was a world of young women who occupied almost all of the seats of the assembly operation, it was always a headache for the upper management, the foremen, and the line leaders, often male, to manage the workers. None of the foremen or line leaders, male or female, assumed that dagongmei were submissive females waiting to be regulated at their will. Complaints about the discipline of dagongmei were frequent when I talked to any supervisor. Indeed, submissiveness, often with an imaginary feminine identity pinned on the workers, needed to be articulated and rearticulated in the everyday language of management to facilitate labor control. Here are a few vignettes used to invoke sexualized bodies that I recorded from management:

> *Shun* (foreman of line C): Mei, you're a girl, how can you speak to me like this? Didn't your parents teach you how to be a woman? Do you speak to your father like this?

> *Hong* (assistant manager): Rough voice, rough *qi* [energy], don't you want to marry yourself out? Behave yourself, since you're still a young girl.

> *Li* (foreman of line A): Girl, do you have ears? You never follow exactly what I tell you to do. Where is your heart? Gone with your lover?

> *He-chuan* (foreman of line B): Mei, don't you know you're a girl? You should treat the work more tenderly. How many times do I have to remind you?

> *He-chuan* (foreman of line B): Look at yourself, like a *nanren po* [butch woman]. Can't you learn to be like a woman?

Such remarks were often heard in the Meteor workplace, particularly when workers' discipline had to be tightened. What is especially interesting was that in the eyes of management their identity as laborer was less important than their identity as female. The regulation of gender was invoked when labor control was at stake. The workers were often reminded of their femaleness: "You are a girl." As a girl in the process of becoming a woman, one should behave as the culture required: submissive, obedient, industrious, tender, and so on. The underlying implications were: "You are a girl, you should be obedient enough to do what the management tells you to do. You are a girl, you should not be defiant to your superior by speaking in a loud voice. You are a girl, you are going to marry someone, serve someone, so you had better train yourself to behave properly. You should take care of the job you do as you one day will take care of your family. As a girl you are going to be a woman, a wife and a mother of men."

The ascription of these feminine attributes to a woman and the regulation of a woman's behavior did not, of course, concern her future life in general. Rather, her future life as a wife and as a mother was deployed for the present technologizing of bodies as docile labor. As Judith Butler (1993, 1) puts it, "sex/gender" not only functions as a norm but is part of a regulatory practice that produces the bodies it governs, that is, whose regulatory force is made clear as a kind of productive power, the power to produce the bodies it controls.

Also of note is that maleness was posited as a degraded opposite in warnings to the workers: "You should not act like a boy, a boy is lazy and troublesome, careless and rough. Otherwise, you can't marry yourself out." Maleness was thus articulated as an oppositional and inferior sexual attribute that a woman should not have if she wanted to become a good female and thus a good worker. [. . .]

Despite the implication that maleness was supposedly contradictory to dagong-mei self-esteem and self-identity, it always seemed that those who possessed the power to speak were free of gender constraints. When Hechuan, our foreman, condemned workers for manly behavior, he seemed to forget that he himself was a man. It was so naturally practiced that nobody could cast any doubt on the legitimate correspondence between being a female and a good worker. Discursive power was not only pervasive, but also elusive. Further, those who held regulatory power tried hard to create anxieties among the targets of their condemnation—they would be shamed if they, as girls, behaved like boys. "Dividuals," as Marilyn Strathern (1988, 19) states, were often taken as individual wholes, and one could only choose or be forced to choose, either as a female or as a male.

No internal ambivalence inside the individual is allowed; femaleness and maleness were created as a fundamental binary opposition in human beings. The women workers, however, cared less about being unable to get married than about not living up to the imaginary feminine. They could seldom fight back if their foremen or line leaders attacked their sexuality as being too male. They were induced to fear any evidence of their own gender ambiguity or perversity. Gender thus became a means of discipline and self-discipline, invoked so that they would learn to police themselves. The feminine was not only imagined and inscribed but also self-desired, and its mirroring other was the opposite sex—male (Irigaray 1977, 25). In this way, dagongmei was never only a subject of power, but an object of one's own desire.

Sexual Division of Labor

Femininity was always imagined and linked to performance as a good worker. But women workers in the Meteor plant knew quite well that in the pyramidal hierarchy inside the workplace, the female, not the male, was the inferior sex. While they might not fully understand how their femininity was articulated, imagined, and engineered time and again in everyday disciplinary practices, they knew well that the division of labor was rigidly segregated by sex. Out of more than five hundred workers in the workplace, about 75 percent were female. They were predominant on the assembly lines, and were placed in all kinds of work processes: assembling components, screwing, air seasoning, soldering, molding, function testing, quality control, and packaging. Above them were men as their foreman, their managers, and their director. Meteor was a world of women, but not for women. No matter how often they were reminded not to be mannish—"don't behave like a boy"—it was the male who had the power and status, with a higher wage and more benefits. Women workers in the workplace had to live up to the ambivalent realities construed by disciplinary discourses, daily language, and institutionalized power, which often were inherently split and self-contradictory.

The worlds of management and assembly workers were strongly stratified along sexual lines. The management strata were not entirely men but were males and masculinized females. In the eyes of the line women the top level of management was a world of masculinity—cool, deep, and untouchable. Although two managers and three supervisors were female, they were all taken as men or as being "as capable as men." The director, Mr. Zhou, and the four managers—Mr. Li of the engineering department, Mr. Wu of the production department, Miss Tang of the quality control department, and Miss Ren of the material stock department—were all from Hong Kong. As in all of the large foreign-owned corporations in China, the most important posts were not given to the mainland Chinese. Mr. Zhou, the founder of Meteor, had a firm and disciplined paternalistic image. He was an untouchable authoritarian figure in the workplace, especially for the women workers on the production lines. He seldom appeared on the shop floor except when accompanied by representatives of Western businesses touring the company. If he did show up on his own, it meant a serious problem had occurred.

Mr. Li, who was over fifty years old, was a Hong Kong–born professional; he could not speak Mandarin well. In charge of the engineering department, which was full of male university graduates, he was seen in the eyes of the women workers as a somewhat respectable person of expertise and knowledge. Mr. Wu, in his early forties, had immigrated to Hong Kong in 1987. He was one of the first generation of university graduates when China resumed university education after the Cultural Revolution. He was hired for the important position of production department manager because of his particular background. According to Mr. Wu, the production department was the largest section of the company and thus its heart. It had more than 350 workers, and managing it well required someone who was not a mainland Chinese but knew how to manage mainland Chinese workers. "The bosses thought I was an expert in Chinese and knew how to control the mainland workers' psychology," Mr. Wu said to me one day. After graduating from the Economics Department at Nanjing University, he first worked as an accountant in a state-owned enterprise in Nanjing. In 1985 he was promoted to secretary, the highest position in the enterprise. However, he chose to leave China because status and power could no longer satisfy him, and he was looking for a higher living standard in Hong Kong.

Miss Tang was employed as the quality control manager, probably because she looked like a man and was sufficiently strong and authoritarian. There was a widespread rumor that she was a lesbian, and nobody could control the gossip about her throughout the workplace. People called her "Mr. Tang" to her face and *nanren tou* (man head) behind her back. The manager of material stock, Miss Ren, was a stout mother type who had left her husband and son in Hong Kong to work in Shenzhen. As with other Hong Kong staff members, she had to stay in Shenzhen during the week and could only go home on Saturday afternoon, whereupon she had to return to Shenzhen very early on Monday morning. Mr. Zhou told me he preferred to find men from Hong Kong to take up managerial posts in Shenzhen, because men carried less of the family burden. Women, even when they were strong like Miss Ren, still considered their families as their first concern.

For production line women in their everyday sexual fantasies, the engineering department was the place that conjured up dreams and desires. In the department, all positions—engineers, technicians, work analysts, and machinists—were occupied by men. These men appeared young, handsome, urbane, and professional, and most important of all they often had urban hukou and hence higher social status. As such, they filled the women's dreams of escaping rural poverty and moving up the social ladder. Rumors would enthusiastically spread throughout the workplace if an engineer dined with a production line woman, or if they went out together to see a film. But these sexual fantasies were full of ambivalent feelings in the everyday struggles when the women had to confront these men as the ones in power and in charge of their daily production. The electronic engineers were the people who designed the operation of the assembly lines and decided how each work process on the line should run. The work analysts studied and determined the time, speed, and pay rate of the line. The technicians and machinists would maintain and repair the conveyor belts and all of the machines and tools. Orders and production designs were then sent to the production department, which undertook the actual daily operation of production.

Under Mr. Wu, Tin and Shen were the assistant managers in charge of the production lines and the bonding department, respectively. These two men were also university graduates from big cities, with qualifications that the women dared not envy. On the shop floor it was actually Tin and Shen who held direct control of production and thus the highest authority over the female line operators. It was thus clear that the entire production process was under the control of men, who gave orders and decided the work speed and wages for the women. No one complained about male authority in the workplace because gender issues were subsumed by rural-urban differences and educational level. In the eyes of line women, Tin and Shen were not only male but urban born and highly educated, and as such it seemed difficult to organize any fundamental challenge to male power in the workplace, in spite of the fact that spontaneous and momentary resistances to male authority were frequent in the women's daily lives.

The assembly operators, although predominantly female, were not a homogeneous group. They were categorized into three grades: the basic operators concentrated on the job; the second-grade operators were competent in at least three jobs; and the first-grade operators knew almost all the jobs and could be moved up and down the line as required. Some of the first-grade operators were called "flyers" because they were trained for all of the work processes and could be called up for any position in the event of absence. Most of the time assistant line leaders were chosen from among the ranks of these "flyers," who were considered capable and experienced and who dared to speak out. "It is difficult to find the right people for leaders among the line girls. Girls are so talkative when they crowd together. But at work, they are so timid and afraid to criticize the others," Tin tried to explain when I asked why management was dominated by males.

Men were not totally excluded from the assembly lines, but over 90 percent of the positions were occupied by women. As usual, assembling tiny electronic components was often considered women's work because it required patience, care, sharp eyes, and nimble fingers. At Meteor the management emphasized that the reality was that they did not have a totally submissive workforce under control. While upper management would typically imagine women to be more submissive, attentive, dexterous, and thus more reliable than men, the middle-level management, nearer to the actual shop floor, often held different views.

Due to the sexual segregation of jobs, the wage system, organized on a hierarchical basis, was also favorable to male workers. Male staff had a more stable form of wage, and the average wage of male workers at Meteor was about 30 percent higher than that of female workers. Furthermore, the uniforms and overalls worn at the factory helped to symbolize and draw the laboring bodies into the world of sexual hierarchies. Men and women, in different work positions, were put in different types and colors of uniforms and overalls. Management by color, understood as a new workplace management practice, signified position, status, and power. Except for the director, everybody—managers, office staff, shop floor staff, and workers—were asked to be properly uniformed.

But there were great differences between those who wore uniforms and those who wore overalls. The male engineers and technicians had to wear white shirts, whereas the male supervisors had blue shirts and the female supervisors blue dress sets. Shirts and dress sets were formally recognized as uniforms, clearly articulating the symbols and representations of power that belonged to the management strata. Despite the fact that the foremen and line leaders might sometimes be considered representatives of management, they nevertheless were dressed in overalls rather than uniforms, although in a different color, yellow, from that of the operators, who were dressed in white and blue. Operators on the quality control lines wore white overalls, symbolizing a slightly higher status than the production line operators in blue. Uniforms and overalls thus marked the line differentiating between managerial staff and basic workers, male and female, and controller and controlled, and the gender hierarchies were covertly revealed and reproduced in uniforms and overalls. Women, either consciously or unconsciously, came to a realization of themselves as an inferior sex with a degraded body when they put on a pair of blue overalls and worked on the shop floor.

Perverted Bodies

Dagongmei as an obedient and submissive social body was, in spite of everything, merely a hegemonic imaginary: although powerful enough, it was often contradicted in real-life struggles. The technology of power over female bodies was often self-defeating or sometimes even impotent. This impotence of the all-powerful matrix of power and language was, for example, acutely revealed when the factory disciplinary machine repeatedly failed to co-opt Fatso's sexual identify. Fatso was always a headache for management. She refused to feminize herself, and she openly acted butch. She was quick to air grievances and express her opinions when she saw unreasonable arrangements or unfairness. But she was loved as well as loathed by our line leader and foreman. She often worked faster than anyone else on the line and thus was able to help the others when their work was piling up. She rarely asked for sick leave; rather, she often helped to take women suffering from menstrual pain or other bodily discomfort to the restroom or the hospital. It was considered inappropriate for male supervisors to touch the female body, especially when the woman was menstruating. Everybody knew Fatso's important role on our line, and thus the regulation of sex did not work on her. This is not to say that the disciplinary machine completely failed to regulate her behavior, but to do so it needed to resort to other strategies.

Although she had to face much gossip and innuendo, Fatso insisted on having her own way: "I don't mind that people say that I'm mannish. I don't like girls to be timid, screaming, and fussing all the time." Fatso liked to make friends with the men rather than the women in the factory, and she often went out with male workers to see films or videos with violent and heroic plots. Women's talk at night, the most common entertainment after working, did not particularly attract her because she often thought that women gossiped and murmured too much. Young women in the workplace, on the other hand, accepted her as butch and treated her as a boy. They came to her when they needed help. In this case, body, sex, and identify, had no one-to-one correspondence; for Fatso, neither body nor sex could provide legitimacy for sexual identify. Her sexual identify was not yet split, but ambivalent and somewhat different.[5]

A Fight

The ideal construct of dagongmei as a docile feminized body was further disrupted and shattered in my mind when one day I witnessed a terrible scene. It was a winter night, windy and cold. At 10:00, after overtime, I went with Fatso back to the dormitory, dragging my exhausted body. Fatso told me she would queue up for hot water for me to bathe, and she told me to have a few minutes of rest in bed. Every night we would struggle over whether or not to bathe, especially on cold nights. If we decided in favor of the bath, we needed to queue up for hot water, sometimes for more than half an hour. At the end of our dorm rooms was a room with a big stove that heated water between ten and twelve at night. Because hot water was provided within limited hours, women frequently helped relatives, fellow villagers, and good friends to wait for hot water. Sometimes one person would bring four or five buckets from the long queue. Needless to say, queue jumping happened from time to time and squabbles and arguments followed. It was a site of contestation.

When we entered the dormitory gate, approaching the stove room, I heard loud noises and surmised it was an argument. Fatso screamed: "They are fighting, they are fighting with each other!" We ran to the spot, where two groups of women were wrestling. In a rage, one woman hit the other woman's face with great strength; the other woman fought back by pulling her opponent's hair. As Fatso tried to stop the fighting, she was forcefully pushed away by a thin young woman. I stood still, terribly frightened by the violence.

I couldn't sleep that night, haunted by how it was that these women could engage in such violence. Violence is often believed to be a male attribute; that is, that it belongs only to men and does not happen except among men. But this fierce women's fight disrupted my thoughts. It seemed silly to ask why these young women could act as brutal and aggressive as boys. It was also senseless to think about "human nature" as such. Forced to live in a harsh and inhuman environment, these women did not know how long they could tolerate such a life. Suspicion, quarreling, and even fighting were ways to release grievances, especially those suppressed for a long time. It was the outside environment that acted on the subject. What was the point if I retreated back to the "inside" of the subject, the "nature" of a human being, male or female? Violence is a performance of social relationship, embedded in specific historical and social contexts and often gendered in nature. Yet, it is never sexually prescribed.

The fighting women were all dismissed by the factory the next morning, without any investigation of who might be right or wrong. These workers all knew factory discipline and they all knew this fact: they did not behave like girls but rather like unruly boys or animals. Defiant bodies were punished and, again, they were disciplined through the discourse of sex and gender.

[. . .]

Gossip and Romance

One night I was invited to eat soup with a Cantonese group. The women were all from Qingyuan, the poorest rural area in Guangdong Province, and they all worked in the quality control department. During our meal gossip and rumor flowed naturally and wildly and, as on many occasions, came to focus on Miss Tang, the manager of quality control, who was from Hong Kong.

Qing started gossiping about Miss Tang: "I saw her eating with her girlfriend in the McDonald's."

"When? Did you see her girlfriend? Is she pretty?" all the other women asked.

"Last Sunday. I could only see the side of her face, you know, I dared not enter. I looked from the glass wall. I guess she doesn't look bad. Very well dressed and thick make-up. Dong told me that one day she saw them walking in the street. Her girlfriend was taller than her," Qing answered.

"But Tang looks quite handsome, doesn't she?" Bin said.

"Wow, somebody is secretly in love with our Tang!" Qing teased, and all the women laughed.

Bin responded instantly, "What rubbish are you talking? Will I love a person who is so harsh to us? I think because she treats people so hard and so emotionlessly, that's why she became abnormal. Can I love a pseudo man, who is in fact a woman? Can I?"

We continued to laugh despite Bin's explanation. A woman named Hua cackled "Why not? She is rich, powerful, and handsome. I bet if she chooses you, we can all get promoted. Please do sacrifice yourself!"

"But how can a woman love a woman? I am asking seriously. How can two women have sex? Can they give birth to a baby?" Bin turned her head to me, expecting an answer and trying to divert attention from herself. Unwilling to intervene in their talk, I simply said, "They can have sex, but they can't have a baby that way."

Qing added, "I saw a magazine one day. It said that in Western countries they have a lot of gays and lesbians who don't care about social and family pressure and insist on getting married to each other."

"How strange! They can marry. But it's good for them, isn't it?" another woman named San said.

"But it's still a pity they can't give birth to a baby. I think a woman's life can't be complete without going through marriage and the delivery of babies," Bin muttered.

"Oh, Bin, your thoughts are a little bit outdated. Today, who will care about the stuff of delivering sons? Happiness is more important!" Qing responded.

"Yet finding a good man is still important, isn't it?" Hua asked.

"Oh, Hua, you are dating somebody, aren't you? When are you going to marry him?" Bin asked back. All of us chuckled again and Hua blushed.

"I still have no idea. I don't want to go back home too early. But last New Year when I was back home, the man's family had already asked my father. Last month, my boyfriend came to visit me. He tried to convince me to come back home too." Hua spoke in an embarrassed tone.

"What a lucky woman! You must have done a lot of good things in your previous life. By the way, will you have sex before your married life?" Qing teased again, and we all fell into chuckles.

Hua instantly flushed and shouted, "I won't, I won't!"

"My father would beat me to death if he knew I had that relation with a man in the city," the quiet San murmured.

"Oh, I don't think it is wrong. If I really love a man, I don't mind," Qing raised her tone, a naughty expression on her face.

"Ah, what a liberated woman!" All the girls turned to laugh at Qing and the joking continued.

Gossip, jokes, and laughter centered on the topics of sex and love helped us to cope with the difficult and tedious factory life. Gossip and laughter demonstrated the power of the female workers, however minimal, to tease the patriarchal and capitalist orders. As Paul Willis (1981, 29) puts it, "having a laff" is a way to defeat boredom and fear, to ease the hardship and brutality of life, and thus is a way out of almost anything. "Having a laff" was clearly a weapon of the weak in fighting against the alienation of work and the subsumption of labor to capital. The factory daughters learned that sexuality was political and something they could decide to manipulate or not. Becoming sexually involved with someone in management, if one were willing, was a possible way to get promotion and gain advantages. Like labor, sexuality was something that belonged to the workers but could be manipulated and subsumed into the logic of capital. Sexual relationships between male supervisors and female line workers were not absent in the Meteor workplace, although they were frowned on heavily by all those not involved. Dating and sexual relations were often seen as advantageous and functional, but in the end futile, if not evil.

Another focus for gossip was the love affair between Gen, one of the supervisors in the production department, and Jing, now the secretary of the department. People kept telling me that Jing was only a line worker before she knew Gen, and that she was a nice, humble person before. But now she was completely proud and seldom talked even to her ethnic-kin group. At one point, a worker remarked to me: "You see the thick make-up, nobody is stronger than her. I am sure I won't want to learn from her, selling sex in exchange for a higher position."

Despite some bias, there were genuine social and cultural reasons for the workers to worry about any love and sexual relations they might have. First, if the man were an urban citizen, his family probably would not accept a woman of rural origin. Second, if both sides came from different provinces, the woman's family might not approve of the affair either. No family wanted their daughter to marry far away, unless they were really poor. Third, there were many rumors in the workplace that once a woman got pregnant, the man would run away and there would be no hope of finding him. It was an anonymous industrial world, not a communal village where everybody knew each other. Tragedy came once the man ran away and the woman's pregnancy was noticed by her company. Losing a job and not daring to go back home, the woman would be left alone to face her misfortune. Most women thought that it was not worth exchanging sex for short-term interest because in the end it could ruin one's whole life.

Gossip and laughter nevertheless were more than a weapon that was deployed to poke fun at the management. Jokes, laughter, and rumors were exactly where the women workers played out their gender subjectivities. Having a laugh was about having their views and ideas on sex, love, and marriage exchanged and voiced, and therefore helped to suture their female identities. During joking and laughing, women were more capable of articulating their feelings and emotions, albeit conflicting and ambivalent, such as love and hatred, desire and fear, dream and anxiety. For example, there was Bin who thought a woman could not be complete without getting married and giving birth to babies. There was Hua who took marriage as an important life path for women. But there was also Qing who said sex for happiness should be acceptable. Feelings and emotions expressed in the talking and joking were all part of a process of sexualization (Hearn and Parkin 1987). They were how women colluded in playing themselves out as sexualized subjects.

Consumerist Desire and the Modern Self

[. . .]

In the workplace, the women workers dreamed of consumption even as they labored, as if the dreaming spurred them on despite their mood. Dagongmei consuming practices contested the assumption that consumption was an "individualizing project" invested in, by, and for capital. In the workplace, the women shared with equal enthusiasm the satisfaction and frustration of shopping as well as work. Instead of keeping them separated, consumption bound them into a collectivity through their shared dreams and desires to become a new kind of gendered subject. "Dressing up" is perhaps the most common of these practices. Returning to their workplaces after a day of shopping, they could not wait to display their transformed selves wearing newly purchased T-shirts and jeans. For those who had worked in the city for a year or two, the urban environment with its many shops was attractive. In the evenings, they returned to their dormitories where they talked excitedly about fashion and make-up and where they could find the best buys. The desire to transform themselves and have a new look was what drew them together.

Their change in appearance was pivotal to them in the workplace. As mentioned earlier, the managerial class mocked the dagongmei's "coarse hands and feet," an abject subject bearing the stigma of rural backwardness. One could not help but notice how much time they spent on their fingernails, painting them with shiny colors to make them look more glamorous. Another obsession was with products that promised to whiten their skin, darkened from long exposure to the sun while laboring in the fields back home. One had to be light skinned to be a city dweller, and thus whitening lotions and creams were among their favorite purchases. A new look and a fresh identity were not only desired but could be realized by actively working on their appearance. A rebirth could be achieved through a consumption practice that functioned as a technology of the self. Through this means, they could realize for themselves "a great leap forward" out of rurality.

[. . .]

In this rapidly transforming period old cultural practices; new urban cosmopolitan models, pressures, and norms from the rural society; and desires and pursuits in a modern yet anonymous industrial world are all mixed up yet work together to invoke new female subjects and sexual bodies. There are no fixed boundaries and stable reference frames, no harbors in which new subjects can take refuge. We can say that Maoist China aimed only at producing an asexual subject—*tongzhi*; a unified subject embodied with the same will as the state socialist production. No class, no gender. Reform China, however, within a global project of capital, shows interest in resexualizing the subject, most notably a new dagong subject tailored to meet the new international division of labor. In the workplace, while the homogeneous construct of sexuality seemed the dominant mode, alternative models like Miss Tang, new ideas from Hong Kong, Taiwan, Japan, and the West, new experiences of urban life, and all kinds of contradictory ideas and behaviors, are nurtured and contribute to constituting fluid, shifting, and decentered female subjects. While some of the women escaped from their rural families to work in the global factory, thus hoping to elevate themselves to being modern subjects by staying in the city, many of them would soon realize that the toil of factory work was only an alienation from which there was no rescue; some of them even dreamed of marrying out and hoped to return home as an escape from factory work. Women workers in contemporary China are induced to live with conflicting feelings, emotions, and subjectivities, far from their own making.

These Chinese dagongmei, however, were manipulated by capital not only to be turned into efficient industrial producers, but they themselves desired to become fetish subjects as elements of the project of subject and of power. As Marx (1954) has said, the production process is an alienating process, in which women and men turn themselves into objects and confront themselves as something hostile and alien. In the process of consumption, then, women and men strive to redeem their alienation and achieve a sense of satisfaction through consumption. The harder they work, the more they want to spend. The more they desire to spend, the harder they need to work—thereby mirroring the dyadic relationship between production and consumption. The desire to be rid of poverty and to become modern gendered subjects is articulated together with the desire to consume commodities. Young female workers in the factory shared the same passion for purchasing lipsticks, whitening creams, trendy watches, jeans, and T-shirts, just to name a few items. These objects conjured up new desiring subjects who only were to discover themselves still trapped in a politics of identity and difference. [. . .]

Notes

1. While Foucault dealt with the body and sexuality, he has been criticized for not paying adequate attention to the gendered nature of disciplinary techniques on the body, or to a sexually differentiated body that is necessary for certain types of mechanisms or apparatuses (see McNay 1992).

2. See also the stories by An Zi (1993) in the volume *Qingchun xuyu: Dagongzai dagongmei Qingjian* (The dialogue of youth: Love letters of working sons and working daughters).

3. See Li Xiaojiang's two representative books on feminist politics in China: *Xiawa de tansuo* (Eve' search) (1988) and *Xing gou* (Gender gap) (1989).

4. Research on women and work shows that the advent of multinational capital and the industrialization of developing countries leads to the disintegration of traditional morality and the growth of a pornography culture. See also Ong 1987; and Truong 1990.

5. For more on ambivalence in sexuality, see Moore 1994.

CHAPTER 25

Breadwinners No More

MASCULINITY IN FLUX

Michele Ruth Gamburd

"He's good-hearted guy, but what a fool!" Priyanthi exclaimed, laughing, as we sat in her living room three days after her return to Sri Lanka from two years' work as a domestic servant in the Middle East. Any money her alcoholic husband had, she told me, he spent right away: "Today he's like a white man, tomorrow like a beggar." Every time she came home from abroad, she found only the four walls of their house remaining; during her last trip, he even sold the kitchen knives. Nonetheless, Priyanthi radiated an affectionate, good-humored conviction that she could reform her husband and build a better life for her four sons with the money she had earned abroad.

When Sri Lankan village women like Priyanthi leave their families to work abroad, their men remain at home, often unemployed and subsisting on the money their wives remit. The migration of these married women has expanded common notions of motherhood in Sri Lanka to include long absences from home. At the same time, female migration has reconfigured male gender roles in an often uncomfortable fashion. Many men feel a loss of self-respect and dignity when their wives become breadwinners. Such men only reluctantly take over the "women's work" of child care and cooking; if possible, they arrange to have female relatives assume these duties instead, in accordance with strongly felt local gender roles. Scenarios that circulate in television shows, newspaper articles, and local gossip suggest that uneducated, slothful husbands waste the money their wives earn abroad and turn to alcohol to drown their sorrows. Representations of delinquent, emasculated men appear in these stories in tandem with images of promiscuous, selfish, pleasure-seeking women who neglect their husbands and children.

The prevalence of migration, itself a response to high unemployment in Sri Lanka, has introduced new social and economic realities in villages like Naeaegama, where Priyanthi lives. In so doing, migration also forces villagers to violate old gender norms and to generate new ideals. This sort of change affects the gut-level, commonsense conceptions of how the world is organized that Raymond Williams calls "structures of feeling."[1]

In Sri Lanka, many people believe that women should stay at home and tend their families while men earn a living for the household. Local poverty and scarce job opportunities for men, however, drive many women to migrate for work. In the Naeaegama area in 1997, 90 percent of all migrants were women. Of the migrant women, 30 percent were single, and 70 percent were married, separated, or divorced. Most of the women in this latter group had at least one child, and approximately half had husbands who contributed regularly to their household income; the other half had husbands who were under- or unemployed. Despite the relatively high proportion of employed husbands, many villagers lump together all the husbands of migrant women as lazy spendthrifts.

Common local stereotypes devalue these husbands' competence as breadwinners and as lovers. A number of housemaids in Naeaegama told me that "Arab people say that Sri Lankan men must be 'donkeys' because they send their wives abroad." The phrase carries two sets of implications. First, it emphasizes Sri Lankan men's inability to provide for their families. Second, the phrase implies that Sri Lankan women are not sexually satisfied with their husbands; if they were, they would not travel to the Middle East (and, presumably, sleep with Arab men). These images of Sri Lankan men rest on certain popular assumptions about migrant women: "If they can't eat grapes and apples, they go abroad. If they can't eat cheese and butter, they go abroad," runs one common adage. Grapes and apples, luxury fruits imported from abroad, signify a life of leisure and affluence. Cheese and butter, also luxury products, signify a rich and satisfying sexual life. This remark suggests that migrant women, dissatisfied with their lives and husbands in Sri Lanka, travel abroad in search of more gratifying economic and sexual situations.

When my research associates, Siri and Sita, and I repeated the story about Arab men calling Sri Lankan men "donkeys" to people I interviewed, it often sparked a lively conversation. Many people, after a moment's contemplation, replied by detailing their financial situations. Some slightly shamefacedly, some matter-of-factly, cited poverty as the reason women went abroad. A family, they explained, could not make ends meet on a man's wages as a casual laborer. Migrant women did not seek anything as fancy as "grapes and apples"; they merely hoped to support their families above the poverty line. Fewer respondents addressed the implicit suggestion of sexual impotence. Pradeep, an articulate young man, bounced his two-year-old son on his knee and replied that he knew and trusted his wife. Despite his hard work, his family could not afford to buy land, build a house, and start a business on his salary alone. If he could save the money his wife sent from abroad and build a house, and if she came home without being unchaste, that would prove he was not a donkey.

Despite the widespread awareness of such pragmatic concerns as local poverty and economic opportunities abroad, negative stereotypes continue to circulate, stigmatizing local men whose wives migrate for their inability to live up to older gender ideals. Both the stereotype of the Sri man as a "donkey" and the pragmatic discussions of poverty reflect the slow, difficult, and often painful negotiation of changing gender roles and family structures.

Alcohol: Group Bonding and Masculinity

In Naeaegama, alcohol is a business, a medicine, a pleasure, a necessity, and a mark of masculinity. Drinking, an exclusively male activity and a sign of wealth (however fleeting), preoccupies many of the under- and unemployed village men. When families do not prosper from female migration to the Middle East, villagers often blame husbands who quit work and take up drinking in their wives' absence. At once scornful and tolerant of such husbands, villagers commonly tut, "He sits idly, drinks, and wastes." Asked why these men indulge in such behavior, several villagers suggested that the men sought to emulate the rich landowners of the previous generation. One village notable explained to me: "It is good to be rich and look idle; in the absence of riches, idle will suffice." Hard work, particularly physical labor, carries significant stigma in the village; light skin, clean white clothing, and a sweatless brow indicate leisure, high status, or at the very least a respectable office job out of the burning sun.

Alcohol is the despair of many a wife, and the basis of community among drinking buddies. When a migrant woman comes home, her husband often demands money to buy drinks for himself and to improve his status by buying rounds for poorer male friends and relatives. Some Naeaegama women anticipate these requests by bringing home prestigious foreign liquor they purchase at duty-free shops. Although they enable their husbands' drinking, these women nevertheless seek to limit it. Blame for bad male behavior—such as gambling, smoking, drinking, and womanizing—often falls on the absent wife, without whose control a husband, considered constitutionally incapable of controlling his baser urges, drifts helplessly into bad habits and bad company. Frequently, however, patterns of drinking, wasteful spending, and failure to prosper predate, and even prompt, female migration. While women are considered responsible for disciplining their families and regulating household finances, they often have little authority to enforce their will, especially while they are abroad.

Drinking norms in Sri Lankan villages do not resemble Western norms of social drinking or before-dinner cocktails. At weddings, funerals, and other mixed-sex get-togethers, the host often "runs a bottle" of hard liquor out of a back room that most of the male guests visit surreptitiously, becoming progressively drunker as the event proceeds. While drinking, men do not eat, because food reduces the "current" or high. This style of drinking spans social classes. I once attended a university dinner party where I learned (a little too late) that respectable unmarried women rarely lingered at such functions past seven or eight in the evening. While their wives (and two uncomfortable female Western academics) huddled together in one room, married and unmarried men drank bottle after bottle in another until, around ten or eleven in the evening, the host decided to serve dinner. Immediately after eating, the visitors departed, most in cars driven by drunken men. Men strove to get as drunk as possible as quickly as possible; drinking to excess was the norm, not the exception.

The production, distribution, and consumption of alcohol form a significant component of the village economy. A bottle of the legal hard liquor, arrack, costs roughly what a manual laborer might earn in a day; in 1994 a bottle of the officially distilled arrack costs Rs 118 (US$2.36), while a laborer's daily wage was between Rs 100 and Rs 125 (US$2–$2.50). In 1994, one village outfit that offered wages of 150 Sir Lankan Rupees (Rs)—US$3—a night, with free food and drink, went into production twice a week, running three stills all night, each requiring six people's constant attention. Including production crews, complicit landowners and law enforcement officers, and distribution networks, this distillery, one of several in the area, directly involved more than fifty people. Women, who rarely if ever touch liquor, constantly pressure their husbands to spend money on items for family consumption rather than on alcohol. To save money, most local men drink *kasippu*, the local moonshine. A bottle of *kasippu*, a fruit, yeast, and sugar-based fractionally distilled liquor, cost about Rs 60 (US$1.20) in 1994. Despite their families' debts and hunger, many men spend a great deal on alcohol, and some work for local *kasippu* manufacturers who operate stills at night in remote, wooded places.

Alcohol provides a strong basis for social allegiance and identity. Drinking groups often form around a particular *kasippu* producer. Heavy drinkers adopt the values and norms of their groups, which tolerate, even encourage, such activities as gambling, stealing, rape, and assault. Anthropologist Jonathan Spencer glosses *lajja* as shame, shyness, and social restraint—all essential ingredients of good public behavior. He glosses *lajja-baya* as "shame-fear," particularly the fear of ridicule and public humiliation. Those who drink are thought not to know *lajja* or *baya*. Spencer notes, "It is assumed that people who drink alcohol will no longer be in control of their actions and [will be] easily aroused to anger, which would be likely to spill out in physical violence, given the opportunity."[2] Shifting groups of local men, usually of similar age and status, gather regularly to drink, surreptitiously visiting a distribution center or purchasing a bottle to take to a private location. Often those with money spot drinks for those without, who return the favor at a later date.

[...]

For men whose incomes are eclipsed by those of their wives, or who fail to make the most of their wives' salaries, alcohol provides relief from personal responsibility. An extenuating condition that can be entered whenever needed, drunkenness provides the perfect alibi for poor judgment or socially unacceptable behavior.[3] Responsibility falls on the alcohol for any foolish actions and on the absent wife for the drinking itself. With prosperity in the village resting primarily on female migration to the Middle East, involvement with *kasippu* production and distribution provides poor men with alcohol, money, community, political clout, and a means to reassert the male power and respect lost in the face of women's new economic role. Drinkers thus emulate the idle rich of prior generations and reject the work ethic of the contemporary wealthy.

Meaning in the Making:
Rukmini and Ramesh

Although many families hope to save a female migrant's earnings for large purchases, such as buying land and building a house, in many cases supporting the family on the husband's wages while putting the wife's earnings aside proves difficult. Men can pursue sporadic, grueling physical labor for very low wages—or they can dip into their wives' remittances. Many men in the Naeaegama area choose to rely on the money their wives earn abroad to finance their daily needs. The following case presents a fairly typical example of voluntary male underemployment and the concomitant use of a migrant woman's wages for family consumption. In a series of interviews, family members struggled to explain to me and to themselves their lack of improvement despite seven years of work abroad. In the process, they wrestled with the meaning of their continued poverty, and with its effect on individual and family identity.

Siri and I interviewed Hema, an elderly woman of a lower caste, and her son Ramesh. Ramesh's wife, Rukmini, was then working abroad as a housemaid. Rukmini, about thirty years old, had spent most of the previous seven years abroad. During the four years Rukmini worked in Jordan, she sent her money to her mother, who was supposed to look after her daughter. But Rukmini's mother had no stable home. She visited all of Rukmini's siblings, staying roughly six weeks with each, and spending lavishly with the checks Rukmini sent. The next time Rukmini went abroad, she left her daughter with Hema, her mother-in-law, instead. While Siri, Hema, Ramesh, and I sat in the shade of Hema's unfinished cement house, Siri half-jokingly explained to me in that Rukmini did not send money to her husband Ramesh, an infamous drinker and gambler. Once the ice was broken, Hema took over the story, explaining that she had told Rukmini not to send the money but to keep it herself. Ramesh's gambling and drinking left nothing even to support himself and his daughter, Hema recounted. Ramesh had taken credit with many local stores, and he now owed interest-bearing debts to several moneylenders.

Hema suggested that if Ramesh could earn money for himself and his daughter, his wife could save all of her salary, and the family could then buy land and build a house, as they had originally planned. Sober and embarrassed, Ramesh said nothing to contradict his mother. I asked him about his work. He said he made about Rs 125 (US$2.50, considered a good salary locally) a day doing physical labor, and more than that when he drummed for ceremonies. Silently contradicting the impression that all of his wife's earnings had evaporated, Ramesh took me into the two-room clay house where he, his mother, father, daughter, and several brothers all lived, and he showed us a crowded collection of furniture he had bought with Rukmini's remittances.

When she returned to the village in mid–April 1994, I asked Rukmini to come meet with me at Siri's house for an interview. Usually I spoke with people in their homes, but at that time Rukmini and Ramesh were living in a six-by-twelve-foot lean-to built against the new cement wall of Hema's unfinished house. Unexpectedly, Ramesh accompanied his wife to the interview. Moreover, he was drunk. Siri tried to take Ramesh aside while Sita and I talked to Rukmini. Occasionally, however, Ramesh approached or interjected. When he did so, palpable tension pervaded the interview. Rukmini seemed barely able to finish a sentence. When I asked her about the gifts she had brought back from the Middle East, Ramesh declared that Rukmini had given him a shirt but that he had gotten his sarong for himself. She replied that she had given him a shirt, shoes, and cigarettes.

The full story explained Rukmini's barbed remark. Rukmini had given Ramesh a new pair of sandals, a pack of prestigious foreign cigarettes, and a new shirt. But when the police raided the illegal coconut beer brewery where Ramesh had gone to drink, he ran through a drainage canal toward the ocean. The canal muck claimed his new sandals, and the salt water ruined the pack of cigarettes in his shirt pocket. Rukmini mentioned that she had also brought her husband twelve beers and two whiskey bottles, all of which he had already consumed. But even if he drank, Ramesh retorted to Rukmini, at least he saved her clothing. Siri, Sita, and I assume that he was comparing himself favorably with the husband of another village migrant, who had sold his wife's dresses during her absence.

When Siri had persuaded Ramesh to walk in the garden, I asked Rukmini if she planned to go back to the Middle East. She intended to go back "no matter what," Rukmini replied. She said she was fed up with her husband's habits. There was no use earning money when he was drinking, she lamented, speaking very quickly. Some of the money Rukmini had just brought home had gone to settle Ramesh's debts and to finance drinking and gambling binges. Although she liked to come home to see her daughter, problems with her husband "unsettled her mind." Ramesh never listened to her, Rukmini complained, instead "he breaks things and wastes and drinks." Her variation on the common trope—"He sits idly, drinks, and wastes"—emphasized her dismay at Ramesh's destructive behavior, which she judged worse even than indolence and dissipation.

Ramesh returned to the porch. Reaching for a neutral topic, but inadvertently stumbling into a minefield, I asked Rukmini what had been the worst time in her life. It started after she got married, she replied. Ramesh exclaimed, "Really?" They talked heatedly about a fight several years earlier that had ended with both of them filing separate complaints at the police station at the junction—a common conclusion to serious village disputes. Ramesh accused his wife of abandoning their daughter and neglecting her wifely duties. Silenced, Rukmini picked up an umbrella from the table, examining it with great care. Center stage and unchecked, Ramesh delivered a monologue about himself and how hard he had been working for the family's sake. Siri and Sita made no effort to translate his tirade, and I stopped taking notes. Rukmini slouched low in her cane armchair, turning slightly away from her husband. I caught her eye and winked. Suddenly she sat up straight and relaxed physically, telling Ramesh to go home so that she could answer my questions.

[. . .] Although for the most part they accept men's right to dominate the public transcript, women make ample use of other opportunities to communicate their opinions.[4]

That afternoon on the porch, Rukmini and Ramesh each attempted to control the narrative, influence judgments, and shape appraisals. Theirs was a struggle over meaning in the making, as each attempted to define his or her own agency, identity, and self-worth with respect to the story of their family's failure to prosper. By including himself in my invitation to talk, and by excluding Rukmini from the conversation when he could, Ramesh sought to prevent his wife (and me) from portraying Rukmini as the household's decision-maker and breadwinner. Ramesh wanted to be thought of as part of a team, even as a leader, instead of as deadweight, or as someone who "sits at home idle, eating while his wife works." In his monologue, he sought to retell the story of what happened to all the money Rukmini had sent home, simultaneously reworking his own image in my eyes and in his own.

[. . .]

Rukmini had asked a doctor for medicine to stop Ramesh's drinking, but the doctor would only write a prescription to Ramesh himself. Hema suggested asking the alcohol distributors not to sell Ramesh liquor. Although Rukmini still had some money in the bank (and she and her baby both wore gold necklaces), she said that the family had trouble making ends meet on Ramesh's earnings. She did not want to dip into her savings for daily expenses because she wanted to have a large coming-of-age ceremony for her oldest daughter. Fanning herself and her baby under the hot tin roof, Rukmini said that sometimes she thought she would have been better off not going abroad at all; if her husband "had a brain" she could have "brought the family up," but Rukmini wondered if her small plot of land and modest house were worth eight years of hard work abroad.

Back in 1994, I had asked Rukmini how she envisioned her life in another ten years. She said that she would like her whole family to live in a nice house of their own. My research associate greeted this aspiration with skepticism. In 1997, however, villagers voiced different opinions. Despite adversity and a wasteful husband, Rukmini did indeed live in her own home. Although small, the land and house counted as improvement in the eyes of the Naeaegama villagers, and they demonstrated that despite his heavy drinking, Ramesh had not wasted all of the money his wife earned abroad.

Women's Work

Migration has forced men and women in Sri Lankan villages to renegotiate gender roles regarding not only whether a woman can respectably work abroad but also who will take care of a migrant woman's duties and responsibilities in the home she leaves behind. Despite the large number of under- and unemployed husbands in the village, only four or five families of around ninety I interviewed admitted that men had taken over more than the bare minimum of housework. In all but one of these cases, the men in question held other jobs as well, and they shared the domestic duties with female relatives.

In Sri Lankan villages, the gendered division of labor clearly marks child care and cooking as female activities. Most men would feel their sense of masculinity threatened if they took on household chores or cared for young children. Carla Risseeuw writes of a rural Sri village near Naeaegama:

> Men cannot "stoop down" in the widest sense, without experiencing severe emotional stress. . . . The principle that he is "higher" than a woman, and more specifically his wife, permeates the actions, thoughts and emotions of both men and women. . . . Handling dirt, feces, cleaning toilets, being impure, doing repetitive, relatively less prestigious work, which often lacks the status of work as such or "prestige" of the proximity of danger, is the female expression of the principle of gender hierarchy.[5]

Most of the men and women in Naeaegama accept this division as just, and they judge themselves and others according to it.

Migrants generally told me that they left their children in the care of their mothers or mothers-in-law, but in my daily interactions in the village, I noted more male participation in child care than people reported. Priyanthi, the Naeaegama migrant introduced earlier, left her four sons in the care of her husband and his father while she was abroad. Such men and their families often glossed over men's housework in order to preserve a masculine image. Since Priyanthi's husband, Ariyapala, held a well-paying job at the hospital, he was somewhat sheltered from village ridicule when he took on his wife's work. But in an interview, Ariyapala somewhat defensively explained his assumption of domestic duties as a pragmatic solution to Priyanthi's absence. Ariyapala's heavy drinking also reaffirmed his masculine identity. The few men who did take over their migrant wives' domestic chores both challenged and reaffirmed older gender roles.

Joker, Simpleton, Freethinker: Lal

Indrani and her husband, Chandradasa, belonged to a new elite in the Naeaegama area. They were considered one of the most successful village families involved with the migration of labor to the Middle East. Indrani worked for the same family in Doha, Qatar, for twelve years, earning a very generous salary, Chandradasa worked as a security officer at a hotel near Colombo, returning home for two weekends a month. The couple saved and spent both spouses' salaries wisely. In Indrani's and Chandradasa's absence, Chandradasa's mother and brother took care of their five children and supervised the construction of their new house. Although Indrani named her mother-in-law the primary guardian for her children, the older woman's arthritis severely restricted her movements. The children's uncle Lal, a colorful village character, did the lion's share of the cooking and housekeeping.

Lal lived across the road from Siri's house, where I stayed, and he drew drinking water from the well in our garden. Members of our household replied to the greetings Lal called out every time he entered the compound with teasing comments and questions. About the state of the meal Lal was preparing, Siri invariably asked, "Is the [cooking] course over?" For a man to study cooking in school would be only slightly more astounding than to find him cooking at all. In a world of simple structural reversals, when the house-worker leaves to earn a living, one might expect the former breadwinner to do the housework. In Naeaegama, however, in most cases other women, not men, took over "feminine" chores, with grandmothers and aunts looking after the children. Lal, a man who for the past twelve years had cooked, kept house, fetched water, done laundry and shopping, and taken care of children, was the source of some astonishment and amusement in the village.

Many villagers associate full male adulthood with having a wife and a stable job. Lal had neither. At his mother's insistence, Lal had reluctantly married some years before I met him. His beautiful wife asked him to move to her relatives' home in the capital; when he refused, she found work in the Middle East and never returned to the village. Although he was fairly sure that she had come home safely, Lal had no desire to visit her relatives in the city or to see her again.

Lal had worked as a laborer and as an office clerk, but he had not held a job since he was hit by a van while walking on the side of the road a number of years previous. He had no wish to return to work and no ambition to start a business. His mother, who had persuaded him to marry in the first place, thought that he should do so again. Quoting a proverb, Lal said," The man who is hit with the firebrand from the fire is afraid even of the firefly" (the local equivalent of "Once bitten, twice shy"). When his mother died and all of his family duties were fulfilled, Lal figured, he would become a priest. In the meantime, when his sister-in-law Indrani left for Qatar, Lal and his mother moved in with Chandradasa to look after the couple's children. The fact that Lal was single, lacked a salaried job, and devoted attention to chores often thought of as women's work caused a number of chuckles in the village.

Curious about Lal's sexuality, two village notables arranged to question him informally. One afternoon Lal, who was nearly illiterate, asked Siri's father, the local Justice of the Peace, to help him write a letter to the Graama Seevaka, the local government administrator, asking to be put on a list to receive aid from a local nongovernmental organization. In jest, the Justice of the Peace wrote a completely unsuitable letter, telling the Graama Seevaka the stark truth—that Lal lived in a good cement house with electricity and a television set. (Lal's official residence, a collapsing clay hut, formed the basis of a subsequent, successful application.) Unable to read the letter, Lal took it to the Graama Seevaka, who laughed and said, "This won't do at all," and suggested that he and Lal both go talk to the Justice of the Peace.

Siri overheard the conversation. The Justice of the Peace and the Graama Seevaka teasingly but somewhat cruelly peppered Lal with questions about his long-absent wife, asking if he had sent her cards and sweets in the Middle East. They also asked about Lal's sex life. In a village where everyone knew everyone else's business, there was not even the hint of a rumor suggesting that Lal might be actively homosexual; several other men were known to be so. The Justice of the Peace and the Graama Seevaka merely determined that Lal did not know "which end was up." Having satisfied their curiosity, the Justice of the Peace wrote a suitable letter for the Graama Seevaka and gave it to Lal, who went home to start the evening meal.

Lal's calm, slow, joking manner made him a hard target for teasing. He was the only male recipient of government aid who waited in line with the women to collect food at the local cooperative store. When villagers mocked his feminine behavior, Lal regaled them with humorous stories about his finicky taste in groceries; those who attempted to laugh at him found themselves instead laughing with him about the dead gecko in the rice bag and the dried fish so smelly it must have been fertilizer. He met comments on his domesticity with exaggerated stories about the latest crises in the kitchen, the rough quality of a new soap, and the price of beans. His complaints were uniformly within his domestic role, not about it. He created an ambiguous self-image, as something between a simpleton with no understanding of his failure to fulfill a man's proper role and a freethinker, impervious to criticism, who held a singularly different set of values. That opacity, along with his nonstop wit, allowed Lal to carve out a unique space for himself as a man whose sole job was women's work. The good-humored probing of the Graama Seevaka and the Justice of the Peace indexed at once the community's awareness of Lal's unusual behavior, and its baffled but amused acceptance.

When I spoke with Lal in 1997, he expressed some ambivalence about his domestic role. At one point he said that he needed to be "bailed out of jail" and set free from the kitchen; a little later, he noted with pride that his family preferred his cooking to Indrani's. When Indrani cooked, Lal recounted, Chandradasa and the children could tell. "*Bappa* [uncle] didn't cook this," the children would say, with gestures that indicated that they did not like the food. Lal said that his sister-in-law made coconut milk by machine; he scraped coconuts the old-fashioned way, generating a richer milk. Her curries had a foreign taste; his had a better flavor. Neighbors had asked Lal why he still cooked when Indrani was home for a visit. He said that he would like to find a job, but Indrani and his mother had asked him not to leave. If he no longer took care of the family, Indrani would have to give up her job and look after her mother-in-law, a prospect neither of the strong-willed women viewed with pleasure. I asked Lal if he were ashamed or shy (*lajja*) about the work he did. Suddenly completely serious, he held his head up very straight and said that one should never be ashamed of the work one does to eat or drink. He took care of his mother, the house, and the children, and he did not try to hide what he did. He said he was ready to do any job that came his way, either men's work or women's work. He was not ashamed.

While Indrani's migration had changed household gender roles for both Lal and Chandradasa, only Lal's behavior drew extensive village comments. Although Chandradasa took over some of the household chores during his infrequent visits, for the most part his job as a security guard kept him out of the domestic sphere, at the same time reaffirming his breadwinner role. In contrast, Lal's daily routine included many activities commonly thought of as women's work; he lacked any other form of regular employment to reaffirm his masculinity; he had no wife or family of his own; and he did not drink alcohol. When a local committee arranged to resurface the paved road that led into the village, Lal, who had worked in road construction in the past, eagerly volunteered for the overtly masculine job. I believe he sought both the modest paycheck and the highly visible change of gender role.

Lal's ambiguous gender position complemented the new status and prestige Indrani's accumulated wealth gave her in the village. Indrani and Chandradasa contributed yearly to a large ceremony at a popular local shrine, spending over Rs 5,000 (US$100) on food and decorations. Contributing lavishly to community projects elevated the prestige and social standing of villagers; for Indrani and Chandradasa, this entitled them to positions of authority in community politics and temple decision-making formerly monopolized by wealthy, high-caste, elite families. Several days after her return from the Middle East in 1993, Indrani received an invitation from three village youths to "open" a community food distribution event. Indrani accepted the offer and also made a generous contribution. Indrani's financial capital metamorphosed into prestige, symbolic capital, respect, and renown. Watching each other cynically for signs of returning poverty, villagers often recognized that wealth was difficult to maintain. Patrons who sustained their positions for a significant length of time, as Indrani and Chandradasa have, were recognized in the village as people who had truly prospered.

How Lal and Indrani would negotiate the transformation of their roles when Indrani returned permanently to the village remained to be seen. In 1997, returning home for a vacation for the first time in four years, Indrani displayed no desire to relieve Lal of the household chores. Having spent lavishly for her daughter's coming-of-age ceremony, Indrani insisted (against her husband's will) on returning overseas to continue earning money for the family. Many villagers felt that she should have stayed home to look after her daughter instead. Indrani countered that she had spent all of her money on improving her house and holding a grand ceremony for her daughter. Now that they were older, her children needed money for their schooling. She added that she had promised to fund the construction of a new cement house where Lal and his mother would move when Indrani returned from abroad for good. The family also needed money for further improvements on their own house and to start a business, perhaps a small shop.

Indrani's prolonged absence changed not only Lal's social position but also her own. Like many migrant women, she no longer fit into village society the same way she had before she left. Though her primary motivation for migrating was economic, issues of identity, independence, and torn loyalties also impinged on her decision. Like Lal, Indrani seemed ambivalent about assuming the housewife's role in her Sri Lanka home.

Conclusion

When women migrate to the Middle East, gender roles and power relations change in the villages they leave behind. The preceding cases illustrate both the world that could once be taken for granted and the challenges that now face older patterns of behavior. Ramesh, Lal, and Chandradasa, three village men associated with female migrants, all asserted their masculinity differently: Ramesh through idleness and alcohol, Chandradasa through work and wealth, and Lal through a playful self-parody of his feminizing housekeeping role.

Ramesh's drinking, his braggadocio, and his deliberate cultivation of the idle life challenged Rukmini to prosper despite her husband, not with his help. Membership in the drinking group affirmed Ramesh's masculinity, assuaged his shame or guilt (*lajja*) for not improving his family's social status, and provided the economic and social community he may have missed in his wife's absence. Chandradasa, by comparison, found his identity in hard work away from home. The cooperative and trusting relationship he shared with his wife gave him control not only of his own salary but also of the money she earned abroad. Willingly remitted for the construction of their house, her pay enhanced both spouses' standards of living and prestige in the village.

Lal, who took on all of the domestic chores in Indrani's absence, encountered daily teasing about his cooking and household work, but he met these remarks with unfailing good humor. Because he lacked other employment, Lal brought villagers face to face with the possibility of men taking over not just individual chores but entire social roles vacated by migrant women. Lal's behavior projected a crisis in gender categories. He generated a powerful mixture of laughter and unease by assuming a traditionally domestic role as his sister-in-law moved out into the international labor market.

Notes

1. Raymond Williams, *Marxism and Literature* (Oxford: Oxford University Press, 1977), 132.

2. Jonathan Spencer, *A Sinhala Village in a Time of Trouble* (Delhi: Oxford University Press, 1991), 169–72.

3. Hans Olav Fekjaer, *Alcohol and Illicit Drugs: Myths and Realities* (Colombo, Sri Lanka: IOGT Alcohol and Drug Information Centre, 1993).

4. James Scott, *Domination and the Arts of Resistance: Hidden Transcripts* (New Haven: Yale University Press, 1990).

5. Carla Risseeuw, *Gender Transformation, Power, and Resistance among Women in Sri Lanka: The Fish Don't Talk about the Water* (New Delhi: Manohar, 1991), 271.

CHAPTER 26

Thailand: Because She Looks Like a Child

Kevin Bales

When Siri wakes it is about noon. In the instant of waking she knows exactly who and what she has become. As she explained to me, the soreness in her genitals reminds her of the fifteen men she had sex with the night before. Siri is fifteen years old. Sold by her parents a year ago, her resistance and her desire to escape the brothel are breaking down and acceptance and resignation are taking their place.

In the provincial city of Ubon Ratchitani in northeastern Thailand, Siri works and lives in a brothel. About ten brothels and bars, dilapidated and dusty buildings, line the side street just around the corner from a new Western-style shopping mall. Food and noodle vendors are scattered between the brothels. The woman behind the noodle stall outside the brothel where Siri works is also spy, warder, watchdog, procurer, and dinner-lady to Siri and the other twenty-four girls and women in the brothel.

The brothel is surrounded by a wall with iron gates meeting the street. Within the wall is a dusty yard, a concrete picnic table, and the ubiquitous spirit house, a small shrine that stands outside all Thai buildings. A low door leads into a windowless concrete room that is thick with the smell of cigarettes, stale beer, vomit, and sweat. This is the "selection" room (hong du). On one side of the room are stained and collapsing tables and booths; on the other side is a narrow elevated platform with a bench that runs the length of the room. Spotlights pick out this bench, and at night the girls and women sit here under the glare while the men at the tables drink and choose the one they want.

Passing through a door at the far end of the bench, the man follows the girl past a window where a bookkeeper takes his money and records which girl he has taken. From there he is led to the girl's room. Behind its concrete front room the brothel degenerates even further into a haphazard shanty warren of tiny cubicles where the girls live and work. A makeshift ladder leads up to what may have once been a barn. The upper level is now lined with doors about five feet apart opening into rooms of about five by seven feet that hold a bed and little else.

Scraps of wood and cardboard separate one room from the next, and Siri has plastered her walls with pictures and posters of teenage pop stars cut from magazines. Over

367

her bed, as in most rooms, there also hangs a framed portrait of the king of Thailand; a single bare light bulb hangs above. Next to the bed a large tin can holds water; there is a hook nearby for rags and towels. At the foot of the bed next to the door some clothes are folded on a ledge. The walls are very thin and everything can be heard from the surrounding rooms: a shout from the bookkeeper echoes through them all whether their doors are open or not.

After rising at midday, Siri washes herself in cold water from the single concrete trough that serves the twenty-five women of the brothel. Then, dressed in a T-shirt and skirt, she goes to the noodle stand for the hot soup that is a Thai breakfast. Through the afternoon, if she does not have any clients, she chats with the other girls and women as they drink beer and play cards or make decorative handicrafts together. If the pimp is away the girls will joke around, but if not they must be constantly deferential and aware of his presence, for he can harm them or use them as he pleases. Men coming in the afternoon are the exception, but those that do tend to have more money and can buy a girl for several hours if they like. A few will even make appointments a few days ahead.

At about five, Siri and the other girls are told to dress, put on their makeup, and prepare for the night's work. By seven the men are coming in, purchasing drinks and choosing girls, and Siri will have been chosen by one or two of the ten to eighteen men who will buy her that night. Many men choose Siri because she looks much younger than her fifteen years. Slight and round faced, dressed to accentuate her youth, she might be eleven or twelve. Because she looks like a child she can be sold as a "new" girl at a higher price, about $15, which is more than twice that charged for the other girls.

Siri is very frightened that she will get AIDS. Long before she understood prostitution she knew about HIV, as many girls from her village returned home to die from AIDS after being sold into the brothels. Every day she prays to Buddha, trying to earn the merit that will preserve her from the disease. She also tries to insist that her clients use condoms, and in most cases she is successful as the pimp backs her up. But when policemen use her, or the pimp himself, they will do as they please; if she tries to insist, she will be beaten and raped. She also fears pregnancy, and like the other girls she receives injections of the contraceptive drug Depo-Provera. Once a month she has an HIV test, and so far it has been negative. She knows that if she tests positive she will be thrown out of the brothel to starve.

Though she is only fifteen Siri is now resigned to being a prostitute. After she was sold and taken to the brothel, she discovered that the work was not what she thought it would be. Like many rural Thais, Siri had a sheltered childhood and she was ignorant of what it meant to work in a brothel. Her first client hurt her and at the first opportunity she ran away. On the street with no money she was quickly caught, dragged back, beaten, and raped. That night she was forced to take on a chain of clients until the early morning. The beatings and the work continued night after night until her will was broken. Now she is sure that she is a bad person, very bad to have deserved what has happened to her. When I commented on how pretty she looked in a photograph, how like a pop star, she replied, "I'm no star; I'm just a whore, that's all." She copes as best she can. She takes a dark pride in her higher price and in the large number of men who choose her. It is the adjustment of the concentration camp, an effort to make sense of horror.

In Thailand prostitution is illegal, yet girls like Siri are sold into sex slavery by the thousands. The brothels that hold these girls are but a small part of a much wider sex industry. How can this wholesale trade in girls continue? What keeps it working? The answer is more complicated than we might think; Thailand's economic boom, its macho culture, and its social acceptance of prostitution all contribute to it. Money, culture, and society blend in new and powerful ways to enslave girls like Siri.[1]

Rice in the Field, Fish in the River, Daughters in the Brothel

Thailand is a country blessed with natural resources and sufficient food. The climate is mild to hot, there is dependable rain, and most of the country is a great plain, well-watered and fertile. The reliable production of rice has for centuries made Thailand a large exporter of grains, as it is today. Starvation is exceedingly rare in its history and social stability very much the norm. An old and often-repeated saying in Thai is "There is always rice in the fields and fish in the river." And anyone who has tried the imaginative Thai cuisine knows the remarkable things that can be done with those two ingredients and the local chili peppers.

If there is one part of Thailand not so rich in the necessities of life, it is the mountainous north. In fact, that area is not Thailand proper; originally the kingdom of Lanna, it was integrated into Thailand only in the late nineteenth century. The influence of Burma here is very strong—as are the cultures of the seven main hill tribes, which are distinctly foreign to the dominant Thai society. Only about a tenth of the land of the north can be used for agriculture, though what can be used is the most fertile in the country. The result is that those who control good land are well-off; those who live in the higher elevations, in the forests, are not. In another part of the world this last group might be called hillbillies, and they share the hardscrabble life of mountain dwellers everywhere.

The harshness of this life stands in sharp contrast to that on the great plain of rice and fish. Customs and culture differ markedly as well, and one of those differences is a key to the sexual slavery practiced throughout Thailand today. For hundreds of years many people in the north, struggling for life, have been forced to view their own children as commodities. A failed harvest, the death of a key breadwinner, or any serious debt incurred by a family might lead to the sale of a daughter (never a son) as a slave or servant. In the culture of the north it was a life choice not preferred but acceptable, and one that was used regularly. In the past these sales fed a small, steady flow of servants, workers, and prostitutes south into Thai society.

Religion helped provide two important justifications for such sales of daughters. Within the type of Buddhism followed in Thailand, women are regarded as distinctly inferior to men. A woman cannot, for example, attain enlightenment, which is the ultimate goal of the devout. On the ladder of existence women are well below men, and only if she is especially careful might a woman hope to be reborn as a man in her next life. Indeed, to enter this incarnation as a woman might indicate a particularly disastrous and sinful previous life. In the advice recorded as his own words, Buddha warns his disciples about the danger of women: they are impure, carnal, and corrupting. Within these Buddhist writings prostitution is sanctioned; the vihaya, or rules for monks, lists ten kinds of wives, the first three of which are "those bought for money, those living together voluntarily, those to be enjoyed or used occasionally."[2] Within these beliefs is no notion of sex as a sin; instead, sex is seen as an attachment to the physical and natural world, the world of suffering and ignorance. The implication is that if you must have sex, have it as impersonally as possible.

Thai Buddhism also carries a central message of acceptance and resignation in the face of life's pain and suffering. The terrible things that happen to a person are, after all, of an individual's own making, recompense for the sins of this life or previous lives. Whatever happens is a person's fixed destiny, his or her karma. To achieve the tranquility necessary for enlightenment, a person must learn to accept quietly and completely the pain of this life. For some Thai children the pain of this life includes forced prostitution. They may struggle against the abuse they suffer, but most come to resign themselves, living out a psychology of slavery that we will explore in this chapter.

A religious belief in the inferiority of girls is not the only cultural rule pressing them into slavery. Thai children, especially girls, owe their parents a profound debt, an obligation both cosmic and physical. Simply to be born is a great gift, then to be fed and raised another; and both require a lifetime of repayment. Girls in Thailand have always been expected to contribute fully to their family's income and to service their debt of obligation. In extreme cases this means being sold into slavery, being sacrificed for the good of their family. At the same time some parents have been quick to recognize the money to be realized from the sale of their children.

The small number of children sold into slavery in the past has become a flood today. This increase reflects the enormous changes in Thailand in the past fifty years as the country goes through the great transformation of industrialization—the same process that tore Europe apart over a century ago. If we are to understand slavery in Thailand we must understand these changes as well, for like so many other parts of the world, Thailand has always had slavery, but never before on this scale and never before as the new slavery.

One Girl Equals One Television

The economic boom of the past twenty years (which crashed in 1997) had a dramatic impact on northern villages. While the center of the country, around Bangkok, rapidly industrialized, the north was left behind. Prices of food, land, and tools all increased as the economy grew, but the returns for rice growing and other agricultural work were stagnant, held down by government policies guaranteeing cheap food for factory workers in Bangkok. Yet visible everywhere in the north is a flood of consumer goods—refrigerators, televisions, cars and trucks, rice cookers, air conditioners—all of which are extremely tempting. Demand for these goods is high as families try to join the ranks of the prosperous. As it happens, the cost of participating in this consumer boom can be met from an old source, one that has also become much more profitable: the sale of children.

In the past, daughters were sold in response to a serious family financial crisis. Under the threat of losing their mortgaged rice fields and faced with destitution, a family might sell a daughter to redeem its debt, but for the most part daughters were worth about as much at home as workers as they would realize when sold. Modernization and economic growth have changed all that. Now parents feel a great pressure to buy consumer goods that were unknown even twenty years ago; the sale of a daughter might easily finance a new television set. A recent survey in the northern provinces found that of the families who sold their daughters, two-thirds could afford not to do so but "instead preferred to buy color televisions and video equipment."[3] And from the perspective of parents who are willing to sell their children, there has never been a better market.

The brothels' demand for prostitutes is rapidly increasing. The same economic boom that feeds consumer demand in northern villages lines the pockets of laborers and workers of the central plain. Poor economic migrants from the rice fields now work on building sites or in new factories earning many times what they did on the land. Possibly for the first time in their lives, these laborers can do what more well-off Thai men have always done: go to a brothel. The purchasing power of this increasing number of brothel users strengthens the call for northern girls and supports a growing business in procurement and trafficking in girls.

Siri's story was typical. A broker, a woman herself from a northern village, approached the families in Siri's village with assurances of well-paid work for their daughters. Siri's parents probably understood that the work would be as a prostitute—since they knew that other girls from their village had gone south to brothels. After some negotiation they were paid 50,000 baht ($2,000) for Siri, a very significant sum for this family of rice farmers.[4] This exchange began the process of debt bondage that is used to enslave the girls. The contractual arrangement between the broker and parents requires that this money be repaid by the daughter's labor before she is free to leave or is allowed to send money home. Sometimes the money is treated as a loan to the parents, the girl being both the collateral and the means of repayment. In such cases the exorbitant interest charged on the loan means there is little chance that a girl's sexual slavery will ever repay the debt.

Siri's debt of 50,000 baht rapidly escalated. Taken south by the broker, Siri was sold for 100,000 baht to the brothel where she now works. After her rape and beating Siri was informed that the debt she must repay, now to the brothel, equaled 200,000 baht. In addition, Siri learned of the other payments she would be required to make, including rent for her room at 30,000 baht per month as well as charges for food and drink, fees for medicine, and fines if she did not work hard enough or displeased a customer.

The total debt is virtually impossible to repay, even at Siri's higher rate of 400 baht. About 100 baht from each client is supposed to be credited to Siri to reduce her debt and pay her rent and other expenses; 200 goes to the pimp and the remaining

100 to the brothel. By this reckoning, Siri must have sex with 300 men a month just to pay her rent, and what is left over after other expenses barely reduces her original debt. For girls who can charge only 100 to 200 baht per client, the debt grows even faster. This debt bondage keeps the girls under complete control as long as they seem to the brothel owner and pimp worth having. Violence reinforces the control and any resistance earns a beating as well as an increase in the debt. Over time, if the girl becomes a good and cooperative prostitute, the pimp may tell her she has paid off the debt and allow her to send small sums home. This "paying off" of the debt usually has nothing to do with an actual accounting of earnings but is declared at the discretion of the pimp, as a means to extend the profits to be made by making the girl more pliable. Together with rare visits home, money sent back to the family operates to keep her at her job.

Most girls are purchased from parents as Siri was, but for others the enslavement is much more direct. Throughout Thailand agents travel to villages offering work in factories or as domestics. Sometimes they bribe local officials to vouch for them or they befriend the monks at the local temple to gain introductions. Lured by the promise of good jobs and the money that the daughters will send back to the village, the deceived families send their girls with the agent, often paying for the privilege. Once they arrive in a city, the girls are sold to brothels where they are raped, beaten, and locked in. Still other girls are simply kidnapped. This is especially true of women and children who have come to visit relatives in Thailand from Burma or Laos. At bus and train stations gangs watch for women and children that can be snatched or drugged for shipment to brothels.

Direct enslavement by trickery or kidnapping is not really in the economic interest of the brothel owners. The steadily growing market for prostitutes, the loss of girls due to HIV infection, and the especially strong demand for younger and younger girls make it necessary for brokers and brothel owners to cultivate village families so that they might buy more daughters as they come of age. In Siri's case this meant letting her maintain ties with her family and ensuring that after a year or so she sent a monthly postal order for 10,000 baht to her parents. The monthly payment is a good investment, since it encourages Siri's parents to place their other daughters in the brothel as well. Moreover, the young girls themselves become willing to go, when older sisters and relatives returning for holidays bring stories of the rich life to be lived in the cities of the central plain. Village girls lead a sheltered life, and the appearance of women only a little older than themselves with money and nice clothes is tremendously appealing. They admire the results of this thing called prostitution with only the vaguest notion of what it is. Recent research found that young girls know that their sisters and neighbors have become prostitutes, but when asked what it means to be a prostitute their most common answer was "wearing Western clothes in a restaurant."[5] Drawn by this glamorous life, they put up little opposition to being sent away with the brokers to swell an already booming sex industry.

By my own conservative estimate there are perhaps 35,000 girls like Siri enslaved in Thailand. Remarkably, this is only a small proportion of all prostitutes. The actual number of prostitutes, while unknown, is certainly much higher. The government states that there are 81,384 prostitutes in Thailand—but that official number is calculated from the number of registered (though still illegal) brothels, massage parlors, and sex establishments. Every brothel, bar, or massage parlor we visited in Thailand was unregistered, and no one working with prostitutes believes the government figures. At the other end of the spectrum are the estimates put forward by activist organizations such as the Center for the Protection of Children's Rights. These groups assert that there are over 2 million prostitutes. I suspect that this number is too high in a national population of 60 million. My own reckoning, based on information gathered by AIDS workers in different cities, is that there are between half a million and one million prostitutes.

Of this number only about one in twenty is enslaved. Most become prostitutes voluntarily, though some start out in debt bondage. Sex is sold everywhere in Thailand—barber shops, massage parlors, coffee shops and cafes, bars and restaurants, nightclubs and karaoke bars, brothels, hotels, and even temples traffic in sex. Prostitutes range from the high-earning "professional" women who work with some autonomy, through the women working by choice as call girls or in massage parlors, to the enslaved rural girls like Siri. Many women work semi-independently in bars, restaurants, and nightclubs—paying a fee to the owner, working when they choose, and having the power to decide whom to take as a customer. Most bars or clubs could not use an enslaved prostitute like Siri, as the women are often sent out on call and their clients expect a certain amount of cooperation and friendliness. Enslaved girls service the lowest end of the market: the laborers, students, and workers who can afford only the 100 baht per half hour rate. It is low-cost sex in volume, and the demand is always there. For Thai men, buying a woman is much like buying a round of drinks.

[. . .]

Millionaire Tigers and Billionaire Geese

Who are these modern slaveholders? The answer is anyone and everyone: anyone, that is, with a little capital to invest. The people that *appear* to own the enslaved prostitutes—the pimps, madams, and brothel keepers—are in fact usually just employees. As hired muscle, pimps and their helpers provide the brutality that controls women and makes possible their commercial exploitation. Although they are just employees, the pimps do rather well for themselves. Often living in the brothel, they receive a salary and add to that income from a number of scams; for example, food and drink are sold to customers at inflated prices and the pimps pocket the difference. Much more lucrative is their control of the price of sex. While each woman has a basic price, the pimps size up each customer and pitch the fee accordingly. In this way a client may pay two or three times more than the normal rate and all of the surplus goes to the pimp. In league with the bookkeeper, the pimp systematically cheats the prostitutes of the little that is supposed to be credited against their debt. If they manage the sex slaves well and play all of the angles, pimps will easily make ten times their basic wage—a great income for an ex-peasant whose main skills are violence and intimidation, but nothing compared to the riches to be made by the brokers and the real slaveholders.

The brokers and agents that buy girls in the villages and sell them to brothels are only short-term slaveholders. Their business is part recruiting agency, part shipping company, part public relations, and part kidnapping gang. They aim to buy low and sell high, while maintaining a good flow of girls from the villages. Brokers are equally likely to be men or women and usually come from the regions in which they recruit. Some will be local people dealing in girls in addition to their jobs as police officers, government bureaucrats, or even schoolteachers. Positions of public trust are excellent starting points for buying young girls. In spite of the character of their work they are well respected. Seen as job providers and sources of large cash payments to parents, they are well known in their communities. Many of the women brokers were once sold themselves, spent some years as prostitutes, and now, in their middle age, make a living by supplying girls to the brothels. These women are walking advertisements for sexual slavery. Their lifestyle and income, their Western clothes and glamorous sophisticated ways, point to a rosy economic future for the girls they buy. That they have physically survived their years in the brothel may be the exception—many more young women come back to the villages to die of AIDS—but the parents tend to be optimistic. Whether these dealers are local people or traveling agents, they combine the business of procuring with other economic pursuits. A returned prostitute may live with her family, look after her parents, own a rice field or two, and buy and sell girls on the side. Like the pimps, they are in a good business, doubling their money on each girl within two or three weeks, but like the pimps, their profits are small compared to those of the long-term slaveholders.

The real slaveowners tend to be middle-aged businessmen. They fit seamlessly into the community, and they suffer no social discrimination for what they do. If anything, they are admired as successful, diversified capitalists. Brothel ownership is normally only one of many business interests for the slaveholder. To be sure, a brothel owner may have some ties to organized crime, but in Thailand organized crime includes the police and much of the government. Indeed, the work of the modern slaveholder is best seen not as aberrant criminality but as a perfect example of disinterested capitalism. Owning the brothel that holds young girls in bondage is simply a business matter. The investors would say that they are creating jobs and wealth. There is no hypocrisy in their actions, for they obey an important social norm: earning a lot of money is a good enough reason for anything. Of course, the slaveholder living in a middle-class neighborhood would display no outward sign of his work. His neighbors would know that he was a business-man, a successful one, and respect him for that. To look too closely into someone else's affairs is a serious affront in Thai culture: "mind your own business" (yaa suek) is one of the strongest retorts in the Thai language. So the slaveholder gains all of the benefits of exploiting and abusing young girls with no social repercussions.

[. . .]

Disposable Bodies

Girls are so cheap that there is little reason to take care of them over the long term. Expenditure on medical care or prevention is rare in the brothels, since the working life of girls in debt bondage is fairly short—two to five years. After that, most of the profit has been drained from the girl and it is more cost-effective to discard her and replace her with someone fresh. No brothel wants to take on the responsibility of a sick or dying girl.

Enslaved prostitutes in brothels face two major threats to their physical health and to their lives: violence and disease. Violence—their enslavement enforced through rape, beatings, or threats—is always present. It is the typical introduction to their new status as sex slaves. Virtually every girl interviewed repeated the same story: after being taken to the brothel or to her first client as a virgin, any resistance or refusal was met with beatings and rape. A few girls report being drugged and then attacked; others report being forced to submit at gunpoint. The immediate and forceful application of terror is the first step in successful enslavement. Within hours of being brought to the brothel, the girls are in pain and shock. Like other victims of torture they often go numb, paralyzed in their minds if not in their bodies. For the youngest girls, with little understanding of what is happening to them, the trauma is overwhelming. Shattered and betrayed, they often have little clear memory of what has occurred.

After the first attack the girl has little resistance left, but the violence never ends. In the brothel, violence and terror are the final arbiters of all questions. There is no argument, there is no appeal. An unhappy customer brings a beating, a sadistic client brings more pain; in order to intimidate and cheat them more easily, the pimp rains down terror randomly on the prostitutes. The girls must do anything the pimp wants if they are to avoid being beaten. Escape is impossible. One girl reported that when she was caught trying to escape, the pimp beat her and then took her into the viewing room; with two helpers he then beat her again in front of all the girls in the brothel. Afterward she was locked into a room for three days and nights with no food or water. When she was released she was immediately put to work. Two other girls who attempted escape told of being stripped naked and whipped with steel coat hangers by pimps. The police serve as slave-catchers whenever a girl escapes; once captured, girls are often beaten or abused in the police station before being sent back to the brothel. For most girls it soon becomes clear that they can never escape, that their only hope for release is to please the pimp and to somehow pay off their debt.

In time, confusion and disbelief fade, leaving dread, resignation, and a separation of the conscious link between mind and body. Now the girl does whatever it takes to reduce the pain, to adjust mentally to a life that means being used by fifteen men a day. The reaction to this abuse takes many forms: lethargy, aggression, self-loathing and suicide attempts, confusion, self-abuse, depression, full-blown psychoses, and hallucinations. Girls who have been freed and taken into shelters are found to have all these. Rehabilitation workers report that the girls suffer emotional instability; they are unable to trust or form relationships, to readjust to the world outside the brothel, or to learn and develop normally. Unfortunately, psychological counseling is virtually unknown in Thailand, as there is a strong cultural pressure to keep any mental problems hidden, and little therapeutic work is done with girls freed from brothels. The long-term impact of this experience is unknown.

A clearer picture can be drawn of the physical diseases that the girls accumulate. There are many sexually transmitted diseases, and prostitutes contract most of them.

Multiple infections reduce the immune system and make it easier for infections to take hold. If the illness affects their ability to have sex it may be dealt with, but serious chronic illnesses are often left untreated. Contraception often harms the girls as well. Some slaveholders administer contraceptive pills themselves, continuing them without any break and withholding the monthly placebo pills. Thus the girls stop menstruating altogether and work more nights in the month. Some girls are given three or four contraceptive pills a day; others are given Depo-Provera injections by the pimp or the bookkeeper. The same needle might be used for injecting all of them, passing HIV from girl to girl. Most girls who become pregnant will be sent for an abortion. Abortion is illegal in Thailand so this will be a backstreet operation, with all the obvious risks. A few women are kept working while they are pregnant, as some Thai men want to have sex with pregnant women. When the child is born it can be taken and sold by the brothel owner and the woman put back to work.

Not surprisingly, HIV/AIDS is epidemic in enslaved prostitutes. Thailand now has the highest rate of HIV infection in the world. Officially, the government admits to 800,000 cases, but health workers insist there are at least twice that many. Mechai Veravaidya, a birth control campaigner and expert who has been so successful that mechai is now the Thai word for condom, predicts there will be 4.3 million people infected with HIV by 2001.[6] The epidemic has passed beyond the high-risk groups of sex workers and drug users, who now have infection rates as high as 90 percent in some areas. The group with the greatest increase in HIV infection today are wives exposed through their husbands' visits to prostitutes. In some rural villages where the trafficking of girls has been a regular feature, the infection rate is over 60 percent. Recent research suggests that the younger the girl, the more susceptible she is to HIV due to the lack of development of the protective vaginal mucous membrane. In spite of the distribution of condoms by the government, some brothels do not require their use. Many young girls understand little about HIV and how it is contracted. Some feel that using condoms is too painful when they have to service ten to fifteen men a night. In fact, the abrasion of the vagina brought on by repeated sex with condoms can increase the chances of HIV infection when unprotected sex next occurs. Even in brothels where condoms are sold or required, girls cannot always force men to use them. Most northern villages house young girls and women who have come home from the brothels to die of AIDS. There they are sometimes shunned and sometimes hounded out of the village. There are a few rehabilitation centers run by charities and the government that work with ex-prostitutes and women who are HIV-positive, but they can take only a tiny fraction of those in need. Outside the brothel there is no life left for most of these women, and some will stay in the brothel even when they have the chance to leave.

Notes

1. Siri is, of course, a pseudonym; the names of all respondents have been changed for their protection.

2. I. B. Horner, *Women under Primitive Buddhism* (London: Routledge, 1930), 43.

3. "Caught in Modern Slavery: Tourism and Child Prostitution in Thailand," Country Report Summary prepared by Sudarat Sereewat-Srisang for the Ecumenical Consultation held in Chiang Mai in May 1990.

4. Foreign exchange rates are in constant flux. Unless otherwise noted, dollar equivalences for all currencies reflect the rate at the time of the research.

5. From interviews done by Human Rights Watch with freed child prostitutes in shelters in Thailand, reported in Jasmine Caye, *Preliminary Survey on Regional Child Trafficking for Prostitution in Thailand* (Bangkok: Center for the Protection of Children's Rights [CPCR], 1996), 25.

6. Mechai Veravaidya, address to the International Conference on HIV/AIDS, Chiang Mai, September 1995. See also Gordon Fairclough, "Gathering Storm," *Far Eastern Review* (September 21, 1995): 26–30.

Going Against the Tide: Gender Discrimination in Male-Dominated Construction Field (© International Labour Organization)

Part VII

GENDERED DISCRIMINATION AT WORK

Does overt gender discrimination at work still exist in the United States, and if so, what are the causes? What does the evidence say? According to the U.S. Equal Employment Opportunity Commission (EEOC), 15 percent more charges of discrimination were filed with the EEOC in 2008 than in the previous year, with $376 million recovered for its victims. The most frequently filed charges were allegations of discrimination based on race and sex and allegations of retaliation (EEOC 2009).

Discrimination is defined by the courts as the unequal treatment of persons or groups based on race, ethnicity, and/or gender. Title VII of the Civil Rights Act of 1964 is the primary legislative protection under which sex bias has been litigated in the United States. According to Title VII, it is unlawful for employers to discriminate in hiring, promotion, and compensation, and to further segregate or classify employees on the basis of race, sex, ethnicity, color, religion, or national origin.

There are two fundamental aspects of employment discrimination: "disparate treatment" and "disparate impact." "Disparate treatment" was defined by the U.S. Supreme Court in 1977 as an instance in which "the employer simply treats some people less favorably than others because of their race, color, religion, sex, or national origin. . . ." "Disparate impact" was defined by the court as ". . . employment practices [rules and procedures] that are facially neutral in their treatment of different groups, but that in fact fall more harshly on one group than another, and cannot be justified by business necessity" (Lindgren and Taub 1977). The courts have required proof of intent to discriminate in cases of employment discrimination.

There are several interpretations of the cause or lack thereof of discrimination in employment, some of which are addressed in previous chapters. Prominent among these are: 1) functionalist theory, 2) conflict theory, 3) taste-based discrimination, 4) statistical discrimination, 5) competence-based vs. sexual-desire dominance theory, and 6) unconscious bias theory. The readings in Part VII address these approaches.

Functionalist theory disregards the potential role of discrimination as an explanation for the unequal distribution of individuals and groups in the workplace or labor market as a whole. Functionalism suggests that individual workers occupy different positions in the workplace based on their personal choices, inherent ability, and work effort. Inequality according to this perspective "functions" to motivate the best and the brightest to strive for the top positions in society and allows the least qualified to occupy the least desirable positions (Davis and Moore 1945).

Conflict theorists argue that dominant groups seek to intentionally discriminate against subordinate groups in order to enhance their own position in the world of work (Edwards 1979). Those groups (white males), who benefit from systems of inequality with greater access to desirable occupations, jobs, promotions, and income, "protect their privilege by using the resources they control to exclude members of subordinate groups" (Reskin 2000). Dual labor market theorists describe the mechanisms by which conflict theory operates in labor markets. They maintain that there is both a primary and a secondary labor market. In the former, employers offer high wages, job stability, mobility, and benefits to primarily white males, while in the secondary labor market, employers offer low wages, job instability, poor work conditions, and minimal benefits to primarily women, nonwhites, and immigrants. Lack of adequate education, training, child care, and employment networks additionally prohibit women and minorities from gaining access to the primary labor market (Doeringer and Piore 1971).

Mainstream economists, such as Gary Becker, argue that discrimination in the workplace is due to the individual employer's "taste for discrimination." In other words, an employer's personal preference to maintain a social and psychological distance from a particular group he or she dislikes (e.g., women, gays, or racial minorities) will influence whom he or she ultimately hires. Becker argues that competition decreases discrimination. If a business employed primarily minorities and produced a better product or service, that firm would avoid discriminating between races and genders in terms of wages and jobs (Becker 1971).

"Statistical discrimination" differs from "taste for discrimination" in that the former concept refers to employers who use group stereotypes as a proxy for individual productivity in the hiring process. An employer might choose not to hire a woman, for example, based on the statistical probability that women as a group take more time off from work than men for child-related issues. When an employer calculates a prospective employee's potential productive work life with statistics about her gender, regardless of her past work history, she is being treated unfairly (Kirschenman and Neckerman 1991).

Two primary explanations of sexual harassment, a form of sex discrimination, include the "sexual-desire dominance" paradigm and the "competence-based" paradigm (Schultz 1998). Sexual harassment is a form of sex discrimination, prohibited under Title VII of the Civil Rights Act of 1964, because it creates adverse conditions of employment on the basis of sex. The "sexual-desire dominance" approach suggests that sexual harassment is comprised of unwanted male sexual advances toward women due to inappropriate male sexual desire in the workplace. Supervisors with greater power and control in the workplace demand sex from subordinates in exchange for the right to work, gain promotions, and secure raises, a quid pro quo form of sexual harassment.

The "competence-based" paradigm, in contrast, views sexual harassment as that form of sex discrimination where men seek to maintain the most highly rewarded forms of work for themselves by persistently denigrating women's competence and undermining their confidence. According to this theory, sexual desire has nothing to do with sexual harassment. Rather, a "hostile work environment" is created to impede a woman's ability to perform her work as an equal member of the workplace (Schultz 1998).

"Unconscious bias" theory is the final approach addressed by the readings in Part VII. This approach suggests that all individuals attempt to organize the complexities of life by using techniques that simplify the incoming data. This entails the categorization of information, the use of stereotypes, preferences for in-group members, and the use of bias in individuals' interpretation of reality (Fiske 1998, quoted in Reskin 2000). These techniques are portrayed as unconscious "shortcuts" that individuals take without premeditation, regardless of a person's group preference or desire to maintain power over another group.

Barbara Reskin, in "Unconsciousness Raising," suggests that statistical discrimination, conflict theory, and dual labor market explanations have proven insufficient in understanding employment discrimination. Instead, she and others (Bielby 2003) argue for what they believe to be a more discerning analysis that reveals how and why discrimination works. They suggest that this more refined approach, located in the field of cognitive psychology, takes into account that individuals maintain "unconscious biases." Such biases include the fact that individuals tend to favor others most like themselves and to exclude those who are different, the group that becomes the "out-group." Since white males hold the majority of positions of authority in the American workplace, the "unconscious bias" theory suggests that minorities and women become out-group members because of their physical and cultural differences from those in power. Such unconscious bias "probably contributes to the devaluation of jobs that are predominantly female and . . . minority" (Reskin 2000). Part of this unconscious process is automatic stereotyping and making assumptions about individuals based on their group membership, according to Reskin.

This inadvertent process becomes discriminatory when employers use their unconscious biases to render decisions on hiring, firing, and promotions. If the unconscious stereotype of women is nurturing rather than assertiveness, then the underlying assumption is that women would generally not make strong executive hires.

Tyson Smith and Michael Kimmel's analysis of employment discrimination law in "The Hidden Discourse of Masculinity in Gender Discrimination Law" exemplifies the "unconscious bias" framework in their analysis of employment discrimination law. In using various court cases to illustrate their argument, Smith and Kimmel assert that employment discrimination law has "essentialized" men, portraying them in stereotypic ways: all men seek power, are emotionally impermeable, inexpressive, and aggressive, and engage in risk taking. Presumably, the judges in these cases exhibited their own unconscious biases when rendering their judgments.

In the 1988 case *EEOC v. Sears, Roebuck and Co.,* the court reinforced the essentialist notions of masculinity and femininity by stating that "men prefer the dog-eat-dog world of high risk competition in commission sales" and are not interested in spending time with family, while female employees are "more interested in [selling] product lines like clothing, jewelry and cosmetics . . . with no commission," due to their alleged "fear of . . . cutthroat competition, and increased pressure and risk associated with commission sales."

Another case, *United States v. Virginia,* which the Supreme Court heard in 1996, involved the Civil Rights Division of the U.S. Department of Justice versus Virginia Military Institute (VMI). VMI, an all-male, state-supported, military educational institution, was sued for excluding female students, violating women's right to equal protection. When the federal government told the school to open its doors to women, VMI claimed its mission was to produce leaders in military and civilian society, accomplished through the "'adversative methodology,' in which physical rigor, mental stress . . . absence of privacy, [and] minute regulation of behavior . . ." were necessary. This learning technique was deemed unsuitable for women, whose presence would interfere with the all-male bonding necessary to this process. Smith and Kimmel claim that the court neglected to refer to the voluminous research that demonstrates the "adversative method" is not appropriate for most men, let alone women, and generally results in exaggerating the socially constructed notion of natural male superiority. In sum, the judges in these cases exhibited their unconscious gender biases when rendering their decisions.

Ivy Kennelly argues for the salience of the "statistical discrimination" approach in "'That Single Mother Element': How White Employers Typify Black Women." She documents the way in which white employers in Atlanta, Georgia, have used statistical discrimination to denigrate black women's position in the labor market. Although some stereotypes are completely erroneous, others are based on empirical evidence about the group. The problem with using these data, argues Kennelly, is that white employers can misuse statistics about a group characteristic by applying it to every individual within that group. For example, the stereotype that black women are more likely to be single mothers than white women is in fact based on empirical evidence when calculating the percentage of single mothers in each group. However, discrimination emerges when employers use this statistic as a proxy for all potential individual black women workers' productivity. Kennelly found that employers have utilized "statistical discrimination" to suggest that black women make poor workers because they subordinate paid work to their children's needs. Ironically, Kennelly found that this same stereotype has also been used obversely to highlight the fact that black women are highly responsible workers.

When one interviewer asked an employer if in fact black men have a similar level of absenteeism as black women, the employer responded affirmatively, although he attributed this to "low self-esteem," not single parenthood. Although some employer stereotypes about black women workers are positive, such as the fact that parenting obligations render them good workers, the author maintains that white employers have overwhelmingly constructed negative views of African American women workers based on statistical discrimination processes.

Susan Eisenberg's piece, "Marking Gender Boundaries: Porn, Piss, Power Tools," and Margaret Talbot's article, "Men Behaving Badly," both illustrate legal scholar Vicky Schultz's "competence based paradigm" on sexual harassment. Susan Eisenberg describes the ways in which women in nontraditional jobs, such as electricians, carpenters, pipe fitters, and other manual laborers, at predominantly male work sites are virulently discriminated against. In one instance, a male coworker dropped a sledgehammer on a woman's hard hat as she worked below him on the scaffolding. In another instance, pornographic photographs papered the walls of the work site. When the male workers were told to remove them, even more photos appeared the following day. In yet another instance, an ironworker pushed a female construction worker down an embankment, and she landed face-first in the mud. There is a plethora of other examples in this selection that illustrate how women's confidence and competence were deliberately undermined to rid male-dominated occupations of female coworkers.

Schultz argues that some men engage in intentional hostile environment sex discrimination in order to secure both economic and gender superiority for themselves. Central to essentialist concepts of masculinity is the male as breadwinner, the one with the most prestigious job. This enables him to fulfill the role of the head of his own household and gain a foothold in the world of politics, as economic power assures political power. Hence, sexual harassment in the form of a hostile environment is used to eliminate women from male arenas of power (Schultz 2000).

Sexual harassment as discrimination becomes even more complex when men create a hostile environment for other males on the job. Margaret Talbot writes of several such cases. It wasn't until 1998, however, that the Supreme Court ruled in the case of Joseph Oncale, a straight man with a diminutive physical stature, that pervasive same-sex conduct that creates a hostile or abusive work environment constitutes sexual harassment. Oncale worked at Sundowner Offshore Services on a Chevron U.S.A. oil platform in the Gulf of Mexico and was severely harassed by other straight men on the job. On one occasion, one of Oncale's supervisors placed his genitals on Oncale's neck. On another occasion, the supervisor forced a bar of soap into Oncale's anus while coworkers restrained him in the shower at the work site. They called him a homosexual and threatened him with rape. In this extremely hostile work environment, Oncale quit his job. This example illustrates the way in which sexual harassment is used to undermine another's man's competence and confidence, in order to reserve the "manly" jobs for "manly men." The essentialist construct of masculinity as large, aggressive, dominant, and sexualized was used to intimidate a small-framed, nonaggressive male and force him from the workplace.

These readings illustrate the myriad of ways in which to understand gender discrimination and the ways in which it continues to function in the workplace.

CHAPTER 27

Unconsciousness Raising

Barbara Reskin

Although women have made unprecedented headway in the work world over the last 30 years, it has been slow going. The pay gap between the sexes has narrowed by about a half a cent a year, the decline in sex segregation stalled in the 1990s, and women's share of executive jobs has only been inching up. In short, equal opportunity remains out of reach for most women.

In the past, discrimination against employed women was commonplace. No doubt, several bushels full of bad apples still intentionally discriminate, but overt, intentional discrimination almost disappeared after it was outlawed. Unfortunately, a second type of discrimination, one outside the reach of the law, persists across American workplaces. This discrimination originates in unconscious mental processes that systematically distort the way we see other people. In order to deal with a constant barrage of stimuli, our brains are wired to reflexively categorize and stereotype people, often in ways that we would consciously reject. All but impossible to detect in ourselves, these unconscious reactions are normally outside of our control. While they are largely invisible, their consequences are not: They systematically disadvantage women—and minorities—at work.

Although individuals cannot banish the automatic unconscious distortions that limit women's careers, employers can minimize their discriminatory effects through personnel policies that reduce managers' discretion, such as formalizing hiring and promotion practices, holding managers accountable for fair decisions, encouraging employees to identify with groups in which membership is not associated with gender, and actively compensating for unconscious biases. Many employers would readily implement these reforms if they understood the consequences when cognitive errors go unchecked. However, most employers do business as usual unless something in their external environment forces them to change. Until we change the environment in which businesses operate, our unconscious biases will block women's and minorities' rise to the top.

Automatic Stereotyping

Unconscious distortions harm the career prospects of working women (and minorities) through stereotyping and ingroup favoritism. Stereotypes automatically associate in our minds group membership (e.g., male) and traits (e.g., aggressive). While most people consciously stereotype some groups (for example, the assumption that someone with a youthful or unsophisticated appearance lacks savvy about the world, or that someone from the South harbors conservative racial attitudes), automatic stereotypes occur outside our conscious awareness and may involve beliefs that we consciously reject.

Societies pass on a body of shared cultural "knowledge" to their members, and this knowledge includes the content of stereotypes associated with particular groups (e.g., skinheads, fundamentalists, immigrants, politicians). As a result, most people can accurately describe the content of stereotypes, regardless of whether or not they accept them as accurate. And apparently simply knowing these stereotypes leads our unconscious minds to draw on them, linking group membership with stereotypical attributes or behaviors. These automatic implicit associations have survival value. Because we cannot consciously consider each new bit of information our senses pick up, responding without conscious thought to some categories of stimuli (e.g., the sudden appearance of a snarling dog or a person who looks dangerous) frees up cognitive resources for other tasks. Similarly, automatic stereotypes about the sex or color of a person we encounter may help us to quickly size up a situation. Of course, to the extent that our stereotypes are not valid, we will size it up incorrectly.

The cognitive efficiency of automatic stereotyping makes it all the more tenacious. We process stereotype-consistent information more readily than inconsistent information. And anything that taxes our attention—multiple demands, complex tasks, time pressures—increases the likelihood of our stereotyping. For example, research subjects assigned to complete a sentence could obey an instruction to avoid sexist statements when they had ample time. But under time pressure (or more generally, with multiple cognitive demands), their statements were more sexist than those of a control group. The experimenter's admonition against sexism actually "primed" the subjects' unconscious sexist stereotypes, making them especially likely to come to mind. Similarly, we tend to believe and recall evidence consistent with our stereotypes (including untrue "evidence") and dismiss evidence that challenges them. Thus, automatic cognitive distortion in our evaluation of evidence makes it hard for us to sort out valid from mistaken beliefs.

The unconscious beliefs most people harbor about women cast doubt on women's suitability for high-level jobs. For example, women are stereotypically viewed as less oriented to their careers and more oriented to their families than men are. They are also seen as too nurturing to effectively manage subordinates or head-to-head competition and too risk-averse to succeed in business. Automatic sex stereotypes block women's access to high-level jobs, especially in predominantly male work settings, by affecting the tasks supervisors assign to women and men, biasing their evaluations, and influencing the attributions they make for the successes and failures of workers of each sex.

For women who hold or aspire to customarily male positions, stereotyping is especially problematic because sex stereotypes for women are inconsistent with stereotypes about ideal job holders. As a result, predominantly male work settings put women in a double-bind. Conforming to societal stereotypes about how women should behave prevents their fitting the stereotype of the ideal worker, while satisfying the stereotype of the ideal worker violates prescriptive stereotypes about how women should behave. For example, Ann Hopkins, who successfully sued Price Waterhouse for denying her partnership despite her exemplary performance, was described by one partner as "overly aggressive, unduly harsh, and difficult to work with," while another encouraged her to adopt a more feminine appearance. In sum, Price Waterhouse did not promote her because she could not fill the mutually exclusive stereotypes of woman and Price Waterhouse partner.

Ingroup Favoritism

The machinations of our unconscious minds create another hurdle for women's access to top jobs. Within seconds of meeting a person, our brains automatically categorize them as someone like ourselves (a member of our ingroup; "us") or unlike ourselves (a member of our outgroup; "them"). Like stereotyping, automatically categorizing others is functional in a complex world. Because we categorize people immediately, we do so based on visible, and often surprisingly irrelevant, attributes. (People's inclination to classify all others into ingroups and outgroups was first observed among boys whose only visible difference was whether their shirt was red or blue.) Thus, whether we view others as "us" or "them" often depends on their sex.

Two processes associated with "us-them" categorization pose problems for women's advancement. First, having categorized someone as like or unlike us, we extrapolate to other characteristics, assuming that ingroup members generally resemble us and outgroup members differ. Second, we automatically favor ingroup members. We trust them more than other persons, attribute positive traits to them while ignoring their negative characteristics, prefer to cooperate rather than to compete with them, evaluate them more positively than others, cut them more slack when their performance falls short, and favor them when distributing rewards.

In settings in which men hold most top-level positions, ingroup favoritism limits women's likelihood of advancement. The career benefits from belonging to the "old boys' network" involve both conscious and unconscious ingroup favoritism. For example, when one female CEO asked her previous boss for a promotion, "he looked . . . flabbergasted" and then explained, "The guy I've got up there now has been my running partner, and it's taken me two years to get him to that position." Her boss's explanation suggests that he implicitly assumed that someone who shared his gender and interest in running also shared his executive ability. In similar situations in which women who were passed over for promotion sued (for example, *Foster v. Dalton* in 1995 and *Brandt v. Shop 'n Save Warehouse Foods* in 1997), the courts have acknowledged that "such actions are unfair from the standpoint of the plaintiff and persons of [their] sex," but concluded that they do not violate antidiscrimination laws. Because the courts interpret antidiscrimination law as applying only to intentional discrimination, it is legal for men to favor their buddies (usually male) over people they don't socialize with (almost all women and people of color).

Another upshot of the assumption that ingroup members resemble us and outgroup members don't is that the latter are unlikely to come to mind for career-building opportunities. And if they do, they bring the baggage of "themness" with all its implicit associations. As another CEO told a researcher, "We [had] talked about having a woman [on the bank's board] . . . but had been unable to settle on someone who we thought could make a major contribution."

The daily effects of automatic stereotyping and ingroup favoritism may be small: being excluded, passed over, or denied credit. But over time, micro acts of unintentional discrimination lead members of ingroups to accumulate advantages not available to outgroup members. The disparities this produces are as consequential as those of intentional, overt acts of discrimination.

Stemming Discrimination through Structure

The unconscious, reflexive nature of stereotyping and ingroup favoritism makes unequal opportunity for women an everyday occurrence. But when the laws of nature or of the mind lead to predictable, but undesirable outcomes, we often try to prevent it ahead of time. For example, because we know that automobile accidents can lead to serious injury or death, we require manufacturers to install seatbelts. Similarly, to suppress the bias that predictably results from automatic cognitive distortions, employers need to implement personnel practices that are analogous to seatbelts in preventing unintended disparate outcomes.

My favorite example of a preventive structure comes from a study of how symphony orchestras started to include women. Until the 1970s, Claudia Goldin and Cecilia Rouse report, virtually all the musicians in major symphony orchestras were male. In the auditions that symphonies used to select musicians, judges could see as well as hear the candidates. Moreover, the auditions were unapologetically subjective: Judges were not constrained by prespecified criteria. And those selected were almost always male. We can't know why this happened, but when symphony orchestras began to put auditioners behind a screen, thereby concealing their sex, symphonies increasingly hired women. The screen both curbed intentional discrimination and prevented any unconscious stereotypes and ingroup favoritism from having discriminatory effects on women applicants.

Although there are few settings in which applicants' sex can be concealed, the impact of blind auditions illustrates the importance of structures for reducing discrimination. The subjective and unstructured decision-making invites bias. Consider Home Depot, which began as a close-knit, predominantly male company in which people hired or promoted their buddies. The company's hiring and promotions practices remained informal as it expanded, and women's exclusion from management eventuated in a class-action lawsuit. In keeping with the consent decree that settled the lawsuit, Home Depot completely revamped its hiring and promotions practices. The new employment structure included computer or telephone kiosks in every store for people to apply for jobs and specify their qualifications and job preferences. When managers posted openings, they automatically received a list of all qualified applicants. By standardizing all facets of the matching process, Home Depot curtailed managers' discretion, reducing the likelihood that managers' conscious or unconscious ingroup favoritism or sex stereotypes would affect job assignments or promotions.

Simply reducing managerial discretion by formalizing personnel practices does not ensure a level playing field, however. Accountability is another key factor in reducing biases in judgments. Managers must know they will be held accountable for the criteria they use, the accuracy of the information they use in personnel decisions, the procedures by which they make those decisions, and their consequences for gender and race equality. For instance, experimental subjects charged with recommending teaching assistants were less likely to recommend candidates of their own race and sex when they had been told that the decision-making process would be public than when they believed their decisions would be kept secret. But, importantly, when decision-makers are under time pressure (which is presumably most of the time), knowing that they will be held accountable does not suppress automatic cognitive biases. For accountability to be effective, departing from specified procedures must have tangible consequences. Home Depot, for example, fired managers who hired staff outside the computerized system.

Employers can also reduce the discriminatory impact of ingroup favoritism by promoting the formation of mixed-sex ingroups by employees. One option is integrating work teams, thereby encouraging workers to categorize coworkers on bases other than their sex, such as teams, projects, or divisions. Organized competition between work groups, for instance, encourages team-based ingroups, which then discourages stereotyping because people tend to see their teammates as individuals.

In sum, micro acts of discrimination occur every day in most workplaces as a result of automatic cognitive processes that are largely outside of our awareness, much less our conscious control. The pervasive and automatic nature of these unconscious biases makes it almost impossible to prevent their helping men's careers and harming women's, even when firms implement structures to minimize bias and hold managers accountable for using them. This means that ensuring an equal-opportunity workplace may require consciously taking gender into account in job assignments and promotions. This could take the form of gender-conscious recruiting, such as targeting traditionally female labor pools or proactively identifying women who are likely candidates for advancement; or gender-conscious hiring, which explicitly treats sex as a "plus factor" in deciding among qualified applicants. The latter approach is legal only for firms that have admitted past exclusionary treatment.

External Pressure

The *raison d'être* of work organizations is not to prevent discrimination, but to produce a service or product. And few organizational leaders, particularly in the private sector, take their positions primarily to create a more just society. As a result, reducing the discriminatory effect of automatic cognitive errors almost always takes a back seat to productivity and the career growth of top executives.

Widespread problems within a firm—such as high turnover among women professionals—can lead firms to change their personnel policies. But usually the impetus for change comes from outside the firm, in adverse publicity regarding its treatment of women or minorities, lawsuits charging discrimination, or oversight by regulatory agencies. For example, the Office for Federal Contract Compliance Programs monitors and regulates employers' compliance with presidential executive orders mandating nondiscrimination and affirmative action by federal contractors. Although the likelihood of losing a contract is minuscule, employees of federal contractors look more like America than those of noncontractors. Likewise, the outcome of discrimination lawsuits can influence the personnel practices not only of the firm under consent decree—like Home Depot—but also of other firms in the same industry or labor market. It is not easy to prevail in sex discrimination cases, however. Ann Hopkins succeeded in her lawsuit against Price Waterhouse only because the partners in the firm expressed conscious sex stereotypes. If their decision had been distorted only by their unconscious stereotypes, she would not have been able to prove sex discrimination.

The legal environment can also make a difference on women's outcomes in more subtle ways. For instance, a study by Doug Guthrie and Louise Roth showed that the more equal employment opportunity laws in a corporation's home state and the more progressive the federal appellate courts in the corporation's district, the more likely it was to have a female CEO. The policy stance of a region, a state, or a local labor market can affect women's access to top jobs through the message it sends to corporations about the consequences of disobeying discrimination laws. It can also affect women's representation in the candidate pool by encouraging or discouraging them from pursuing opportunities in various kinds of careers. And because women, like men, pursue the best jobs open to them, a favorable legal and regulatory environment will attract women to opportunities.

The logical conclusion of this analysis—that regulatory agencies should require firms to curb the consequences of automatic stereotyping and ingroup favoritism—is likely to be controversial. But organizations rarely implement genuine reform without external pressures; and in the absence of a political sea change along with a broader legal conception of discrimination, equal opportunity is likely to take place one firm at a time. Leveling the playing field more quickly will require pressure on lawmakers and regulators to address both conscious and unconscious barriers to women's inclusion.

CHAPTER 28

The Hidden Discourse of Masculinity in Gender Discrimination Law

Tyson Smith and Michael Kimmel

The relationship among difference, sameness, and equality is one of the founding relationships of liberal democracies. It was an assumption made by John Locke that different talents, motivations, and abilities would lead to different outcomes, that is, to unequal economic and social consequences. Meritocracies presume different inputs and outputs: the harder you work, the more able you are, the higher you will rise. The inequalities at the end of the road are the natural outcomes of differences. By contrast, equality has often been confused with sameness. In the 1950s, for example, images of economic equality often caricatured Russian communists as all looking and acting (and thinking) exactly the same, while attacks on racial and gender equality played on fears of widespread miscegenation and androgyny. Difference, we are told, leads to inequality; equality means sameness.

In the United States, the relationship among difference, sameness, and equality has also been the foundation of efforts to rectify discrimination based on race and sex. The Fourteenth Amendment of the U.S. Constitution guarantees "equal protection under the law," and on this clause an entire antidiscrimination edifice has been built. Equal protection is generally considered to have two meanings: one cannot treat "alikes" as if they were unalike, nor can one treat "unalikes" as if they were alike (see, e.g., MacKinnon 1987). Equality therefore has two meanings, and this duality has provided the foundation for a wide range of discrimination cases.

Treating the same as if they were different is the basis for most sex and race discrimination cases. The landmark 1954 case, *Brown v. Board of Education*, struck down the concept of "separate but equal" on the premise that affording disparate treatment (difference) to those who are the same is a form of discrimination. Since then the courts have accorded race "strict scrutiny." This means that in all functionally relevant categories blacks and whites must be viewed as the same, and therefore any discrimination based on race would be seen as treating equals as if they were different.

Yet the courts do not grant gender strict scrutiny; rather, gender receives "intermediate scrutiny," which means that under certain very limited conditions gender discrimination may withstand equal-protection scrutiny. In such cases the discrimination must first be based on real differences between women and men (not stereotypes); second, such discrimination must be functionally relevant to the fulfillment of the task (the bona fide occupational qualification [BFOQ]); and finally, there must be "compelling state interest" in the maintenance of the discrimination. These criteria were spelled out in a series of cases. In *Griggs v. Duke Power Co.* (1971), the court found that practices that affect women in a discriminatory way are in violation of Title VII of the Civil Rights Act (1964) unless those practices are necessary to running a business operation (see also *Frontiero v. Richardson* [1973] and *Mississippi University for Women v. Hogan* [1982]).

Nor, however, can you treat unalikes as alike or treat different people the same. For example, child labor laws presume that adults and children are functionally unalike categories and that workplace reforms can be geared toward one without an injury to basic premises of equality and fairness. In sexual harassment cases, the traditional standard of harassment—"would a reasonable *person* find the behavior objectionable?"— has been replaced by a "reasonable *woman* standard" (*Ellison v. Brady* 1991; emphasis added). Recognizing that women are different from men, the question is not whether some abstract person would find it objectionable but whether a woman would find it so. We cannot treat people as if their personal backgrounds or social characteristics were inconsequential. In one recent case, a twelve-year-old girl who was a catcher on her central Florida Little League team was prohibited from playing because she did not wear a protective cup, and the league rules, ungendered as they are, require that "all catchers must wear a protective cup." So since she did not wear one, she could not play. She went to the Little League commission but lost the decision. After losing the decision, she wore it on her ankle (Pacenti 1997).

Many commentators have observed that this dual definition of equality—treating alikes alike and treating unalikes unalike—has put the target population, the population that is injured by the discrimination, in a certain legal bind. Sometimes they must minimize difference in order to be treated equally (i.e., the same); at other times they must maximize difference in order to be treated equally (i.e., differently). For example, efforts to gain access to the workplace must emphasize that female workers are no different from male workers, while other cases maintain that pregnant female workers are indeed different from male workers.

This has put women—and gays and lesbians—in a difficult position, best expressed in the title of a law review article by feminist theorist Jewelle Gomez: "Repeat after Me: We Are Different. We Are the Same" (Gomez 1986). But rarely, if ever, is the comparative question fully articulated. Different from whom? The same as whom?

The answer is: men. In all these cases men serve as the unexamined norm against which women are measured. Where women have sought access, they are to be treated no differently from how men are treated. Where women have sought to acknowledge the specificity of their experiences, they are to be treated differently from how men are treated. But how are men to be treated? What are men like in the first place? These questions are assumed but never answered.

Efforts to end gender discrimination have enlarged the scope of women's activity and successfully changed stereotypic definitions of femininity with an understanding of variation and diversity among women. The courts have demonstrated in their more recent record of cases related to gender that there are various ways to construe the meaning of womanhood; not all women are mothers, and not all women are workers. Many women are nurturing and caring; however, some are interested in military combat and uninterested in having children. Meanwhile, the courts have stuck to a one-dimensional understanding of masculinity; its definition has been reified into one normative construction, anchored by traditional stereotypes.

[. . .]

Stereotypes about Masculinity

Gender discrimination is not permitted when it is based on stereotypes and not on real differences, however, in practice, this mandate appears to apply only to women. When men are considered, the courts often rely on very traditional and stereotypic definitions of masculinity.

This traditional normative construction of Western masculinity consists of several elements, cleverly codified by Robert Brannon and Deborah David (1975) in the mid-1970s and barely modified since then. These include, first, "No Sissy Stuff"—the relentless repudiation of the feminine; second, the "Big Wheel"—masculinity implies wealth, power, and status; third, the "Sturdy Oak"—emotional impermeability, inexpressiveness, and reliability in a crisis; and finally, "Give 'em Hell"—daring, risk taking, and aggression. Textbooks on men's lives (see, e.g., Doyle 1989) use these elements as organizational framing devices; psychological inventories of gender identity disaggregate them into a series of adjectives associated with masculinity, including *aggressive, ambitious, analytical, assertive, athletic, competitive, dominant, forceful, independent, individualistic, self-reliant, self-sufficient,* and *strong.*

At the same time, social scientists have come to think of masculinities in a very different way, based on the differences among men. We understand that what constitutes masculinity varies across cultures, over time, throughout the life course, and among a variety of different groups of men at any one time. Thus a young white working-class heterosexual male is likely to conceive of manhood quite differently than an elderly middle-class African American gay male. These differences can, for example, explain variations in access to power and privilege, as well as variations in relationships to women. The pluralized term *masculinities* has come into use to underscore these differences. (See, e.g., Brod 1994; Kimmel 1994, 1995; Connell 1995; but see also Hearn 1996 for a critique of how the term *masculinities* may also obscure power dynamics among various definitions.)[1]

[. . .]

We maintain that the invisibility of masculinities in legal discourse about gender will reveal how gender-nonconforming men are misunderstood, disregarded, and dismissed, and also how the normative standard of masculinity ends up harming both women and men.

[. . .]

Can Women Be (like) Men?
Three Cases of Sex Discrimination

EOC V. SEARS, ROEBUCK & CO.

In 1986, the Equal Employment Opportunity Commission (EEOC) brought to trial a charge that Sears, Roebuck and Co. (Sears) was practicing a nationwide pattern of sex discrimination. The allegation claimed that Sears was discriminatory because the company failed to hire women applicants for commission selling on the same basis as male applicants and because it failed to promote female noncommission salespersons into commission sales on the same basis as it promoted male noncommission salespersons into commission sales. In its defense, Sears claimed that commission sales was a high-risk job category, for which qualifications included physical vigor, drive, and aggression (*EEOC v. Sears, Roebuck & Co.* [1986]).

The case was notable because at trial both sides relied on feminist historians as expert witnesses (Milkman 1986; Scott 1988). Testifying for Sears, Rosalind Rosenberg argued that the paucity of women in commission sales reflected women's choices, not a pattern of employer discrimination. Women and men are different, she argued; they have "different interests, goals and aspirations" and, therefore, make different choices (Rosenberg 1986, 757). "Women tend to be more relationship-centered and men tend to be more work-centered" (763). Women are "less competitive" than men (763). As a result, women generally prefer to sell soft-line products (apparel, housewares, or accessories) on a noncommission basis; they tend to be more interested than men in the social and cooperative aspects of the workplace (*EEOC v. Sears, Roebuck & Co.*, 1308).

Alice Kessler-Harris, testifying for the EEOC, argued that the question was not whether this represented women's choices but working women's choices—that is, working women worked for similar reasons as men did, and they were therefore likely to make the same choices as working men about where to work. Kessler-Harris did not argue that women were the same as men; instead, she used historical evidence to show far more variety in the jobs that women actually took than Rosenberg assumed. She argued that economic considerations usually offset the effects of socialization in women's attitudes to employment; wages were an incentive to take new, demanding, or atypical positions. (Had Sears offered the higher wages to its noncommission jewelry salespeople, we believe that men would have streamed into the positions, having found a sudden interest in precious and semiprecious stones.) Opportunity creates demand, not vice versa. Finally, Kessler-Harris argued that Sears's causal chronology was backward and that job segregation by sex was the consequence of employer preferences, not employee choices (Scott 1988). Instead, "substantial numbers of women have been available for jobs at good pay in whatever field those jobs are offered, and no matter what the hours. Failure to find women in so-called nontraditional jobs can thus only be interpreted as a consequence of employers' unexamined attitudes or preferences, which phenomenon is the essence of discrimination" (Kessler-Harris 1986, 779).

But the courts agreed with Rosenberg. The decision from the Seventh Circuit Court found that "women were generally more interested in product lines like clothing, jewelry, and cosmetics that were sold on a noncommission basis, than they were in product lines involving commission selling like automotives, roofing and furnaces. The contrary applied to men. . . . Women's lack of interest in commission selling included a fear or dislike of what they perceived as cutthroat competition, and increased pressure and risk associated with commission sales. Noncommission selling, on the other hand, was associated with more social contact and friendship, less pressure and less risk" (*EEOC v. Sears, Roebuck & Co.* [1988], 320–21). Since women were neither as interested in nor as qualified for commission selling as men were, any disparities were the product of real gender preferences and not employer policies (322).

While various court decisions reinforced stereotypes about women, they also reinforced stereotypes about men. In its qualifications for various positions, Sears listed being socially dominant, aggressive, and having a willingness to travel and be away from home as criteria for commission sales jobs for high-end consumer durables. The question before the courts was whether women could embody those characteristics. But the courts' logic assumed that men must exhibit them.

The courts, we can deduce, held that women "prefer" less competitive and less risky positions, where cooperation and gossip are the norm; the courts assumed that men "prefer" the dog-eat-dog world of high-risk competitive commission sales. Women, the courts believed, would choose their families over their work, so they would not want to work longer hours and be away from home. Men, by contrast, the courts assumed, have no real interest in family contact, so they would have no trouble with being away from home for long periods of time.

When legal arguments attempt to explain or justify how women are different from men, the implication is that what they are *not* is what men *are*. So when Rosenberg depicted women as humane and nurturing, focused on relationships, and averse to capitalist virtues such as competition, she painted men as competitive and motivated by self-interest: possessive individualists (Williams 1996, 626). In the Sears case the courts' decisions institutionalized difference, relying on stereotypes of both women and men.

UNITED STATES V. VIRGINIA (VMI)

In 1990 the Civil Rights Division of the U.S. Department of Justice filed a suit against the state of Virginia and the Virginia Military Institute (VMI), an all-male state-supported military-type educational institution, for possible constitutional violation of the Fourteenth Amendment of the U.S. Constitution. The suit claimed that VMI's all-male admissions policy violated women's right to equal protection, and the U.S. government demanded that VMI become coeducational. The institute denied this charge and claimed that its unique educational methodology served vital state interests.

The educational mission of VMI is to produce "citizen-soldiers, educated and honorable men who are suited for leadership in civilian life and who can provide military leadership when necessary" (*VMI* II [1992], 893–94). To accomplish this, the institution utilizes what it calls an "adversative methodology," emphasizing "physical rigor, mental stress, absolute equality of treatment, absence of privacy, minute regulation of behavior, and indoctrination of values. The process is designed to foster in VMI cadets doubts about previous beliefs and experiences and to instill in cadets new values which VMI seeks to impart" (1421).

In 1991 a high school student in South Carolina named Shannon Faulkner applied and was admitted to the Citadel, having removed identification on her high school records that she was a woman. (As the Citadel had also previously been an all-male institution, there was no place on its application form that asked the applicant's sex.) When she was subsequently rejected because of her sex, she brought suit against the Citadel, also a state-supported all-male military-type institution.

On the surface, the VMI and Citadel cases were about the constitutionally protected rights of women to equal educational opportunity. Questions at trial centered around the appropriateness for women of the "adversative" educational methodology employed by both schools and the physiological and psychological differences between women and men that might prevent women from succeeding at VMI. A further set of questions involved the consequences for men if women were to be admitted. The Citadel and VMI argued that an all-male environment was essential to the fragile but imperative male bonding that was the foundation of cadet life at the schools.[2]

The district court agreed with VMI. The judge found that "key elements of the adversative VMI educational system, with its focus on barracks life, would be fundamentally altered and the distinctive ends of the system would be thwarted, if VMI were forced to admit females and to make changes necessary to accommodate their needs and interests" (VMI I [1991], 1413). Thus, admitting women would yield a catch-22—it would so alter the structure of the education that women's admission would immediately transform the school into another institution. Women's very entry would prevent them from getting the education they sought.

On appeal, the Court of Appeals for the Fourth Circuit reversed the district court decision on liability. The appeals court claimed that while VMI's educational methodology is "pedagogically justifiable," the state had not offered any justification as to why it offered such a program to men only. The appeals court then remanded the case back to the district court for a hearing on remedy, offering essentially four possible courses of action: VMI could close, go private (and thus forgo federal money), admit women, or find some way to offer women the educational benefits that VMI offers to men (VMI II [1992]). It was this last option that VMI chose, though the Fourth Circuit Court had warned in the Citadel case that "in the end, distinctions in any separate facilities provided for males and females may be based on real differences between the sexes, both in quality and quantity, so long as the distinctions are not based on stereotyped or generalized perceptions of differences" (VMI III [1993], 232). In choosing to provide a similar option for women, VMI proposed to establish a comparable program at Mary Baldwin College, a small private all-women's college in nearby Staunton, Virginia. The Virginia Women's Institute for Leadership (VWIL) was to offer women a military component to their education, including rigorous physical training and Reserve Officer Training Corps (ROTC), all in a single-gender educational environment. However, VWIL would be significantly different: while VMI would continue to use its adversative method of total immersion into rigid hierarchies, VWIL was to be a more nurturing and supportive educational atmosphere; each school would use the educational methodology most "appropriate" for the gender of its students (VMI IV

[1994]). This was not to be a case of "separate but equal," VMI claimed, but rather a case of "distinct but superior."[3]

While the district court and circuit courts were persuaded by this sleight of hand, the U.S. Supreme Court offered a stinging near-unanimous ruling against VMI: VWIL was but a "pale shadow" of VMI (*VMI V* [1996], 2285). The Citadel's board of visitors voted to admit women the day after the Supreme Court ruling; VMI's board considered raising the money to go private but ultimately voted nine to eight to admit women later that season.

In essence, the Supreme Court (and the district court in South Carolina) found that there were no substantive physical differences that would prevent some women from succeeding under VMI's adversative method. While the two sides bickered over whether rigorous physical training coupled with ruthless harassment and hazing by upperclassmen was "appropriate" for women, both quietly assumed that such an educational methodology was perfectly appropriate for men. The remedial plan developed by VMI, for example, claimed that the adversative model "is developmentally unsuitable for the vast majority of female students" (*VMI V* [1996], 4) but that it is "conducive to the development of confidence and self-esteem" in men (*VMI V* [1996], 5). And while the courts ruled that it was neither more nor less appropriate for women, no one thought to refer to any number of studies of educational preferences that have consistently found that the adversative methodology is not appropriate for most men.

What was in question was simply whether women could "want" to undergo such brutal and unpleasant educational experiences, not whether such experiences themselves contradicted all available evidence from educational research. Men, of course, could experience it and, perhaps, should want to—if they were real men.[4]

The adversative method's chief result was to exaggerate socially constructed differences between women and men, to naturalize those differences, and to reinforce male superiority as normal and natural. One highly decorated Citadel cadet who testified on behalf of Faulkner underscored this process. "I came out of the Citadel thinking that I was automatically fundamentally more superior than half of the human race," he said in deposition. "Why?" he was asked: "Because every time I did anything wrong at the Citadel someone made a point of telling me that I was, with expletives, a woman, you're weak, why don't you go to a woman's school, you belong in a woman's school. What is the matter, are you having your period? Why can't you do the push-ups? Are you a woman? Why don't we go get a skirt for you? That's why" (Vergnolle 1993, 84).

In a sense, the VMI and Citadel cases revolved around whether or not women could come to VMI and the Citadel and become men. Neither side ever raised the question of what that model of masculinity looked like and the appropriateness of that model for men.

PRICE WATERHOUSE V. HOPKINS (1989)

After five years as a senior manager at the accounting firm Price Waterhouse, Ann Hopkins was proposed for partnership in 1982—the only woman among eighty-eight candidates proposed that year. She had outperformed her competition, successfully securing more contracts than any other candidate, and had been instrumental in securing a $25 million State Department contract for the firm. Her supporters called her work "outstanding" and praised her "deft touch . . . strong character, independence and integrity" (*Price Waterhouse v. Hopkins* [1989], 1782). Despite this, her candidacy for partnership was deferred, and she was subsequently informed that she would not be reproposed. She brought a sex discrimination suit under Title VII of the Civil Rights Act of 1964.

At trial, testimony was offered that Hopkins was "sometimes overly aggressive, unduly harsh, difficult to work with and impatient with staff" (*Price Waterhouse v. Hopkins* [1989], 1782). Evaluations of her work included comments that she was "macho" and that she "overcompensated for being a woman." Several criticized her use of profanity, and one advised that she take "a course at charm school." One of her supporters had advised her to "walk more femininely, talk more femininely, dress more femininely, wear make up, have her hair styled, and wear jewelry" (*Price Waterhouse v. Hopkins* [1989], 1117).

Traditionally, legal scholars have seen the Price Waterhouse case as encapsulating the double bind of working women: to the extent that they act like men in the workplace they are seen as competent but not as feminine, while to the extent that they are seen as feminine in the workplace they are not seen as competent. Workplace success is coded as "masculine," so that, as the workplace proverb has it, a man is unsexed by failure and a woman is unsexed by success.

But what does this decision imply about men? The criteria used by Price Waterhouse and reinforced by the courts is that women should not be aggressive, profane, impolite, impatient, and harsh, while men *must* be. Hopkins was denied partnership because she acted too masculine. But what is the image of masculinity that is assumed by the courts?

The courts, in this case, also used gender stereotypes about men and then set them as a gauge by which to evaluate women. Implicit in the courts' decisions were guidelines for following the codes of hegemonic masculinity. What about the men who were denied partnership? Were they insufficiently aggressive, domineering, or rude? Were they polite and genteel in their manner of speech? Did they treat staff with respect and kindness?

While the VMI and Sears cases asked the question about whether women *could* be men in order to gain access to arenas coded as masculine, Hopkins asks whether women *must* be men in order to do so. As long as traits, attitudes, and behaviors are coded as gendered, then women who are "too masculine" and men who are "not masculine enough" will be negatively valued.

Women Need Special Protection, but Men Do Not: [Two] Cases of Differential Treatment

INTERNATIONAL UNION, UAW V. JOHNSON CONTROLS (1991)

This class action suit challenged Johnson Controls's policy barring female employees, except those whose infertility was medically documented, from jobs involving actual or potential lead exposure exceeding the Occupational Health and Safety Administration (OSHA) standard. In 1982 the company had shifted from a policy of warning women to a policy of barring women from positions that involved battery manufacturing. Johnson Controls, a manufacturer of lead-based batteries, argued that its exclusionary (fetal protection) policy fell within the safety exception to the BFOQ. The policy stated that "women who are pregnant or who are capable of bearing children will not be placed into jobs involving lead exposure or which could expose them to lead through the exercise of job bidding, bumping, transfer or promotion rights" (*International Union, UAW v. Johnson Controls* [1991], 1200). The Court of Appeals for the Seventh Circuit became the first appellate court to hold that a fetal protection policy directed exclusively at women could qualify as a BFOQ.

The Supreme Court reversed that decision, concluding that Johnson Controls did not establish a BFOQ. The Supreme Court posed the question as "whether an employer, seeking to protect potential fetuses, may discriminate against women just because of their ability to become pregnant" (*International Union, UAW v. Johnson Controls* [1991], 1202). Instead, relying on the Pregnancy Discrimination Act—in 1978, section 701 of the Civil Rights Act of 1964 was amended to prohibit sex discrimination on the basis of pregnancy—the court affirmed that pregnant employees "shall be treated the same for all employment related purposes" as nonpregnant employees similarly situated with respect to their ability or inability to work (*International Union, UAW v. Johnson Controls* [1991], 1206). Thus, the court concluded that "women as capable of doing their jobs as their male counterparts may not be forced to choose between having a child and having a job" (1206).

On the face of it, this case reprimanded a company for trying to satisfy its "obligations under federal law to provide a safe workplace simply by kicking out fertile women" (Stone 1990, 48). Women, the courts reasoned, should be allowed to choose whether to expose themselves to the dangers posed by lead. Men, on the other hand, are simply *expected* to do so.

The Supreme Court's opinion was unequivocal that the bias in Johnson Controls's policy was "obvious. Fertile men, but not fertile women, are given a choice whether they wish to risk their reproductive health for a particular job" (*International Union, UAW v. Johnson Controls* [1991], 1202). However, this is not true. The majority opinion is wrong because of the testimony offered by Donald Penney. Penney, a male employee who testified on behalf of the United Auto Workers, had requested a leave of absence to lower his lead-level exposure because he intended to become a father. Yet the company denied his request.

While the court did note testimony that "lead-caused genetic damage to both sperm and egg cells can be passed on to the fetus," such evidence was used only to prove that women and men were being treated differently (Levit 1998, 76). This oversight in Justice Harry Blackmun's opinion makes clear that men's role in reproductive health is nonexistent. Denying men's ability to avoid exposure to workplace hazards, while requiring it of women, is a form of sex discrimination itself (1998, 77).

[...]

The court's dismissal of the health of an adult male worker implies that men are expendable. It is therefore a Pyrrhic victory for women to have sued successfully for the right to be subjected to the same workplace hazards that men experience (Levit 1998, 77).

The health of workers' offspring should be the concern of employers, employees, and the courts. Yet when the courts have intervened in fetal protection policies, they have frequently wielded this protection selectively and, thus, defined women's behavior and roles as mothers. Fortunately, the *UAW v. Johnson Controls* decision challenged these stereotypes and expectations of women. However, the *UAW* decision was a missed opportunity to examine the stereotypes of men that were embedded in this employer's policy. How else can we explain a fetal protection policy that puts women in their fifties and sixties in safe jobs but lets young men hold jobs that endanger their offspring? (Stone 1990, 53).

[. . .]

SAME-SEX SEXUAL HARASSMENT: *GOLUSZEK V. H. P. SMITH* (1988)

But what of men who do not conform to that stereotypic view of masculinity and male sexuality? Are they to be afforded constitutional protection? For some time, the answer from the bench was a resounding "no." But a recent case (*Oncale v. Sundowner Offshore Services, Inc.* [1996]), which we will discuss in our conclusion, may offer some signs of hope. Prior to the Supreme Court decision in the *Oncale* case, though, same-sex harassment as gender harassment received no judicial notice.

In 1988, Anthony Goluszek brought a sexual harassment suit against his employer, H. P. Smith, under Title VII of the Civil Rights Act of 1964. Goluszek worked as an electronic maintenance mechanic at H. P. Smith, a paper manufacturer, in Illinois. He was a single male and lived with his mother. The court found that he was sexually very unsophisticated, with "little or no sexual experience," and was "abnormally sensitive to comments pertaining to sex" (*Goluszek v. H. P. Smith* [1988], 1452). In his nearly all-male workplace, he was constantly harassed by fellow workers.[5]

Goluszek's night supervisor told him that he needed to "get married and get some of that soft pink smelly stuff that's between the legs of a women." The following year, 1979, Goluszek reported a complaint to the same supervisor about a comment referring to a female coworker who "fucks." The supervisor's response was that if "Goluszek did not fix a machine, they would get Carla Drucker to fix Tony [Goluszek]. . . . Operators periodically asked Goluszek if he had gotten any 'pussy' or had oral sex. . . . [They] showed him pictures of nude women, told him they would get him 'fucked,' accused him of being gay or bisexual, and made other sex-related comments. The operators also poked him in the buttocks with a stick" (*Goluszek v. H. P. Smith* [1988], 1453–54).

When Goluszek confronted his fellow employees and demanded that supervisors take some action, they dismissed their sexual comments as "mere 'shop talk.'" This undisputedly hostile environment continued and went unabated for several years. During the same time period Goluszek began to receive warnings, reprimands, and suspensions for tardiness and missed work, which eventually led to grounds for his release. He sued for sexual harassment, retaliatory discharge, and discrimination based on national origin.

The court sided with Goluszek's employers and threw out claims of same-sex sexual harassment. The U.S. District Court granted summary judgment to H. P. Smith on the sexual harassment and national origin claims (although it found some grounds for the retaliation claim). The district court claimed that Title VII was designed to remedy discrimination "stemming from an imbalance of power and an abuse of that imbalance by the powerful which results in discrimination against a discrete and vulnerable group" (*Goluszek v. H. P. Smith* [1988], 1456). Since men are not a vulnerable group, no sexual harassment could be said to have occurred. Had Goluszek been a woman, no doubt H. P. Smith would have taken action to alleviate the harassment. But as a man, he was not protected.

Making Masculinities Visible

When is a man not a man? When he's not a "real" man is when other men challenge his masculinity. In the Goluszek case, the courts condoned the harassment because Goluszek was a male who was mistreated because he was insufficiently manly, which is not constitutionally protected. Because he was a man biologically meant that he could not seek protection, despite the fact that he was not a "real" man.

To us, however, what is interesting is that, in so ruling, the court inscribes a certain vision of masculinity as the norm—physically aggressive, sexually crude and repulsive, predatory, nonrelational, vulgar, and violent. Any man who refuses to go along with this vision of sexuality has no remedy under law for what happens to him. "Goluszek may have been harassed 'because' he is a man," the district court opined, "but that harassment was not of a kind which created an anti-male environment in the workplace" (*Goluszek v. H. P. Smith* [1988], 1456). Yet the harassment did create an "anti-male environment"—at least for males who do not conform to a stereotypic definition of masculinity and male sexuality. The court here normalizes that stereotype so that any behavior that falls outside the stereotype's boundaries is no longer counted as male.

[. . .]

The anomaly of rejecting same-sex sexual harassment becomes clearer if we add one hypothetical fact to either the *Polly v. Houston Lighting and Power Company* (1993) or *Goluszek v. H. P. Smith* (1988) case. Assume that a female employee had witnessed the events that occurred and filed a claim of sexual harassment based on the hostile work environment. If the same events had occurred and were simply witnessed by a woman, the woman probably would have a cognizable claim for a sexually hostile work environment. Thus, while the female bystander could recover for sexual harassment, the direct male victim would not have a remedy (Levit 1998, 117).

By claiming that same-sex sexual harassment could occur if the person being harassed were gay, the courts further confused sexual desire with sexual harassment because of gender. It matters not at all whether the harassers were heterosexual or homosexual, and it is surely not the case that such harassment was motivated by lust—the two criteria the courts seem to have used in opposite-sex harassment cases (see Coombs 1999, 125). But surely gender is what underlies the harassment of Goluszek and Polly—not the sexual desires of the harassers or the targets (see, e.g., Gruber and Morgan

2004). Goluszek and Polly were gender nonconformists, acting in nonstereotypical ways that embody the very multiplicity of masculinities that social and behavioral sciences have been documenting. These two cases were cases of gender harassment in which the harassers acted as a form of gender police, punishing those who transgress the hegemonic stereotypes (Brake 1999). The courts reinforced those stereotypes by arguing that the targets of such harassment deserved what they got.

Yet there are signs that the Supreme Court, at least, has begun to acknowledge a multiplicity of masculinities and that those who do not conform to stereotypical notions of gender may themselves be entitled to constitutional protection. The Supreme Court's decision in *Oncale v. Sundowner Offshore Services, Inc.* (1998) provides a final case in point and suggests a hopeful direction in which such legal cases may proceed.

In August 1991, Joseph Oncale was employed by Sundowner Offshore Services as a deckhand worker on an offshore oil rig. Only men were employed on the rig. Crew members spent up to seven straight days on the rig and then received seven days off. Early on in Oncale's employment, his supervisor and others began making sexual comments and threatened to rape him. Eventually, they assaulted him. One man placed his penis on the back of Oncale's neck; another shoved a bar of soap into his buttocks. After his complaints were ignored by the company, Oncale quit in fear of further sexual assault. The district court and circuit courts found no grounds for a same-sex sexual harassment case, stating, "Mr. Oncale, a male, has no cause of action under Title VII for harassment by male coworkers" (*Oncale v. Sundowner Offshore Services, Inc.* [1996], app. 106).

The Supreme Court reversed in 1998 and, for the first time, found that sexual harassment may indeed occur among members of the same sex. In a short, unanimous opinion, Justice Antonin Scalia, speaking for the court, made clear that members of a group may, indeed, discriminate against members of that same group and that sexual harassment need not be motivated by sexual desire to be understood as sexual harassment (i.e., harassment on the basis of sex).

It is premature to argue that the *Oncale v. Sundowner* decision represents a transformation of legal attitudes, auguring an era in which multiple masculinities may be acknowledged and gender nonconformity might be protected. But the decision throws into stark relief the ways in which prior courts, by refusing to acknowledge multiple masculinities, assumed and therefore reified a narrow, outdated, and indeed defamatory definition of masculinity.

We have tried to demonstrate how a one-dimensional understanding of masculinity has deleterious consequences for not only men but women, too. The consequences for women are numerous; at the bare minimum, this understanding assumes that women will—and should—continue to shoulder child-care responsibilities while remaining ever vigilant against male sexual aggression.

The assumption that this stereotypical definition of masculinity—sexually omnivorous and predatory, violent and aggressive, risk taking and emotionally disconnected, and uninterested in family life and in health—is the "normal" way for men to behave reproduces inequalities based on gender, both between women and men and among men. Until the courts can fully embrace these multiple masculinities, they will remain an unsafe harbor for both women and "other" men who do not conform to the hegemonic form of masculinity.

Notes

1. We are aware of the difficult political terrain on which arguments about "masculinities" take place. The disaggregation of masculinities often obscures the ways in which gender power is organized between women as a group and men as a group. While we share these concerns, we cannot address this issue here.

2. Several expert witnesses supported VMI's position. David Riesman, e.g., argued that VMI's adversative method would be "inappropriate" for women. Women, he claimed, are "not capable of the ferocity requisite to make the program work" (Riesman deposition [*VMI* II (1992), 66]. He said this despite ample evidence from prisons, military academies, and the military itself that such assumptions are fallacious. Were women to be admitted, he feared "real psychological trauma if they went through the rat program" (66). Another expert, Richard C. Richardson, claimed that "you could not design an experience that was more hostile to the success of women than the one that exists there because of the fact that it exists to maximize the development of men and it does that extremely well" (Richardson deposition [*VMI* II (1992), 75]).

3. *VMI* II 1992, 3. The Citadel had also come up with its own parallel program, the South Carolina Institute for Leadership (SCIL), to be housed at Converse College, a small, private women's college in Spartanburg, three hundred miles from Charleston. This program, Elizabeth Fox-Genovese, an expert witness for VMI and the Citadel, argued, was "designed to respond optimally to the specific educational needs of most women" (Fox-Genovese affidavit [*VMI* II (1992), 3]).

4. Men who did not appreciate the rigors of the adversative method could not be said to be men at all. One mother of a Citadel cadet was asked if some male cadets did not appreciate the brutal hazing of the adversative method. Mrs. Young said, "I think some pansies leave. I think some jocks who think they deserve special treatment leave because they're just—they think they deserve special treatment and they didn't get it" (Young 1993, 126).

5. In another case, *Polly v. Houston Lighting and Power Company* (1993) (and *IBEW, Local Union No. 66 v. Houston Lighting and Power Co.* [1997]), the plaintiff, Norman Polly, made similar allegations of same-sex sexual harassment and employer indifference. Polly was employed by Houston Lighting as a member of a traveling group of repairmen. He was repeatedly harassed by fellow employees who berated him with homophobic taunts and grabbed and squeezed his genitals; one forced a broom handle against his rectum. Polly was fired for failing to report to work as ordered. He had already filed three charges of sexual harassment with the EEOC. He brought suit against Houston Lighting. The company, in turn, sued his union, which had demanded Polly's reinstatement at an arbitration hearing.

CHAPTER 29

"That Single-Mother Element"

HOW WHITE EMPLOYERS TYPIFY BLACK WOMEN

Ivy Kennelly

Many employers assess their workforces with gendered and racialized imagery that can put groups of workers and applicants at a disadvantage in the labor market. Based on 78 interviews with white employers in Atlanta, the author reveals that some employers use a complex but widely shared stereotype of Black working-class women as single mothers to typify members of this group. These employers use this single-mother image to explain why they think Black women are poor workers, why they think Black women are reliable workers, and why they think Blacks are poorly prepared for the labor market. In focusing on these white employers' claims, the author concentrates not on the well-documented outcomes of labor market discrimination, such as differential rates of pay and promotion, but on how employers construct and use the images that may form the basis of it. This is especially relevant amid current attacks on affirmative action programs.

Affirmative action programs in the United States have come under attack recently as many citizens and politicians argue that racial-ethnic minorities now have the same chances of making it as do whites. A Black woman who walks through the door of the human resources department, according to affirmative action foes, has an equal or possibly even better chance of getting the job as the white woman who comes in after her, and they both have the same or better chances as the white man who comes in the next day. According to this argument, any "preferences" for racial-ethnic minorities in employment constitute discrimination against whites.

One of the many important factors that such attacks disregard is that the overwhelming majority of those who make decisions about whom to hire are white. A substantial literature documents that while whites no longer largely subscribe to beliefs that racial-ethnic minorities are inherently inferior to them, whites continue to harbor racist beliefs and make racist decisions largely based on perceived economic threat (Berg 1984; Bobo and Kluegel 1993; Bobo and Suh 1996; Farley et al. 1994; Feagin and Vera 1995; Frankenberg 1993; Sears 1988). In addition, research indicates that both men and women tend to evaluate women lower than men on a number of valued characteristics, even in the absence of evidence to substantiate such evaluations (Eagly and Wood 1982; Reskin 1988). This suggests that chances are, in fact, not equal in the aforementioned employment scenario. Potential and current employees still have to deal with the perceptions of white employers regarding their race and gender, as well as their sexuality, age, religion, class, and ability.

[. . .]

[. . .] Few studies, however, document the content of opinions held specifically by employers. Existing studies that have investigated this issue (Moss and Tilly 1991, 1995; Neckerman and Kirschenman 1991; Wilson 1996) have primarily focused on employers' views of Black men compared to white men, which has provided a beginning for our understanding of how employers think about race. However, these studies have not considered that employers' views of men are, in fact, also gendered. They have not satisfactorily answered or even asked important questions about how employers' views of Black men may differ from their views of Black women and how these gendered, racialized views contribute to the unique disadvantage of different groups in the labor market.

In this article, I examine the images some white employers use to construct claims about Black women in the labor market.[1] These images are largely stereotypical and can be used negatively. I demonstrate that the dynamics of these white employers' typifications of women and of Blacks differ from their images of Black women, indicating that this group may stand at a unique disadvantage to all other racial and gender groups.

I illustrate how some white employers use a complex but widely shared stereotype of Black working-class women as single mothers to typify members of this group. In somewhat contradictory ways, white employers use this image to explain (1) why they think Black women are poor workers, (2) why they think Black women are reliable workers, and (3) why they think Blacks—women and men—are poorly prepared for the labor market. Their construction of these claims may be based in part on evidence from what they see in their firms, but their views are colored by generalized cultural stereotypes about Black women. Because they may use these images of a group to predict and assess the behavior of individuals, employers' typification of Black women as single mothers may provide the basis for discrimination.

In focusing on white employers' claims about Black womanhood, I concentrate not on the well-documented outcomes of labor market discrimination, such as differential rates of pay and promotion, but on how employers construct and use the images that may form the basis of it. Because these employers have the power to hire, fire, pay, and promote, their claims can be important for Black women's life chances. While I do not have data to link white employers' images of Black women with their employment decisions regarding members of this group, I argue that the evidence that shows that these images exist is compelling in itself. My analysis is focused on the previously unexplored intricacies of the single-mother image as used by some white employers.

[. . .]

Stereotypes as the Basis for Claims

STEREOTYPES AND STATISTICAL DISCRIMINATION

Stereotypes can have deleterious effects for employees and potential employees. If employers subscribe to stereotypes, whether they are gross overgeneralizations or derived more closely from evidence, they may use these views about groups of people to predict the behavior of individuals. Economists have identified the process of using characteristics associated with groups as substitutes for information about individuals as "statistical discrimination" (Aigner and Cain 1977; Bielby and Baron 1986; Kirschenman and Neckerman 1991; Moss and Tilly 1991; Thurow 1975). Basow argues that

> even when a generalization is valid (that is, it does describe group averages), we still cannot predict an individual's behavior or characteristics. Stereotypes, because they are more oversimplified and more rigidly held than such generalizations, have even less predictive value. (1986, 3)

Thus, stereotypes are not required to be false. For example, even if employers know that a higher percentage of Black women than white women are single mothers—27.1 percent and 4.5 percent, respectively (U.S. Bureau of the Census 1995)[2]—they may still use this information in a stereotypical way that generates inequality. To assume that each Black woman who applies for an entry-level job at a firm is probably a single mother and make employment decisions based on that assumed status is to stereotype and engage in statistical discrimination.

Another example of how employers may stereotype individuals based on the characteristics associated with the group to which they belong involves women and rates of turnover. "If women have higher turnover rates, and employers know this, then, based on this gender difference in turnover, they may engage in statistical discrimination" (England and Browne 1992, 35) by not hiring women, not paying women as much as men, not promoting women as rapidly as men, or firing women more readily than men. This example indicates that employers assume that "workers will conform to the average performance of others with the same ascriptive characteristics" (Folbre 1994, 21). Yet, the assumptions they make are often not correct; women as a group have turnover rates similar to men when controls for type of job and cohort are introduced (Lynch 1991; Price 1977; Waite and Berryman 1985). Using assumptions, whether erroneous or empirically based, about group characteristics as a proxy for individual productivity is a powerful tool employers use to make decisions about workers.

STEREOTYPES OF WOMEN, BLACKS, AND BLACK WOMEN

Black feminists have identified many of the stereotypes about Black women that are prevalent in U.S. culture. These include reliance on welfare, sexual promiscuity, "emasculating" tendencies, and single motherhood (Collins 1990; Davis 1981; Essed 1991;

Guy-Sheftall 1990; hooks 1981; Marshall 1996; Mink 1990; Morton 1991; Mullins 1994; Roberts 1994; Sims-Wood 1988; Weitz and Gordon 1993; Wilkinson 1987). Other scholars have identified a similarly negative list of associations with Black men in white U.S. culture: shiftlessness, aloofness, laziness, and involvement with crime, gangs, and drugs (Hacker [1992] 1995; Kirschenman and Neckerman 1991; Majors and Mancini Billson 1992; West 1993; Wilson 1987, 1996).

These negative stereotypes flourish in part because whites in the United States have a history of viewing Blacks "as an undifferentiated mass of people" (Fordham and Ogbu 1986) without individual characteristics or identities, Negative stereotypes of white women as a group are less easy to identify, since white women are less likely than Black women to be seen as a monolithic group and are also less likely to be viewed negatively in this majority-white culture. Identifying negative stereotypes of white men as a group is difficult as well for the same reasons. This is not to say that no negative stereotypes of white men and women exist, but only that such stereotypes that combine whites' gender and race are less common and less all-encompassing than those of Black women and men.

Stereotypes, both negative and positive, influence the thinking and decision making of employers (Berg 1984). For example, employers tend to think about women in the workforce as mothers (Hochschild 1997). As Sokoloff explains, "Once in the labor market, women—all women—are treated as mothers—former, actual, or potential" (1980, 216–17).[3] The cultural image of motherhood, which is not a stereotypically negative image, can still be used by employers in a negative way. Sokoloff argues that if a woman in the labor force has children,

> The rationalization given is that she will be unreliable because of the need to be absent if her children are sick. This apologia persists despite the fact that male turnover and absenteeism rates are similar to women's, the crucial difference being that women have traditionally left the market for lack of child care and other family services, while men have left a particular job for personal advancement. Men's reasons for leaving are always more acceptable, for men are understood as workers; women, on the other hand, are understood as mothers. (1980, 219)

This demonstrates how employers construct an image of women in the workplace using the stereotypes surrounding motherhood as some of their primary defining characteristics. Men who work outside the home for pay may also be fathers, but no stereotypes prompt employers to fear that men's parental roles threaten their productivity.

Employers' images of women as mothers tend to be a disadvantage to women for at least three reasons. First, the image is used negatively, as employers associate it with a weak commitment to paid work. Second, employers do not readily evoke a fatherhood image for men and assume that men with children are worse workers than men without children.[4] Finally, the assumption that all women workers are plagued by the burdens and responsibilities of motherhood is inaccurate. While a large percentage of women in the paid labor force do have children under the age of 18, 75.3 percent do not (U.S. Department of Commerce 1996).[5] Despite this, employers who assume that women in their workplaces are mothers who are less committed workers than men are allowing this stereotype to influence the way they think about members of their workforces. [. . .]

In addition to the stereotype of women as mothers who tend to be late to and absent from work, employers evoke racial stereotypes as sincere fictions. Kirschenman and Neckerman (1991) and Wilson (1996) demonstrate how employers subscribe to common stereotypes of Black men as lazy, dishonest, involved with drugs, and lacking a work ethic. Different from the way they take motherhood—a generally positive culture image—and make it negative, employers grab onto the overwhelmingly negative stereotypes that U.S. white culture perpetuates about Black men. Employers are able to list the characteristics they associate with Black men, which they have adopted from the larger racist white culture, and discuss why they feel justified in not hiring Black men because of such characteristics (Kirschenman and Neckerman 1991; Moss and Tilly 1995).

Employers conceivably also evoke racial stereotypes of Black women, although employers' stereotypes of Black women have been given much less scholarly attention than those of Black men. Collins (1990) and Mullins (1994) argue that the image of the matriarch surrounds Black women and relates to their experiences in both the home and the paid labor market. The matriarch, according to Collins (72), is a single Black working woman with children. The image of the matriarch also carries the connotation of an "overly aggressive, unfeminine" woman who spends "too much time away from home" working. She is "the 'bad' Black mother" who has to work so much that she "cannot properly supervise her children and is a major contributing factor to her children's school failure" (74). Collins (1990) and Mullins (1994) suggest that this controlling image, sustained by those with the power to define it, is dangerous because it puts the responsibility and blame for the perceived deficiencies in all African Americans, especially men, directly onto Black women. hooks also speaks to the issue of the "sexist/racist representations that would have everyone believe that black women are responsible for the many dilemmas black families are facing. Black women are blamed for poverty, joblessness, black male aggression, and violence both inside and outside the home" (1995, 82-83).

[. . .]

Methods and Data

The data I use were collected in Atlanta as part of an extensive project, the Multi-City Study of Urban Inequality.[6] Study design involved three components: interviews of household respondents, a telephone survey of employers, and face-to-face interviews with employers.

The household interviews were conducted with a stratified, random sample of residents in the summer and fall of 1993.[7] Each respondent in the household interviews was asked to name her or his occupation and employer and, if unemployed, the place she or he last worked.[8] The employers for the telephone survey were drawn randomly from a list of employers named by each household respondent who had a job requiring no more than a high school degree.[9] Another random sample was then drawn from the list of employers who had completed the telephone survey, and these employers were interviewed in person in more depth. The data for this article come from the in-depth, face-to-face interviews with white employers from the metropolitan Atlanta sample.[10]

[. . .]

The Typification of Black Women

Many white employers typified Black women as single mothers, an image constructed largely from existing cultural stereotypes and conservative rhetoric rather than from information about particular employees and applicants. To contextualize how these employers used this image, I briefly discuss their perceptions of women and Blacks in general. I then discuss how these white employers' typifications of Black women are both related to and unique from their images of women (implicitly assumed to be white) and Blacks (implicitly assumed to be men).

IMAGES OF WOMEN

As the literature suggests, one of the most pervasive images white employers held is the woman worker as mother, a role that employers often further associated with tardiness and absenteeism. For example, one human resources manager at an insurance company that is composed of almost half men and half women stated,

> If I look at our attendance record I would in fact not doubt that the people who have been documented and who have been terminated for attendance reasons were women, and those people are primarily out not because they're ill, but because kids are ill or the husband is ill or the parent. (White man, human resources manager, insurance company)

This employer indicated that women—not men—had problematic attendance rates and speculated that women had family responsibilities that detracted from their paid work duties so much that they needed to be fired. Constructing an image of women in which their assumed motherhood is a large liability in the labor market, he left little room for the possibility that women may have been absent for reasons other than family or that men may have ever needed to be off the job for family reasons.

In another example, the interviewer asked a supervisor of clerical workers if the company's hiring procedures had changed any in the past few years, to which the supervisor responded,

> Yes, because there's some questions you can't ask when you're interviewing, you know. Years ago you could ask them anything, you know. "Are you pregnant? Do you have children? Do you have someone to keep your children while you are at work? Are your children sick often?" You can't ask those questions anymore. (White woman, supervisor, insurance company)

This supervisor of employees in a woman-dominated occupation clearly defined motherhood as part of womanhood and alluded to the potential problems this conflation can bring to her workforce.

These examples suggest that women's family responsibilities are one of the primary concerns employers had about women workers. Forty-two percent of white employers, without prompting from interviewers, brought up the images of motherhood and family when they talked about women. Employers often made these characterizations of women as mothers without empirical knowledge of their actual family situations. For example, the employer who wanted to know about her women applicants' pregnancies and day care situations was talking about women whom she had not yet even met. White employers' construction of the image of women applicants and workers as mothers, and their concern over the problems that motherhood entails in their workplaces, has the potential to damage women's chances in the labor market.

Seven white employers, three of whom worked for the same company, brought up the notion of family in conjunction with men. The most common comments these employers made were about men having to monetarily support their families, and just one of these employers indicated that men's familial roles could be problematic. Clearly, many white employers' images of parenthood and the effects of parenthood on paid labor market responsibilities differ along gender lines.

IMAGES OF BLACKS

White employers in Atlanta characterized Black workers negatively in well over two-thirds of the interviews, with images regarding time, skills, education, laziness, and belligerence. For example, an employment manager at a very large organization made this remark regarding Black employees, who made up 58 percent of the sample job, data entry workers: "I have noticed maybe a slight difference in the perception of time. Tardiness, a certain degree of tardiness seems more acceptable" (White woman, employment manager, educational institution). This is not simply her observation that members of one group work differently than members of another group; it is an evocation of a common stereotype that Blacks are generally late. Throughout the interview, this employment manager also stressed that she only processes employees' applications and does not "deal with them [the employees] directly," which makes her perception about employee norms somewhat suspect. An administrative specialist in the same organization explained why she thought Blacks were not faring well in the labor market:

> It goes back to just education issues, that a lot of Blacks are maybe only getting through high school. And whether it is because of economic issues or whether they just don't have the drive, or y'know, a variety of factors. But they don't pursue, I guess, y'know, being more educated than just being able to get by. (White woman, admininstrative specialist, educational institution)

This employer subscribed to another stereotype, that of Blacks' laziness and lack of motivation, as one of the primary causes for their lack of advancement in the labor market. In these examples, employers were doing more than simply reporting empirical differences in Black and white workers' levels of productivity. They were invoking stereotypes to make claims that helped them explain the deficiencies they perceive in Blacks. Interestingly, both of these employers said that they had very little day-to-day contact with employees, but both were in the position to make hiring decisions about them.

Many white Atlanta employers also expressed their irritation with what they perceived as Black workers' tendency to complain, cause problems, and cry "Discrimination!" For example, when asked if she noticed any differences between Black and white workers, one area director for teachers' aides, a job filled only by women, responded,

> The insubordination, and what I would almost say belligerence, is maybe more prevalent in Blacks than in whites. I think my Black employees definitely question much more management than my white employees do. . . . I have more Black employee, Black complaints than any other type of complaints. They love to complain about their manager. . . . They're more likely to call and complain either about their manager or new company policies or procedures or something they've been asked to do. And they're also more likely to say to me that, it's because they're Black. (White woman, area director, child care center)

This employer, one of two white supervisors over a workforce that is 75 percent Black, emphatically expressed her irritation with Black employees' insistence on "bringing race" into every issue. Throughout the rest of the interview, she repeatedly defended the decisions she had made that only Black employees had questioned, which indicated her unwillingness to consider the validity of their concerns. The other supervisor at this organization also commented at length on how she was "constantly getting this racial stuff thrown in my face" (White woman, branch manager, child care center). "It just seems like every time you turn around," she said, "they want to blame things on racial issues." This manager noted that she planned to make some changes in their hiring practices so that they would have "more kind of a 50/50 thing" of white and Black employees as compared to the 25/75 ratio they had at the time of the interview.

Another employer similarly described the workplace as a venue for Black employees to express belligerence. This employer, a branch manager of pest control sales representatives, 78 percent of whom are Black, said this when asked about differences between Black and white workers:

> Well obviously the answer is that Black workers don't work as good as the white workers. I have less trouble out of my white people than my Black. Ninety percent of the problems I have with employees are with the Black employees. . . . The productivity is down. They're harder to manage. They won't come in on time. They come up with silly excuses not to be to work. . . . They come up with all these . . . well, that's the court-goingest people

> I've ever seen in my life. . . . Like I said, white guys really don't cause me
> any problem. They do what I tell them to do. The Black guys don't, so I
> have to write them up on a corrective action report and then the first thing
> they say to me is, "Why didn't you write so and so up on it? . . . Well you
> don't reprimand this white guy for doing this? Why did you reprimand me,
> because I'm Black?" and that kind of thing. (White man, branch manager,
> pest control service)

This characterization of Black employees who do not work hard, cause trouble, are late, lie, and then "use race" to try to compensate for those things is probably the strongest example from the interviews of white employers using stereotypes to construct a negative image of Blacks. Moreover, this example highlights white employers' resistance to believing that Blacks ever experience racial discrimination. [. . .]

IMAGES OF BLACK WOMEN

Not separate from some white employers' images of women and Blacks, but still distinct, are their typifications of Black women. Some white employers stereotype women workers as mothers, regardless of the women's actual parental status. Many also typify Black workers as having a number of very negative attributes, such as laziness, poor education, and a tendency to lie. An interesting point about these typifications is that they do not explicitly refer to Black women even though Black women are members of each group. The absence of specific references to Black women in employers' discussions of these two groups led me to look further in the data for those specific references.

One head cashier provided an excellent example of how some employers' perceptions of Black women may be distinctive from their perceptions of women in general (i.e., white women). Regarding the cashiers she supervised, 3 of whom were men and 27 of whom were women, she found that "*Men* are more dependable. . . . They don't have as many emotional problems. They're not as emotional and they're, y'know, they seem to be able to come to work more. . . . Women are a little bit harder to work with" (White woman, head cashier, grocery store). Then, when asked about differences between Black men and Black women specifically, she said, "Between those two . . . I think the *women* are a little bit more dependable. . . . They do most, most of the work." Her perception of Black women was vastly different from the first group of women to enter her mind: white women. This example underscores the need to pay specific attention to the ways employers view Black women.

Almost a quarter of the white respondents (24 percent) explicitly used the single-mother image at some point in their interviews when referring to Black women. An example of an employer using this type of imagery is a superintendent who hired elementary school instructional aides, a job filled solely by women.

> We are pressed to find minority workers in the work force. . . . I think your
> typical white instructional aide that comes to us has a four-year degree.
> And [we get] a large number of Black single-parent applicants who are not

as skilled . . . not educated. (White man, superintendent for personnel, elementary school)

This respondent talked about white applicants and employees without making any reference to their family situations, yet he said that the Black applicants he gets are unskilled single mothers. This statement reveals the melding of single motherhood with Black women in his claims and a further assumption that single mothers are unskilled and uneducated.

In an additional 12 percent of the interviews, employers linked Black women with single motherhood less explicitly than in the example above. For example, an employer may have talked about the topic of race by referring to differences between workers from the "inner city" and the "suburbs," using these words as code words for Black and white. The employer may have then talked about how it is difficult to find employees in the inner city (meaning among Blacks) because of the high percentage of single mothers there who are on welfare and do not work for pay. Employers in these implicit instances did not always put "Black woman" and "single mother" in the same sentence, but throughout interviews they made the connections.

White employers referred to white women, or women generally, as single mothers in only a handful of interviews, while they made these explicit and implicit associations of Black women and single motherhood in more than one-third of the interviews. In no cases did employers talk about either Black men or white men having sole responsibility for children.

It is important to note that no questions about single motherhood were included on the interview instrument. Employers brought up this imagery on their own, often in conjunction with explicit questions about race.[11] [. . .]

One manager of laundry workers, all of whom were Black and three-fourths of whom were women, provided an example of this association when he brought up the idea of family structure. The interviewer had asked him if he was happy with his available workforce, and he said he was not, because of the "family structure" in the inner city. Then he directly related family structure to the job performance of Black women. The interviewer asked him, "Does that have an impact, does family structure have an impact on, on their job performance?" He replied, "I think it's everything. I think it's the major thing that we have here that's a problem." When asked why, he proceeded to say,

> Well, right off the bat you've got a, a child care problem. With a single mother, there's a, a child care problem. Of course obviously there's a big financial problem. . . . You're gonna have a, experience a higher absenteeism rate and tardiness rate because of the fact that the children obviously are very important and come first and there's a whole set of things that happen where the mother has to be, ah, y'know, off her job for one reason or another. So you have a workforce where it's, it's a high rate of absenteeism. (White man, laundry/valet manager, hotel)

This employer clearly stated that the biggest problem with his workforce was the poor job performance of Black women, whom he could not distinguish from single mothers.

Then the interviewer asked him if he had the same type of problems, like absenteeism, from men. He replied,

> Well, I have. The, I realize that for the most part the men are not tied down with, with the kids. I know that. But yes, we have, have the same type of problems as far as basic work habits and coming to work with the men as we do with the ladies, but it's for a different set of reasons I believe. [Interviewer: Do you have any idea what their reasoning is?] Well I think black male has a very low self-esteem level. (White man, laundry/valet manager, hotel)

This employer, then, said that he observed the same absenteeism problems in men and women. But he stated that the biggest problem in his workforce was not the Black men's absenteeism, which he related to their self-esteem, but Black women's, because of their assumed single-mother family structure. This indicates that even when employers simply state their perception of facts, such as absenteeism rates, they construct claims often using stereotypical images to explain these facts. This process can result in an overwhelmingly negative typification of Black women, which can put individual Black women at a unique disadvantage in the labor market.

[. . .]

Single Black mothers: the root of Black problems. When asked why they believed Blacks may be doing poorly in the labor market, many white employers asserted that Blacks lack certain necessary elements, such as education and morality. Employers often speculated that these perceived deficiencies were the result of being raised by single mothers. While it is true that a larger percentage of Black children are raised by single mothers—54.2 percent compared to 17.9 percent of white children (Bennett 1995)—it is unlikely that white employers who made this claim about Black workers actually knew which Black workers were and were not raised by women heads of household, and that they were able to directly compare levels of labor market success with family type.

About 55 percent of white employers who typified Black women as single mothers brought up this image in the context of poor mothering skills. Yet, this third and most commonly used image of Black women, the mothers of the Black workforce, reveals a striking paradox that affects Black women not only as the mothers but also as workers. Half of the employers who made claims about the poor mothering skills of Black single mothers also said that Black single mothers are poor workers because they are off work too often attending to their children's needs. Regardless of what these employers actually knew about these women's lives and responsibilities at home, they made judgments about Black women's adequacy in their public and private roles based on the stereotypes associated with Black single motherhood. [. . .]

An example of the paradox in which Black women are seen as both poor workers and poor mothers comes from a plant manager of 70 percent Black and 30 percent white women order processors. He talked about "single families," "single-parent families," and "single-parent moms" interchangeably. He also talked about space and race in a related way, using the terms "inner city," and "Black" as proxies for one another, and he spoke about single mothers only in the context of the problems of the inner city. When asked to identify the single biggest problem with his workers, he replied, "I'd say single-parent moms. [Interviewer: Why?] Missing work. . . . When somebody's sick they've got to go." This comment, within the context of his discussion of the deficiencies in the inner city, identifies Black single mothers as the weakest part of his workforce because of their family responsibilities. [. . .]

> The people that I want, it would be hard to get those people to come downtown. And when we get into the inner city, in my opinion, work values change because you're talking about people that are primarily raised in a single family. Very poor environment, don't have a role model that shows them that work is good, that you should do your very best and a good job no matter where it is or who it's for. (White man, plant manager, manufacturing plant)

[. . .]

Conclusion

[. . .]

Stereotypes of Black women as single mothers, because of cultural assumptions about single motherhood as an inherently negative state, can make the positive characteristics of individual Black women (and of single mothers) invisible. It is likely that these stereotypes are also shaped by class, since professional Black women may be less susceptible than Black women in entry-level positions to employers' assumptions about their need for money, their responsibilities outside work, and their values. White employers' creation of claims about racial, gender, and class groups, such as entry-level Black women, seems less about assessing the actual characteristics of individuals in those groups than it is about maintaining inequality. No matter what characteristics one-third of white employers in this sample used to assess Black women, the resulting typification was overwhelmingly negative, leaving Black women with few acceptable alternatives of action.

[. . .]

Notes

1. I purposely use the term *Black* rather than *African American* because I am focusing on white employers' images of members of this racial group. Since the Black persons to whom I refer were not able to report their own race, and the possibility exists that they may have origins other than Africa, I avoid using the term African American throughout the text.

2. These numbers only reflect women ages 15 to 44 in the population since data are not available for older groups. Also, these are percentages of never-married mothers and do not reflect divorced or separated women with children (U.S. Bureau of the Census 1995).

3. Although employers assume that their women employees are mothers, they have been very reluctant to restructure their workplaces in ways that would allow parents to better balance their home and paid labor market duties (Hochschild 1997).

4. If anything, employers who have taken men's fatherhood into account have historically used it in a positive way for men, as a rationale to pay men a "family wage" (Gerson 1993; Hartmann 1976).

5. This is not to suggest that workplaces do not need to undergo major structural changes to accommodate the needs of parents in the workforce. It is simply to say that employers who assume that women are mothers are incorrect, and since this assumption can disadvantage individual women, it is problematic.

6. This study was also conducted in Boston, Detroit, and Los Angeles.

7. In the Atlanta Metropolitan Area, 1,529 interviews were completed, 829 with Black residents, 651 with white residents, and 49 with residents of other races, reflecting an overall completion rate of 75 percent. This represents an oversampling of Black and low-income households.

8. Before drawing the sample for the employer telephone surveys from this list of firms, the researchers eliminated any firms named by household respondents who reported having jobs that required more than a high school education. They also dropped firms where the respondent's occupation was only a "negligible proportion of the firm's workforce—for example, a custodian in an insurance company" (Kirschenman, Moss, and Tilly 1992, 18). The sample for the employer telephone survey was then drawn from the remaining firms named.

9. In the summer of 1994, 269 employer telephone surveys were completed, with a completion rate of 60 percent.

10. The counties included in the Atlanta Metropolitan Area include Clayton, Cobb, DeKalb, Douglas, Fayette, Fulton, Gwinett, Henry, and Rockdale. Before drawing this final sample, firms that had been named by household respondents and contacted for the telephone survey were stratified into nine categories (cells) by occupation (service with public contact, service without public contact, and blue collar or manual) and by whether the firm had gone through either a change in location, technology, or work organization. Following the precedent set by Kirschenman and Neckerman (1991), the firms were stratified by these three occupational categories to isolate different occupational groups. Change in location, technology, or work organization was used as a stratifying variable because of Multi-City Study of Urban Inequality researchers' hypotheses that part of the increase in employers' requirements for skills is due to changing composition of firms (Kirschenman, Moss, and Tilly, 1992).

11. In two interviews, the interviewer did bring up the term *single mother* even though it was not included on the interview instrument. The interviewer noticed that parts of these two employers' accounts seemed to contain allusions to single mothers, which prompted her to ask for confirmation. In one case, this was confirmed; the employer had been talking about single mothers without using the term. In the other case, the interviewer's hunch was not confirmed. Since I am primarily concerned in this project with how employers, themselves, bring up this image, I do not count these two cases among those in which white employers typified Black women in terms of single motherhood.

CHAPTER 30

Marking Gender Boundaries: Porn, Piss, Power Tools

Susan Eisenberg

I don't worry about the ones who say things to me. That quiet person with that very controlled anger is the one I worry about. You can feel the anger, they don't have to voice it, you know it's there.

And those are sometimes the ones who try to be the nicest to you. You have to watch them.   .

—Gay Wilkinson, Boston

Close to eleven on a Friday morning, the steward was walking around the 44-story job collecting $2 each from the roughly sixty electricians on the site to celebrate the general foreman's fiftieth birthday with a drinking party in the shack. The party would start at lunchtime and extend into the afternoon. A stripper would be performing.

I was, at that point, less than a year out of my time.

Several of the new journeywomen in my local, including myself, and several of our business agents had only recently gone through a training together on sexual harassment. Earlier that week a highly publicized rape in the Boston area—on a poolroom table at Big Dan's Tavern—had called public attention to sexual violence. And it was the same week as International Women's Day. Ignoring the situation didn't feel like an option.

The steward told me that I didn't have to contribute or come to the party. I countered that, if the steward was organizing a celebration of the GF's birthday, it should be done so that everyone could participate. And I explained why I didn't think there should be a drinking party with a stripper on a union jobsite. "Just because we have to take you in," the steward said, "doesn't mean anything has to change because you're here."

I knew I didn't want to go to the party or be working on the job that afternoon. I told my foreman I was going home. Before leaving, I called the union hall and told my business agent that

I was walking off the job and why. He asked what the other two female electricians there thought. I said that since both were apprentices and more vulnerable, I hadn't talked with them. He explained that, given how late it was, there wasn't really anything he could do. I said I understood. And I went home. Expecting the party to go on.

Monday morning on the bus ride to work, I learned from a woman plumber who worked on the site that, after I'd left on Friday, my business agent had asked the steward to cancel the party and return everyone's money. My breath caught. I was surprised and impressed that the hall had acted, but I knew there would be retribution.

—Susan

On jobsites the behavior of those in authority—the foreman or general foreman representing the contractor (though they are also union members) and the steward representing the union—set a tone and an example for the crew to follow, and strongly affected a tradeswoman's sense of her welcome and safety. On her first job as an apprentice carpenter Lorraine Bertosa felt protected.

I remember my first foreman literally saying to the guys, "Watch how you talk." He said that in the first week I was on the jobsite. He was one of these guys that felt confident himself, wasn't out to prove anything. It was fine that women were there. A really unbelievable guy to get as a first foreman. If you were willing, then he was willing to meet you halfway He would say to the guys, "Don't talk like that. You can't talk like that around here" (cuss words, certain things they were saying). I think that pressure came directly from the office, from the contractor. We want to keep these women.

Where contractors and unions did not make such a clear commitment to "keep these women," new tradeswomen were less fortunate. Co-workers, foremen, or stewards who felt that women did not belong in the industry at times expressed that opinion through words, actions, or silence. Before affirmative action brought government support for a more diverse workforce, harassment, ranging from petty to criminal, had been a standard means to discourage those who strayed across the industry's gender and racial boundaries. It did not end when the government regulations began.

Tradeswomen were sharp observers, and most perceived themselves to be on their own in handling any hostility. They worried that requesting assistance could as likely bring retribution as help. Given the imbalance of power, many women put blinders on, kept their focus on the day's work, and waited for a bad situation to end by itself. Women, especially those unfamiliar with the safety practices of tools and equipment, were particularly vulnerable on their first jobs. Not only were they green, but they were not yet sworn into union membership. Probationary periods could range from a few months to two years, for those entering under special affirmative action guidelines. Kathy Walsh was sent driving on a wild goose chase looking for the foreman on her first day at work—hazing that might have happened to any new apprentice. But on her second day, when she knew where she was going, the ironworker who'd verbally expressed his resentment about having a woman on the job expressed those feelings again, this time physically.

> Everybody parked up on top of this embankment. It was about forty feet down to where we were working, very steep, and it was muddy and slippery. An ironworker pushed me from behind. And I slid most of the way down that embankment face first.
>
> Getting up from there—I can't remember whether I was crying or not, if I wasn't I was almost—and getting the mud off of my face and out of my tool pouch and going to work that day was one of the hardest things I'd ever done at that point. Mark, the guy that was nice to me, was like *so nice* to me that day. He gave the guy shit about it, and he came down as quick as he could and helped me get up. At the end of the day he said, "I don't know anybody that wouldn't have walked away at that point. You just keep it up, and fuck these guys." My first day I slammed my hand in the car door. My second day I went down face first down a muddy forty-foot embankment.
>
> The job lasted for about two weeks. They laid me off and I was like—*uh*. I think I made it back to my car before I started crying.

Loyalty by trade is very strong in construction. Workers generally spend coffee breaks and lunch: carpenters with carpenters, ironworkers with ironworkers, painters with painters. For a journeyman of one trade to push down an apprentice of another trade is highly unusual, because normally the full crew would rally to defend *their* apprentice. Attacks on women put men in the position of choosing between male bonding and union or trade solidarity. Only one of the carpenters came to Kathy's assistance. When she reported back to her apprenticeship coordinator after the layoff, she never mentioned the ironworker's action, or the tacit approval of most of her crew. "I was totally intimidated by the whole process, all of it. We didn't even join the union until we had at least 600 hours in."

The behavior of the union representatives a tradeswoman happened to encounter was critical to shaping her expectations of whether or not the union would assist her in handling harassment or discrimination. Although MaryAnn Cloherty would return to union construction years later and complete her apprenticeship with a different local, she quit the first time around. She was a second-year apprentice on a job where having a steward on the site only added to her problems.

> There was a lot of pornography on the job, and when I would complain about it they would take it down and they would put up more. Crotch shots, legs spread, blown up. I mean there was a crotch shot that was blown up that was at least three feet by five feet. I walked by it for three days, I didn't know what it was. I did not know what it was until I was on the other side of the picture and I saw a whole series of porno shots. I realized what the other shot must be. That was when I complained.
>
> The offending stuff came down. And then the next day the whole jobsite was littered with it.

There was a union steward who was the worst offender. I really felt like
there was nowhere to go. My steward when I first arrived on the job said,
"Put your tools over here." After I put my tools down he said, "One thing
you got to understand is, I used to throw gooks from helicopters in Vietnam." I didn't know what was that supposed to mean to me. I think he was
trying to scare me or intimidate me or paint himself as a big ogre. I didn't
really think I could relate to this guy.

A skilled construction worker must be able to climb scaffolding, use power tools,
lift heavy objects, and perform countless other tasks that are inherently dangerous.
But like driving a car on a freeway, they can be accomplished with relative safety
given proper training, support, and equipment. Just as a student driver wouldn't feel
comfortable in high-speed traffic accompanied by a driving instructor who was threatening, someone learning to splice live wires, walk an I-beam, or maneuver their way
through the obstacle course of a construction site needed to trust their supervision in
order to focus on the actual task at hand.

As a first-year apprentice plumber in Boston, Maura Russell was sent to a new
building under construction, a good opportunity to see a project from the ground up.
On the crew, though,

One guy was really a very sick fella. One day we were both carrying a length
of 6- or 8-inch cast iron pipe. It was a stage of the underground, and he
was on one end and I was on the other. We were carrying it from one place
to a trench on another part of the job. We were walking by this one big
pit that had all this rebar, reinforcing bar, sticking up in various patterns
because they were going to be pouring a floor and also have some starts for
some columns.

He gave me a shove with that pipe so that I went down into that pit with
the pipe—which is heavy pipe. And it was really lucky—luck had a lot to
do with it—that I landed on my feet, still holding the pipe. That I did not
end up in a perforated sandwich, with the pipe on top of me, landing on a
lot of that rebar which was vertical. I can still see him standing at the top of
that pit with his little Carhartt jacket and reflector shades and Arctic CAT
hat looking down. And with his little psycho voice saying, "Gotta watch
out. You could get killed around here."

He was really creepy.

I'd be pouring lead in a pit, in a trench. It's a sunny day. This is totally
outside. All of a sudden, cloud. And there'd be this Dick—which was his
name, actually—totally bending over me, blocking the sun and whisper-
ing in my ear in his little creepy voice, "Watch out that you don't get any
water in that lead. It could pop up and you'd get a face full of lead and that
wouldn't be too pretty, would it?"

Rather than bring the danger she felt from this journeyman to the attention of any authority, Maura just dodged him as best she could. She recognized the box he had her in—it
was her word against his. And what's wrong with his warning her to be careful? And who
wouldn't believe that a green girl apprentice simply lost her balance carrying heavy pipe?

Women who had no reason to perceive the union as offering them protection, but were still committed to staying in the trade, often chose not to report even very serious harassment. Karen Pollak had applied to several Kansas City unions over the years before affirmative action regulations created an opening in the Carpenters. Having learned the trade from her grandfather, she passed the journeyman's test. She was allowed to enter as a first-year apprentice. Despite the opportunity to hire a skilled mechanic at apprentice rate, it was a year before a contractor would hire her. On her first day on the job as an apprentice carpenter, she could have reported her treatment to the union. Or to the police. Committed to keeping the job, she chose instead the silence she felt was required.

Since none of the carpenters wanted to work with her, Karen was partnered with a laborer who was "none too happy to be working with me. He was trying to do everything he could to drive me crazy. I lost him for several hours in the afternoon. I couldn't find him." Assigned to put in insulation at the edge of the building, Karen was given a safety belt that was too large for her. She eventually just left it "hooked up onto one of the lines, but it was laying over the edge of the floor." When the superintendent found her still working later that afternoon, he told her he'd assumed she'd fallen and died. While the super was admonishing her for not wearing the belt,

> I look down and the laborer that I was paired up to was taking a sledgehammer and just demolishing my little red Volkswagen. It was like, "What did I do?" Well, he explained to me that we don't drive Communist cars onto union parking lots.
>
> I couldn't leave my tools at work, because the gang boxes were full. I'm over in the middle of nowhere, with no way to get home and I can't leave my tools. So I just put my toolbox on my shoulder and we hitched a ride. This farmer picked me up alongside of the road about a half mile from the jobsite. I got home, though, several hours later than I should have. And the husband was real upset. He was like, "Where's your car?" That was the nicest car that we owned. "Well, we don't have it anymore." "What do you mean, we don't have it anymore?" And then I explained. And it was like, "Well, you have to press charges against this guy. You can't let him do this shit to you." "No, I can't do that. You don't understand. I *will* get pushed off the building. You can't do those things."
>
> I eventually got it towed home. We used parts off of it. I had nice seats and a nice shifter. But as far as the car—he had taken a cutting torch and cut the frame. I would assume it would have to be on work time, because I had the car at lunchtime. When I went back to work from lunch, it was fine.
>
> After getting chewed out by this superintendent because I had left my safety belt and it was hanging over the edge of the floor and he thought that I had died, it was like, "Did you even go down to see if I was there?" "No, I just figured I'd worry about it when I got down there." Well, that told me where I stood. So that's why I was not going to press charges on my little Volkswagen. We just gritted our teeth and went on and bought a really old Volkswagen, and took and drove it to work. But from then on I parked it two or three blocks away from the jobsite.

These were real strong-valued people. It was not a union-made car and it represented to them, definitely I had to be a communist. I was driving a Volkswagen. I was a woman wanting to be a carpenter. So I had to be. That was my first day of work. Welcome to the real world.

Asking for help was not necessarily a more useful response, as Yvonne Valles learned. Attracted by the opportunity to work with her hands and the hope that she'd be able to buy a home once she made a journey level painter's salary, she was an eager first-year apprentice. She joined painters hanging vinyl wallpaper at a hotel in Los Angeles, and within the first two weeks faced harassment from her foreman.

I'm still kind of traumatized by the second job I got. The foreman on the job was a real jerk. Him and a couple of the other painters would always be talking real dirty about women all the time. They used to leave magazines of naked women in the bathroom that I'd use. They'd leave the book wide open and it would show. They'd think it was funny. They were harassing from day one.

There was a young kid apprentice that was about 18 years old. My foreman used to talk verbally abusive to him, call him a dickhead and all kinds of names. With me, I heard him making a crack one time, called me a dyke. Anyway, he was always bragging on breaks. He'd be talking to the guys, but I could overhear him because we'd eat in the same room. I mean, where was I going to go eat lunch? He used to pick up prostitutes. He'd be saying, I'm going to see so-and-so tonight.

One day, I was hanging up some wallpaper and he came to me, I was kneeling down. He goes, "Hey, you want to see some pictures of my girl-friend?" And I said, "No." He said, "Oh, come on, I'm training her to be an apprentice, too. Don't you want to see some pictures of how I train my apprentices?" I said, "No, why don't you just leave me alone?"

So anyway, I was kneeling down, spreading the wallpaper on the walls. All of a sudden he stuck a Polaroid picture in front of my face and he goes, "Look." And I looked. And he starts laughing.

It was a picture of a young woman laying down with her legs open and she had what they call in wallpapering a seam roller. It's got a little handle with the roller on it, you lay the seams down flat with that to get the air bubbles out. She had the handle inside her vagina. And he starts, "Yeah, that's how I train my apprentices."

Oh, man. I just said, "Get out of here, I don't want to see that!" I was really upset. I went home that day and I called the apprenticeship school and I told the head of the apprentice school, "I got a problem on the job. I'm being harassed and I just want you to know what's going on."

I told him about it, and I started crying 'cause I was really humiliated. He says, "Oh, gee, I'm sorry," and "That asshole," and he goes, "Yvonne, it's not always going to be like that." He says, "I'll talk to him."

But nothing ever happened. He had told me too, "You know, Yvonne, I can report this but it might not be good for you."

I said, "Well, there's only one thing I'm afraid of. I've heard that women that file lawsuits against their companies, they end up getting blackballed.

I wouldn't want to have that mark against me." He said, "That's true, that could happen."

They don't care. They want to discourage you. It's like contractors have this attitude, from what I've heard, if a woman sues them—fine, they won't hire any more women at all.

I hated that guy. He was disgusting. He used to ask me if I'd want to snort some cocaine with him after work. I just kept my mouth shut because I needed the job. I needed to pay my rent, so I just tolerated it.

Any new worker wants to make the workplace more comfortable by developing congenial relationships with co-workers. Yet as Melinda Hernandez, a new electrical apprentice learned, friendliness could set off an invisible minefield.

On that job there was an apprentice—he wasn't a piece of shit, he was *the* piece of shit of life, the lowest of the low. But I didn't know this, see. He came off very nice. He happened to be Puerto Rican, too.

And he says, "Oh, it's nice to have a girl working side by side, why don't we hang out one day? We'll go out to dinner after work." So I didn't know. "It's just dinner. What's the big thing? What, are you afraid of me or something?" But he came off very nicely, so I said, All right. Maybe I can make a friend, you know, in the industry starting out.

So we went to dinner, and after dinner he wanted to go out dancing or whatever. And I said, "No, you know, I told you that I have someone, that I'm involved."

To make a long story short, that Monday we went to work, I think he told everybody what every man wants to hear—that we got intimate (and that's a very refined word coming from this character, okay). He did me, you know.

He became very nasty, openly, verbally cursing a lot, talking about who he screwed the night before to the men. And I'm sitting in the men's locker because the women weren't given their own locker. One day he actually brought in pornographic material, pictures that he had taken of a woman close up, with a flashlight. The reason I know this was because he was describing to them the pictures when I was in the room. And they were laughing. But none of them ever took a stand. I thought in their minds they figured, Well, it's not my daughter, or it's her own kind, it's a Puerto Rican just like her doing it to her. It's not us. Whatever it was, they justified it. Nobody ever said anything. And I remember there was a guy in the room that was sitting in the corner, he was a born-again Christian, reading a Bible.

I got up and I walked out, I just stepped out of the room. I realized that I was in for a long haul, because that was my first job. Wow, you know, what a drag. But I hoped. I had high hopes that things would get better.

Family support was key for Cheryl Camp when she faced hostility on her second job. The knowledge that her union rotated apprentices to a different shop every six months meant that even if treatment didn't improve, it would at least end. And the fact that men on her first job had been particularly supportive helped her ride through the hard times.

There was an electrician on the job, a younger guy, too. And a minority, he was black. He went out of his way to harass me. It really irritated him to know that there was a female electrician on the job. And plus, I was an apprentice. He had gone through the trainee program and, you know, there was a stigma always attached to the people that came through the trainee program. I can't repeat the things that he said. He had the filthiest mouth, I mean really filthy the things that he would say. And then he would describe his outings the night before with ladies of the night and go off into really intricate details of his endeavors and make sure that I could hear every single word. If I was walking someplace, he would start walking behind me and making rude comments about how women are.

What I really hated was, all the guys on the job knew that he was doing this to me, that he was harassing me. And no one intervened and talked to him to tell him, Why don't you back off and leave her alone. They knew that I was new, that I was an apprentice, and as an apprentice you're supposed to be seen and not heard, you're lower than whale crap. You really aren't supposed to have anything to say to a journeyman as an apprentice, other than asking questions, *if* they allow you to ask questions. I really don't think that they even considered my feelings in the matter. When I told them that I was taking him up on charges for harassment, they told me, Well, this is just the way he is, and don't let it bother you. But that's impossible for it not to bother you.

There was another female on this job. She was a plumber, but we didn't work in the same area. He was harassing her too, but her husband is also a plumber, so he straightened him out so he didn't say anything else to her. But I had no one to intervene for me. And he was the type of individual that you could not just approach personally, and say, why don't you just back off and leave me alone. It was the foreman that came through and ended up having him apologize to me. He ignored me after that.

I was under so much stress with him, from what he was saying and the way that he made me feel every day, I was ready to quit the trade at that time. My mother talked to me and was saying, "Well, Cheryl, you don't remember what your ultimate goals are. You wanted to finish this and see it through. You know the first shop that you worked for was so great and the guys were different there, so it's not going to always be this way. Just bear with it and try to see it through and it could get better." My mom was a real source of comfort.

The effect of a harasser's action was compounded when others on the job knew about it but did not intervene—as though he were acting on their behalf. Contractors and unions tended to underestimate the gravity of harassment and in some instances even condoned the behavior, tacitly or explicitly. Institutional procedures for prevention or punishment were rare.

Acts of passive aggression could cause serious injury without anyone's seeming to be responsible. Although with an inexperienced worker it might be difficult to distinguish between a true accident and an intended one, it was the responsibility of the supervising journeyman to look out for an apprentice's safety, and the responsibility of the training program to properly prepare apprentices. Karen Pollak saw the failure to train apprentices in the proper use of power tools not as some malevolent attack on women, but merely as the result of assuming that apprentices knew how to use them, which had traditionally been true. Karen had been trained to use a skill saw safely when she was five or six years old (by her grandfather, who showed the grandchildren his missing finger). But other female apprentices received

> Lots and lots of injuries. Eye injury. Feet. Hands. We had a woman that lost three fingers. Because no one told her how to use the table saw. Another one was cutting stakes out on the jobsite, cut off her whole hand. All because no one took the time to really, really explain that these things can hurt you. I knew how to use the tools. I had an unfair advantage to a lot of the women. Basically what they taught you was how to put the saw blade into the saw and make sure that the guard worked, if there was a guard. That was about it.
>
> They would say to the woman that it happened to, See? I told you, you should have stayed home. A broom wouldn't do that to you. And then they would make it a point that *you knew* that someone had gotten hurt.
>
> They told me when the lady cut her hand off. She was using a big radial arm saw, a 16-incher, out on the jobsite. She had put her hand down to hold the material. The material started to move. The saw got bound. And somehow or another her hand got back behind the saw, so it pulled itself right back across her. They were able to save it, but she didn't have full function of her hand. It's not the same. And never will be. That's something that could have been easily prevented.

Even if it began as an unintentional oversight, once women started to experience so many injuries, an adjustment should have been quickly made to incorporate power tool safety into the training. Instead, the pattern of accidents became not only proof that women didn't belong, but an amulet to frighten women into leaving.

Some job situations had the feel of trench warfare. Men who wanted to drive women out; women who were determined to stay. Knowledge of tools and experience at the trade did not prevent an "accident" that broke Karen Pollak's nose, when a journeyman did not want her—not only a woman, but a Cherokee Indian—working with him.

> I had a sledgehammer dropped on me. This was a job that they had to have a woman. And they needed a minority. It was like, Give me a black woman or somebody who I can mark as a double and then I only have to have one of them. It was just a little tiny library for the University of Kansas Medical Center.
>
> We were down in the hole and I was stripping forms. The guy above me was on the next set of scaffolding working on the next layer. I kept noticing that hairpins, which are a form-type hardware, would fall down and hit the hardhat. Every once in a while it'd hit the bill and knock the hat off. You'd bend over and pick the hat up, look up and go, "Can't you be careful?" "Yep, I just dropped it, sorry."
>
> The superintendent had yelled at him about something. I was standing below and he was going, "Well, make *her* do it. She doesn't do anything."

"She's stripping. That's all she's here to do."

I was going, "Well, I'm willing to learn. I can handle doing more things than just pulling nails."

"Nah. Not with me you're not." At lunchtime, the foreman said that I was going to go help him after lunch.

He got up on top of the wall before I did. He was standing up on the scaffolding he had just built. I was just starting to climb up the form. BAM! The sledgehammer hit me, it rang my bell.

It was like, Okay, that *could* have been an accident. He throws the rope down. I hook up the sledgehammer and he pulls it back up. I make sure I'm away from the rope. If he happens to slip again, no problem.

For some odd reason, he didn't nail down his scaffolding like you're supposed to do. He told me he did. I stepped on the far end of the board and the scaffolding went smack with the board right in the face. Straight down, back into the hole.

The hole had mud in it. And water. I had hip waders on earlier that day stripping it out. It was an ugly sight. I had broke my nose. The superintendent comes over and says, "Well, this isn't going to work. He doesn't really want you up there."

"Oh, I just thought it was an accident that the sledgehammer fell."

"Probably was on his part, Karen."

"And that's why he didn't nail down the boards, huh?"

"Well, maybe he was getting ready to move them over to the next set of scaffolding."

"Right. He knew I was climbing up there."

I stayed on the bottom and stripped. He would drop things if I was underneath him. I soon got the idea, Stay away from him.

The wisdom of Karen's response—to outwit her journeyman's efforts to injure her while keeping up production—is made clear by the actions of the superintendent who both represents the contractor on the job and belongs to the union. The journeyman responsible for her safety not only drops a sledgehammer and other objects on her, but lies to her about the scaffolding being nailed down, resulting in her fall and broken nose. Rather than laying off the journeyman or bringing him up on charges in the union, the super accommodates his wishes. All three understand the same unspoken ground rules: not only is it acceptable to refuse to work with a woman, it is acceptable to communicate that refusal through actions which, out on the street, could result in prosecution for assault and battery with a dangerous weapon.

Harassment could result not only in a stressful work environment or physical injury but also in economic costs, both short- and long-term. It was not unusual for a tradeswomen to be transferred or laid off after attention was called to harassment. Barbara Trees found that her skill training was also affected.

I was a second-year apprentice working for this contractor doing ceilings—the concealed kind, the hard kind of ceiling—and I was really trying to learn them. The bar isn't revealed, you don't see it, so they're kind of complicated. I wasn't finding it easy to begin with. I was up on the Baker [staging] by myself and the electricians opened up the computer floor around me. They opened up enough tiles so I couldn't move my Baker. I said to them, "You know, I need to move this Baker. Will you put back those tiles?" They just wouldn't do it.

I'd be working on a Baker and they'd be having their coffee break and I would hear my name fairly continuously. "Barbara . . . Barbara . . . Barbara . . . " I got sick of it, so I called over to them and I said, "Is there something you want to say to me?" And, "Oh, no, no, there's nothing we want to say to you."

That was really all it took.

I went home that night and I came back into work the next morning and these guys obviously had written on my Baker in letters a foot high, "PROPERTY OF THE CUNT." I didn't know what to do about it. I didn't really think there was anything I *could* do about it. But what happened is that my sub-foreman came over and he saw it. I didn't really want him to see it or anything. I was embarrassed, actually. So he says, "What's this?" I said, "Well, I think those electrician guys wrote this on here, you know, because we had words yesterday." He says, "Well, we can't have this. I'll speak to the foreman." I was really surprised by his reaction. I felt he was trying to help me.

So the foreman came over to me and asked me what happened. And he said, "We can't have other trades harassing our carpenters. We're going to have a meeting of all the trades later in the day. I'll let them know that they can't do this." I thought, you know, this sounded good, this sounded like what he was supposed to say to me.

I guess they had the meeting and what happened is that I was transferred out of there. They just decided that I was too much trouble. I remember as I walked down the street I passed one of those electrician guys and he almost tried to hide in the building. He saw me and he kind of put his eyes down. I think he must have realized what he had done.

This was my introduction to how they help you out. This guy was so sincere —Oh, we can't have them harassing our carpenters, we're not going to put up with this. I remember thanking him, thinking, This is really great.

Whenever I see ceilings now, I sort of panic. I actually kind of get a cold sweat going. I started to realize what it's from is that the two opportunities I had to learn ceilings both ended where I was laid off or taken off the job. I still feel bad about this. That was my chance to learn.

So this is what happens. Your training suffers. You feel guilty. You don't know what you did wrong. You're feeling like kind of an awful person. And you don't learn your ceilings.

A tradeswoman who changed contractors or crews—particularly if she bounced between situations where co-workers were friendly and fair and situations where she faced hostility and humiliation—could find it hard to build self-confidence and gain her bearings as a developing mechanic. Like many tradeswomen, Helen Vozenilek, an apprentice electrician in Albuquerque, struggled to understand the cause of harassment, looking for how she might prevent or avoid it.

I made the shithouse walls. It was something like, FUCKING LESBIAN ELECTRICIAN BITCH. I somehow knew that had to be me. You know, process of elimination.

On that job, the steward was terrible. I don't think he liked women. It was just a bad collection of people. You know how men can get—when they're alone, they're fine, they're actually brothers? And then they get in a group and they're just beasts? I think that was the situation there. They sort of got beastly.

I did feel really harassed there and I didn't quite get it. I remember going home a couple of nights and just crying myself to sleep. I think the steward had talked to me that day, said they were going to run me off or something— and it was like, I didn't get it. The hardest thing is the capriciousness, not knowing what you did or what you were being held responsible for, or irresponsible for.

Some of the men who saw tradeswomen as invaders of their domain marked territory with graffiti, pornography, or bodily fluids. Although Irene Soloway, a New York City carpenter, "really didn't experience a great deal of sexual harassment,"

I had one incident that upset me for quite a while, which was a job that I was determined to do well on and keep. After six months of coming in every day, I took a day off. When I came back, the shanty had porno pictures all over it, real disgusting ones.

The foreman and I didn't get along. It turned out his brother had spent the entire day plastering the shanty on company time. I really was truly shocked, because I had been on the job for six months and pornography was not an issue. So I felt it was terribly personal. It's like, you don't even know where to look! The men were all sitting on their benches and I knew that they weren't comfortable with it, either. I mean, you have a shanty that's clean and decent, you have your little nail and your little hook and your little lunch, and then one day you come in and it's—you know, open cunts all over the wall. It made a lot of people uncomfortable, but I knew that nobody would say a word. I had a screaming fight with the foreman outside the shanty. I was a second-year apprentice.

The reason why I had a problem with the foreman in the first place was because I told him, in front of a group of men, "I'm an apprentice, I'm not an animal, and if you want to call me, I have a name." He used to call black people Nigger, you know. I guess he must have called me Girl. He was furious with me and he told me so in no uncertain terms. And then this happened. I ended up being sent off the job, and I never felt that I had any retribution for that.

They sent me to another job and then two days later I got laid off. So they sort of diffused it that way. I always felt I had to find some like really, really remarkable way to turn the situation around. You think you have to deal with this on your own and you have to be able to stay in the industry, you know. That was my philosophy. I always thought of how would I turn this around and have him be shocked and upset and angry. Which is stupid. I mean, he's the boss. I'm not. So you can't turn it around in that way, in a personal way. But that was the way I used to think.

As an apprentice plumber, Maura Russell never had the opportunity to work with another woman in her trade. On one job with several hundred workers, though, she was able to work with two other tradeswomen, an electrician and a taper, building apartments for the elderly.

> We hung around together, which was really nice. But they have a hard time with women getting together on the jobs.
>
> There was one time when the three of us were having lunch in K—'s car. This one guy who was there just for two days, an asphalt contractor putting in the parking lot, came over to where we were eating our lunch and pissed on the side of the car. Quite unbelievable. Looking at him coming over, at first I thought his truck must be parked next to us. And then K— is like, "Wait a minute! Is he doing what I think he's doing?" Really.
>
> He'd left by this point. We convinced K— that what she should do is talk to the super. The guy's in his truck and he denies it. K— says, "Oh, bullshit, you did this." At which point, the super went insane that she swore. And just said, "If you talk like that, you don't deserve to be treated like a lady."
>
> He was just going to walk away and not deal with it. And that was the point at which K— took out her little Swiss Army knife and told the guy that she would slash his tires if he didn't apologize. He'd been laughing at the incident, which is what really enraged her. He finally did say, "Oh, I'm sorry, I'm sorry, I'm sorry."
>
> She said, "No. You got out of the car to piss on my car, and now you have to get out to apologize."
>
> So he did. He was angry at that point that he was compelled to do that. And the super was jumping up and down livid, like she was a maniac. He didn't want her on his job anymore. He went running to the trailer to call her company to get her fired (which he was unsuccessful in doing).
>
> But that incident later, we joked, would become that she had a ten-inch knife or something to this guy's throat—and it has pretty much gone around the circuit like that. But that was definitely, Talk like a lady if you expect to be treated like one.
>
> Laborer boss said that to me later in the day, "My wife, she just would have turned her head."
>
> Really.

Although, for women, responding in kind to harassment could bring on more trouble, Maura was sure that if there had been three men in that car,

> They would absolutely have pummeled him. And what would the super have done about that? He would have turned his little head. He would have expected that. Oh, they would have gone insane if something like that had happened to a man.
>
> That was really quite an interesting statement of, You're not welcome. Gross, really gross.

Hostility could be triggered by small acts of self-empowerment. Like three women sitting together in a car. Or a woman becoming more assertive. Doubly vulnerable, as an African American woman, Gloria Flowers found that her worst harassment came when she decided to speak up for herself, after she reached "a point where I wanted to have some respect, I wanted to be talked to like I had some sense."

Towards the end of my apprenticeship I was really catching the blues. That last year, I said to myself, I'm not taking this crap anymore. I'm going to start telling some of these guys off. Well, that was the worst thing I could have done. It's almost like, when you get revenge, it's not as sweet as you think it's going to be.

That last year was my worst year by far. I remember this super telling me, maybe I shouldn't have gotten in the trade. "Why don't you just give up and give out?"

I fell out with a lot of the guys. Some of the guys I had liked previously, we ended up just rubbing each other the wrong way. They started rotating me, working me every other week. At the time I didn't know it was because they wanted to lay me off and couldn't figure out a way to really do it.

This one job I was on, the Ohio Bell Building, downtown Cleveland, there was this black guy on the job, he hated my guts for some reason. He had problems with women, he was like in his third or fourth marriage. That was the worst, the darkest period, I have to say, because he got physically abusive.

He pushed me, physically pushed me down stairs when nobody was watching, in a sub-basement. I remember being so mad and so hurt, I wanted to kill that guy. But he was a body builder, he was really built.

A lot of times they had raffles for different things on the jobs. It just so happened that on this job—I don't know why this happened to me, God was trying to show me something—they were raffling a .357 magnum. I don't know what made this guy ask me if I was interested that particular day. Generally I had my little blinders on. I was kind of kept in the dark on a lot of things.

But that particular time—and feeling the way I was feeling—I wanted in on that raffle. I remember coming home. I talked to a girlfriend about it, and she said, Pray about it, and don't do nothing stupid. You can't take on no man, blah, blah, blah.

She really brought me back down to the ground. I prayed about it and it ended up working out. He got laid off, and I got laid off shortly thereafter.

That guy wanted to hurt me. He did. I never told any of the guys about it because, you know, they didn't care. That job had gone sour for me. None of the guys wanted to have anything to do with me on that particular job because I just wasn't taking any stuff.

Accidents set up against women or people of color were particularly insidious. When "successful" they accomplished two things: eliminating or frightening the target, and framing them to look incompetent, not only as individuals but, by extension, as a representative of their gender or race. As an apprentice electrician, Nancy Mason learned to be extra cautious, in case work was sabotaged.

I was deliberately set up, actually, on two occasions. Once I had circuits turned on when I was trimming out receptacles in a high-rise office space. I don't know who turned the circuits on. And another time I'd been hooking up fire alarm exit signs and I went back to check some. I was up at a light exit sign, and someone had actually tied the ground wire into the hot wire on the other end of the Scotchlok and as I was taking it out, someone turned it on and it blew up in front of me.

I did not get hurt, but obviously someone was hoping I probably would have, or gotten scared or whatever. Those incidents both happened, I think, when I was a fourth-year apprentice. I was getting pretty tuned in to always checking stuff with my own meter. But the turning on the circuit while I was at that exit sign was probably the most dangerous thing, because of the higher voltage. It was a 277 situation.

Bernadette Gross, who went through her carpentry apprenticeship in Seattle, was on many jobs where "the object was to buck me off, and I rode them like that. It was like, I'm not going anywhere." But harassment, even when handled, carried an additional personal cost—to one's sense of trust in other people. On a job early in her apprenticeship, Bernadette fell from a ladder that was not properly secured.

I was up on a second story framing a window, and the ladder wasn't tied off and it slid from under me.

I had a sheet of plywood dropped on my hardhat. I mean, it hit my hardhat really hard. I was bent over and it could have broke my back, really—and there was just never anything done.

At that time I didn't have sense enough to think that someone had set out to hurt me. Just later on, it was like putting it all together. I was still pretty new, right? And then, I never had that many accidents after that. In my second year, I knew better. If somebody told me to go up a ladder, I'd check it, you know. But in life, it took me a long time to believe that people had malice in their heart. I always believed that they were sort of going their way and you got in the way and they knocked you over. It wasn't anything that they set out to say, I'm going to knock her over, you know.

But I found out that there were people who did, you know, sit down and plot that. It's kind of a hard blow for me.

Such experiences happened to women who graduated from apprenticeship programs. They cast an ironic light on the common explanation for those who did not, the new women apprentices who quit after only a day, a month, or a year, the ones who supposedly "found it wasn't for them."

CHAPTER 31

Men Behaving Badly

Margaret Talbot

When you work at a car dealership, you spend a lot of time standing around, but that does not mean you relax. How can you, with the manager constantly hovering over you and the strains of "We Will Rock You" or some other sales-meeting anthem ricocheting around your brain? You've got to be on, you've got to be pumped, you've got to be ready to pursue a car that noses into the lot, and then be standing right there, hand extended, when the wary customer steps out.

Body language is vital. Philip Reed, a writer who last year posted a diary on the Internet about his stint as a car salesman, described a seminar in which he was taught how to shake hands—with a "slight pulling motion" that represents "the beginning of your control over the customer." Reed observed that the car salesmen he worked with shook hands with one another often, too, practicing for "Mr. Customer" and "staying loose." There was also a lot of "high-fiving, fist-bumping, back-slapping and arm-squeezing" and during slow periods a lot of "tie-pulling, wrestling and shadowboxing."

And a fair amount of free-floating, adrenalized aggression. "At car dealerships, there's a lot of downtime," says Jean Clickner, a lawyer with the Equal Employment Opportunity Commission in Pittsburgh. "You work 12-hour days, and there's a lot of waiting around for customers. At the same time, there's big money to be made and a lot of pressure to make a deal, and when you're the one selling cars, you feel you can do no wrong." Clickner, who has represented several aggrieved car salesmen, sums up the problem this way: "Sometimes the guys get slap-happy." Car dealerships, in other words, are one of those American workplaces where masculinity and job performance are straightforwardly equated, which makes them fun for some men and not at all for others.

Consider what happened, back in the late 90's, at Burt Chevrolet in Denver, where two swaggering sales managers named Terry Franks and Jay Gaylord held sway for a time, and in unreconstructed style. It was apparently their habit, for example, to address salesmen as "little girls" or "whores." They would upbraid a guy by asking if he used tampons or tease him by saying that he had "to squat" when he urinated. The managers publicly derided struggling salesmen as "queers" or "steers"—because "steers

432

try; bulls get the job done." To motivate the troops during sales meetings, they showed raunchy video clips, including one depicting a bull stepping on the genitals of a rodeo cowboy. Gaylord signaled his boredom with what a subordinate was saying to him by simulating masturbation while the employee talked. He grabbed at male employees' genitals, sometimes making contact, sometimes not, but mainly (or so it seemed to the men who got used to jumping out of his way or even running when they saw him) hoping to make them flinch.

The reason we know about any of these antics is that 10 of the salesmen at Burt Chevrolet ultimately decided to register their objections. And to do so they chose what might seem to be an unusual means. With the help of the E.E.O.C., they filed a sexual-harassment lawsuit charging the car dealership with creating a hostile environment that discriminated against them as men. It was, in their case, an effective weapon: two years ago, the E.E.O.C. won a $500,000 settlement (and a promise to implement mandatory sexual-harassment training) from Burt Chevrolet, which had already fired the two managers in question.

The idea that by being raunchy, men might be discriminating against other men is not an intuitive one. Indeed, not all of the guys involved in the Burt Chevrolet suit realized "that this was discrimination at first," says Mia Bitterman, one of the E.E.O.C. lawyers who handled the case. "But they certainly did not enjoy being afraid to bend over at the water fountain because they didn't know what was coming. And they were certainly embarrassed that anything like this could have happened to them."

Most people asked to envision a sexual-harassment complaint from a man would probably think of "Disclosure"-like scenarios starring rapacious female bosses in pin-striped Armani. Maybe, when reminded that men can file sexual-harassment suits against other men, they might think of a gay boss coming on to a subordinate. Both kinds of cases do occur (the latter more often than the former), but judging from law journals and court documents, they do not represent the typical harassment claim brought by men. A more common case involves heterosexual men, often in blue-collar and service-industry jobs, who object to the "hostile environment" created by the behavior of other heterosexual men.

Since 1992 the percentage of sexual-harassment charges filed by men with the E.E.O.C. and state agencies has been increasing steadily, to 13.7 percent in 2001, from 9.1 percent in 1992. A total of 2,120 such cases were filed last year. (The most common kind of harassment case by far still involves a woman accusing a male co-worker or supervisor.) Men's claims of harassment often center on what is considered "horseplay," or what Bruce McMoran, an employment lawyer in Tinton Falls, N.J., describes as "bullying, hazing, adolescent kinds of behavior."

Sexual-harassment lawsuits are not obvious or straightforward or even particularly sensible solutions to the problem of men treating one another badly at work (or expecting other men to like their crude jokes), but they seem to be the solution we have hit upon. Often the men who are targeted and later bring claims of harassment are the weakest of the herd—younger, smaller or more effeminate than the men they work with. But this is not always the case. Sometimes a big guy who is a seasoned worker is picked on anyway, maybe because he's new to the job or quick to register his distaste for his workplace's particular rituals of boredom and aggression.

At a Harbert-Yeargin construction site in Jackson, Tenn., where Joseph Carlton worked as a pipe welder in 1996, for example, there was a lot of what the men who worked there referred to as "goosing." This could mean poking or pinching a guy anyplace on his body, but more often it meant swatting or grabbing his genitals. Carlton was goosed on two occasions soon after he took the job—once, he claimed, in a sneak attack while he was wearing his welding helmet—and he did not care for it. His attacker, he said, was his crew chief, Louis Davis, and Davis's modus operandi struck Carlton as a curious way to get to know a new employee. As Carlton testified in court: "I meet a man, I shake his hand. I don't reach down and touch him in his personal area."

Carlton was not some weedy college boy. "Joe's a big, good-looking country guy, maybe 6-foot-5 and 250 pounds," says his lawyer, Michael Weinman. "The secretaries in my office called him the Marlboro Man." Carlton wanted the job at the Jackson site because it was close to his girlfriend's home. And he was used to horsing around—he had put in plenty of hours at construction sites and shipyards. Goosing, though, was not something he cared to put up with at work. "I like to weld," Carlton testified. "That's what I've always done. And I like to do a good job at it. But I ain't never had nobody grab me."

Carlton complained to a supervisor at the site, who did not reprimand Davis but who did transfer Carlton out of Davis's crew. By then, though, some of Carlton's co-workers had heard about his complaints. To make fun of him, Carlton said, they started to "grab each other" and "hunch on each other" whenever they saw him. It made work miserable in a new way. When Carlton got on a truck to be transported around the site, he said, everybody else would jump off, "like I had the plague." Finally, Carlton decided that he had no choice but to quit. The E.E.O.C., which investigated Carlton's claim of sexual harassment, found three other employees who told similar stories about life at Harbert-Yeargin, where workers built and repaired machinery for a food-processing factory. In the spring of 1999, the matter went to trial.

The proceeding was a curious three-day semantics-fest involving fraught and detailed discussions of the terms "goosing" and "horseplay." Carlton testified that when he worked in a shipyard in Newport News, Va., he would "horseplay a bit at lunchtime," but to him that meant doing something like covering a colleague's welding visor with black tape. It wasn't the same as some guy, out of the blue, grabbing another guy's crotch.

On the stand, Louis Davis denied goosing Carlton below the belt and said he didn't recall doing it to other men. But he added that at Harbert-Yeargin somebody probably was goosed "every day." You goosed some men, he said, because they were "goosey"—prone to startled reactions—and it was funny to see them jump. Davis said that he "probably" would have goosed the three women who worked in the office if he had been around them more often and "if they was goosey." He allowed, however, that he did not think he would goose the women below the belt.

Carlton was not the only employee to testify about high jinks at the plant. Tony Warren told the court that he drew the line when Davis started twisting his nipples and had felt compelled to tell him that he "didn't mind cutting up a bit" but "didn't go for stuff like that." An instrument fitter named Terry Dotson said he put up with goosing—

his tormentors, he said, were a couple of contract electricians known as Smurf and Possum—but he never really got used to it. He wanted to hit Possum when he grabbed him "down there," but Possum was an old man, and besides, Dotson didn't want to get fired for fighting. Sometimes he thought getting startled like that when you were working on, say, the pipe-threading machine, and trying your best to concentrate, might be dangerous—he'd seen guys get their sleeves ripped off their arms on that particular machine. But luckily, he testified: "I never did get hung up in any equipment or anything. It was just—I don't know. It was just the aggravation of having to put up with it."

Given the distribution of the work force today, it's not surprising that some male-on-male sexual harassment takes place not in blue-collar strongholds but in the retail world and, in particular, in the fluorescently lit vastness of suburban superstores. Sometimes in these cases you find men who are offended by an almost perkily demeaning atmosphere, one in which the insults are sexual in tone mostly because there just aren't that many insults to choose from in the English language. A lot of these harassers deride men by comparing them to women. Variations on "bitch," which is so ubiquitous as to have lost its capacity to shock, if not its payload of contempt, abound. As in, "Come here, cashier bitch." As in, "You talk like a bitch." Even "sweetheart" can sound nasty if uttered in a certain tone of voice. Much of the rhetorical and gestural language of male-on-male sexual harassment is borrowed directly from adolescent rituals that have been around for decades: wedgies, pants-yanking, rabbit punches to various parts of the body. They all thrive on restlessness, a sense of unfair containment, the itch to make something—anything—happen. Sexual insults are the ones lying around and the easiest to pick up when you're bored with cranky customers and their cranky kids and feel like messing with somebody's mind, just getting a response out of somebody, even if it's to something really dumb. But in that kind of atmosphere—minimum-wage miles-of-aisles tedium—men and women often aren't treated all that differently. The culture is hardly masculinist. And that complicates a sexual-harassment case.

When Christopher Lack worked the cash register at the Wal-Mart in Beckley, W.Va., for example, his boss, James Bragg, was a tenacious kidder. Bragg had a few favorite expressions, and he liked to toss them around the store, where he was an assistant manager and Lack was a salesclerk back in the mid-90's. "Spank you very much" was the play on words Bragg favored for his telephone sign-off; "penis butter and jelly sandwiches" was his lunchtime joke; and "Oh, my rod!" was his preferred exclamation when he saw an attractive woman. Lack, who eventually brought suit against Bragg and Wal-Mart for sexual harassment, testified that Bragg wore him down with crass double-entendres, often delivered in front of customers or co-workers. Once, when Lack was helping a customer, Bragg came up to the counter and said, "I need a small bag, and not the one between your legs." When Lack called Bragg over so that he could, for example, authorize a refund, Bragg would say, "I'm coming, Chrissy" in a "real sexual" tone, Lack charged. At the store Christmas party one year, Bragg sidled up to Lack and a group of co-workers, grabbed his own crotch and said, "Hey, Chris, here's your Christmas present." Lack tried complaining to Bragg but claimed that Bragg did not stop and indeed retaliated by saddling him with a more punishing work schedule. "You can say it's horseplay, and men are all alike, but not all men are

Neanderthals," says Sharon Iskra, the lawyer who represented Lack. "Chris was this decent, likable guy in his 20's. He was married, had a couple of kids and needed a job but didn't want to put up with this kind of thing."

[. . .]

Complaints like the ones brought by Carlton and Lack represent a peculiar development for sexual-harassment law and especially for the concept of "hostile environment." Feminist legal scholars first introduced the idea of a hostile environment in the 80's, in response to the fact that a lot of workplace harassment consisted not of bluntly quid pro quo sexual solicitations (sleep with me, and I'll give you a promotion) but of sexual jokes and vulgarity. Since women were presumed to be more offended by coarse behavior than men were, a workplace in which such joking was the norm was discriminatory by definition—and a violation of civil rights law, as opposed to a violation of sensibility or privacy or taste.

The hostile-environment idea has always been problematic, however, as the legal scholar Rosa Ehrenreich, among others, has pointed out. Rather than assuming that workplace harassment is wrong because women are human beings and all human beings deserve to be treated with dignity, it assumes that women are somehow "uniquely vulnerable to men," as Ehrenreich puts it. And the reason they are is that men are supposedly "always vulgar and loutish," or that women supposedly "have 'special' sensitivities and rights that men do not share." But the hostile-environment concept becomes even more dubious if it turns out that a growing number of men do share some of the same sensitivities, even when they work in blue-collar settings, which some courts have held to a lower standard.

And the truth is that male-against-male claims sit uneasily within the framework of sexual-harassment law, even as they expose, in their own peculiar way, some of the persistent weaknesses of that framework. Before 1998, it was not at all clear whether same-sex harassment was even actionable. Harassment law as we knew it owed a great deal to the feminist legal scholar Catherine MacKinnon's gloss on Title VII, the provision of the 1964 Civil Rights Act prohibiting discrimination based on race, religion and sex. Starting in the 1970's, MacKinnon began elaborating an argument that sexual advances in the workplace constitute discrimination against women, the historically subordinated sex and the one most often on the receiving end of such advances.

But this neat division—men as harassers, women as victims—did not hold for long. Indeed, by the mid-90's, the courts were besieged with male-on-male harassment cases, the very last sort of cases that either the drafters of Title VII or its feminist interpreters had ever envisaged. There was some legal precedent for allowing that members of the same race could discriminate against one another. "Because of the many facets of human motivation," the Supreme Court declared in 1977, "it would be unwise to presume as a matter of law that human beings of one definable group will not discriminate against members of their group." But this still left the status of same-sex discrimination, let alone harassment, ambiguous. Between 1992 and 1997, four different federal appeals courts, asked to determine whether same-sex harassment was actionable, came up with four different answers. The Fourth Circuit ruled that same-sex Title VII claims were actionable only if the accused harasser was homosexual and could therefore be motivated by sexual desire. The Eighth Circuit ruled that men could prove they had been sexually harassed by other men if they could show that women were not subject to the same debasing treatment. Since the treatment in question in that case was "bagging"—a variation on goosing that targets the testicles—anatomical literalism carried the day. Women didn't have testicles, ergo only men could be bagged, ergo men were bagged "because" of their sex and in violation of Title VII.

The Seventh Circuit, in a 1997 case known as *Doe v. City of Belleville*, drew a sweeping conclusion allowing for same-sex harassment cases of many kinds. Title VII was sex-neutral, the court ruled; it didn't specifically prohibit discrimination against men or women. Moreover, the judges argued, there was such a thing as gender stereotyping, and if someone was harassed on that basis, it was unlawful. This case, for example, centered on teenage twin brothers working a summer job cutting grass in the city cemetery of Belleville, Ill. One boy wore an earring, which caused him no end of grief that particular summer—including a lot of menacing talk among his co-workers about sexually assaulting him in the woods and sending him "back to San Francisco." One of his harassers, identified in court documents as a large former marine, culminated a verbal campaign by backing the earring-wearer against a wall and grabbing him by the testicles to see "if he was a girl or a guy." The teenager had been "singled out for this abuse," the court ruled, "because the way in which he projected the sexual aspect of his personality"—meaning his gender—did not conform to his co-workers' view of appropriate masculine behavior."

Meanwhile, the Fifth Circuit, in *Garcia v. Elf Atochem*, issued an equally sweeping declaration of the opposite bent. Garcia complained that while working at a chemical-processing factory in Texas, a plant foreman continually grabbed him and "made sexual motions from behind." But the judges ruled that same-sex claims of harassment, even those with "sexual overtones," did not fall under Title VII, which in their view addressed only "gender discrimination."

When, in 1998, the Supreme Court set about resolving these formidable differences, it took up the case of Joseph Oncale, a roustabout on an offshore oil rig whose co-workers had selected him for various sex-related humiliations. Not all sexual conduct in the workplace was unlawful, the court emphasized. It had, first of all, to be "sufficiently severe or pervasive" to "alter the conditions of the victim's employment." Just as important, it had to be demonstrated that "members of one sex are exposed to disadvantageous terms or conditions of employment to which members of the other sex are not exposed," thereby establishing discrimination "because of sex." (In other words, the workplace would have to be one in which men were the victims of harassment but not women.) If these conditions were met, the court ruled, same-sex harassment was indeed actionable. There was no language in Title VII suggesting otherwise.

In same-sex harassment cases, the court elaborated, a plaintiff could prevail in one of three ways. He could present credible evidence that the alleged harasser was a homosexual and therefore motivated by sexual desire. He could present evidence that the harasser was animated by "a general hostility" to men in the workplace (or, if the plaintiff was a woman harassed by a woman, to women in the workplace). Finally, he could show evidence of differential treatment of the sexes in a place where people of both sexes worked.

[. . .]

[The] knotty logic behind the Supreme Court's ruling has had some peculiar unintended consequences, including the fostering of a rather perverse "equal-opportunity harasser" defense. Following the court's argument that same-sex harassment is an actionable offense only when there is disparate treatment of the sexes in a workplace, then a workplace boor who treats men and women with the same contempt is off the hook. The idea that you can defend yourself by being equally awful to both sexes is "just dumb," says David Sherwyn, a law professor at Cornell. "It couldn't be what anyone wanted out of this." Yet even Sherwyn has written that "employers are well advised to raise the prospect of such a defense in any litigation and in settlement talks."

In fact, the equal-opportunity-harasser defense has been argued successfully. In the 2000 case *Holman v. Indiana*, for instance, a husband and wife working for the state's Department of Transportation charged that the same supervisor sexually harassed them both. He asked the wife to go to bed with him and gave her negative job evaluations when she rejected him. But he was also accused of "grabbing the husband's head while asking for sexual favors," then getting back at him for not complying by opening his locker and throwing away his belongings. The Seventh Circuit Court of Appeals rejected both the husband's and the wife's claims (and exonerated their boss-from-hell) on the basis that "conduct occurring equally to members of both genders cannot be discrimination 'because of sex.'" The Supreme Court declined to consider the case on appeal.

Christopher Lack, the former Wal-Mart employee, eventually fell afoul of the same paradox. A jury in West Virginia awarded him $80,000 in damages after a brief trial in April 1996. But an appeals court overturned Lack's victory in February 2001. He had not proved that he was subject to discrimination as a man, the court concluded, because he had proved all too well that his boss was an indiscriminate jerk. Bragg, the appeals court said, was a "vulgar and offensive supervisor, obnoxious to men and women alike." Even Joe Carlton—the welder who didn't like being goosed—ran into similar trouble. A jury in Tennessee found in Carlton's favor in 1999 and awarded him $300,000. But a federal appeals court overturned the verdict in September 2001. "Since the conduct complained of in many of these sexual-harassment cases is so offensive," wrote Judge Ralph Guy, "a sense of decency initially inclines one to want to grant relief." But Guy overturned the decision because, in his view, the E.E.O.C. had failed to prove that Carlton's harasser discriminated against men. Even though Louis Davis had never goosed women at Harbert-Yeargin, he might well have had there been more of them in goosing range. Besides, Guy argued, it could hardly be said that Davis was motivated by a general hostility to men in the workplace. "Mr. Davis liked nothing better than to have men in the workplace," he reasoned. "If not, who else would he roughhouse with?" (The E.E.O.C. recently asked for a rehearing of the case, though Carlton himself reached a settlement with Harbert-Yeargin.)

The case law is made all the more confusing by the fact that while some male victims of sexual harassment were clearly chosen because they are gay, sexual orientation is not covered by Title VII, and anyone who claims harassment on that basis, no matter how terrible the facts of the case, has no recourse. One way to get around this is to argue that a man was harassed not because he is a homosexual but because he is "effeminate" or "walks like a woman" or wears an earring or lives with his mother and is therefore a victim of what is known as gender stereotyping. Sometimes he is or does one or more of these things and is heterosexual, like the teenager who worked at the Illinois cemetery. And sometimes he is gay, in which case he stands the best chance of winning if he has never acknowledged at work that he is gay.

Earlier this year, for instance, a judge allowed a Boston postal carrier named Stephen Centola to proceed with his Title VII claims case against his employer. Centola had been taunted by co-workers who demanded to know if he had AIDS yet and left pictures of Richard Simmons in pink hot pants and a sign that read "Heterosexual Replacement on Duty" in his work space. Centola is homosexual, but because he had not said so at work, the judge found sufficient evidence to support his claim that his co-workers had "punished him for being impermissibly feminine." Surely one interpretation of such a ruling is that it pays to stay closeted at work. Deborah Zalesne, a CUNY law professor, sums up the problem this way: "Basically, if your harasser is gay, you stand a good chance of winning a same-sex harassment case. If you are gay, you lose."

But even this basic rule of thumb is subject to strange variations. Last month a federal appeals court in San Francisco overturned two earlier rulings dismissing the claims of a gay butler named Medina Rene who said he was harassed on the job at the MGM Grand Hotel in Las Vegas. Rene claimed that he had been repeatedly poked in the behind and forced to look at pictures of men having sex. In a 7-4 ruling by the Ninth Circuit Court of Appeals, Judge William A. Fletcher declared that a worker's sexual orientation is "irrelevant" in Title VII cases. By Fletcher's lights, the simple fact that the physical assaults Rene claimed to have endured had "a sexual nature" made them discrimination, and actionable under federal law. But Fletcher's reading was a highly idiosyncratic interpretation of Title VII. And the dissenting judges recognized this, concluding that however "appalling" the behavior alleged, it did not constitute a violation of federal antidiscrimination law. Meanwhile, two of the judges who sided with Fletcher offered a very different reason: Rene had a legitimate case not because the teasing he suffered was sexual in tone and content but because he had been gender-stereotyped. Of course, this argument raises its own questions: Does gender stereotyping cover cases in which the man harassed is straight-acting but gay or only those in which the victim, to put it bluntly, acts like a queen but doesn't say he's gay? The only thing made clear by the Rene ruling is that sexual-harassment law is messier and less coherent than ever.

Of course, when you're a man in the midst of making a sexual-harassment charge against another man, you're probably not thinking all that much about the vexed doctrine behind it. You probably couldn't care less about the historical contradictions of sexual-harassment law. Mostly you're thinking about how angry you felt at work and about how relieved you are to have a way of legally avenging yourself.

Not long ago I spent an afternoon with Joseph DePronio, a graphic designer from Buffalo, N.Y., who recently became a plaintiff in a same-sex harassment suit. DePronio is a handsome, angular 35-year-old with close-shaved hair, alert green eyes and the half-hopeful, half-exasperated manner of somebody who has always been a little more serious than the people around him. Since he has been struggling with the weird burden of his lawsuit, that divide has become even sharper. Relatives tease him about the case at family parties, trotting out some choice smutty lines. Though DePronio has a sense of humor, that kind of ribbing doesn't go over well with him these days. He got himself a T-shirt this summer whose slogan sums up his mood: "I Get Enough Exercise Just Pushing My Luck."

DePronio's wife, Tina, is a hairdresser whose fingernails that day were painted with sparkly silver stripes. She had the air of a naturally effervescent person good-heartedly striving for a more somber tone. We sat in their living room, watching their 3-year-old son, Joey, zip around in his Spider-Man costume. For a while we talked about Joe's love of drawing, and how he'd wanted to be an artist for as long as he could remember. As a teenager he painted big portraits of his favorite rock bands: Black Sabbath, Motley Crue, Kiss. When he was older he had a job in Sarasota, Fla., turning architectural blueprints of new mini-malls and the like into drawings that clients could relate to—complete with brightly attired families and puffy trees. But eventually DePronio found that he had a particular knack for designing large-scale signs: billboards, neon logos, multiplex marquees. He was delighted when, in 1999, a company called U.S. Signs recruited him for a job in its small office right outside Buffalo, DePronio's hometown. But it was in that office that his life took an unexpected, and unwelcome, turn into Neil LaBute territory.

Throughout the seven months he worked there, DePronio says, a U.S. Signs employee named Corey Perez filled DePronio's e-mail in-box with lurid material ranging from off-color jokes to hard-core porn. (The complaint filed on DePronio's behalf by the E.E.O.C. says that there were "200 to 300" such messages; DePronio says that those were just the ones he was able to retrieve and that in fact there were about 1,000.) Since Perez was a senior account representative who brought in clients and assigned work to DePronio, DePronio often felt obliged to open Perez's e-mail, which might contain information he needed to know. But while DePronio says he told Perez several times that he found the dirty jokes and images offensive, Perez laughed off his protests and once sent him an e-mail message that said, "You love it sweet cheeks." Perez would not comment for this article on any of DePronio's specific allegations, saying only that "the truth will come out at the trial."

That afternoon at his home, while Tina shooed Joey away, DePronio sat down at his computer and flipped through dozens of what he said were Perez's e-mail messages. We're all used to unwanted e-mail about hot teenagers and to tasteless jokes sent to us and 50 other close personal friends. But this was, I must say, an extremely outré archive, sort of like the fever dream of somebody who had been locked up since childhood with a steady supply of Bourbon Street novelty items and "Girls Gone Wild" videos. There was a Ricky Martin cartoon adorned with dancing penises. A picture labeled "the perfect woman" showed a naked female body with two crotches and no head. There was a joke about something called "the girlfriend remote," containing buttons marked "PMS: Off," "Bra: Off," "Voice: Off." There were a number of nudie photographs—old, young, fat, anorexic, male, female—and several explicit video clips of sexual acts. And on and on, into the far reaches of grossness.

"Look, I'm 35, I'm not naïve," DePronio said, after he turned off the computer. "I know what's out on the Internet. And I'm not an angel. I'm a normal person. I'm not going to sit here and say I've never seen a pornographic video. But this was in my office. This was my work. What if a woman—somebody I work with, a client—walks in and sees what's on my screen? What's she going to think? What's she going to do? I think some of this is offensive to women." He paused for a moment, looking genuinely puzzled. "I mean, is it just me, or is this really not funny?"

For a long time, DePronio did not think of Perez's behavior as sexual harassment. He thought of it as something he could stop by saying repeatedly that he didn't like it; he thought of it as a bewildering and embarrassing daily annoyance that put him in a lousy mood at work and at home too and made him rue the day he moved back to Buffalo. For several months he didn't even tell Tina about it —wouldn't she figure he was inviting this kind of e-mail somehow?—and that made him feel worse, detached from everybody around him. Perez sent many of the same e-mail messages to a couple of other people who worked in the office, including one woman. "I felt they kind of accepted it," DePronio said. "I was the one who wasn't going along."

What changed his mind, and made him start thinking about his experience under the rubric of sexual harassment, was what happened after he wrote a letter to the company president detailing his complaints about Perez. At first DePronio was told to work from home. A month later the company laid him off, saying it no longer had enough work for him. (DePronio says—and the E.E.O.C. has charged—that he was laid off in retaliation for his complaints.) On the Internet he found a New York lawyer named Jonathan Bernstein, who recommended a lawsuit. At the E.E.O.C. office in New York they hooked up with a young lawyer named Raechel Adams, who found the fact that this was harassment mainly by e-mail particularly interesting. DePronio hoped that the suit—when it is finally over, that is; for these things can drag on for years—would help him feel better about an episode in his life that had left him demoralized and depressed.

But when I talked to him over the summer he wasn't so sure. "Will it help?" he said. "Who knows? A big part of me would still have preferred if there had been some way to sit down and talk with somebody at the company and end it that way without lawyers and everything."

For several years now, legal scholars and others have been arguing that sexual-harassment law is deeply flawed. After "almost two decades of litigation," as Kathryn Abrams, a feminist legal scholar, has written, it is a doctrine still riddled with "inconsistencies, exclusions and misunderstandings." It is hardly self-evident, even this late in the game, for instance, why sexual overtures should be conceived of as a form of discrimination. As Jeffrey Rosen, who writes widely about legal issues, has observed: "Discrimination usually implies some form of contempt for a class of people being singled out for disadvantageous treatment as a consequence of their shared characteristics. Unwanted advances, by contrast, often involve a man's attraction to a particular woman because of her unique characteristics."

The explanations usually offered for thinking of sexual harassment as a civil rights violation are each in their own way unsatisfying. Is harassment discrimination, Rosa Ehrenreich asks, "because a man who propositions a female employee would presumably not have propositioned a male employee, and thus the propositioned woman has been treated differently than her male colleagues because of her sex? Is it because sexual harassment is motivated by hostility to the presence of women in the workplace? Is it because, in a context of patriarchy and sexual violence against women, the mere presence of sexuality in the workplace, however motivated, is inherently threatening to women and prevents them from enjoying their work and succeeding on the same basis as men?"

The first explanation relies on a limited and formalistic notion of equality. The second neglects the fact that while sexual harassment may be motivated by hostility to women in the workplace, it frequently is not. (It may, for instance, be motivated by attraction to a particular person.) The third offers a paternalistic view of women as paradigmatic victims in need of protection from all forms of sexual expression.

In her critiques of harassment law, Vicki Schultz, a Yale law professor, points out that the emphasis on the specifically sexual content of harassment is unfortunate in two ways. On the one hand it ignores other kinds of unequal treatment that may in fact be more damaging: male supervisors refusing to provide required training or work materials to women, declaring that no woman could ever do the job in question, announcing that women are dumb. (In cases involving all of these examples, courts have declined to consider them harassment.) And on the other hand it can induce companies to clamp down on any hints of sexuality in the workplace, including friendly banter in which women might willingly engage. We've all heard the stories of sexual-harassment codes gone way overboard: the Miller brewing company executive fired for retelling the "Seinfeld" joke about the woman whose name rhymed with "clitoris"; the teaching assistant whose desktop photo of his scantily clad wife elicited a hostile-environment complaint. The prevailing legal view of harassment is "both too narrow and too broad," to Schultz's mind. "Too narrow because the focus on rooting out unwanted sexual activity has allowed us to feel good about protecting women from sexual abuse while leading us to overlook equally pernicious forms of gender-based mistreatment. Too broad because the emphasis on sexual conduct has encouraged some companies to ban all forms of sexual interaction, even when those do not threaten women's equality on the job."

But even when it is not stretched to absurd extremes, sexual-harassment law has become a clumsy substitute for manners. Useful and important as it has been in opening up some workplaces to women and in reminding employers not to treat their offices as private dating pools, sexual-harassment doctrine and the threat of a lawsuit cannot replace informal codes of civil behavior. Yet we often seem to expect them to, pinning our hopes for fixing workplace relations between the sexes—and now within them—on litigation, as we pin so many of our hopes for social regeneration.

If these problems have been in evidence for some time now, though, the increase in male-on-male sexual-harassment cases makes them much starker. It underscores the intellectual incoherency of the whole doctrine. It raises the awkward problem of the equal-opportunity harasser. It wreaks havoc with the notion, so central to sexual-harassment law till now, that sexual expression in the workplace hurts women more than men. It casts into bold relief the absence of sexual orientation from Title VII's list of protected characteristics.

And when sexual-harassment law is extended to men accusing other men, it assumes that motivations for noxious behavior are straightforward—hostility to men in the workplace, for instance—when they are more likely weird, involuted and mysterious. Goosing, to take one example, might seem to be the very simplest, or at least simple-minded, of acts. (It only really makes sense when gooser and goosee are 12-year-olds.) But its motivations are, in their own way, fairly complex: boredom, repressed attraction, a need to humiliate a co-worker out of personal dislike or to establish one's dominance, even a sense that participants are perpetuating—don't laugh—a tradition.

It is equally hard to demonstrate that gender stereotyping—a provocative but slippery notion—motivates harassment. As Joseph Carlton's case shows, not all male victims fail to conform, in any clear-cut way, to their harassers' norms of masculinity. And attributing harassment to "hostility to men" in the workplace seems an even thinner reed. You could imagine a situation in which, say, a man employed in a nail salon might feel oppressed by his female co-workers. But most charges of sexual harassment brought by men are probably not brought against women, and the typical case seems to involve a mostly male workplace. [. . .] It may be possible to handle more of them through mediation and to prevent others by recognizing that not all men, white-collar or blue-collar, share the same sensibilities.

More broadly, the whole paradigm of sexual harassment, and in particular its anchoring in discrimination law, is due for reconsideration. Sometimes sexual harassment is discrimination: sexual humiliation can be part of a concerted campaign to keep women out of a workplace, for instance. But often the harm it does is less to one's equal standing as a man or a woman than to one's dignity or autonomy, regardless of sex. Rosa Ehrenreich has argued that it makes more sense to think of sexual harassment as a harm to dignity—a concept that tort law has long recognized—than as a form of discrimination. Harassment may occur in a context of discrimination against women, but the harm it inflicts is something different, she observes. The harm is its violation of "each individual's right to be treated with the respect and concern that is due to her as a full and equally valuable human being"—and, in practical terms, to do one's job to the best of one's ability. Many cases now brought under Title VII could instead come under tort laws, like those proscribing battery (which is defined, broadly, as "a harmful or offensive contact with a person" made with intent), assault, intentional infliction of emotional distress and invasion of privacy. One objection to this approach is that there would be less money to be won, since victims would often be going after the individuals who tormented them rather than after deep-pocketed companies that employed them. That doesn't necessarily seem to be a bad thing, though, especially if it discourages frivolous or opportunistic suits.

"Actions that would humiliate, torment, threaten, intimidate, pressure, demean, frighten, outrage or injure a reasonable person are actions that can be said to injure an individual's dignitary interests and, if sufficiently severe, can give rise to causes of action in tort," Ehrenreich writes. Often these concepts come far closer to the facts of sexual-harassment cases than the concept of discrimination does. This approach has the virtue of preserving the legitimacy and coherency of antidiscrimination law while still recognizing that bad things happen between people at work, some of which may be susceptible to legal remedies. All discrimination entails harm to dignity, but not all harm to dignity is discrimination.

[. . .]

Considering Care: Child Plays in the Day Care Center of a Swedish IKEA as Parents Shop (AFP/Getty Images)

Part VIII

FAMILY, GENDER, AND WORK

How do gender, class, race, and family intersect with work? Do working parents necessitate the destruction of family? How do different classes, ethnicities, and societies negotiate the difficult waters of sustaining family and work? Some argue that the "traditional" middle-class nuclear family in America has deteriorated due to an overall culture of narcissism and individualism, which has led women into the workforce to fulfill their own personal needs, at the expense of their family (Popenoe 1995). David Popenoe, for example, cites increased rates of divorce, child neglect, violence, substance abuse, and juvenile delinquency as the effects of this phenomenon. He suggests that women's workforce participation has contributed to the downfall of the nuclear family, as he maintains that women in "traditional" heterosexual families have served to "civilize men," providing them with the moral and emotional instruction needed for family stability (1995).

Family historians such as Stephanie Coontz disagree with Popenoe's interpretation, arguing that 1) the idyllic notion of the nuclear family is an inaccurate historical portrayal of American families, and 2) women have always worked. Coontz asserts that the nuclear families of the 1950s were part of a unique postwar decade in America, in which trends from the previous hundred years were temporarily reversed. Divorce rates fell and fertility rates increased, but other social problems persisted. The peak year for nuclear families in America was 1960, at 45 percent, but births to unmarried women tripled between 1940 and 1958. Unmarried women routinely left home to give birth and put their children up for adoption (Coontz 2000).

Coontz documents changes that have occurred within contemporary families, noting some misconceptions. The proportion of American women who remain single throughout their lives today is less than it was at the end of the nineteenth century. In addition, although divorce was infrequent in the nineteenth and early twentieth centuries, marriages were often terminated due to the death of a spouse. Today marriages often end in divorce, but Coontz argues this is partially attributable to longer life spans and longer marriages (2000).

Many contemporary American family transformations reflect global trends. Nuclear families comprise less than 25 percent of all families in the United States (Benfer 2007); however, increased divorce rates can be found in many other postindustrial Western societies. Of all marriages in 1990, 517 per 1000 ended in divorce in the United States; 441 per 1000, in Sweden; 425 per 1000, in the UK; 384 per 1000, in Canada, 321 per 1000, in France; and 270 per 1000, in Germany (Cherlin 2005). The largest change in the American family has been the rise in same-sex unmarried partner households, with a 314 percent increase between 1990 and 2000 (Smith and Gates 2001).

Birth rates to unmarried women are also global in nature. As of 2007, 40 percent of births in the United States were by unmarried women, up from 34 percent in 2002. A global survey by the U.S. Centers for Disease Control and Prevention found that the highest unmarried birth rates were in Scandinavian nations: 66 percent of births in Iceland were by unmarried women, 55 percent in Sweden, 54 percent in Norway, and 46 percent in Denmark (*The Editors* 2009).

Are these changes in family form solely attributable to working women? Mainstream economists, such as Gary Becker, argue that women's increased participation in the labor force and increased economic independence have rendered marriage less economically necessary and, therefore, a less desirable option for women (Becker 1991). Sociologist William Julius Wilson found that stable male employment is correlated with higher rates of marriage among inner-city African Americans. Due to the shrinking work-force opportunities, reduced labor-force participation, and the declining wage rates of inner-city males, women find these men less suitable as marriage partners (Wilson 1997). Conservative social scientist Charles Murray argues that the generous American welfare system prior to the 1996 Welfare Reform Act was responsible for inhibiting marriage, as women could choose welfare over marriage (Murray 1994).

Others such as Coontz maintain that neither welfare nor working women are responsible for the fraying of family; rather, a lack of adequate family employment policy is. Throughout most of human history both women and men have worked to contribute to the family economy. Not only was productive work by mothers and fathers compatible with family life, she argues, but it strengthened it. "Neither Native American, African American, nor white [American] women were seen as economic dependents" (Coontz 2000).

The change in family/work status occurred in the United States during the early 1800s, when capitalist production for local exchange and wage labor supplanted self-employment and farming. Men and older children began to work outside the home in centralized workplace locations, and women remained home to transform purchased goods into items the family could use. This remained the status for white working-class women until the 1920s, when child labor declined and there was a concomitant rise in women as co-providers. The problem, Coontz asserts, is that wage labor did not accommodate family needs.

The readings in Part VIII examine varied family transformations as different racial, class, and ethnic groups respond to difficult changing political and economic realities. Arlie Hochschild illustrates Coontz's conclusion that wage labor does not accommodate family needs in her piece entitled "The Administrative Mother," based on her fieldwork at the fictitious Americo, an American corporation. Vicky King, a middle-class white female manager at Americo, struggled with the competing demands of her own nuclear family and work. Her personal experience reflects 2009 data that show 74 percent of American parents do not feel they have enough time for their children. She attempted to rectify the situation by creating a flexible, family-friendly workplace for her staff. She judged her employees' performance by the work they produced, not by the number of hours they were clocked in. She pursued alternatives for them, such as flextime, job sharing, and on-site day care, in her attempts to create a family-friendly worksite.

King's own husband engaged in more parenting time than she did in order to ameliorate her time crunch. He was subsequently belittled by their friends and family for doing atypical gendered work. He eventually responded to the criticism by cutting back on family time, which forced the family to rely more on unrelated child caregivers. Although King was able to transform work for her employees, she was not able to benefit from it herself due to her demanding managerial role.

Tracey Reynolds writes about entirely different family/work experience of working-class Afro-Caribbean women in the UK in "Black Mothering, Paid Work and Identity." She argues that unlike the white British female experience, working-class Afro-Caribbean women have always incorporated work into their status as mothers due to three factors: 1) the historical experience of slavery, 2) British colonialism in the Caribbean, and 3) the economic migration of black women from the Caribbean during the postwar period. Afro-Caribbean women have always worked, both during and after slavery.

Post-emancipation conditions for Afro-Caribbean men consisted of discrimination, low wages, and unemployment, necessitating that black women (often mothers) engage in wage work as well. The British government recruited both men and women from its territories in the 1940s to work as cheap, flexible migrant labor in public transportation, the national health services, and manufacturing; and they did.

Because of these factors, working-class Afro-Caribbean mothers consistently engaged in paid work, and employment became integral to their socially constructed notions of motherhood. In contrast, "traditional" middle-class western notions of "good mothering," derived from the nineteenth-century "cult of domesticity" belief system, instructed mothers to stay home with children. Economic realities, plus racial discrimination, prohibited this construct for Afro-Caribbean women. Most of the parenting was actually carried out by Afro-Caribbean grandmothers and fathers, for whom steady work was less easy to attain.

Pierrette Hondagneu-Sotelo's "Families on the Frontier: From Braceros in the Fields to Braceras in the Home" discusses another socially constructed concept of family, as it intersects with economic conditions of the global economy. From the late nineteenth century until 1964, Mexican, Chinese, Japanese, and Filipino men were recruited by the United States as cheap immigrant laborers for work in mining, agriculture, and the railroads. In the late twentieth and early twenty-first centuries, Filipina and Indian immigrant women were recruited into nursing work. Caribbean, Mexican, and Central American women emanating from countries whose economies remained weak due to the former destabilizing processes of colonization, immigrated to the United States primarily for domestic work. As American women moved deeper into the paid workforce, and formal child-care provisions remained unavailable, immigrant women filled the child-care niche, which was previously served by African American women.

Because Latina immigrants perform live-in domestic work, which entails all aspects of social reproduction, such as child rearing, cooking, cleaning, shopping, transporting, and washing, the working-class braceras ("pairs of arms") have no time or place to care for their own families. They are forced to leave their own children to send money to the grandmothers, fathers, and "godmothers" who raise their children back home. Some children even risk their lives crossing the border to be with their mothers in the United States, only to discover that their mother's work generally precludes her from spending time with them. While middle-class American professional women struggle with the "time bind," so, too, do the Latina women who work for them, to a far greater extent.

Are there contemporary solutions to the problem of combining wage work with family needs? Janet Gornick and Marcia Meyers examine potential solutions to some of the conflicts delineated in the other readings in Part VIII, albeit with slightly different emphases, in their piece, "More Alike than Different: Revisiting the Long-Term Prospects for Developing 'European Style' Work/Family Policies in the United States." Rather than viewing working women as a potential cause of family deterioration, the authors found that the European Union (EU) nations have created a strategy to accommodate all classes of working parents.

Some EU countries encourage young mothers to spend more time with their children. Austria, the Czech Republic, Finland, and Hungary provide up to three years of paid leave for mothers. Germany provides a "parent's salary" to encourage women to stay home with their young children. Other countries emphasize the importance of preschool education. New Zealand and the Nordic countries provide subsidized child care and preschool, encouraging young children to enter schools. In eight of the European countries studied, over 70 percent of the children aged three to five are in publicly financed preschool programs. Still others such as the Scandinavian countries provide increased incentives for fathers to spend more time caring for their children. Universal health care is also available to citizens of EU countries.

America, in contrast, provides no statutory paid leave for parents, only 12 weeks of unpaid leave for maternity, paternity, or serious family illness through the Family and Medical Leave Act (FMLA). The U.S. spends only 0.2 percent of its GDP on public support for child care, compared to 1.3 percent in France, and 2.7 percent in Denmark. Only 6 percent of American children aged one and two are enrolled in publicly financed preschools, and just over 50 percent aged three to five are in a preschool program.

Despite the persistence of occupational sex segregation and lower wages for women in European workplaces, the family-work policies they have implemented have served to generate increased female employment, fertility, and time for parenting. Rather than blame working mothers for the fraying of the family, EU policies have strengthened family by addressing the work/care conundrum, simultaneously benefiting parents, children, the state, and employers—lessons the U.S. might well heed.

CHAPTER 32

The Administrative Mother

Arlie Russell Hochschild

A day in the life of Vicky King revealed a paradox. She was known among managers as a strong advocate of flexible schedules. Her division had won awards for reducing errors and decreasing the time between orders and shipments over the previous three years, and this success gave her the confidence to go out on a limb on the question of time. Unlike Bill Denton, she judged most of her 150 workers by their work, not by the hours they put in. I asked her how many in her plant could work irregular or shorter schedules without a loss of efficiency. To my amazement, she answered, "85 percent." She explained,

> I need 15 percent core workers who work regular hours or longer. If benefits for part-timers were prorated, there would be no cost—in money or efficiency— to splitting one job into two, or two jobs into three, or instituting flextime. It would probably increase the plant's efficiency. Workers would have to redesign their jobs, that's all. I'm all for it.[1]

Yet, paradoxically, Vicky herself lived the hard-driving, tightly scheduled, long-hours work life of Bill Denton. The only difference was that Bill Denton had his wife to care for children and home. Vicky had a son, a daughter, and an obliging husband who had no magical solutions to the problem of too much work and too little time at home. More than almost anyone at Amerco, she stood staunchly for the right to flexible, shorter hours. One afternoon she asked me,

> Did you ever see that film *Nine to Five*? Remember in the end how the women set up on-site daycare, they come and go on flextime? They job-share. And the business actually runs better because it's based on trust and flexibility. I loved that film. That's my vision.

But to be credible as an executive, Vicky worked inflexible, long hours. Her stand on time was family friendly; her life was centered on work.

People instinctively liked Vicky. A tall, lanky forty-five-year-old woman with gray-ing blond hair, she walked the halls of Amerco with great long strides and laughed with gusto. She typically wore a linen skirt suit, a jacket with modest shoulder pads, and a pastel-colored blouse loose around the chest. This style reflected neither the latest fashions nor her personal taste but Amerco managerial norms in dress, which changed from time to time, informally and collectively.

As with many of Amerco's rising male stars, Vicky's career success held great personal meaning for her. She had grown up in a small Midwestern family that was always on the financial edge. Her father ran a grocery store, and her mother was a housewife who was chronically anxious about the possibility of bad news, and usually unprepared when it actually arrived. After Vicky left home for college, her mother called at the end of each semester fretfully warning that the money would soon run dry and Vicky would have to drop out. With scholarships, jobs, and pluck, Vicky nonetheless put herself through engineering school. In the position she held at Amerco, she continually turned her mother's behavior inside out. If her mother waited for calamity to strike before acknowledging its existence, Vicky predicted problems with uncanny accuracy and made plans to avert them. Predict and avert, that's what she did for a living.

Happily married on a second try to Kevin, she had an eight-year-old son and a four-year-old daughter. Vicky and Kevin shared the "second shift," but under the increasing demands of two long-hour careers, that shift was becoming an ever smaller part of their life.

For Vicky, work was a well-ordered, high-pressure world in which she could blossom as a competent, helpful "mother." She created a homey atmosphere within a buzzing larger community, where all sorts of small dramas unfolded. Work was interesting to do, be in, and watch. Vicky was not exactly avoiding her home, but she worked hard to limit its pull on her life. She reported candidly on her return to work six weeks after the birth of her first child:

> People said to me, "You only took six weeks maternity leave?" I answered, "Gee, guys, that was six weeks I didn't have anybody to talk to. My friends are at work. The things that interest me are at work. My stimulation is at work. I am *delighted* to come back."

Vicky measured parenting, as Bill Denton did, by how well her children were doing, not how much time she spent with them. Unlike Bill, however, she did not define her involvement in terms of numbers of athletic events or school plays attended. Just as Vicky brought a maternal presence to the office, so she brought administrative skill to mothering Kevin Jr. and Janey. She was often calling to make arrangements with gym and piano teachers, a playground director, and two babysitters. During the week, she was an out-sourcing mom; she only became a hands-on mom on sunny weekends at the family's mountain cottage. But despite her heroic efforts to be a mother-manager, she often felt she was coming up short. "I have never felt this out of control in my entire career," Vicky told me one day. "I came home from a business trip and looked at a note I'd left for Cammy [the babysitter] to pick up Kevin Jr. at a different time on the weeks he's in camp. I had the wrong month *and* the wrong week. I said to myself, 'Oh my God, I'm slipping at work and home. There's no more left.'"

What was the solution to the Kings' time scarcity? Had they lived in China, grandparents might be raising their children while she and her husband did "productive labor." Had they lived in a Ghanaian village, her sister might have pitched in while she sold goods at the market. In the New England of the 1800s, Kevin Jr. might have been placed as a millwright's apprentice in a neighboring family short of boys. But in this town in the middle of America in the 1990s, no such options were available. Vicky's parents lived far away, and Kevin's were not disposed to help out much. The Kings' babysitter was a bright, ambitious college student who was planning to move on toward her own career soon. In the end, Vicky and Kevin were it, and they were hiring a great deal of help.

Vicky wore the same ten-hour time-uniform Bill Denton did, and added to such a schedule her role as domestic manager. However, she had no choice but to let go of the other jobs Bill's wife did—entertaining friends, cultivating a garden, doing needlepoint, looking in on elderly relatives, or volunteering to raise funds for the local school. The needlepoint Vicky could do without, but visiting her aged aunt—well, she wished she had the time to do that.

Bill Denton and Vicky King, male and female executives, fit a larger pattern. According to a 1990 Amerco survey, top-payroll men like Bill put in slightly longer hours at work than did their female counterparts, but adding together work at office and home, the "Bills" put in seventy-five hours a week while the "Vickys" put in ninety-six.[2]

Women who work also find that their efforts to balance job and family can place them in direct conflict with mothers who stay home. To arrange for Kevin Jr. to get to school, for example, Vicky called on a neighboring stay-at-home mom, Beverly, whose son, also eight, was one of Kevin Jr.'s playmates. Vicky suggested the boys set out at 8 a.m. each morning, as Vicky's job started at 8:15 a.m. and school at 8:30 a.m. Rolling her eyes, Vicky recalled,

> Beverly told me, "Can't we just talk by phone at 8 a.m. each morning to figure out how to get the kids to school? Sometimes I like to let him sleep in. Sometimes he wants to go early." Then Beverly snapped and the truth came out: "*I decided to stop working so I could have* flexibility. I'm not giving that up now to accommodate *your* schedule!"

Beverly had reluctantly renounced her career in order to stay home with her child. Perhaps, like the hapless farmer's son in the LaFontaine fable, she secretly feared she had traded a fine cow for an old donkey, and the donkey for a hen. Now a stick was being offered for the hen, and she was determined to refuse that "stick"—that strict eight o'clock departure.

Beverly had adopted a homemaker's sense of child time. She was building spacious temporal castles around the early events of her child's life, starting with the moment he was to wake up. Holding down a career, to her, meant locking a child in a temporal prison, walled in by the rigid demands of work life. If a woman wanted to be a good mother, not a prison warden, she should give up her career, Beverly thought.

Vicky thought the problem was Beverly's. The 8 a.m. send-off was, as she saw it, the beginning of a happy day, not prison life, for Kevin Jr. Being a good mother meant knowing when her son's sailboat painting was coming home from after-school painting class, hearing about his playground friends and foes, not necessarily sitting home, awaiting his arrival. It was staying in touch with her son by phone, being responsible for having his needs met, even if she wasn't the one meeting them. Being a good mother meant choosing the right day camp and the right babysitter for her children. If Beverly's time with her child was less planned, more flexible, slower paced, more like time in a late-nineteenth-century haven from industrialism, such time for Vicky was a little more like time at work.

Vicky and Beverly had fallen on opposite sides of a strange temporal dividing line for women—ten-hour days on the one hand, no-hour days on the other. Until now, the two had been friends, mother to mother. Vicky quickly smoothed over the small immediate crisis but, wary now, arranged for Kevin Jr. to walk to school with the son of another working mom, an ally on her side of the line. Now the two working mothers and their sons were friends, while Beverly and Vicky seldom talked.

Vicky's husband Kevin King, was a tall, lean, affable man with an active dental practice in town. He wanted to be a full-fledged father to his children, but he worried that he might be using parenting as an escape from a conflict he faced in his career. If, to Vicky, work had been a way out of a childhood of emotional constriction and economic uncertainty, Kevin's work felt like an ill-marked path through a series of booby traps. The son of a respected orthodontist, Kevin carried on in the same profession, but his father found fault with him at nearly every turn. Kevin took refuge from this criticism in an avocation. A gifted artist, he began to paint soulful, wind-torn landscapes that he exhibited in local art shows, to which his father paid short, dutiful visits.

Meanwhile, his wife rose higher and higher at Amerco. For Kevin, each of Vicky's steps up was a source of pride, but also of unease. He enjoyed her energy and shared her joy, but one evening at a Lion's Club dinner during which members were good-naturedly "taxed" for some new piece of luck, Kevin was "taxed" for Vicky's latest promotion. His fellow Lions ribbed him, "Now you can retire, Kevin. Let Vicky bring in the money." He took it in good humor, but that night as they were dropping off to sleep, he asked Vicky with more anxiety than he meant to betray, "When do you think all this talk will die down?"

Vicky's success created a dilemma for Kevin, but one so disguised by a happy marriage and two beautiful children that he felt he had no right to complain. The children needed more parental time, and frankly he, Kevin, *could* spend more time with them. But it was still remarkably hard in a midwestern town in the 1990s for a man like Kevin to get the public approbation he felt he deserved for all he did at home. In the eyes of other people being a father was very different from being a mother. Devoted as he was to his children, spending more time with them only made it harder to improve his public identity. Yet he knew that to expand his practice would lead to still more criticism from his father.

Faced with Vicky's rise and his own anxieties about public perception, Kevin began half-consciously to match Vicky, work commitment for work commitment. If

Vicky had an unavoidable 5 to 6:30 p.m. meeting every Tuesday night for a month, Kevin would find that in his new position at the Lions he couldn't say no to any of their Wednesday evening discussions of finances. If Vicky had to travel in November, Kevin found reason to travel the following February. It wasn't exactly competition; it was matching. As Kevin saw it, this matching kept them even in the eyes of the world if he was home as much as Vicky, but not a second more. In this way, time spent at home came to signal weakness, not only to outsiders but within the marriage itself. And the family lost out.

By contrast, at work, Vicky put the force of her being behind the principle of flexible management and evaluation by results. If Bill Denton and others like him claimed that time, results, and credit were an indissoluble package, Vicky firmly disagreed whenever the chance arose. A fresh, rested dynamo, she insisted, "could cut through a pile of work like a sushi chef fan-chopping mushrooms." Why, she would ask, reward the guy who takes the longest time to do the job?

Vicky had learned about certain half-hidden practices at Amerco by listening to colleagues from other divisions discuss requests for time off. Two "high potential" men had asked their supervisor for a year off to travel around the world and do underwater photography of Australian coral reefs. "I want them back," their supervisor had explained sheepishly, "so we gave an 'educational' leave."

If supervisors could make such large exceptions for "high potential men," Vicky pointed out, why couldn't they offer flexible schedules to parents who wanted to pick up their kids at 4:30 p.m. instead of 5:30 p.m.? So Vicky started collecting exceptions—"coral reefs," she called them. Dan Danforth was known to clear his calendar regularly between 11 a.m. and 1 p.m. to do real estate deals. He didn't *ask* his boss, but his boss knew and because Dan was prodigious worker didn't complain. That qualified as a kind of coral reef. To enhance the cohesion of the Arnerco sales teams, the various regional divisions went out for afternoon golf games from 1 to 5 p.m. about six times a year, always just before they took off on their road trips. Secretaries drove the golf carts, packed cold sodas in ice chests, cheered good shots. The trips were solemnly defended as an aid to cooperation and had become a custom, "almost work" but also another kind of coral reef.

If you looked hard enough, there were others as well. In 1975, Amerco had instituted a "40 percent system," whereby an employee could "retire" at age fifty, fifty-five, or sixty-five and then work 40 percent of his or her previous time. As one plant manager noted, "The 40 percent plan is very successful. We get their expertise. They get the balance they want." "Why," Vicky wondered, "couldn't Amerco implement a plan for young parents that it already successfully applied to older men?"

With her collection of coral reefs in mind, one day over lunch Vicky began to argue with Bill about the ways in which time and work were linked. Bill claimed that the sheer amount of time people were in their offices at Amerco did something for the workplace. Vicky lived according to that belief, but she didn't embrace it. After all, what was work? "Employees talked about it as if their jobs were clear, solid, defined," Vicky told me. But how much of a manager's job, she wondered, was simply being a good daddy to fatherless workers? And how necessary was this sort of work? Was it in fact work at all?

Without long expanses of time at the office, Bill claimed, the Amerco workplace wouldn't hum. To make it hum, inevitably one had to tend to human relationships. A well-functioning football team is basically a set of smoothly meshing relationships, Bill argued, and those relationships need nurturing, and this nurturing takes time. Bill staunchly defended his role as homemaker at work; while Vicky questioned the whole idea that there should be any equivalent at work to planting the garden, mowing the lawn, or playing with the kids—the very activities she was forced to curtail or eliminate at home. At home, of course, it was usually men who questioned the necessity of keeping the house tidy, the windows washed, the bathtub clean. It was men who promoted a strategy of "needs reduction." Now Vicky was intent on applying the same criteria to Bill Denton's "housekeeping" at work. By dessert, though far from a resolution, they had made a truce on this issue, and talk turned to children's impossibly difficult science projects, camping adventures, and other topics that affirmed their common ground.

The Unfinished Dance

At home, Vicky was locked in another struggle that refused to resolve itself—this time with her four-year-old daughter Janey. At work, Vicky was fighting to convince Bill that work and productivity were separate, that one could accomplish as much or more without being a ten-or eleven-hour player. At home, Janey was making her own case to Vicky that she needed the time for which Vicky was arguing.

The summer had seemed especially busy, and Janey-Vicky time had been unusually limited. During the week, Janey was enrolled in day camp. Her mornings began at 7 a.m. when Vicky woke her and helped her dress in preparation for her 7:30 a.m. day camp departure. Cammy, the babysitter, picked Janey and her brother up from camp at 5 p.m. and sometimes took them both out for dinner, not arriving home until 7 p.m. This had been fairly typical of Janey's Monday-through-Friday life. On Saturdays the family threw away the clock and drove off to their mountain vacation cottage for the weekend. At least that was the idea. But the previous weekend Janey had stayed with cousins while her parents had had a much needed, long awaited, night alone together. Vicky, whose job took her out of town from time to time, had also been away for a number of days in the last few weeks. This, as Vicky freely admitted, was pushing the idea of quality time to Janey's limit.

On this Thursday evening, when Cammy and the children came in, they found four adults—Mommy, Daddy, and two guests (I was one)—in the kitchen. Kevin Jr. skipped in to report on his day's activities. Janey hung back, clutching her blanket. "Mommy," she mumbled, clearly disgruntled to see us there. Only Mommy could greet her. Gradually, coaxed by both parents, Janey inched into the kitchen. Cammy smoothly and sympathetically filled in episodes from Janey's day that Janey refused to report. Addressing both children and adults, she gracefully bridged the gap. Later Vicky told me, "Cammy is real management material. I'm going to try to get her a job at Amerco."

During the adults' dinner, Janey was "invited" to take a toy out to the screen porch "where there's more room," and later still, she was urged to try out the swings in the backyard. After a short swing, however, Janey was back again, standing silently by her mother's chair.

Suddenly, as dinner was ending, to everyone's pleasant surprise, Janey announced that she wanted to do a dance. Her father rose from the table, went to the record player in the living room, and put on Janey's favorite dance music. Janey stood facing us, as from a stage. All eyes were on her—her hopeful parents, the polite guests, the helpful babysitter, and her "good" brother. She waited a few moments, then began. She danced a series of twirls to the right, then a series of twirls to the left. Then, looking directly at her mother, she collapsed on the floor in a heap of tangled limbs. "Go on," her mother urged gently. "Don't stop in the middle." The guests held their expectant half-smiles. It seemed the whole world waited and that somewhere a giant clock was ticking. Finally, Janey stood up. Again time stretched out while she remained motionless. "Okay," said her father reasonably, "if you don't want to finish the dance, then I'll have to turn off the music. You have one last chance to finish the dance." No, the dance was half-done but Janey *was* finished.

Cammy, who had positioned herself to protect the dinner party from the children, but also to allow for some check-in time with the parents suggested: "I think Janey is t-i-r-e-d." After reasoning with Janey, disregarding her, then reasoning again, Vicky put her napkin down with gentle deliberation, rose from the table, and drew Janey out of sight, though not fully out of earshot. Janey let go a mighty protest: "*Why? . . . Early . . . Want to . . . Not fair!*"

We could hear Vicky replying in firm, soothing tones that sounded like well-worn steps up a ladder: "*If you . . . then I . . . We have to . . . We always . . .*" Taking the brunt of her daughter's ire, Vicky gently picked Janey up and carried her off to bed. Tomorrow, after all, was another busy day with another early start.

What was going on? Was Janey's unfinished dance simply the kind of thing kids do sometimes? Or was Janey perhaps saying, "I know you'd like me to perform well in front of your guests, but if you won't give *me* time, then I won't give *you* time, and I won't finish my dance." Maybe Janey was staging a kind of sit-down strike against a speedup on the domestic factory floor: "More quality time! More quality time!"

In the King household, both parents felt they were equally committed to doing the second shift. But Vicky spent more time coping with the children's resentment at having so little time with their parents. Vicky often tried to explain to Janey her view that love should not be measured by time spent together. She suggested that summer weekdays were mainly for work and day camp, while weekends were the appropriate time for them to relax as a family. The time for love, of course, was *all* the time, whether they were with each other or not. From Janey's point of view, though, week-days, even at a day camp she liked, were too long. The result—for Vicky—was a lengthy first shift, an expeditious second shift, and an unacknowledged third shift, in which she desperately tried to make up emotionally for her child's unhappiness over a lack of family time.

Vicky was urging Janey to accept a promissory note against future parental payment. The bargain was this: If you're a good girl and "do your job" by being on your own from Monday through Friday, I promise to give you a great deal of attention on the weekend.

This bargain raised a new set of questions, though: How did Janey feel about this arrangement, and what could her mother do to influence her feelings? Given the fact that the situation was not likely to change, how should both mother and daughter deal with their feelings? A surprising amount of Vicky's scarce parenting time was spent working out answers to these abiding questions, or simply fending the questions off. In the meantime, Vicky was teaching Janey how to live on time credit. "If Mommy works now," Janey was learning, "she owes me play time later." But just how much time did Mommy owe Janey, and where was it to be and when? These issues remained to be negotiated. And Janey, young as she was, was mastering the art of bill collecting.

Vicky King was leading a work life that resembled Bill Denton's; but without a wife like his to call on, she was passing on the temporal costs of her career to her children, one of whom was fighting back. By the time Vicky rejoined the group at the dinner table, the storm was over. Everyone was quick to agree that Janey was t-i-r-e-d, her usual sort of crankiness at the end of a long day. Her brother had adapted himself better to his parents' long work hours. He did extremely well in school, which seemed proof in itself that all was well. His mother told me contentedly, "Kevin Jr.'s a good boy." His father agreed, and the babysitter, now retreating to the kitchen, left behind her vote, "Yes, he is. Janey was just tired." But did the unfinished dance tell a different story?

Notes

1. Amerco offered full benefits to employees working thirty hours or more a week.

2. At Amerco, the highest-paid (A-payroll) mothers in dual-earner marriages averaged fifty hours at work and forty-five caring for children and home (for A-payroll men, the figures were fifty-three and twenty-five). Such women came in second in overall hours of work, after factory laborers who are single mothers. The third longest hours (ninety-four hours a week) are worked by mothers married to nonworking spouses. However, it's not simply the number of hours but the control one has over them that counts. See, for example, R. Karesek, "Lower Health Risk with Increased Job Control among White-Collar Workers," *Journal of Organizational Behavior* 11 (1990), 171–85.

CHAPTER 33

Black Mothering, Paid Work and Identity

Tracey Reynolds

Paid work, in particular full-time paid work, is a major characteristic of black[1] mothers' lives in Britain. In 1997, for instance, the Commission for Racial Equality (1997) reported that 77.3% of black women were in some form of full-time employment and that a high rate of economic activity by these women has remained fairly consistent over the years. This has led to several commentators writing in the field to claim that black women's roles as workers is valued over and above their maternal reproductive status (see Breugel 1989; Lewis 1993; King 1995). This article develops such a claim concerning black women's primary status as workers by investigating how specific cultural, historical, and structural, economic factors determine a strong work status among black women in Britain today and create specific employment experiences for these women.

Research Background

The article explores the employment experiences of twenty black mothers in order to consider the rationales that inform their decision to undertake full-time paid work. From 1996 to 1997 I interviewed each of these mothers on separate occasions as part of my doctoral thesis. The thesis, a qualitative piece of research, investigates the mothering and family experiences of African-Caribbean women in Britain from the post-war period (late 1940s onwards) through to the present day. In particular, it addresses the way in which race, notions of cultural identity and racism create collective mothering experiences despite generation and social class differences between the mothers (see Reynolds 1999). The interviews with the mothers took place in London, primarily because the region has the largest black population in Britain. The research sample (twenty mothers) is relatively small. [. . .]

All the mothers interviewed were either in heterosexual relationships, with partners of African-Caribbean origin or were single-mothers who had children by an African-Caribbean male.[2] [. . .] [T]en of the mothers had "traditional" relationships: married or

459

co-habiting in long-term stable relationships. The remaining ten mothers in the study were either single-mothers, with the male partner completely absent from their lives or had "visiting" relationships. [. . .] [M]y own research (Reynolds 1999) suggest, that in many low-income black households, the father may be actively involved in family life. However, economic constraints (such as unemployment or low paid employment) prevent him from living in the household on a full-time basis.

[. . .]

Cultural and Economic Rationales for Paid Work Among Black Mothers

[. . .] It is suggested that [the] centrality to paid work is a consequence of black women's status under slavery, British colonialism in the Caribbean and economic migration of black women to Britain from the Caribbean during the post-war era. What connects each of these distinctive historical moments to each other is that black women in each of these instances are socially positioned as workers. Black women irrespective of a mothering status were expected to work alongside their men folk. Slavery, where black women acted as free labour, first removed women's (also black men's) "human" status and instead conceptualized them as "mules" and "work-horses" (Gutman 1976; Mohammed 1988).[3] Black women were not only constructed as human chattel but they were judged purely on their reproductive labour capacities.[4] Work to emerge from the USA, exploring the implications of colonial slavery illustrate the dichotomous relationship of man/woman, work/home and dominant/subordinate dominant ideological patterns of Western societies, were not applicable to the slavery experiences of black men and women. Angela Davis (1981), for example, sums up the significance of slavery in creating black women's unique position as workers:

> The enormous space that work occupies in Black women's lives today follows a pattern established during the very earliest days of slavery. As slaves, compulsory labor overshadowed every other aspect of women's existence. It would seem, therefore, that the starting point for any exploration of Black women's lives under slavery would be an appraisal of their role as workers. (Davis 1981, 5)

Herbert Gutman's (1976) study of African-American life in the USA also returns to slavery to explain black women's role as workers in contemporary society. He argued that slavery produced a cumulative effect for black people, that is, structural oppression and systems of inequality and disadvantage that in turn affected black men's ability to earn a sufficient wage for his family. Black families had to culturally adapt themselves to survive this and a primary survival strategy involved black communities culturally adapting themselves to accommodate the socio-economic need for black women (including mothers) to work outside the home. Christine Barrow's (1996) work investigating black families in the Caribbean presents a similar argument. She suggests that black women's actions as workers is regarded as a "positive response to adverse circumstances of poverty and unemployment especially amongst males" (65).

Britain's colonialism in the Caribbean further strengthened claims regarding black women's work status (Shepherd et al. 1995). This culminated in the introduction of government policy during the late 1940s to actively recruit black women and men from the region to Britain and thus act as a source of cheap and flexible migrant labour. Black women were recruited to key public services that were suffering from an acute labour shortage at the time: the National Health Service, manufacturing industries, public transport and public utility services (Breugel 1989; Lewis 1993; Bhavnani 1994). One striking aspect of this recruitment pattern of black women was that a "significant number" (Bryan et al. 1985, 43) of black women who arrived in Britain to take up full-time paid work were themselves mothers with young children or women who became mothers within a few short years. This finding is supported by my own research where eight out of ten first-generation mothers who migrated to Britain, and who also worked full-time arrived with young children or had had children within the first five years of arrival. Black mothers' entry into Britain as workers directly contradicted the popular discourse of the time that advocated notions of the "good mother" whose central location is in the home with their primary role as domestic homemaker, nurturer and carer (Kathryn Woodward 1997).

There is evidence to suggest that the legacy concerning black women's status as workers still exists today. Black women continue to represent the highest proportion of women in full-time employment. This fact has remained unchanged since statistical data first emerged during the early 1980s to measure ethnic differences in women's labour market participation (Bhavnani 1994). Furthermore, black mothers themselves still continue to view their work status as part of a longstanding cultural practice. In my study, one mother Michele, when discussing her own relationship to paid work, surmises:

> **Michele:** Why I work is not something that I have really thought about. My mother worked, my grandmother worked and my fore-mothers before that, so I don't see why I should be any different. I would imagine that it is the same thing for most black women too. Certainly the black women that I know, their mothers and even their grandmothers have also worked and so I don't think what I'm saying about my family is that unusual.
>
> [Michele, age 28, single-mother—occupation: legal secretary]

[. . .] [B]oth black men's and women's subordinate location within the labour market on account of race and gender discrimination act as key factors in encouraging black mothers towards full-time employment.

Today in Britain, for instance, there is a high rate of unemployment for black men specifically and across the black community in general. Recent findings indicate that black men are more than twice as likely to be unemployed as compared to white men (Richard Berthoud 1999). Research by the Moyenda Project (1997) found that the high rate of black male unemployment has indirectly contributed towards maintaining high rates of black women in full-time paid work. Indeed, one of the mothers in the study presented her choice to work full-time as an outcome of her partner's inability to find employment:

> **Denise:** At one stage both of us were unemployed. I decided it would be easier for me to find work and he would stay at home and take care of our son because I feel that it is a lot easier for a black woman than a black man in this country to get a job. Companies would rather take a black woman over a black man and that's the main reason why you have so many black men out there drawing dole money.
> [Denise, age 22—living with partner hairdresser]

Even in instances where black men are in full-time employment, lower earnings and greater job insecurity compared to their white male counterparts, across all sectors of the labour market (Modood 1997)[5] ensure black men's financial contribution cannot always, on its own, adequately sustain family and household expenditure. The working mothers to whom I spoke, in partnered relationships (married/living together), stated that one of the main reasons they remained in full-time employment was to cover the financial deficit of their husband's salary. One working mother:

> **Zora:** his wages are not enough for all of our bills and so I feel I have no choice but to go out to work so that all of our bills can be covered.
> [Zora, age 26, living with partner—occupation: housing officer]

Anita, a married mother expresses a similar viewpoint:

> **Anita:** We depend more on my salary if not more than his because I earn a little more than "David." His money covers most of the household expenses like the electricity, gas, his car repayment for instance and my money goes on the mortgage, shopping, my car repayment, nursery fees and buying things that the children need. I have thought about staying at home but that's a dream. Realistically speaking there's no way that his salary alone, his money would be able to do everything.
> [Anita, age 43, married—occupation: university lecturer]

There is no doubt that the high proportion of lone-mother households prevalent among black families in Britain has also contributed towards black mothers' work status. Over half (51 percent) of the total number of African-Caribbean families in Britain are single-parent households (Modood 1997; Goulbourne and Chamberlain 1999). All but one of the single-mothers in my study chose full-time work over unemployment or part-time hours because it offered them the only viable option to maintaining some degree of economic freedom and financial independence. One single-mother comments:

> **Jamilla:** I am determined not to rely on welfare because it's a trap. They only give you so much money and they expect you to live on that but of course you can't live on the pittance they give you, and so you go into debt. Getting up and going to work every morning is hard but it's the only way

I know to have a comfortable life and to be able to afford the things that I want to do.

> [Jamilla, age 25, single-mother—occupation:
> special needs teaching assistant]

Financial contributions from "absent"[6] spouses towards childrearing and other domestic costs in some instances provide single mothers with an alternative source of income. However, the level of financial support that the single-mothers in the study received from these men varied according to individual circumstances, and it was also largely dependent on the father's current relationship, his employment status and the level of contact he had with the mother and his children. In 1991 Children Support Agency [CSA], was set up to increase the financial contribution of "absent" fathers towards their families. However, this agency, in reality, has had little effect on these single-mothers' lives because they were reluctant to involve the CSA in their financial arrangements with the "absent" father. Instead, these single-mothers preferred to make their own private financial arrangements with these men or receive no financial support from him at all. Their reluctance to report their children's fathers to the CSA was based on the justifiable fear that societal institutions (of which the CSA is one example) pathologize and criminalize black men. Such economic constraints facing black mothers mean that even if they do support the "traditional" Western ideal of mothering—that is to remain at home with their children while their male partner assumes sole or primary responsibility for household family provision (Richardson 1993; Ribbens 1995)—these ideals take second place to the economic realities that they encounter.

Recent statistics by the Commission for Racial Equality (1997) show that black women work longer hours, and engage in higher rates of full-time employment (77 percent at a minimum thirty-five working hours per week) than white women (56 percent at a minimum thirty-five working hours). Importantly, for white women the number of women in full-time employment has more than doubled in rate over the last thirty years. Yet, for black women, their working hours have remained virtually unchanged from the late 1970s, when the figure was 74 percent (Jones 1984). There is a far greater tendency for white women with children of school age and younger to work part-time (40 percent) whereas the rate for part-time employment among black women is much lower (Dale and Holdsworth 1998). [. . .] [T]he proportion of black mothers working part-time is as low as 12 percent in London (Owen 1994). In comparable jobs across all sectors of the labour market, black women earn disproportionately less than their black male and white male and female counterparts (Bhavnani 1994). While it is true that an increasing minority of black women are entering professional and managerial occupations (5 percent), the vast majority of black women (69 percent) are positioned on the lower rungs of the occupational ladder (Modood 1997). Moreover, the jobs they are concentrated in tend to be administrative and other non-manual posts that offer lower pay and little opportunity for career (and with it salary) advancement (Bhavnani 1994). One primary outcome of black women's subordinate location in the labour market is that black women have to work longer hours (hence greater rates of full-time employment) or remain in a post for longer continuous years in order to earn similar rates of pay to other social groups.

The employment activity of black mothers and their high rates of employment suggest that paid work is a central aspect of their mothering despite the fact that unemployment is becoming an increasing phenomenon for young black women (including mothers) in Britain. In speaking to the mothers it was common for them to identify paid work and mothering practices (the emotional and physical care and nurturing of the child) as two interlocking and interdependent functions:

> **Zora:** I don't see them as separate things—I work so I can be a mother. If I didn't work, I wouldn't be able to take care of them [children] properly, or take care of their needs, so I wouldn't really be doing my job properly as a mother if I didn't go to work.
>
> [Zora, age 26, living with partner—housing officer]

> **TR**: Do you think that going out to work is an important part of being a good mother?
>
> **Joy:** Most definitely yes, it's very important to me, knowing that I'm out there working for my family.
>
> [Joy, age 39, single mother—government administrative officer]

Both of Zora's and Joy's comments implicitly convey an understanding of "good" mothering being dependent upon their ability to financially support their families through paid work. This supports similar work on black women in the USA (such as Hill Collins 1994) and Britain (Duncan and Edwards 1999) that identify the "mother/ worker" status as being "good mothering" for black women. Interestingly, such comments as expressed by Zora and Joy are in opposition to traditional Western ideologies of mothering and employment that present the two as separate, and often incompatible, gendered entities (Richardson 1993). Their perceptions of "good mothering" concerning paid work and mothering as two interlocking functions present a distinctive alternative to the idealized and normative representation of the "good mother"—the mother who remains at home to care for her children, in particular during the children's formative years (Woodward 1997). Recent debates concerning maternal employment in Britain recognize that "gendered moral rationalities" on maternal employment remain rooted in this idealized notion of "good mothering." As a consequence mothers who work full-time are perceived as "morally wrong," irrespective of whether or not they work because of economic considerations (see Duncan and Edwards 1999).

This Western idealized notion of "good mothering" has to some extent influenced black mothers' views concerning working mothers. Two of the mothers whom I interviewed openly questioned the culturally accepted practice of working mothers and they also voiced a desire to change their working practices in order that they can have more time at home with their children:

> **Melanie:** I don't know where it says that we [black women] are automatically expected to keep working all of the time. It just seems to be the done thing for black women. Given the chance I would stay at home with my baby son. Also I like the bit with my daughter coming home from school

where I could be home when she's there. So, what I would like to do is set up my own nursery. Or if it costs too much maybe I could set up a child-minding service at home. That way I'll be able to choose my own hours and have more time for them [children].

[Melanie, age 29, single-mother—inland revenue officer]

Lydia: There is that expectation and pressure that comes, more from within the black community, that as a good black mother, then you work to pro-vide for your family. However, if I could afford it then I would be at home with my family, although I would have to probably find something to fill my days. I could do some form of charity work and help other children who are sick or disabled. Or I could make things such as little arts and crafts and sell them to raise money for a charity. That would be really good.

[Lydia, age 28, single-mother—clerical officer]

Two other mothers in the study also offer retrospective accounts of their own child-hood in order to reflect upon the way in [which] their own working mothers negatively impacted on their childhood:

Melanie: When we were younger my mum was at work all the time. She used to do shifts so it just depends on if she was on early shift or late shift, but she wasn't at home from four o'clock or whatever time school finishes and you sort of notice the difference. We missed out on a lot of things be-cause our mum was always working. We didn't go anywhere. We didn't go brownies or anything. We even had to beg just to go to church (laughing).

[Melanie, age 29, single-mother—inland revenue officer]

Jamilla: Going back to my childhood, I do remember thinking I wish my mum was there to take me to school and pick me up. I went to a childmin-der, she used to take me to school. In the mornings my mum and dad used to leave for 7:30 a.m. and I used to go over there first to have breakfast, it was only when I got big that I could cater for myself. I did miss not having a mum there when I woke up in the mornings to make breakfast for me and send me off to school and be there when I got back from school. I want to have a kind of job, I don't know if it's possible, where I could be there first thing in the morning and last thing—you know drop them off at school and pick them up. I just missed that in my childhood and I want to have that for my daughter.

[Jamilla, age 25, single-mother—special needs teaching assistant]

Melanie, Lydia and Jamilla appear to speak the language of the Western "gendered moral rational" discourse concerning "good" mothering and celebrate these ideals. Indeed, the latter two accounts and, in particular, Melanie's account, also imply a "maternal deprivation model" (O'Brien 1997) of full-time working mothers. How-ever, despite the mothers' claims to want to remain at home with their children, all of them in their accounts consider the option of doing activities that would take them outside the home. Lydia, for example, speaks of a desire to do charity work. Jamilla and Melanie want employment opportunities that offer flexible working patterns. The fact that these mothers still consider the option of some form of work (either paid or charity work) suggest that these mothers do not completely reject all elements of the black cultural practice of working mothers. It also reveals the implicit tension black mothers commonly experience in balancing Western ideas [of] mothering alongside [. . .] their own cultural expectations.

Working Mothers and Childcare

Black mothers' work status produces childcare implications. In terms of the first-generation mothers who arrived in Britain during the post-war period, the occupations that they were primarily congregated in, such as nursing and manufacturing industries, were worked on a shift system. Elyse Dodgson's (1984) study of black women's family life during this period shows that the shift system of working perversely helped to facilitate these women's childcare and domestic arrangements, despite the long and unsocial hours of work that they did. Working on a shift system meant that black mothers could arrange to work different shifts [from] their partner (and others involved with childcare), leaving someone available to care for their children at different times of the day and night. The mothers were particularly forced to depend upon their own family members and their social networks because white childminders would often refuse to care for black children (Dodgson). The other forms of childcare options available to these mothers included sending for relatives, usually the women's own mother, from the Caribbean to care for the children, or alternatively sending young children back to the Caribbean to be cared for by family members (see Goulbourne and Chamberlain 1999). Black mothers who could not afford the cost of sending their children back to the Caribbean or bringing a relative to Britain depended upon their husbands to play a key role in child care. As one first-generation mother recollects:

> **Enid:** The jobs we did meant that I worked nights and my husband worked in the day. After work I would rush home to get my children's breakfast ready and then my husband would leave for work. In the afternoons we would eat together and then I would leave for work and he would care for them until the next morning when I arrived back home.
> [Enid, age 68, first-generation mother—retired nurse]

Black men's prominent position as carers remains largely undocumented, and they continue to be represented as absent or marginal from family life. The research work by Goulbourne and Chamberlain (1999) and my own research (Reynolds 2000) are some of the few attempts to re-insert black fathers into constructions of the black family.

In comparing the childcare options available to black mothers today with black mothers during these early post-migration days then on a theoretical level black mothers today have more childcare resources available to them. Thirteen mothers in the study with pre-school children or children of school age used some form of formal childcare service, such as childminders, nurseries, work crèche, after-school club and holiday play schemes.

The demand for childcare provision far outnumbers the supply in Britain (Cohen and Fraser 1991). Research findings by Burghes and Brown (1995) also indicate that the race, social class and occupational status of working mothers largely determine their access to childcare. Social class and occupational status certainly influenced the mothers' childcare choices and options in the study. Those black mothers with professional occupations and levels of high income have the easiest time with their childcare arrangements. For instance, one mother, [. . .] a Director of a mental health trust on a relatively high income employed a live-in nanny to care for her children. Another high income working mother, employed as a lawyer, has a childminder who assists in getting her children ready for school in the mornings, taking the children to and from school and caring for them at the end of the school day until the parents arrive home. Unsurprisingly, those black mothers with lower incomes had a more difficult time accessing affordable childcare provisions. Their experiences mirrored those of many low-income mothers across all ethnic and racial groups (Daycare Trust 1997). Childcare costs comprise the largest proportion of monthly expenditure for all the working single-mothers in the study. **Nizinga,** one single-mother, comments:

> At the end of the month she [daughter] is starting nursery. It's going to break my bank.

> **TR:** Can I ask you how much it will cost you?

> **Nizinga:** £347 a month but my mum is going to help me out otherwise I couldn't afford it on my own.

> [Nizinga, age 31, single-mother—university administrator]

Black grandmothers are the primary childcare source for the working mothers [on the weekend]. One reason for this is that demographically the black population in Britain is a relatively young one with 75 percent of black women under the age of sixty-five years (Owen 1997). As a result, black grandmothers are unlikely to act as primary childcare providers during the working week because they themselves are likely to be in full-time employment.

The Impact of Black Female Unemployment on Black Mothers' Work Status

Of course, not all black mothers are in full-time employment. Increasingly, high rates of unemployment, traditionally the preserve of black men is now starting to impact on young black women too. Recent CRE figures (1997) place unemployment for all minority ethnic women between the ages of 16 and 24 years at 30 percent compared with 12.5% of white women. Within this minority ethnic group of 16–24 years old, black women represent 37 percent of unemployed women.

[. . .] Sharon, a single mother of 19, and the only mother in the study who is unemployed, encountered the barrier of a lack of available free nursery places for low-income mothers in seeking employment. As a consequence she felt that it was more beneficial to remain at home and care for her own children instead of securing employment with low wages that do not adequately cover the cost of childcare.

[. . .] The current Labour government is to some extent working to redress this issue and also shift "gendered moral rationalities" for welfare dependent single-mothers towards maternal employment instead of a moral reasoning that mothers should be at home with young children (see Duncan and Edwards 1999). In 1998 the New Deal Initiative for Lone-Parents was introduced to encourage single-mothers away from welfare state dependency and towards self-sufficiency through paid employment. [. . .]

Black Mothers in the Labour Market: "Mother-ism, Racism and Sexism"

Despite black women's long work history in Britain's labour market, they have enjoyed a less than successful relationship in it (see Westwood and Bhachu 1988; Williams 1989; Lewis 1993). The intersecting factors of racism, sexism and "mother-ism" have all impacted on black mothers' relationship to work. The term "mother-ism," first introduced by Heather Joshi (1991) highlights the way in which employers discriminate against working mothers based on their mothering status and continue to remain sceptical in their attitudes towards them. The following comment by, Michele, clearly depicts the way in which "mother-ism," has combined with the racism and sexism to constrain black mothers' employment choices:

> **Michele:** I was the first black woman the firm ever took on. What made it worse was that I was a mother, a single-mother and so they made certain assumptions about me. When I first started the firm put me on three months probation. It wasn't probation to see if I could do the job, they wanted to see if I would dash home because my childcare arrangements were not sorted. I never had to leave the office because of childcare arrangements. When there was another vacancy going in our department, they got another mother. I gave them the incentive to choose somebody else who was a single-mother, another black girl, but her childcare arrangements were not sorted and she left after a period of time. Then my boss went back to, "I don't want another mother, I want somebody who hasn't got any children." [sic]
> [Michele, age 28, single-mother—legal secretary]

As the above quotation by Michele indicates traditional expectations of mothering still underpin employers' attitudes to working mothers. In many instances being a mother, in particular a single-mother with young children, can act as a significant barrier to securing employment, or inhibit promotional prospects for those mothers already in work (Joshi 1991). For black mothers (as the previous quotation illustrates) there lies the additional burden of being the "first" and "only" black woman within the organization alongside being the "first" and "only mother." The interlocking experiences of racism, sexism, and "mother-ism" encountered by working black mothers also make it difficult to determine which of these factors, are most influential affecting their employment conditions and working practices.

[. . .] Today, most black women are employed in public administration: central and local government (40 percent); and retail and distribution (22 percent) (Bhavnani 1994). Within these occupations vertical segregation exists because black women are over-represented in the lower paid and lower status posts across these employment sectors. For example, in the public administration sector, a large employer of black women, black women are disproportionately employed as junior clerical/administrative workers (69 percent) and their presence as senior managers is virtually negligible (a slight increase from 1 percent in 1982 to 4 percent in 1997) (Modood 1997).

The "glass ceiling" cuts across all sectors of the labour market to limit black women's promotion prospects and the opportunity to enter specific areas of employment (Phizacklea 1988). For those black women in professional and managerial positions the career choices and opportunities for career advancement that they face are narrowly defined. For example, an early study (Reynolds 1997) indicates that [. . .] black women predominantly secure [management posts] that have a majority of black client users.[7] Chris Ham (1991) analysis of race and gender in the National Health Service also point to the prevalence of black female senior managers in the least glamorous "Cinderella" health care services such as geriatric care and mental health. To suggest, however, black women are always marginalized or even "ghettoized" into making their employment choices denies their agency. Five of the mothers in the study that were employed in professional posts—a teacher, lawyer, social worker, academic lecturer; mental health director—identified that they actively sought out employment in predominantly "black areas" or with a high proportion of black client users. [. . .]

Conclusion

To conclude, there is evidence that black mothers' long employment history in Britain is shaped by interlocking cultural and economic factors. Historically and culturally black mothers in Britain, along with black mothers in the Caribbean and the USA, have been constructed as workers. These women possess a mother/worker status. The historical experience of slavery, colonialism and economic migration, within a British context, shows black mothers' economic labour capacity for work is a primary status.

For black mothers today a tension exists in balancing this mother/worker status against the discriminatory conditions that they face as part of their daily working lives and the desire for greater personal choice and freedom in their working practices. Within the study this has translated itself into increasing numbers of black women considering employment options that would take them out of full-time paid employment (but not necessarily situate them in the home as full-time carers). Other mothers have sought to resolve this tension by actively looking for employment opportunities that allows them to "give back" to the wider black community and act as positive role models for others. In reality economic constraints limit these options for many black mothers and they continue to work in work settings in which racism, sexism and mother-ism is an everyday aspect of paid work.

Notes

1. For the purpose of this article the term "black" refers specifically to people of African-Caribbean descent.

2. Recent figures suggest that nearly 50 percent of black men and 30 percent of black women are in mixed-raced relationships in Britain (see Berthoud, 1999). The fact the sample comprised families with exclusively male-female partnerships is indicative of the mothers' own personal networks and the sample is not meant to be representative of the population as a whole.

3. Not all theorists agree with this point. Nnaemeka (1997), for example, identifies a high work activity among black women in pre-slavery societies.

4. This includes black women's fertility and reproductive capacities. As black slave women they were positioned as "breeders" whose role was also to reproduce a future workforce (Davis 1981).

5. There was strong variation within this group varied according to individual circumstances such as level of educational attainment. Those African-Caribbean men with degrees have a far less risk of unemployment compared to those men with only a secondary school education and little or no formal qualifications. However, overall as a group the average risk of unemployment was high and those African-Caribbean men with degrees had a considerably higher risk of unemployment in comparison with white men with similar academic qualifications (Berthoud 1999).

6. The men who shared a "visiting" relationship with mothers in the study (i.e., not living within the household on a full-time basis) also come under this category.

7. A case in point being Lambeth Council, London, England who appointed the first African-Caribbean woman as Chief Executive of the borough of Lambeth which has the highest proportion of African-Caribbean people within a local population in Britain (Owen 1997).

CHAPTER 34

Families on the Frontier

FROM BRACEROS IN THE FIELDS TO
BRACERAS IN THE HOME

Pierrette Hondagneu-Sotelo

[. . .]

Gendered Labor Demand and Social Reproduction

Throughout the United States, a plethora of occupations today increasingly rely on the work performed by Latina and Asian immigrant women. Among these are jobs in downgraded manufacturing, jobs in retail, and a broad spectrum of service jobs in hotels, restaurants, hospitals, convalescent homes, office buildings, and private residences. In some cases, such as in the janitorial industry and in light manufacturing, jobs have been re-gendered and re-racialized so that jobs previously held by U.S.-born white or black men are now increasingly held by Latina immigrant women. Jobs in nursing and paid domestic work have long been regarded as "women's jobs," seen as natural outgrowths of essential notions of women as care providers. In the late twentieth-century United States, however, these jobs entered the global marketplace, and immigrant women from developing nations around the globe were increasingly represented in them. In major metropolitan centers around the country, Filipina and Indian immigrant women make up a sizable proportion of HMO nursing staffs—a result due in no small part to deliberate recruitment efforts. Caribbean, Mexican, and Central American women increasingly predominate in low-wage service jobs, including paid domestic work.

This diverse gendered labor demand is quite a departure from patterns that prevailed in the western United States only a few decades ago. The relatively dramatic transition from the explicit demand for *male* Mexican and Asian immigrant workers to demand that today includes women has its roots in a changing political economy. From the late nineteenth century until 1964, the period during which various contract-labor programs were in place, the economies of the Southwest and the West relied on primary, extractive industries. As is well-known, Mexican, Chinese, Japanese, and Filipino immigrant workers, primarily men, were recruited for jobs in agriculture, mining, and railroads. These migrant workers were recruited and incorporated in ways that mandated their long-term separation from their families of origin.

As the twentieth century turned into the twenty-first, the United States was once again a nation of immigration. This time, however, immigrant labor is not involved in primary, extractive industry. Agribusiness continues to be a financial leader in the state of California, relying primarily on Mexican immigrant labor and increasingly on indigenous workers from Mexico, but only a fraction of Mexican immigrant workers are employed in agriculture. Labor demand is now extremely heterogeneous and is structurally embedded in the economy of California (Cornelius 1998). In the current period, which some commentators have termed postindustrial, business and financial services, computer and other high-technology firms, and trade and retail prevail alongside manufacturing, construction, hotels, restaurants, and agriculture as the principal sources of demand for immigrant labor in the western United States.

As the demand for immigrant women's labor has increased, more and more Mexican and (especially) Central American women have left their families and young children behind to seek employment in the United States. Women who work in the United States in order to maintain their families in their countries of origin constitute members of new transnational families. And because these arrangements are choices that the women make in the context of very limited options, they resemble apartheid-like exclusions. These women work in one nation-state but raise their children in another. Strikingly, no formalized, temporary contract-labor program mandates these separations. Rather, this pattern is related to the contemporary arrangements of social reproduction in the United States.

Why the Expansion in Paid Domestic Work?

[. . .]

The exponential growth in paid domestic work is due in large part to the increased employment of women, especially married women with children, to the underdeveloped nature of U.S. childcare centers, and to patterns of U.S. income inequality and global inequalities. National and global trends have fueled this growing demand for paid domestic services. Increasing global competition and new communications technologies have led to work speed-ups in all sorts of jobs, and the much-bemoaned "time bind" has hit professionals and managers particularly hard (Hochschild 1997). Meanwhile, normative middle-class ideals of child rearing have been elaborated (consider the proliferation of soccer, music lessons, and tutors). At the other end of the age spectrum, greater longevity among the elderly has prompted new demands for care work.

[. . .]

Social reproduction consists of those activities that are necessary to maintain human life, daily and intergenerationally. This includes how we take care of ourselves, our children and elderly, and our homes. Social reproduction encompasses the purchasing and preparation of food, shelter, and clothing; the routine daily upkeep of these, such as cooking, cleaning, and laundering; the emotional care and support of children and adults; and the maintenance of family and community ties. The way a society organizes social reproduction has far-reaching consequences not only for individuals and families, but also for macro-historical processes (Laslett and Brenner 1989).

Many components of social reproduction have become commodified and outsourced in all kinds of new ways. Today, for example, not only can you purchase fast-food meals, but you can also purchase, through the Internet, the home delivery of customized lists of grocery items. Whereas mothers were once available to buy and wrap Christmas presents, pick up dry cleaning, shop for groceries, and wait around for the plumber, today new businesses have sprung up to meet these demands—for a fee.

[. . .]

Global Trends in Paid Domestic Work

Just as paid domestic work has expanded in the United States, so too it appears to have grown in many other postindustrial societies, in the "newly industrialized countries" of Asia, in the oil-rich nations of the Middle East, in Canada, and in parts of Europe. In paid domestic work around the globe, Caribbean, Mexican, Central American, Peruvian, Sri Lankan, Indonesian, Eastern European, and Filipina women—the latter in disproportionately large numbers—predominate. Worldwide, paid domestic work continues its long legacy as a racialized and gendered occupation, but today, divisions of nation and citizenship are increasingly salient.

The inequality of nations is a key factor in the globalization of contemporary paid domestic work. This has led to three outcomes. (1) Around the globe, paid domestic work is increasingly performed by women who leave their own nations, their communities, and often their families of origin to do the work. (2) The occupation draws not only women from the poor socioeconomic classes, but also women who hail from nations that colonialism has made much poorer than those countries where they go to do domestic work. This explains why it is not unusual to find college-educated women from the middle class working in other countries as private domestic workers. (3) Largely because of the long, uninterrupted schedules of service required, domestic workers are not allowed to migrate as members of families.

Nations that "import" domestic workers from other countries do so using vastly different methods. Some countries have developed highly regulated, government-operated, contract-labor programs that have institutionalized both the recruitment and the bonded servitude of migrant domestic workers. Canada and Hong Kong provide paradigmatic examples of this approach. Since 1981 the Canadian federal government has formally recruited thousands of women to work as live-in nannies/housekeepers for Canadian families. Most of these women came from Third World countries in the 1990s (the majority came from the Philippines, in the 1980s from the Caribbean), and once in Canada, they must remain in live-in domestic service for two years, until they obtain their landed immigrant status, the equivalent of the U.S. "green card." [. . .]

Similarly, since 1973 Hong Kong has relied on the formal recruitment of domestic workers, mostly Filipinas, to work on a full-time, live-in basis for Chinese families. Of the 150,000 foreign domestic workers in Hong Kong in 1995, 130,000 hailed from the Philippines, and smaller numbers were drawn from Thailand, Indonesia, India, Sri Lanka, and Nepal (Constable 1997, 3). [. . .] Filipina domestic workers in Hong Kong are controlled and disciplined by official employment agencies, employers, and strict government policies. Filipinas and other foreign-born domestic workers recruited to Hong Kong find themselves working primarily in live-in jobs and bound by two-year contracts that stipulate lists of job rules, regulations for bodily display and discipline (no lipstick, nail polish, or long hair; submission to pregnancy tests; etc.), task timetables, and the policing of personal privacy. Taiwan has adopted a similarly formal and restrictive government policy to regulate the incorporation of Filipina domestic workers (Lan 2000).

In this global context, the United States remains distinctive, because it takes more of a laissez-faire approach to the incorporation of immigrant women into paid domestic work. No formal government system or policy exists to legally contract foreign domestic workers in the United States. Although in the past, private employers in the United States were able to "sponsor" individual immigrant women who were working as domestics for their green cards using labor certification (sometimes these employers personally recruited them while vacationing or working in foreign countries), this route is unusual in Los Angeles today. Obtaining legal status through labor certification requires documentation that there is a shortage of labor to perform a particular, specialized occupation. In Los Angeles and in many parts of the country today, a shortage of domestic workers is increasingly difficult to prove. And it is apparently unnecessary, because the significant demand for domestic workers in the United States is largely filled not through formal channels of foreign recruitment but through informal recruitment from the growing number of Caribbean and Latina immigrant women who are *already* legally or illegally living in the United States. The Immigration and Naturalization Service, the federal agency charged with enforcement of migration laws, has historically served the interests of domestic employers and winked at the employment of undocumented immigrant women in private homes.

As we compare the hyper-regulated employment systems in Hong Kong and Canada with the more laissez-faire system for domestic work in the United States, we find that although the methods of recruitment and hiring and the roles of the state in these processes are quite different, the consequences are similar. Both systems require the incorporation as workers of migrant women who can be separated from their families.

The requirements of live-in domestic jobs, in particular, virtually mandate this. Many immigrant women who work in live-in jobs find that they must be on call during all waking hours and often throughout the night, so there is no clear line between working and nonworking hours. The line between job space and private space is similarly blurred, and rules and regulations may extend around the clock. Some employers restrict the ability of their live-in employees to receive phone calls, entertain friends, attend evening ESL classes, or see boyfriends during the workweek. Other employers do not impose these sorts of restrictions, but because their homes are located in remote hillsides, suburban enclaves, or gated communities, live-in nannies/housekeepers are effectively restricted from participating in anything resembling social life, family life of their own, or public culture.

These domestic workers—the Filipinas working in Hong Kong or Taiwan, the Caribbean women working on the East Coast, and the Central American and Mexican immigrant women working in California—constitute the new braceras. They are literally "pairs of arms," disembodied and dislocated from their families and communities of origin, and yet they are not temporary sojourners. In the section that follows, I suggest some of the dimensions of this phenomenon and present several illustrative career trajectories.

The New Braceras and Transnational Motherhood

What are the dimensions of this phenomenon that I refer to as the new braceras and the new forms of transnational motherhood? Precise figures are not available. No one has counted the universe of everyone working in private paid domestic work, which continues to be an informal sector—an "under the table" occupation. Accurately estimating the numbers in immigrant groups that include those who are poor and lack legal work authorization is always difficult. Several indicators, however, suggest that the dimensions are quite significant. My nonrandom survey of 153 Latina immigrant domestic workers, which I conducted at bus stops, at ESL evening classes, and in public parks where Latina nannies take their young charges, revealed the following. Approximately 75 percent of the Latina domestic workers had children of their own, and a startling 40 percent of the women with children had at least one of their children "back home" in their country of origin.

[. . .]

[A]n estimated 40 to 50 percent of Central American and Mexican women leave their children in their countries of origin when they migrate to the United States. They believe the separation from their children will be temporary, but physical separation may endure for long, and sometimes undetermined, periods of time. Job constraints, legal-status barriers, and perceptions of the United States as a dangerous place to raise children explain these long-term separations. [. . .]

Private domestic workers who hail primarily from Mexico, Central America, and the Caribbean hold various legal statuses. Some, for example, are legal, permanent residents or naturalized U.S. citizens, many of them beneficiaries of the Immigration Reform and Control Act's amnesty-legalization program, which was enacted in 1986. Most Central American women, who prevail in the occupation, entered the United States after the 1982 cutoff date for amnesty-legalization, so they did not qualify for legalization. Throughout the 1990s, a substantial proportion of Central Americans either remained undocumented or held a series of temporary work permits, granted to delay their return to war-ravaged countries.

Their precarious legal status as an "illegal" or "undocumented immigrant" discouraged many immigrant mothers from migrating with their children or bringing them to the United States. The ability of undocumented immigrant parents to bring children north was also complicated in the late 1990s by the militarization of the U.S.-Mexico border through the implementation of various border-control programs (such as Operation Gatekeeper). As Jacqueline Hagan and Nestor Rodriguez compellingly show, the U.S.-Mexico border has become a zone of danger, violence, and death. This not only made it difficult to migrate with children, it also made it difficult to travel back and forth to visit family members "back home." Bound by precarious legal status in the United States, which might expose them to the risk of deportation and denial of all kinds of benefits, and by the greater danger and expense in bringing children to the United States, many immigrant mothers opted not to travel with their children or send for them. Instead, they endure long separations.

Many immigrant parents of various nationalities also view the United States as a highly undesirable place to raise children. Immigrant parents fear the dangers of gangs, violence, drugs, and second-rate schools to which their children are likely to be exposed in poor, inner-city neighborhoods. They are also appalled by the way immigration often weakens generational authority. As one Salvadoran youth put it, "Here I do what I please, and no one can control me" (Menjivar 2000, 213).

Even mothers who enjoyed legal status and had successfully raised and educated their children through adolescence hesitated to bring them to this country. They saw the United States as a place where their children would suffer job discrimination and economic marginalization. As one Salvadoran domestic worker (who had raised her children on earnings predicated on her separation from them) exclaimed when I spoke with her at an employment agency: "I've been here for 19 years. I've got my legal papers and everything, but I'd have to be crazy to bring my children here. All of them have studied for a career, so why would I bring them here? To bus tables and earn minimum wage? So they won't have enough money for bus fare or food?" (Hondagneu-Sotelo and Avial 1997).

Although precarious legal status and perceptions of the United States as an undesirable place in which to raise children are important in shaping transnational family forms, the constraints of paid domestic work, particularly those that are typical in live-in work, virtually mandate family separations.

[. . .]

When I met, Carmen Velasquez, a thirty-nine year-old Mexicana, [she] was working as a live-in nanny-housekeeper, in charge of general housekeeping and the daily care of one toddler, in the hillside suburban home of an attorney and schoolteacher. Carmen, a single mother, had migrated alone to California ten years before, leaving behind her three children when they were four, five, and seven years old. Since then, she had seen them only in photographs. The children were now in their teens. She regularly sent money to the children and communicated by letters and phone calls with them and her three *comadres* (co-godmothers), who cared for one of the children each in Mexico.

Carmen had initially thought that it would be possible for her to maintain these arrangements for only a short while. She knew she could work hard and thought that working as a live-in domestic worker would enable her to save her earnings by not paying rent or room and board. But, as she somberly noted, "Sometimes your desires just aren't possible."

A series of traumatic events that included incest and domestic violence prompted her migration and had left her completely estranged from the father of her children, her parents, and her siblings. With only the support of her female comadres in Mexico, and assisted by the friend of a friend, she had come north "without papers," determined to pioneer a new life for herself and her children.

Her first two live-in jobs, in which she stayed for a total of seven years, included some of the worst arrangements I have had described to me. In both cases, she worked round-the-clock schedules in the homes of Mexican immigrant families, slept on living room couches or in hallways, and earned only $50 a week. Isolated, discouraged, and depressed, she stayed in those jobs out of desperation and lack of opportunity.

In comparison with what she had endured, she expressed relative satisfaction with her current live-in job. Her employers treated her with respect, paid $170 a week, gave her a separate bedroom and bathroom, and were not, she said, too demanding in terms of what they expected of her. Unlike the workdays of many other live-in nannies/housekeepers, her workday ended when the *señora* arrived home at 5 p.m. Still, when I asked whether she now had plans to bring her children to Los Angeles, she equivocated.

She remained vexed by the problem of how she could raise her children in Los Angeles and maintain a job at the same time. "The *señora* is kind and understanding," she said, "but she needs me here with the baby. And then how could I pay the rent, the bus fare to transport myself? And my children [voice quivering] are so big now. They can't have the same affection they once had, because they no longer know me. . . ." As psychologist Celia Jaes Falicov (2004) underscores [. . .], there are many losses incurred with migration and family reunification. Women such as Carmen sacrifice to provide a better life for their children, but in the process, they may lose family life with their children.

Some women *do* successfully bring and reintegrate their children with them in the United States, but there are often unforeseen costs and risks associated with this strategy. Erlinda Castro, a Guatemalan mother of five children, came to the United States in 1992. She left all five children behind in Guatemala, under the care of the eldest, supervised by a close neighbor, and joined her husband in Los Angeles. She initially endured live-in domestic jobs. These jobs were easy to acquire quickly, and they enabled her to save on rent. After two years, she moved into an apartment with her husband and her sister, and she moved out of live-in domestic work into housecleaning. By cleaning different houses on different days, she gained a more flexible work schedule, earning more with fewer hours of work. Eventually, she was able to send money for two of the children to come north.

The key to Erlinda's ability to bring two of her children to the United States was her shift in domestic employment from live-in work to housecleaning. According to my survey results, Latina immigrant mothers who work in live-in nanny/housekeeping jobs are the most likely to have their children back home (82 percent) than are women who work cleaning houses. And mothers who clean different houses on different days are the least likely to have their children in their countries of origin (24 percent).

Bringing children north after long periods of separation may entail unforeseen "costs of transnationalism," as Susan Gonzalez-Baker suggests. Just as migration often rearranges gender relations between spouses, so too, does migration prompt challenges to familiar generational relations between parents and offspring. In the following section, I draw some parallels between these rebellions of gender and generation.

Braceros and Their Wives, Braceras and Their Children: Rebellions of Gender and Generation

The Bracero Program, the institutionalized contract-labor program that authorized the granting of five million contracts to Mexican agricultural workers, most of them men, remained in place from 1942 to 1964. This program, like earlier contract-labor programs that recruited Mexican, Filipino, and Chinese men to work in the western and southwestern United States, incorporated men as pure workers, not as human beings enmeshed in family relationships. Mandated by formal regulations, but made possible by patriarchal family culture and male-dominated social networks, this pattern of male-selective migration remained in place for many years following the end of the Bracero Program (Hondagneu-Sotelo 1994). This pattern is still not uncommon.

In many families, however, this migration pattern prompted gender rebellion among the wives of braceros. Many wives of braceros and other Mexican immigrant men working in the United States after the end of the program sought to migrate to the United States, and many of them did so in the face of resistance from their husbands. Elsewhere, I have detailed some of these processes and have referred to this pattern as "family stage migration" (Hondagneu-Sotelo 1994). In many instances, Mexican women worked hard to persuade their husbands to help them migrate to the United States, and when this failed, many of them turned to their own social-network resources to accomplish migration. Although patriarchal practices and rules in families and social networks have persisted, labor demand has changed in ways previously outlined in this chapter, and now both women and men creatively reinterpret normative standards and manipulate the rules of gender. As they do, understandings about proper gendered behavior are reformulated, and new paths to migration are created.

Just as wives have followed their husbands north, so too are children today following their mothers to California and other states. *Los Angeles Times* investigative journalist Sonia Nazarrio told me that every year the INS captures approximately five thousand unaccompained minors traveling illegally across the U.S.-Mexico border. Because this figure does not include those who are apprehended and choose voluntary deportation within 72 hours, and those who are never apprehended, Nazarrio believes that the number of unaccompanied minors migrating to the United States from Central America and Mexico each year may be as high as forty to fifty thousand. She estimates that about half are coming to be reunited with their mothers.

In some cases, these are the children of mothers who, after having established themselves financially and occupationally, have sent money for the children's migration. These children and youths enter either accompanied by smugglers or through authorized legal entry. In other cases, these are children who have run away from their grandmothers, paid caregivers, or fathers. In both cases, the children and youths face tremendous dangers, and fatalities are not unheard of. Nazarrio reports that many of them travel north by hopping moving trains, risking life and limb as they embark and disembark, and that they are victimized, robbed, and raped by roving bandits and thugs and by delinquent gang members who are returning north after having been deported. After the 1996 immigration law imposed new restrictions on criminal aliens—even on legal immigrants falsely convicted of crimes (a common practice in Los Angeles, which was victimized by a corrupt police force in the 1990s)—many immigrants were deported. Members of tough Los Angeles street gangs, such as Mara Salvatrucha or the 18th Street Gang, have been deported to El Salvador, Guatemala, and Mexico, and they too are traveling on these northbound trains back to California. Meanwhile, children and other minors are trekking northward for the first time, in hopes of being reunited with their mothers and other family members.

What happens once these children are reunited with their mothers? A short honeymoon may occur upon reunification, but long periods of discord typically follow. Once in the United States, the children are apt to blame their mothers for the economic deprivation and the emotional uncertainty and turmoil they have experienced. They may express contempt and disrespect for their mothers. The emotional joy of reunification that they may have anticipated quickly sours when they realize their mothers are off working for hours, and they may feel betrayed when they discover that their mothers have new husbands and children. Competition with new half-siblings forms part of the backdrop through which they reintegrate. And finally, their mothers' long workdays leave them on their own for a good portion of their waking hours. In one case reported by Menjivar (2000, 209), a Salvadoran mother brought her daughter to San Francisco, only to have Child Protective Services take her daughter and deem her an unfit mother for working seventy hours a week. Many of the children and youths miss their grandmothers, or whoever was their primary caregiver during their formative years, and feel neglected and rejected by family in the United States. Many, indeed, wish to return to their homeland.

Conclusion

What do these developments mean for a twenty-first century research agenda on Latino families? Clearly, they force us to rethink monolithic understandings of Latino families, familism, and sentimentalized notions of motherhood. There are also many remaining empirical questions about the impact of these transnational processes on children and youth. How does the length of separation affect processes of adaptation? How does the age at which the children are reunited with their "bracera" mothers affect family social relations? How do these migration processes affect adolescent identity and school performance? Answering questions such as these will require incorporating children and youths into research as active agents in migration.

The trajectories described here pose an enormous challenge to those who would celebrate any and all instances of transnationalism. These migration patterns alert us to the fact that the continued privatization of social reproduction among the American professional and managerial class has broad repercussions for the social relations among new Latina immigrants and their families. Similarly, strong emotional ties between mothers and children, which we might dismiss as personal subjectivities, are fueling massive remittances to countries such as El Salvador and the Philippines. Our most fundamental question remains unanswered: Who will continue to pick up the cost of raising the next generation? Surely, we can hope for a society wherein Latina immigrant women and children are not the first to bear those costs.

CHAPTER 35

More Alike than Different

REVISITING THE LONG-TERM PROSPECTS FOR
DEVELOPING "EUROPEAN-STYLE" WORK/FAMILY
POLICIES IN THE UNITED STATES

Janet C. Gornick and Marcia K. Meyers

[...]

Balancing Parenthood and Employment: Common Problems, Divergent Solutions

Working parents in the United States and Europe face a number of similar challenges. One of the most pressing is the need for adequate time for both employment and caregiving. In the U.S. and in each of the eight major European welfare states that we studied—Denmark. Finland, Norway, Sweden, Belgium, France, Germany and the Netherlands—a large proportion of parents are balancing time in the labor market with child caregiving. As of the middle-to-late 1990s, in the U.S. and in each of these European countries, over 90 percent of married/cohabiting fathers and at least half of all mothers worked for pay. In Belgium and France, as in the U.S., about two-thirds of mothers were employed; in the Nordic countries, between 75 and 85 percent of mothers worked outside the home. While American dual-earner couples spent the longest hours (jointly) working for pay—on average, 80 hours a week—employed couples in these European countries, with the exception of the Netherlands, spent about 70 or more hours each week in employment (authors' calculations, based on Luxembourg Income Study data). With most parents in the labor market, often for long hours, families in all of these countries face the questions of "who will care for the children?" and "at what cost?" in terms of income and career advancement.

Parents on both continents are also grappling with divisions of labor within the family. As in the U.S., issues of gender equality in paid work and caregiving are also prominent in European gender politics and research. This is especially evident in the Nordic countries and in the Netherlands. Divisions of labor command attention partly because substantial gender differentials persist in labor market attachment; mothers still earn much less than half of family earnings in all of these European countries as well as in the United States. Married/cohabiting mothers take home just over a third of family earnings in the Nordic countries, and between a quarter and a third in Belgium, France, and in the U.S.—and even less in Germany and in the Netherlands (authors' calculations, based on Luxembourg Income Study data). And while men are now assuming a larger share of unpaid care work in the home—largely because women's hours of unpaid work have declined in recent years—gender inequalities in unpaid caregiving work remain substantial in all of these countries (Gornick and Meyers 2003).

European and American parents clearly have shared challenges. Everywhere, parents need time for caregiving. Parents in all of these countries grapple with where to place their children during hours that parental care is not available. They face potentially high financial costs whether they take temporary caregiving breaks from employment or purchase substitute care. And parents in all of these countries have complex decisions to make when allocating paid and unpaid work between partners.

Despite the commonality of problems, solutions in the U.S. could hardly be more different than those in place in much of Europe. Although there is variability across these European welfare states, each of them has established public programs that support employed parents—programs that are almost entirely absent in the United States.

With regard to family leave, all eight of these European welfare states have national-level public policies mandating access to various forms of leave. All grant mothers job protection and wage replacement around the time of childbirth and during children's first year of life; all grant fathers leave rights through paternity or parental leave schemes, usually with pay; all grant temporary periods of paid leave—or "leave for family reasons"—that allow brief breaks to respond to routine or unexpected caregiving demands (see Gornick and Meyers 2003 for details). In sharp contrast to the situation in Europe, the U.S. has enacted no national law that grants any paid leave to parents[1] and only five states pay any maternity benefits (as part of temporary disability insurance).[2] Outside the five states with disability laws in place, American parents have access to paid leave to the extent that their employers voluntarily provide it. As of the mid-1990s, only 43 percent of American women who were employed during their pregnancies received any paid leave during and after childbirth through either public provisions or voluntarily provided employer benefits—including maternity pay, sick pay, and/or vacation pay (Smith et al. 2001). A recent survey of personnel managers revealed that only about 7 percent of employers offer fathers paid paternity leave (Office of Personnel Management 2001).

Parents in Europe and the U.S. also experience extremely different institutional arrangements for child care and early education. As with family leave, there is variability across Europe but in each of these eight welfare states, young children across the income spectrum are cared for in extensive systems of publicly supported ECEC [Early Childhood Education Care]. In the U.S., only about 6 percent of children aged one and two are cared for in publicly financed and regulated child care programs, compared to one-fifth of children in this age group in France and Finland, over a third in Norway, nearly half in Sweden and about three-quarters in Denmark. In the U.S. just over half of children aged three to five are in public preschool programs (and most of these are five-year-olds in kindergarten), compared to 70 percent or more in the countries in our study. In these European countries, families' access to care, especially for children over age three, is usually guaranteed through legal entitlements. The quality of care is assured through national standards and high levels of required training, and commensurate compensation, for providers. Public financing spreads the costs of care to both reduce the burden on individual families and to equalize out-of-pocket expenditures across families at different income levels. In these countries, parents of the "under threes" generally pay according to sliding scales; preschool programs for children aged three and older typically charge no fees at all (see Gornick and Meyers 2003 for details).

On nearly every dimension, the current patchwork in the U.S. of highly privatized ECEC arrangements and multiple federal, state, and local policies lags behind the major European welfare states. American parents' access to ECEC depends largely on their private resources and on what local private markets produce. Despite recent expansions of means-tested child care subsidies, and of pre-kindergarten programs in some states, only a fraction of low-income families receive child care assistance. Both high- and low-income families often incur high costs when purchasing private care, and these costs are particularly burdensome for the lowest-income families if they do not receive subsidies. Despite high private costs, quality is uneven, due to weak public oversight and the minimal educational preparation of ECEC workers. The costs and uncertain quality of child care in the U.S. have troublesome implications for children, who may experience less than optimal or even neglectful care. And the pressure to minimize costs has produced a large, highly feminized, and poorly paid child care workforce.

European Family Policy: Models for the U.S.?

[. . .] [I]f resources are measured by tax revenues as a share of GDP, they are substantially higher in most European countries; compare the European Union (EU) average of 42 percent to approximately 30 percent in the U.S. (OECD 2003a). However, per capita GDP is higher in the U.S. than in most European countries—in 2002, approximately U.S. $36,000 compared to the EU average of U.S. $26,000. The absence of a substantial package of work/family reconciliation policies in the U.S. is a problem of political will, not one of insufficient resources. All of these countries are among the richest in the world.

Revisiting the Accepted Wisdom

[. . .]

"AMERICANS PREFER MARKET SOLUTIONS TO GOVERNMENT PROVISIONS"

American political culture is universally characterized as individualist, meaning that Americans tend to believe in the capacity of unfettered free enterprise to achieve social goals.

That individualism is combined with a weak orientation—compared with Europeans—toward hierarchy, where hierarchists value order, security, and predictability, and thus tend to trust established powers, including public bureaucracies. American political culture also values equality but—consonant with the anti-statist individualism—American egalitarian goals embrace equality of opportunity rather than of outcome (see Kingdon 1999 for a synthesis of literature on this point). The crucial claims, for our purposes, are that while Americans value the idea of equal opportunity, they prefer that the distribution of social welfare be left to labor markets and consumer markets.

American skepticism, in the view of the authors, is both cause and consequence of a century of limited policy effort and anti-statist public rhetoric; this does appear to be at odds with a major expansion of social policy. At the same time, there are reasons to believe that American political culture would not be hostile to European models for work/family policy. A careful assessment of American attitudes and welfare state exceptionalism suggests that both are more accurately characterized by incompleteness and selectivity than by overall meagerness. Americans find some public programs to be especially objectionable, in particular, "welfare" programs for the non-employed poor (see, for example, Page and Shapiro 1992, Gilens 1999). Not surprisingly, this is the area in which the U.S. provides remarkably little by comparative standards. Yet other public programs have historically received strong support from the American public and provisions are generous when compared to those in the major European welfare states. Lockhart (1991) identifies the two most salient examples: "[T]he United States spends a relatively high proportion of GNP on public education, and American social security provisions for the elderly (OASI and HI) are similar to the provision made by most advanced societies. So the United States shares aspects of well-developed social policy with other advanced welfare states" (515).

[...]

When asked directly, the majority of U.S. parents are more alike than different from parents in other industrialized countries in their support for specific policies. According to data from the 1994 International Social Survey Programme (ISSP), as many as 85 percent of American parents in working families believe that employed women should receive paid maternity leave, close to the 90 to 98 percent who express similar views in our comparison countries. Sixty-three percent of U.S. parents also believe that working parents should get financial benefits for child care, a share that is similar to that in most of our comparison countries in Europe (authors' calculations, based on ISSP data). [...] Large majorities support paid family leave and they want it to be publicly financed (National Parenting Association 1998, Zero to Three 2000); Americans also express support for government assistance with child care (Lake Sosin Snell Perry 1998; Wall Street Journal/NBC 1998) and after-school programs (Mott Foundation 1998).

"THE UNITED STATES IS TOO DIVERSE TO SUPPORT UNIVERSAL POLICIES"

Many critics argue that other transatlantic political differences are simply too great to allow fruitful policy transfer to the U.S. from most of Europe. It is often said that the extent of racial, ethnic and national diversity is the most important difference between the U.S. and other wealthy countries. Indeed, the U.S. population is remarkably diverse; nearly 10 percent of U.S. residents were not born in the country and just over one quarter are African-American, Hispanic, Asian/Pacific Islander, and/or Native American. Some identify this as a fundamental barrier in the U.S. to policy development along European lines, arguing that the generosity of the European welfare states is possible only because the populations in these countries are so homogeneous.

[. . .]

Although formidable, there are also compelling reasons to believe that these cleavages are not an insurmountable barrier to lesson-drawing on work/family policies. American social policy history itself provides some encouragement as it indicates that it is possible to mobilize broad support for redistributive policies, especially for policies outside the public assistance rubric. As we noted earlier, social insurance for the elderly is the most striking example of the political resiliency of redistributive policy. Social security pensions for the elderly have become more inclusive over time and the redistributive structure of benefits has survived years of heated debate and efforts to restructure and privatize the basic provisions.

The European experience provides further encouragement. Although generous social welfare provisions in Europe are often credited to the homogeneity of the population, a number of European countries have levels of immigration that are similar to or even higher than the level in the United States. In most of the countries in this study, between about 5 and 9 percent of residents are foreign, rates approaching the 10 percent of the population who are foreign-born which has been reported in the United States (OECD 2001a).[3] Nearly all European countries face complex ethnic and linguistic diversity, but this diversity has not prevented them from maintaining inclusive social programs that serve legal immigrants, and racial and ethnic minorities. Rather than dividing the population, the extension of social rights to all residents is intended to promote inclusion.

Universal preschool programs are particularly notable in this regard. A survey by the Organization for Economic Cooperation and Development (OECD: 2001b) of public ECEC policies in Europe notes, for example, that several of the countries covered in this study—including Belgium, Denmark, Finland, the Netherlands, Norway, and Sweden—have adopted policies explicitly aimed at "increasing access to early childhood services for immigrant and ethnic minority groups in order to expose children and families to the language and traditions of mainstream society, and provide opportunities for parents to establish social contacts and networks" (25). Some American observers have reported with amusement that the *école maternelle* provides children with lessons on French culture, including distinctions among French cheeses. But these lessons reflect, in part, the commitment to extend preschool to all children in France in order to promote social solidarity. And nearly all immigrant parents choose to enroll their children.

Immigration is growing all across Europe (OECD 2001a). Both large and small welfare states are grappling with the arrival of even greater numbers of immigrants, refugees, asylum seekers, and economic migrants. As populations are becoming more heterogeneous, there are signs of political strain and polarization along ethnic and nativity lines. These strains are most evident in the rise of anti-immigrant and other explicitly racist political movements in many of the European democracies. To date, however, this political polarization has not translated into either wholesale or selective reductions in social benefits in these countries. All of the countries studied in this article continue to provide generous social benefits and continue to provide them inclusively. While some European countries have trimmed some social programs—most notably old age pensions, unemployment insurance, and disability pensions—these restructurings have not had the effect of exacerbating racial, ethnic or class divides via social policies. The basic structures and functions of the social welfare states remain strong in the face of growing population diversity, in part because their inclusive structures create broad political support.

"AMERICAN PARENTS WANT MORE 'FREEDOM OF CHOICE'"

Skeptics about lesson-drawing often point to another dimension on which the U.S. appears exceptional: the salience of individual choice. In cross-national terms, Americans do appear to be remarkably concerned about the protection of individual choice and freedom from government interference. Critics often suggest that the highly centralized and standardized policy approaches of Europe would be a mismatch for a society in which individuals expect to exercise choice in the consumption of everything from athletic shoes to their children's education.

In the area of family policy, these concerns are often related to the issues of diversity considered above. While it is all well and good for French children to attend the same preschool program and learn about national cheeses, some argue, American parents want to be free to choose the type of care that their children receive. In *The Advancing Nanny State*, Darcy Olsen (1997), of the conservative Cato Institute, warns that the creativity of private and community solutions "should not be replaced with a set of rigid standards, which run roughshod over the individual needs of parents and children. As parents know, every child has unique needs that cannot be met by a uniform code" (1997).

Americans are justifiably sensitive about their right to preserve their own beliefs and cultural practices and this sensitivity is particularly acute on family issues. But families within diverse societies share common challenges and dilemmas. Problems of balancing work and family are often portrayed as the concern of high-achieving, two-career families. In reality, the time squeeze on parents, the difficulty of finding high-quality child care, and the social and economic penalties that women incur by assuming the majority of child caregiving, are not unique to affluent or poor, white or black, native-born or immigrant, gay or straight families. They cut across the lines of class, race, ethnicity, and sexual preference. Mishel, Bernstein and Schmidt (2001), for example, find that African-American married couples work longer hours than their white counterparts within every income quintile, while Gornick and Meyers (2003) report that gender differences in parental caregiving are nearly the same at all educational levels and in all income quartiles.

Successful policies that would help reduce these challenges can be broadly inclusive, without violating the rights of families and communities to determine the precise shape of policy provisions. Casting European-style social policies as inconsistent with these goals is misleading for at least two reasons.

First, although the policies we have described are generally national in terms of authorizing legislation and financing, they are flexible enough to allow individuals and communities to tailor them to their own preferences. In the case of family leave, for example, parents in most of the Nordic countries have a nationally established and financed entitlement to a set period of leave. They have enormous flexibility, however, in scheduling their use of that leave. Parents may elect to use all their benefits within the first months after childbirth, or they may stretch their leave out over a period of several years, combining part-time employment with part-time leave. In some countries, such as Finland, they may even elect to take their benefits in the form of leave or subsidized child care. [. . .]

A second and more compelling reason to question the claim that European systems provide less choice is the reality that the "choices" of many American parents are profoundly constrained by economic and other circumstances. In many respects, U.S. parents have, *fewer* choices than their European counterparts because minimal and fragmented social provisions do not extend parental choice so much as they force parents to choose among undesirable alternatives. The lack of paid family leave and subsidized child care forces difficult choices for many families. In the absence of mandated leave provisions, most parents face the choice of returning to work 12 weeks after childbirth or quitting their jobs. In the absence of affordable child care, they are compelled to choose between reducing their working hours to care for their own children or lowering their effective earnings by purchasing substitute child care (see Gornick and Meyers 2003 for a detailed discussion of constraints on American parents' choices).

"AMERICANS WOULD NEVER BE WILLING TO PAY FOR THESE BENEFITS"

Perhaps the common objection to European-style family policy is the price tag. Skeptics of lesson-drawing often argue that Americans would simply be unwilling to tax themselves at the levels necessary to provide comprehensive, universal social provisions. Americans prefer private solutions, in part, because they distrust redistributive government programs. The challenge of mobilizing support for new taxes to assist working families would be considerable. But public financing for education provides an encouraging precedent in terms of both the magnitude of expenditures and the political feasibility of public financing.

It is true that the tax burden in the U.S. is lighter than in the countries that have been compared in this study. In the U.S., total tax receipts account for 30 percent of GDP, compared to 54 percent in Sweden, 45 to 49 percent in Belgium, Denmark, Finland, and France, and 38 to 41 percent in Germany, the Netherlands, and Norway. Americans pay less in taxes than their counterparts in much of Europe, and the current political climate suggests that policies that cut taxes resonate with Americans, whatever the fiscal consequences.

It is also true that comprehensive family leave and ECEC would require substantial public outlays. But the outlay is less than might be expected. Even the highest-providing countries in this study devote a surprisingly small share of their GDPs to these programs. Sweden, with arguably the most extensive benefits, spends about 2.5 percent of its GDP on family leave and ECEC; Denmark and Finland each spend just under 2 percent of GDP; France, with somewhat less extensive leave benefits, spends about 1.3 percent.[4] The U.S. currently spends about one-tenth of these amounts: approximately 0.2 percent of its GDP on publicly financed child care and a negligible amount on publicly paid leave.

Americans are generally reluctant to increase their tax burden. But would Americans be willing to tax themselves to provide these specific public benefits? As noted above, there is considerable evidence that Americans want government to do more in the areas of family leave and ECEC. And Americans have shown themselves willing to contribute to social insurance programs and to pay taxes for another form of support to children and families: public education. Although the U.S. is a laggard in many areas of social welfare spending, it was one of the early leaders in extending public education to all children. The U.S. continues to invest heavily in the education of its children, spending about 3.4 percent of GDP on primary and secondary public education (OECD 2002).

Relative to what the U.S. currently spends on public education, what would it cost to extend the generous Swedish package of family leaves and ECEC to families with younger children in the U.S.? If the package of benefits cost the same amount in real per capita dollars in the U.S., providing generous family leaves would require about 0.4 percent of GDP; extending ECEC to the levels of provision in Sweden would translate into another approximately 1.0 percent of GDP (assuming the 0.2 percent already spent in the U.S.). Together, these benefits would require an investment that is equivalent to 1.7 percent of the U.S. GDP; that is about one-half of what is currently committed to public primary and secondary education as a share of GDP.[5]

[. . .]

"THESE POLICIES HAVE NEGATIVE EFFECTS ON FAMILY STRUCTURE"

European-style policies that provide assistance specifically to families with children raise questions, in the minds of many, about unintended effects on fertility and family formation. In the European context, these questions arise from concerns about *declining* fertility and the possibility that work/family policies are actually contributing to falling birthrates—if, say, many wives are choosing employment now rather than bearing two or three children because paid work has become so attractive. In the U.S. context, the concern is different; critics suggest that generous social welfare policies could *increase* fertility and non-marriage, particularly among non-employed mothers.

The European debate about family formation has been motivated largely by the problem of declining fertility. In most of the European countries, as in nearly all high-income countries, rising childlessness and shrinking family size have pushed the total fertility rate (TFR)[6] below the replacement level of 2.1 births per woman. While fertility remains relatively near replacement level (1 .7 or higher) in a number of European countries—including Denmark. Finland, France, and Norway—in others, the TFR has dropped to below 1.5. Particularly worrisome cases include Germany, where the TFR is 1.3, and Italy, where it has fallen to 1.2 (U.S. Bureau of the Census 2002). If current patterns are not reversed, countries with very low fertility will face serious social, economic, and cultural dislocations in the future.

These trends have prompted some observers to argue that policies such as those described here may have contributed to the destabilization of the European family by pushing and/or pulling women into the labor market and away from childbearing. In fact, contemporary variation within Europe suggests that if work/family reconciliation policies have behavioral effects, the[y] are likely to operate in the direction of increasing fertility. The Australian demographer Peter McDonald (2000a, b) argues that two distinct fertility scenarios are possible in countries that provide women with substantial opportunities in both education and labor market entry. In countries where it is feasible to blend employment and childbearing, without major losses in labor market status and earnings, many women will choose both paid work and parenting. In countries where it is (more) difficult to combine motherhood and employment, because of conservative family cultures combined with weak social policies, large numbers of women will forgo childbearing. Although other factors are influential as well, these predictions are consistent with variation across the European countries. Countries with the most generous work/family programs and highest levels of female employment—including the Nordic countries and France—are among those experiencing the least decline in fertility; fertility crises are most severe in countries with less fully developed work/family policies.[7]

While it is tempting to draw a causal inference, this finding is correlational. [. . .] Although there is limited evidence that European family policies have had either a positive or negative effect on fertility, these policies have often been framed in pronatalist terms in European policy debates. Although pronatalism is only one of several motivations for European family policy, that pronatalism raises particularly grave concerns about policy-borrowing in the minds of some American observers. While Europeans have worried that generous social programs may contribute to a decline in fertility, many Americans have been preoccupied by the possibility that these same programs could raise fertility among certain vulnerable populations. In the U.S., where rates of single parenthood are already exceptionally high, many of the most vocal critics of social policy aimed at families with children have argued that any generous social benefits available to single parents create incentives for (or at least increase the economic feasibility of) non-marital childbearing. While some worry about high-income single parents, the most pressing concerns are raised about single women with no ties, or limited ties, to paid work.

Although the employment disincentives of cash assistance programs are well established, particularly for mothers, the empirical evidence linking social policies to non-marital childbearing is at best inconsistent (for reviews, see Moffitt 1990, Acs 1995, Peters et al. 2001). Policy effects, where they have been found, appear to operate through choices about marriage and living arrangements rather than through choices about childbearing. Significantly, virtually all of this research has examined the effects of cash assistance for the non-employed and, more recently, of child support enforcement. And it has concentrated on women with very weak ties to the labor market.

These studies suggest no persuasive theoretical reason, or empirical evidence, to suggest that the policies that we consider here—family leave and ECEC—would increase childbearing among single women who are not attached to employment. The extent to which supportive work/family policies would contribute to the formation of single-parent households in the U.S. remains unknown. Work/family policies could make single parenthood more economically feasible. It is equally possible, however, that these policies—by extending support to married as well as single parents and by extending benefits equally to mothers and to fathers—would increase the attractiveness of marital childbearing and create new incentives for fathers to remain connected to their children.

[. . .]

Conclusion: The Prospects for Family Policy Lesson-Drawing in the U.S.

[. . .]

In his recent work, *America the Unusual*, political scientist John Kingdon is openly optimistic about the prospects for American social policy reform in the near term:

> The United States, like many other countries, is facing a set of new problems that may overwhelm our customary ways of thinking about the proper role of government and may prompt us to think in new directions. . . . As we continue the process of increasing global interdependence, we may find that we will not necessarily be forced to make a stark choice between American-style relatively unfettered capitalism and European-style social programs and economic interventions. . . . A happy medium may be possible if we are willing to consider pragmatically, in the light of experience, what works and what does not. (1999, 96–100)

In the U.S., that "happy medium" could be a policy package of paid family leave and early childhood education and care modeled after the most progressive of the European countries. Explicit lesson-drawing about work/family policies in Europe might advance policy development in the United States while avoiding the "pretensions of meta-policy models" that, as DeLeon and Resnick-Terry (1998) caution, undermined earlier generations of lesson-drawing efforts.

Notes

1. U.S. national law grants workers in establishments with 50 or more employees 12 weeks a year of *unpaid* leave.

2. Since 2002, one state. California, pays partial wage replacement for six weeks to eligible fathers.

3. The U.S. generally counts "foreign-born," as opposed to "foreign," as all persons born in the U.S. are granted citizenship. European countries generally count the "foreign," which includes both foreign-born and those born in the country but not naturalized.

4. These cost estimates are based on expenditures reported in Gornick and Meyers (2003). Across these countries, total ECEC expenditures are generally three to five times higher than family leave expenditures.

5. We calculated this as follows. We converted Swedish per capita spending on leave and ECEC into U.S. dollars (adjusting for differences in purchasing parity). We multiplied per capita spending by the total U.S. population to arrive at estimated total spending and then converted that to a share of U.S. GDP. That is equivalent to estimating these expenditures as the share of GDP that they capture in Sweden (2.5 percent) and adjusting that 2.5 percent downward to account for the differences in GDP per capita—that is, multiplying 2.5 by (Sweden's per capita GDP/U.S.'s per capita GDP). In fact, the two methods produce exactly the same result: these programs would cost about 1.7 percent of U.S. GDP.

6. The total fertility rate (TFR) is defined as the average number of births each woman would have if she were to live through her reproductive years and bear children at each age at the rates observed in the current period (OECD 2001a).

7. Whereas in 1980 total fertility rates and women's employment rates were negatively correlated across the OECD countries, that cross-sectional relationship changed over time. By the late 1990s there was a positive correlation between fertility and women's employment (Sleebos 2003).

Microcredit: Creating Economic Opportunity and Independence Among Impoverished Women in LDCs (© International Labour Organization)

Part IX

A SAMPLE OF POLICY ALTERNATIVES

While there are many policies that address inequalities in the gendered global economy, Part IX of this volume puts forward two perspectives: 1) the "individualist" and 2) the "structural." The former perspective suggests that inequality can be transformed by modifying individual behaviors through reward and punishment in public policy. The structural perspective suggests, in contrast, that inequality can be eradicated only through change in broader economic, social, and political institutions.

The "individualist" perspective is put forward by Nobel Peace Prize winner Muhammad Yunus, an economist and the founder of the Grameen Bank of Bangladesh. In his piece, entitled "The Stool Makers of Jobra Village," Yunus describes his concept of "microcredit," lending small sums, of less than one hundred dollars, to poor rural women belonging to "loan circles" in less-developed countries (LDCs). The loan recipients are primarily involved in small-scale, informal-sector entrepreneurship or piecework, making and selling baskets, stools, clothes, and rugs, farming fish, raising cattle, or assembling toys and electronic components. Each individual is required to repay her own loan. If she defaults, the entire loan circle is held liable or becomes ineligible for future loans. The Grameen Bank claims a 95 percent rate of repayment of loans.

Critics argue that this neoliberal, individualist solution to female poverty may help a few but cannot overhaul the massive poverty in LDCs, caused by the structural constraints of globalization, where indigenous peoples have lost their land rights, essential services have been privatized, and cutbacks have taken place in health, education, and welfare—all of which engender and reproduce poverty among women in developing countries. Critics maintain that the weakness of microcredit is its focus on transforming the individual behaviors of the disenfranchised, rather than on the broader structural conditions that have created their disenfranchisement. The behavior modifications advocated by the individualist perspective include strengthening the work ethic, obtaining an education, limiting the number of births, and taking personal responsibility for one's status. Improving these individual behaviors should be rewarded by the market, according to this perspective. This may prove difficult as long as some microlenders reap huge profits off of the poor, sometimes charging 25 to 50 percent annual interest rates (Feiner and Barker 2006).

Despite such criticism, a World Bank report states that ten years of microlending to the poorest of the poor in Bangladesh has significantly improved the lives of over six million individuals, empowering women in particular, as they gain greater control over their resources, decision-making power, and access to participation in public life. Journalist Sheryl Nance Nash reports that microfinance currently involves about ten thousand lenders and fifty million borrowers around the world (Nash 2005). Ninety percent of the borrowers are women; and of these, 99 percent report increased incomes of over 15 percent, an increased supply of food and clothing, and better housing, with 88 percent able to send their children to school. Fifty-five percent now own land (World Bank 2007).

Martha Nussbaum advocates a structural solution to decreasing gendered inequality in the global workplace. In "Women's Education: A Global Challenge," she argues that the institution of education must be overhauled and made available to the world's girls and women; economic growth is not enough. She proposes intervention by well-known international development organizations to eradicate local and national corruption in less-developed countries, focusing in part on the elites that have pilfered state funds allocated to schools. In addition, she advocates abolishing school fees imposed upon the poor, necessitated by the "structural adjustments" required of debtor nations by the World Bank and the International Monetary Fund. Additionally, she argues that international development agencies must work to end the institutions of the dowry and child marriage, both of which act to prohibit the education of females.

Nussbaum decries the gross gender inequality in literacy rates around the world: male literacy rates surpass female literacy rates by 15 percent or more in one-quarter of the world's countries. Some of the countries with the worst female literacy rates are Pakistan at 30 percent, Nepal at 22.8 percent, Bangladesh at 29.3 percent, Senegal at 26.7 percent, and Niger at 7.9 percent. Such illiteracy condemns women to limited, unskilled employment options, rendering them perpetually dependent on others for their economic survival. This leaves illiterate women and female children vulnerable in both the market and the family. Illiterate females lack bargaining power due to their inability to make substantial financial contributions to the family, placing them at risk for denied access to food and medical care. Nussbaum claims that literacy would empower women economically, politically, and socially by enabling them to gain access to adequate work, credit, and the legal system, and to accrue knowledge of their rights. Further, the greater the level of literacy, the fewer births poor women have, enhancing their financial well-being and that of their children.

Nussbaum acknowledges that the system of gendered illiteracy is perpetuated by poor families themselves, who educate their boys first when given the choice, due to greater employment opportunities for males. Thus she argues for policies that will enable mandatory universal education to flourish, in order to stop the cycle of gender inequality. Literacy will allow women and girls to realize their personal economic and human potential, enhancing the economic development and political stability of entire regions.

Another structural solution to gender, race, and ethnic inequality in the workplace and society as a whole is the policy of affirmative action. Shannon Harper and Barbara Reskin's article, "Affirmative Action at School and on the Job," details how the American program of affirmative action was initially established in schools to rectify the gross racial inequality in the United States and was later amended to include women. This program was designed to promote the aggressive integration of racial, gender, and ethnic groups (protected classes) that had historically been excluded from access to the social, political, and economic institutions of mainstream society. Although a source of controversy, as well as success, in the United States and around the world, affirmative action programs have been introduced in countries as varied as India and Britain, the former Soviet Union and China, as well as Nigeria, Malaysia, New Zealand, Pakistan, and Sri Lanka among others (Sowell 2005).

In 1964 the United States Congress passed the Civil Rights Act to end discrimination against individuals in employment, public accommodation, voting, housing, education, and other facets of society, in response to the organized unrest of the Civil Rights movement. Shortly thereafter, President Lyndon Johnson issued Executive Order 11246, known as affirmative action, requiring federal contractors to take aggressive, preemptive "affirmative actions" to ensure that qualified applicants from the protected classes are recruited, educated, employed, and promoted.

Arguments for affirmative action programs are based on three general principles: compensatory justice, distributive justice, and social utility. Compensatory justice suggests that affirmative action is necessary to compensate members of protected classes for past injustices. Distributive justice advocates proportional representation of protected classes throughout all strata of society. Social utility purports that enhancing the education, employment, and participation of members of the protected classes benefits society as a whole, increasing the number of taxpayers, professional and political leaders, thinkers, and contributors to overall community well-being. Arguments against affirmative action are based on the principle of reverse discrimination, the underlying premise being that white males are unfairly discriminated against by the policy of affirmative action.

Currently, women workers remain clustered in a narrow range of lower-paid, lower-status jobs in the United States and around the world. Although the number of female politicians, firefighters, police officers, construction workers, and college presidents has increased substantially in the United States since the 1970s, in the year 2000 women still comprised only 3 percent of firefighters, 8 percent of state and local police officers, 1.9 percent of construction workers, 11.8 percent of college presidents, and 3–5 percent of senior position holders in major corporations in the United States. In private industry, 65 percent of American officials and managers were white men, while 24.8 percent were white women, 6.5 percent were minority men, and 3.8 percent were minority women (Feminist Majority Foundation 2000).

Despite the persistence of inequality in the workplace, reverse discrimination reared its head in a controversial 2009 discrimination lawsuit, the firefighters' case *Ricci v. DeStefano* in New Haven, Connecticut. The city of New Haven decided to change its promotion procedures for firefighters and instituted a written exam for promotions in 2003, instead of using the criteria of demonstrated leadership ability or experience. Of the forty-one applicants who took the exam for captain, eight were black; of the seventy-seven applicants who took the exam for lieutenant, nineteen were black. None of the African Americans scored high enough on the written exam to be promoted, and only two of the Hispanics did.

The city of New Haven withdrew the exam, based on its "disparate impact": it affected one racial group differently from another. This triggered a cry of reverse discrimination from white firefighters who had done well on the exam. These firefighters sued the city of New Haven, and the court ruled in favor of the city. The case went to appeal, and the Court of Appeals for the Second Circuit refused to reverse the original district court judge's ruling that the exam had a disparate impact. The case then went all the way to the Supreme Court, which overturned the Second Circuit's ruling in a 5–4 decision, declaring that to ignore the exam violated Title VII of the Civil Rights Act of 1964. Clearly, the struggle for affirmative action in the American workplace is far from over.

The last structural solution to gender inequality that Part IX addresses is the "dual earner/dual carer" approach to the problem working mothers face: the double shift—spending thirty extra days per year on child and household work after their paid workday (Hochschild 1989). Janet Gornick and Marcia Meyers explain in "Support for Working Families" that by 2001 almost 85 percent of American mothers who worked prior to the birth of their first child returned to work before their child's first birthday. Despite an increase in mother's labor market participation rates over the past four decades, mothers continue to work a double shift: in 1998 they spent approximately the same amount of time with their children as mothers did in 1965. However, they spend less time on sleep, housework, and leisure activities. This begs the question, what is the best way to insure gender equality for working mothers?

One solution to the gendered problem of the "double shift" is the "universal breadwinner" perspective, which suggests that the state should facilitate women's role in the workplace by providing for working mothers' needs, such as ensuring quality public child care. Alternatively, the "caregiver parity" view suggests that working women must be granted remuneration, as well as time for caregiving at home, through generous maternity pay and other benefits. Gornick and Meyers argue that the weakness of these two approaches is that they assume maternal caregiving only and don't address paternal caregiving. The authors call for a "gender-neutral" approach, in which the state supports both mothers and fathers in their market and caregiving roles, what Rosemary Crompton calls the "dual earner/dual carer" perspective.

Such an approach has been adopted by many European welfare states, as discussed in the previous chapter, most generously in Scandinavia. In Norway either parent can take fifty-two weeks of family leave with 80 percent of their wages replaced after the birth or adoption of a child. In Sweden parents can share a full year of leave with nearly complete wage replacement and three additional months of leave at a lower rate of pay. Swedish parents can also opt for a reduced workweek of six-hour days at a lower rate of pay until their youngest child is eight years old, to accommodate the child's school schedule. One-third to one-half of children under three are in some form of publicly sponsored full-day day care in Sweden and Denmark, and approximately 82 percent of those between the ages three and five are as well. These child-care services are funded by national, state, and regional governments.

Although fathers in the European welfare states use only 10 percent of their allotted paid parental-leave time, rendering a gender imbalance in the system, Gornick and Meyers argue this must change to achieve gender parity. The private sphere of care and the public sphere of work are interrelated. As long as women predominate in the former arena, men will benefit from the latter. The authors argue societies must attain gender integration within each sphere to achieve overall equality.

The policy proposals discussed in this chapter offer only a small sampling of ways to rectify the unequal gendered conditions of work in the global economy. These readings are intended to trigger debate and the construction of new solutions to the continued and ever-changing gendered inequality in the workplace.

CHAPTER 36

The Stool Makers of Jobra Village

Muhammad Yunus

In 1976, I began visiting the poorest households in Jobra to see if I could help them directly in any way. There were three parts to the village: a Muslim, a Hindu, and a Buddhist section. When I visited the Buddhist section, I would often take one of my students, Dipal Chandra Barua, a native of the Buddhist section, along with me. Otherwise, a colleague, Professor H. I. Latifee, would usually accompany me. He knew most of the families and had a natural talent for making villagers feel at ease.

One day as Latifee and I were making our rounds in Jobra, we stopped at a run-down house with crumbling mud walls and a low thatched roof pocked with holes. We made our way through a crowd of scavenging chickens and beds of vegetables to the front of the house. A woman squatted on the dirt floor of the verandah, a half-finished bamboo stool gripped between her knees. Her fingers moved quickly, plaiting the stubborn strands of cane. She was totally absorbed in her work.

On hearing Latifee's call of greeting, she dropped her bamboo, sprang to her feet, and scurried into the house.

"Don't be frightened," Latifee called out. "We are not strangers. We teach up at the university. We are neighbors. We want to ask you a few questions, that is all."

Reassured by Latifee's gentle manner, she answered in a low voice, "There is nobody home." She meant there was no male at home. In Bangladesh, women are not supposed to talk to men who are not close relatives.

Children were running around naked in the yard. Neighbors peered out at us from their windows, wondering what we were doing.

In the Muslim sections of Jobra, we often had to talk to women through bamboo walls or curtains. The custom of *purdah* (literally, "curtain" or "veil") kept married Muslim women in a state of virtual seclusion from the outside world. It was strictly observed in Chittagong District.

As I am a native Chittagonian and speak the local dialect, I would try to gain the confidence of Muslim women by chatting. Complimenting a mother on her baby was a natural way to put her at ease. I now picked up one of the naked children beside me, but he started to cry and rushed over to his mother. She let him climb into her arms.

"How many children do you have?" Latifee asked her.

"Three."

"He is very beautiful, this one," I said.

Slightly reassured, the mother came to the doorway, holding her baby. She was in her early twenties, thin, with dark skin and black eyes. She wore a red sari and had the tired eyes of a woman who labored every day from morning to night.

"What is your name?" I asked.

"Sufiya Begum."

"How old are you?"

"Twenty-one."

I did not use a pen and notepad, for that would have scared her off. Later, I only allowed my students to take notes on return visits.

"Do you own this bamboo?" I asked.

"Yes."

"How do you get it?"

"I buy it."

"How much does the bamboo cost you?"

"Five taka." At the time, this was about twenty-two cents.

"Do you have five taka?"

"No, I borrow it from the *paikars*."

"The middlemen? What is your arrangement with them?"

"I must sell my bamboo stools back to them at the end of the day as repayment for my loan."

"How much do you sell a stool for?"

"Five taka and fifty poysha."

"So you make fifty poysha profit?"

She nodded. That came to a profit of just two cents.

"And could you borrow the cash from the moneylender and buy your own raw material?"

"Yes, but the moneylender would demand a lot. People who deal with them only get poorer."

"How much does the moneylender charge?"

"It depends. Sometimes he charges 10 percent per week. But I have one neighbor who is paying 10 percent per day."

"And that is all you earn from making these beautiful bamboo stools, fifty poysha?"

"Yes."

Sufiya did not want to waste any more time talking. I watched as she set to work again, her small brown hands plaiting the strands of bamboo as they had every day for months and years on end. This was her livelihood. She squatted barefoot on the hard mud. Her fingers were callused, her nails black with grime.

How would her children break the cycle of poverty she had started? How could they go to school when the income Sufiya earned was barely enough to feed her, let alone shelter her family and clothe them properly? It seemed hopeless to imagine that her babies would one day escape this misery.

Sufiya Begum earned two cents a day. It was this knowledge that shocked me. In my university courses, I theorized about sums in the millions of dollars, but here before my eyes the problems of life and death were posed in terms of pennies. Something was wrong. Why did my university courses not reflect the reality of Sufiya's life? I was angry, angry at myself, angry at my economics department and the thousands of intelligent professors who had not tried to address this problem and solve it. It seemed to me the existing economic system made it absolutely certain that Sufiya's income would be kept perpetually at such a low level that she would never save a penny and would never invest in expanding her economic base. Her children were condemned to live a life of penury, of hand-to-mouth survival, just as she had lived it before them, and as her parents did before her. I had never heard of anyone suffering for the lack of *twenty-two cents*. It seemed impossible to me, preposterous. Should I reach into my pocket and hand Sufiya the pittance she needed for capital? That would be so simple, so easy. I resisted the urge to give Sufiya the money she needed. She was not asking for charity. And giving one person twenty-two cents was not addressing the problem on any permanent basis.

Latifee and I drove back up the hill to my house. We took a stroll around my garden in the late-afternoon heat. I was trying to see Sufiya's problem from her point of view. She suffered because the cost of the bamboo was five taka. She did not have the cash necessary to buy her raw materials. As a result, she could survive only in a tight cycle—borrowing from the trader and selling back to him. Her life was a form of bonded labor, or slavery. The trader made certain that he paid Sufiya a price that barely covered the cost of the materials and was just enough to keep her alive. She could not break free of her exploitative relationship with him. To survive, she needed to keep working through the trader.

Usurious rates have become so standardized and socially acceptable in Third World countries that the borrower rarely realizes how oppressive a contract is. Exploitation comes in many guises. In rural Bangladesh, one *maund* (approximately 37 kilograms) of husked rice borrowed at the beginning of the planting season has to be repaid with two *maunds* at harvest time. When land is used as security, it is placed at the disposal of the creditor, who enjoys ownership rights over it until the total amount is repaid. In many cases, a formal document such as a *bawnanama* establishes the right of the creditor. According to the *bawnanama*, the creditor usually refuses to accept any partial payment of the loan. After the expiration of a certain period, it also allows the creditor to "buy" the land at a predetermined "price." Another form of security is the *dadan* system, in which traders advance loans against standing crops for purchase of the crops at predetermined prices that are below the market rate. Sufiya Begum was producing her bamboo stools under a *dadan* arrangement with a *paikar*.

In Bangladesh, the borrowing is sometimes made for specific and temporary purposes (to marry off a daughter, to bribe an official, to fight a court case), but sometimes it is necessary for physical survival—to purchase food or medication or to meet some emergency situation. In such cases, it is extremely difficult for the borrower to extricate himself or herself from the burden of the loan. Usually the borrower will have to borrow again just to repay the prior loan and will ultimately wind up in a cycle of poverty like Sufiya. It seemed to me that Sufiya's status as a bonded slave would only change if she could find that five taka for her bamboo. Credit could bring her that money. She could then sell her products in a free market and charge the full retail price to the consumer. She just needed twenty-two cents.

The next day I called in Maimuna Begum, a university student who collected data for me, and asked her to help me make a list of people in Jobra, like Sufiya, who were dependent on traders. Within one week, we had a list prepared. It named forty-two people, who borrowed a total of 856 taka—less than 27 dollars.

"My God, my God. All this misery in all these families all for of the lack of twenty-seven dollars!" I exclaimed.

Maimuna stood there without saying a word. We were both sickened by the reality of it all.

My mind would not let this problem lie. I wanted to help these forty-two able-bodied, hard-working people. I kept going around and around the problem, like a dog worrying a bone. People like Sufiya were poor not because they were stupid or lazy. They worked all day long, doing complex physical tasks. They were poor because the financial institutions in the country did not help them widen their economic base. No formal financial structure was available to cater to the credit needs of the poor. This credit market, by default of the formal institutions, had been taken over by the local moneylenders. It was an efficient vehicle; it created a heavy rush of one-way traffic on the road to poverty. But if I could just lend the Jobra villagers the twenty-seven dollars, they could sell their products to anyone. They would then get the highest possible return for their labor and would not be limited by the usurious practices of the traders and moneylenders.

It was all so easy. I handed Maimuna the twenty-seven dollars and told her, "Here, lend this money to the forty-two villagers on our list. They can repay the traders what they owe them and sell their products at a good price."

"When should they repay you?" she asked.

"Whenever they can," I said. "Whenever it is advantageous for them to sell their products. They don't have to pay any interest. I am not in the money business."

Maimuna left, puzzled by this turn of events.

Usually when my head touches the pillow, I fall asleep within seconds, but that night sleep would not come. I lay in bed feeling ashamed that I was part of a society that could not provide twenty-seven dollars to forty-two skilled persons to make a living for themselves. It struck me that what I had done was drastically insufficient. If others needed capital, they could hardly chase down the head of an economics department. My response had been ad hoc and emotional. Now I needed to create an institutional answer that these people could rely on. What was required was an institution that would lend to those who had nothing. I decided to approach the local bank manager and request that his bank lend money to the poor. It seemed so simple, so straightforward. I fell asleep.

The next morning I climbed into my white Volkswagen beetle and drove to my local branch of the Janata Bank, a government bank and one of the largest in the country. Janata's university branch is located just beyond the gates of the campus on a stretch of road lined with tiny stores, stalls, and restaurants where local villagers sell students everything from betel nuts to warm meals, notebooks, and pens. It is here that the rickshaw drivers congregate when they are not ferrying students from their dormitories to their classrooms. The bank itself is housed in a single square room. Its two front windows are covered with bars and the walls are painted a dingy dark green. The room is filled with wooden tables and chairs. The manager, sitting in the back to the left, waved me over.

"What can I do for you, sir?"

The office boy brought us tea and cookies. I explained why I had come. "The last time I borrowed from you was to finance the Three Share Program in Jobra village. Now I have a new proposal. I want you to lend money to the poor people in Jobra. The amount involved is very small. I have already done it myself. I have lent twenty-seven dollars to forty-two people. There will be many more poor people who will need money. They need this money to carry on their work, to buy raw materials and supplies."

"What kind of materials?" The bank officer looked puzzled, as if this were some sort of new game whose rules he was not familiar with. He let me speak out of common respect for a university head, but he was clearly confused.

"Well, some make bamboo stools. Others weave mats or drive rickshaws. If they borrow money from a bank at commercial rates, they will be able to sell their products on the open market and make a decent profit that would allow them to live better lives. As it is now, they work as slaves and will never manage to get themselves out from under the heel of the wholesalers who lend them capital at usurious rates."

"Yes, I know about *mahajons* [moneylenders]," the manager replied.

"So I have come here today because I would like to ask you to lend money to these villagers."

The bank manager's jaw fell open, and he started to laugh. "I can't do that!"

"Why not?" I asked.

"Well," he sputtered, not knowing where to begin with his list of objections. "For one thing, the small amounts you say these villagers need to borrow will not even cover the cost of all the loan documents they would have to fill out. The bank is not going to waste its time on such a pittance."

"Why not?" I said. "To the poor this money is crucial for survival."

"These people are illiterate," he replied. "They cannot even fill out our loan forms."

"In Bangladesh, where 75 percent of the people do not read and write, filling out a form is a ridiculous requirement."

"Every single bank in the country has that rule."

"Well, that says something about our banks then, doesn't it?"

"Even when a person brings money and wants to put it in the bank, we ask him or her to write down how much she or he is putting in."

"Why?"

"What do you mean, 'Why?'"

"Well, why can't a bank just take money and issue a receipt saying, 'Received such and such amount of money from such and such a person?' Why can't the banker do it? Why must the depositors do it?"

"Well, how would you run a bank without people reading and writing?"

"Simple, the bank just issues a receipt for the amount of cash that the bank receives."

"What if the person wants to withdraw money?"

"I don't know . . . there must be a simple way. The borrower comes back with his or her deposit receipt, presents it to the cashier, and the cashier gives back the money. Whatever accounting the bank does is the bank's business."

The manager shook his head but did not answer this, as if he did not know where to begin.

"It seems to me your banking system is designed to be anti-illiterate," I countered.

Now the branch manager seemed irritated. "Professor, banking is not as simple as you think," he said.

"Maybe so, but I am also sure that banking is not as complicated as you make it out to be."

"Look, the simple truth is that a borrower at any other bank in any place in the world would have to fill out forms."

"Okay," I said, bowing to the obvious. "If I can get some of my student volunteers to fill out the forms for the villagers, that should not be a problem."

"But you don't understand, we simply cannot lend to the destitute," said the branch manager.

"Why not?" I was trying to be polite. Our conversation had something surreal about it. The branch manager had a smile on his face as if to say he understood that I was pulling his leg. This whole interview was humorous, absurd really.

"They don't have any collateral," said the branch manager, expecting that this would put an end to our discussion.

"Why do you need collateral as long as you get the money back? That is what you really want, isn't it?"

"Yes, we want our money back," explained the manager. "But at the same time we need collateral. That is our guarantee."

"To me, it doesn't make sense. The poorest of the poor work twelve hours a day. They need to sell and earn income to eat. They have every reason to pay you back, just to take another loan and live another day! That is the best security you can have—their life."

The manager shook his head. "You are an idealist, Professor. You live with books and theories."

"But if you are certain that the money will be repaid, why do you need collateral?"

"That is our bank rule."

"So only those who have collateral can borrow?"

"Yes."

"It's a silly rule. It means only the rich can borrow."

"I don't make the rules, the bank does."

"Well, I think the rules should be changed."

"Anyway, we do not lend out money here."

"You don't?"

"No, we only take deposits from the faculty members and from the university."

"But don't banks make money by extending loans?"

"Only the head office makes loans. We are here to collect deposits from the university and its employees. Our loan to your Three Share Farm was an exception approved by our head office."

"You mean to say that if I came here and asked to borrow money, you would not lend it to me?"

"That is right." He laughed. It was evident the manager had not had such an entertaining afternoon in a long time.

"So when we teach in our classes that banks make loans to borrowers, that is a lie?"

"Well, you would have to go through the head office for a loan, and I don't know what they would do."

"Sounds like I need to talk to officials higher up."

"Yes, that would be a good idea."

As I finished my tea and got ready to leave, the branch manager said, "I know you'll not give up. But from what I know about banking, I can tell you for sure that this plan of yours will never take off."

A couple of days later, I arranged a meeting with Mr. R. A. Howladar, the regional manager of the Janata Bank, in his office in Chittagong. We had very much a repeat of the conversation I had with the Jobra branch manager, but Howladar did bring up the idea of a guarantor, a well-to-do person in the village who would be willing to act on behalf of the borrower. With the backing of a guarantor, the bank might consider granting a loan without collateral.

I considered the idea. It had obvious merit, but the drawbacks seemed insurmountable.

"I can't do that," I explained to Howladar. "What would prevent the guarantor from taking advantage of the person whose loan he was guaranteeing? He could end up a tyrant. He could end up treating that borrower as a slave."

There was a silence. It had become clear from my discussions with bankers in the past few days that I was not up against the Janata Bank per se but against the banking system in general.

"Why don't I become guarantor?" I asked.

"You?"

"Yes, can you accept me as guarantor for all the loans?"

The regional manager smiled. "How much money are you talking about?"

To give myself a margin of error and room to expand, I answered, "Altogether probably 10,000 taka ($300), not more than that."

"Well," he fingered the papers on his desk. Behind him I could see a dusty stack of folders in old bindings. Lining the walls were piles of similar pale blue binders, rising in teetering stacks to the windows. The overhead fan created a breeze that played with the files. On his desk, the papers were in a state of permanent fluttering, awaiting his decision.

"Well," he said. "I would say we would be willing to accept you as guarantor up to that amount, but don't ask for more money."

"It's a deal."

We shook hands. Then something occurred to me. "But if one of the borrowers does not repay, I will not step in to honor the defaulted loan."

The regional manager looked up at me uneasily, not certain why I was being so difficult.

"As guarantor, we could force you to pay."

"What would you do?"

"We could start legal proceedings against you."

"Fine. I would like that."

He looked at me as if I were crazy. That was just what I wanted. I felt angry. I wanted to cause some panic in this unjust, archaic system. I wanted to be the stick in the wheels that would finally stop this infernal machine. I was a guarantor, maybe, but I would not guarantee.

"Professor Yunus, you know very well we would never sue a department head who has personally guaranteed the loan of a beggar. The bad publicity alone would offset any money we might recover from you. Anyway, the loan is such a pittance it would not even pay for the legal fees, much less our administrative costs of recovering the money."

"Well, you are a bank, you must do your own cost-benefit analysis. But I will not pay if there is any default."

"You are making things difficult for me, Professor Yunus."

"I am sorry, but the bank is making things difficult for a lot of people—especially those who have nothing."

"I am trying to help, Professor."

"I understand. It is not you but banking rules I have a quarrel with."

After more such back and forth, Howladar concluded, "I will recommend your loan to the head office in Dhaka, and we will see what they say."

"But I thought you as regional officer had the authority to conclude this matter?"

"Yes, but this is far too unorthodox for me to approve. Authorization will have to come from the top."

It took six months of writing back and forth to get the loan formalized. Finally, in December 1976, I succeeded in taking out a loan from the Janata Bank and giving it to the poor of Jobra. All through 1977, I had to sign each and every loan request. Even when I was on a trip in Europe or the United States, the bank would cable or write to me for a signature rather than deal with any of the real borrowers in the village. I was the guarantor and as far as the bank officials were concerned I was the only one that counted. They did not want to deal with the poor who used their capital. And I made sure that the real borrowers, the ones I call the "banking untouchables," never had to suffer the indignity and demeaning harassment of actually going to a bank.

That was the beginning of it all. I never intended to become a moneylender. I had no intention of lending money to anyone. All I really wanted was to solve an immediate problem. Out of sheer frustration, I had questioned the most basic banking premise of collateral. I did not know if I was right. I had no idea what I was getting myself into. I was walking blind and learning as I went along. My work became a struggle to show that the financial untouchables are actually touchable, even huggable. To my great surprise, the repayment of loans by people who borrow without collateral has proven to be much better than those whose borrowings are secured by assets. Indeed, more than 98 percent of our loans are repaid. The poor know that this credit is their only opportunity to break out of poverty. They do not have any cushion whatsoever to fall back on. If they fall afoul of this one loan, they will have lost their one and only chance to get out of the rut.

CHAPTER 37

Women's Education: A Global Challenge

Martha C. Nussbaum

She mixes the cowdung with her fingers. It is gooey, smelly; she deftly mixes it with hay; and some bran; then she tries to stand up on the slippery floor of the cowshed and skids; slowly she regains her balance, goes outside with her basket and deftly pats cowdung cakes on the walls, on tree-trunks. . . . When dry her mother uses them for cooking. . . . She does a myriad other kaleidoscopic activities. The economy would not survive without her—at least not the economy of the poor: the girl child.

While she is doing all this what is her brother doing? Studying and getting his books ready for school.

The girl child thus remains outside education.

—Viji Srinivasan, director of Adithi (Patna, Bihar, India),
in its monthly newsletter

The right to education flows directly from the right to life and is related to the dignity of the individual.

—*Supreme Court of India, Unnikrishnan*
J.P. v. State of Andhra Pradesh[1]

It is late afternoon in the Sithamarhi district of rural Bihar, in northeastern India. Bihar is an especially anarchic state, with a corrupt government, a problematic infrastructure, and few services for the poor. Roads are so bad that even a Jeep cannot go more than twenty miles per hour; thus it has taken us two days to go what must be a relatively short distance from the capital city of Patna to this area near the Nepalese border. We arrive to find little in the way of public education but a lot of activity provided by a local branch of the Patna-based nongovernmental organization (NGO) Adithi, founded and run by Viji Srinivasan, whose dynamic organization is one of the most influential advocates for women's education in this difficult region.[2]

The girls of the village, goatherds by day, are starting school. They come together in a shed, all ages, to attend the Adithi literacy program. In some regions of India, most notably Kerala, the state government has been highly effective in promoting literacy for both boys and girls. Here in Bihar, the state government, run from jail by demagogue Laloo Prasad Yadav, fails to deliver essential services to the poor, so most education for the rural poor is pieced together in this way.[3] Viji and I sit on the ground to watch the class, which, like the one-room schoolhouses I read about as a child in stories of the American West, covers all levels and subjects at once, with about fifteen students. Somehow, it all seems to work, through the resourcefulness and responsiveness of the teachers, themselves poor rural women who have been assisted by Adithi's programs.

Viji, who has worked in women's development for almost forty years, began to run Adithi in 1988. It currently helps more than twenty-five thousand women and children in rural Bihar. After the math and the reading comes drama: the girls proudly present for Viji and me a play that they have improvised and recently performed for their entire village, about a young man who refuses to demand a dowry when he marries. (Dowry is a major cause of women's poor life chances in India, both because it defines a girl child as a drag on family resources and because it can later be used as the occasion for extortionate demands for more, frequently involving domestic violence and even murder.) The girls play all the roles; one big tough girl, whose six-foot stature gives surprising evidence of good nutrition, takes special pleasure in acting the young man's villainous father, greedy for dowry. (This area of rural Bihar has a female-male ratio of 75 to 100, giving strong indication of unequal nutrition and health care; girls in school do better because their families expect that they may bring in an income.) At last, young love and good sense triumph: the couple get married and go their own way, and no money changes hands. Even the groom's parents say that this way is better. The girls giggle with pleasure at the subversive thing they have cooked up. One little girl, too young for the play, sits by the window, her hair lit up by the setting sun. On her slate she draws a large and improbable flower. "Isn't she wonderful?" Viji whispers with evident zest.

[. . .]

Women's education is both crucial and contested. A key to the amelioration of many distinct problems in women's lives, it is spreading, but it is also under threat, both from custom and traditional hierarchies of power and from the sheer inability of states and nations to take effective action.

[. . .]

Education and Women's Capabilities

Despite a constant focus on women's education as a priority in global discussions of human rights and quality of life, and in the efforts of activists of all sorts and many governments, women still lag well behind men in many countries of the world, even at the level of basic literacy. In many countries, male and female literacy rates are similar. These include virtually all the countries that the *Human Development Report, 2001 (HDR)* of the United Nations Development Programme identifies as countries of "high human development," because most of these nations have close to 100 percent literacy, at least as measured by data supplied by the countries themselves (UNDP 2001).[4] But relative male-female equality can also be found in many poorer nations, such as Trinidad and Tobago, Panama, Russia, Belarus, Romania, Thailand, Colombia, Venezuela, Jamaica,[5] Sri Lanka, Paraguay, Ecuador, the Dominican Republic, South Africa, Guyana, Vietnam, Botswana, and Lesotho.[6]

There are, however, forty-three countries in which male literacy rates are higher than the female rate by fifteen percentage points or more. Since the *HDR* lists 162 nations, this means more than one-fourth of the nations in the world. These nations include India, Syria, Turkey, Pakistan, Nepal, Bangladesh, Nigeria, Sudan, and in general most, though not all, of the poorer nations of Africa.[7] (China's gap is 14.5 percent, so it barely avoids being part of the group of 43.) In absolute terms, women's literacy rates are below 50 percent in India, Bangladesh, Pakistan, Nepal, Egypt, and the preponderant number of the nations listed in the "low human development" category.[8] Some of the lowest rates are Pakistan at 30 percent, Nepal at 22.8 percent, Bangladesh at 29.3 percent, Yemen at 23.9 percent, Senegal at 26.7 percent, Gambia at 28.5 percent, Guinea-Bissau at 18.3 percent, Burkina Faso at 13.3 percent, and Niger at 7.9 percent.

If we now turn to secondary education, the gaps are even more striking. Moreover, as is not generally the case with basic literacy, the gaps are actually growing: in twenty-seven countries the secondary school enrollment of girls declined between 1985 and 1997. And this happened, as the *HDR* stresses, during a time of rapid technological development, in which skills became ever more important as passports to economic opportunity (UNDP 2001, 15). Finally, although data on university enrollments of women are not presented in the *HDR*, it is evident that, in many nations, women form a small fraction of the university population.

Why should we think that this matters deeply? Is not all this emphasis on literacy an elite value, possibly not relevant to the lives that poor working people are trying to lead? Approximately in January 1988, Rajiv Gandhi came to Harvard to deliver a large public lecture about the achievements of his administration. Questioned by some Indian students about why he had done so little to raise literacy rates, he replied, "The common people have a wisdom that would only be tarnished by literacy." Why was this answer so ill received by the Indians in the audience, and (more importantly) why was it a bad answer?

First of all, let us get rid once and for all of the idea that literacy is a value that is peculiarly "Western." Women all over the world are struggling to attain it, and some of the biggest success stories in the area of literacy are non-Western stories. Kerala, for example, raised literacy rates to virtually 100 percent for both boys and girls—by virtue of intense government concern, creative school designing, and other things that I shall later discuss. That is a staggering achievement given Kerala's poverty, and it is supported with joy and energy by girls and women.

We can add that most women in developed countries do not have to struggle to become literate: it is foisted upon them. So we do not really know how deeply we value it, or whether we could, in fact, fight for it, the way women in India and other developing countries do every day, often at risk to safety and even life. But perhaps we can see even more clearly why literacy is not a parochial value if we begin to ponder the connections between literacy and other capabilities for which women are striving all over the world.

If there was a time when illiteracy was not a barrier to employment, that time has passed. The nature of the world economy is such that illiteracy condemns a woman (or man) to a small number of low-skilled types of employment. With limited employment opportunities, a woman is also limited in her options to leave a bad or abusive marriage. If a woman can get work outside the home, she can stand on her own. If she is illiterate, she will either remain in an abusive marriage for lack of options, or she may leave and have nothing to fall back on. (Many sex workers end up in sex work for precisely this reason.) While in the family, an illiterate woman has a low bargaining position for basic resources such as food and medical care because her exit options are so poor and her perceived contribution to the success of the family unit is low.[9] Where women have decent employment options outside the home, the sex ratio tends to reflect a higher valuation of the worth of female life.

Literacy is, of course, not the only key factor in improving women's bargaining position: training in other marketable skills is also valuable, though literacy is more flexible. Property rights that give women access to credit and programs that give them credit even in the absence of real property are also highly significant.[10]

Because literacy is connected in general with the ability to move outside the home and to stand on one's own outside of it, it is also connected to the ability of women to meet and collaborate with other women. Women may, of course, form local face-to-face networks of solidarity, and they ubiquitously do. But to participate in a larger movement for political change, women need to be able to communicate through mail, e-mail, and so forth.

More generally; literacy very much enhances women's access to the political process. We can see this very clearly in the history of the *panchayats*, or local village councils, in India. In 1992, India adopted the seventy-second and seventy-third amendments to the Constitution, giving women a mandatory 33 percent reservation in the *panchayats*.[11] (Elections take place by rotation: in each cycle, a given seat is designated as a woman's seat, and the woman's seat shifts from cycle to cycle.) This move, of course, had intrinsic significance. Increasing women's literacy by itself would not have produced anything like a 33 percent result, as we can see from the United States, where women still hold only 13 percent of the seats in Congress. But in order for this result to be truly effective, making women dignified and independent equals of males, literacy has to enter the picture. According to extensive studies of the *panchayat* system by Niraja Jayal and Nirmala Buch, women are persistently mocked and devalued in the *panchayats* if they are illiterate. (Jayal and Buch note that illiterate men do not suffer similar disabilities.)[12] Women often campaign as stand-ins for husbands who can no longer hold their seats—and their independence is greater if they are literate, able thus to have greater independent access to information and communications. As a woman seeks to contest a non-reserved seat (sometimes running against her own husband), her chances are clearly enhanced if she can move as a fully independent actor in society, with access to communications from memos to national newspapers.[13] Literacy is crucial in this transition. Buch finds that one of the biggest changes brought about by the new system is a greater demand on the part of women for the education of their daughters—so that they can take their place as equals in the new system. While this finding shows us that we should not push for literacy in isolation from other values such as political participation—for here it is the fact of greater participation that drives the demand for literacy, not the reverse—it does show us that the two are allies.

[. . .]

Literacy is crucial, too, for women's access to the legal system. Even to bring a charge against someone who has raped you, you have to file a complaint.[14] If your father or husband is not helping you out and some legal NGO does not take on your case, you are nowhere if you cannot read and write—and, indeed, more than that. For you need an education that includes basic knowledge of the political and legal process in your own nation. Many NGOs in India spend a lot of time helping uneducated women bring their complaints, and individual educated women often do this as a kind of voluntary public service. But obviously enough, more such work could be done if more people could do it!

These concrete factors suggest some less tangible connections. Literacy (and education in general) is very much connected to women's ability to form social relationships on a basis of equality with others and to achieve the important social good of self-respect. It is important, as well, to mobility (through access to jobs and the political process), to health and life (through the connection to bodily integrity and exit options)—in short, to more or less all of the "capabilities" that I have argued for as central political entitlement.[15]

Especially important is the role that female education has been shown to have in controlling population growth. No single factor has a larger impact on the birth rate: for as women learn to inform themselves about the world they also increasingly take charge of decisions affecting their own lives. And as their bargaining position in the family improves through their marketable skills, their views are more likely to prevail.[16]

[. . .]

Thinking about the intrinsic value of basic education makes us see that what should be promoted—and what good activists typically promote—is not mere rote use of skills; it is an inquiring habit of mind and a cultivation of the inner space of the imagination. The girls in Bihar did not just drill on their sums and write letters on their slates. They gave plays, sang, and told stories. They used imagination to address their predicament, and this use of the imagination was woven into the entire educational process. This is typical of the approach of good NGOs in this area—unless entrenched social forces block their efforts. One day in January 2000, I went with activist Sarda Jain to visit a girls' literacy project in rural Rajasthan, several hours from Jaipur. This is the region of India in which child marriage (illegal) is the most common. Large groups of girls are married off at ages four or six. Although they do not live with their husbands until age twelve or so, their course in life is set. Their parents must keep them indoors or watch over them constantly to guard their purity, so that they can not really play outside like little boys. In addition, the parents know that these girls will not support them in their old age—they already "belong" to another family. So their development and health are typically neglected. The program I was visiting, run by an NGO called Vishaka, gives basic literacy and skills training to girls between the ages of six and twelve, that is, before they go to live with their husbands and while they are doing either domestic work or goatherding.[17] On this particular day, the girls from many different villages were coming together for testing in a large group. Sarda said to me, "I don't want to see the sums on their slates. I want to see the look in their eyes." The girls duly appeared—all dolled up in their women's finery, unable to move freely, faces partly covered. The expected presence of strangers had made their parents costume them so as to assume their role as wives. They were physically unable to dance. Sarda was profoundly disappointed, for she interpreted the demeanor and appearance of the girls as a sign that all their training was merely skin deep and would not survive in their new lives as married women, as an inner shaping of their mental world.

My argument about the role of education in developing central human capabilities in no sense implies that, without education, women do not have selves worthy of respect or basic human dignity. We may acknowledge that the absence of education involves a blighting of human powers without at all denying that the person who has been so blighted retains a basic core of human equality that grounds normative claims of justice. Indeed, in the capabilities approach it is precisely the presence of human dignity that gives rise to a claim that core human capacities should be developed, as an urgent issue of justice. Thinking about how to reconcile the recognition of dignity with the recognition that life's accidents can deform and deeply mar human powers is a very difficult matter, one that political philosophy has not yet resolved in a fully satisfactory way.[18] But it does seem clear that we can respect basic human capacities (what I elsewhere call "basic capabilities") without denying that the failure to support them (by nutrition, health care, education, etc.) can blight them in a serious way, by denying them a full development that is essential to the person's ability to live a life worthy of human dignity. The uneducated woman is likely to be a woman whose human powers of mind have been seriously underdeveloped, in just the way that the starving and powerless workers whom Marx describes in the *Economic and Philosophical Manuscripts* ([1844] 1982) are cut off from the fully human use of their faculties.

[. . .]

Resistance to Women's Education

If all this is so, why should women's education encounter any resistance at all? Why should not the whole world agree that it is an urgent priority? Of course, at this point we encounter resistance of an obvious sort from entrenched custom and power. I have stressed that women's education is revolutionary; it is a key to many other sources of power and opportunity. It is therefore not at all surprising that people who resist extending these other sources of power and opportunity to women typically oppose women's education, or at least its extension. Sometimes this opposition takes an extreme form, as it did in Afghanistan under the Taliban. Often, it takes a less extreme form, but it is real enough.[19]

[. . .]

Sometimes, however, resistance comes from sheer economic necessity. Thus, many individual parents who have no objection to educating girls and boys on a basis of equality may be able to afford to educate only one of their children (in the sense that they will need to keep some at home to do the housework or send some out to do unpaid work such as herding or even wage work). In many cultural circumstances, existing employment opportunities dictate that the one educated must be a boy because his overall employment opportunities are greater and education is a necessary passport to these.[20] So the neglect of female education may be a matter of survival for parents in many parts of the world. This sort of resistance must be addressed, and I shall get to that point in my next section.

[. . .]

Solving the Problem

The worldwide crisis of female education has multiple dimensions. In part, it is a problem of poverty and cannot be stably solved without raising the living standard of the poor in each nation. In part, the data indicate, it is a separate problem, whose solution requires special, focused action. Action aimed at raising the education level of women and girls has, in turn, several distinct elements. Both nations and states within nations must get involved, and rich nations must support the efforts of poorer nations.

To see the importance of intelligent state action, we need only consider the case of Kerala, frequently discussed in the development literature.[21] A relatively poor state in India, it has nonetheless achieved 99 percent literacy for both boys and girls in adolescent age groups. Several factors play a role here. The history of matrilineal property transmission and matrilocal residence makes female life take on, from the start, a greater worth in the eyes of parents than it seems to have in many parts of the nation. Thus, while the sex ratio in the nation as a whole is plummeting, as a result of access to sex-selective abortion, and has now reached the alarming figure of 85 women to 100 men, the sex ratio in Kerala is 102 women to 100 men, just what demographers say one should expect if equal nutrition and health care are present. Education for women, moreover, is a tradition with a long history in Kerala. In the seventeenth century, Jesuit missionaries began campaigning for literacy for both boys and girls, and this influence had an important effect.

But these historical factors are only a part of the story. For much of its history since independence, Kerala has had a democratically elected Marxist government that successfully pursued an ambitious plan of land reform, crucial to the empowerment of the poor, and that has pushed hard for both health services and education. Some of the techniques the government has used to increase literacy—besides aggressive campaigning in every region—are the provision of a nutritious school lunch for children, which offsets much of the lost income for parents who depend on child labor, and flexible school hours, which allow working children and children who help their parents in the home to enroll in school.

There is no reason in principle why these excellent ideas cannot be followed elsewhere. (Indeed, a Supreme Court decision late in 2002 has now ordered all states to adopt Kerala's program of providing a nutritious school lunch, and there is evidence that this directive is being implemented.) All too often, what happens is that local officials are corrupt and take the education money without establishing schools or teachers are corrupt and take government money without showing up.

National governments are also a large part of the solution. Sen and Dréze show dramatically how India and China diverged after India's independence. The two nations had similar literacy rates in 1947; fifty-five years later, China has 76.3 percent adult literacy for women and 91.7 percent for men, by contrast to India's 45.4 percent and 68.4 percent.[22] Another useful contrast is Sri Lanka, a nation geographically and ethnically close to India, which by now has achieved adult literacy rates of 89.0 percent for women and 94.4 percent for men. Clearly one of the key failures of Nehru's plan for the new nation was an insufficient emphasis on basic education. This fact is now generally recognized.

[. . .]

The enormous worldwide problem of female education cannot, however, be solved by domestic policies in each nation alone. Adithi's projects in the Sithamarhi district alone have received support from Swiss and Dutch development agencies. In general, women's literacy projects in India receive assistance from a wide range of international development agencies, prominently including those of Sweden, Norway, and the Netherlands. International charities such as OXFAM (with its branches in various countries), UNICEF, and others play a role. [. . .]

Well-intentioned donors must be vigilant, for many India-related charities in the United States are fronts that funnel money to Hindu-right organizations that engage in anti-Muslim violence.[23] The India Development and Relief Fund (IDRF), which claims to have various attractive purposes, is actually a front organization for the RSS (the paramilitary right-wing organization loosely connected to the governing Bharatiya Janata Party). One of the front organizations on the Indian side, recipient of IDRF money; is actually called Sewa Bharati, a name that is similar to that of SEWA, the Self-Employed Women's Association, one of the most impressive NGOs working on women's issues. There are many other such cases. United States money is behind the recent genocide of Muslim men and the mass rapes of Muslim women in the state of Gujarat: in evidence presented to the U.S. Commission on International Religious Freedom, Najid Hussain, a professor at the University of Delaware, estimated that nine of every ten dollars used to foment religious violence in Gujarat came from the United States.[24] Some such donors know what they are doing: unfortunately, many wealthy Indian Americans are staunch supporters of such causes. But there is reason to believe that much of the money is given in ignorance. Kanwal Rekhi, chair of the IndUS Entrepreneurs (an organization of South Asian business people), wrote in the *Wall Street Journal*: "Many overseas Indian Hindus, including some in this country, finance religious groups in India in the belief that the funds will be used to build temples and educate and feed the poor of their faith. Many would be appalled to know that some recipients of their money are out to destroy minorities (Christians as well as Muslims) and their places of worship" (Rekhi and Rowen 2002).[25] I recommend either giving directly to some Indian NGO that one knows well (and forfeiting the U.S. charitable deduction) or giving to OXFAM, which does not make India a particular focus but which does good work wherever it operates and does enough in India to make those who care particularly about that nation content.

Today overall, as is the case with world poverty and need generally, the nations of the developed world are doing too little to support the education of the world's women. [. . .] Money invested in education, we say, is money well spent. An educated workforce is a more productive and stable workforce. Women who are educated contribute to economic development and the political stability of the entire region.[26]

Notes

1. All India Reports 1993 SC 2178. The court is referring to an interpretative tradition according to which Article 21 of the Constitution (the analogue of our Fourteenth Amendment), which stipulates that no person may be deprived of "life or liberty" without due process of law, should be interpreted broadly, so as to include within the concept of life the idea of a life with human dignity. This tradition has therefore also held that the right to life includes the right to livelihood.

2. Adithi had to begin by creating teaching materials. India has 385 or so languages, seventeen official, and many with no written traditions. The poor are often simply unable to obtain an education if their only language is one in which education is not offered.

3. Laloo Prasad Yadav's wife, Rabri Devi, was running the state officially, given that he had been jailed for corruption (a grain/bribery scandal). Shortly after this time, a state of national emergency was declared in Bihar, and the state was put under the direct governance of the national government for a month or two, not long enough to effect any real change. I cannot resist adding one point connected to my earlier writing. In several papers, most recently "Human Capabilities, Female Human Beings" (Nussbaum 1996), I criticized a paper by anthropologist Frédérique Marglin that attacked the practice of smallpox vaccination in India on the grounds that it had eradicated the cult of Sittala Devi, the goddess to whom one prays in order to avert smallpox. I can now announce that Sittala Devi is alive and well in Bihar. Indeed, she flourishes under the patronage of Laloo Prasad Yadav, who believes that she cured him from a liver ailment. I have seen her beauteous shrine in a slum in Patna, surrounded by the signs of Laloo's neglect of his civic duties.

4. Countries in this group that show a striking male-female disparity (more than five percentage points) include Singapore, Hong Kon, Brunei Darussalam, Bahrain, and Kuwait. Lest we think that the "Arab States" are systematically depriving women, the United Arab Emirates and Qatar show a higher literacy rate for women than for men. The sheikh of the United Arab Emirates is a vigorous supporter of female education and is also opening a coeducational liberal arts university that recently offered a position to one of my graduate students who specializes in feminism and environmental ethics.

5. Jamaica, although relatively poor (78 on the Human Development Index [HDI]), actually shows 90.3 percent female literacy and 82.4 percent male literacy.

6. In Lesotho, women allegedly have 93.3 percent literacy as against only 71.7 percent for men, so there is really a large gender gap, but in the atypical direction.

7. Kenya, which barely gets into the "medium" rather than "low human development" group, does unusually well on education, with 74.8 percent literacy for women, 88.3 percent for men.

8. The most striking exception at the bottom of the HDI is Zambia, with 70.2 percent female literacy, 84.6 percent male literacy.

9. See Sen 1991.

10. See Agarwal 1994; 1997.

11. See Nussbaum 2004.

12. See Buch 2000 and Jayal 2000; I am also greatly indebted to Zoya Hasan (2000).

13. See "Sex, Laws, and Inequality: What India Can Teach the United States" (Nussbaum 2002b), where I discuss one such case and the history in general. (*Caveat lector*: the publishers, in their infinite wisdom, removed reference to teaching the United States from my title when they put it on the cover of the journal, calling it simply "Sex, Laws, and Inequality: India's Experience.")

14. Called, in India a "First Information Report" (FIR), these documents must be initiated by the victim: thus in India law-enforcement agencies all on their own typically do not initiate criminal prosecution.

15. See Nussbaum 2000 and 2003a. The list of capabilities, as published in Nussbaum 2000, is presented as an appendix to the present article.

16. See Sen 1996. Presented as a working document at the Cairo Population meeting, Sen's paper strongly influenced their conclusions. For a more general discussion of women's bargaining position and the factors affecting it, see Agarwal 1997.

17. Vishaka is famous in India because it was the plaintiff in one of the landmark sexual harassment cases (*Vishaka v. Rajasthan*, discussed in Nussbaum 2002b and also in Nussbaum 2003c). The Vishaka case is not the one I call "problematic": it is a promising example of the creative use of international documents in crafting domestic law. The Supreme Court held, in this case, that the guidelines on sexual harassment in the Convention on the Elimination of All Forms of Discrimination against Women (CEDAW) were binding on the nation through its ratification of the treaty.

18. See Nussbaum 2002a, 2002c.

19. On the history of this resistance in Bengal, a region marked by early progressive efforts to educate women, see Bagehi 1997. Bagehi describes the way in which the language of purity and nationalism was used to oppose women's literacy.

20. Interestingly, although this is the most common situation for poor parents in India, it is not so for the Muslim minority. Muslim men typically have poorer job opportunities than do Hindu men, both because of poverty and because of discrimination. Muslim parents do not press hard for the education of boys where they believe that the boy's job opportunities are in low-paying jobs that do not require education. In this situation, parents frequently continue the education of their daughters and send their sons out to work.

21. See Drèze and Sen 1995; in the companion volume of field studies (Drèze and Sen 1997), see the field study of Kerala by V. K. Ramachandran.

22. These are data for 2000, cited in the *Human Development Report, 2002* (UNDP 2002), 223–24.

23. For discussion of this problem, with references, see Nussbaum 2003b.

24. For data, see references in Nussbaum 2003b and also A. K. Sen 2002.

25. The authors suggest that Indian President Atal Bihari Vajpayee should label such causes terrorist and thus strike a blow against this covert funding of violence.

26. Buch's (2000) study shows that women's presence in *panchayats* has increased expenditure on health, especially child health, and other aspects of the welfare of the poor, as contrasted with other goals that might contribute less to the long-term security and well-being of the region.

CHAPTER 38

Affirmative Action at School and on the Job

Shannon Harper and Barbara Reskin

[...]

In the 1960s and 1970s, policy makers responded to the Civil Rights movement and the pervasive race discrimination that had produced it by implementing programs to foster minorities' inclusion in major U.S. institutions. In K–12 schools, these included court-ordered busing and magnet schools. Selective public and private colleges and universities voluntarily implemented race-based outreach, explicitly considering race in admission and funding decisions. Governments at the city, state, and federal levels set aside a proportion of public contracts for minority- and female-run firms. Executive orders (EOs) required government contractors and government agencies to assess and address minorities' and women's underrepresentation. Some employers not covered by these regulations voluntarily undertook positive steps to make jobs accessible to a wider range of workers. Restrictions on congressional redistricting sought to end practices that had excluded blacks from the political process. Although these activities involved different actors operating in different societal spheres using different tactics and under the auspices of different regulatory bodies, all represented positive actions to promote racial and gender inclusion. In short, all constitute affirmative actions.

Affirmative action (AA) involves the "remedial consideration of race, ethnicity, or sex as a factor . . . in decision making . . ." to integrate institutions (Leiter and Leiter 2002, 1). Organizations pursue AA by changing how they distribute scarce opportunities, sometimes directly redistributing those opportunities in part on the basis of membership in an underrepresented group. Observers distinguish between "hard" and "soft" AA. The former directly considers group membership in allocating opportunities; the latter increases inclusion without taking race or sex into account (Malamud 2001). A more useful classification by Oppenheimer (1989) better reflects the range of affirmative activities. At one extreme are strict quotas that make race or sex a deciding factor. At the other are affirmative commitments not to discriminate. Between these are preference systems that give minorities or women some edge over white men; self-examination activities in which organizations review whether and why minorities or women are underrepresented in certain slots, and if they are, how to achieve a more balanced representation; and outreach plans that increase minorities' and women's representation in the pool from which applicants are chosen. AA activities are also classified by whether they were mandated or voluntarily implemented and whether the organization is a public or private entity—distinctions with implications for which practices are permissible.

[...]

Prohibited Characteristics and Protected Groups

Like antidiscrimination laws, AA aims to end discriminatory exclusion. The logic and implementation of the two approaches differ sharply, however. Legislators passed the 1964 Civil Rights Act (CRA) to end discrimination that "violate[s] clear and uncontroversial norms of fairness and formal equality" (Sturm 2001). Antidiscrimination law provides a mechanism for recompensing individual victims and changing the behavior of discriminating organizations. It is enforced primarily through complaints by persons who believe they have suffered discrimination based on a prohibited characteristic, usually race, color, national origin, religion, sex, or disability (Reskin 2001, 580). Although law makers understood that the law's object was to end discrimination against people of color, the CRA's injunction against discrimination made discrimination against a white person or a black person on the basis of race equally illegal.

Shortly after Congress passed the CRA, President Lyndon Johnson issued an EO to ensure nondiscrimination against minorities by federal contractors. The enforcement agency interpreted Johnson's order as requiring contractors to take active steps to prevent discrimination. The EO obliged contractors to act preemptively to identify and eliminate discriminatory barriers (Graham 1992). Thus, whereas antidiscrimination laws offer redress to individuals after they experienced discrimination, AA regulations aim to protect members of groups vulnerable to exclusion, thereby preventing discrimination from occurring.

CREATING PROTECTED GROUPS

Although the primary objective of AA was to protect African Americans, Johnson's EO followed Title VII in creating other "official minorities" (i.e., protected groups). Thus, the CRA and the 1965 and 1967 EOs listed race, color, national origin, creed, and sex. Of course, these characteristics define groups that have been included (e.g., men) as well as excluded (e.g., women). Because the goal of the EO was to require federal contractors to actively protect members of groups that had customarily been excluded, the EO in effect protected Asians, but not whites; Mexican Americans, but not Italian Americans; women, but not men (Leiter and Leiter 2002). Groups' inclusion depended on whether they were "analogous to blacks" (Skrentny 2002, 90). This operationalization of the EO has precipitated resentment toward AA. [...]

Affirmative Action in Education

[...]

HIGHER EDUCATION

Until the 1960s, most college students were white Protestants from middle- or upper-class families (Bowen and Bok 1998, Lemann 1999, Orfield 2001, 4). In 1960, only 2% of students in northern colleges and universities were black (Coleman 1966, 443), and of the 146,000 African American college students, over half attended all-black colleges (Thernstrom and Thernstrom 1997, 389). The more prestigious the school, the fewer blacks on campus (1997, 390). Twenty-two states legally mandated racially segregated education, and ending segregation at some schools took a decade-long legal struggle.

By the late 1960s and early 1970s, however, many selective schools[1] had undertaken AA, voluntarily recruiting students from underrepresented groups (Astin and Oseguera 2004, 322). [...] The University of California (UC), for example, created "special action" admissions with lower cutoffs for minorities (Douglass 2001, Skrentny 2002, 166). By the 1970s, racial preferences were the norm in selective schools and existed for nonblack minorities. White women were not included in most of these programs (except for athletics); ending sex discrimination had been sufficient to end women's exclusion (Skrentny 2002, 168).

However, race-based preferences by public universities violated the Equal Protection Clause of the 14th Amendment as well as Title VI of the 1964 CRA, which barred educational institutions from discriminating. In 1978, the Supreme Court addressed this issue in *Bakke v. Regents of the University of California*, a challenge to admissions at the UC Davis Medical School by a white man. The Court ruled that a public school could not give categorical preferences on the basis of race except to remedy past discrimination (Davis's Medical School was new). Justice Powell opined that diversity was a "compelling state interest," signaling that states could use AA to foster diversity, as long as they assessed each application individually. Bakke told other universities that racial preferences were legal and even provided a legal rationale for them. Thereafter, the use of race preferences increased (Douglass 2001, 123, 127; Welch and Gruhl 1998).

The turning point for AA in higher education came almost 20 years after *Bakke*, in 1995 when the UC regents barred UC from taking into account race, religion, sex, color, ethnicity, or national origin.[2] One year later, Californians passed a referendum abolishing the use of these characteristics in public education or employment. Washington State voters followed suit in 1998, and in 2000 Florida ended AA in higher education. Meanwhile, the Federal Appellate Court for the Fifth District overruled *Bakke* after the University of Texas Law School's separate admissions standards for whites and minorities were challenged (*Hopwood v. Texas* 1996). Subsequently, the Supreme Court clarified its stance on race-sensitive practices in two cases against the University of Michigan. In a case against Michigan's law school (*Grutter v. Bollinger*

2003), the Court reaffirmed *Bakke*, holding that diversity is a compelling state interest that warrants transgressing from the Equal Protection Clause. However, in *Gratz v. Bollinger* (2003), it struck down the undergraduate school's practice of automatically adding points to minorities' admission scores. Thus, universities may consider race to enhance diversity, but only as part of individualized assessments of each applicant. States barred from using race-sensitive AA have sought ways to maintain minority enrollment. California, Texas, Florida, and Colorado took advantage of high levels of secondary school segregation in implementing plans that guaranteed admission to a fixed percentage of top-ranked graduates from every high school.

Some have proposed using class-based AA to preserve racial and ethnic diversity (Kahlenberg 1996). Class-based AA is legal and in keeping with a tradition of considering class in admissions, either in needs-based financial aid, the consideration of economic disadvantage in recruiting or admissions, or legacy preferences (Carnevale and Rose 2003). Public support for class-based AA depends on how it is structured. Only a minority of Americans support preference for a low-income applicant whose scores are "slightly worse" than those of a high-income applicant (2003, table 3.8). Although class-based AA would broaden educational opportunity and increase economic diversity, the racial composition of the poor means that it could not maintain the levels of minority representation generated by race-based AA (Kane 1998b; Wilson 1999, 97, 99).

IMPACT OF AFFIRMATIVE ACTION IN HIGHER EDUCATION

AA has substantially increased the numbers of students of color in selective colleges and universities (Holzer and Neumark 2000; Leiter and Leiter 2002, 140), and whites' share—but not their numbers—of slots has fallen (Kane 1998b, 438). Nonetheless, black and Hispanic students remain underrepresented in selective institutions, and whites increasingly outnumber minorities among college graduates (U.S. Bureau Census 2004).

Some observers have suggested that AA puts minority students in competition with better prepared whites, raising minorities' dropout rate (Cole and Barber 2003; Thernstrom and Thernstrom 1997, 388). In fact, attending more selective schools raises minorities' graduation rates compared with their counterparts at nonselective schools (Bowen and Bok 1998; Brown et al. 2003, 116). Also, schools that implemented stronger forms of AA had higher minority retention rates than schools whose implementation was weaker (Hallinan 1998, 749). After graduating, AA beneficiaries get good jobs and serve their communities at similar rates as whites (Bowen and Bok 1998; Kane 1998a, 19, 43; Kane 1998b, 445).

One avenue for assessing the impact of AA is to examine the effect of eliminating it. After California and Washington voters ended race and sex preferences in state-run education or employment, applications to UC and the University of Washington fell, apparently because the elimination of AA sent a negative signal to minorities regarding their welcome (Chambers et al. 2005; Wierzbicki and Hirschman 2002). Texas's post-Hopwood percentage plan lowered blacks' and Hispanics' share of admitted applicants

11 and 8 percentage points, respectively, despite substantial outreach. In addition, blacks' share and Hispanics' share of University of Texas enrollees fell by one fifth and one seventh, respectively (Tienda et al. 2003).

Two principal strategies have reduced the impact of banning racial preferences: expanding admissions criteria to incorporate applicants' personal challenges and background characteristics (Leiter and Leiter 2002, 155) and targeted recruiting. Both strategies are costly (as are individualized assessments of every application that Gratz requires). Leiter and Leiter (155) claim that universities have employed a third strategy: "deft fiddling." Sander (2003) hypothesizes that "backdoor admission" allowed UC Berkeley to increase its number of minorities the year after California's ban on AA was implemented. Despite universities' back-door or front-door tactics, minority enrollments have fallen at schools that ended AA (Brown et al. 2003, 114; Leiter and Leiter 2002, 155; Tienda et al. 2003).

Research on law schools indicates that AA has substantially increased minority representation in legal education and the legal profession (Lempert et al. 2000, Wightman 1997); that bar-exam passage does not differ for minorities admitted through AA and those accepted solely on the basis of their grades and LSAT scores (Leiter and Leiter 2002, 140; Alon and Tienda 2003); and that the post-law-school differences between these two groups are minor (Lempert et al. 2000). However, Sander (2004) claims that ending AA would increase the number of African American lawyers. Although fewer blacks would enter law school, he predicts that a higher proportion would pass the bar. Re-analysis of Sander's data led Chambers et al. (2005) to the opposite conclusion: Ending AA at elite law schools would reduce African Americans' representation from 7% to 1%–2% (lower if their application rates declined when they learned that they would be among a tiny minority). Chambers et al. (2005) project that if law schools stopped considering race in admissions, blacks would all but disappear not only from elite law schools but also from law faculty, federal law clerkships, and top law firms.

AFFIRMATIVE ACTION IN HIGHER EDUCATION AND DIVERSITY

In *Bakke* and *Grutter*, the Supreme Court concluded that states had a compelling interest in racial diversity in higher education. Corporate America, the military, and some academic associations submitted amicus briefs indicating their agreement. Of the little research that has examined the effects of diversity on students' educational experiences, some suggest that it benefits all students in their intergroup relations and ability to understand others' perspectives (Gurin 1999; Orfield and Whitla 2001; Whitla et al. 2003). According to a retrospective study of University of Michigan graduates, students who interacted with diverse peers had a greater sense of commonality with members of other ethnic groups, were more likely to have racially or ethnically integrated lives five years after graduating, and more often reported that their undergraduate education had helped prepare them for their current job (Gurin 1999). The strongest evidence for the impact of diversity comes from an experiment in which white students were randomly assigned a white or minority roommate. Assignment to a minority roommate led to more contact and greater comfort with members of other races and more support for AA policies at the year's end (Duncan et al. 2003). These results are consistent with Allport's (1954) contact hypothesis, which holds that sustained, institutionally supported contact among people of different races reduces prejudice when these people are interdependent and of equal status. Diversity does not necessarily increase contact, however. Several observers have commented on racial segregation on campus, and a longitudinal survey of 159 schools indicates that increased minority presence on campus reduces white students' sense of community (Leiter and Leiter 2002, 151). In sum, although preliminary evidence suggests that diversity may affect students' attitudes, almost no rigorous evidence supports this conclusion (Holzer and Newmark 2000).

Affirmative Action in Employment

Congress mounted an attack on race discrimination in 1964 when it passed the omnibus CRA. Title VII of the CRA prohibited discrimination on the basis of race, color, creed, or sex in all aspects of employment. The enactment of the CRA was acclaimed by the media as a huge victory for the Civil Rights movement, for Lyndon Johnson, and for African Americans (Graham 1990).

AA was created in a very different way, unheralded, and with few expectations. Since 1941, every president had banned race discrimination by federal (or defense) contractors through an EO, thereby repaying political debts to African Americans without a fight with Congress (Skrentny 1996). Johnson's 1965 EO followed this pattern; in fact, it simply copied a 1961 EO issued by Kennedy. Both orders required federal contractors to refrain from discriminating at every stage of the employment process and to take positive steps—that is, affirmative action—to ensure that they treated workers equally, regardless of their race.[3] Johnson's AA differed from Kennedy's in two important ways. First, in 1967, he amended his EO to include women as a protected group. Second, his administration established an enforcement agency—the Office of Federal Contract Compliance (OFCC, later OFCCP) that could debar contractors who failed to comply with AA requirements (although it rarely took such action).

AA is required of only a subset of employers. In the private sector, only large companies with substantial government contracts must practice AA; these employ about 30 million persons (Office of Federal Contract Compliance 2002). (In comparison, Title VII applies to all employers with at least 15 employees, which covers an estimated 80 million employees [US EEOC 2004].) As is discussed below, many employers voluntarily practice some type of AA.

Since the late 1940s, federal agencies have also been under EOs requiring active steps to ensure nondiscrimination. Federal agencies took AA more seriously only after Congress passed the 1972 Equal Employment Opportunity Act, which required AA (Kellough 1992). In 2000, approximately 3.5 million federal jobs were subject to this law (U.S. Bureau Census 2000). Additionally, state EOs and statutes require many state agencies to practice AA.

DEFINING THE BOUNDARIES OF AFFIRMATIVE ACTION

[. . .]

A number of judicial decisions have helped shape the boundaries of AA in employment, and the changing political slant of the federal judiciary has affected which practices are legal (Reskin 1998). For instance, the Court has restricted most uses of hard AA in employment. It has ruled that private employers may voluntarily implement hard AA without violating Title VII, provided that the preferences are temporary and do not interfere excessively with the rights of members of the majority (*United Steel Workers v. Weber* 1979). The Equal Protection Clause subjects similar AA efforts by public employers to a higher level of judicial scrutiny. To justify race-based preferences, the Court requires a compelling state interest and a narrowly tailored remedy. In contrast, it holds remedial sex-based preferences to an intermediate level of scrutiny (see *Johnson v. Santa Clara County Department of Transportation* 1987; Malamud 2001, 314–29). The Supreme Court applied strict scrutiny to AA in federal contracting in *Adarand v. Pena* (1995), overruling the use of race in awarding government contracts.

Judicial enforcement of Title VII has created the most controversial form of AA—court-ordered hiring or promotion quotas to remedy blatant and longstanding discrimination. Although court-ordered quotas are rare (Burstein 1991), they draw considerable attention. The Supreme Court has upheld such quotas as long as they are narrowly tailored, serve a compelling state interest, and take into account the rights of members of the majority (Bruno 1995, 13).

The legislative branch has also stepped in periodically to define or limit acceptable AA. During the 1970s, Congress endorsed AA by designating Vietnam veterans and the handicapped as protected groups. In the latter case, AA goes beyond increased outreach and recruitment to require that employers provide "reasonable accommodations" for the functional limitations of disabled workers (U.S. Department of Labor, Office of Disability Employment Policy 2003).

EMPLOYERS' PRACTICES

The extra efforts that AA has required of contractors vary, ranging from conducting utilization analyses, outreach and recruitment, and active monitoring of employment patterns to—for a brief period in the late 1960s—using quotas. Since 1971, the OFCCP has required large nonconstruction contractors to annually produce AA plans based on a utilization analysis of their employment of women and minorities relative to the relevant labor pool. The plans must include goals and timetables for addressing substantial disparities revealed in the analysis (Bruno 1995, 8). Companies are not required to meet their goals, but if audited they must be able to show they made a good faith effort to do so.

[. . .]

The intensity of employers' AA efforts has varied with the politics of AA. The number of firms with AA or equal employment opportunity (EEO) offices grew in the

1970s and early 1980s (Dobbin et al. 1993). With declining political support for AA and increasing attention to the diversity of the future workforce, many employers replaced voluntary AA programs with "diversity management" (Ryan et al. 2002), and by 1998, three quarters of Fortune 500 companies had diversity programs and 88% tried to "hire for diversity in some way" (Ryan et al. 2002). Although diversity initiatives ostensibly move beyond race and sex, recruitment efforts are most often targeted at blacks, Hispanics, and women, and less at older workers or persons for whom English is a second language (Ryan et al. 2002).

THE IMPACT OF AFFIRMATIVE ACTION IN EMPLOYMENT

The limited knowledge of which employers practice AA and what they are doing in its name hampers assessing the impact of AA in employment. Also, AA's effects may be confounded with those of antidiscrimination laws and with increasing human capital among minorities and women. The bulk of research on the impact of AA has been quantitative and cross-sectional, although a detailed ethnography of AA in the Army showed how one organization created an effective program (Moskos and Butler 1996). Additional ethnographic studies of how AA is practiced in other workplaces would be illuminating.

The impact of AA in employment among federal contractors depends almost entirely on OFCCP's enforcement of the EO requiring AA. OFCCP enforcement has varied over the agency's lifetime, roughly coincident with presidential administrations. The effects of AA have also differed across protected groups. In the years from its birth to 1973, a period of weak enforcement, AA raised black men's—but not women's—employment in unskilled jobs in contractor firms relative to noncontractors (Heckman and Payner 1989; Leonard 1991; Smith and Welch 1984). Enforcement efforts escalated between 1974 and 1980, resulting in a rapid rise in the employment of black women by federal contractors (Welch 1989). Black men continued to be employed at higher rates by contractors than by noncontractors, and this difference showed up in white-collar and skilled craft jobs as well as blue-collar jobs (Leonard 1990; 1991). The wages of both black men and women rose in this period. Blacks' increased representation in white-collar and skilled craft jobs is consistent with AA's reduction in race and perhaps sex segregation. However, some employers have used race- and sex-based job assignments to cater to a minority or female market or clientele, creating occupational ghettos (Collins 1997; Durr and Logan 1997; Malamud 2001). This practice simultaneously opens jobs to the excluded and segregates them, ultimately limiting their opportunities (Frymer and Skrentny 2004, 722).

Further establishing that enforcement is necessary for effective AA, compliance reviews, explicit goals, and sanctions have been instrumental in increasing minority employment (Leonard 1990). Some employers have admitted that they would not have implemented programs "to increase fairness" without the risk of sanctions or the possibility of incentives (Hartmann 1996). With conservatives in the White House during the 1980s, enforcement declined, ending the advantage for minorities and women employed by federal contractors over those employed by noncontractors (Leonard 1990; Stephanopoulos and Edley 1995).

Underlying the strong effect of enforcement is the importance of organizational commitment to AA. Researchers have shown that the commitment of top leaders is a key determinant of AA outcomes (Baron et al. 1991). People in charge are positioned to alter organizational practices because they can influence the way things are done and obtain conformity through reward systems (Konrad and Linnehan 1995; N. DiTomaso, unpublished paper). Consider the Army's AA experience. The Army's commitment to racial equality throughout the ranks while maintaining standards meant that it provided training to ensure that the persons it promoted were qualified. The dual commitment to standards and racial equality enabled the Army to achieve both, while winning acceptance of its AA efforts (Moskos and Butler 1996, 71–72). In sum, AA has improved minorities' and women's positions in the labor market. Although the sources and estimated strengths of these effects have varied, they do not appear to have resulted from quotas (Leonard 1990) or come at the cost of lower productivity (Holzer and Neumark 2000).

In addition to affecting workers' distribution across jobs, AA promoted changes in labor markets and employers' practices. Few employers changed their employment practices or implemented new structures in response to Title VII and AA until 1971, when the OFCCP imposed utilization analyses as a monitoring tool (Kelly and Dobbin 1998). Firms began to change after the OFCCP outlined how it would monitor contractors and the Supreme Court accepted the disparate-impact theory of discrimination in *Griggs v. Duke Power* (1972), which expanded the legal meaning of discrimination to include neutral employment practices with an unjustified and adverse impact on protected groups (Stryker 2001). They scrutinized personnel practices and created EEO and AA structures and practices. These included targeting recruitment and establishing special training programs for women and minorities (Kelly and Dobbin 1998). When government and judicial support for AA waned in the 1980s and 1990s, the structures remained initially because they rationalized employment decisions (Kelly and Dobbin 1998) and later because they served as tools to promote and manage diversity (Kelly and Dobbin 1998, Ryan et al. 2002). Importantly, as AA transformed organizations, it was increasingly "rooted in strategies to maximize the[ir] performance" (Frymer and Skrentny 2004, 721).

Societal Responses to Affirmative Action

ATTITUDES ABOUT AFFIRMATIVE ACTION

The creation of protected groups collided with the ideologies of equal opportunity and meritocracy (but see Berg 2001). As Patterson (1997, 148) puts it, many viewed AA as "collective remediation in a heterogeneous society traditionally accustomed to a highly individualistic ethic." Critics charge that in creating group rights, AA compromises the principle of merit-based allocation, discriminates against innocent persons, fosters inefficiency, harms its intended beneficiaries, and perpetuates racism by making color relevant (Leiter and Leiter 2002; 233; Thernstrom and Thernstrom 1997).

Levels of support for AA depend on the specific policy mentioned (Krysan 2000). Within employment, the degree of approval for race-conscious AA (i.e., racial preferences) is far lower than that for race-neutral AA (outreach, mentoring). Surveys that find little support for AA tend to ask about practices that are illegal and rare (Kravitz et al. 1997). For at least two decades, corporations have almost universally supported AA because it protects them from discrimination lawsuits and because they see a need for a diverse workforce (Leiter and Leiter 2002, 86).

Because many white males are excluded from AA's benefits, we would expect racial differences in support for AA. Overall, whites are less supportive of AA than blacks. Support for racial preferences in hiring and promotion decisions is significantly higher among blacks than whites, and the race gap is even larger with respect to support for quotas in college admissions (Schuman et al. 1997). However, researchers have cautioned against exaggerating black-white differences in support for AA (Bobo 2001; Swain 2001; Wilson 1999). Disapproval of AA is not simply a matter of opposition to racial equality. The majority of Americans support racial equality, but support drops significantly if government intervention is involved (Schuman et al. 1997). However, Kinder and Sanders (1996) claim that the white-black gap in support for AA has widened. Contributing to the gap is the disparity in whites' and blacks' beliefs about how much blacks remain disadvantaged in American society (Davis and Smith 1996).

Although opponents frame their disapproval of AA in terms of fairness, survey data cast doubt on the claim that whites' opposition to AA stems from their commitment to meritocracy. The more committed whites are to the belief that hard work should be rewarded, the more positive their attitudes toward AA (Bobo 2001).[4] From analyzing social surveys, Bobo concludes that whites' opposition to AA resides in their sense of group-based entitlement. Group identification is consistent with the much greater support among blacks for AA for native-born blacks than for recent immigrants that Swain et al. (2001) observed in focus groups. Swain and colleagues also found that Latinos' level of support for AA was closer to blacks' and that Asian Americans' level was closer to whites'. As Patterson (1997, 159) argues, AA invokes the sense of group position for both excluded groups and groups that are already securely in: Both tend to support policies that will advantage them.

Others oppose preferences because they believe they harm beneficiaries (Steele 1991). Whether preferences reduce self-esteem depends on whether recipients of group-based preferences believe they were selected solely on the basis of their group membership. If they do, then beneficiaries' self-evaluations suffer. If beneficiaries believe they were selected on the basis of both personal merit and group membership, their self-esteem does not suffer (Major et al. 1994). Others, of course, may stigmatize individuals whom they believe are beneficiaries of preferences.

Although better information may not dispel the criticisms of many opponents, opposition to AA is based, at least in part, on several misconceptions. Most people are presumably unaware that different legal standards govern AA in higher education, federal contracting, and voluntary AA in employment. Across these spheres, the prevalence of race-conscious AA varies from considerable in higher education to minimal in employment. The visibility of race-conscious AA in higher education has probably led Americans to assume that AA in employment is also race conscious. The media and the public have largely ignored the differences between these various forms of AA (Duster 1998; Patterson 1997; Stryker et al. 1999), sometimes even equating AA and quotas (L. Bobo, personal communication).

The existence of open preferences for minorities has probably led whites to over-state AA's prevalence, to believe that AA limits their own opportunities, and to con-clude that AA prioritizes minority group status over qualifications (Davis and Smith 1996; Reskin 1998; Royster 2003). Surveys show that Americans believe that minority preferences in employment are rampant (Davis and Smith 1996). This perception is not supported by either the law or the body of empirical evidence attesting to the persistence of race and sex discrimination in employment (Bertrand and Mullainathan 2004; Kirschenmann and Neckerman 1991; Pager 2003; Turner et al. 1991).

Public opinion can exert an important influence on political action (Burstein 1998). As we discuss below, politicians have manipulated public opinion and public misunderstanding about AA to further their interests.

CHALLENGES TO AFFIRMATIVE ACTION

Opposition to AA has taken the form of legal activism, voice, and exit. Organized opposition, initiated by a small number of actors, has relied primarily on two tacks: judicial challenges and referenda to eliminate AA. Voter referenda ended AA in public employment and education in California and Washington but at the time of this writ-ing have not succeeded in other states. Opponents have had some success in using the courts to challenge the explicit use of race in decision making by public agencies in apparent violation of the Equal Protection Clause. For example, the appellate court decision in *Hopwood* against the University of Texas and the more recent *Gratz* deci-sion against the University of Michigan have been important precedents, influencing the admissions process at all public universities (Aldave 1999, 314). Indeed, in the wake of the *Gratz* decision, the threat of costly lawsuits prompted several public and private universities that had considered race for scholarships or academic enrichment programs to end such programs or open them to all comers (Malveaux 2004).

[. . .]

Challenges to AA in employment reach the courts (and the media) through a differ-ent path. They are initially filed as discrimination complaints under Title VII of the CRA or state antidiscrimination agencies. Even at the complaint stage, just a small minority of race discrimination charges come from whites—between 1991 and 2001, just 6% (Hirsh and Kornrich 2004), and the EEOC rejected the overwhelming majority of reverse-discrimination complaints as unfounded (Blumrosen 1996). The low prevalence of race discrimination complaints by whites is consistent with the small proportion of whites who report having been harmed by AA (Davis and Smith 1996). A few cases that have gone to court have had the support of a union or a men's rights group (Faludi 1991), but orga-nized opposition to AA in employment has emerged primarily in the political sphere.

POLITICIZATION OF AFFIRMATIVE ACTION

AA's basis in group rights can easily be translated into a political tool. The political influence of various ascriptive groups has created opportunities for politicians, and politicians have regularly tried to exploit AA for political gain by supporting or opposing it (Skrentny 2002, 86). As noted above, politicians have responded to pressure from various constituencies to be included as protected groups under AA programs.

In several other instances, AA has been used to polarize voters. Political calculations regarding his prospects in the 1964 election contributed to Johnson's commitment to AA (Skrentny 1996). Nixon supported a scheme known as the "Philadelphia Plan" in part because he saw a political benefit in implementing what amounted to hiring quotas for blacks in white-run unions in an attempt to divide the traditional Democratic base (Anderson 2004, 138). The ensuing controversy delivered the union vote to Nixon. Reagan ran for office partly on the basis of his opposition to AA. Although he did not end AA for federal contractors, his administration did not enforce AA regulations.

Public opinion can also exert an important influence on political action (Burstein 1998). As discussed above, public attitudes toward AA are based in part on misperceptions about the content of AA policies. Politicians have occasionally contributed to the confusion about what AA actually entails, as when Senator Orrin Hatch (1994) equated AA with quotas:

> I want to emphasize that affirmative action means quotas or it means nothing. It means discrimination on the basis of race or sex. It does not mean remedial education [or] special programs for the disadvantaged. . . . It has nothing to do with equality of opportunity. . . . Affirmative action is about equality of results, statistically measured. . . . All distinctions [between quotas and "goals," "targets," and "timetables"] dissolve in practice.

[. . .]

Conclusions

Substantial disparities remain among whites, Asians, Hispanics, and African Americans in the quality of colleges they attend, the proportions who graduate, their labor force participation and unemployment rates, their distribution across neighborhoods and occupations, and their earnings (Darity and Mason 1998; Jaynes and Williams 1989; Massey and Denton 1993; Reskin 2001; 2002). Social scientists have debated whether group-based AA is the appropriate way to address these disparities. Commentary on both sides is readily available (Bergmann 1996; Crosby 2004; Glazer 1975; Orfield and Kurlaender 2001; Patterson 1997; Sowell 1972; Thernstrom and Thernstrom 1997; Tienda et al. 2003). Most of the supportive commentary emphasizes persistent or even growing disparities. Commentators who oppose AA acknowledge that disparities persist, but they support other remedies (often increasing minorities' human capital) or argue that in overriding meritocratic distribution AA's costs outweigh the benefits.

In the early years of AA, government decision makers and judicial decisions viewed it as temporary. As antidiscrimination regulations eradicated discrimination from U.S.

institutions, they expected the need for AA to disappear. As AA integrated organizations, network recruitment would maintain inclusion. Better jobs for minorities would produce more competitive minority college applicants in the next generation. Over time the effects of helping provide initial access into these institutions would multiply.

Research does not support these scenarios. Many AA efforts have succeeded in opening new opportunities to women and minorities in both education and employment. However, these gains have often been contingent on active enforcement and administrative support of AA, neither of which has been consistently present for AA. Public schools became more racially integrated during busing but have now returned to their pre-busing segregation levels. Minority college enrollments increased with hard AA, but fell in states that abolished AA. Federal contracting firms provided better opportunities for women and minorities than noncontractors only as long as the OF-CCP enforced the EO. California public agencies whose budgets depended on greater integration became more integrated at the same time that nontargeted agencies became more segregated (Baron et al. 1991).

Meanwhile, the terms of the debate have literally changed. Declining support for AA has led employers and universities to pursue the more innocuous goal of diversity. Although diversity programs may or may not seek to provide access to members of protected groups, like AA they emphasize group membership. In this respect, the debate over AA reflects fundamental tensions about the relationship between underrepresentation and inequality.

The intense attention to AA in the United States has diverted scholars from other countries' efforts to include the formerly excluded.[5] Several nations have implemented some form of AA, although many differ radically from American AA. This diversity both over time and cross-nationally can be seen as an extended natural experiment with substantial variation across spheres, protected groups, implementation, and public and political responses. Despite this wealth of information, Hochschild's (1995) assessment still holds: "[T]he debate over the empirical consequences of affirmative action . . . is striking for its high ratio of claims to evidence" (100). There is every reason to believe that AA will be topical for some time to come. Both social science and public policy stand to gain from additional scholarly analyses.

Notes

1. Selective colleges and universities are defined as those in the top quintile of selectivity in admissions standards.

2. By this time, Congress had endorsed AA in education by authorizing scholarships targeted to women and minorities (Stephanopoulus and Edley 1995, section 10.1).

3. Kennedy also launched "Plans for Progress" to encourage employers to voluntarily pursue AA. The program's primary effect was to demonstrate that voluntary AA did not increase minorities' access to good jobs, at least in the early 1960s (Anderson 2004, 64–65).

4. Individuals who strongly supported meritocracy were less opposed to AA when there was evidence of discrimination (Son Hing et al. 2002).

5. See Darity and Nembhard (2000); Sowell (2004); Teles (1998) for discussions of AA in other nations. Space limits prevent our discussing AA in other societies.

CHAPTER 39

Support for Working Families

Janet C. Gornick and Marcia K. Meyers

Four decades of steady growth in female employment have gone a long way toward closing the job gap between women and men in the industrialized countries. One of the most striking changes in Europe and the United States has been the rise in employment among mothers with young children. Nearly 85 percent of U.S. mothers employed before childbearing now return to work before their child's first birthday. Although this is an encouraging trend from the perspective of gender equality in the marketplace, it is raising a new and difficult question about arrangements in the home: If everyone is working in the market, who is caring for the children?

Many parents in the industrialized countries find themselves navigating uncertain new terrain between a society that expects women to bear the primary responsibility for caring in the home and a society that expects, and increasingly requires, all adults to be at work in the market. Mothers and fathers are struggling to craft private solutions to this problem. But rather than resolving the question of who will care for children when everyone is on the job, these private solutions often exacerbate gender inequality, overburden the parents, and ultimately lead to poor-quality child care.

Although such problems are not unique to the United States, they may be more acute in this country because families have access to so little public support. The nation's policy makers and opinion leaders have been preoccupied in recent years with the promotion of "family values." Compared with most of Europe, however, this country provides exceptionally meager help to children, their parents, and the workers—mostly women—who care for other people's children. And despite the current preoccupation with getting everyone—particularly poor mothers—into the work force, the United States does much less than European countries to remove employment barriers for women with young children.

The Problem of Private Solutions

One private solution to child care adopted by many parents in the United States is the combining of parental caregiving and part-time employment. Because the parents who work reduced hours are overwhelmingly mothers—only 42 percent of American women work full-time year round—this solution exacerbates gender inequality in both the market and the caring spheres. Part-time work schedules, career interruptions, and intermittent employment relegate many women to the least remunerative and reward-ing jobs; and these employment patterns contribute to wage penalties that persist long after the children are grown. In dual-parent families with children below school age, married mothers' labor-market income accounts for, at most, a third of families' total labor-market income across the industrialized countries; in the United States, it ac-counts for only one quarter.

Another private solution is the combining of substitute care for children and full-time parental employment. Although this works well for some families, many others find themselves overburdened by the demands of the market and the home. Women in particular often work the equivalent of a double shift, combining full-time paid work with unpaid caregiving. In a recent article in *Demography,* Suzanne Bianchi concludes that despite the increase in mothers' labor-market activities, their time spent with their children remained nearly constant between 1965 and 1998. Where do employed mothers get the time? The data suggest that they do less of everything else, including housework, volunteering, engaging in leisure activities, and sleeping.

More parental employment also means children spend much more time in sub-stitute care. Recent increases in the use of child care in the United States have been particularly sharp for children below age one, 44 percent of whom are now in some form of nonparental child care. The extensive reliance on substitute child care imposes a heavy financial burden, consuming as much as 35 percent of household income for poor working families. It also raises concerns about the quality of care in children's youngest and most developmentally sensitive years. These concerns are particularly acute in the United States, where experts conclude that nearly two-thirds of the mostly private nonparental child care settings provide only fair-to-poor care.

The private-child-care solution to the work-family dilemma creates another, often overlooked problem: It impoverishes a large, low-wage child care work force dominated by women. Child care workers in the United States are among the most poorly paid members of the work force, averaging less than $7 per hour in earnings and usually working without employment benefits or realistic opportunities for career advancement.

While parents in the United States are left largely to their own devices, parents in most European welfare states can count on child care and parental-leave benefits to help them juggle work in the market and in the home. Although these policies have not fully resolved the problems of gender inequality and parental overburdening, they provide encouraging lessons about how government can help parents strike a balance between caring and earning.

Key to realizing greater gender equality in both the workplace and the home is recognizing that mothers and fathers alike deserve support in their market and care-giving roles. For a number of years, feminist scholars in Europe and the United States have debated the meaning of a woman-friendly welfare state. A universal-breadwinner perspective calls for welfare-state provisions that support and equalize women's employment attachments—for example, by providing extensive public child care. An opposing caregiver-parity perspective calls for provisions that grant women "the right to time for care" and remunerate women for care work performed in the home through generous maternity pay and other caregiver benefits.

Neither perspective fully resolves the tension between work and family life while promoting gender equality. Both fail to provide a satisfying vision of the welfare state—in part because they do not address the issue of fathers as caregivers. Women's widespread assumption of greater market responsibilities has not been equally matched by fathers' assumption of child care responsibilities in the home. Although men's involvement in caregiving appears to be on the rise, Bianchi estimates that married fathers in the United States spent just 45 percent of the time their wives spent on caregiving in 1998—an increase of only 15 percentage points since 1965.

A bridge between the universal-breadwinner and caregiver-parity perspectives may lie in social policies that promote what British welfare-state scholar Rosemary Crompton calls the "dual earner/dual carer" society. This is a society in which men and women engage symmetrically in both paid work in the labor market and caregiving work in the home. Central to the dual earner/dual carer solution is the recognition that *both* mothers and fathers should have the right and opportunity to engage in market and caregiving work without incurring poverty in terms of money or time. For families with very young children (say, younger than age three), mothers and fathers would have the right to take substantial time off from market work to care for their children, without loss of income. For families with children from age three to school age, both parents would have the right to engage in flexible and reduced-hour employment, and they would have access to affordable, high-quality substitute child care.

This solution assumes that men would re-allocate substantial portions of time from the labor market to the home while their children are young. Hence, as American political theorist Nancy Fraser has suggested, "men [would] become more like women are now" in the allocation of their time.

The sweeping transformations of market and gender relations necessary to achieve a gender-egalitarian dual earner/dual carer society are obviously not imminent. But the steep rise in maternal employment in recent years and the more modest rise in men's caregiving time suggest that some form of dual earner/dual carer arrangement is already the reality for many families in the industrialized world. Given this reality, what can government do to help such families now and to promote greater gender equality in the future? The United States is arguably a leader in rhetorical support for the family and for equal employment opportunities—but it's a clear laggard in making the rhetoric meaningful. U.S. policy makers could take a lesson from the European welfare states, which finance extensive parental leaves during the earliest years of children's lives and provide high-quality early-childhood education and care services for older preschool children. Increasingly, these countries also incorporate incentives that encourage men to assume a larger share of caregiving work in the home.

Family Leave

Although their family support programs vary substantially, nearly all of the industrialized welfare states provide generous maternity, paternity, or other parental leave during the first year of childhood, typically funded through some combination of national sickness, maternity, and other social-insurance funds. The most substantial leave benefits are provided in two Scandinavian countries that have consolidated maternity, paternity, and other parental-leave schemes. Norwegian parents are entitled to share 52 weeks of leave with an 80 percent wage replacement (or 42 weeks with full wage replacement) following the birth of a child, while Swedish parents can share a full year of leave with nearly full wage replacement, followed by three additional months at a lower rate. Most continental European countries provide somewhat shorter maternity leaves—usually three to five months—but they pay relatively high replacement rates: 80 percent to 100 percent.

Even beyond the child's first birthday, parents in some European countries have rights to partial leave and reduced-hour employment. In Denmark, for example, mothers have a right to 28 weeks of maternity leave after childbirth with high wage replacement, and fathers have a right to two weeks of paternity leave; once these leaves are exhausted, the parents can share 10 weeks of parental leave with high wage replacement, and then each parent is entitled to 13 weeks of child care leave at 80 percent of the parental-leave benefit level. Finnish parents can choose to stay on leave for up to three years while receiving a low, flat-rate benefit. And Swedish parents have the right to work as little as six hours per week, with job protection, until their children are eight years old.

Although generous leave policies have economic and social benefits for families with very young children, they can create new forms of gender inequality. The total percentage of paid parental-leave days taken by fathers amounts to less than 10 percent across the European welfare states and less than 3 percent in many. Because leaves are taken overwhelmingly by mothers, many women pay a price for their long absences from the labor market in the form of lost human capital and career advancement.

Several of the Scandinavian countries are addressing the gender gap in parental-leave taking by creating incentives for fathers to take the leave to which they are entitled. The most critical of these incentives is high wage-replacement rates. Because men tend to have higher wages than women, in the absence of full wage replacement it often makes economic sense for couples to decide that the mother should withdraw from the labor market. The 80 percent to 100 percent wage-replacement rates in most of the European countries reduce the economic disincentive for fathers to take full advantage of leave benefits.

A second important gender-equalizing policy is the granting of individual or nontransferable leave benefits to fathers as well as to mothers. In Norway and Sweden, four weeks of parental leave are reserved explicitly for fathers; in Denmark fathers have a right to two weeks of paternity leave. In all three countries, leave time reserved for the father but not taken is lost to the family. These "use or lose" provisions encourage parents to participate more equally in leave-supported caregiving. The Scandinavian welfare states have taken active steps to promote fathers' use of leave benefits. In the late 1990s, the Swedish government engaged in a public campaign to educate employers and unions about how fathers' parental leave can be good not just for families but for work organizations and society. Norwegian policy expert Anne Lise Ellingsaeter reports that in her country government officials are now pushing fatherhood onto the political agenda: "While employment for women was the main issue of policies in the 1980s," she suggests, the 1990s brought in "the caring father, and thus the domestication of men." The emphasis on fathers is expanding beyond the Scandinavian countries as well. Italy, for example, instituted use-or-lose days in 2000.

The European welfare states also provide instructive lessons about how to finance parental-leave benefits. Nearly all of the European leave programs are funded through either social-insurance schemes or general tax revenues. None relies on mandating employers to provide wage replacement for their own employees. Those countries in which social-insurance funds draw heavily on employer contributions do not "experience-rate"—that is, adjust contributions to reflect the number of leave takers at the firm level. These financing mechanisms reduce employer resistance by spreading the cost among employers and by supplementing employer contributions with general revenue funds. By reducing the cost to individual employers, these mechanisms also minimize the risk that employers will discriminate against potential leave takers who might otherwise be seen as unusually expensive employees.

How costly are these leave schemes? Spending on maternity, paternity, and parental leave is substantial and is rising in nearly all the European welfare states. Costs relative to population and gross domestic product (GDP) are surprisingly modest, however. As of the middle 1990s, annual family leave expenditures per employed woman (in 1990 U.S. dollars) were about $900 in Sweden and Finland, and about $600 to $700 in Norway and Denmark. France spent a more moderate $375 per employed woman. The higher-spending Scandinavian countries invested approximately 0.7 percent to 1.0 percent of GDP in family leave, while France spent 0.35 percent.

Child Care

The European welfare states provide another critical form of support for dual earner/ dual carer families and for gender equality in the form of high-quality, public early-childhood education and care. They have developed two distinct models. The model in the Scandinavian countries is an integrated system of child care centers and organized family-day-care schemes serving children from birth to school age, managed by social-welfare or educational authorities. Nearly all employed parents have access to a place in the public child care system with little or no waiting time, and enrollment rates are high. In Sweden and Denmark, for example, one-third to one-half of children under age three are in some form of full-day, publicly supported care, along with 72 percent to 82 percent of children between the ages of three and five.

The model developed by the continental countries of France and Belgium is a two-phase system of child care. For younger children, full-day child care centers (*creches*) and some publicly supervised family-day-care schemes are provided under the authority of the social-welfare system. Beginning at age two and a half or three, children are served in full-day preprimary programs, the *écoles maternelles,* within the educational system. Enrollment of young children in *creches* is high (30 percent in Belgium and 24 percent in France); it's nearly universal in the *écoles maternelles* for preschool-age children.

Although a large child care sector would seem to be unambiguously positive for gender equality in employment, it can exacerbate inequality if it impoverishes women who work as child care providers. In the European countries, although the child care sector is also mainly women, a large share of child care workers are public-sector employees. As such, they benefit from the good public-sector wages and benefits common in Europe. Relatively high wages for child care workers are tied to high standards for the education and training of child care professionals, who are typically required to have three to five years of vocational or university training. Higher educational standards have benefits that extend beyond the economic welfare of female child care workers. They also increase the quality of care that children receive.

Like leave benefits, early-childhood education and care services in European countries are financed largely by the government. Funding is provided by national, state or regional, and local authorities, with the national share typically dominant in services for preschool-age children. Care for very young children and, to a lesser extent, for preschool children is partially funded through parental co-payments that cover an average of 15 percent to 25 percent of costs. Because co-payments are scaled to family income, lower-income families typically pay nothing and more affluent families pay no more than 10 percent to 15 percent of their income.

Child care expenditures are large and growing in the European welfare states but—like leave expenditures—are modest in per capita terms. Total spending on direct child care in the mid-1990s was about $2,000 per child under age 15 in Sweden and Denmark; it served a large share of all children under the age of seven and many school-aged children in after-school care. In France expenditures totaled a little over $1,000 per child under age 15; they served nearly all three-to-five-year-olds and about one-quarter of children under age three. These investments in early-childhood education and care constituted about 1.6 percent to 2.2 percent of GDP in Sweden and Denmark, and about 1 percent in France.

On all fronts, the United States lags behind Europe to a remarkable extent. The United States stands out as one of only a few countries in the entire world that fail to provide any national program of paid maternity leave. Until 1993 this country lacked even job protections for women at the time of childbirth. With the passage of the Family and Medical Leave Act (FMLA), workers in firms with at least 50 employees were granted rights to 12 weeks of unpaid, job-protected leave each year for childbirth or adoption or to care for a seriously ill family member. The exclusion of small firms leaves an estimated one-half of the U.S. work force without even this rudimentary benefit. Additionally, the absence of wage replacement presents an obvious problem: The congressionally established U. S. Commission on Leave reports that 64 percent of employees who need but do not take FMLA-based leave indicate that they cannot afford the loss of wages.

Some families in the United States receive short periods of paid leave through employer-based disability benefits. Five states provide public Temporary Disability

Insurance (TDI) programs. Because the Pregnancy Discrimination Act applies to these programs, new mothers have a right to short periods of paid leave if they have either private or public disability benefits. As of the early 1990s, however, only an estimated one-quarter of U.S. working women had coverage under these laws. The Institute for Women's Policy Research found that weekly benefits paid through the TDI programs average only $170 to $200 and that the duration of benefit claims ranged from five to 13 weeks.

The United States also stands out among industrialized countries for its paucity of public child care assistance. Unlike most of Europe, it has never embraced a national system for universal provision, funding, or regulation of early-childhood education and care. More than 40 percent of American children under age five spend 35 hours or more per week in nonparental care, and another 25 percent spend 15 to 35 hours.

Substitute care in this country is overwhelmingly private in both provision and financing. The U.S. government spends about $200 on direct child care assistance per child under age 15—about one-tenth of the spending in Sweden and one-fifth of that in France. Assistance is provided through two primary mechanisms: (1) means-tested subsidies, available on a limited basis for low-income families with employed parents, and (2) early-childhood education programs (mostly through the means-tested Head Start program) and state prekindergarten programs. Children in the United States now routinely start public school at a young age; about one-half of four-year-olds and 89 percent of five-year-olds are in (usually) part-day prekindergarten or kindergarten programs. But as few as 5 percent of children age three and younger, and of older pre-school children outside prekindergarten and kindergarten, are in any form of publicly subsidized or provided care.

Some observers justify miserly child care expenditures in the United States by pointing to tax benefits for families who use child care. The federal government and several state governments exempt a portion of child care expenses from personal income taxes. While the federal Child and Dependent Care Credit is now used by a large number of families, low-income families with no tax liability receive no benefits, and the actual benefit for others is low. As of the mid-1990s, the federal tax credit expenditures totaled about $47 per child under the age of 15.

Unfortunately, the United States gets what it pays for. Minimally regulated private-child-care arrangements provide uneven and generally low-quality care. A research team from the National Institute of Child Health and Human Development recently estimated that only 11 percent of child care settings for children age three and younger meet standards for "excellent" care. In part, quality is poor because the care is provided by a minimally educated and inadequately trained work force. According to data collected by Marcy Whitebook of the Center for the Child Care Workforce, some 22 percent to 34 percent of teachers in regulated child care centers and family child care settings do not have a high school diploma; Ellen Galinsky, president of the Families and Work Institute, reports that in unregulated family-and-relative child care settings, between 33 percent and 46 percent of caregivers have not completed high school.

Child care providers are a poorly educated work force in large part because families cannot afford to pay more highly trained professionals. Full-time child care for a four-year-old averages between $3,500 and $6,000 per year—more than college tuition at many state universities. Yet despite this expense, child care workers often earn poverty-level wages. Whitebook estimates that they earn an average of $6.12 per hour—slightly less than parking lot attendants and one-third the average salary of flight attendants.

Many of these poorly paid child care workers are women of color. And many are immigrants from developing countries who are in search of better economic prospects—and who often leave the care of their own children to even poorer women in their home country. [See Arlie Russell Hochschild, "The Nanny Chain," *TAP,* January 3, 2000.]

Although the European welfare states could teach the United States much about child care, they have not completely solved the dilemma of providing gender-egalitarian support for dual earner/dual carer families. The supply of child care for children under age three is very limited in many countries, and for older preschool children in some. Also, both short- and longer-term leaves are still used overwhelmingly by mothers. A fully egalitarian package of family support policies is not completely realized even in the progressive Scandinavian countries, but there at least the framework for such policies is in place.

[. . .]

References

Part I: Origins of the Gendered Division of Labor

Engels, Frederick. *The Origin of the Family, Private Property and the State*, edited by Eleanor Burke Leacock. New York: International Publishers, [1942] 1972.

"Global Employment Trends for Women 2004." International Labor Organization, 2004. http://www.ilo.org/public/english/employment/strat/download/trendsw.pdf. (20 March 2009)

Chapter 1: The Problem of Sex/Gender and Nature/Nuture by Anne Fausto-Sterling

Annandale, E. "Gender and Health Status: Does Biology Matter?" In *Debating Biology*, edited by S. J. Williams, L. Birke, and G. Bendelow. New York: Routledge, 2003.

Birke, A. "Shaping Biology: Feminism and the Idea of the 'Biological.'" In *Debating Biology*, edited by S. J. Williams, L. Birke, and G. Bendelow. New York: Routledge, 2003.

Butler, J. *Gender Trouble: Feminism and the Subversion of Identity*. New York: Routledge, 1990.

Byne, W., S. Tobet, and Linda A. Mattiace, et al. "The Interstitial Nuclei of the Human Anterior Hypothalamus: An Investigation of Variation with Sex, Sexual Orientation and HIV Status." *Hormones and Behavior*, no. 40 (2001): 86–92.

Cheah, P. "Mattering." *Diacritics* 26, no. 1 (1996): 108–39.

Davis, B. E., R. Y. Moon, H. C. Sachs, and M. C. Ottolini. "Effects of Sleep Position on Infant Motor Development." *Pediatrics* 102, no. 5 (1998): 1135–40.

Fausto-Sterling, A. *Myths of Gender: Biological Theories about Women and Men*. New York: Basic Books, 1992.

———. *Sexing the Body: Gender Politics and the Construction of Sexuality*. New York: Basic Books, 2000.

Kraus, C. "Naked Sex in Exile: On the Paradox of the 'Sex Question' in Feminism and Science." *National Women's Studies Association Journal* 12, no. 3 (2000): 151–77.

Le Grand, R., C. J. Mondloch, D. Maurer, H. P. Brent. "Early Visual Experience and Face Processing." *Nature*, no. 410 (2001): 890.

LeVay, S. "A Difference in Hypothalamic Structure between Heterosexual and Homosexual Men." *Science*, no. 253 (1991): 1034–37.

Nader, K., G. E. Schafe, and J. E. Le Doux. "Fear Memories Require Protein Synthesis in the Amygdala for Reconsolidation after Retrieval." *Nature*, no. 406 (2000): 722–26.

Oyama, S. *Evolution's Eye: A System's View of the Biology-Culture Divide.* Durham: Duke University Press, 2000.

Ruble, D., and C. L. Martin. "Gender Development." Pp. 933–1016 in *Social, Emotional and Personality Development*, edited by N. Eisenberg. New York: Wiley, 1998.

Russett, C. E. *Sexual Science: The Victorian Construction of Womanhood.* Cambridge: Harvard University Press, 1989.

Thelen, E., and L. B. Smith. *A Dynamic Systems Approach to the Development of Cognition and Action.* Cambridge: MIT Press, 1994.

Udry, J. R. "Biological Limits of Gender Construction." *American Sociological Review* 65, no. 3 (2000): 443–57.

Wahlsten, D. "Insensitivity of the Analysis of Variance to Heredity-Environment Interaction." *Behavior and Brain Sciences*, no. 13 (1990): 109–61.

Wizemann, T. M., and M. L. Pardue, eds. *Exploring the Biological Contributions to Human Health: Does Sex Matter?* Washington, DC: National Academy Press, 2001.

Chapter 2: "Night to His Day": The Social Construction of Gender" by Judith Lorber

Acker, Joan. "Hierarchies, Jobs, and Bodies: A Theory of Gendered Organizations." *Gender & Society* 4 (1990): 139–58.

Almquist, Elizabeth M. "Labor Market Gendered Inequality in Minority Groups." *Gender & Society* 1 (1987): 400–414.

Amadiume, Ifi. *Male Daughters, Female Husbands: Gender and Sex in an African Society.* London: Zed Books, 1987.

Ariès, Philippe. *Centuries of Childhood: A Social History of Family Life*, translated by Robert Baldick. New York: Vintage, 1962.

Austad, Steven N. "Changing Sex Nature's Way." *International Wildlife* 29, (May–June 1986).

Barkalow, Carol, with Andrea Raab. *In the Men's House.* New York: Poseidon Press, 1990.

Bem, Sandra Lipsitz. *The Lenses of Gender: Transforming the Debate on Sexual Inequality.* New Haven: Yale University Press, 1993.

Bernard, Jessie. *The Female World.* New York: Free Press, 1981.

Bernstein, Richard. "France Jails 2 in Odd Case of Espionage." *New York Times,* May 11, 1986.

Bérubé, Allan. "Marching to a Different Drummer: Gay and Lesbian GIs in World War II." In *Hidden from History: Reclaiming the Gay and Lesbian Past*, edited by Martin Bauml Duberman, Martha Vicinus, and George Chauncey, Jr. New York: New American Library, 1989.

Bettelheim, Bruno. *Symbolic Wounds: Puberty Rites and the Envious Male.* London: Thames and Hudson, 1962.

Biersack, Aletta. "Paiela 'Women-men': The Reflexive Foundations of Gender Ideology." *American Ethnologist* 11 (1984): 118–38.

Birdwhistell, Ray L. *Kinesics and Context: Essays on Body Motion Communications.* Philadelphia: University of Pennsylvania Press, 1970.

Blackwood, Evelyn. "Sexuality and Gender in Certain Native American Tribes: The Case of Cross-gender Females." *Signs* 10 (1984): 27–42.

Bolin, Anne. "Transsexualism and the Limits of Traditional Analysis." *American Behavioral Scientist* 31 (1987): 41–65.

———. *In Search of Eve. Transsexual Rites of Passage.* South Hadley, Mass.: Bergin & Garvey, 1988.

Bourdieu, Pierre. *The Logic of Practice.* Stanford, Calif.: Stanford University Press, [1980] 1990.

Brody, Jane E. "Benefits of Transsexual Surgery Disputed as Leading Hospital Halts the Procedure." *New York Times,* October 2, 1979.

Butler, Judith. *Gender Trouble: Feminism and the Subversion of Identity.* New York and London: Routledge, 1990.

Chodorow, Nancy. *The Reproduction of Mothering.* Berkeley: University of California Press, 1978.

Cixous, Hélène, and Catherine Clément. *The Newly Born Woman.* Translated by Betsy Wing. Minneapolis: University of Minnesota Press, [1975] 1986.

Cockburn, Cynthia. *Machinery of Dominance: Women, Men and Technical Know-how.* London: Pluto Press, 1985.

Collins, Patricia Hill. *Black Feminist Thought: Knowledge, Consciousness, and the Politics of Empowerment.* Boston: Unwin Hyman, 1990.

Connell, R. [Robert] W. *Gender and Power: Society, the Person, and Sexual Politics.* Stanford, Calif.: Stanford University Press, 1987.

Coser, Rose Laub. "Cognitive Structure and the Use of Social Space." *Sociological Forum* 1 (1986): 1–26.

Davies, Christie. "Sexual Taboos and Social Boundaries." *American Journal of Sociology* 87 (1982): 1032–63.

de Beauvoir, Simone. *The Second Sex.* Translated by H. M. Parshley. New York: Knopf, 1953.

Devor, Holly. "Gender Blending Females: Women and Sometimes Men." *American Behavioral Scientist* 31 (1987): 12–40.

———. *Gender Blending: Confronting the Limits of Duality.* Bloomington: Indiana University Press, 1989.

Dollimore, Jonathan. "Subjectivity, Sexuality, and Transgression: The Jacobean Connection." *Renaissance Drama*, n.s. 17 (1986): 53–81.

Douglas, Mary. *Natural Symbols.* New York: Vintage, 1973.

Durova, Nadezhda. *The Calvary Maiden: Journals of a Russian Officer in the Napoleonic Wars.* Translated by Mary Fleming Zirin. Bloomington: Indiana University Press, 1989.

Eichler, Margrit. "Sex Change Operations: The Last Bulwark of the Double Standard." In *Feminist Frontiers II*, edited by Laurel Richardson and Verta Taylor, New York: Random House, 1989.

El Dareer, Asma. *Woman, Why Do You Weep? Circumcision and its Consequences.* London: Zed Books, 1982.

Epstein, Cynthia Fuchs. *Deceptive Distinctions: Sex, Gender and the Social Order.* New Haven: Yale University Press, 1988.

Faderman, Lillian. *Odd Girls and Twilight Lovers: A History of Lesbian Life in Twentieth-Century America.* New York: Columbia University Press, 1991.

Foucault, Michel. *The Archeology of Knowledge and the Discourse on Language.* Translated by A.M. Sheridan Smith. New York: Pantheon, 1972.

Freeman, Lucy, and Alma Halbert Bond. *America's First Woman Warrior: The Courage of Deborah Sampson*. New York: Paragon, 1992.

Frye, Marilyn. *The Politics of Reality: Essays in Feminist Theory*. Trumansburg, NY: Crossing Press, 1983.

Garber, Marjorie. *Vested Interests: Cross-dressing and Cultural Anxiety*. New York and London: Routledge, 1992.

Garfinkel, Harold. *Studies in Ethnomethodology*. Englewood Cliffs, N.J.: Prentice-Hall, 1967.

Gilmore, David D. *Manhood in the Making: Cultural Concepts of Masculinity*. New Haven: Yale University Press, 1990.

Goffman, Erving. "The Arrangement Between the Sexes." *Theory and Society* 4 (1977): 301–33.

———. "Felicity's Condition." *American Journal of Sociology* 89 (1983): 1–53.

Gramsci, Antonio. *Selections from the Prison Notebooks*. Translated and edited by Quintin Hoare and Geoffrey Nowell Smith. New York: International Publishers, 1971.

Greenblatt, Stephen. *Shakespearean Negotiations: The Circulation of Social Energy in Renaissance England*. Berkeley: University of California Press, 1987.

Groce, Stephen B., and Margaret Cooper. "Just Me and the Boys? Women in Local-Level Rock and Roll." *Gender & Society* 4 (1990): 220–29.

Haraway, Donna. "Animal Sociology and a Natural Economy of the Body Politic. Part I: A Political Physiology of Dominance." *Signs* 4 (1978): 21–36.

———. "Investment Strategies for the Evolving Portfolio of Primate Females." In *Body/Politics: Women and the Discourses of Science*, edited by Mary Jacobus et al. New York: Routledge, 1990.

Howard, Jean E. "Crossdressing, the Theater, and Gender Struggle in Early Modern England." *Shakespeare Quarterly* 39 (1988): 418–41.

Hwang, David Henry. *M Butterfly*. New York: New American Library, 1989.

Jacobs, Sue-Ellen, and Christine Roberts. "Sex, Sexuality, Gender, and Gender Variance." In *Gender and Anthropology*, edited by Sandra Morgen. Washington, D.C.: American Anthropological Association, 1989.

Jay, Nancy. "Gender and Dichotomy." *Feminist Studies* 7 (1981): 38–56.

Kando, Thomas. *Sex Change: The Achievement of Gender Identity Among Feminized Transsexuals*. Springfield, Ill.: Charles C. Thomas, 1973.

Kondo, Dorinne K. *Crafting Selves: Power, Gender, and Discourse of Identity in a Japanese Workplace*. Chicago: University of Chicago Press, 1990a.

———. "*M. Butterfly*: Orientalism, Gender, and a Critique of Essentialist Identity." *Cultural Critique*, no. 16 (Fall 1990b): 5–29.

Lancaster, Jane Beckman. *Primate Behavior and the Emergence of Human Culture*. New York: Holt, Rinehart and Winston, 1974.

Laqueur, Thomas. *Making Sex: Body and Gender from the Greeks to Freud*. Cambridge, Mass.: Harvard University Press, 1990.

Lévi-Strauss, Claude. "The Family." In *Man, Culture, and Society*, edited by Harry L. Shapiro, New York: Oxford, 1956.

———. *The Elementary Structures of Kinship*. Translated by J. H. Bell and J. R. Von Sturmer. Boston: Beacon Press, [1949] 1969.

Lightfoot-Klein, Hanny. *Prisoners of Ritual: An Odyssey into Female Circumcision in Africa*. New York: Harrington Park Press, 1989.

MacCormack, Carol. P. "Nature, Culture and Gender: A Critique." In *Nature, Culture and Gender*, edited by Carol P. MacCormack and Marilyn Strathern. Cambridge, England: Cambridge University Press, 1980.

Matthaei, Julie A. *An Economic History of Women's Work in America.* New York: Schocken, 1982.

Mencher, Joan. "Women's Work and Poverty: Women's Contribution to Household Maintenance in South India." In *A Home Divided: Women and Income in the Third World*, edited by D. Dwyer and J. Bruce. Stanford: Stanford University Press, 1988.

Money, John, and Anke A. Ehrhardt. *Man & Woman, Boy & Girl.* Baltimore, Md: Johns Hopkins University Press, 1972.

Morris, Jan. *Conundrum.* New York: Signet, 1975.

Nanda, Serena. *Neither Man Nor Woman: The Hijiras of India.* Belmont, Calf.: Wadsworth, 1990.

New York Times. "Musician's Death at 74 Reveals He Was a Woman," February 2, 1989.

Ortner, Sherry B. "Is Female to Male as Nature is to Culture?" In *Woman, Culture and Society*, edited by Michelle Z. Rosaldo and Louise Lamphere. Stanford, Calif.: Stanford University Press, 1974.

Ortner, Sherry B., and Harriet Whitehead, eds. *Sexual Meanings: The Cultural Construction of Gender and Sexuality.* Cambridge, England: Cambridge University Press, 1981.

Paige, Karen Ericksen, and Jeffrey M. Paige. *The Politics of Reproductive Ritual.* Berkeley: University of California Press, 1981.

Palmer, Phyllis. *Domesticity and Dirt: Housewives and Domestic Servants in the United States, 1920–1945.* Philadelphia: Temple University Press, 1989.

Papanek, Hanna. "Family Status Production: The 'Work' and 'Non-work' of Women." *Signs* 4 (1979): 775–81.

———. "To Each Less Than She Needs, From Each More Than She Can Do: Allocations, Entitlements and Value." In *Persistent Inequalities: Women and World Development*, edited by Irene Tinker. New York: Oxford University Press, 1990.

Raymond, Janice G. *The Transsexual Empire: The Making of the She-male.* Boston: Beacon Press, 1979.

Reskin, Barbara F. "Bringing the Men Back In: Sex Differentiation and the Devaluation of Women's Work." *Gender & Society* 2 (1988): 58–81.

Rogers, Mary F. "They Were All Passing: Agnes, Garfinkel, and Company." *Gender & Society* 6 (1992): 169–91.

Rubin, Gayle. "The Traffic in Women: Notes on the Political Economy of Sex." In *Toward an Anthropology of Women*, edited by Rayna R[app] Reiter. New York: Monthly Review Press, 1975.

Rugh, Andrea B. *Reveal and Conceal: Dress in Contemporary Egypt.* Syracuse, N.Y.: Syracuse University Press, 1986.

Scott, Joan Wallach. *Gender and the Politics of History.* New York: Columbia University Press, 1988.

Smith, Dorothy E. *The Everyday World as Problematic: A Feminist Sociology.* Toronto: University of Toronto Press, 1987a.

———. *The Conceptual Practices of Power: A Feminist Sociology of Knowledge.* Toronto: University of Toronto Press, 1990.

van der Kwaak, Anke. "Female Circumcision and Gender Identity: A Questionable Alliance?" *Social Science and Medicine* 35 (1992): 777–87.

van Gennep, Arnold. *The Rites of Passage.* Translated by Monika B. Vizedom and Gabrielle L. Caffee. Chicago: University of Chicago Press, 1960.

Walker, Molly K. "Material Reactions to Fetal Sex." *Health Care for Women International* 13 (1992): 293–302.

West, Candace, and Don Zimmerman. "Doing Gender." *Gender & Society* 1 (1987): 125–51.

Whitehead, Harriet. "The Bow and the Burden Strap: A New Look at Institutionalized Homosexuality in Native North America." In *Sexual Meanings: The Cultural Construction of Gender and Sexuality*, edited by Sherry B. Ortner and Harriet Whitehead. Cambridge, England: Cambridge University Press, 1981.

Wikan, Unni. *Behind the Veil in Arabia: Women in Oman*. Baltimore, Md.: Johns Hopkins University Press, 1982.

Williams, Christine L. *Gender Differences at Work: Women and Men in Nontraditional Occupations*. Berkeley: University of California Press, 1989.

Williams, Walter L. *The Spirit and the Flesh: Sexual Diversity in American Indian Culture*. Boston: Beacon Press, 1986.

Yanagisako, Sylvia Junko, and Jane Fishburne Collier. "Toward a Unified Analysis of Gender and Kinship." In *Gender and Kinship: Essays Toward a Unified Analysis*, edited by Jane Fishburne Collier and Sylvia Junko Yanagisako. Berkeley: University of California Press, 1987.

Zelizer, Viviana A. *Pricing the Priceless Child: The Changing Social Value of Children*. New York: Basic Books, 1985.

Chapter 4: Montagnais Women and the Jesuit Program for Colonization by Eleanor Leacock

Bailey, Alfred Goldsworthy. *The Conflict of European and Eastern Algonkian Cultures, 1504–1700*. Toronto: University of Toronto Press, 1969.

Burgesse, J. Allan. "The Woman and the Child among the Lac-St-Jean Montagnais." *Primitive Man* 17, no. 102 (1944): 1–19.

Leacock, Eleanor. "The Montagnais 'Hunting Territory' and the Fur Trade." *American Anthropological Association Memoirs* 78 (1954).

——. "Matrilocality in a Simple Hunting Economy (Montagnais-Naskapi)." *Southwestern Journal of Anthropology* 11 (1955): 31–47.

——. "Status Among the Montagnais-Naskapi of Labrador." *Ethnohistory* 5 (1958): 200–09.

——. "The Montagnais-Naskapi Band." In *Contributions to Anthropology: Band Societies*, edited by David Damas. National Museums of Canada Bulletin 228. Ottawa: Queens Printer for Canada, 1969.

——. "The Montagais-Naskapi of the Seventeenth Century: Social Relations and Attitudes, from the Relations of Paul Le Jeune." In *Subarctic* edited by June Helm. Handbook of North American Indians, vol. 6. Washington: Smithsonian Institution, 1981.

Leacock, Eleanor, and Jacqueline Goodman, "Montagnais Marriage and the Jesuits in the Seventeenth Century: Incidents from the Relations of Paul Le Jeune." *Western Canadian Journal of Anthropology* 6, no. 3 (1976): 77–91.

Murphy, Robert F., and Julian H. Steward. "Tappers and Trappers: Parallel Processes in Acculturation." *Economic Development and Cultural Change* 4 (1955): 335–55.

Strong, William Duncan. "Cross-cousin Marriage and the Culture of the Northeastern Algonkian." *American Anthropologist* 31 (1929): 277–88.

Thwaites, R. G., ed. *The Jesuit Relations and Allied Documents*, 71 vols. Cleveland: Burrows Brothers Co., 1906.

Turner, Lucien. *Ethnology of the Ungava District, Hudson Bay Territory*. 11th Annual Report, Bureau of American Ethnology, 1894.

Part III: Gender, Wages, and Inequality

Cartmill, Randi S. "Occupational Sex Segregation in Global Perspective: Comparative Analyses of Developed and Developing Nations." CDE Working Paper 99–12; Center for Demography and Economy, University of Wisconsin-Madison, 1999.

Institute for Women's Policy Research. "The Gender Pay Gap by Occupation." IWPR Publication #C350a, 2009. <http://www.docstoc.com/docs/5681750/The-Gender-Pay-Gap-Report-April-2009> (24 July 2009).

Stolberg, Sheryl Gay. "Obama Signs Equal Pay Legislation," Politics Section, *New York Times*, January 29, 2009.

Chapter 11: The Social Organization of Toy Stores by Christine L. Williams

Abelson, Reed. "States Are Battling against Wal-Mart over Health Care." *New York Times*, November 1, 2004, A1, A13.

Acker, Joan. "Hierarchies, Jobs, Bodies: A Theory of Gendered Organizations." *Gender & Society* 4 (1990): 139–58.

Burawoy, Michael. *Manufacturing Consent*. Chicago: University of Chicago Press, 1980.

Cohen, Lizabeth. *A Consumers' Republic: The Politics of Mass Consumption in Postwar America*. New York: Knopf, 2003.

Collins, Patricia Hill. *Black Feminist Thought*. New York: Routledge, 2000.

Ehrenreich, Barbara. *Nickel and Dimed: On (Not) Getting By in America*. New York: Metropolitan Books, 2001.

Folbre, Nancy. *The Invisible Heart: Economics and Family Values*. New York: New Press, 2001.

Freeman, Carla. *High Tech and High Heels in the Global Economy: Women, Work, and Pink Collar Identities in the Caribbean*. Durham, NC: Duke University Press, 2000.

Glazer, Nona. *Women's Paid and Unpaid Labor: The Work Transfer in Health Care and Retailing*. Philadelphia: Temple University Press, 1993.

Greenhouse, Steven. "Abercrombie & Fitch Accused of Discrimination in Hiring." *New York Times,* June 17, 2003, AI, A20.

Hochschild, Arlie. *The Managed Heart: Commercialization of Human Feeling*. Berkeley: University of California Press, 1983.

Hondagneu-Sotelo, Pierrette. *Doméstica: Immigrant Workers Cleaning and Caring in the Shadows of Affluence*. Berkeley: University of California Press, 2001.

Hossfeld, Karen. "Their Logic against Them: Contradictions in Sex, Race, and Class in Silicon Valley." Pp. 149–78 in *Women Workers and Global Restructuring*, edited by Kathryn Ward. Ithaca, NY: ILR Press, 1990.

Kessler-Harris, Alice. *A Woman's Wage*. Lexington: University of Kentucky Press, 1990.

Leidner, Robin. *Fast Food, Fast Talk: Service Work and the Routinization of Everyday Life*. Berkeley: University of California Press, 1993.

Lichtenstein, Nelson. *State of the Union: A Century of American Labor*. Princeton, NJ: Princeton University Press, 2002.

Loe, Meika. "Working for Men: At the Intersection of Power, Gender, and Sexuality." *Sociological Inquiry* 66 (1996): 399–421.

McCall, Leslie. *Complex Inequality: Gender, Class and Race in the New Economy*. New York: Routledge, 2001.

Milkman, Ruth. *Farewell to the Factory: Auto Workers in the Late Twentieth Century*. Berkeley: University of California Press, 1997.

National Association for the Advancement of Colored People. "Retail Industry Receives 'D' Grade for Diversity." http://www.naacp.org/news/2003/2003-07-15-3.html> (9 Dec. 2003).

Newman, Katherine S. *No Shame in My Game*. New York: Knopf, 1999.

Project on Disney. *Inside the Mouse*. Durham, NC: Duke University Press, 1995.

Reskin, Barbara, and Patricia Roos. *Job Queues, Gender Queues*. Philadelphia: Temple University Press, 1990.

Ritzer, George. *McDonaldization: The Reader*. Thousand Oaks, CA: Pine Forge Press, 2002.

Salzinger, Leslie. "Manufacturing Sexual Subjects: 'Harassment,' Desire and Discipline on a Maquiladora Shop Floor." *Ethnography* 1, no. 1 (2000): 67–92.

———. *Genders in Production: Making Workers in Mexico's Global Factories*. Berkeley: University of California Press, 2003.

Talwar, Jennifer Parker. *Fast Food, Fast Track: Immigrants, Big Business, and the American Dream*. Boulder, CO: Westview Press, 2002.

U. S. Bureau of Labor Statistics. "Median Usual Weekly Earnings of Full-time Wage and Salary Workers by Detailed Occupation and Sex." 2002. <http://ftp.bls.gov/pub/special.requests/lf/aat39.txt.html> (9 Dec. 2003).

———. "Household Data Annual Averages. 18. Employed Persons by Detailed Industry, Sex, Race, and Hispanic or Latino Ethnicity." 2004. <http://www.bls.gov/cps/cpsaat18.pdf.html> (6 April 2005).

Williams, Christine L. *Gender Differences at Work: Women and Men in Nontraditional Occupations*. Berkeley: University of California Press, 1989.

———. *Still a Man's World: Men Who Do "Women's Work."* Berkeley: University of California Press, 1995.

Wrigley, Julia. *Other People's Children*. New York: Basic Books, 1995.

Part IV: Gender, Management, and the Professions

The Economist. "The Conundrum of the Glass Ceiling," July 21, 2005.

Gilligan, Carol. *In a Different Voice: Psychological Theory and Women's Development*. Cambridge, MA: Harvard University Press, 1982.

Groves, Nancy. "From Past to Present: The Changing Demographics of Women in Medicine." *Ophthalmology Times* (February): 2008.

Ripley, Amanda. "Who Says a Woman Can't Be Einstein?" *Time Magazine* (February 27, 2005). http://www.time.com/time/magazine/article/0,9171,1032332,00.html (24 June 2009).

Schonberger Andrea, and Sabine Schonberger. "Bridging the Gap." *Time Magazine*, January 22, 2006.

UN Report. "The World's Women 2000: Trends and Statistics." UN Statistics Division Report, 2000. http://unstats.un.org/unsd/Demographic/products/indwin/wwpub2000.htm (21 January 2008).

U.S. Department of Labor. Employment and Earnings, Annual Averages Table 39, "Median Weekly Earnings of Full Time Wage and Salary Workers by Detailed Occupation and Sex," 2007. http://www.bls.gov/cps/cpsaat39.pdf (21 May 2009).

U.S. EEOC. "Diversity in Law Firms." 2003. http://www.eeoc.gov/stats/reports/diversitylaw/index.html#status (18 June 2008).

Wirth, Linda. "Breaking Through the Glass Ceiling: Women in Management." International Labor Office, 2002. http://www.gouvernement.lu/salle_presse/actualite/2002/02/04jacobsbiltgen/wirth.pdf (11 May 2008).

Chapter 13: The Impact of Hierarchical Structures on the Work Behavior of Women and Men by Rosabeth Moss Kanter

Bartol, Kathryn M. "Male Versus Female Leaders: The Effect of Leader Need for Dominance on Follower Satisfaction." *Academy of Management Journal* 17 (June 1974): 225–33.

———. "The Effect of Male Versus Female Leaders on Follower Satisfaction and Performance." *Journal of Business Research* 3 (January 1975): 33–42.

Bartol, Kathryn M., and D. Anthony Butterfield. "Sex Effects in Evaluating Leaders." Working Paper #74–10. School of Business Administration, University of Massachusetts, 1974.

Bennis, Warren G, Norman Berkowitz, Mona Affinito, and Mary Malone. "Reference Groups and Loyalties in the Outpatient Department." *Administrative Science Quarterly* 2 (1958b): 481–500.

Blau, Peter M., and W. Richard Scott. *Formal Organizations*. San Francisco: Chandler, 1962.

Bonjean, Charles M., Grady D. Bruce, and Allen J. Williams Jr. "Social Mobility and Job Satisfaction: A Replication and Extension." *Social Forces* 46 (June 1967): 492–501.

Bowman, G. W., N. B. Worthy, and S. A. Greyser. "Are Women Executives People?" *Harvard Business Review* 43 (July-August 1965): 14–30.

Burns, Tom. "The Reference of Conduct in Small Groups: Cliques and Cabals in Occupational Milieux." *Human Relations* 8 (1955): 467–86.

Chinoy, Ely. *Automobile Workers and the American Dream*. New York: Doubleday, 1955.

Cohen, Arthur R. "Upward Communication in Experimentally Created Hierarchies." *Human Relations* 11 (1958): 41–53.

Constantini, Edmond, and Kenneth H. Craik. "Women as Politicians: The Social Background, Personality, and Political Careers of Female Party Leaders." *Journal of Social Issues* 28, no. 2 (1972): 217–36.

Crowley, Joan E., Teresa E. Levitan, and Robert P. Quinn. "Seven Deadly Half-truths about Women." *Psychology Today* 6 (April 1973): 94–96.

Crozier, Michael. *The World of the Office Worker*. Translated by David Landau. Chicago: University of Chicago Press, (1965) 1971.

Cussler, Margaret. *The Woman Executive*. New York: Harcourt Brace, 1958.

Davis, Keith. *Human Relations at Work.* New York: McGraw-Hill, 1967.

Day, D. R., and R. M. Stodgill. "Leader Behavior of Male and Female Supervisors: A Comparative Study." *Personnel Psychology* 25 (1972): 353–60.

Dubin, Robert. "Industrial Workers' Worlds." *Social Problems* 3 (January 1956): 131–42.

Epstein, Cynthia Fuchs. *Woman's Place: Options and Limits on Professional Careers.* Berkeley: University of California Press, 1970.

Gardner, Burleigh B. *Human Relations in Industry.* Chicago: Richard D. Irwin, 1945.

Goodstadt, Barry E., and Larry A. Hjelle. "Power to the Powerless: Focus of Control and the Use of Power." *Journal of Personality and Social Psychology* 27 (July 1973): 190–96.

Goodstadt, B., and D. Kipnis. "Situational Influences on the Use of Power." *Journal of Applied Psychology* 54 (1970): 201–17.

Grunker, William J., Donald D. Cooke, and Arthur W. Kirsch. *Climbing the Job Ladder: A Study of Employee Advancement in Eleven Industries.* New York: Shelley and Co., 1970.

Hennig, Margaret. "Career Development for Women Executives." PhD diss., Harvard Business School, 1970.

Hetzler, Stanley A. "Variations in Role-playing Patterns among Different Echelons of Bureaucratic Leaders." *American Sociological Review* 20 (December 1955): 700–6.

Homall, Geraldine M. "The Motivation to be Promoted among Non-Exempt Employees: An Expectancy Theory Approach." Master's thesis, Cornell University, 1974.

Hurwitz, Jacob I., Alvin F. Zander, and Bernard Hymovich. "Some Effects of Power on the Relations among Group Members." In *Group Dynamics,* edited by D. Cartwright and A. Zander. New York: Harper and Row, 1968.

Johnston, Ruth. "Pay and Job Satisfaction: A Survey of Some Research Findings." *International Labour Review* 3 (May 1975): 441–49.

Kanter, Rosabeth Moss. "The Problems of Tokenism." Working Paper, Center for Research on Women in Higher Education and the Professions, Wellesley College, 1975a.

———. "Women and the Structure of Organizations: Explorations in Theory and Behavior." In *Another Voice: Feminist Perspectives on Social Life and Social Science*, edited by M. Millman and R. M. Kanter. New York: Doubleday, 1975b.

———. "Research Styles and Intervention Strategies: An Argument for a Social Structural Model." *Signs: A Journal of Woman in Culture and Society* 2 (Spring 1976a). And in *Women and the Workplace*, edited by M. Blaxall and B. Reagan. Chicago: University of Chicago Press, 1976a.

———. *Men and Women of the Corporation.* New York: Basic Books, 1993.

Laird, Donald A., and Eleanor C. Laird. *The Psychology of Supervising the Working Woman.* New York: McGraw-Hill, 1942.

Langer, Elinor. "Inside the New York Telephone Company." In *Women at Work*, edited by W. L. O'Neil. Chicago: Quadrangle, 1970.

Laws, Judith Long. "Work Aspirations in Women: False Leads and New Starts." *Signs: A Journal of Women in Culture and Society* 2 (Spring 1976) and in *Women and the Workplace*, edited by M. Blaxall and B. Reagan. Chicago: University of Chicago Press, 1976.

Levenson, Bernard. "Bureaucratic Succession." Pp. 362–75 in *Complex Organizations: A Sociological Reader*, edited by A. Etzioni. New York: Holt, Rinehart and Winston, 1961.

Lirtzman, Sidney I. and Mahmoud A. Wahba. "Determinants of Coalitional Behavior of Men and Women: Sex Roles or Situational Requirements?" *Journal of Applied Psychology* 56, no. 5 (1972): 406–11.

Marcus, Philip M., and James S. House. "Exchange between Superiors and Subordinates in Large Organizations." *Administrative Science Quarterly* 18 (1973): 209–22.

Mayer, Kurt B., and Sidney Goldstein. "Manual Workers as Small Businessmen." Pp. 537–50 in *Blue Collar World,* edited by A. Shostak and W. Gomberg. Englewood Cliffs, New Jersey: Prentice-Hall, 1964.

Merton, Robert K. *Social Theory and Social Structure.* New York: Free Press, 1968.

Pelz, Donald C. "Influence: A Key to Effective Leadership in the First-line Supervisor." *Personnel* 29 (1952): 3–11.

Pennings, J. M. "Work-value Systems of White-collar Workers." *Administrative Science Quarterly* 15 (1970): 397–405.

Purcell, Theodore V. *Blue Collar Man: Patterns of Dual Allegiance in Industry.* Cambridge: Harvard University Press, 1960.

Riesman, David. "Introduction." In *Automobile Workers and the American Dream* by Ely Chinoy. New York: Doubleday, 1955.

Roethlisberger, F. J. and William J. Dickson. *Management and the Worker.* Cambridge: Harvard University Press, 1939.

Rosen, Benson and Thomas H. Jerdee. "The Influence of Sex-role Stereotypes on Evaluations of Male and Female Supervisory Behavior." *Journal of Applied Psychology* 5, no. 1 (1973): 44–48.

Rousell, Cecile. "Relationship of Sex of Department Head to Department Climate." *Administrative Science Quarterly* 19 (June 1974): 211–20.

Sikula, Andrew F. "The Uniqueness of Secretaries as Employees." *Journal of Business Education* 48 (Fall 1973): 203–5.

Stein, Barry A. "Patterns of Managerial Promotions." Working Paper, Center for Research on Women in Higher Education and the Professions, Wellesley College, 1976.

Tannebaum, Arnold S. *Social Psychology of the Work Organization.* Belmont, California: Wadsworth, 1966.

Tannenbaum, Arnold S., Bogdan Kavcic, Menachem Rosner, Mino Vianello and Georg Wieser. *Hierarchy in Organizations: An International Comparison.* San Francisco: Jossey-Bass, 1974.

Thibaut, John W. and Henry W. Riecken. "Authoritarianism, Status, and the Communication of Aggression." *Human Relations* 8 (1955): 95–120.

Tichy, Noel. "An Analysis of Clique Formation and Structure in Organizations." *Administrative Science Quarterly* 18 (1973): 194–207.

Uesugi, Thomas K. and W. Edgar Vinacke. "Strategy in a Feminine Game." *Sociometry* 26 (1963): 35–88.

Vinacke, Edgar W. "Sex Roles in a Three-person Game." *Sociometry* 22 (December 1959): 343–60.

Chapter 14: Women and Men as Litigators: Gender Differences on the Job by Jennifer Pierce

American Bar Association. *Model Code of Professional Responsibility and Code of Judicial Conduct.* Chicago, Ill.: National Center for Professional Responsibility and the American Bar Association, 1982.

Bay, Monica. "Poll: Sex Bias Pervades State's Legal Profession." *The Recorder,* September 13, 1989, 1.

Benjamin, Jessica. *The Bonds of Love: Psychoanalysis, Feminism and the Problems of Domination.* New York: Pantheon Books, 1989.

Brown, Lyn, and Carol Gilligan. *Meeting at the Crossroads: Women's Psychology and Girl's Development*. Cambridge, Mass.: Harvard University Press, 1992.

Butler, Katy. "Women Lawyers Still Complain of Bias." *San Francisco Chronicle,* December 4, 1989, A3.

Coser, Rose Laub. "Laughter among Colleagues." *Psychiatry* 23 (February 1960): 81–90.

Epstein, Cynthia Fuchs. *Women in Law*. 3rd ed. Urbana: University of Illinois Press, 1993.

———. *Women in Law.* 2nd ed. New York: Anchor Books, 1983.

Fishman, Pamela. "Interaction: The Work Woman Do," *Social Problems* 25, no. 4 (April 1978): 397–406.

Gilligan, Carol. *In A Different Voice: Psychological Theory and Women's Development*. Cambridge, Mass.: Harvard University Press, 1982.

Harragan, Betty. *Games Mother Never Taught You: Corporate Gamesmanship for Women*. New York: Warner Books, 1977.

Hazard, Geoffrey. "Male Culture Still Dominates the Profession." *National Law Journal* (December 19, 1988): 13.

Hochschild, Arlie. "Inside the Clockwork of Male Careers." In *Women and the Power to Change,* edited by Florence Howe. New York: McGraw Hill, 1975.

Jack, Dana, and Rand Jack. *Moral Visions and Professional Decisions: The Changing Values of Women and Men Lawyers*. New York: Cambridge University Press, 1989.

———. "Women Lawyers: Archetypes and Alternatives." In *Mapping the Moral Domain: A Contribution of Women's Thinking to Psychological Theory and Education*, edited by Carol Gilligan, J. Ward, and J. Taylor. Cambridge, Mass.: Harvard University Graduate School of Education, 1988.

Jordan, Hallye. "ABA Head Urges Peer Pressure." *San Francisco Banner,* March 22, 1989, 3.

Kanter, Rosabeth Moss. "Reflections on Women and the Legal Profession: A Sociological Perspective," *Harvard Women's Law Journal* 1, no. 1 (Spring 1978): 1–22.

———. *Men and Women of the Corporation*. New York: Basic Books, 1977.

Lewin, Tamar. "Women Say They Face Obstacles as Lawyers." *New York Times*, December 4, 1989, A21.

MacCorquodale, Patricia, and Gary Jensen. "Women in the Law: Partners of Tokens?" *Gender & Society* 7, no. 4 (December 1993): 582–93.

Margolick, David. "Curbing Sexual Harassment in the Legal World." *New York Times,* November 9, 1990, B11

Morello, Karen. *The Invisible Bar: The Woman Lawyer in American, 1638 to the Present*. New York: Random House, 1986.

National Law Journal. "What America Really Thinks About Lawyers," (October 1986): 1.

Rhode, Deborah. *Justice and Gender: Sex Discrimination and the Law*. Cambridge, Mass.: Harvard University Press, 1989.

———. "Perspectives on Professional Women." *Stanford Law Review* 40 (May 1988): 1163–1207.

Rosenberg, Janet, Harry Perlstadt, and William Phillips. "Now We That Are Here: Discrimination, Disparagement and Harassment at Work and the Experience of Women Lawyers." *Gender & Society* 7, no. 3 (September 1993): 415–33.

Salaman, Linda. "Progress for Women? Yes? But . . . " *American Bar Association Journal,* (April 1, 1988): 18.

Spangler, Eve, Marsha Gordon, and Ronald Pipkin. "Token Women: An Empirical Test of Kanter's Hypothesis." *American Journal of Sociology* 84, no 1 (July 1978): 160–70.

Stacey, Judith. *Brave New Families.* New York: Basic Books, 1991.

Strachan, Nell. "A Map for Women on the Road to Success." *American Bar Association Journal* (May 1984): 94–96.

West, Candace, and Don Zimmerman. "Doing Gender." *Gender & Society* 1, no.2 (June 1987): 125–51.

Williams, Christine. *Gender Differences at Work: Women and Men in Nontraditional Occupations.* Berkeley and Los Angeles: University of California Press, 1989.

Chapter 15: The Glass Escalator: Hidden Advantages for Men in the 'Female' Professions by Christine L. Williams

Bielby, William T., and James N. Baron. "A Woman's Place Is with Other Women: Sex Segregation Within Organizations." In *Sex Segregation in the Workplace: Trends, Explanations, Remedies*, edited by Barbara Reskin. Washington D.C.: National Academy Press, 1984: 27–55.

Blum, Linda M. *Between Feminism and Labor: The Significance of the Comparable Worth Movement.* Berkeley and Los Angeles: University of California Press, 1991.

Carothers, Suzanne C., and Peggy Crull. "Contrasting Sexual Harassment in Female-dominated and Male-dominated Occupations." Pp. 220–27 in *My Troubles are Going to have Trouble with Me: Everyday Trials and Triumphs of Women Workers*, edited by Karen B. Sacks and Dorothy Remy. New Brunswick, N.J.: Rutgers University Press, 1984.

Cohn, Samuel. *The Process of Occupational Sex-Typing.* Philadelphia: Temple University Press, 1985.

Ehrenreich, Barbara, and Deirdre English. *For Her Own Good: 100 Years of Expert Advice to Women.* Garden City, N.Y.: Anchor Press, 1978.

Epstein, Cynthia Fuchs. *Women in Law.* New York: Basic Books, 1981.

———. *Deceptive Distinctions: Sex, Gender and the Social Order.* New Haven, Conn.: Yale University Press, 1988.

———. "Workplace Boundaries: Conceptions and Creations." *Social Research* 56 (1989): 571–90.

Freeman, Sue J. M. *Managing Lives: Corporate Women and Social Change.* Amherst, Mass.: University of Massachusetts Press, 1990.

Grimm, James W., and Robert N. Stern. "Sex Roles and Internal Labor Market Structures: The Female Semi-professions." *Social Problems* 21 (1974): 690–705.

Hardcastle, D.A. "The Social Work Labor Force." Austin, Texas: School of Social Work, University of Texas, 1987.

Hodson, Randy, and Teresa Sullivan. *The Social Organization of Work.* Belmont, Calif.: Wadsworth Publishing Co., 1990.

Jacobs, Jerry. *Revolving Doors: Sex Segregation and Women's Careers.* Stanford, Calif.: Stanford University Press, 1989.

Kanter, Rosabeth Moss. *Men and Women of the Corporation.* New York: Basic Books, 1977.

Kessler-Harris, Alice. *A Woman's Wage: Historical Meanings and Social Consequences.* Lexington, Ky.: Kentucky University Press, 1990.

Lorber, Judith. *Women Physicians: Careers, Status, and Power.* New York: Tavistock, 1984.

Martin, Susan E. *Breaking and Entering: Police Women on Patrol.* Berkeley, Calif.: University of California Press, 1980.

———. "Think like a Man, Work like a Dog, and Act like a Lady: Occupational Dilemmas of Policewomen." Pp. 205–23 in *The Worth of Women's Work: A Qualitative Synthesis*, edited by Anne Statham, Eleanor M. Miller, and Hans O. Mauksch. Albany N.Y.: State University of New York Press, 1988.

Phenix, Katharine. "The Status of Women Librarians." *Frontiers* 9 (1987): 36–40.

Reskin, Barbara. "Bringing the Men Back In: Sex Differentiation and the Devaluation of Women's Work." *Gender & Society* 2 (1988): 58–81.

Reskin, Barbara, and Heidi Hartman. *Women's Work, Men's Work: Sex Segregation on the Job.* Washington, D.C.: National Academy Press, 1986.

Reskin, Barbara, and Patricia Roos. *Job Queues, Gender Queues: Explaining Women's Inroads into Male Occupations.* Philadelphia: Temple University Press, 1990.

Schmuck, Patricia A. "Women School Employees in the United States." Pp. 75–97 in *Women Educators: Employees of Schools in Western Countries*, edited by Patricia A. Schmuck. Albany, N.Y.: State University of New York Press, 1987.

Schreiber, Carol. *Men and Women in Transitional Occupations.* Cambridge, Mass.: MIT Press, 1979.

Spencer, Anne, and David Podmore. *In a Man's World: Essays on Women in Male-dominated Professions.* London: Tavistock, 1987.

Strauss, Anselm L. *Qualitative Analysis for Social Scientists.* Cambridge, England: Cambridge University Press, 1987.

U.S. Bureau of the Census. *Detailed Population Characteristics,* Vol. 1, Ch. D. Washington, D.C.: Government Printing Office, 1980.

U.S. Congress, House. *Civil Rights and Women's Equity in Employment Act of 1991 Report.* (Report 102–40, Part I.) Washington, D.C.: Government Printing Office, 1991.

U.S. Department of Labor. *Employment and Earnings.* Bureau of Statistics. Washington, D.C.: Government Printing Office, January 1991.

Williams, Christine L. *Gender Differences at Work: Women and Men in Nontraditional Occupations.* Berkeley, Calif.: University of California Press, 1989.

Yoder, Janice D. "Women at West Point: Lessons for Token Women in Male-dominated Occupations." Pp. 523–37 in *Women: A Feminist Perspective*, edited by Jo Freeman. Mountain View, Calif. Mayfield Publishing Company, 1989.

York, Reginald, O., H. Carl Henley, and Dorothy N. Gamble. "Sexual Discrimination in Social Work: Is it Salary or Advancement?" *Social Work* 32 (1987): 336–40.

Zimmer, Lynn. "Tokenism and Women in the Workplace." *Social Problems* 35 (1988): 64–77.

Chapter 16: Black Mobility in White Corporations: Up the Corporate Ladder but Out on a Limb by Sharon M. Collins

Braverman, Harry. *Labor and Monopoly Capital: The Degradation of Work in the Twentieth Century.* Albany: State University of New York Press, 1973.

Chicago Reporter. "Annual Corporate Survey." December 2–6, 1983.

———. "Annual Corporate Survey." January 7–10, 1986.

Chicago Urban League. *Blacks in Policy-Making Positions in Chicago.* Chicago: Chicago Urban League, 1977.

Collins, Sharon M. *Black Corporate Executives: The Making and Breaking of a Black Middle Class*. Philadelphia: Temple University Press, 1977.

Doeringer, Peter B., and Michael J. Piore. *Internal Labor Markets and Manpower Analysis*. Lexington, Mass.: D.C. Heath, 1971.

Farley, Reynolds. *Blacks and Whites: Narrowing the Gap?* Cambridge: Harvard University Press, 1984.

Farley, Reynolds, and Walter R. Allen. *The Color Line and the Quality of Life in America*. New York: Russell Sage, 1987.

Freeman, Richard. *The Black Elite*. New York: McGraw-Hill, 1976a.

———. *The Over-Educated American*. New York: Academic Press, 1976b.

———. "Black Economic Progress after 1964: Who Has Gained and Why." Pp. 247–95 in *Studies in Labor Markets*, edited by S. Rosen. Chicago: University of Chicago Press, 1981.

Ghiloni, Beth W. "The Velvet Ghetto: Women, Power, and the Corporation." Pp. 21–36 in *Power Elites and Organizations*, edited by G. William Domhoff and Thomas R. Dye. Newbury Park, Calif.: Sage, 1987.

Heidrick and Struggles, Inc. *Chief Personnel Executives Look at Blacks in Business*. New York: Heidrick and Struggles, Inc., 1979.

Hermstein, Richard J., and Charles Murray. *The Bell Curve: Intelligence and Class Structure in American Life*. New York: Free Press, 1994.

Irons, Edward, and Gilbert W. Moore. *Black Managers in the Banking Industry*. New York: Praeger, 1985.

Jones, Edward W. "Black Managers: The Dream Deferred." *Harvard Business Review* (May–June 1986): 84–89.

Kanter, Rosabeth Moss. *Men and Women of the Corporation*. New York: Basic Books, 1977.

Korn/Ferry. *Korn/Ferry International's Executive Profile: A Survey of Corporate Leaders in the Eighties*. New York: Korn/Ferry International, 1986.

———. *Korn/Ferry International's Executive Profile: A Decade of Change in Corporate Leadership*. New York: Korn/Ferry International, 1990.

Kraiger, Kurt, and J. Kevin Ford. "A Meta-analysis of Ratee Race Effects in Performance Ratings." *Journal of Applied Psychology*, 70 (1985): 56–63.

Landry, Bart. *The New Black Middle Class*. Berkeley, Calif.: University of California Press, 1987.

Murray, Charles. *Losing Ground: American Social Policy 1950–1980*. New York: Basic Books, 1984.

National Opinion Research Center, Chicago. *Closing the Gap: Forty Years of Economic Progress for Blacks*. Santa Monica, Calif.: Rand Corporation, 1986.

Nkomo, Stella M., and Taylor Cox, Jr. "Factors Affecting the Upward Mobility of Black Managers in Private Sector Organizations." *The Review of Black Political Economy* 78 (1990): 40–57.

Reskin, Barbara F. *Job Queus, Gender Queus: Explaining Women's Inroads into Male Occupations*. Philadelphia: Temple University Press, 1990.

Reskin, Barbara F., and Patricia Roos. "Status Hierarchies and Sex Segregation." Pp. 71–81 in *Ingredients for Women's Employment Policy*, edited by Christine Bose and Glenna Spite. Albany: State University of New York Press, 1987.

Smith, James P., and Finis R. Welch. "Longer Trends in Black/White Economic Status and Recent Effects of Affirmative Action." Paper prepared for Social Science Research Council Conference at the National Opinion Research Center, Chicago, 1983.

Sowell, Thomas. "The Economics and Politics of Race." Transcript from "The Firing Line" program. Taped in New York City on November 1983 and telecast later by PBS.

Theodore, Nikolas C., and D. Garth Taylor. *The Geography of Opportunity: The Status of African Americans in the Chicago Area Economy.* Chicago: Chicago Urban League, 1991.

Thurow, Lester. *Generating Inequality.* New York: Basic Books, 1975.

Tomaskovic-Devey, Donald. *Gender and Racial Inequality at Work: The Sources and Consequences of Job Segregation.* Ithaca, N.Y.: ILR Press, 1993.

U. S. Bureau of Census. *Occupational Characteristics.* Series PC(2)–7A. Washington, D.C.: The Bureau of Census, 1960.

———. *Occupational Characteristics.* Series PC(2)–7A. Washington, D.C.: The Bureau of Census, 1973.

U. S. Department of Labor. *Report on the Glass Ceiling Initiative.* Washington, D.C.: U. S. Department of Labor, 1990.

Chapter 17: Gender and Labor in Asian Immigrant Families by Yen Le Espiritu

Akast, D. "Cruller Fates: Cambodians Find Slim Profit in Doughnuts." *Los Angeles Times*, March 9, 1993, sec. D:1.

Blumenberg, E., and P. Ong. "Labor Squeeze and Ethnic/racial Composition in the U.S. Apparel Industry." Pp. 309–27 in *Global Production: The Apparel Industry in the Pacific Rim*, edited by E. Bonacich, L. Cheng, N. Chinchilla, N. Hamilton, and P. Ong. Philadelphia: Temple University Press, 1994.

Bonacich, E. "Asians in the Los Angeles Garment Industry." Pp. 137–63 in *The New Asian Immigration in Los Angeles and Global Restructuring*, edited by P. Ong, E. Bonacich, and L. Cheng. Berkeley: University of California Press, 1994.

Bonacich, E., M. Hossain, and J. Park. "Korean Immigrant Working Women in the Early 1980s." Pp. 219–47 in *Korean Women in Transition: At Home and Abroad*, edited by E. Yu and E. H. Philipps. Los Angeles: California State University, Center for Korean-American and Korean Studies, 1987.

Chai, A. Y. "Freed from the Elders but Locked into Labor: Korean Immigrant Women in Hawaii." *Women's Studies* 13 (1987): 223–34.

Chen, H. S. *Chinatown No More: Taiwan Immigrants in Contemporary New York.* Ithaca, NY: Cornell University Press, 1992.

Cho, S. "Asian Pacific American Women and Racialized Sexual Harassment." Pp. 164–73 in *Making More Waves: New Writing by Asian American Women*, edited by E. Kim, L. Villanueva, and Asian Women United of California. Boston: Beacon, 1997.

Clement, W., and J. Myles. *Relations of Ruling: Class and Gender in Postindustrial Societies.* Montreal, Canada: McGill-Queen's University Press, 1994.

Curtis, R. "Household and Family in Theory on Equality." *American Sociological Review* 51 (1986): 168–83.

Dhaliwal, A. K. "Gender at Work: The Renegotiation of Middle-class Womanhood in a South Asian-owned Business." Pp. 75–85 in *Reviewing Asian America: Locating Diversity*, edited by W. L. Ng, S.-Y. Chin, J. S. Moy, and G. Y. Okihiro. Pullman: Washington State University Press, 1995.

Donato, K. M. "Understanding U.S. Immigration: Why Some Countries Send Women and others Send Men." Pp. 159–84 in *Seeking Common Ground: Multidisciplinary Studies of Immigrant Women in the United States*, edited by D. Gabbacia. Westport, CT: Greenwood, 1992.

Donnelly, N. D. *Changing Lives of Refugee Hmong Women.* Seattle: Washington University Press, 1994.

Duleep, H., and S. Sanders. "Discrimination at the Top: American-born Asian and White Men." *Industrial Relations* 31, (1993): 416–32.

Espiritu, Y. L. *Filipino American Lives.* Philadelphia: Temple University Press, 1995.

Fawcett, J. T., and R. W. Gardner. "Asian Immigrant Entrepreneurs and Non-Entrepreneurs: A Comparative Study of Recent Korean and Filipino Immigrants." *Population and Environment* 15 (1994): 211–38.

Gardner, R, B. Robey, and P.C. Smith, eds. "Asian American: Growth, Change, and Diversity." *Population Bulletin* 40, no. 4 (1985).

Glenn, E. N. *Issei, Nisei, War Bride: Three Generations of Japanese American Women at Domestic Service.* Philadelphia: Temple University Press, 1986.

Gold, S. "Chinese-Vietnamese Entrepreneurs in California." Pp 196–226 in *The New Asian Immigration in Los Angeles and Global Restructuring,* edited by P. Ong , E. Bonacich, and L. Cheng. Philadelphia: Temple University Press, 1994.

Green, S. *Silicon Valley's Women Workers: A Theoretical Analysis of Sex-segregation in the Electronics Industry Labor Market.* Honolulu, HI: Impact of Transnational Interactions Project, Cultural Learning Institute, East-West Center, 1980.

Hondagneu-Sotelo, P. *Gendered Transition: Mexican Experiences in Immigration.* Berkeley: University of California Press, 1994.

Hood, J. G. *Becoming a Two Job Family.* New York: Praeger, 1983.

Hossfeld, K. "Hiring Immigrant Women: Silicon Valley's 'Simple Formula.'" Pp. 65–93 in *Women of Color in U.S. Society,* edited by M. Baca Zinn and B. T. Dills. Philadelphia: Temple University Press, 1994.

Hune, S., and K. Chan. "Special Focus: Asian Pacific American Demographic and Educational Trends." In *Minorities in Education* (Report No. 15), edited by D. Carter and R. Wilson. Washington, DC: American Council on Education, 1997.

Irby, C., and E. M. Pon. "Confronting New Mountains: Mental Healthy Problems among Male Hmong and Mien Refugees." *Amerasia Journal* 14 (1988): 109–18.

Kanjanapan, W. "The Immigration of Asian Professionals to the United States: 1988–1990." *International Migration Review* 29 (1995): 7–32.

Katz, N., and D. Kemnitzer. "Women and Work in Silicon Valley: Options and Futures." In *My Troubles Are Going to Have Trouble with Me: Everyday Trials and Triumphs of Women Workers,* edited by K. B. Sacks and D. Remy. New Brunswick, NJ: Rutgers University Press, 1984.

Kibria, N. *Family Tightrope: The Changing Lives of Vietnamese Americans.* Princeton, NY: Princeton University Press, 1993.

Kim, K. C., and W. M. Hurh. "Ethnic Resource Utilization of Korean Immigrant Entrepreneurs in the Chicago Minority Area." *International Migration Review* 19 (1985): 82–111.

———. "The Burden of Double Roles: Korean Wives in the U.S.A." *Ethnic and Racial Studies* 11 (1988): 157–67.

Light, I., and E. Bonacich. *Immigrant Entrepreneurs: Koreans in Los Angeles, 1965–1982.* Berkeley: University of California Press, 1986.

Lim, L. Y. C. "Capitalism, Imperialism, and Patriarchy: The Dilemma of Third-World Women Workers in Multinational Factories." Pp. 70–91 in *Women, Men, and the International Division of Labor,* edited by J. Nash and M. P. Fernàndez-Kelly. Albany: State University of New York Press, 1983.

Loo, C., and P. Ong. "Slaying Demons with a Sewing Needle: Feminist Issues for Chinatown's Women." *Berkeley Journal of Sociology* 27 (1982): 77–88.

Loucky, J., M. Soldatenko, G. Scott, and E. Bonacich. "Immigrant Enterprise and Labor in the Los Angeles Garment Industry." Pp. 345–61 in *Global Production: The Apparel Industry in the Pacific Rim,* edited by E. Bonacich, L. Cheng, N. Chinchilla, N. Hamilton, and P. Ong. Philadelphia: Temple University Press, 1994.

Louie, M. C. "Immigrant Asian Women in Bay Area Garment Shops: 'After Sewing, Laundry, Cleaning and Cooking, I Have No Breath Left to Sing.'" *Amerasia Journal* 18 (1992): 1–26.

Lowe, L. "Work, Immigration, Gender: Asian 'American' Women." Pp. 267–77 in *Making More Waves: New Writing by Asian American Women,* edited by E. Kim, L. Villanueva, and Asian Women United of California. Boston: Beacon, 1997.

Luu, V. "The Hardship of Escape for Vietnamese Women." Pp. 60–72 in *Making Waves: An Anthology of Writings by and about Asian American Women,* edited by Asian Women United of California. Boston: Beacon, 1989.

May, L. "Asians Looking to Broaden Horizons: Immigrants Prosper but Hope to Venture Outside the 'Business Ghetto.'" *Los Angeles Times,* February 2, 1987.

Mazumdar, S. "General Introduction: A Woman-centered Perspective on Asian American History." Pp. 1–22 in *Making waves: An Anthology by and about Asian American Women,* edited by Asian Women United of California. Boston: Beacon, 1989.

Min, P. G. "Korean Immigrant Wives' Overwork." *Korea Journal of Population and Development* 21 (1992): 23–36.

———. "Korean Americans." Pp. 199–231 in *Asian Americans: Contemporary Trends and Issues,* edited by P. G. Min. Thousand Oaks, CA: Sage, 1995a.

———. "An Overview of Asian Americans." Pp. 10–37 in *Asian Americans: Contemporary Trends and Issues,* edited by P. G. Min. Thousand Oaks, CA: Sage, 1995b.

———. *Caught in the Middle: Korean Communities in New York and Los Angeles.* Berkeley: University of California Press. 1996.

———. *Changes and Conflicts: Korean Immigrant Families in New York.* Needham Heights, MA: Allyn and Bacon, 1998.

Morokvasic, M. "Birds of Passage are Also Women." *International Migration Review* 18 (1984): 886–907.

Ong, P. "Chinatown Unemployment and the Ethnic Labor Market." *Amerasia Journal* 11 (1984): 35–54.

Ong, P. , and T. Azores. "Health Professionals on the Front Line." Pp. 139–63 in *The State of Asian Pacific America: Economic Diversity, Issues, and Policies,* edited by P. Ong. Los Angeles: LEAP Asian Pacific American Public Policy Institute and University of California at Los Angeles Asian American Studies Center, 1994a.

———. "The Migration and Incorporation of Filipino Nurses." Pp. 164–95 in *The New Asian Immigration in Los Angeles and Global Restructuring,* edited by P. Ong, E. Bonacich, and L. Cheng. Philadelphia: Temple University Press, 1994b.

Ong, P., and E. Blumenberg. "Scientists and Engineers." Pp. 165–89 in *The State of Asian Pacific America: Economic Diversity, Issues, and Policies,* edited by P. Ong. Los Angeles: LEAP Asian Pacific American Public Policy Institute and University of California at Los Angeles Asian American Studies Center, 1994.

Ong, P., and S. Hee. "Economic Diversity." Pp. 31–56 in *The State of Asian Pacific America: Economic Diversity, Issues, and Policies,* edited by P. Ong. Los Angeles: LEAP Asian Pacific American Public Policy Institute and University of California at Los Angeles Asian American Studies Center, 1994.

Ong, P., and K. Umemoto. "Life and Work in the Inner-city." Pp. 87–112 in *The State of Asian Pacific America: Economic Diversity, Issues, and Policies,* edited by P. Ong. Los Angeles: LEAP Asian Pacific American Public Policy Institute and University of California at Los Angeles Asian American Studies Center, 1994.

Park, K. "Impact of New Productive Activities on the Organization of Domestic Life: A Case Study of the Korean American Community." Pp. 140–50 in *Frontiers of Asian American Studies,* edited by G. Nomura, R. Endo, S. Sumida, and R. Leong. Pullman: Washington State University Press, 1989.

Pedraza, S. "Women and Migration: The Social Consequences of Gender." *Annual Review of Sociology* 17 (1991): 303–25.

Pesquera, B. M. "'In the Beginning He Wouldn't Lift a Spoon:' The Division of Household Labor." Pp. 181–95 in *Building with Our Hands: New Directions in Chicana Studies*, edited by A. de la Torre and B. M. Pesquera. Berkeley: University of California Press, 1993.

Pessar, P. R. *The Pilipinos in America: Macro/micro Dimensions of Immigration and Integration.* Staten Island, NY: Center for Migration Studies, 1984.

Pressner, H. "Shift Work and Child Care among Young Dual-earner American Parents." *Journal of Marriage and the Family* 50 (1988): 133–48.

Romero, M. *Maid in the U.S.A.* New York: Routledge, 1992.

Rong, X. L., and J. Preissle. "The Continuing Decline in Asian American Teachers." *American Educational Research Journal* 34 (1997): 267–93.

Siegel, L., and H. Borock. *Background Report on Silicon Valley* (Prepared for the U.S. Commission on Civil Rights). Mountain View, CA: Pacific Studies Center, 1982.

Snow, R. "The New International Division of Labor and the U.S. Workforce: The Case of the Electronics Industry." In *Women, Men, and the International Division of Labor*, edited by J. Nash and M. P. Fernàndez-Kelly. Albany: State University of New York Press, 1986.

Tienda, M., and K. Booth. "Gender, Migration, and Social Change." *International Sociology* 6 (1991): 51–72.

Ui, S. "Unlikely Heroes: The Evolution of Female Leadership in a Cambodian Ethnic Enclave. Pp. 161–77 in *Ethnography Unbound*, edited by M. Burawoy. Berkeley: University of California Press, 1991.

U. S. Bureau of the Census. *Statistical Abstract of the United States,* 112th ed. Washington, DC: Government Printing Office, 1992.

U. S. Bureau of the Census. *We the American Asians.* Washington, DC: Government Printing Office, 1993.

Welaratna, U. *Beyond the Killing Fields: Voices of Nine Cambodian Survivors in America.* Stanford, CA: Stanford University Press, 1993.

Williams, M. "Ladies on the Line: Punjabi Cannery Workers in Central California." Pp. 148–59 in *Making Waves: An Anthology of Writings by and about Asian American Women,* edited by Asian Women United of California. Boston: Beacon, 1989.

Wong, M. "Chinese Sweatshops in the United States: A Look at the Garment Industry." *Research in Sociology of Work: Peripheral Workers* 2 (1983): 357–79.

Yamanaka, K., and K. McClelland. "Earning the Model-minority Image: Diverse Strategies of Economic Adaptation by Asian-American Women." *Ethnic and Racial Studies* 17 (1994): 79–114.

Yoon, I. J. *On My Own: Korean Businesses and Race Relations in America.* Chicago: Chicago University Press, 1997.

Zhou, M., and J. R. Logan. "Returns on Human Capital in Ethnic Enclaves: New York City's Chinatown." *American Sociological Review* 54 (1989): 809–20.

Part V: Gender and Low-Waged Work

Butler, Judith. *Gender Trouble: Feminism and the Subversion of Identity.* London: Routledge, 1990.

Sacks, Karen. "Toward a Unified Theory of Class Race and Gender." *American Ethnologist* 16, no. 3 (1989): 534–50.

Chapter 18: The Interlocking of Gender with Nationality, Race, Ethnicity and Class: The Narratives of Women in Hotel Work by Amel Adib and Yvonne Guerrier

Adkins, L. *Gendered Work: Sexuality, Family and the Labour Market.* Buckingham: Open University Press, 1995.

Alfieri, A. V. "Critical Race Theory: The Cutting Edge" (book reviews). *California Law Review* 85, no. 5 (1997): 1647–86.

Ashforth, B. E., and G. E. Kreiner. "'How Can You Do It?': Dirty Work and the Challenge of Constructing a Positive Identity." *Academy of Management Review* 24, no.3 (1999): 413–35.

Bagguley, P. *Flexibility, Restructuring and Gender: Changing Employment in Britain's Hotels.* Lancaster Regionalism Group: University of Lancaster, 1987.

Bagguley, P. "Gender and Labour Flexibility in Hotel and Catering." *The Service Industries Journal* 10 (1990): 737–47.

Brah, A. *Cartographies of Diaspora: Contesting Identities.* London: Routledge, 1996.

Butler, J. *Gender Trouble: Feminism and the Subversion of Identity.* London: Routledge, 1990.

Cockburn, C. *Brothers.* London: Pluto Press, 1983.

Collinson, D. L. *Managing the Shopfloor: Subjectivity, Masculinity and Workplace Culture.* Berlin: Walter de Gruyter, 1992.

Collinson, D. L., and J. Hearn. "Naming Men as Men: Implications for Work Organization and Management." *Gender Work and Organization* 1, no. 1 (1994): 2–22.

Collinson, D. L., and J. Hearn. "'Men' at 'Work': Multiple Masculinities/Multiple Workplaces." Pp. 61–76 in *Understanding Masculinities: Social Relations and Cultural Arenas,* edited by Ghaill MMa. Buckingham: Open University Press, 1996.

Crenshaw, K., N. Gotanda, G. Peller, and T. Kendall, eds. *Critical Race Theory: The Key Writings That Formed the Movement.* New York: New Press, 1995.

Delgado, R., ed. *Critical Race Theory: The Cutting Edge.* Philadelphia: Temple University Press, 1995.

Delphy, C., and D. Leornard. *Familiar Exploitation: A New Analysis of Marriage in Contemporary Western Societies.* Oxford: Polity, 1992.

Edwards, P., D. Collinson, and G. Della Rocca. "Workplace Resistance in Western Europe: A Preliminary Overview and a Research Agenda." *European Journal of Industrial Relations* 1, no. 3 (1995): 283–316.

Franzosi, R. "Narrative Analysis—Or Why (and How) Sociologists Should Be Interested in Narrative." *Annual Review of Sociology* 24, no. 1 (199?): 517–55.

Gherardi, S. *Gender, Symbolism and Organizational Cultures.* London: Sage, 1995.

Goffman, E. *The Presentation of Self in Everyday Life.* London: Penguin, 1959.

Guillaumin, C. *Racism, Sexism, Power and Ideology.* London: Routledge, 1995.

Hall, E. "Smiling, Deferring and Flirting: Doing Gender by Giving 'Good Service.'" *Work and Occupations* 20, no. 4 (1993): 452–71.

Hall, S. "Introduction: Who Needs 'Identity'"? Pp. 1–17 in *Questions of Cultural Identity,* edited by S. Hall and P. du Gay. London: Sage, 1996a.

Hall, S. "New Ethnicities." Pp. 441–49 in *Stuart Hall: Critical Dialogues in Cultural Studies*, edited by D. Morley and K-H Chen. London: Routledge, 1996b.

Hochschild, A. *The Managed Heart*. Berkeley: University of California Press, 1983.

Hughes, E. C. *Men and Their Work*. Glencoe, IL: Free Press, 1958.

Hughes, K. D., and V. Tadic. "'Something to Deal with': Customer Sexual Harassment and Women's Retail Service Work in Canada." *Gender, Work and Organization* 5, no. 4 (1998): 207–19.

Jermier, J., D. Knights, and W. Nord, eds. *Resistance and Power in Organizations*. London: Sage, 1994.

Kinnaird, V., U. Kothari, and D. Hall. "Tourism: Gender Perspectives." In *Tourism: A Gender Analysis* edited by V. Kinnaird and D. Hall. Chichester: John Wiley and Sons, 1994.

Leidner, R. *Fast Food Fast Talk: Service Work and the Routinization of Everyday Life*. Berkeley: University of California Press, 1993.

Lucas, R. *Managing Employee Relations in the Hotel and Catering Industry*. London: Cassell, 1995.

Novarra, V. *Men's Work, Women's Work*. London: Marion Boyars, 1980.

Pollert, A. *Girls, Wives, Factory Lives*. London: Macmillan Press, 1981.

Purcell, K. "Equal Opportunities in the Hospitality Industry: Custom and Credentials." *International Journal of Hospitality Management* 12, no. 2 (1993): 127–40.

Said, E. *Orientalism*. New York: Vintage, 1978.

Walby, S. *Patriarchy at Work*. Cambridge: Polity Press, 1986.

Chapter 19: "Outsider Within" the Station House: The Impact of Race and Gender on Black Women Police by Susan E. Martin

Acker, Joan. "Hierarchies, Jobs and Bodies: A Theory of Gendered Organizations." *Gender & Society* 4 (1990): 139–58.

Bloch, Peter D., and Deborah Anderson. "Policewomen on Patrol: Final Report." Washington, D.C.: Urban Institute, 1974.

Christopher, Warren, J. A. Arguelles, R. Anderson, W. R. Barnes, L. F. Estrada, Mickey Kantor, R. M. Mosk, A. S. Ordin, J. B. Slaughter, and R. E. Tranquada. Report of the Independent Commission on the Los Angeles Police Department, 1991.

Collins, Patricia H. "Learning from the Outsider Within: The Sociological Significance of Black Feminist Thought." *Social Problems* 33, (1986): 14–32.

———. *Black Feminist Thought: Knowledge, Consciousness and the Politics of Empowerment*. New York: Routledge, 1990.

Dill, Bonnie T. "The Dialectics of Black Womanhood." *Signs* 4 (1979): 543–55.

Fyfe, James. "Police Personnel Practices." *Baseline Data Report* 18, no. 6. Washington, DC: International City Management Association, 1986.

Glenn, Evelyn N. "From Servitude to Service Work: Historical Continuities in the Racial Division of Paid Reproductive Labor." *Signs* 18 (1992): 1–43.

Hall, Elaine J. "Waitering/Waitressing: Engendering the Work of Table Servers." *Gender & Society* 7 (1993): 329–46.

Harlan, Sharon L., and Brigid O'Farrell. "After the Pioneers: Prospects for Women in Non-Traditional Blue Collar Jobs." *Work and Occupations* 9 (1982): 363–386.

Horne, Peter. *Women in Law Enforcement*, 2nd ed. Springfield, Ill.: Charles C. Thomas, 1980.

Hunt, Jennifer. "The Development of Rapport through Negotiation of Gender in Field Work Among Police." *Human Organization* 43 (1984): 283–96.

———. "The Logic of Sexism among Police." *Women and Criminal Justice* 1 (1990): 3–30.

Kanter, Rosabeth M. *Men and Women of the Organization*. New York: Basic Books, 1977.

Leinen, Stephen. *Black Police, White Society*. New York: New York University Press, 1984.

Martin, Susan E. *"Breaking and Entering": Policewomen on Patrol*. Berkeley, Calif.: University of California Press, 1980.

———. *On the Move: The Status of Women in Policing*. Washington, D.C.: Police Foundation, 1990.

Milton, Catherine. *Women in Policing*. Washington, D.C.: Police Foundation, 1972.

Palmer, Phyllis. "White Women/Black Women: The Dualism of Female Identity and Experience in the United States." *Feminist Studies* 9 (1983): 151–71.

Pike, Diane L. "Women in Police Academy Training: Some Aspects of Organizational Response." Pp. 261–80 in *The Changing Roles of Women in the Criminal Justice System: Offenders, Victims, and Professionals*, 2nd ed., edited by Imogene Moyer. Prospect Heights, Ill.: Waveland Press, 1991.

Reskin, Barbara, and Patricia Roos. *Job Queues, Gender Queues: Explaining Women's Inroads into Male Occupations*. Philadelphia: Temple University Press, 1990.

Scarborough, Cathy. "Conceptualizing Black Women's Employment Experiences." *Yale Law Journal* 98 (1989): 1457–78.

Sulton, Cindy, and Roi Townesy. *A Progress Report on Women in Policing*. Washington, D.C.: Police Foundation, 1981.

Swerdlow, Marion. "Men's Accommodations to Women Entering a Nontraditional Occupation: A Case of Rapid Transit Operatives." *Gender & Society* 3 (1989): 373–87.

Westley, William. *Violence and the Police*. Cambridge: M.I.T. Press, 1970.

Williams, Christine. "The Glass Escalator: Hidden Advantages for Men in the 'Female' Professions." *Social Problems* 39 (1992): 253–66.

Zimmer, Lynn. *Women Guarding Men*. Chicago: University of Chicago Press, 1986.

———. "Tokenism and Women in the Workplace: The Limits of Gender Neutral Theory." *Social Problems* 35 (1988): 64–77.

Chapter 21: Myths of Docile Girls and Matriarchs: Local Profiles of Global Workers by Carla Freeman

Beechey, Veronica. *Unequal Work*. London: Verso, 1987.

Besson, Jean. "Reputation and Respectability Reconsidered: A New Perspective on Afro-Caribbean Peasant Women." In *Women and Change in the Caribbean*, edited by Janet Momsen. Bloomington: Indiana University Press, 1993.

Braverman, Harry. *Labor and Monopoly Capitalism*. New York: Monthly Review Press, 1974.

Catanzarite, Lisa, and Myra Strober. "Gender Recomposition of the Maquiladora Workforce." *Industrial Relations* 32 (1993): 133–47.

Durant-Gonzalez, Victoria. "The Realm of Female Familial Responsibility." In *Women and the Family, Women in the Caribbean Project*, vol. 2, edited by Joycelin Massiah. Cave Hill, Barbados: Institute of Social and Economic Research, University of the West Indies, 1982

Freeman, Carla. "Localizing Informatics: Situating Women and Work in Barbados." In *High Tech and High Heels in the Global Economy: Women, Work, and Pink-Collar Identities in the Caribbean*. Durham: Duke University Press, 2000.

Fröbel, Folker, Jürgen Heinrichs, and Otto Kreye. *The New International Division of Labour*. Cambridge: Cambridge University Press, 1980.

Hall, Stuart. "The Local and the Global: Globalization and Ethnicity." In *Culture, Globalization, and the World System*, edited by Anthony King. Binghamton: Department of Art and Art History, State University of New York, 1991.

Hartmann, Heidi. "The Historical Roots of Occupational Segregation: Capitalism, Patriarchy, and Job Segregation by Sex." In *Women and the Workplace*, edited by Martha Blaxall and Barbara Reagan. Chicago: University of Chicago Press, 1976.

Harvey, David. *The Conditions of Postmodernity*. Oxford: Blackwell, 1989.

Henderson, Jeffrey, and Manuel Castells, eds. *Global Restructuring and Territorial Development*. London: Sage, 1987.

Hodge, Merle. "Introduction." Erna Prodber, *Perceptions of Caribbean Women: Towards a Documentation of Stereotypes*. Cave Hill, Barbados: Institute of Social and Economic Research, University of the West Indies, 1982.

Miller, Daniel. *Modernity: An Ethnographic Approach: Dualism and Mass Consumption in Trinidad*. Oxford: Berg, 1994.

Miller, Errol. *Men at Risk*. Kingston: Jamaica Publishing House, 1991.

Moses, Yolanda. "Female Status, the Family, and Male Dominance in a West Indian Community." *Signs* 3, no. 1 (1977): 142–53.

Olwig, Karen Fogg. "The Migration Experience: Nevisian Women at Home and Abroad." In *Women and Change in the Caribbean*, edited by Janet Momsen. Bloomington: Indiana University Press, 1993.

Peña, Devon. "Tortuosidad: Shop Floor Struggles of Female Maquiladora Workers." In *Women on the U.S.-Mexico Border: Responses to Change*, edited by Vicki L. Ruiz and Susan Tiano. Winchester, England: Allen and Unwin, 1987.

Pyde, Peter. "Gender and Crab Antics in Tobago: Using Wilson's Reputation and Respectability." Paper presented to the American Anthropological Association Conference, New Orleans, November 1990.

Pyle, Jean Larson. *The State and Women in the Economy: Lessons from Sex Discrimination in the Republic of Ireland*. Albany: State University of New York Press, 1990.

Safa, Helen I. "Women and Industrialization in the Caribbean." In *Women, Employment, and the Family in the International Division of Labour*, edited by Sharon Stichter and Jane L. Parpart. Philadelphia: Temple University Press, 1990.

———. *The Myth of the Male Breadwinner: Women and Industrialization in the Caribbean*. Boulder, Colo.: Westview Press, 1995.

Senior, Olive. *Working Miracles: Women's Lives in the English-Speaking Caribbean*. Bloomington: Indiana University Press, 1991.

Sklair, Leslie. *Sociology of the Global System*. Baltimore: Johns Hopkins University Press, 1991.

———. *Assembling for Development: The Maquila Industry in Mexico and the United States*. San Diego: Center for U.S.-Mexican Studies, University of California, 1993.

Stolcke, Verena. "The Exploitation of Family Morality: Labor Systems and Family Structure on Sao Paulo Coffee Plantations, 1850–1979." In *Kinship, Ideology, and Practice in Latin America*, edited by R. T. Smith. Chapel Hill: University of North Carolina Press, 1984.

Sutton, Constance. "Cultural Duality in the Caribbean." *Caribbean Studies* 14, no. 2 (1974): 96–101.

Tilly, Louise A., and Joan W. Scott. *Women, Work, and Family*. New York: Holt, Rinehart and Winston, 1978.

Ward, Kathryn B., and Jean Larson Pyle. "Gender, Industrialization, Transnational Corporations and Development: An Overview of the Trends." In *Women in the Latin American Development Process*, edited by Christine E. Bose and Edna Acosta-Belen. Philadelphia: Temple University Press, 1995.

Westwood, Sallie. *All Day, Every Day: Factory and Family in the Making of Women's Lives*. Urbana: University of Illinois Press, 1985.

Wilson, Peter H. "Reputation and Respectability: A Suggestion for Caribbean Ethnography." *Man* 4 no. I (1969): 70–84.

Yelvington, Kevin. *Producing Power: Ethnicity, Gender, and Class in a Caribbean Workplace*. Philadelphia: Temple University Press, 1995.

Part VI: Gender and the Global Division of Labor

Hart-Landsberg, Martin. "Neoliberalism: Myths and Reality." *Monthly Review* 57, no. 11 (April 2006).

Norberg, Johan. "Three Cheers for Global Capitalism." *The American Enterprise*, June 1, 2004.

UNIFEM. [UN Development Fund for Women]. "Progress of the World's Women 2009." http://www.unifem.org/progress/2008 (24 June 2009).

U.S. Department of State. "Trafficking in Persons Report." 2007. http://www.humantrafficking.org/uploads/publications/2007_TIP_Report.pdf (30 May 2009).

Waldman, Amy. "Sri Lankan Maids Pay Dearly for Perilous Jobs Overseas." *New York Times*, May 8, 2005.

Chapter 22: New World Domestic Order by Pierrette Hondagneu-Sotelo

Baker, Susan Gonzalez, Frank D. Bean, Augustin Escobar Latapi, and Sidney Weintraub. "Immigration Policies and Trends: The Growing Importance of Migration from Mexico." Pp. 81–109 in *Crossings: Mexican Immigration in Interdisciplinary Perspectives*, edited by Marcelo Suarez-Orozco, Cambridge, Mass.: Harvard University Press, 1998.

Beecher, Catharine E., and Harriet Beecher Stowe. *The American Woman's Home: or, Principles of Domestic Science, Being a Guide to the Formation and Maintenance of Economical, Healthful, Beautiful, and Christian Homes*. New York: J. B. Ford, 1869.

Beneria, Lourdes, and Martha Roldan. *The Crossroads of Class and Gender: Industrial Homework, Subcontracting, and Household Dynamics*. Chicago: University of Chicago Press, 1987.

Camarillo, Albert. *Chicanos in a Changing Society: From Mexican Pueblos to American Barrios in Santa Barbara and California, 1848–1930*. Cambridge, Mass.: Harvard University Press, 1979.

Chang, Grace. "Undocumented Latinas: The New 'Employable Mothers.'" Pp. 259–85 in *Mothering: Ideology, Experience, and Agency*, edited by Evelyn Nakano Glenn, Grace Chang, and Linda Rennie Forcey. New York: Routledge, 1994.

Chinchilla, Norma Stoltz, and Nora Hamilton. "Ambiguous Identities: Central Americans in Southern California." Working Paper 14, Chicano/Latino Research Center, University of California, Santa Cruz, 1997.

Clarke-Stewart, Alison. *Daycare.* Rev. ed. Cambridge, Mass.: Harvard University Press, 1993.

Colen, Shellee. "'Just a Little Respect': West Indian Domestic Workers in New York City." Pp. 171–94 in *Muchachas No More: Household Workers in Latin America and the Caribbean,* edited by Elsa M. Chaney and Mary Garcia Castro, Philadelphia: Temple University Press, 1989.

Coutin, Susan Bibler. "From Refugees to Immigrants: The Legalization Strategies of Salvadoran Immigrants and Activists." *International Migration Review* 32 (1998): 901–25.

de Oliveira, Orlandina. "Empleo femenino en México en tiempos de recession economica: Tendencias recientes." Pp. 31–54 in *Mujer y crisis: Respuestas ante la recesión,* edited by Neuma Aguilar. Caracas: Editorial Nueva Sociedad, 1990.

Deutsch, Sarah. *No Separate Refuge: Culture, Class, and Gender on an Anglo-Hispanic Frontier in the American Southwest, 1880–1940.* New York: Oxford University Press, 1987.

Flanigan, James. "State's Economy Booming Again—With a Difference." *Los Angeles Times,* May 18, 1997, AI, A31.

Garcia, Mario. *Desert Immigrants: The Mexicans of El Paso, 1880–1920.* New Haven: Yale University Press, 1981.

Glenn, Evelyn Nakano. *Issei, Nisei, Warbride.* Philadelphia: Temple University Press, 1986.

———. "From Servitude to Service Work: Historical Continuities in the Racial Division of Women's Work." *Signs* 18 (1992): 1–43.

Glenn, Evelyn N., Grace Chang, and Linda Forcey, eds. *Mothering: Ideology, Experience and Agency.* New York: Routledge, 1994.

Gordon, Larry. "Economy's Rise Pulls the Richest Along with It." *Los Angeles Times,* June 27, 1998, AI, A20.

Gotanda, Neil. "A Critique of 'Our Constitution Is Color-Blind.'" *Stanford Law Review* 44 (1991): 1–68.

Hagan, Jacqueline Maria. *Deciding to Be Legal: A Maya Community in Houston.* Philadelphia: Temple University Press, 1994.

Hondagneu-Sotelo, Pierrette. *Gendered Transitions: Mexican Experiences of Immigration.* Berkeley: University of California Press, 1994.

———. "Working 'without Papers' in the U.S.: Toward the Integration of Legal Status in Frameworks of Race, Class, and Gender." Pp. 101–25 in *Women and Work: Race, Class, and Ethnicity,* edited by Elizabeth Higginbotham and Mary Romero. Beverly Hills, Calif.: Sage, 1997.

Hondagneu-Sotelo, Pierrette, and Ernestine Avila. "'I'm Here, But I'm There': The Meanings of Latina Transnational Motherhood." *Gender and Society* 11 (1997): 548–71.

Ibarra, Maria Luz. "Mexican Immigrant Women and the New Domestic Labor." *Human Organization* 59, no. 4 (2000): 452–67.

Jonas, Suzanne, n.d. "Transnational Realities and Anti-Immigrant State Policies: Issues Raised by the Experiences of Central American Immigrants and Refugees in a Trinational Region." Working Paper 7, Chicano/Latino Research Center, University of California, Santa Cruz.

Kaplan, Elaine Bell. "'I Don't Do No Windows': Competition between the Domestic Worker and the Housewife." Pp. 92–105 in *Competition: A Feminist Taboo?* edited by Valerie Miner and Helen E. Longino, New York: Feminist Press, 1987.

Katzman, David M. *Seven Days a Week: Women and Domestic Service in Industrializing America.* Urbana: University of Illinois Press, 1981.

Kim, Claire Jean. "The Racial Triangulation of Asian Americans." *Politics and Society* 27 (1999): 103–36.

Liddick, Betty. "A Critical Game of Hide and Seek: Plight of the Foreign Domestics." *Los Angeles Times,* June 8, 1973a, B4.

———. "The Domestics—A Quest for Clout." *Los Angeles Times,* March 19, 1973b, BI.

Lopez, David E., Eric Popkin, and Edward Telles. "Central Americans: At the Bottom, Struggling to Get Ahead." Pp. 279–304 in *Ethnic Los Angeles*, edited by Roger Waldinger and Mehdi Bozorgmehr. New York: Russell Sage Foundation, 1996.

Mahler, Sarah J. *American Dreaming: Immigrant Life on the Margins*. Princeton: Princeton University Press, 1995.

Massey, Douglas S., Rafael Alarcon, Jorge Durand, and Humberto Gonzalez. *Return to Aztlan: The Social Process of International Migration from Western Mexico*. Berkeley: University of California Press, 1987.

Mendez, Jennifer Bickham. "Of Mops and Maids: Contradictions and Continuities in Bureaucratized Domestic Work." *Social Problems* 45 (1998): 114–35.

Menjivar, Cecilia. "The Intersection of Work and Gender: Central American Immigrant Women and Employment in California." *American Behavioral Scientist* 42 (1999): 601–27.

Myers, Dowell, and Cynthia J. Cranford. "Temporal Differentiation in the Occupational Mobility of Immigrant and Native-Born Latina Workers." *American Sociological Review* 63 (1998): 68–93.

Olivio, Antonio. "Salvadorans Stake Their Claim in Southland Political Game." *Los Angeles Times*, April 11, 1999, B1, B8.

Omi, Michael, and Howard Winant. *Racial Formation in the United States: From the 1960s to the 1980s*. 2nd ed. New York: Routledge, 1994.

Parreñas, Rhacel Salazar. "Migrant Filipina Domestic Workers and the International Division of Reproductive Labor." *Gender and Society* 14 (2000): 560–80.

Powers, Marilyn. "Occupational Mobility of Black and White Women Service Workers." Paper presented at the Second Annual Women's Policy Research Conference, Institute for Women's Policy Research, Washington, D.C., 1990.

Repak, Terry A. *Waiting on Washington: Central American Workers in the Nation's Capital*. Philadelphia: Temple University Press, 1995.

Richmond, Anthony. *Global Apartheid: Refugees, Racism, and the New World Order*. Toronto: Oxford University Press, 1994.

Rollins, Judith. *Between Women: Domestics and Their Employers*. Philadelphia: Temple University Press, 1985.

Romero, Mary. *Maid in the U.S.A.* New York: Routledge, 1992.

Sassen, Saskia. *The Global City: New York, London, Tokyo*. Princeton: Princeton University Press, 1991.

Stone, Deborah. "Valuing 'Caring Work': Rethinking the Nature of Work in Human Services." Typescript, Radcliffe Public Policy Institute, April, 1998.

Sutherland, Daniel. *Americans and Their Servants: Domestic Service in the United States from 1800 to 1920*. Baton Rouge: Louisiana State University Press, 1981.

Thorne, Barrie, and Marilyn Yalom. Rethinking the Family. Boston: Northeastern University Press, 1992.

Ulloa, Roxana Elizabeth. "De indocumentados a cuidadanos: Caracteristicas de los salvadorenos legalizados en Estados Unidos." Typescript, Facultad Latinoamericana para las Ciencias Sociales (FLACSO-El Salvador), 1998.

Waldinger, Roger. "Ethnicity and Opportunity in the Plural City." Pp. 445–70 in *Ethnic Los Angeles*, edited by Roger Waldinger and Mehdi Bozorgmehr. New York: Russell Sage Foundation, 1996.

Wong, Sau-ling C. "Diverted Mothering: Representations of Caregivers of Color in the Age of 'Multiculturalism.'" Pp. 67–91 in *Mothering: Ideology, Experience, and Agency*, edited by Evelyn Nakano Glenn, Grace Chang, and Linda Rennie Forcey. New York: Routledge, 1994.

Wrigley, Julia. *Other People's Children*. New York: Basic Books, 1995.

Chapter 23: Trope Chasing: Making a Local Labor Market by Leslie Salzinger

Baerresen, Donald. *The Border Industrialization Program of Mexico*. Lexington, Mass.: Heath Lexington Books, 1971.

Baird, Peter, and Ed McCaughan. *Beyond the Border*. New York: North American Congress on Latin America, 1979.

Brannon, Jeffery, and William Lucker. "The Impact of Mexico's Economic Crisis on the Demographic Composition of the Maquiladora Labor Force." *Journal of Borderlands Studies* 4, no. I (1989): 39–70.

Carrillo, Jorge. *Conflictos laborales en la industria maquiladora*. Tijuana: Centro de Estudios Fronterizos del Norte de México, 1985.

Carrillo, Jorge, and Alberto Hernandez. *Mujeres fronterizas en la industria maquiladora*. Tijuana: Centro de Estudios Fronterizos del Norte de México, 1985.

Carrillo, Jorge, and Miguel Angel Ramírez. "Maquiladoras en la frontera norte: Opinión sobre los sindicatos." *Frontera Norte* 2, no. 4 (1990): 121–52.

Catanzarite, Lisa, and Myra Strober. "The Gender Recomposition of the Maquiladora Labor Force." *Industrial Relations* 32, no. I (1993): 133–47.

Centro de Orientación de la Mujer Obrero, A.C. (COMO). n.d. *Manual de la mujer obrera*. Ciudad Juárez: COMO.

Cruz Piñeiro, Rudolfo. "Mercados de trabajo y migración en la frontera: Tijuana, Ciudad Juárez, Nuevo Laredo." *Frontera Norte* 2, no. 4 (1990): 61–93.

De la O Martínez, María Eugenia. "Reconversión industrial en la industria maquiladora electrónica: Cuatro estudios de caso participación femenina en Ciudad Juárez, Chihuahua." Unpublished manuscript, Tijuana, 1991.

———. "Y Por eso Se Llaman Maquilas . . . La configuración de las relaciones laborales en la modernización: Cuatro estudios de plantas electrónicas en Ciudad Juárez." Ph.D. dissertation, Colegio de México, Mexico City, 1997.

De la Rosa Hickerson, Gustavo. "La contratación colectiva en las maquiladoras: Analisis de un caso de sobreexplotación." Professional thesis, Universidad Autónoma, Escuela de Derecho, Ciudad Juárez, 1979.

Desarrollo Económico de Ciudad Juárez. *Ciudad Juárez en cifras*. Ciudad Juárez: Desarrollo Económico, 1991.

Fernández-Kelly, María Patricia. *For We Are Sold, I and My People: Women and Industry in Mexico's Frontier*. Albany: State University of New York Press, 1983.

Gambrill, Mónica. "Composición y conciencia de la fuerza de trabajo en las maquiladoras: Resultados de una encuesta y algunas hipótesis interpretivas." Pp. 106–24 in *La frontera del norte*, edited by Roque González Salazar. Mexico City: Colegio de México, 1981.

Iglesias Prieto, Norma. *La flor más bella de la maquiladora*. Mexico City: Secretaría de Educación Pública and Centro de Estudios Fronterizos del Norte de México, 1985.

Instituto Nacional de Estadística, Geografia e Informática (INEGI). *Estadística de la industria maquiladora de exportación, 1975–1988*. Mexico City: INEGI, 1990.

———. *Estadística de la industria maquiladora de exportación, 1979–1989*. Mexico City: INEGI, 1991.

———. *Estadística de la industria maquiladora de exportación, 1990–1995*. Mexico City: INEGI, 1996.

Jiménez Betancourt, Rubí. "Participación femenina en la industria maquiladora: Cambios recientes." Pp. 393–424 in *Fuerza de trabajo femenina urbana en México*, 2nd ed., edited by

Jennifer Cooper, Teresita de Barbarieri, Teresa Rendón, Estela Juárez, and Esperanza Tuñon. Mexico City: UNAM, 1989.

Kopinak, Kathryn. "Living the Gospel through Service to the Poor: The Convergence of Political and Religious Motivations in Organizing Maquiladora Workers in Juárez, Mexico." *Socialist Studies: A Canadian Annual* 5 (1989): 217–45.

Lutz, Nancy Melissa. "Images of Docility: Asian Women and the World Economy." Pp. 57–73 in *Racism, Sexism and the World-System,* edited by Joan Smith et al. New York: Greenwood, 1988.

Martínez, Oscar. *Border Boom Town: Ciudad Juárez since 1848.* Austin: University of Texas Press, 1978.

Pearson, Ruth. "Male Bias and Women's Work in Mexico's Border Industries." Pp. 133–63 in *Male Bias in the Development Process,* edited by Diane Elson. Manchester: Manchester University Press, 1991.

Peña, Devon. *The Terror of the Machine: Technology, Work, Gender, and Ecology on the U.S.-Mexican Border.* Austin: University of Texas Press, 1997.

Reygadas, Luis. *Un rostro moderno de la pobreza: Problemática social de las trabajadoras de las maquiladoras de Chihuahua.* Chihuahua: Ediciones Gobierno de Estado de Chihuahua, 1992.

Safa, Helen. "Runway Shops and Female Employment: The Search for Cheap Labor." Pp. 58–71 in *Women's Work: Development and the Division of Labor by Gender,* edited by Eleanor Leacock and Helen Safa. South Hadley, Mass.: Bergin and Garvey, 1986.

Shaiken, Harley. *Mexico in the Global Economy: High Technology and Work Organization in Export Industries.* San Diego: University of California Center for U.S.-Mexican Studies, 1990.

Sklair, Leslie. *Assembling for Development: The Maquila Industry in Mexico and the United States.* San Diego: Center for U.S.-Mexican Studies, UCSD, 1993.

Standing, Guy. "Global Feminization through Flexible Labor." *World Development* 17, no. 7 (1989): 1077–95.

Tiano, Susan. "Maquiladoras in Mexicali: Integration or Exploitation?" Pp. 77–102 in *Women on the U.S.-Mexico Border: Responses to Change,* edited by Vicki Ruiz and Susan Tiano. Boston: Allen and Unwin, 1987a.

———. "Women's Work and Unemployment in Northern Mexico." Pp. 17–39 in *Women on the U.S.-Mexico Border: Responses to Change,* edited by Vicki Ruiz and Susan Tiano. Boston: Allen and Unwin, 1987b.

Van Waas, Michael. "The Multinational's Strategy for Labor: Foreign Assembly Plants in Mexico's Border Industrialization Program." Ph.D. dissertation, Stanford University, 1981.

———. 1982. "Multinational Corporations and the Politics of Labor Supply." *The Insurgent Sociologist* II, no. 3 (1982): 49–57.

Vila, Pablo. "Gender and the Overlapping of Region, Nation and Ethnicity on the U.S.-Mexico Border." In *Border Ethnographies,* edited by Pablo Vila. Minneapolis: University of Minnesota Press, 2003.

Wolf, Diane. "Daughters, Decisions and Domination: An Empirical and Conceptual Critique of Household Strategies." *Development and Change* 21 (1990): 43–74.

Young, Gay, and Beatriz Vera. "Extensive Evaluation of Centro de Orientación de la Mujer Obrera, A.C. in Ciudad Juárez." Unpublished manuscript, Inter-American Foundation, Ciudad Juárez, 1984.

Yudelman, Sally. *Hopeful Openings: A Study of Five Women's Development Organizations in Latin America and the Caribbean.* West Hartford: Kumarian Press, 1987.

Chapter 24: Imagining Sex and Gender in the Workplace by Pun Ngai

An, Zi. *Qingchun xuyu: Dagongzai dagongmei qingjian* [The dialogue of the youth: Love letters of the working boys and working girls]. Shenzhen: Haitian Chubanshe, 1993.

Baudrillard, Jean. 1993. *Symbolic Exchange and Death*. London: Sage, 1993.

Butler, Judith. *Gender Trouble: Feminism and the Subversion of Identity*. London: Routledge, 1990.

———. *Bodies That Matter: on the Discursive Limits of "Sex."* London: Routledge, 1993.

Croll, Elisabeth. *Changing Identities of Chinese Women*. London: Zed; Hong Kong: Hong Kong University Press, 1995

Evans, Harriet. *Women and Sexuality in China*. London: Polity, 1997.

Foucault, Michel. *The History of Sexuality; Volume 1: An Introduction*. New York: Vintage, 1978.

Hearn, Jeff, and Wendy Parkin. *"Sex" and "Work": The Power and Paradox of Organization Sexuality*. London: Wheatsheaf Books, 1987.

Irigaray, Luce. *This Sex Which Is Not One*. Ithaca: Cornell University Press, 1977.

Li, Xiaojiang. *Xiawa de tansuo* [Eve's search]. Henan: Henan remin chubanshe, 1988.

———. *Xing gou* [Gender gap]. Beijing: Sanlian Shudian, 1989.

Marx, Karl. *Capital*. Vol. 1. Moscow: Progress Publishers, 1954 [1865].

McNay, Lois. *Foucault and Feminism: Power, Gender, and the Self*. Oxford: Polity, 1992.

Moore, Henrietta L. *A Passion for Difference: Essays in Anthropology and Gender*. Cambridge: Polity, 1994.

Ong, Aihwa. *Spirits of Resistance and Capitalist Discipline: Factory Women in Malaysia*. Albany: State University of New York Press, 1987.

Shen, Tan. "A Special Economic Zone Cannot Take Care of Dagongmei's Love." *Shenzhen Ren*, October 1994.

Strathern, Marilyn. *The Gender of Gift: Problems with Women and Problems with Society in Melanesia*. Berkeley: University of California Press, 1988.

Truong, Thanh-Dam. *Sex, Money, and Morality: Prostitution and Tourism in Southeast Asia*. London: Zed, 1990.

Willis, Paul. *Learning to Labor*. New York: Columbia University Press, 1981.

Part VII: Gendered Discrimination at Work

Becker, Gary S. *The Economics of Discrimination*. Chicago: University of Chicago Press, 1971.

Bielby, William T. "Can I Get a Witness? Challenges of Using Expert Testimony on Cognitive Bias in Employment Discrimination Litigation." *Employment Rights and Employment Policy Journal* 7, no. 2 (2003): 377–400. Symposium issue on "Litigating the Glass Ceiling and the Maternal Wall: Using Stereotyping and Cognitive Bias Evidence to Prove Gender Discrimination."

Davis, Kingsley, and Wilbert E. Moore. "Some Principles of Stratification." *American Sociological Review* 10 (1945): 242-49.

Doeringer, Peter B., and Michael J. Piore. *Internal Labor Markets and Manpower Analysis*. Lexington, Mass: Heath, 1971.

Edwards, Richard. *The Contested Terrain: The Transformation of the Workplace in the Twentieth Century*. Basic Books, 1979.

Equal Employment Opportunity Commission. "EEOC Reports Job Bias Charges Hit Record High of over 95,000 in Fiscal Year 2008." http://www.eeoc.gov/press/3-11-09.html (10 August 2009).

Kirschenman, Joleen, and Kathryn M. Neckerman. "'We'd Love to Hire Them, But . . .': The Meaning of Race for Employers." In *The Urban Underclass*, edited by Christopher Jencks and Paul E. Peterson. Washington, DC: Brookings Institution, 1991.

Lindgren, Ralph J., and Nadine Taub. *The Law of Sex Discrimination*. St. Paul, MN: West Publishing Company, 1977.

Reskin, Barbara F. "The proximate causes of employment discrimination." *Contemporary Sociology* 29 (2000): 319–328.

Schultz, Vicki. "Reconceptualizing Sexual Harassment." *Yale Law Journal* 107, no. 6 (1998).

Chapter 28: The Hidden Discourse of Masculinity in Gender Discrimination Law by Tyson Smith and Michael Kimmel

Brake, Deborah. "The Cruelest of the Gender Police: Student-to-Student Sexual Harassment and Anti-gay Peer Harassment under Title IX." *Georgetown Journal of Gender and the Law* 1 (Fall 1999): 37–108.

Brannon, Robert, and Deborah David, eds. *The Forty-nine Percent Majority*. Reading, MA: Addison-Wesley, 1975.

Brod, Harry. "Some Thoughts on Some Histories of Some Masculinities: Jews and Other Others." Pp. 82–96 in *Theorizing Masculinities*, edited by Harry Brod and Michael Kaufman. Thousand Oaks, CA: Sage, 1994.

Brown v. Board of Education. 1954. 347 U.S. 483.

Connell, R. W. *Masculinities*. Berkeley: University of California Press, 1995.

Coombs, Mary. "Title VII and Homosexual Harassment after Oncale: Was It a Victory?" *Duke Journal of Gender Law and Policy* 6, no. 1 (1999): 113–50.

Doyle, James A. *The Male Experience*. Dubuque, IA: Brown, 1989.

EEOC v. Sears, Roebuck & Co. 1986. 628 F. Supp. 1264 (N. D. III.).

———. 1988. 839 F.2d 302 (7th Cir.), 320–21.

Ellison v. Brady. 1991. 924 F.2d 872 (9th Cir.).

Frontiero v. Richardson. 1973. 411 U.S. 677.

Goluszek v. H. P. Smith. 1988. 697 F. Supp. 1452.

Gomez, Jewelle. "Repeat after Me: We Are Different. We Are the Same." *NYU Review of Law and Social Change* 14, no. 4 (1986): 935–41.

Griggs v. Duke Power Co. 1971. 401 U.S. 424.

Gruber, James, and Phoebe Morgan, eds. *In the Company of Men: Male Dominance and Sexual Harassment*. Boston: Northeastern University Press, 2004.

Hearn, Jeff. "Is Masculinity Dead? A Critique of the Concept of Masculinity/Masculinities." Pp. 202–17 in *Understanding Masculinities*, edited by Máirtin Mac an Ghaill. Buckingham: Open University Press, 1996.

IBEW, Local Union No. 66 v. Houston Lighting and Power Co. 1997. 117 S. Ct. 2480.

International Union, UAW v. Johnson Controls, Inc. 1991. 111 S. Ct. 1196.

Kessler-Harris, Alice. "Written Testimony of Alice Kessler-Harris." U.S. District Court for the Northern District of Illinois, Eastern Division, no. 79-C-4373. In *Signs: Journal of Women in Culture and Society* 11, no. 4 (1986): 767–79.

Kimmel, Michael. "Masculinity as Homophobia: Fear, Shame and Silence in the Construction of Gender Identity." Pp. 119–41 in *Theorizing Masculinities*, edited by Harry Brod and Michael Kaufman. Thousand Oaks, CA: Sage, 1994.

———. *Manhood in America: A Cultural History.* New York: Free Press, 1995.

Levit, Nancy. *The Gender Line: Men, Women, and the Law.* New York: New York University Press, 1998.

MacKinnon, Catharine A. *Feminism Unmodified: Discourses on Life and Law.* Cambridge: MA: Harvard University Press, 1987.

Milkman, Ruth. "Women's History and the Sears Case." *Feminist Studies* 12, no. 2 (1986): 375–400.

Mississippi University for Women v. Hogan. 1982. 458 S. Ct. 718.

Oncale v. Sundowner Offshore Services, Inc. 1996. 83 F.3d 118 (5th Cir.).

———. 1998. 523 U.S. 75.

Pacenti, John. "The Catcher and the Cup." *Augusta Chronicle*, May 23, 1997. http://augustachronicle.com/stories/052397/spo_girlcatcher.html (21 Oct 2004).

Polly v. Houston Lighting and Power Company. 1993. 825 F. Supp. 135 (U.S. District Court for Southern District of Texas, Houston Division).

Price Waterhouse v. Hopkins. 1989. 109 S. Ct. 1775.

Rosenberg, Rosalind. "Offer of Proof Concerning the Testimony of Rosalind Rosenberg." U.S. District Court for the Northern District of Illinois, Eastern Division, no. 79-C-4373. In *Signs* 11, no. 4 (1986): 757–66.

Scott, Joan W. "Deconstructing Equality vs. Difference: The Uses of Poststructural Theory for Feminism." *Feminist Studies* 15, no. 2 (1988): 237–54.

Stone, Deborah A. "Fetal Risks, Women's Rights: Showdown at Johnson Controls." *American Prospect* 1, no. 3 (1990): 43–53.

Vergnolle, Ron. Deposition of Ron Vergnolle, witness for the plaintiff in *Johnson v. Jones*, 1993. 42 F.3d 1385 (4th Cir.).

VMI I. 1991. 766. F. Supp. 1407 (W.D. Va.).

VMI II. 1992. *United States v. Commonwealth of Virginia*, 976 F.2d 890 (4th Cir.).

VMI III. 1993. 10 F.3d 226 (4th Cir.).

VMI IV. 1994. 852 F. Supp. 471 (W.D. Va.).

VMI V. 1996. *United States v. Virginia*, 518 U.S. 515, 116 S. Ct. 2264.

Williams, Joan. "Deconstructing Gender." Pp. 624–35 in *Applications of Feminist Legal Theory to Women's Lives*, edited by D. Kelley Weisberg. Philadelphia: Temple University Press, 1996.

Young, E. Deposition of E. Young in *Faulkner v. Jones*, 1993. 10 F.3d 226 (4th Cir.), 126.

Chapter 29: "That Single Mother Element": How White Employers Typify Black Women by Ivy Kennelly

Aigner, Dennis J., and Glen C. Cain. "Statistical Theories of Discrimination in Labor Markets." *Industrial Labor and Relations Review* 30 (1977): 175–87.

Basow, Susan A. *Gender Stereotypes: Traditions and Alternatives.* 2nd ed. Monterey, CA: Books/Cole, 1986.

Bennett, Claudette E. *The Black Population in the United States: March 1994 and 1993.* U.S. Bureau of the Census, Current Population Reports, P20–480. Washington, DC: Government Printing Office, 1995.

Berg, David N. "Objectivity and Prejudice." *American Behavioral Scientist* 27 (1984): 387–402.

Bielby, William T., and James N. Baron. "Men and Women at Work: Sex Segregation and Statistical Discrimination." *American Journal of Sociology* 91 (1986): 800–37.

Bobo, Lawrence, and James R. Kluegel. "Opposition to Race-targeting: Self-interest, Stratification Ideology, or Racial Attitudes?" *American Sociological Review* 58 (1993): 443–64.

Bobo, Lawrence, and Susan Suh. "Racial Attitudes and Power in the Workplace: Do the Haves Differ from the Have-nots?" Working paper. Department of Sociology, University of California, Los Angeles, 1996.

Collins, Patricia Hill. *Black, Feminist Thought: Knowledge, Consciousness, and the Politics of Empowerment.* New York: Routledge, 1990.

Davis, Angela Y. *Women, Race and Class.* New York: Random House, 1981.

Eagly, Alice H., and Wendy Wood. "Inferred Sex Differences in Status as a Determinant of Gender Stereotypes about Social Influence." *Journal of Personality and Social Psychology* 43 (1982): 915–28.

England, Paula, and Irene Browne. "Trends in Women's Economic Status." *Sociological Perspectives* 35 (1992): 17–51.

Essed, Philomena. *Understanding Everyday Racism: An Interdisciplinary Theory.* Newbury Park, CA: Sage, 1991.

Farley, Reynolds, Charlotte Steeh, Maria Krysan, Tara Jackson, and Keith Reeves. "Stereotypes and Segregation: Neighborhoods in the Detroit Area." *American Journal of Sociology* 100 (1994): 750–80.

Feagin, Joe R., and Hernan Vera. *White Racism: The Basics.* New York: Routledge, 1995.

Folbre, Nancy. *Who Pays for the Kids? Gender and the Structures of Constraint.* New York: Routledge, 1994.

Fordham, Signithia, and John U. Ogbu. "Black Students' School Success: Coping with the 'Burden of Acting White.'" *Urban Review* 18 (1986): 176–206.

Frankenberg, Ruth. *White Women, Race Matters: The Social Construction of Whiteness.* Minneapolis: University of Minnesota Press, 1993.

Gerson, Kathleen. *No Man's Land: Men's Changing Commitments to Family and Work.* New York: Basic Books, 1993.

Guy-Sheftall, Beverly. *Daughters of Sorrow: Attitudes toward Black Women, 1880–1920.* Brooklyn, NY: Carlson, 1990.

Hacker, Andrew. *Two Nations: Black and White, Separate, Hostile, Unequal.* New York: Ballantine, [1992] 1995.

Hartmann, Heidi. "Capitalism, Patriarchy, and Job Segregation by Sex." In *Women and the Workplace*, edited by Martha Blaxall and Barbara Reagan. Chicago: University of Chicago Press, 1976.

Hochschild, Arlie Russell. *Time Bind: When Work Becomes Home and Home Becomes Work.* New York: Henry Holt, 1997.

hooks, bell. *Ain't I a Woman: Black Women and Feminism.* Boston: South End, 1981.

———. *Killing Rage: Ending Racism.* New York: Henry Holt, 1995.

Kirschenman, Joleen. "Gender within Race in the Labor Market." Paper presented at the Urban Poverty and Family Life Conference, University of Chicago, 1991.

Kirschenman, Joleen, Philip Moss, and Chris Tilly. "Employers, Hiring, and Urban Inequality: A Multi-city Interview Study." Research proposal submitted to the Russell Sage Foundation, 1992.

Kirschenman, Joleen, and Kathryn M. Neckerman. "'We'd Love to Hire Them, but . . .': The Meaning of Race for Employers." In *The Urban Underclass*, edited by Christopher Jencks and Paul E. Peterson. Washington, DC: Brookings Institution, 1991.

Lynch, Lisa M. "The Role of Off-the-Job Training vs. On-the-Job Training for the Mobility of Women Workers." *American Economic Review* 81 (1991): 151–56.

Majors, Richard, and Janet Mancini Billson. *Coolpose: The Dilemmas of Black Manhood in America*. New York: Touchstone, 1992.

Marshall, Annecka. "From Sexual Denigration to Self-respect: Resisting Images of Black Female Sexuality." In *Reconstructing Womanhood, Reconstructing Feminism: Writings on Black Women*, edited by Delia Jarrett-Macauley. London: Routledge, 1996.

Mink, Gwendolyn. "The Lady and the Tramp: Gender, Race, and the Origins of the American Welfare State." In *Women, the State, and Welfare*, edited by Linda Gordon. Madison: University of Wisconsin Press, 1990.

Morton, Patricia. *Disfigured Images: The Historical Assault on Afro-American Women*. New York: Greenwood, 1991.

Moss, Philip, and Chris Tilly. "Why Black Men are Doing Worse in the Labor Market: A Review of Supply-side and Demand-side Explanations." Working paper. Social Science Research Council, New York, 1991.

———. "'Soft' Skills and Race: An Investigation of Black Men's Employment Problems." Working Paper No. 80. Russell Sage, New York, 1995.

Mullins, Leith. "Images, Ideology, and Women of Color." In *Women of Color in U.S. Society*, edited by Maxine Baca Zinn and Bonnie Thornton Dill. Philadelphia: Temple University Press, 1994.

Neckerman, Kathryn M., and Joleen Kirschenman. "Hiring Strategies, Racial Bias, and Inner-city Workers." *Social Problems* 38 (1991): 433–47.

Price, James L. *The Study of Turnover*. Ames: Iowa State University Press, 1977.

Reskin, Barbara F. "Bringing the Men Back In: Sex Differentiation and the Devaluation of Women's Work." *Gender and Society* 2 (1988): 58–81.

Roberts, Diane. *The Myth of Aunt Jemima: Representations of Race and Region*. New York: Routledge, 1994.

Sears, David O. "Symbolic Racism." In *Eliminating Racism: Profiles in Controversy*, edited by Phyllis A. Katz and Dalmas A. Taylor. New York: Plenum, 1988.

Sims-Wood, Janet L. "The Black Female: Mammy, Jemima, Sapphire, and Other Images." In *Images of Blacks in American Culture: A Reference Guide to Information Sources*, edited by Jesse Carney Smith. New York: Greenwood, 1988.

Sokoloff, Natalie J. *Between Money and Love: The Dialectics of Women's Home and Market Work*. New York: Praeger, 1980.

Thurow, Lester C. *Generating Inequality*. New York: Basic Books, 1975.

Tomaskovic-Devey, Donald. *Gender and Racial Inequality at Work: The Sources and Consequences of Job Segregation*. Ithaca, NY: ILR Press, 1993.

U.S. Bureau of the Census. *Current Population Survey*. P20–499, July. U.S. Department of Commerce, Economics and Statistics Administration, 1995.

U.S. Department of Commerce. *Statistical Abstract of the United States 1996*. Washington, DC: Bureau of the Census, 1996.

Waite, Linda, and Sue E. Berryman. *Women in Nontraditional Occupations: Choice and Turnover*. RAND Report R–3106–FF. Santa Monica, CA: RAND, 1985.

Weitz, Rose, and Leonard Gordon. "Images of Black Women among Anglo College Students." *Sex Roles* 28 (1993): 19–34.

West, Cornel. *Race Matters*. New York: Vintage, 1993.

Wilkinson, Dorris Y. "The Doll Exhibit: A Psycho-cultural Analysis of Black Female Role Stereotypes." *Journal of Popular Culture* 21 (1987): 19–29.

Wilson, William Julius. *The Truly Disadvantaged: The Inner City, the Underclass, and Public Policy*. Chicago: University of Chicago Press, 1987.

———. *When Work Disappears: The World of the New Urban Poor*. New York: Knopf, 1996.

Part VIII: Family, Gender, and Work

Becker, Gary. *A Treatise on the Family*. Cambridge, MA: Harvard University Press, 1991.

Benfer, Amy. "The Nuclear Family Takes a Hit." 2007. http://archive.salon.com/mwt/feature/2001/06/07/family_values/index.html (20 May 2008).

Cherlin, Andrew. "American Marriage in the Early 21st Century." *The Future of Children* 15, no. 2 (2005): 33–55.

Coontz, Stephanie. *The Way We Never Were: American Families and the Nostalgia Trap*. New York, NY: Basic Books, 2000.

The Editors. "A New Trend in Motherhood." Room for Debate, A Running Commentary on the News, *New York Times*, May 17, 2009. http://roomfordebate.blogs.nytimes.com/2009/05/17/a-new-trend-in-motherhood (22 July 2009).

Murray, Charles. *Losing Ground: American Social Policy 1950–1980*. New York, NY: Basic Books, 1994.

Popenoe, David. "The American Family Crisis." *National Forum: The Phi Kappa Phi Journal*, Summer, 1995.

Smith, David, and Gary Gates. "Gay and Lesbian Families in the United States, Same Sex Unmarried Partner Households." The Urban Institute, August 22, 2001. http://www.urban.org/publications/1000491.html (21 January 2007).

Wilson, William Julius. *When Work Disappears*. Random House Vintage Books, 1997.

Chapter 33: Black Mothering, Paid Work and Identity by Tracey Reynolds

Barrow, C. *Family in the Caribbean: Themes and Perspectives*. London: James Currey Publishing, 1996.

Berthoud, R. *Young Caribbean Men and the Labour Market: A Comparison with Other Ethnic Groups*. London: Joseph Rowntree Foundation, 1999.

Bhavnani, R. *Black Women in the Labour Market: A Research Review*. London: Equal Opportunities Commission, 1994.

Breugel, I. "Sex and Race in the Labour Market." *Feminist Review* 32 (Summer 1989): 49–68.

Bryan, B., S. Dadzie, and S. Scafe. *The Heart of the Race: Black Women's Lives in Britain*. London: Virago, 1985.

Burghes, L., and M. Brown. *Single Lone Parents: Problems, Prospects and Policies*. London: Family Policies Studies Centre, 1995.

Cohen, B., and N. Fraser. *Childcare in a Modern Welfare State*. London: Institute of Public Policy Research, 1991.

Commission for Racial Equality [CRE]. *Employment and Unemployment Factsheet*. London, 1997.

Dale, A., and C. Holdsworth. "Why Don't Minority Ethnic Women in Britain Work Part-time?" In *Part-Time Prospects*, edited by J. O'Reilly and C. Fagan. London: Routledge, 1998.

Davis, A. *Women, Race and Class*. London: Women's Press Ltd., 1981.

Daycare Trust. *Childcare Disregard in Family Credit, Who Gains?* London: Daycare Trust, 1997.

Dodgson, E. *Motherlands: West Indian Women in Britain in the 1950s*. Oxford: Heinemann, 1984.

Duncan, S., and R. Edwards. *Lone Mothers: Paid Work and Gendered Moral Rationalities*. Basingstoke: Macmillan, 1999.

Goulbourne, H., and M. Chamberlain. "Living Arrangements, Family Structure and Social Change of Caribbeans in Britain." *ESRC Population and Household Change for Research*. Swindon: Economic Social Research Council, 1999.

Gutman, H. *The Black Family in Slavery and Freedom 1750–1925*. New York: Vintage, 1976.

Ham, C. *Health Policy in Britain*. London: Macmillan, 1991.

Hill Collins, P. "Shifting the Centre: Race, Class and Feminist Theorizing about Motherhood." In *Mothering: Ideology, Experience and Agency*, edited by E. Glenn, G. Chang, and L. Forcey. California: Routledge, 1994.

Jones, T. *Ethnic Minorities in Britain*. London: Policy Study Institute, 1984.

Joshi, H. "Sex and Motherhood as Handicaps in the Labour Market." In *Women's Issues in Social Policy*, edited by M. MacClean and D. Groves. London: Routledge, 1991.

King, M. "Black Women's Labour Market Status: Occupational Segregation in the United States and Britain." *Review of Black Political Economy* 24, no. 1 (1995): 23–43.

Lewis, G. "Black Women's Employment and the British Economy." In *Inside Babylon: The Caribbean Diaspora in Britain*, edited by W. James and C. Harris. London: Verso, 1993.

Modood, T. *Ethnic Minorities in Britain*. London: PSI, 1997.

Mohammed, P., ed. *Gender in Caribbean Development*. Women and Development Studies Project, Trinidad: University of the West, 1988.

Moyenda Project. *Family and Survival Strategies: Moyenda Black Families Report*. London: Joseph Rowntree Foundation, 1997.

Nnaemeka, O. *The Politics of (M)othering: Womanhood, Identity and Resistance in African Literature*, London: Routledge, 1997.

O'Brien, M. "Missing Mum." *Panorama*. British Broadcasting Corporation, (February 3, 1997).

Owen, D. *Ethnic Minority Women and the Labour Market: Analysis of the 1991 Census*. London: EOC, 1994.

Owen, D. "A Demographic Profile of Caribbean Households and Families in Great Britain." *ESRC Populations and Household Change Research Programme*. Swindon: Economic and Social Research Council, 1997.

Phizacklea, A. "Gender, Racism and Occupational Status." In *Gender Segregation at Work*, edited by S. Walby. Milton Keynes: Open University Press, 1988.

Reynolds, T. "The (Mis)Representation of the Black (Super)Woman." In *Black British Feminism*, edited by H. Mirza. London: Routledge, 1997.

———. "African-Caribbean Mothering: Reconstructing a 'New' Identity." Unpublished Ph.D. at South Bank University, London, 1999.

———. "Caribbean Fathers in Family Lives." In *Caribbean Families in the Trans-Atlantic World*, edited by H. Goulbourne and M. Chamberlain. London: Macmillan, 2000.

Ribbens, J. *Mothers and Their Children: A Feminist Sociology of Childrearing*. London: Macmillan, 1995.

Richardson, D. *Women, Motherhood and Childrearing*, London: Macmillan, 1993.

Shepherd, V., B. Brereton, and B. Bailey. *Engendering History: Caribbean Women in a Historical Perspective*. London: James Curry Publishing, 1995.

Westwood, S., and P. Bhachu, eds. *Enterprising Women: Ethnicity, Economy and Gender Relations*. London: Routledge, 1988.

Williams, Fiona. *Social Policy, A Critical Introduction*. London: Polity Press, 1989.

Woodward, K. "Motherhood, Identities, Meanings and Myths." In *Identity and Difference*, edited by K. Woodward. Keynes: Open University Press, 1997.

Chapter 34: Families on the Frontier: From Braceros in the Fields to Braceras in the Home by Pierrette Hondagneu-Sotelo

Bakan, Abigail B., and Daiva Stasiulis. "Foreign Domestic Worker Policy in Canada and the Social Boundaries of Modern Citizenship." In *Not One of the Family: Foreign Domestic Workers in Canada*, edited by Abigail B. Bakan and Daiva Stasiulis. Toronto: University of Toronto Press, 1997.

Constable, Nicole. *Maid to Order in Hong Kong: Stories of Filipina Workers*. Ithaca and London: Cornell University Press, 1997.

Cornelius, Wayne. "The Structural Embeddedness of Demand for Mexican Immigrant Labor: New Evidence from California." In *Crossings: Mexican Immigration in Interdisciplinary Perspectives*, edited by Marcelo M. Suárez-Orozco. Cambridge, MA: Harvard University, David Rockefeller Center for Latin American Studies, 1998.

Falicov, Celia Jaes. "Ambiguous Loss: Risk and Resilience in Latino Immigrant Families." Pp. 197–206 in *The New Immigration: An Interdisciplinary Reader*, edited by Desiree Baslian Qin, Margaret E. Hertzig, and Marcelo Suárez-Orozco. New York: Routledge, 2004.

Hagan, Jacqueline, and Mestor Rodriguez. "Resurrecting Exclusion: The Effects of 1996 U.S. Immigration Reform on Communities and Families in Texas, El Salvador, and Mexico." In *Latinos: Remaking America*, edited by Marcelo M. Suárez-Orozco and M. Paez. Berkeley: University of California Press, 2002.

Hochschild, Arlie. *The Time Bind: When Work Becomes Home and Home Becomes Work*. New York: Metropolitan Books, Henry Holt, 1997.

Hondagneu-Sotelo, Pierrette. *Gendered Transition: Mexican Experiences of Immigration*. Berkeley: University of California Press, 1994.

Hondagneu-Sotelo, Pierrette, and Ernestine Avila. "'I'm Here, But I'm There': The Meanings of Latina Transnational Motherhood." *Gender and Society* 11 (1997): 548–71.

Lan, Pei-chia. "Global Divisions, Local Identities: Filipina Migrant Domestic Workers and Taiwanese Employers." Dissertation, Northwestern University, 2000.

Laslett, Barbara, and Johanna Brenner. "Gender and Social Reproduction: Historical Perspectives." *Annual Review of Sociology* 15 (1989): 381–404.

Menjivar, Cecilia. *Fragmented Ties: Salvadoran Immigrant Networks in America*. Berkeley: University of California Press, 2000.

Chapter 35: More Alike than Different: Revisiting the Long-Term Prospects for Developing "European-Style" Work/Family Policies in the United States by Janet C. Gornick and Marcia K. Meyers

Acs, Gregory. "Does Welfare Promote Out of Wedlock Childbearing?" In *Welfare Reform: Analysis of the Issues*, edited by Isabel V. Sawhill. Washington, DC: The Urban Institute, 1995.

DeLeon, Peter, and Phyllis Resnick-Terry. "Comparative Policy Analysis Déjá Vu All Over Again?" *Journal of Comparative Policy Analysis: Research and Practice* 1, no. 1 (1998): 9–22.

Gilens, Martin. *Why Americans Hate Welfare: Race, Media, and the Politics of Antipoverty Policy.* Chicago, Ill: The University of Chicago Press, 1999.

Gornick, Janet C., and Marcia K. Meyers. *Families That Work: Policies for Reconciling Parenthood and Employment.* New York: Russell Sage Foundation, 2003.

Kingdon, John W. *America the Unusual.* New York: St. Martin's/Worth, 1999.

Lake Sosin Snell Perry. "Polls Indicate Widespread Support for Increased Investment in Child Care." 1998. http://cdfweb.vwh.net/childcare/cc_polls.html (18 Jan. 2002).

Lockhart, Charles. "American Exceptionalism and Social Security: Complementary Cultural and Structural Contributions to Social Policy Development." *The Review of Politics*, (Summer 1991): 510–29.

McDonald, Peter. "Gender Equity, Social Institutions and the Future of Fertility." *Journal of Population Research* 17, no. 1 (2000a): 1–16.

———. "Gender Equity in Theories of Fertility Transition." *Population Development Review* 26, no. 3 (2000b): 427–39.

Mishel, Lawrence, Jared Berstein, and John Schmidt. *The State of Working America: 2000–2001.* Ithaca, NY: Cornell University Press, ILR Press, 2001.

Moffitt, Robert. "The Effect of the U.S. Welfare System on Marital Status." *Journal of Public Economics*, 41 (1990): 101–24.

Mott Foundation. "Polls Indicate Widespread Support for Increased Investment in Child Care." 1998. http://cdfweb.vwh.net/childcare/cc_polls.html (18 Jan. 2002).

National Parenting Association. "Family Matters: A National Survey of Women and Men Conducted for the National Parenting Association." 1998. http://nationalpartnership.org/survey/survey1.html (26 Sept. 2001).

OECD (Organization for Economic Cooperation and Development). *Society at a Glance: OECD Social Indicators.* Paris: OECD, 2001a.

———. *Starting Strong: Early Childhood Education and Care.* Paris: OECD, 2001b.

———. "Education at a Glance." 2002. http:www.cvm.qc.ca/agecvm/dossiers/OECD/TABLES/B (18 Jan. 2003).

———. *OECD in Figures: Statistics on the Member Countries.* Paris: Organization for Economic Cooperation and Development, 2003.

Office of Personnel Management. "Paid Parental Leave." 2001. http://www.opm.gov/oca/leave/HTML/ParentalReport.htm (19 Aug. 2002).

Olsen, Darcy. "The Advancing Nanny State." *Cato Policy Analysis*, October 23, 1997. http://www.cato.org/pubs/pas/pa-285.html

Page, Benjamin, and Robert Y. Shapiro. *The Rational Public*. Chicago, Ill: University of Chicago Press, 1992.

Peters, H. Elizabeth, Robert Plotnick, and Se-Ook Jeong. "How Will Welfare Reform Affect Childbearing and Family Structure Decisions?" Institute for Research on Poverty Discussion paper No. 1239–01. University of Wisconsin, Madison, Wisconsin, 2001.

Sleebos, Joelle. "Low Fertility Rates in OECD Countries: Facts and Policy Responses." OECD Social, Employment, and Migration Working Paper #15. Organization for Economic Cooperation and Development, Paris, France, 2003.

Smith, Kristen, Barbara Downs, and Martin O'Connell. "Maternity Leave and Employment Patterns: 1961–1995." *Current Population Reports* (2001): 70–79, 1–21.

U.S. Bureau of the Census. International Database Summary Demographic Data. 2002. http://www.census.gov/ipc/www/idbsum.html (9 Jan. 2003).

Wall Street Journal/NBC. "Polls Indicate Widespread Support for Increased Investment in Child Care." 1998. http://cdfweb.vwh.net/childcare/cc_polls.html (19 Jan. 2002).

Zero to Three. *What Grown-Ups Understand About Child Development: A National Benchmark Survey*. Washington, DC: ZERO TO THREE: National Center for Infants, Toddlers and Families, 2000.

Part IX: A Sample of Policy Alternatives

Feiner, Susan, and Drucilla Barker. "Microcredit and Women's Poverty." *Dollars and Sense*. 2006. http://www.dollarandsense.org/archives/2006/1106feinerbarker.html (17 July 2009).

Feminist Majority Foundation. "Affirmative Action: Expanding Employment Opportunities for Women." 2000. http://74.125.47.132/search?q=cache:6K7wdnsTTwQJ:feminist.org/other/ccri/aafact2.html+affirmative+action:+expanding+employment+opportunities+for+women&cd=1&hl=en&ct=clnk&gl=us&client=firefox-a (1 July 2009).

Hochschild Arlie. *The Second Shift: Working Families and the Revolution at Home* with Anne Machung. New York, NY: Viking Press, [1989] 2003.

Nash, Sheryl Nance. "Microfinance Interest Rates Attract Mega-Banks." Women's eNEWS. July 12, 2005. http://www.womensenews.org/article.cfm/dyn/aid2446 (15 July 2009).

Sowell, Thomas. *Affirmative Action Around the World*. New Haven, CT: Yale University Press, 2005.

The World Bank. "10 Years of World Bank Support for Microcredit in Bangladesh." 2007. http://web.worldbank.org/WBSITE/EXTERNAL/COUNTRIES/SOUTHASIAEXT0,,contentMDK:21153910~pagePK:2865106~piPK:2865128~theSitePK:223547,00.html (17 July 2009).

Chapter 37: Women's Education: A Global Challenge by Martha C. Nussbaum

Agarwal, Bina. *A Field of One's Own: Gender and Land Rights in South Asia*. Cambridge: Cambridge University Press, 1994.

———. "'Bargaining' and Gender Relations: Within and Beyond the Household." *Feminist Economics* 3, no. 1 (1997): 1–51.

Bagehi, Jasodhara. *Loved and Unloved: The Girl Child in the Family*. Calcutta: Stree, 1997.

Buch, Nirmala. *From Oppression to Assertion: A Study of Panchayats and Women in M. P., Rajasthan and U. P.* New Delhi: Centre for Women's Development Studies, 2000.

Drèze, Jean, and Amartya Sen. *India: Economic Development and Social Opportunity*. Delhi: Oxford University Press, 1995.

———, eds. *Indian Development: Selected Regional Perspectives*. Delhi: Oxford University Press, 1997.

Hasan, Zoya. "Women's Reservations and the 'Politics of Presence.'" Paper presented at the annual meeting of the American Philosophical Association, Eastern Division, New York, 2000.

Jayal, Niraja Gopal. "Gender and Decentralization." Unpublished manuscript, Centre for the Study of Law and Governance, Jawaharal Nehru University, New Delhi, India, 2000.

Marx, Karl. "Economic and Philosophical Manuscripts." Pp. 87–196 in *Marx's Concept of Man*, edited by Erich Fromm, translated by T. B. Bottomore. New York: Continuum, (1844) 1982.

Nussbaum, Martha. "Human Capabilities, Female Human Beings." Pp. 61–105 in *Women, Culture and Development*, edited by Martha Nussbaum and Jonathan Glover. Oxford: Oxford University Press, 1996.

———. *Women and Human Development: The Capabilities Approach*. Cambridge: Cambridge University Press, 2000.

———. "'Mutilated and Deformed': Adam Smith on the Material Basis of Human Dignity." A lecture in memory of Tamara Horowitz, presented at the University of Pittsburgh, April 5, 2002(a). Unpublished, part of a book in progress titled *The Cosmopolitan Tradition* under contract to Yale University Press.

———. "Sex, Laws, and Inequality: What India Can Teach the United States." *Daedalus* (Winter 2002[b]): 95–106.

———. "The Worth of Human Dignity: Two Tensions in Stoic Cosmopolitanism." Pp. 31–49 in *Philosophy and Power in the Graeco-Roman World: Essays in Honour of Miriam Griffin*, edited by Gillian Clark and Tessa Rejak. Oxford: Oxford University Press, 2002c.

———. "Capabilities as Fundamental Entitlements: Sen and Social Justice." *Feminist Economics* 9, no. 2–3 (2003[a]): 33–59.

———. "Genocide in Gujarat." *Dissent* (Summer 2003[b]): 61–69.

———. "The Modesty of Mrs. Bajaj: India's Problematic Sexual Harassment Law." In *Directions in Sexual Harassment Law*, edited by Catharine MacKinnon and Reva Siegel. New Haven, Conn.: Yale University Press, 2003c.

———. "India, Sex Equality, and Constitutional Law." In *Constituting Women: The Gender of Jurisprudence*, edited by Beverly Baines. Cambridge: Cambridge University Press, 2004.

Nussbaum, Martha, and Amartya Sen. "Introduction." Pp. 1–8 in *The Quality of Life*, edited by Martha Nussbaum and Amartya Sen. Oxford: Clarendon, 1993.

Rekhi, Kanwal, and Henry S. Rowen. "India Confronts Its Own Intolerance." *Wall Street Journal*, May 21, 2002.

Sen, A. K. (not the same person as Amartya K. Sen). "Deflections to the Right." Speech. 2002. http://mail.sarai.net/pipermail/reader-list/2002-August/001653.html

Sen, Amartya K. "Gender and Cooperative Conflicts." Pp. 123–49 in *Persistent Inequalities: Women and World Development*, edited by Irene Tinker. Oxford: Clarendon, 1991.

———. "Fertility and Coercion." *University of Chicago Law Review* 63, no. 3 (1996): 1035–62.

United Nations Development Programme (UNDP). *Human Development Report, 2001: Making New Technologies Work for Human Development* (HDR). Oxford: Oxford University Press, 2001.

———. *Human Development Report, 2002: Deepening Democracy in a Fragmented World (HDR)*. Oxford: Oxford University Press, 2002.

Chapter 38: Affirmative Action at School and on the Job by Shannon Harper and Barbara Reskin

Aldave, B. B. "Affirmative Action and the Ideal of 'Justice for All.'" *Research in Social Stratification and Mobility* 17 (1999): 303–17.

Allport, G. *The Nature of Prejudice*. Cambridge, MA: Addison-Wesley, 1954.

Alon, S., and M. Tienda. "Hispanics and the 'Misfit' Hypothesis: Differentials in College Graduations Rates by Institutional Selectivity." Presented at Color Lines Conference, Cambridge, MA., 2003.

Anderson, T. H. *The Pursuit of Fairness*. New York: Oxford University Press, 2004.

Astin, A.W., and L. Oseguera. "The Declining 'Equity' of American Higher Education." *Review of Higher Education* 27 (2004): 321–41.

Baron, J. N., B. S. Mittman, and A. E. Newman. "Targets of Opportunity: Organizational and Environmental Determinants of Gender Integration within the California Civil Service, 1979–1985." *American Journal of Sociology* 96 (1991): 1362–401.

Berg, I. "Race, Stratification, and Group-based Rights." Pp. 115–41 in *The Problem of the Century*, edited by E Anderson and D Massey. New York: Sage, 2001.

Bergman, B. R. *In Defense of Affirmative Action*. New York: Basic Books, 1996.

Bertrand, M., and S. Mullainathan. "Are Emily and Greg More Employable than Lakisha and Jamal? A Field Experiment on Labor Market Discrimination." *American Economics Review* 94 (2004): 991–1013.

Blumrosen, A. W. *Declaration*. Statement Submitted to Supreme Court of California in Response to Proposition 209, September 26, 1996.

Bobo, L. "Race, Interest, and Belief about Affirmative Action." Pp. 191–213 in *Color Lines: Affirmative Action, Immigration, and Civil Rights Options for America*, edited by J. D. Skrenty. Chicago: University of Chicago Press, 2001.

Bowen, W. G., and D. Bok. *The Shape of the River: Long-Term Consequences of Considering Race in College and University Admissions*. Princeton, NJ: Princeton University Press, 1998.

Brown, M. K., M. Carnoy, E. Currie, T. Duster, and D. B. Oppenheimer, et al. *Whitewashing Race : The Myth of a Color-Blind Society*. Berkeley: University of California Press, 2003.

Bruno, A. "Affirmative Action in Employment." *Congressional Research Service Reports 95–165 GOV*. Library of Congress, Washington, DC, 1995.

Burstein, P. "'Reverse Discrimination' Cases in Federal Courts: Mobilization by a Countermovement." *Sociological Quarterly* 32 (1991): 511–28.

———. *Discrimination, Jobs, and Politics*. Chicago: University of Chicago Press, 1998.

Carnevale, A. P., S. J. Rose. "Socioeconomic Status, Race/Ethnicity, and Selective College Admissions." *Research Report,* Century Foundation, New York, 2003. http://www.tcf.org/Publications/Education/carnevale_rose.pdf

Chambers, D. L., T, Clydesdale, W. C. Kidder, and R. O. Lempert. "The Real Impact of Eliminating Affirmative Action in American Law Schools." *Stanford Law Review* 57, no. 6 (2005): 1855–98.

Cole, S., and E. Barber. *Increasing Faculty Diversity: The Occupational Choices of High Achieving Minority Studies*. Cambridge, MA: Harvard University Press, 2003.

Coleman, J. S., E. Q. Campbell, C. J. Hobson, J. McPartland, and A. M. Mood, et al. *Equality of Educational Opportunity*. Washington, DC: Department of Health Education and Welfare, 1966.

Collins, S. M. *Black Corporate Executives: The Making and Breaking of a Black Middle Class*. Philadelphia, PA: Temple University Press, 1997.

Crosby, F. *Affirmative Action Is Dead: Long Live Affirmative Action*. New Haven, CT: Yale University Press, 2004.

Darity, W. A., and P. L. Mason. "Evidence on Discrimination in Employment: Codes of Color, Codes of Gender." *Journal of Economic Perspectives* 12 (1998): 63–90.

Darity, W. A., and J. G. Nembhard. "Racial and Ethnic Inequality: The International Record." *American Economic Review* 90 (2000): 308–11.

Davis, J. A, and T. W. Smith. *General Social Surveys, 1972–1996*. Chicago: National Opinion Research Center, 1996.

Dobbin, F., J. R. Sutton, J. W. Meyer, and W. R. Scott. "Equal Opportunity Law and the Construction of Internal Labor Markets." *American Journal of Sociology* 99 (1993): 396–427.

Douglass, J. A. "Anatomy of a Conflict: The Making and Unmaking of Affirmative Action at the University of California." Pp. 118–44 in *Color Lines: Affirmative Action, Immigration, and Civil Rights Options for America*, edited by J. D. Skrenty. Chicago: University of Chicago Press, 2001.

Duncan, G. J., J. Boisjoly, D. M. Levy, M. Kremer, and J. Eccles. "Empathy or Antipathy? The Consequences of Racially and Socially Diverse Peers on Attitudes and Behaviors." Working Paper, Institute for Policy Research, Northwestern University, 2003.

Durr, M., and J. R. Logan. "Racial Submarkets in Government Employment: African American Managers in New York State." *Sociological Forum* 2 (1997): 353–70.

Duster, T. "Individual Fairness, Group Preferences, and the California Plan" Pp. 111–34 in *Race and Representation: Affirmative Action*, edited by R. Post and M. Rogin. New York: Zone Books, 1998.

Faludi, S. *Backlash*. New York: Crown Publishing Group, 1991.

Frymer, P., and J. D. Skrentny. "The Rise of Instrumental Affirmative Action: Law and the New Significance of Race in America." *Connecticut Law Review* 36 (2004): 677–723.

Glazer, N. *Affirmative Discrimination: Ethnic Inequality and Public Policy*. New York: Basic Books, 1975.

Graham, H. D. *The Civil Rights Era: Origins and Development of National Policy*. New York: Oxford University Press, 1990.

———. "The Origins of Affirmative Action: Civil Rights and the Regulatory State." *Annals of the American Academy of Political and Social Science* 523 (1992): 50–62.

Gurin, P. "The Compelling Need for Diversity in Education." *Michigan Journal of Race and Law* 5 (1999): 363–425.

Hallinan, M. T. "Diversity Effects on Student Outcomes: Social Science Evidence." *Ohio State Law Journal* 59 (1998): 733–54.

Hartmann, H. "Who Has Benefited from Affirmative Action in Employment?" Pp. 77–96 in *The Affirmative Action Debate*, edited by G. E. Curry. Cambridge, MA: Addison-Wesley, 1996.

Hatch O. "Loading the Economy." Pp. 261–67 in *Equal Employment Opportunity*, edited by P. Burstein. New York: Aldine de Gruyter, 1994.

Heckman, J. J., and B. S. Payner. "Determining the Impact of Federal Antidiscrimination Policy on the Economic Status of Blacks: A Study of South Carolina." *American Economics Review* 79, no. 1 (1989): 138–77.

Hirsh, C. E., and S. Kornrich. "The Context of Discrimination: The Impact of Firm Conditions on Workplace Race and Sex Discrimination." Presented at Annual Meeting of the American Sociological Association, San Francisco, CA, 2004.

Hochschild, J. *Facing Up to the American Dream.* Princeton, NJ: Princeton University Press, 1995.

Holzer, H., and D. Neumark. "Assessing Affirmative Action." *Journal of Economic Literature* 308 (2000): 483–568.

Jaynes, G. D., and R. M. Williams, eds. *A Common Destiny.* Washington, DC: National Academic Press, 1989.

Kahlenberg, R. D. *The Remedy: Class, Race, and Affirmative Action.* New York: Basic, 1996.

Kane, T. "No Alternatives: The Effects of Color-blind Admissions in California." Pp. 33–50 in *Chilling Admissions,* edited by G. Orfield and E. Miller. Cambridge, MA: Harvard Education Publishing Group, 1998a.

Kane, T. "Racial and Ethnic Preferences in College Admissions." Pp. 431–56 in *The Black-White Test Score Gap,* edited by C. Jencks and M. Phillips. Washington, DC: Brookings Institute, 1998b.

Kellough, J. E. "Affirmative Action in Government Employment." *The Annuals of the American Academy of Political and Social Sciences* 523 (1992): 117–30.

Kelly, E., and F. Dobbin. "How Affirmative Action became Diversity Management: Employer Response to Antidiscrimination Law, 1961 to 1996." *American Behavioral Scientist* 41, no. 7 (1998): 960–84.

Kinder, D. R., and L. M. Sanders. *Divided by Color.* Chicago: University of Chicago Press, 1996.

Kirschenmann, J., and K. M. Neckerman. "'We'd Love to Hire Them but . . .': The Meaning of Race for Employers." Pp. 203–34 in *The Urban Underclass,* edited by C. Jencks and P. E. Peterson. Washington, DC: Brookings Institute, 1991.

Konrad, A. M. and F. Linnehan. "Formalized HRM Structures: Coordinating Equal Employment Opportunity or Concealing Organizational Practices?" *Academic Management* 38 (1995): 787–820.

Kravitz, D. A., D. A. Harrison, M. E. Turner, E. L. Levine, and W. Chaves, et al. *Affirmative Action: A Review of Psychological and Behavioral Research.* Washington, DC: Society for Industrial and Organizational Psychology, 1997.

Krysan, M. "Prejudice, Politics, and Public Opinion." *Annual Review of Sociology* 26 (2000): 135–68.

Leiter, S., and W. M. Leiter. *Affirmative Action in Antidiscrimination Law and Policy: An Overview and Synthesis.* Albany: SUNY Press, 2002.

Lemann, N. *The Big Test: The Secret History of American Meritocracy.* New York: Farrar, Straus & Giroux, 1999.

Lempert, R. O., D. L. Chambers, and T. K. Adams. "Michigan's Minority Graduates in Practice." *Law and Social Inquiry* 25 (2000): 395–506.

Leonard, J. "The Impact of Affirmative Action Regulations and Equal Employment Law on Black Employment." *Journal of Economic Perspective* 4 (1990): 47–63.

Leonard, J. "The Federal Anti-bias Effort." Pp. 85–113 in *Essays on the Economics of Discrimination,* edited by E. P. Hoffman. Kalamazoo, MI: W.E. Upjohn Institute of Employment Research, 1991.

Major, B., J. Feinstein, and J. Crocker. "Attributional Ambiguity of Affirmative Action." *Basic and Applied Social Psychology* 15 (1994): 113–41.

Malamud, D. C. "Affirmative Action and Ethnic Niches: A Legal Afterword." Pp. 313–45 in *Color Lines: Affirmative Action, Immigration, and Civil Rights Options for America,* edited by J. D. Skrenty. Chicago: University of Chicago Press, 2001.

Malveaux, J. "Know Your Enemy: The Assault on Diversity." *Black Issues in Higher Education* 21 (2004): 32–33.

Massey, D. S., and N. A. Denton. *American Apartheid*. Cambridge, MA: Harvard University Press, 1993.

Moskos, C. C., and J. S. Butler. *All That We Can Be: Black Leadership and Racial Integration the Army Way*. New York: Basic Books, 1996.

Office of Federal Contract Compliance. *Facts on Executive Order 11246—Affirmative Action*, 2002. http://www.dol.gov/esa/regs/compliance/ofccp/aa.htm

Oppenheimer, D. "Distinguishing Five Models of Affirmative Action." *Berkeley Women's Law Journal* 4 (1989): 42–61.

Orfield, G. "Schools More Separate: Consequences of a Decade of Resegregation." Cambridge, MA: Final Report Harvard University Civil Rights Project, 2001. http://www.civilrights project.harvard.edu/research/deseg/separate_schools01.php

Orfield, G., and M. Kurlaender, eds. *Diversity Challenged: Evidence on the Impact of Affirmative Action*. Cambridge, MA: Harvard University Civil Rights Project, 2001.

Orfield, G., and D. Whitla. "Diversity and Legal Education: Student Experiences in Leading Law Schools." Pp. 143–74 in *Diversity Challenged: Evidence on the Impact of Affirmative Action*, edited by G. Orfield and M. Kurlaender. Cambridge, MA: Harvard University Civil Rights Project, 2001.

Pager, D. "The Mark of a Criminal Record." *American Journal of Sociology* 108 (2003): 937–75.

Patterson, O. *The Ordeal of Integration*. Washington, DC: Civitas, 1997.

Reskin, B. F. *The Realities of Affirmative Action*. Washington, DC: American Sociological Association, 1998.

———. "Discrimination and Its Remedies." Pp. 567–600 in *Sourcebook on Labor Market Research: Evolving Structures and Processes*, edited by I. Berg and A. Kalleberg. New York: Plenum, 2001.

———. "Rethinking Employment Discrimination." Pp. 218–44 in *The New Economic Sociology: Developments in an Emerging Field*, edited by M. F. Guillen, R. Collins, P. England, and M. Meyer. New York: Russell Sage, 2002.

Royster, D. A. *Race and the Invisible Hand*. Berkeley: University of California Press, 2003.

Ryan, J., J. Hawdon, and A. Branick. "The Political Economy of Diversity: Diversity Programs in Fortune 500 Companies." *Sociology Research Online* 7, no. 1, 2002. http://www.socresonline .org.uk/7/1/ryan.htm

Sander, R. H. "Colleges Will Just Disguise Racial Quotas." *Los Angeles Times*, June 30, 2003.

———. "A Systemic Analysis of Affirmative Action in Law Schools." *Stanford Law Review* 57 (2004): 367–483.

Schuman, H., C. Steeh, L. D. Bobo, and M. Krysan. *Racial Attitudes in America: Trends and Interpretations*. Cambridge, MA: Harvard University Press, 1997.

Skrentny, J. D. *The Ironies of Affirmative Action: Politics, Culture, and Justice in America*. Chicago: University Chicago Press, 1996.

———. *The Minority Rights Revolution*. Cambridge, MA: Harvard University Press, 2002.

Smith, James P., and Finis Welch. "Affirmative Action and Labor Markets." *Journal of Labor Economics* 2:2 (April 1984).

Son Hing, L. S, D. R. Bobocel, and M. P. Zanna. "Meritocracy and Opposition to Affirmative Action: Making Concessions in the Face of Discrimination." *Journal of Personality and Social Psychology* 83 (2002): 493–509.

Sowell, T. *Black Education*. New York: David McKay, 1972.

———. *Affirmative Action Around the World: An Empirical Study*. New Haven, CT: Yale University Press, 2004.

Steele, S. *The Content of Our Character*. New York: Harper Perennial, 1991.

Stephanopoulos, G., and C. Edley. *Affirmative Action Review. A Report to the President*. Washington, DC: U.S. Government Printing Office, 1995.

Stryker, R. "Disparate Impact and the Quota Debates: Law, Labor Market Sociology, and Equal Employment Policies." *Sociological Quarterly* 42 (2001): 13–46.

Stryker, R., M. Scarpellino, and M. Holtzman. "Political Culture Wars 1990s Style: The Drum Beat of Quotas in Media Framing of the Civil Rights Act of 1991." *Research in Social Stratification and Mobility* 17 (1999): 33–106.

Sturm, S. "Second Generation Employment Discrimination: A Structural Approach." *Columbia Law Review* 101 (2001): 458–568.

Swain, C.M. "Affirmative Action: Legislative History, Judicial Interpretations, Public Consensus." Pp. 318–47 in *America Becoming: Racial Trends and Their Consequences*, edited by N. J. Smelser, W. J. Wilson, and F. Mitchell. Washington, DC: National Academy Press, 2001.

Swain, C. M., K. R. Greene, and C. M. Wotipka. "Understanding Racial Polarization on Affirmative Action: The View from Focus Groups." Pp. 214–37 in *Color Lines: Affirmative Action, Immigration, and Civil Right Options for America*, edited by J. D. Skrentny. Chicago: University Chicago Press, 2001.

Teles, S. M. "Why Is There No Affirmative Action in Britain?" *American Behavioral Scientist* 41, no. 7 (1998): 1004–27.

Thernstrom, S., and A. Thernstrom. *America in Black and White*. New York: Simon & Schuster, 1997.

Tienda, M., K. T. Leicht, T. Sullivan, M. Maltese, and K. Lloyd. "Closing the Gap? Admissions and Enrollments at the Texas Public Flagships Before and After Affirmative Action." Working Paper No. 2003–01. Office of Population Research, Princeton University, 2003. http://www.texastop10.princeton.edu/publications/tienda012103.pdf

Turner, M. A., M. Fix, and R. J. Struyk. "Opportunities Denied, Opportunities Diminished: Race Discrimination in Hiring." Working Paper. Urban Institute, Washington, DC., 1991.

U.S. Bureau of the Census. *QT–P25. Class of Worker by Sex, Place of Work, and Veteran Status: 2000*. http://factfinder.census.gov

———. *Statistical Abstract of the United States*. 2004. http://www.census.gov/prod/www/statistical-abstract-04.html

U.S. Department of Labor, Office of Disability Employment Policy. *Affirmative Action and People with Disabilities*. 2003. http://www.dol.gov/odep/pubs/ek98/affirmat.htm

U.S. EEOC. *Indicators of Equal Employment Opportunity—Status and Trends*. Washington, DC: U.S. Equal Employment Opportunity Commission, 2004.

Welch, F. "Affirmative Action and Discrimination." Pp. 153–89 in *The Question of Discrimination: Racial Inequality in the U.S. Labor Market*, edited by S. Schulman, and W. Darity Jr. Middletown, CT: Wesleyan University Press, 1989.

Welch, S., and J. Gruhl. "Affirmative Action and Minority Enrollments in Medical and Law Schools." *Ohio State Law Journal* 59 (1998): 607–732.

Whitla, D. K., G. Orfield, W. Silen, C. Teperow, C. Howard, and J. Reede. "Educational Benefits of Diversity in Medical School: A Survey of Students." *Academy of Medicine* 78 (2003): 460–66.

Wierzbicki, S., and C. Hirschman. "The End of Affirmative Action in Washington State and Its Impact on the Transition from High School to College." Presented at the Annual Meeting of Population Association of America, Atlanta, GA, 2002.

Wightman, L. F. "The Threat to Diversity in Legal Education: An Empirical Analysis of the Consequences of Abandoning Race as a Factor in Law School Admission Decisions." *New York University Law Review* 72 (1997): 1–53.

Wilson, W. J. *Bridge Over the Racial Divide*. Berkeley: University of California Press, 1999.

Credits

"The Problem with Sex/Gender and Nature/Nurture" by Anne Fausto-Sterling. From *Debating Biology*, ed. Simon Williams et al. Copyright © 2003, Routledge. Reprinted with permission of Taylor & Francis Ltd.

"'Night to His Day': The Social Construction of Gender" by Judith Lorber. From *Paradoxes of Gender*. Copyright © 1994, Yale University Press. Reprinted with permission of Yale University Press.

"Culture, Gender, and Math" by Luigi Guiso, Ferdinando Monte, Paola Sapienza, and Luigi Zingales. From *Science,* May 30, 2008. Copyright © 2008, The American Association for the Advancement of Science.

"Montagnais Women and the Jesuit Program for Colonization" by Eleanor Leacock. From *Women and Colonization*, ed. Mona Etienne and Eleanor Leacock. Copyright © 1980, J. F. Bergin Publishers, Inc. Reprinted with permission of Greenwood Publishing Group, Inc.

"Capitalism, Patriarchy, and Job Segregation by Sex" by Heidi Hartmann. From *SIGNS*, vol. 1, no. 3, 1976. Reprinted with permission of University of Chicago Press.

"Women's Work and the Family in Nineteenth-Century Europe" by Joan W. Scott and Louise A. Tilly. From *Comparative Studies in Society and History*, vol. 17, no. 1, 1975. Reprinted with permission of Cambridge University Press.

"Housewifery: Household Work and Household Tools under Pre-Industrial Conditions" by Ruth Schwartz Cowan. From *More Work for Mother*. Reprinted with permission of Perseus Books Group.

Index

matriarch/matriarchy, 294, 296–97, 299–300, 408
Mayer, Kurt B., 167
M Butterfly (Hwang), 21
McBride, Theresa, 71
McDonald, Peter, 488
McFarland, Hannah, 100
McJobs, 136
McKinnon, Catherine, 436
medicine, women in, 159
memory, nature of, 13
men: absent spouses of, financial support by, 463; citizenship rights, 150; labor legislation protecting, 106–7, 116; maintaining women's inferiority in the labor market, 54–62; stereotypic assumptions about Sri Lankan, 356; unemployed, 302n19, 308, 355–65; valuing the work of, 29–30. *See also* fathers; husbands
men in the female professions: conclusion, 208–10; glass ceilings and walls, 161; in hiring, 198–200; homosexuals, 326; introduction, 195–98; maquiladora industries, 301n6, 327–28, 331–34; media representation and, 209–10; from outsiders, 206–8; supervisors and female colleagues, 201–6
men's work, valuing, 29–30
mentors, 201–2
The Merchant of Venice (Shakespeare), 177
Merton, Robert K., 165, 168
Meteor factory, 342–43, 344–48
Mexican American women, 317
Mexican immigrants, male, 307, 313
Mexican women, 326
Mexico, 301n6, 307, 325–34
Meyers, Marcia K., 485
MGM Grand Hotel, 439
microcredit, 493–94, 499–507
microelectronics industry, 235–36
middle-class, emergence of, 84
Middle East, transnational workers in the, 308
migration: braceros, 307, 313, 320, 325–26, 477–78; of Caribbean women, 306, 312–14; female-first pattern, 230–31; gender relations and, 226; generational rebellions and, 476, 477–79; motherhood and, 319–21, 355, 359, 362, 448, 472,

475–77; of Sri Lankan women, 308, 355–65
military, U.S., 526
Miller, Lucinda, 100
Min, P. G., 230
Mishel, Lawrence, 485
Montagnais-Naskapi, Le Jeune's program to convert and civilize, components of: converts behavior, 44–49; education of the children in, 41, 48–49; European family structure introduced, 40–42; introduction, 3–4, 39–42; long-range impact, 47–52; marriage, changing the structure of, 43–47; permanent settlements, 41; punishment principle, introducing, 41
Montagnais-Naskapi society: children, love for, 41; children in, 41, 45, 48–49; economy and decision making, 42–43, 49–52; egalitarianism in, 42–43; ethics, 49–50, 52; female-male relations, 40–41, 45–47, 48, 51–52; marital structures, 42, 43–47; shamans, 52; women in, 40–42, 44–47, 51–52
morality/moral development, 43, 185
Morris, James/Jan, 2, 17–18, 25–26
motherhood, 116, 150, 152, 407
mother-ism, 467–68
mothers: good, concept of, 28, 320, 447, 454–55, 461, 464–65; identity, interlocking relationship of gender with, 243–44; job protections for, 69–70, 244, 399, 497, 536–37; single, 152–53, 488–89; single and black, 414–15, 462–63; transnational, 319–21, 355, 359, 362, 448, 472, 475–77; union protections for, 281–82, 284. *See also* working mothers
motivation theory, 168
Muller, Viana, 58, 59
Muller v. Oregon, 70, 107, 112
Multitext, 289
Murray, Charles, 446
Muslim women, 499–500

naked sex, 8
National Organization for Women (NOW), 279
National Woman's Party (NWP), 283
nature/nurture debate, 2–3, 10–14
Nazarrio, Sonia, 478

About the Editor

Dr. Jacqueline Goodman is a professor of sociology and director of Women's and Gender Studies at the State University of New York, Potsdam College. She has been teaching courses on work, gender, inequality, and human rights for twenty years. She has contributed articles to the book series *Studies in Law, Politics and Society* and to the *American Journal of Economics and Sociology*. She is the author of *Health Care's Forgotten Majority: Nurses and Their Frayed White Collars* and of a forthcoming book on women and family law. Dr. Goodman lives in Canton, New York, with two children.

About the Book

Central to all our lives, work affects our status in the state, the family, and the economy. This comprehensive reader examines the myriad ways in which work—whether it is well-paid, unpaid, or underpaid—profoundly influences our roles in both the public and private spheres. Jacqueline Goodman has selected a key set of essays that examine influential arguments on such central themes as (1) the origins of the gendered division of labor; (2) historical trends and economic transformations that affect and are affected by women's position in market and non-market work; (3) the effects of occupational and job segregation by sex on status, pay, and promotion; (4) the ways in which formal and informal organizational culture shape and in turn are shaped by gender in professional and managerial positions; (5) class consciousness among wage-earning men and women; (6) the different forms of gender discrimination that women and men face in the workplace; (7) the problems working parents face and the ways in which different societies, subcultures, and genders cope; and (8) alternative approaches to improving the lives of working women and their families in the global economy. With its rich interdisciplinary perspective, this text is ideal for courses in sociology, political science, anthropology, and women's and gender studies.